ETHICS
Theory and Practice

FIFTH EDITION

Jacques P. Thiroux

BAKERSFIELD COLLEGE

PRENTICE HALL, Englewood Cliffs, New Jersey 07632

Library of Congress Cataloging-in-Publication Data

Thiroux, Jacques P.
    Ethics: theory and practice / Jacques P. Thiroux.—5th ed.
      p. cm.
    Includes index.
    ISBN 0-02-419921-4 (pbk.)
    1. Ethics. 2. Ethical problems. I. Title.
BJ1012.T47 1995
170—dc20   93-37365
                                    CIP

Editors: Ted Bolen/Maggie Barbieri
Editorial Assistant: Meg McGuane
Production Supervisor: Jeff Chen
Production Managers: Alex Odulak and Fran Drago
Cover Designer: Robert Freese

Copyright © 1995 by Prentice-Hall, Inc.
A Simon & Schuster Company
Englewood Cliffs, New Jersey 07632

Previous editions copyright © 1977, 1980, 1986, and 1990.

Printed in the United States of America

10 9 8 7 6 5 4 3 2 1

ISBN 0-02-419921-4

Prentice-Hall International (UK) Limited, *London*
Prentice-Hall of Australia Pty. Limited, *Sydney*
Prentice-Hall Canada Inc., *Toronto*
Prentice-Hall Hispanoamericana, S.A., *Mexico*
Prentice-Hall of India Private Limited, *New Delhi*
Prentice-Hall of Japan, Inc., *Tokyo*
Simon & Schuster Asia Pte. Ltd., *Singapore*
Editora Prentice-Hall do Brasil, Ltda., *Rio de Janeiro*

Dedicated to Emily,
my loving wife

Preface to the Fifth Edition

For the first time since I have been doing revisions to *Ethics: Theory and Practice*, I did not add any new chapters because after four editions, most contemporary moral issues have been covered, and any new issues that have come up in recent years usually fall into the major categories I have already established (for example, sexual harassment comes into play mostly in business ethics). The book is still fairly evenly divided into "theory" (Chapters 1–7) and "practice" (Chapters 8–15). Since ethical issues and contemporary situations change every day, I have had to bring the theories and cases up to date in many areas, such as abortion; allowing someone to die, mercy death, and mercy killing; business ethics; and bioethics.

Among additions to the fifth edition is a section in Chapter 3 on Virtue Ethics, which is not a new theory, having originated with Aristotle, but which is having a moderate revival among some ethicists. In Chapter 9, "Allowing Someone to Die, Mercy Death, and Mercy Killing," many changes had to be made to reflect the medical and legal advances in this area, such as the greater significance of persistent vegetative state (PVS), the passing of the Patient Self-Determination Act (PSDA) by the government in 1990, and the revision of advanced directives (living wills, the California Natural Death Act Declaration, and most importantly, the Durable Power of Attorney for Health Care [DPAHC]). In addition, the famous (or infamous) activities of Derek Humphry and Dr. Jack Kevorkian in right-to-die issues are discussed and two new cases presented.

In Chapter 10, on abortion, I have added the new chorionic villus sampling (CVS) method of determining genetic information of embryos in utero, which may be used much earlier in pregnancy than the older amniocentesis method; I also added a history of abortion in America, the recent U.S. Supreme Court decision on abortion, and a more specific description of what occurs at each stage of gestation of the conceptus. In Chapter 13, on bioethics, I have added a section on confidentiality and its problems, especially in the area of AIDS. In Chapter 14, on business ethics, I have added a section on sexual harassment in the workplace and two cases involving severe sexual harassment. In Chapter 15, on environmental ethics, I have presented possible arguments from the New Testament of the Bible that may be interpreted to support acting morally toward the environment, and I have also added a new appendix on how Humanitarian Ethics would deal with ethics and the environment.

In all chapters, bibliographies have been expanded and updated, and the glossary has been expanded to include new terms added to the text, such as PVS and CVS. All of the instructor aids are still present, including chapter objectives, detailed chapter summaries, review and discussion questions for Chapters 1–7 and review questions and case discussions for Chapters 8–15, and appendixes that demonstrate the ways in which my ethical system deals with the moral issues presented in the various chapters.

My thanks go to the many students and instructors who have used the book and who have been kind enough to give me suggestions and criticisms; to the reviewers of the book; to my editors, Maggie Barbieri and Ted Bolen, and the production supervisor, Jeff Chen, all of whom have been extremely helpful and patient with me in this revision; and lastly, to my wife, Emily, who has always been supportive and helpful during revisions. I hope that instructors and students continue to find my book clear and helpful in their struggle to deal earnestly with ethical theory and issues.

J.P.T.

Contents

Two Ways of Approaching Rights and Obligations in Business.
The Moderate Position. Justice, Truth Telling, and Honesty in
Business. Ethical Issues in Business. Sexual Harassment. Cases
for Study and Discussion. Chapter Summary. Exercises for
Review. Notes. Supplementary Reading.

♦ CHAPTER 15

Environmental Ethics   437

Objectives. Key Terms. Nature and Morality. Environmental
Ethical Issues. Our Attitude Toward Nature and What Lies
Behind It. Arguments for Use and Exploitation of the Natural
Environment. Arguments Against the Use and Exploitation of
Nature. Moderate Position. Criteria for Animal Rights. Ways
of Dealing with Animal Rights. Use of Animals for Food. Use of
Animals for Experimentation. Killing Animals for Sport. Pro-
tection of Endangered Species. Conclusion. Cases for Study
and Discussion. Chapter Summary. Exercises for Review.
Notes. Supplementary Reading.

Appendixes

ETHICS

What Is Morality?

Objectives

After you have read this chapter you should be able to

1. Define philosophy and explain the relationship of ethics to it.
2. Define key terms concerning ethics or morality.
3. Explain the various approaches to the study of morality.
4. Understand what morality is and how it differs from aesthetics, nonmoral behavior, and manners.
5. Understand to whom morality applies.
6. Have some idea of where morality comes from.
7. Distinguish between morality and the law.
8. Distinguish between morality and religion.
9. Understand why human beings should be moral.

What Is Philosophy and Ethics' Relationship to It?

Philosophy literally means love of wisdom, the Greek words *philia* meaning love or friendship, and *sophia* meaning wisdom. Philosophy is concerned with basically three areas: *Epistemology* (the study of knowledge), *metaphysics* (the study of the nature of reality), and *ethics* (the study of morality), which will be our major concern in this book.

Epistemology deals with the following questions: What is knowledge? What are truth and falsity, and to what do they apply? What is required for someone to actually *know* something? What is the nature of perception, and how reliable is it? What are logic and logical reasoning, and how can human beings attain them? What's the difference between knowledge and belief? Is there anything such as certain knowledge? From time to time throughout this book epistemological questions will be discussed, especially in Chapter 4, which deals with absolutes and truth.

Metaphysics is the study of the nature of reality, asking the questions: What exists in reality and what is the nature of what exists? Specifically, such questions as the following are asked: Is there really cause and effect in reality, and if so, how does it work? What is the nature of the physical world, and is there anything other than the physical, such as the mental or spiritual? What is the nature of human beings? Is there freedom in reality or is everything predetermined? Here again, we will deal with some of these questions throughout the book, but especially in Chapter 4—are there any absolutes or is everything really relative?—and Chapter 5, is there any such thing as freedom, or are all things in reality predetermined?

Ethics, our main concern, deals with what is right or wrong in human behavior and conduct. It asks such questions as what constitutes any person or action being good, bad, right, or wrong, and how do we know (epistemology)? What part does self-interest or the interests of others play in making moral decisions and judgments? What theories of conduct are valid or invalid and why? Should we use principles or rules or laws, or should we let each situation decide our morality? Are killing, lying, cheating, stealing, and sexual acts right or wrong, and why or why not?

As you can see, these three areas are related and at times overlap, but each one is worthy of concentrated study in itself. The major concern in this book, as its title suggests, is ethics, and before going any further, it is important to define some key terms used in any discussion of ethics or morality.

Key Terms

Ethical, Moral, Unethical, Immoral

In ordinary language, we frequently use the words *ethical* and *moral* (and *unethical* and *immoral*) interchangeably; that is, we speak of the ethical or moral person or act. On the other hand, we speak of codes of ethics, but only infrequently do we mention codes of morality. Some reserve terms *moral* and *immoral* only for the realm of sexuality and use the words *ethical* and *unethical* when discussing how the business and professional communities should behave toward their members or toward the public. More commonly, however, we use none of these words as often as we use the terms *good, bad, right,* and *wrong.* What do all these words mean, and what are the relationships between them?

Ethics comes from the Greek *ethos,* meaning character. *Morality* comes from the Latin *moralis,* meaning customs or manners. Ethics, then, seems to pertain to the individual character of a person or persons, whereas morality seems to point to the relationships between human beings. Nevertheless, in ordinary language, whether we call a person ethical or moral or an act unethical or immoral doesn't really make any difference. In philosophy, however, the term *ethics* is also used to refer to a specific area of study—the area of morality, which concentrates on human conduct and human values.

When we speak of people as moral or ethical, we usually mean that they are good people, and when we speak of them as immoral or unethical, we mean that they are bad people. When we refer to certain human actions as moral, ethical, immoral, and unethical, we mean they are right or wrong. The simplicity of these definitions, however, ends here, for how do we define a right or wrong action or a good or bad person? What are the human standards by which such decisions can be made? These are the more difficult questions that make up the greater part of the study of morality, and they will be discussed in more detail in later chapters. The important thing to remember here is that moral, ethical, immoral, and unethical, essentially mean good, right, bad, and wrong, often depending on whether one is referring to people themselves or to their actions.

Characteristics of Good, Bad, Right, Wrong, Happiness, or Pleasure. It seems to be an empirical fact that whatever human beings consider good involves happiness and pleasure in some way, and whatever they consider bad involves unhappiness and pain in some way. This view of what is good has traditionally been called "hedonism." As long as the widest range of interpretation is given to these words (from simple sensual pleasures to intellectual or spiritual pleasures and from sensual pain to deep emotional unhappiness), then it is difficult to deny that whatever is good involves at least some pleasure or happiness, and whatever is bad involves some pain or unhappiness.

One element involved in the achievement of happiness is the necessity of taking the long- rather than the short-range view. People may undergo some pain or unhappiness in order to attain some pleasure or happiness in the long run. For example, we will put up with the pain of having our teeth drilled to keep our teeth and gums healthy so that we may enjoy eating and the general good health that results from teeth that are well maintained. Similarly, people may do very difficult and even painful work for two days in order to earn money that will bring them pleasure and happiness for a week or two.

Furthermore, the term *good* should be defined in the context of human experience and human relationships rather than in an abstract sense only. For example, knowledge and power in themselves are not good unless a human being derives some satisfaction from them or unless they contribute in some way to moral and meaningful human relationships. They are otherwise nonmoral.

What about actions that will bring someone some good but will cause pain to another, such as those of a sadist who gains pleasure from violently mistreating another human being? Our original statement was that everything that is good will bring some person satisfaction, pleasure, or happiness of some kind, but this statement does not necessarily work in the reverse—that everything that brings someone satisfaction is necessarily good. There certainly are "malicious pleasures."

Excellence. William Frankena states that whatever is good will also probably involve "some kind or degree of excellence."[1] He goes on to say that "what is bad in itself is so because of the presence of either pain or unhappiness or of some kind of defect or lack of excellence."[2] Excellence is an important addition to pleasure or satisfaction in that it makes "experiences or activities better or worse than they would otherwise be."[3] For example, the enjoyment or satisfaction gained from hearing a concert, seeing a fine movie, or reading a good book is due, to a great extent, to the excellence of the creators and presenters of these events (composers, performers, directors, actors, writers). Another and perhaps more profound example of the importance of excellence is that if one gains satisfaction or pleasure from witnessing a well-conducted court case and from seeing and hearing the judge and the lawyers perform their duties well, that satisfaction will be deepened if the judge and the lawyers are also excellent people, that is, if they are kind, fair, and compassionate human beings in addition to being clever and able.

Whatever is good, then, will probably contain some pleasure, happiness, and excellence, whereas whatever is bad will probably contain their opposites—pain, unhappiness, and lack of excellence. I am only stating that there will probably be *some* of these elements present. For example, a good person performing a right action might not be particularly happy and might even find what he or she is doing painful, but the recipients of the right action might be made happy by it and the right action might also involve excellence.

Harmony and Creativity. There are two other attributes of "good" and "right" that may add to our definition; they are harmony and creativity on the "good" side and discord, or disharmony, and lack of creativity on the "bad" side. If an action is creative or can aid human beings in becoming creative and, at the same time, help to bring about a harmonious integration of as many human beings as possible, then we can say it is a right action. If an action has the opposite effect, then we can say that it is a wrong action.

For example, if a person or a group of people can end a war between two nations and create an honorable and lasting peace, then a right or good action has been performed. It can allow members of both nations to be creative rather than destructive and can create harmony between both sides and within each nation. On the other hand, causing or starting a war between two nations will have just the opposite effect. Lester A. Kirkendall stresses these points and also adds to what I stated earlier about the necessity of placing the emphasis on what is good or excellent in human experience and relationships.

> Whenever a decision or a choice is to be made concerning behavior, the moral decision will be the one which works toward the creation of trust, confidence, and integrity in relationships. It should increase the capacity of individuals to cooperate, and enhance the sense of self-respect in the individual. Acts which create distrust, suspicion, and misunderstanding, which build barriers and destroy integrity are immoral. They decrease the individual's sense of self-respect and rather than producing a capacity to work together they separate people and break down the capacity for communication.[4]

Two other terms we should define are *amoral* and *nonmoral*.

Amoral

Amoral means having no moral sense, or being indifferent to right and wrong. This term can be applied to very few people. Certain people who have had prefrontal lobotomies tend to act amorally after the operation; that is, they have no sense of right and wrong. And there are a few human beings who, despite moral education, have remained or become amoral. These tend to be found among certain criminal types who can't seem to realize they've done anything wrong. They tend not to have any remorse, regret, or concern for what they have done.

One such example of an amoral person is Gregory Powell, who, with Jimmy Lee Smith, gratuitously killed a policeman in an onion field south of Bakersfield, California. A good description of him and his attitude can be found in Joseph Wambaugh's *The Onion Field*.[5] Another such example is Colin Pitchfork, another real-life character, who raped and killed two young girls in England, and who was described by Wambaugh in *The Blooding*. In that book Wambaugh also quotes from various psychologists on the amoral, psychopathological, sociopathological personality, which is defined as "a person characterized by emotional instability, lack of sound judgment, perverse and impulsive (often criminal) behavior, inability to learn from experience, amoral and asocial feel-ings, and other serious personality defects."[6] He describes "the most important feature of the psychopath . . . as his monumental irresponsibility. He knows what the ethical rules are, at least he can repeat them parrotlike, but they are void of meaning to him."[7] He quotes further: "No sense of conscience, guilt, or remorse is present. Harmful acts are committed without discomfort or shame."[8] Amorality, then, is basically an attitude that some—luckily only a few—human beings possess.

All of this doesn't mean that amoral criminals should not be morally blamed and punished for their wrongdoings. In fact, such people are even more dan-gerous to society than those who can distinguish right from wrong because they are usually morally uneducable. Society, therefore, needs even more protection from such criminals.

Nonmoral

The word *nonmoral* means out of the realm of morality altogether. For example, inanimate objects such as cars and guns are neither moral nor immoral. A per-son using the car or gun may use it immorally, but the things themselves are nonmoral. Many areas of study (for instance, mathematics, astronomy, and physics) are in themselves nonmoral, but because human beings are involved in these areas, morality may also be involved. A mathematics problem is neither moral nor immoral in itself; however, if it provides the means by which a hydro-gen bomb can be exploded, then moral issues will certainly be forthcoming.

In summary, then, the immoral person knowingly violates human moral standards by doing something wrong or by being bad. The amoral person may also violate moral standards because he or she has no moral sense. Something that is nonmoral can neither be good nor bad nor do anything right or wrong because it simply does not fall within the scope of morality.

Approaches to the Study of Morality

Scientific, or Descriptive, Approach

There are two major approaches to the study of morality. The first is *scientific*, or *descriptive*, which is most often used in the social sciences and which, like ethics, deals with human behavior and conduct. The emphasis here, however, is empir-ical; that is, social scientists observe and collect data about human behavior and conduct and then draw certain conclusions. For example, psychologists, after having observed many human beings in many situations, have reached the con-clusion that human beings often act in their own self-interest. This is a descrip-tive, or scientific, approach to human behavior—the psychologists have observed how human beings act in many situations, *described* what they have observed, and drawn conclusions. However, they make no value judgments about what's morally right or wrong, nor do they prescribe how humans ought to behave.

Philosophical Approach

The second major approach to the study of morality is called the *philosophical* approach and consists of two parts.

Normative, or Prescriptive, Ethics. The first part of the philosophical approach deals with norms (or standards) and prescriptions.

Using the example that human beings often act in their own self-interest, normative ethical philosophers would go beyond the description and conclusion of the psychologists and would want to know whether human beings *should* or *ought to* act in their own self-interest. They might even go further and come up with a definite conclusion—for example, "Given these arguments and this evidence, human beings should always act in their own self-interest" (egoism). Or they might say, "Human beings should always act in the interest of others" (altruism), or "Human beings should always act in the interest of all concerned, self included" (utilitarianism). These three conclusions are no longer merely descriptions but *prescriptions*; that is, the statements are *prescribing* how human beings *should* behave, not merely *describing* how they *do*, in fact, behave.

Another aspect of normative, or prescriptive, ethics is that it encompasses the making of moral value judgments rather than just the presentation or description of facts or data. For example, such statements as "Abortion is immoral" or "Lupe is a morally good person" may not *prescribe* anything, but they do involve *normative* moral value judgments, which we all make every day of our lives.

Metaethics, or Analytic Ethics. The second part of the philosophical approach to the study of ethics is called *metaethics* or, sometimes, *analytic ethics*. Rather than being descriptive or prescriptive, this approach is analytic in two ways. First, metaethicists analyze ethical language (for example, what we mean when we use the word *good*). Second, they analyze the rational foundations for ethical systems or the logic and reasoning of various ethicists. Metaethicists do not prescribe anything, nor do they deal directly with normative systems. Instead, they go beyond (a key meaning for the Greek prefix *meta-*), concerning themselves only indirectly with normative ethical systems by concentrating on reasoning, logical structures, and language rather than on content.

It should be noted here that metaethics, although always used to some extent by all ethicists, has become the sole interest of many ethical philosophers in the twentieth century. This may be due in part to the increasing difficulty of formulating a system of ethics applicable to all or even most human beings. Our world, our cultures, and our lives have become more and more complicated and pluralistic, and finding an ethical system that will undergird all human beings' actions is a difficult if not impossible task. Therefore, these philosophers feel that they might as well do what other specialists have done and concentrate on language and logic rather than attempt to arrive at ethical systems to help human beings live together more meaningfully and ethically.

Synthesis of Approaches

At this point, I would like to make a commitment that will permeate this book, and that commitment is to a reasonable synthesis. By synthesis I mean a uniting of opposing positions into a whole in which neither position loses itself completely, but the best or most useful parts of both are brought out through a basic principle that will apply to both. There are, of course, conflicts that cannot be synthesized—you cannot synthesize the German dictator Adolf Hitler's position of genocide with any ethical system that stresses the value of life for all human beings—but many can be. For example, later in the book we will see how the views of atheists and agnostics can be synthesized with those of theists in an ethical system that relates to all of them. We will also discover how two major divergent views in normative ethics—the consequentialist and the nonconsequentialist (these terms will be defined later)—can be synthesized into a meaningful ethical world view.

The point, however, is that a complete study of ethics demands use of the descriptive, the normative, *and* the metaethical approaches. It is important for ethicists to draw on any and all data and on valid results of experiments from the natural, physical, and social sciences. They must also examine their language, logic, and foundations. But it seems to me even more crucial for ethicists to contribute something toward helping all human beings to live with each other more meaningfully and more ethically. If philosophy cannot contribute to this latter imperative, then human ethics will either be decided haphazardly by each individual for himself or by unexamined religious pronouncements. My own commitment, then, is to a synthesis of descriptive, normative, and analytic ethics, with heavy emphasis on putting ethics to use in the human community, which means a heavier emphasis on the normative.

Morality and Its Applications

What Is Morality?

So far, we have discussed terminology and approaches to studying morality, but we have yet to discover exactly what morality is. The full definition of morality, as with other complex issues, will reveal itself gradually as we proceed through this book. In this chapter, however, I will try to make some important distinctions and to arrive at a basic working definition of morality.

Ethics and Aesthetics. There are two areas of study in philosophy having to do with values and value judgments in human affairs. The first is ethics, or the study of morality—what is good, bad, right, or wrong in a *moral* sense. The second is aesthetics, or the study of art and the artistic, of the beautiful and the nonbeautiful—what is good, bad, right, or wrong in art and what constitutes what is beautiful or not beautiful in our lives. There can, of course, be some overlap between the two areas. For example, one can judge Pablo Picasso's painting *Guernica* from an artistic point of view, deciding whether it is beautiful or ugly or whether it constitutes good or bad art in terms of artistic technique. One can also discuss its moral import—that in it Picasso makes moral comments on the cruelty and immorality of war and the inhumanity of people toward one another. Essentially, however, when we say that a person is attractive or homely and when we say that a sunset is beautiful or a dog is ugly or that a painting is great or its style mediocre, we are speaking in terms of aesthetic rather than moral or ethical values.

Good, Bad, Right, and Wrong Used in a Nonmoral Sense. The same words we use in a moral sense are also often used in nonmoral senses. The aesthetic use described previously is one of them. And when, for example, we say that a dog or a knife is good or that a car runs badly, we are often using these value terms (good, bad, and so on) in neither an aesthetic nor a moral sense. In calling a dog good, we do not mean that the dog is morally good or even beautiful; we probably mean that it does not bite or that it barks only when strangers threaten us or that it performs well as a hunting dog. When we say that a car runs badly or that a knife is good, we mean there is something mechanically (but not morally or aesthetically) wrong with the car's engine or that the knife is sharp and cuts well. In short, what we usually mean by such a statement is that the thing in question is good because it can be used to fulfill some kind of function; that is, it is in "good" working order or is trained well.

It is interesting to note that Aristotle (384–322 BC) argued that being moral had to do with the function of a human being, and that in developing his argument he moved from the nonmoral to the moral uses of "good" and "bad." He suggested that anything that was good or bad was so because it functioned well or poorly. He then went on to say that if we could discover what the function of human beings is, then we would know how the terms *good* or *bad* could be applied to humans. Having arrived at the theory that the proper function of human beings was to reason, he concluded that being moral was therefore "reasoning well for a complete life."

Over the years, many questions have been raised concerning this theory. Some question whether Aristotle truly managed to pinpoint the function of humans (for example, some religious sects hold that a human's primary function is to serve God). Others question whether being moral can be directly tied only to functioning. But the point of this discussion is that terms used in moral discourse are also often used nonmorally, and neither Aristotle nor anyone else really meant to say that these terms, when applied to such things as knives, dogs, or cars, have anything directly to do with what is moral or what is ethical.

Morals and Manners, or Etiquette. Manners, or etiquette, is another area of human behavior that is closely allied with ethics and morals, but careful distinctions must be made between these terms. There is no doubt that morals and ethics have a great deal to do with certain types of human behavior. Not all human behavior can be classified as moral, however; some of it is nonmoral, and some of it is social, having to do with *manners*, or etiquette, which are essentially a matter of taste rather than of right or wrong. Often, of course, these distinctions may blur or overlap, but it is important to distinguish as much as we can between nonmoral and moral behavior and that which has to do with manners alone.

Let us take an example from everyday life: An employer gives a secretary a routine business letter to type. Both the act of giving the letter to the secretary and the secretary's act in typing it involve nonmoral behavior. Let us now suppose that the employer uses four-letter words in talking to the secretary and is loud and rude in front of all of the employees in the office. What the employer has done, essentially, is to exhibit poor *manners*; he or she has not really done anything immoral. Swearing and rudeness may be wrong, but they are basically an offense to taste rather than a departure from morality.

Let us now suppose, however, that the contents of the letter would ruin an innocent person's reputation or result in someone's death or loss of livelihood. The behavior now falls into the sphere of morality, and questions must be raised about the morality of the employer's behavior. Also, a moral problem arises for the secretary concerning whether he or she should or should not type the letter. Further, if the employer uses four-letter words to intimidate or sexually harass the secretary, then he or she is being immoral by threatening the employee's sense of personal safety, privacy, integrity, and professional pride.

Nonmoral behavior constitutes a great deal of the behavior we see and perform every day of our lives. We must, however, always be aware that our nonmoral behavior may have moral implications. For example, typing a letter is, in itself, nonmoral, but if typing and mailing it will result in someone's death, then morality enters the picture.

In the realm of manners, behavior such as swearing, eating with one's hands, and dressing sloppily may be acceptable in some situations but is considered bad manners in others. Such behavior would seldom be considered immoral, however. I do not mean to imply that there is *no* connection between manners and morals, only that there is no *necessary* connection between them. Generally speaking, in our society we feel good manners go along with good morals, and we assume that if people are taught to behave correctly in social situations they will also behave correctly in moral situations.

It is often difficult, however, to draw a direct connection between behaving in a socially acceptable manner and being moral. Many decadent members of societies past and present have acted with impeccable manners and yet have been highly immoral in their treatment of other people. It is, of course, generally desirable for human beings to behave with good manners toward one another and *also* to be moral in human relationships. But in order to act morally or to bring to light a moral problem, it may at times be necessary to violate the "manners" of a particular society. For example, several years ago, in many elements of our society it was considered bad manners (and was, in some areas, illegal) for nonwhite people to eat in the same area of a restaurant as white people. In the many sit-ins held in these places, manners were violated in order to point out and try to solve the moral problems of inequality of treatment and denial of dignity to human beings.

Therefore, there may at times be a connection between manners and morals, but one must be careful to distinguish between the two when there is no clear connection. One must not equate, for example, the use of four-letter words in mixed company with rape or murder or dishonesty in business.

To Whom or What Does Morality Apply?

In discussing the application of morality, four aspects may be considered: religious morality, morality and nature, individual morality, and social morality.

Religious Morality. Religious morality refers to a human being in relationship to a supernatural being or beings. In the Jewish and Christian traditions, for example, the first three of the Ten Commandments (see Figure 1–1) pertain to this kind of morality. These commandments deal with a person's relationship with God, not with any other human beings. By violating any of these three commandments, a person could, according to this particular code of ethics, act immorally toward God without acting immorally toward anyone else.

Morality and Nature. Morality and nature refers to a human being in relationship to nature. Natural morality has been prevalent in all primitive cultures, such as that of the Native American, and in cultures of the Far East. More recently, the Western tradition has also become aware of the significance of dealing with nature in a moral manner. Some see nature as being valuable only for the good of humanity, but many others have come to see it as a good in itself, worthy of moral consideration. With this viewpoint there is no question about

The Ten Commandments

1. I am the Lord, your God; do not worship false gods.
2. Do not take the name of God in vain.
3. Keep holy the Sabbath Day.
4. Honor your father and your mother.
5. Do not kill.
6. Do not commit adultery.
7. Do not steal.
8. Do not bear false witness against your neighbor.
9. Do not covet your neighbor's spouse.
10. Do not covet your neighbor's belonging's.

(Exod. 20:1–17)

Figure 1–1. A paraphrased version of the Ten Commandments.

whether a Robinson Crusoe would be capable of moral or immoral actions on a desert island by himself. In the morality and nature aspect, he could be considered either moral or immoral, depending upon his actions toward the natural things around him.

Individual Morality. Individual morality refers to individuals in relation to themselves and to an individual code of morality that may or may not be sanctioned by any society or religion. It allows for a "higher morality," which can be found within the individual rather than beyond this world in some supernatural realm. A person may or may not perform some particular act, not because society, law, or religion says he may or may not, but because he himself thinks it is right or wrong from within his own conscience.

For example, Sophocles' Antigone opposes Creon because of God's higher law; but the Antigone in Jean Anouilh's play opposes Creon not because of God's law, of which she claims no knowledge, but because of her own individual convictions about what is the right thing to do in dealing with human beings, even dead human beings. This aspect can also refer to that area of morality concerned with obligations individuals have to themselves (to promote their own well-being, to develop their talents, to be true to what they believe, and so on). Commandments 9 and 10, although also applicable to social morality, as we shall see in a moment, are good examples of at least an exhortation to individual morality. "Do not covet" would seem to be an internal control of each individual not to even think of stealing a neighbor's goods or spouse. It is interesting to speculate why there are no "don't covet" commandments against killing or lying, for example. At any rate, these commandments would seem to stress an individual as well as a social morality.

Social Morality. Social Morality concerns a human being in relation to other human beings. It is probably the most important aspect of morality in that it cuts across all of the other aspects and is found in more ethical systems than any of the others.

Returning briefly to the desert island example, most ethicists would probably state that Robinson Crusoe is incapable of any really moral or immoral action except toward himself and nature. Such action would be minimal when compared with the potential for morality or immorality if there were nine other people on the island whom he could subjugate, torture, or destroy. Many ethical systems would allow that what he would do to himself is strictly his business "as long as it doesn't harm anyone else."

The most important human moral issues arise for most ethicists when human beings come together in social groups and begin to conflict with one another. Even though the Jewish and Christian ethical systems, for example, importune human beings to love and obey God, both faiths, in all of their divisions and sects, have a strong social message. In fact, perhaps 70 to 90 percent of all of their admonitions are directed toward how one human being is to behave toward others. Jesus stated this message succinctly when He said that the two greatest commandments are to love God and to love your neighbor. These fall equally into the religious and social aspects, but observing the whole of Jesus' actions and preachings, one sees the greater emphasis on treating other human beings morally. He seems to say that if one acts morally toward other human beings, then one is automatically acting morally toward God. This is emphasized in one of Jesus' Last Judgment parables when He says (and I paraphrase), "Whatever you have done to the least of Mine [the lowest human beings], so have you done it to Me." Three of the Ten Commandments are directed specifically toward God, while seven are directed toward other human beings—the social aspect taking precedence. In other religions, such as Buddhism and Confucianism, the social aspect represents almost the total morality, with very little if any focus on the supernatural or religious aspect. Furthermore, everything that is directed toward the individual aspect is also often intended for the good of others in the individual's culture.

Nonreligious ethical systems, too, often stress the social aspect. Ethical egoism, which would seem to stress the individual aspect, says in its most commonly stated form, "*everyone* ought to act in his own self-interest," emphasizing the whole social milieu. Utilitarianism in all of its forms emphasizes the good of "all concerned" and, therefore, is obviously dealing with the social aspect. Nonconsequentialist, or deontological, theories such as Kant's (see Chapter 3) stress actions toward others more than any other aspect, even though the reasons for acting morally toward others are different from those of ethical egoism or utilitarianism. These theories will be dealt with in detail in Chapters 2 and 3. The important thing to note at this point is that most ethical systems, even the most individualistic or religious, will emphasize the social aspect either exclusively or much more than any of the other aspects.

How, then, are we to use these aspects? We may use them as effective distinctions that will allow us to think in the widest terms about the applicability of human ethics. In the spirit of synthesis, however, I would suggest that we hold these distinctions open in unity so that we can accept into a broad human ethics the religious, nature and morality, and the individual aspects, recognizing, nevertheless, that most ethical systems meet in the social aspect. We should, in other words, keep our eyes on the first three aspects while we stand firmly planted in the social aspect, where most human moral problems and conflicts occur.

Who Is Morally or Ethically Responsible? Who can be held morally or ethically responsible for their actions? All of the evidence we have gained to date compels us to say that morality pertains to human beings and only to human beings; all else is speculation. If one wants to attribute morality to supernatural beings, one has to do so on faith. If one wants to hold animals or plants morally responsible for destructive acts against each other or against humans, then one has to ignore most of the evidence that science has given us concerning the instinctual behavior of such beings and the evidence of our own everyday observations.

Recent experimentation with the teaching of language to animals suggests that they could develop some thought processes similar to those of humans. It is even possible that they might be taught morality in the future, as humans are now. If this were to occur, then animals could be held morally responsible for their actions. At the present time, however, most evidence seems to indicate that they, as well as plants, should be classified as either amoral or nonmoral—that is, they should be considered to have no moral sense or to be out of the moral sphere altogether.

Therefore, when we use the terms *moral* and *ethical*, we are using them in reference only to human beings. We do not hold a wolf morally responsible for killing a sheep, or a fox morally responsible for killing a chicken. We may kill the wolf or fox for having done this act, but we do not kill it because we hold the animal *morally* responsible. We do it because we don't want any more of our sheep or chickens killed. At this point in the world's history, only human beings can be moral or immoral, and therefore only human beings should be held morally responsible for their actions and behavior. There are, of course, limitations on when human beings can be held morally responsible, but the question of moral responsibility should not be brought up where nonhumans are involved.

◆————————————————————————————————————

Where Does Morality Come From?

There always has been a great deal of speculation about where morality or ethics comes from. Has it always been a part of the world, originating from some supernatural being or imbedded within nature itself, or is it strictly a product of the minds of human beings? Or is it some combination of two or all three of these? Because morality and ethics deal with values having to do with good, bad, right, and wrong, are these values totally objective—that is, "outside of" human beings? Are they subjective or strictly "within" human beings? Or are they a combination of the two? Let us consider the possibilities.

Values as Totally Objective

There are three ways of looking at values being totally objective:

1. They come from some supernatural being or beings.
2. There are moral laws somehow embedded and found in nature itself.
3. The world and objects in it have value with or without the presence of valuing human beings.

The Supernatural Theory. Some people believe that values come from some higher or supernatural being, beings, or principle—the Good (Plato), the gods (the Greeks and Romans), Yahweh or God (the Jews), God and His Son, Jesus (the Christians), Allah (the Muslims), and Brahma (the Hindus), to name a few. They believe, further, that these beings or principles embody the highest good themselves and that they reveal to human beings what is right or good and what is bad or wrong. If human beings want to be moral (and they are usually encouraged in such desires by some sort of temporal or eternal reward), then they must follow these principles or the teachings of these beings. If they don't, then they will end up being disobedient to the highest morality (God, for example), will be considered immoral, and will usually be promised some temporal or eternal punishment for their transgressions. Or, if they believe in a principle rather than a supernatural being or beings, they will be untrue to the highest moral principle.

The Natural Law Theory. Others believe that morality is somehow embodied in nature and that there are "natural laws" that human beings must adhere to if they are to be moral. (St. Thomas Aquinas, 1225–1274, argued for this as well as for the supernatural basis for morality, and so did Immanuel Kant, 1724–1804.) For example, some people will state that homosexuality is immoral because it goes against "natural moral law"—that is, it is against nature for beings of the same sex to sexually desire or love one another or to engage in sexual acts.

Values as Totally Subjective

In opposition to these arguments, there are those who would argue that morality stems strictly from within human beings. That is, they believe that things can have values and be classed as good, bad, right, or wrong if and only if there is some conscious being who can put value on these things. In other words, if there are no human beings, then there can be no values.

Evaluation of Objective and Subjective Positions

Criticisms of the Supernatural Theory. It is, of course, possible that the supernatural exists and that it somehow communicates with the natural world and the human beings in it. This, however, is only a belief, based on faith, and there is no *conclusive* proof of the existence of a supernatural being, beings, or principle. Also, there are a great number of highly diverse traditions describing such beings or principles. This diversity makes it very difficult to determine exactly what values the beings or principles are trying to communicate and which values, communicated through the many traditions, human beings should accept and follow. All of this does not mean that we should stop searching for the truth or for verification of the possibility of supernaturally based values, but it does mean that it is difficult to establish with any certainty that morality comes from this source.

Criticisms of the Natural Law Theory. On the other hand, we certainly talk about "laws of nature," such as the law of gravity, but if we examine such laws closely, we see that they are quite different from man-made laws having to do with morality or the governing of societies. The law of gravity, for example, says, in effect, that all material objects are drawn toward the center of the earth: If we throw a ball into the air, it will always fall back down to the ground. Sir Isaac Newton discovered that this phenomenon occurred every time an object was subjected to gravity's pull, and he described this constant recurrence by calling it a "law of nature." The key word in this process is "described," for so-called natural laws are *descriptive*, whereas moral and societal laws are *prescriptive*. In other words, the natural law does not say that the ball, when thrown into the air, *should* or *ought to* fall to the ground, as we say that human beings *should not* or *ought not* kill other human beings. Rather, the law of gravity says that the ball *does* or *will* fall when thrown, describing rather than prescribing its behavior.

The question we should ask at this point is, "Are there any natural *moral* laws that *prescribe* how beings in nature should or ought to behave or not behave?" If there are, I do not know what they would be. I mentioned earlier that homosexuality is considered by some to be "unnatural" or "against the laws of nature," a belief that implies the conviction that only heterosexual behavior is "natural." If, however, we examine all aspects of nature, we discover that heterosexuality is not the only type of sexuality that occurs in nature. Some beings in nature are asexual (have no sex at all), some are homosexual (animals as well as humans), and many are bisexual (engaging in sexual behavior with both male and female of the species). Human beings, of course, may wish to *prescribe*, for one reason or another, that homosexual or antiheterosexual behavior is wrong, but it is difficult to argue that there is some "law of nature" that prohibits homosexuality.

Criticisms of Values Existing in the World and Its Objects. Is it feasible or even possible to think of something having a value without there being someone to value it? What value do gold, art, science, politics, or music have without human beings around to value them? After all, except for gold, didn't human beings invent or create them all? It seems, then, almost impossible for values to totally exist in the world and in things themselves.

Criticism of the Subjective Position. Must we then arrive at the position that values are entirely subjective and that the world in all of its aspects would have absolutely no value if there were no human beings living in it? Let us try to imagine objectively a world without any human beings in it. Is there nothing of value in the world and nature—air, water, earth, sunlight, the sea—unless human beings are there to appreciate it? Certainly, whether or not human beings exist, plants and animals would find the world "valuable" in fulfilling their needs. They would find "value" in the warmth of the sun and the shade of the trees, in the food they ate and the water that quenched their thirst. It is true that many things in the world, such as art, science, politics and music, are valued only by human beings, but there are also quite a few things that are valuable whether human beings are around or not. So it would seem that values are not entirely subjective any more than they are entirely objective.

Values as Both Subjective and Objective—A Synthesis. It would seem that at least some values reside outside of human beings, even though perhaps many more are dependent on conscious human beings, who are able to value things. Therefore, it would seem that values are more complex than either the subjective or the objective position can describe and that a better position to take is that values are both objective *and* subjective. A third variable should be added so that there is an interaction of three variables as follows:

1. The thing of value, or the thing valued.
2. A conscious being who values, or the valuer.
3. The context or situation in which the valuing takes place.

17

For example, gold in itself has value in its mineral content and in that it is bright, shiny, and malleable. However, when seen by a human being and discovered to be rare, it becomes—in the context of its beauty and in its role as a support for world finances—a much more highly valued item than it is in itself. Its fullest value, then, depends not only on its individual qualities but on some conscious being who is valuing it in a specific context or situation. Needless to say, gold is one of those things whose value is heavily dependent on subjective valuing. Note, however, that gold's value would change if the context or situation did. For example, suppose someone were stranded on a desert island without food, water, or human companionship but with one hundred pounds of gold. Wouldn't gold's value have dropped considerably given the context or situation in which food, water, and human companionship were missing and which no amount of gold could purchase? This shows how the context or situation can affect values and valuing.

Where Does Morality Come From? A Theory. Values, then, would seem to come most often from a complex interaction between conscious human beings and "things" (material, mental, or emotional) in specific contexts. But how can this discussion help us answer the question of where morality comes from? Any assumptions about the answer to the question of morality's origins certainly have to be speculative. Nevertheless, I believe that by observing how morality develops and changes in human societies, one can see that it has arisen largely from human needs and desires and that it is based on human emotions and reason.

It seems logical to assume that, as human beings began to become aware of their environment and of other beings like them, they found that they could accomplish more when they were bonded together than they could when isolated from one another. Through deep feelings and thoughts, and after many experiences, they decided upon "goods" and "bads" that would help them to live together more successfully and meaningfully. These beliefs needed sanctions, which were provided by high priests, prophets, and other leaders. Morality was tied by these leaders not only to *their* authority but to the authority of some sort of supernatural being or beings or to nature, which, in earlier times, were often considered inseparable.

For example, as I stated earlier, human beings are able to survive more successfully within their environment in a group than they can as isolated individuals. However, if they are to survive as a community, there must be some prohibition against killing. This can be arrived at either by a consensus of all of the people in the community or by action of the group's leaders. The leaders might provide further sanctions for the law against killing by informing the people that some supernatural being or beings, which may or may not be thought to operate through nature, state that killing is wrong.

It is also possible, of course, that a supernatural being or beings who have laid down such moral laws really exist. However, because most of these laws have in fact been delivered to human beings by other human beings (Moses, Jesus, Buddha, Muhammad, Confucius, and others), we can only say for sure that most of our morality and ethics comes from ourselves—that is, from human origins. All else is speculation or a matter of faith. At the very least, I would argue that morality and moral responsibility must be derived from human beings. Furthermore, I believe that people must decide what is right or good and what is wrong or bad by using both their experience and their best and deepest thoughts and feelings and by applying them as rationally and meaningfully as they can. This brings us to the important distinction between customary or traditional and reflective morality.

Customary or Traditional and Reflective Morality

Customary or Traditional Morality

We are all quite familiar with customary or traditional morality because we are all born into it; it is the first morality with which we come into contact. Morality that exists in various cultures and societies is usually based on custom or tradition, and it is presented to its members, often without critical analysis or evaluation, throughout their childhood and adult years. There is nothing necessarily wrong or bad about this approach to training the young of a society and also its members as a whole.

Many customs and traditions are quite effective and helpful in creating moral societies. As I suggested in the previous paragraph, many moral teachings have arisen out of human need in social interaction and have become customs and traditions in a particular society. For example, in order to live together creatively and in peace, one of the first moral teachings or rules has to be about taking human life because, obviously, if life is constantly in danger, then it is very difficult for people to live and work together. However, in order for customs and traditions to be effective and continuously applicable to the members of a society, they must be critically analyzed, tested, and evaluated, and this is where reflective morality comes in.

Reflective Morality

Philosophers in general demand of themselves and others that every human belief, proposition, or idea be examined carefully and critically to ensure that it has its basis in truth. Morality is no different from any other area of philosophic study in this respect. Philosophers do not suggest that custom and tradition be eliminated or thrown out, but they do urge human beings to use reason to examine the basis and effectiveness of all moral teachings or rules, no matter how traditional or accepted they are. In other words, philosophy requires human beings to reflect on their moral customs and traditions to determine whether they should be retained or eliminated. The great Greek philosopher Socrates (470?–399 BC) said, "The unexamined life is not worth living." For morality, a corollary might be, "The unexamined custom or tradition is not worth living by." Therefore, just as people should not accept statements or propositions for which there is no proof or significant logical argument, so they should not accept moral customs or traditions without first testing them against proof, reason, and their experience.

A good example of reflective morality is an examination of the aforementioned Ten Commandments, which many people in Western culture swear by and claim to follow. Interestingly enough, a good many people don't even know what most of them are, with the possible exception of the one against committing adultery, which everyone seems to know, and often cannot even list them in order or otherwise. Further, how many have examined them as I have suggested earlier and realized that they apply to different aspects of morality? How many people realize that the first three commandments apply only to human beings in relationship to a supernatural being or beings, that commandments four through eight apply to their relationships with others, whereas nine and ten basically apply to themselves as individuals?

It is important, then, that all customs, traditions, systems of ethics, rules, and ethical theories be carefully analyzed and critically evaluated before we continue to accept or live by them. Again, we should not reject them out of hand, but neither should we endorse them wholeheartedly unless we have subjected them to careful, logical scrutiny. As you have seen already, and as you will continue to see throughout the remaining chapters of this book, you are strongly encouraged to become reflective in dealing with morality and moral issues.

Morality, Law, and Religion

At this point, it is important that we use reflection to distinguish morality from two other areas of human activity and experience with which it is often confused and of which it is often considered a part: law and religion.

Morality and the Law

The phrase "unjust law" can serve as a starting point for understanding that laws can be immoral. We also have "shysters," or crooked lawyers, who are considered unethical within their own profession. The Watergate conspirators, almost to a man, were lawyers, and the men who tried and judged them were also lawyers. Obviously, morality and law are not *necessarily* one and the same thing when two people can be lawyers, both having studied a great deal of the same material, and one is moral, whereas the other is not. The many protests we have had throughout history against unjust laws, where more often than not the protestors were concerned with "what is moral" or a "higher morality," would also seem to indicate that distinctions must be made between law and morality.

Does all of this mean that there is no relationship between law and morality? Is law one thing that is set down by human beings and morality something else that they live by? Is there no connection between the two? A "yes" answer to these questions would be extremely hard to support because much of our morality has become embodied in our legal codes. All we have to do is review any of our legal statutes at any level of government, and we will find legal sanctions against robbing, raping, killing, and physical and mental mistreatment of others. We will find many other laws that attempt to protect individuals living together in groups from harm and to provide resolutions of conflicts arising from differences—many of them strictly moral—among the individuals composing these groups.

What, then, is the relationship between law and morality? Michael Scriven points out one important difference when he discusses the differences and distinctions among the Ten Commandments, which are some of the earlier laws of Western culture believed by Christians and Jews to have been handed down by God. Scriven distinguishes between the laws against coveting and the laws against killing, stealing, and adultery (see Figure 1–1). There is no way a law can regulate someone's desire for another man's wife or belongings as long as the adulterous act or the act of stealing is never carried out. Therefore, the statements about coveting contained in the Ten Commandments would seem to be moral admonitions of how one should think or maintain one's interior morality, whereas statements against stealing, killing, and adultery are laws, prohibitions against certain human acts that are in some way enforceable.[9]

The law provides a series of public statements—a legal code, or system of dos and don'ts—to guide humans in their behavior and to protect them from harm to their persons and property. Some laws have less moral import than others, but the relationship between law and morality is not equally reciprocal. What is moral is not necessarily legal and vice versa. That is, you can have morally unjust laws, as mentioned earlier. Also, certain human actions may be considered perfectly legal but be morally questionable.

For example, there were laws in certain parts of the United States that sanctioned the slavery of one human being to another, despite the fact that freedom and equality for all human beings is a strong basic principle of most ethical systems. It is an important principle in many societies, in theory if not always in action, and it is an important part of the United States Constitution that each individual within the society ought to have a certain amount of individual freedom and a definite moral equality. (This principle will be discussed more fully later.) If individual freedom and equality are considered moral, then laws preventing such morality must be immoral. In another example, there is no law against a large chain store's moving into an area and selling products at a loss in order to force the small store owners out of business. But many ethicists would make a case for the immorality of an action that would result in harm to the lives of the small store owners and their families.

At times, students in my classes have argued that the only thing keeping them from being immoral is fear of punishment, either from civil authorities, or from an all-powerful God. I cannot argue with them if they really feel that way, if they have such strong urges to kill, steal, and rape. However, many people that I know, including myself, do not kill, steal, or rape—not because of fear of punishment but because they believe these acts to be wrong (for any number of reasons). Even if all laws were abolished tomorrow, they would still consider such acts wrong and, wanting to be moral beings, would not perform them.

It should be obvious, then, that morality is not necessarily based on law. In fact, a study of history would probably indicate the opposite—that morality precedes law, whereas law sanctions morality; that is, law puts morality into a code or system that can then be enforced by reward or punishment. Perhaps the larger and more complex the society, the greater the necessity for laws, but it is not inconceivable that a moral society could be formed having no legal system at all—just a few basic principles of morality and an agreement to adhere to those principles. This is not to suggest that law should be eliminated from human affairs but rather to show that law is not a necessary attribute of morality.

Can law, however, do without morality? It would seem that morality provides the reasons for any significant laws governing human beings and their institutions. What would be the point of having laws against killing and stealing if there were not some concern that such acts were immoral? Very few laws have no moral import. Even laws controlling the incorporation of businesses, which do not seem to have any direct moral bearing on anyone, function at least to ensure fairness to all concerned—stockholders, owners, and employees. I cannot think of any law that does not have behind it some moral concern—no matter how minor or remote.

We can say, then, that law is the public codification of morality in that it lists for all members of a culture what has come to be accepted as the moral way to behave in that culture. Law also establishes what is the immoral way to act, and it sanctions—by its codification and by the entire judiciary process set up to form, uphold, and change parts of the code—the morality that it contains. The corrective for unjust laws, however, is not necessarily more laws but rather valid moral reasoning carried on by the people who live under the code.

Law is a public expression of social morality and is also its sanction. Law cannot in any way replace or substitute for morality, and therefore we cannot arbitrarily equate what is legal with what is moral. Many times the two "whats" will equate exactly, but many times they will not; and indeed many times what is legal will not, and perhaps should not, completely cover what is moral. For example, most ethicists today seem to agree that except for child molestation and forced sexuality of any kind, there should be no laws governing sexuality among consenting adults. Given this view, one can discuss adult sexual morality without bringing in legal issues. To summarize, it should be obvious that law serves to codify and sanction morality, but that without morality or moral import, law and legal codes are empty.

Morality and Religion

Can there be a morality without religion? Must a god or gods exist in order for there to be any real point to morality? If a people are not religious, can they ever be truly moral? And if the answer to these questions is yes, which religion is the real foundation for morality? There seem to be as many conflicts as there are different religions and religious viewpoints.

Religion is one of the oldest human institutions. We have little evidence that language existed in prehistoric times, but we do have evidence of religious practices, which were entwined with artistic expression, and of laws or taboos exhorting early human beings to behave in certain ways. In these earlier times, morality was embedded in the traditions, mores, customs, and religious practices of the culture.

Furthermore, religion served (as it has until quite recently) as a most powerful sanction for getting people to behave morally. That is, if behind a moral prohibition against killing rests the punishing and rewarding power of an all-powerful supernatural being or beings, then the leaders of a culture have the greatest possible sanction for the morality they want their followers to uphold. The sanctions of tribal reward and punishment pale beside the idea of a punishment or reward that can be more destructive or pleasurable than any that one's fellow human beings could possibly administer.

However, because religion may have preceded any formal legal or separate moral system in human history, or because it may have provided very powerful and effective sanctions for morality, does not at all prove that morality must of necessity have a religious basis. It is my contention that for many reasons morality need not, and indeed should not, be based *solely* on religion.

Difficulty of Proving Supernatural Existence. First, in order to prove that one must be religious in order to be moral, we would have to prove conclusively that a supernatural world exists and that morality exists there as well as in the natural world. Even if this could be proved, which is doubtful, we would have to show that the morality existing in the supernatural world has some connection with that which exists in the natural world. It seems obvious, however, that in dealing with morality, the only basis we have is this world, the people who exist in it, and the actions they perform.

One test of the truth of this reason would be to take any set of religious admonitions and ask honestly which of them would be absolutely necessary to the establishment of any moral society. For example, we might make a case for any of the Ten Commandments except the first three (see Figure 1–1). The first three may be a necessary set of rules for a Jewish or Christian community, but if a nonreligious community observed only Commandments four through ten, how, *morally* speaking, would the two communities differ—assuming that the religious community observed all ten of the Commandments? (One could probably find reasons for eliminating some of the other seven Commandments, too, but that is another issue.) I do not mean to imply that morality cannot be founded on religion; it is an obvious empirical fact that it has been, is, and probably will be in the future. I am saying that morality *need* not be founded on religion at all, and I would add that there is a danger of narrowness and intolerance if religion becomes the *sole* foundation for morality.

Nonreligious People Can Be Moral. If we can briefly characterize morality in this world as not harming or killing others and generally trying to make life and the world better for everyone and everything that exists (I will attempt to justify this contention later), and if many human beings do not accept the existence of a supernatural world and yet act as morally as anyone who does, then there must be some attributes other than religious belief that are necessary for one to be moral. (I will discuss what I feel these attributes are in a later chapter.) Although it is obvious that most religions contain ethical systems, it is not true that all ethical systems are religiously based; therefore, there is no *necessary* connection between morality and religion. The very fact that completely nonreligious people (for example, humanist ethicists) can evolve significant and consistent ethical systems is proof of this.

Difficulty of Providing a Rational Foundation. Providing a rational foundation for an ethical system is difficult enough without also having to provide a foundation for the religion that purportedly founds the ethical system. And the difficulty of rationally founding most religious systems is inescapable. It is impossible to prove conclusively the existence of any supernature, afterlife, god, or gods. I will not go into the traditional and modern arguments for the existence or nonexistence of a god or gods here, but will merely state that there is no conclusive evidence that such beings do or do not exist.[10] Therefore, if no evidence is conclusive and none of the arguments' logic is irrefutable, then the existence of a supernatural world, an afterlife, a god, or gods, is at least placed in the category of the unproven. This, of course, does not mean that many people will not continue to believe in their existence, basing their belief on faith, fear, hope, or their reading of the evidence but as a logical foundation for morality, religion is weak indeed.

If one maintains that we are moral (or should be) because a being exists who is all-good or because we will be rewarded or punished in another life, and the existence of these things cannot be proved, then the entire system is based on unproved assumptions. Believing that God or an afterlife exists may make people "feel" better about acting in certain ways. It may also provide powerful sanctions for acting morally or not acting immorally. But it does not provide a valid, rational foundation for morality that can give us reasons, evidence, and logic for acting one way rather than another. Again, as Michael Scriven has stated, "Religion can provide a psychological but not a logical foundation for morality."[11] Can there be any better foundation for morality than religion? Obviously, I think there can be, and I will attempt to present such a foundation later.

Which Religion? Even if religions could be rationally founded, which religion should be the basis of human ethics? Within a particular religion that question is answered, but it is obviously not answered satisfactorily for members of other conflicting religions or for those who do not believe in any religion. Even if the supernatural tenets of religions could be conclusively proved, which religion are we to accept as the true or real foundation of morality? It is certainly true that different religions have many ethical prescriptions in common—for example, not killing—but it is also true that there are many conflicting ones.

Among different sects of Christianity, for example, there are many conflicting ethical statements concerning sex, war, divorce, abortion, marriage, stealing, and lying. How, if they all believe in God and Jesus and their teachings, can there be so many divergent opinions on what is moral or immoral? The obvious answer is that there can be many interpretations of those teachings as set down in the Bible or otherwise passed down through tradition. But what gives a Roman Catholic, for instance, the right to tell a Methodist that his interpretation of Jesus' teachings is wrong? There can be no adjudication here—only referral to passages in the Bible, many of which are open to different interpretations or even to some teaching not held by either of the differing sects. In short, there simply is no rational basis for resolving serious conflicts when they exist.

The difficulty is underscored even more when we consider that people who believe there is no God or supernatural or afterlife (atheists) or people who are not sure (agnostics) are essentially excluded from moral consideration. If such people do not believe, or neither believe nor disbelieve, then how can any of the moral precepts set down within any particular religion have any application to them? They are automatically excluded from the moral sphere created by the ethics of religion. Provisions are, of course, made within each religion for nonbelievers, but these provisions very often involve some sort of eventual conversion to that religion or, frequently, some patronizing statement about loving one's enemies as well as one's friends.

Difficulty of Resolving Conflicts. How do we resolve the conflicts arising from various religiously based ethical systems without going outside of all religions for some more broadly based human system of morality—some wider base from which to make ethical decisions? When such resolutions are successful, it is usually because we have gone beyond any particular religion's ethical system and used some sort of rational compromise or broader ethical system that cuts across all religious and nonreligious lines. I urge that we pursue this approach more strongly and consistently than we have.

Furthermore, I believe that we can establish a system and method by which this can be done. But in order to accomplish this, all people, religious or nonreligious, must be willing to accept an essentially nonreligiously based overall ethical system within which many of their own moral rules and methods can function successfully. My answer to the question of how we resolve moral conflicts without going outside the narrow boundaries of religion is simple—we don't. We must establish a basis for morality from outside religion, but it must be one in which religion is included. This is, I feel, a necessary first step toward a moral society and a moral world. The foregoing statements and questions enable us, at the very least, to see that the relationship between morality and religion is, as Michael Scriven has said, "a very uneasy one indeed."[12]

In summary, then, just what is the connection between religion and morality? The answer is that there is no *necessary* connection. One can have a complete ethical system without mention of any life but this one—no god or gods, no supernatural, no afterlife. Does this mean that to be moral we must avoid religion? Not at all. Human beings should be allowed to believe or disbelieve as long as there is some moral basis that protects all people from immoral treatment at the hands of the religious and nonreligious alike. A religion that advocates the human sacrifice of unwilling participants, for example, would not be moral because it deprives others of their lives. A religion that persecutes all who do not accept its tenets is equally immoral and should not be allowed to exist in that form under a broad moral system. If, however, religions can agree to some broad moral principles and their members can act in accordance with those principles, then they can exist with nonreligious people and still serve their principles meaningfully and well.

One last point about religion and morality is that religion, for most people who are involved with it, is much more than an ethical system. For example, because Christians believe that there is a being far worthier of their love than any being in the natural world, it is their relationship with this being that is of uppermost importance to them, rather than how they act within the natural world. In this sense, religion is more than (or other than) an ethical system.

26

Considering all of the differences that exist among religions and between religionists and nonreligionists, I feel a greater emphasis should be placed on a wider-based morality that allows these differences and personal religious relationships to continue and develop, while at the same time allowing for ethical attitudes and actions toward all. What we need is not a strictly religious or a strictly humanist (atheist) ethics but rather what I choose to call a *humanitarian* ethics, which includes these two extremes and the middle ground as well.

Why Should Human Beings Be Moral?

Before going on to discuss ethical or moral systems in greater detail, there is one last question that I feel must be dealt with in this chapter, and that is, "Why should human beings be moral?" Another way of putting the problem is as follows: Is there any clear foundation or basis for morality—can any reasons be found for human beings to be good and do right acts rather than be bad and do wrong acts? I want to make it clear at the start that the question I am asking is not "Why should *I* or any one individual be moral?" As Kai Nielsen says in his brilliant essay "Why Should I Be Moral?" these are two different questions.[13] The second one is very difficult to answer with any clear, conclusive evidence or logic, but the first one is not.

I have already pointed out the difficulties of founding morality on religion, and especially on religion as a sole factor. However, if a person has religious faith, then he or she does have a foundation for a personal morality, even though this foundation is basically psychological rather than logical in nature. What disturbs me about the use of religion as the foundation of morality is the frequently made assumption that if there is no supernatural or religious basis for morality, then there can be no basis at all. A related, and perhaps deeper, statement is that there can be no real meaning to human life unless there is some sort of afterlife or some other extranatural reason for living. It is obvious that for many individuals this is psychologically true; that is, they feel that their existence has meaning and purpose and that they have a reason for being moral if and only if there is a god, an afterlife, or some sort of religion in their lives. I feel that we must respect this point of view and accept the conviction of the many people who hold it, because that is how they *feel* about life and morality.

It is also obvious, however, that many people do not feel this way. I think it is terribly presumptuous of religious believers to feel that if some people do not have a religious commitment their lives are meaningless, or that such people have no reason for being moral in their actions. But if religion does not necessarily provide a "why" for morality, then what does? Let us assume for the moment that there is no supernatural morality and see if we can find any other reasons why people should be moral.

Enlightened Self-Interest

One can certainly argue from enlightened self-interest that it is, at the very least, generally better to be good rather than bad and to create a world and society that is good rather than one that is bad. As a matter of fact, as we shall see in the next chapter, self-interest is the sole basis of one ethical theory, ethical egoism. I am not, however, suggesting at this point that one ought to pursue one's own self-interest. I am merely presenting the argument that if everyone tried to do and be good and to avoid and prevent bad, it would be in everyone's self-interest. For example, if within a group of people no one killed, stole, lied, or cheated, then each member of the group would benefit. An individual member of the group could say, "It's in my self-interest to do good rather than bad because I stand to benefit if I do, and also because I could be ostracized or punished if I don't." Therefore, even though it is not airtight (as Kai Nielsen's essay illustrates), the argument from enlightened self-interest is a somewhat compelling one.

Argument from Tradition and Law

Related to the foregoing argument is the argument from tradition and law. This argument suggests that because traditions and laws, established over a long period of time, govern the behavior of human beings, and because these traditions and laws urge human beings to be moral rather than immoral, there are good reasons for being so. Self-interest is one reason but another is respect for the human thought and effort that has gone into establishing such laws and traditions and transferring them from one historic period and one culture to another. This can be an attractive argument, even though it tends to suppress questioning of traditions and laws—a kind of questioning that is, I feel, the very touchstone of creative moral reasoning. It is interesting to note that most of us probably learned morality from being confronted with this argument, the religious argument, and the experiences surrounding them. Can't we all remember being told we should or should not do something because God said it was right or wrong, because it was or was not in our own self-interest, or because it is the way we were supposed to act in our family, school, society, and world?

Evolution of the Arguments

All of the arguments put forth are compelling and valid to some extent, provided that free questioning of the moral prescriptions that they have established or that they support is allowed and encouraged. I have already pointed out some of the difficulties with the religious basis for morality, but problems exist with the other two arguments as well. The self-interest argument can be a problem when other interests conflict with it; it is often difficult to convince someone who sees obvious benefits in acting immorally in a particular situation that it is in his or her self-interest to do otherwise. Morality established by tradition and law is problematic because it is difficult both to change and to question successfully. This lack of questioning sometimes encourages blind obedience to immoral practices. It encourages the belief that because something has been done a certain way for hundreds of years, it must be right. (A good example of this type of thinking can be found in Shirley Jackson's excellent, frequently anthologized short story "The Lottery.")

Common Human Needs

Are there any other reasons we can give why human beings should be moral? If we examine human nature as empirically and rationally as we can, we will discover that all human beings have many needs, desires, goals, and objectives in common. For example, people generally seem to need friendship, love, happiness, freedom, peace, creativity, and stability in their lives, not only for themselves but for others, too. It doesn't take much further examination to discover that in order to satisfy these needs, people must establish and follow moral principles that encourage them to cooperate with one another and that free them from fear that they will lose their lives, be mutilated, or be stolen from, lied to, cheated, severely restricted, or imprisoned.

It is my contention, then, that morality has come about because of human needs and through a recognition of the importance of living together in a cooperative and significant way. I am not trying to suggest that all human beings can be convinced that they should be moral, or even that it will always be in each individual's self-interest to be moral. I do believe, however, that the question "Why should human beings be moral?" *generally* can best be answered by the statement that adhering to moral principles enables human beings to live their lives as peacefully, happily, creatively, and meaningfully as is possible.

Morality—A Working Definition

I have said a great deal so far in this chapter about what morality or ethics is not, but I have not yet said what it is. In setting up a working definition, I would say that morality deals basically with humans and how they relate to other beings, both human and nonhuman. It deals with how humans *treat* other beings to promote mutual welfare, growth, creativity, and meaning in a striving for what is good over what is bad and what is right over what is wrong.

In the next two chapters, we will examine two major ethical viewpoints. These contain a number of traditional ethical theories that are concerned not with *why* human beings should be moral, but rather with *how* morality can be attained. There is no point in "starting from scratch" in the study of morality when we can benefit from our own ethical traditions, out of which almost all modern ethical theories have, in one way or another, evolved.

Chapter Summary

I. Philosophy, and ethics' relationship to it
    A. Philosophy literally means the love of wisdom.
    B. It is concerned with three areas of study:
        1. Epistemology—the study of knowledge, belief, truth, falsity, certainty, and perception.
        2. Metaphysics—the study of what exists, the nature of what exists, cause and effect, freedom, and determinism.
        3. Ethics—the study of morality, good, bad, right, wrong, human conduct and behavior in a moral sense, and moral issues.
II. Key terms
    A. *Moral* and *ethical* (and *immoral* and *unethical*) are interchangeable in ordinary language.
        1. Moral means what is good or right.
        2. Immoral means what is bad or wrong.
    B. Characteristics of "good, bad, right, wrong."
        1. "Good" or "right" should involve pleasure, happiness, and excellence and also lead to harmony and creativity.
        2. "Bad" or "wrong" will involve pain, unhappiness, and lack of excellence and will lead to disharmony and lack of creativity.
        3. The terms "good" and "bad" should be defined in the context of human experience and human relationships.
    C. *Amoral* means having no moral sense, or being indifferent to right and wrong.
    D. *Nonmoral* means out of the realm of morality altogether.
III. Approaches to the study of morality
    A. The scientific, or descriptive, approach is used in the social sciences and is concerned with how human beings do, in fact, behave. For example: Human beings often act in their own self-interest.
    B. The philosophical approach is divided into two categories.
        1. The normative, or prescriptive, is concerned with what "should" be or what people "ought to" do. For example: Human beings *ought to* act in their own self-interest.
        2. A second category is concerned with value judgments. For example: "Barbara is a morally good person."

3. Metaethics, or analytic ethics, is analytic in two ways.
   (a) It analyzes ethical language.
   (b) It analyzes the rational foundations for ethical systems or the logic and reasoning of various ethicists.

IV. Morality and its applications
   A. In the course of determining what morality is, some distinctions must be made.
      1. There is a difference between ethics and aesthetics.
         (a) Ethics is the study of morality, or of what is good, bad, right, or wrong in a moral sense.
         (b) Aesthetics is the study of art and the artistic, or of what is good, bad, right, or wrong in art and what constitutes what is beautiful in our lives.
      2. The terms good, bad, right, and wrong can also be used in a non-moral sense, usually in reference to how someone or something functions.
      3. Manners, or etiquette, differs from morality even though the two are related, in that manners is concerned with certain types of social behavior dealing with taste, whereas morality is concerned with ethical behavior.
   B. There are four main aspects related to the application of morality.
      1. Religious morality is concerned with human beings in relationship to a supernatural being or beings.
      2. Morality and nature is concerned with human beings in relationship to nature.
      3. Individual morality is concerned with human beings in relationship to themselves.
      4. Social morality is concerned with human beings in relationship to other human beings. This is the most important category of all.
   C. Evidence exists to help us determine who is morally or ethically responsible.
      1. Recent experimentation with communication with certain animals reveals that in the future animals might be taught to be moral.
      2. At the present time, however, humans and only humans can be considered to be moral or immoral, and therefore only they should be considered morally responsible.

V. Theories addressing where morality comes from
   A. There are three ways of looking at values being totally objective.
      1. Some people believe that values originate with a supernatural being or beings or principle.
      2. Some believe that values are embodied in nature itself—that is, that there are moral laws in nature.

      3. Some believe that the world and the objects in it have values whether or not there are human beings around.

  B. Some hold the theory that values are totally subjective: that morality and values are strictly within human beings and that there are no values or morality outside of them.

  C. One must evaluate these two conflicting positions.

      1. It is possible to criticize the position that values are objective.

         (a) It is difficult to prove conclusively the existence of any supernatural being, beings, or principle and to prove that values exist other than in the natural world.

         (b) There is a difference between "natural laws," which are descriptive, and "moral and societal laws," which are prescriptive, and there is no conclusive evidence that "natural moral laws" exist.

         (c) Is it really possible to think of things of value without someone to value them?

      2. It is possible to criticize the position that values are subjective. Because aspects of the world and nature can be valued whether or not human beings exist, values would not seem to be totally subjective.

  D. Values are both subjective and objective. They are determined by three variables.

      1. The first variable is the thing of value or the thing valued.

      2. The second is a conscious being who values—the valuer.

      3. The third is the context or situation in which the valuing takes place.

  E. Given the belief that values are both subjective and objective, it is possible to construct a theory concerning the origin of morality.

      1. It comes from a complex interaction between conscious human beings and material, mental, or emotional "things" in specific contexts.

      2. It stems from human needs and desires and is based on human emotions and reason.

VI. Customary or traditional and reflective morality

  A. Customary or traditional morality is based on custom or tradition and is often accepted without analysis or critical evaluation.

  B. Reflective morality is the careful examination and critical evaluation of all moral issues whether or not they are based on religion, custom, or tradition.

VII. Morality and the law

  A. Morality is not necessarily based on law.

  B. Morality provides the basic reasons for any significant laws.

   C. Law is a public expression of and provides a sanction for social morality.

VIII. Morality and religion

   A. Morality need not, indeed should not, be based *solely* on religion for the following reasons.

     1. It is difficult to prove conclusively the existence of a supernatural being.

     2. Nonreligious people can be moral, too.

     3. It is difficult to provide a rational foundation for religion, which makes it difficult to provide such a foundation for morality.

     4. If religion were to be the foundation of morality, which religion would provide this foundation and who would decide?

     5. There is a difficulty in resolving the conflicts arising from various religiously based ethical systems without going outside of them.

   B. We need a humanitarian ethics that is neither strictly religious nor strictly humanistic (atheistic) but that includes these two extremes and the middle ground as well.

IX. The importance of determining why human beings should be moral

   A. The question is not, "Why should any one individual be moral?" but rather, "Why should human beings in general be moral?"

   B. Various reasons for being moral have been posited.

     1. Religion, or the supernatural, has been used as the foundation of morality.

     2. It has been argued that enlightened self-interest is the basis for morality.

     3. Tradition and law have been posited as yet another basis for morality.

   C. There are problems with all the reasons given in A and B; therefore, it is my contention that morality has come about because of common human needs and through the recognition of the importance of living together in a cooperative and significant way in order to achieve the greatest possible amount of friendship, love, happiness, freedom, peace, creativity, and stability in the lives of all human beings.

X. A working definition of "morality." Morality or ethics deals basically with human relationships—how humans treat other beings to promote mutual welfare, growth, creativity, and meaning in striving for good over bad and right over wrong.

Exercises for Review

1. In your own words, define the following terms: *moral, immoral, amoral,* and *nonmoral.*

2. What is the difference between descriptive and normative or prescriptive ethics?

3. What is metaethics, or analytic ethics, and how does it differ from descriptive and normative or prescriptive ethics?

4. Explain the four aspects of morality.

5. Why is the social aspect the most important?

6. Do you agree that morality is not necessarily based on the law but that the law gets its real meaning from morality? Why or why not?

7. Give examples of how the law embodies morality.

8. What does it mean to say that the law provides "sanctions" for morality? How does it do this?

9. Do you believe that morality should or should not be based *solely on religion? Why?*

10. Critically examine the Ten Commandments in the following ways:

    (a) Separate them to show how they would fit into any of the four aspects of morality.

    (b) Which commandments are *absolutely necessary* for any society to be moral? Why?

    (c) Which commandments can be enforced legally and which cannot? Why?

11. Do you agree that we need a humanitarian ethics that includes both religious and nonreligious systems? Why or why not?

12. Do you agree with the author's list of characteristics of "good, bad, right, wrong"? If so, explain why in your own words. If not, explain why not. In either case, give any additional characteristics you think these terms have.

13. What are philosophy, epistemology, and metaphysics, and how do they differ from or relate to ethics?

14. What's the difference between customary or traditional morality and reflective morality?

Discussion Questions

1. Critically examine any ethical system or code (for example, a religious code or a code or system from business or any of the professions) and show how each of the dos or don'ts of this code apply to the various aspects of morality.

2. Go to the library or consult other sources at the discretion of your instructor and get a copy of your city's, country's, or state's laws governing a specific area of community activity. Analyze to what extent these laws relate to your community's moral views and standards and in what ways they do so. To what extent are any of the laws nonmoral or moral in their implications?

3. To what extent do you feel that human beings have an obligation to be moral in their dealings and relationships with nature (excluding other human beings) and for what reasons? Give specific examples of such dealings and relationships, and argue your position fully.

4. Do you think that human beings are essentially good, bad, or a combination of both? Why? In a well-organized essay, argue for and bring evidence to support the position you have taken. How does your position affect your approach to morality—for example, should a moral system be strict, clear, and absolutistic or permissive, flexible, and relativistic? (See Chapter 4 and Glossary for a definition of these terms.)

5. Do you believe that morality should or should not be based *solely* on religion? Why? Is it possible to establish a moral system without any reference to religion? If so, how? If not, why not? What could be the basis of such a system if not religion? Describe your position in detail.

6. Examine your own life and try to establish as honestly and accurately as possible where your values have come from.

7. Do you feel that you should always be moral? Why or why not? Do you think that human beings in general should be moral? Why or why not?

Notes

1. William K. Frankena, *Ethics*, 2nd ed. (Englewood Cliffs, N.J.: Prentice-Hall, 1973), 91.

2. Ibid.

3. Ibid.

4. Lester A. Kirkendall, *Premarital Intercourse and Interpersonal Relationships* (New York: Julian Press, 1961), 6.

5. Joseph Wambaugh, *The Onion Field* (New York: Dell, 1973).

6. Jean L. McKechnie, ed., *Webster's New Universal Unabridged Dictionary* (New York: Simon and Schuster, 1979), 1454.

7. Joseph Wambaugh, *The Blooding* (New York: Bantam, 1989), 325.

8. Ibid., 341.

9. Michael Scriven, "Rational Moral Education." Speech delivered at Bakersfield College, February 18, 1971.

10. See John H. Hick, *Philosophy of Religion* (Englewood Cliffs, N.J.: Prentice-Hall, 1973), 16–17, and John Hospers, *An Introduction to Philosophical Analysis* (Englewood Cliffs, N.J.: Prentice-Hall, 1967), 425–90, for a discussion of these arguments from the religious point of view (Hick) and the nonreligious (Hospers).

11. Scriven.

12. Ibid.

13. Kai Nielsen, "Why Should I Be Moral?" In *Problems of Moral Philosophy*, 2nd ed., ed. Paul W. Taylor (Belmont, Calif.: Dickenson, 1972), 539–58.

Supplementary Reading

Addleson, Kathryn P. *Impure Thoughts: Essays on Philosophy, Feminism, and Ethics*. Philadelphia: Temple University Press, 1991.

Almond, Brenda, and Donald Hill, eds. *Applied Philosophy: Morals and Metaphysics in Contemporary Debate*. New York: Routledge, 1991.

Cortese, Anthony J. *Ethnic Ethics: The Restructuring of Moral Theory*. Albany, N.Y.: State University of New York Press, 1990.

Dore, Clement. *Moral Skepticism*. New York: St. Martin's Press, 1991.

Falikowski, Anthony. *Moral Philosophy*. Englewood Cliffs, N.J.: Prentice-Hall, 1990.

Fischer, John M., and Mark Ravizza. *Ethics: Problems and Principles*. San Diego, Calif.: Harcourt, Brace, Jovanovich, 1992.

Frazer, Elizabeth, et al. *Ethics: A Feminist Reader*. Cambridge, England: Blackwell Publishers, 1992.

Harris, C. E., Jr. *Applying Moral Theories*, 2nd ed. Belmont, Calif.: Wadsworth Publishers, 1992.

Hick, John. *Philosophy of Religion*, 3rd ed. Englewood Cliffs, N.J.: Prentice-Hall, 1983.

Hospers, John. *An Introduction to Philosophical Analysis*, 2nd ed. Englewood Cliffs, N.J.: Prentice-Hall, 1967.

Manning, Rita C. *Speaking from the Heart: A Feminist Perspective on Ethics*. Vantage, N.Y.: Rowman, 1992.

Miller, Richard W. *Moral Differences: Truth, Justice, and Conscience in a World of Conflict*. Princeton, N.J.: Princeton University Press, 1992.

Outka, Gene, and John P. Reeder, Jr., eds. *Religion and Morality*. Garden City, N.Y.: Anchor Press/Doubleday, 1973.

Runkle, Gerald. *Ethics: An Examination of Contemporary Moral Problems*. New York: Holt, Rinehart and Winston, 1982.

Scriven, Michael. *Primary Philosophy*. New York: McGraw-Hill, 1966.

Taylor, Paul, W., ed. *Problems of Moral Philosophy*, 2nd ed. Belmont, Calif.: Dickenson, 1972.

Titus, Harold H., Marilyn S. Smith, and Richard Nolan. *Living Issues in Philosophy*, 8th ed. Belmont, Calif.: Wadsworth, 1987.

Wall, George B. *Introduction to Ethics*. Columbus, Ohio: Charles E. Merrill, 1974. Chapter 2.

Wallace, James D. *Moral Relevance and Moral Conflict*. New York: Cornell University Press, 1988.

Wasserstrom, Richard A., ed. *Morality and the Law*. Belmont, Calif.: Wadsworth, 1971.

Consequentialist (Teleological) Theories of Morality

Objectives

After you have read this chapter you should be able to

1. Define the consequentialist (teleological) and nonconsequentialist (deontological) views of morality.
2. Differentiate psychological egoism from ethical egoism and explain both theories.
3. Distinguish the three types of ethical egoism.
4. Describe and critically analyze the two main consequentialist theories, ethical egoism and utilitarianism.
5. Distinguish between the two types of utilitarianism.

In the history of ethics, two major viewpoints emerge: the *consequentialist* (based on or concerned with consequences) and the *nonconsequentialist* (not based on or concerned with consequences). Traditionally these have been called the teological and deontological theories, respectively, but I will refer to them as consequentialist and nonconsequentialist because these words pinpoint the real differences between the two theories.

The two major consequentialist ethical theories are ethical egoism and utilitarianism. They both agree that human beings ought to behave in ways that will bring about good consequences. They differ, however, in that they disagree on who should benefit from these consequences. The ethical egoist essentially says that human beings ought to act in their own self-interest, whereas utilitarians essentially say that human beings ought to act in the interests of all concerned.

Suppose John has a chance to embezzle some funds from the company for which he works. If he is a consequentialist, he will try to predict the consequences of embezzling and not embezzling. If he is an egoistic consequentialist, he will try to predict what will be in his own best interest; if he is a utilitarian consequentialist, he will try to predict what will be in the interest of everyone concerned. On first learning about ethical egoism some people immediately assume that if a person like John adheres to this theory he will embezzle the funds, because doing so will give him money to live a good life and so forth. However, it is interesting to note that both ethical egoists and utilitarians might decide, from their opposite approaches to consequences, not to embezzle the money. Ethical egoists might not think it is in their self-interest to break the law or anger the company and its stockholders or subject themselves to the risk of punishment for their action. Utilitarians, on the other hand, might arrive at the same conclusion, but on the grounds that embezzlement would bring bad consequences to other people involved in the company even though it might bring good consequences to them. Just as egoists and utilitarians might end up acting in the same way for different reasons, so their ethical reasoning is also similar in that they are both concerned with the consequences of any action they are contemplating. It is important now to examine each ethical theory more thoroughly, noting advantages and disadvantages and examining their similarities and differences.

Psychological Egoism

Before discussing ethical egoism in more detail, we should make a distinction between psychological egoism, which is *not* an ethical theory, and ethical egoism. Some ethical egoists have tried to base their egoistic theories on psychological egoism, so it is important to examine whether it is a valid concept and to make sure we know the difference between how people *do* act and how they *should* act. In Chapter 1, I used psychological egoism to point out the difference between the scientific and the normative philosophical approaches to morality: to reiterate, psychological egoism is a scientific, descriptive approach to egoism, whereas ethical egoism is the philosophical-normative prescriptive approach.

Psychological egoism may be divided into two forms. The strong form maintains that people *always* act in their own self-interest—that they are psychologically constructed to do so—whereas, the weak form maintains that people often, but not always, act in their own self-interest. Neither form can operate as a basis for ethical egoism, however. If the strong form is accepted, then why tell people to do what they cannot help doing? If I am psychologically constructed to always act in my own self-interest, what good will it do to tell me that I *should* always act in my own self-interest? As for the weaker form, stating that I often *do* act in my own self-interest has nothing in itself to do with what I *should* do. (This is referred to in ethics as trying to get "an *ought* from an *is*"—there is no logical argument that conclusively proves that because people *are* behaving in certain ways, they *should* do so or continue to do so.) One might be able to show by some rational argument that I should always act in my own self-interest, but that I do so is neither necessary (absolutely necessary) nor sufficient (enough) argument that I should.

What about the truth of the stronger form of the argument? If human beings indeed must act in their own self-interest and cannot do otherwise, then we are condemned to the egoistic position. Is there any conclusive proof that strong psychological egoism holds true? In order to make an all-encompassing, absolute, universal statement using "always" in connection with human motives and behavior, which are both complex and varied, we would have to be able to examine every single human being's motives and behavior before we could prove such a statement conclusively.

It is presumptuous for psychological egoists to argue that I always act in my own self-interest if I can give them an example of even one time when I did not. They certainly can devise a number of ways to show that everything I do is for some reason that is ultimately in my own self-interest. I may tell them, "Look, when I disregarded my own safety and went after the burglar who robbed the store, I was not motivated by any of the reasons you suggest—I simply did it because I thought that what the burglar did was wrong and because I like my boss and did not want to see him robbed." The psychological egoists can insist, in turn, that I *probably* wanted to impress my boss or that I wanted to look like a hero to my girlfriend or that I wanted society's or God's approval. But if I say those motives were not mine, then they are only theorizing, and they cannot parlay such theorizing into an absolutistic theory about all human motives and actions.

Because human beings vary so much in the thoughts, feelings, motives, and reasons related to their actions, it is highly presumptuous to assume that everyone "always" thinks, feels, is motivated, or reasons in one way to the exclusion of all others. This theory, like the theory about the existence of a supernatural, cannot be conclusively proved; indeed, there is some evidence to the contrary.

When all the other arguments fail, as they usually do in defense of psychological egoism, the psychological egoist, in attempting to prove his or her case, often retreats to the position that people always do what they really want to do. According to the egoist, if people "want" to perform a so-called unselfish act, then they are not really being unselfish because they are doing what they actually want to do. But there are problems with this argument. First of all, how can the psychological egoist deal with the fact that we often do *not* want to act unselfishly, but we do so anyway. At times we would really rather do something else, but we feel that we "must" or "have to" do what we don't want to do. Second, the only evidence the psychological egoist has in support of the statement "people always do what they want to do" is that the act was done. But all that this means is that "everyone always does what he or she does," and this really does not give us any information at all about human conduct, nor does it in any way prove that human beings always act only in their own self-interest.

Therefore, it seems to me that we can discount psychological egoism as a basis for ethical egoism. In the strong form it would destroy all morality and is lacking in both evidence and logic, and in either the strong or the weak form it fails to provide a rational foundation for ethical egoism.

Ethical Egoism

What, then, is ethical egoism? It is not necessarily the same thing as selfishness, which might not be in an egoist's self-interest at all. That is, if I am always acting selfishly, people might hate me and generally treat me badly, so it might be more in my self-interest not to be selfish. I might even go so far as to be altruistic in my behavior at least some of the time—when it is in my own self-interest to be so, of course. So, ethical egoism cannot be equated with selfishness, nor should it necessarily be equated with a big ego or being conceited. An egoist might very well be conceited; on the other hand, he or she might appear to be very self-effacing and humble.

Ethical egoism can take three possible forms:

1. *Individual ethical egoism* states that *everyone* ought to act in *my* self-interest.
2. *Personal ethical egoism* states that *I* ought to act in *my own* self-interest but that I make no claims about what anyone else ought to do.
3. *Universal ethical egoism* states as its basic principle that *everyone* should always act in *his or her own* self-interest regardless of the interests of others unless their interests also serve his or hers.

Problems with Individual and Personal Ethical Egoism

There are serious problems with individual and personal ethical egoism in that they apply only to one individual and cannot be laid down for humanity in general. This is a real drawback if one thinks of morality or a moral system as something applicable to all human beings—that is, if one desires to get beyond a strictly individualistic morality, which most moralists do. The problems with promulgating (laying out or setting forth) either of these forms of ethical egoism go deeper than their lack of general applicability, however. It would probably not be in the interest of individual or personal egoists to state their theory at all because they might anger other people, thus thwarting their own self-interest. For this reason, such egoists might have to appear other than they really are or lie about what they really believe, and dishonesty and lying are considered questionable moral actions in most moral theories.

We might also ask if a moral system shouldn't be consistent and if it shouldn't be more than just a theory. If a person has to state one moral theory while knowingly and purposely operating under another, then isn't he or she being inconsistent? And how moral can this moral system be if it cannot be laid out for others to see? Another problem with such individualistic systems is that they fail to take into consideration that human beings are not isolated from each other and that moral and immoral actions of all persons affect other people around them. These two versions of egoism, however, are good only for one person and may not even be beneficial for that individual, especially if anyone else finds out he or she is really operating under such a system. So these views of egoism are not impossible to hold—indeed, you may find, after we finish discussing universal ethical egoism, that they may be the only ones that are really possible—but they are highly suspect as valid moral theories.

Universal Ethical Egoism

Universal ethical egoism is the version of the theory that is most commonly presented by egoists because, like most other ethical theories, it is, as its name states, "universal"—an ethical theory that claims to apply to all human beings. This theory does not state only what *I* should do; rather, it concerns itself with what *all* human beings should do if they want to be moral: They should always act in their own self-interest. Universal ethical egoism is propounded by Epicurus, Ayn Rand, Jesse Kalin, and John Hospers, among others. These philosophers wish to set up an ethical system for all human beings to follow, and they believe that the most ethical viewpoint is for everyone to act in his or her own self-interest.

Problems with Universal Ethical Egoism

Inconsistency. The most devastating attack on universal ethical egoism was made by Brian Medlin in his essay "Ultimate Principles and Ethical Egoism," which Jesse Kalin attempted to refute in his essay "In Defense of Egoism."[1] Medlin put forth some of the same arguments already described here against individual and personal ethical egoism. For example, he stated that the ethical egoist says everyone ought to act in his own self-interest. Suppose, however, that Tom is acting in his own self-interest, which is not in the ethical egoist's (let's call him John) self-interest. Then it would certainly not be in John's interest to tell Tom that he should act in his, Tom's, own self-interest; therefore, John would be at least reticent to state his ethical system and probably wiser under ethical egoism not to state it at all. Let us suppose that John, the ethical egoist, really means that all people should act in their own self-interest, that the greatest good should be done to all concerned by any ethical action, or, as Medlin states it, that John really wants "everyone to come out on top." Isn't John actually proposing some form of utilitarianism (which states that everyone should always act so that the greatest number of good consequences accrue to everyone concerned by the action) rather than egoism? This may make utilitarians happy, but we don't need two names for one ethical theory.

What Is Meant by "Everyone." The problem really becomes critical when we ask exactly what universal ethical egoists mean when they state that *everyone* ought to act in his or her own self-interest. Do they mean that both John and Tom ought to act in their own self-interest when their self-interests conflict? How will this conflict be resolved? Suppose Tom asks John what he should do in the midst of their conflict? Should John tell him to act in his own self-interest even if it means that John will lose out? Universal ethical egoism would seem to advocate this; however, it would obviously not be in John's self-interest to have Tom do so. There is an inconsistency here, no matter what John does, because when self-interests conflict, universal ethical egoism provides for no resolution that will truly be in the interests of everyone.

Difficulty in Giving Moral Advice. Ethical egoism becomes highly questionable, then, when we talk about giving moral advice. Such advice is inconsistent in that John should do what is in his own self-interest but must advise Tom either to act in John's interest or in Tom's. If he advises Tom to act in his, John's, interest, then John is retreating to individual egoism; if he advises Tom to act in his own self-interest, then John is not serving his own interest. Either way, it would seem that the purpose behind ethical egoism is defeated.

Jesse Kalin says that the only way to state universal ethical egoism consistently is to advocate that John should act in his own self-interest and that Tom should act in *his* own self-interest. Everything will then be all right because even though the theory is announced to everyone, and even though John will have to advise Tom that Tom should act in his own self-interest, John need not *want* Tom to act in his own self-interest. It is on this point that Kalin feels he has refuted Medlin, who states that universal ethical egoism is inconsistent because what the egoist *wants* is obviously incompatible—he wants himself to come out on top and he wants everyone else to come out on top, but because interests conflict, he obviously has incompatible wants. Kalin uses the example of John and Tom playing chess: John, seeing that Tom could move his bishop and put John's king in check, believes that Tom *ought* to move his bishop but doesn't *want* him to, need not persuade him to, and indeed "ought to . . . sit there quietly, hoping he does not move as he ought."[2] With this statement, the problem that occurred with individual and personal ethical egoism again arises in universal ethical egoism—that what people *ought* to do cannot be promulgated (that is, presented for all to see). In other words, we again have an ethical theory that has to be a secret one; otherwise, it will, by being stated, violate its own major tenet—self-interest.

Blurring Moral and Nonmoral Use of "Ought" and "Should." We must also examine how Kalin is using "ought" in his example about the chess game. One of the unintentional outcomes of Kalin's essay seems to be a blurring of the distinction between the moral use of "ought" and "should" and a nonmoral use of the two words. In the first chapter, I described the major difference between the scientific and philosophical-normative approaches to morality as the difference between "is" or "do" and "ought" and "should." I also pointed out that the last two words are not always used in a moral sense and indeed may often be used in a nonmoral sense.

For example, if the instructions for assembling a toy say you should put two end bolts and nuts together before putting in the other four, there is no moral import. "Should" here implies, "if you want this toy to work right and want these two pieces of it to fit snugly." There is no moral imperative here unless incorrect assembly of the toy could cost a child's life, for example. Rarely do lives depend on whether games such as chess are won or lost or whether two sides of a toy fit together well. "Should" in these contexts will probably not have any moral ramifications whatsoever.

Evidently, to Kalin at least, moral rules and advice have such superficial application that "should" and "ought" mean no more than they would mean when applied to a game or directions for assembling something. It seems that only the oddest of ethical systems would state many dos and don'ts and say that people "ought" to adhere to them but then hope they don't. Consider what it would mean for John to advise Tom, "You should kill me because I stand in the way of your having my wife, and it is in your self-interest for you to do so, but since it is not in *my* self-interest for you to do so, I hope you don't." It is certainly not incompatible with what John *says* he thinks ought to be, but it is a strange moral system that actually states what its advocate really does not want. It is obvious to me that what John really thinks Tom *should* do is leave John and his wife alone. This means, at best, that universal ethical egoism is highly impractical, and, at worst, that it is a theory that seriously puts into conflict the desires of people for good things and happiness and is some sort of intellectual game, the rules of which humans "ought" to be told to follow. Kalin seems to have shown that the egoist need not want to have others practice what he or she preaches. By doing so, however, Kalin raises the specter of an even wider split between what "ought to be" and what "is."

I, at least, am forced back to Medlin's logic: "But is not to believe that someone should act in a certain way to try to persuade him to do so?" and "Does it make sense to say, 'Of course you should do this, but for goodness sake don't?'"[3] Without this logic, ethical systems are mere abstract ideals that their proponents hope are not actually carried out. What this amounts to, if Kalin is correct, is that universal ethical egoism claims to be a moral system that is actually based on the nonmoral—its rules actually have no more moral import than the rules of a chess game or the directions for assembling a toy.

Inconsistent with Helping Professions. Another criticism of ethical egoism in any of its forms is that it does not fit well as a basis for people who are in the helping professions. It is certainly true that many people are in such professions for their own self-interest to some extent, but the real basis for being a nurse, doctor, social worker, teacher, or minister is to help others, and a highly self-interested attitude would not work well in these professions.

These criticisms would support the contentions of some philosophers that egoism in any of its forms is really not a moral system at all but rather the nonmoral stance from which one asks, "Why should I be moral?"[4] Although not wanting to go that far, I do feel that there are a great many problems with ethical egoism that are not easily resolvable. Therefore, it seems to me to be a highly questionable ethical theory.

Advantages of Universal Ethical Egoism

What conclusions can we draw from this discussion of ethical egoism? Does the theory have any advantages at all?

It's Easier to Determine Self-Interest. One advantage of ethical egoism over theories that advocate doing what is in the interest of others is that it is much easier for individuals to know what their own interests are than it is for them to know what is in the best interest of others. People will not always act in their own self-interest and will certainly make errors in judgment about what is in their self-interest, but they are in a much better position to correctly estimate what they want, need, and should have and do than anyone else is. Also, they have a better chance of assessing their own self-interest than they have of assessing the interest of anyone else.

It Encourages Individual Freedom and Responsibility. Another advantage of universal ethical egoism is that it encourages individual freedom and responsibility. Egoists need only to consider their own self-interest and then take responsibility for their actions. There need be no dependence on anybody else, and one need only seek his or her own self-interest and let others do the same. Therefore, egoists also argue, this means that their theories really fit in best with the United States' capitalist economy.

Limitations to These Advantages. Ethical egoism can work successfully, but it has severe limitations. The theory will work best as long as people are operating in relative isolation, thereby minimizing conflicts among their self-interests. For example, if everyone could have his or her own self-sufficient community and be almost totally independent, then self-interest would work well. However, as soon as individual spheres begin to touch or overlap, and John's self-interest begins to conflict with Tom's, ethical egoism fails to provide the means of resolving these conflicts in such a way that everyone's self-interest is protected or satisfied. Some principle of justice or compromise must be brought in, and it would probably not be in *everyone's* self-interest. At this point egoists must either become utilitarians and concern themselves with the best interests of everyone involved or play their nonmoral game, telling people what they should do but hoping they don't do it.

The real and immediate problem with egoism, however, is that we do not live in self-sufficient communities. We live, rather, in increasingly crowded communities where social, economic, and even moral interdependence is a necessity, and where self-interests conflict constantly and somehow must be compromised. This means that someone's self-interest will be only partially served and, in fact, may not be served at all.

Ayn Rand's Rational Ethical Egoism

The late Ayn Rand (1905–1982), the foremost modern exponent of universal ethical egoism (which she called rational ethical egoism), has said that the self-interests of rational human beings, by virtue of their being rational, will never conflict.[5] I feel that this view is both naive and utopian. No matter how she tries to argue away conflicts of self-interest among rational human beings, observation shows us that they do exist and have to be dealt with. For example, Albert Einstein (1879–1955) and Bertrand Russell (1872–1970), both mathematicians and scientists (Russell was also a philosopher), were totally opposed to the development of atomic weapons. On the other hand, Dr. Edward Teller (b. 1908), the renowned physicist responsible for many of the developments of atomic power, advocates its proliferation. These are not mere differences of opinion: Russell, for example, even went to jail for protesting the docking of American nuclear submarines in England. Not only did Russell think that the development and use of atomic weapons were not in his own self-interest, but he also felt they were not in the interest of human beings in general.

Rand may wish to argue that these men are neither rational nor intelligent, but if so, I would find it difficult to accept her definition of "rational human beings" and "rational self-interest." Furthermore, it is interesting to speculate, along these lines, why Ayn Rand steadfastly refused to support any communities or projects set up under her theories. One such community was the Minerva Project, an island community to be set up without government, and one such project was Libertarianism, a political party that nominated John Hospers as a presidential candidate in 1972 and has run a candidate in every national election since. Neither endeavor received Rand's blessing. One wonders if she was merely dissatisfied with the particular projects or if she realized that her theory was really only a utopian ideal that could not function except in the abstract.

Conclusions

In conclusion, it would seem that people can be ethical egoists with some success only if they advocate some other theory besides ethical egoism and only if they do not tell people that this is what they are doing. As stated earlier, this makes for a questionable ethical theory at worst and an impractical one at best. Considering all of these serious problems, we certainly should not settle on ethical egoism until we have first examined other ethical theories.

◆

Utilitarianism

Utilitarianism is an ethical theory whose principal architects were Jeremy Bentham (1748–1832) and John Stuart Mill (1806–1873). It derives its name from "utility," which means usefulness. The utilitarian says that an act is right (moral) if it is useful in "bringing about a *desirable* or *good* end."[6] It has been more characteristically stated, however, as "Everyone should perform that act or follow that moral rule that will bring about the greatest good (or happiness) for everyone concerned." The reason for mentioning both acting and following rules is that utilitarianism is generally found in two main forms: *act utilitarianism* and *rule utilitarianism*.

Act Utilitarianism

Act utilitarianism essentially says that everyone should perform that act that will bring about the greatest good over bad for everyone affected by the act. Its advocates do not believe in setting up rules for action because they feel that each situation is different and each person is different. Each individual, then, must assess the situation he or she is involved in and try to figure out which act would bring about the greatest amount of good consequences with the least amount of bad consequences, not just for himself or herself, as in egoism, but for everyone involved in the situation.

In assessing the situation, the agent (the person who will be acting or is acting) must decide whether, for example, telling the truth is the right thing to do in *this* situation at *this* time. It does not matter that most people believe that telling the truth is generally a good thing to do; the act utilitarian must decide for the particular situation he or she is in at the moment whether or not it is right to tell the truth. In act utilitarianism, there can be no absolute rules against killing, stealing, lying, and so on, because every situation is different and all people are different. Therefore, all of those acts that may, in general, be considered immoral would be considered moral or immoral by the act utilitarian in relation to whether they would or would not bring about the greatest good over bad for everyone in a particular situation.

Criticisms of Act Utilitarianism

Difficulty of Determining Consequences for Others. There are several criticisms of act utilitarianism. One of them has been mentioned as an advantage for ethical egoism, and that is that it is very difficult to ascertain what would be good consequences for others. Involved in the difficulty of deciding what the consequences are of any action one is about to take is the problem of deciding what is "good" and "right" for others. What may be a good consequence for you may not be good for another, and how are you to tell unless you can ask other people what would be good for them? Very often, of course, there is no time to ask anyone anything; we must simply act the best way we can.

Impracticality of Beginning Anew. Furthermore, there is a certain impracticality in having to begin anew with each situation. In fact, many moralists might question the act consequentialist's belief that each act and each person is completely and uniquely different, claiming that there are many similarities among human beings and their behavior that would justify the laying down of certain rules. For example, critics of act utilitarianism might say that enough persons value their lives so that there should be some rule against killing, even if it has to be qualified (for instance, "Never kill *except* in self-defense"). They might further say that it is a waste of time and even absurd to reassess each situation when there is a choice for killing or not killing; one should simply follow the general rule with any of its valid qualifications. As mentioned earlier, the time factor in moral decision making is often an important one; a person often does not have the time to start from scratch with each new moral problem. In fact, having to constantly begin anew may result in the inability to commit a moral act in time.

The act utilitarian would answer that after experiencing many situations, one learns to apply one's experience to the new situation readily, with a minimum of time wasting, so that one is really not starting from scratch each time. But when people call on past experience and act consistently in accordance with it, aren't they really acting on unstated rules? If they have been in a number of situations in which the moral choice is not to kill another human being and they are now faced with another similar situation, then aren't they really operating under a hidden rule that says, "Never kill another human being in any situation similar to A"? If so, they are rule utilitarians who merely have not announced their rules.

Difficulty of Educating the Young or Uninitiated. One last criticism of act utilitarianism is how one is to educate the young or the uninitiated to act morally if there are no rules or guides to follow except one: that each person must assess what would be the greatest good consequences of each act for each situation that arises. It would seem that in this ethical system everyone has to start afresh as he or she is growing up to discover what is the moral thing to do in each situation as it occurs. This may be all right in the estimation of some philosophers, but it is very difficult, if not impossible, to conduct any type of systematic moral education on this basis.

Rule Utilitarianism

As an answer to many of the act utilitarian's problems, rule utilitarianism was established. In this form, the basic utilitarian principle is not that "everyone should always *act* to bring about the greatest good for all concerned," but rather that "everyone should always establish and follow that rule or those rules that will bring about the greatest good for all concerned." This at least eliminates the problem of having to start anew to figure out consequences for everyone in every situation, and it also provides a set of rules to use in the moral education of the uninitiated.

Rule utilitarians try, from experience and careful reasoning, to set up a series of rules that, when followed, will yield the greatest good for all humanity. For example, instead of trying to figure out whether one should kill or not kill someone else in each situation where this problem might arise, rule utilitarians might form the rule *Never kill except in self-defense.* Their assumption in stating this rule is that except in self-defense, killing will bring about more bad consequences than good for all concerned, both now and probably in the long run. Killing, if allowed in any but the self-defense situation, they might add, would set dangerous precedents. It would encourage more people to take others' lives than they now do, and because human life is basic and important to everyone, not having such a rule would always cause more harm than good to all concerned.

Rule utilitarians obviously believe, unlike their "act" counterparts, that there are enough similar human motives, actions, and situations to justify setting up rules that will apply to all human beings and to all human situations. To the rule utilitarian's way of thinking, it is foolish and dangerous to leave moral actions up to individuals without giving them some guidance and without trying to establish some sort of stability and moral order to society, as opposed to the haphazard, on-the-spot guesswork that seems to be advocated by the act utilitarian.

Criticisms of Rule Utilitarianism

Difficulty of Determining Consequences for Others. Rule utilitarianism has some of the same problems as the act type, especially in the area of trying to determine good consequences for others. This, as I have already mentioned, is a disadvantage that egoism does not share. How can we be sure, given the vast differences among human beings and human situations, that a rule can really be established to cover such diversity and that it will always and truly bring about the greatest good for all concerned? This difficulty is added to the one shared by the egoist and the act utilitarian of trying to determine *all* the consequences for not just one action but all actions and situations occurring under any particular rule. Nonrule moralists argue strongly that there is no rule for which one cannot find at least one exception somewhere along the line, and that by the time you incorporate all of the possible exceptions into a rule, you are really advocating act utilitarianism. Therefore, they argue, you would be better off without rules that cannot apply to all situations you might face.

For example, can the rule *Never kill except in self-defense* actually cover all situations human beings will become involved in? Will it cover abortion, for example? Many antiabortionists think so, stating that in no way can the unborn fetus be considered an aggressor; therefore, it cannot be aborted. Prochoice advocates, on the other hand, either don't consider the fetus a human being or argue for the precedence of the mother's life over the fetus's and believe that there are times when the fetus must be aborted. How, for example, would the rule utilitarian deal with aborting the fetus when the mother's life is endangered not specifically because she's pregnant but for some other reason? The fetus cannot be considered an aggressor, so how can it be aborted in self-defense?

I am not trying to say that rule utilitarians would have such a rule but rather to show how difficult it is to form a rule that will cover all situations without exception. Rule utilitarians can, of course, rate their rules in primary and secondary categories, but the problem continues in whatever category the rule is found. Act utilitarians do not have this problem; they may have trouble justifying a particular action, but at least they have not committed themselves to acting just one way in all situations. They may make a mistake in situation A, but when situation B comes along, they have another chance to judge and act anew without any binding rules to tie them into a series of mistakes.

Cost-Benefit Analysis, or End-Justifies-the-Means, Approach—Problem for Utilitarianism

There is another problem in both forms of utilitarianism, and that is the difficulty of carrying the "useful" aspect of utility too far. Nonutilitarians may ask, for example, whether it is always right to try to achieve "the greatest good for the greatest number." Doesn't this sometimes end up as the greatest good for the majority with some very bad consequences for the minority? Would science, for example, be justified in taking one hundred children and performing painful and eventually fatal experiments on them if the doctors could guarantee the saving of ten million children's lives in the future? Certainly, by number alone, this would be the greatest good for the greatest number, but many moralists would object, saying that each individual is, morally speaking, unique, and therefore no such experiment may ever be performed regardless of how many individuals will be saved by it.

Yet, if we are aiming for the greatest good for everyone, there is the danger of what many call the "cost-benefit analysis," or "end-justifies-the-means," approach to morality; that is, trying to calculate how much effort or cost will bring about the most benefits. This approach also involves us in determining the social worth of individuals in a society, so that those people who are "worth" more to society, such as professional people, are given more benefits (for instance, medical) than those who are not. In other words, sometimes in trying to do the greatest good for the greatest number, we might find ourselves being quite immoral toward a few.

Some moralists, including Immanuel Kant and Ayn Rand, believe that each human being should be considered as an end in himself or herself, never as merely a means. In trying to be fair and just to all members of a society, this would seem to be a more moral approach than merely trying to attain the greatest good for the greatest number. To be sure, there are times when a group of people has to think of the survival of the group rather than of one or two individuals, and then moral decisions have to be made about who gets the "goods" that are in short supply. However, a person who always operates under "the greatest good for the greatest number" ideal very often ignores what is good for everyone.

An example of one of the times when the survival of the group is put before that of a few individuals exists in medicine. During serious disaster, when medical facilities simply cannot handle everyone who is injured, doctors concentrate on those patients whom they know they can save and not on the "hopeless" cases. Furthermore, an injured doctor or nurse who could be put to work would probably be the first to get medical attention because she or he would be able to help save more of the other injured people than a nonmedical person.

These, fortunately, are unusual circumstances, and they require different priorities from more normal situations. To apply the cost-benefit analysis, or end-justifies-the-means, approach to more normal situations, however, is tantamount to treating human beings as if they were some kind of inanimate "product" in a business where one tries to get the most for one's money and thus discards the inferior product. There have been people who have favored this approach, among them Hitler and some other dictators, but most moralists find this an abhorrent and immoral view of humanity.

Conclusions

In conclusion, then, utilitarianism is an improvement over egoism in that it attempts to take into consideration all people concerned by any moral action. At the same time, however, it runs into the difficulty of determining what would be good for others, a difficulty not involved in egoism. In act utilitarianism the problem is that there are no moral rules or guides to go by; a person must decide what is right for all people in each situation he or she faces. In rule utilitarianism, the problem is finding out which rules really cover all human beings and situations, even though this form of utilitarianism avoids the ambiguity of having to start over in each new situation. The last problem with utilitarianism of either kind is that it lends itself to the cost-benefit analysis type of thinking, which is often the result of "the greatest good for the greatest number" kind of morality. Or, in other words, that any end, and especially any good end, justifies any means used to attain it. There is a question among many moralists whether we should only concentrate on consequences or ends and ignore other things such as means or motives when making moral decisions. This issue will be discussed further when Immanuel Kant's Practical Imperative is presented in the next chapter.

Another advantage utilitarianism has over ethical egoism is that it would be much more suitable for people in the helping professions in that it is concerned with the best good consequences for everyone.

◆—————————————————————————

Difficulty with Consequentialist Theories in General

One difficulty inherent in *all* of the consequentialist theories is the necessity of trying to discover and determine as many of the possible consequences of our actions as we can, a difficult task at best. As I have implied, this problem exists both for those who are concerned with self-interest and those who are concerned with the interest of everyone. Obviously, though, it is a greater problem for utilitarians, because they have to concern themselves with how consequences affect people other than themselves. The critic of consequentialist theories would probably say that it is very difficult to assess all of the consequences of any of our actions because we cannot see far enough into the future, nor do we have enough knowledge about what is best for ourselves or for all concerned to make such a judgment.

For example, if one is living under the rule of an incompetent leader, the fastest way to remove such a leader would be to assassinate him. But what would the consequences of such an act be, and how can we calculate the number of good as opposed to the number of bad consequences and do this for ourselves or everyone concerned by the action? Obviously one would certainly end this leader's rule by killing him, but who would come to power next? Would this next person be any better, or would he be worse? Suppose that we knew who would be next and thought he would be a good leader, but that he turned out to be worse than the former leader? And, is it worse to suffer for three or four years under an incompetent leader than to give precedent to the act of assassination, so that when people are dissatisfied, rightly or wrongly, with their leader they feel they can use assassination to remove him? In the case of utilitarianism, because we are concerned with *everyone* involved in the situation, can we assess with any precision what effect our killing or not killing the leader will have on the children of the society and even on its future unborn members? Will we ever really know what *all* of the consequences, present and future, of our act will be? If not, then how can we judge each situation well enough to take the right action?

In an example taken from United States history, could President Harry Truman have foreseen all of the consequences of his decision to drop the atomic bombs on Hiroshima and Nagasaki during World War II? Obviously he could determine the more immediate consequences, such as the shortening of the war and the saving of American lives. But could he have foreseen long-range consequences: the cold war, the development of the hydrogen and neutron bombs, the stockpiling of nuclear weapons to the point of "overkill," the radiation fallout and consequent pollution of the atmosphere, and so on? As this example illustrates, the discovery and determination of the consequences of our acts and rules, either for ourselves or others, is no easy task—and it is not one that can always be accurately or precisely accomplished. But what if we were to set up a moral system without having to consider consequences? If we can decide what is right or wrong on some basis other than consequences, perhaps we can avoid some of the difficulties involved in both egoism and utilitarianism. The next chapter will deal with such theories.

Chapter Summary

I. Two major viewpoints of morality
   A. Consequentialist (teleological) morality is based on or concerned with consequences.
   B. Nonconsequentialist (deontological) morality is not based on or concerned with consequences.

II. Psychological egoism
   A. This is not an ethical theory but a descriptive or scientific theory having to do with egoism.
   B. It appears in two forms, neither of which can operate as a basis for ethical egoism.
      1. The strong form holds that people always act in their own self-interest.
      2. The weak form holds that people often, but not always, act in their own self-interest.
   C. Psychological egoism in its strong form does not refute morality, and in its weak form it does not provide a rational foundation for ethical egoism.

III. Ethical egoism—a philosophical-normative, prescriptive theory
   A. This appears in three forms.
      1. The individual form maintains that everyone ought to act in my self-interest.
      2. The personal form maintains that I ought to act in my own self-interest but that I make no claims about what anyone else ought to do.
      3. The universal form maintains that everyone should always act in his or her own self-interest.
   B. The problem with the first and second forms is that they apply only to one individual and cannot be laid down for humanity in general because doing so would probably not be in the egoist's self-interest.
   C. Universal ethical egoism is the most commonly held version of ethical egoism, but it also has problems.
      1. It is inconsistent in that it is unclear whose self-interest should be satisfied.
      2. What is meant by "everyone" is unclear.
      3. There is difficulty in determining how to give moral advice.
      4. In answering these criticisms, supporters of egoism tend to blur the moral and nonmoral uses of "ought" and "should."
      5. It does not fit well with the helping professions.
   D. Ethical egoism has certain advantages

1. It is easier for egoists to know what is in their own self-interest than it is for other moralists who are concerned about more than self-interest to know what is in the best interest of others.
2. It encourages individual freedom and responsibility and fits in best, according to egoists, with our capitalist economy.
3. It can work successfully as long as people are operating in limited spheres, isolated from each other, thereby minimizing conflicts.

E. Limitations of these advantages.
1. It offers no consistent method of resolving conflicts of self-interests.
2. We do not live in isolated, self-sufficient communities but rather in increasingly crowded communities where social, economic, and moral interdependence is necessary and where self-interests conflict constantly and somehow must be compromised.

IV. Utilitarianism
A. Utilitarianism maintains that everyone should perform that act or follow that moral rule that will bring about the greatest good (or happiness) for everyone concerned.
B. Act utilitarianism states that everyone should perform that act that will bring about the greatest good over bad for everyone affected by the act.
1. The act utilitarian believes that one cannot establish rules in advance to cover all situations and people because they are all different.
2. There are difficulties with this theory.
   (a) It is very hard to ascertain what would be good consequences for others.
   (b) It is impractical to have to begin anew with each situation to decide what would be moral in that situation.
   (c) It is nearly impossible to educate the young or the uninitiated to act morally if there are no rules or guides to follow.
C. Rule utilitarianism states that everyone should always follow the rule or rules that will bring about the greatest number of good consequences for all concerned.
1. The rule utilitarian believes that there are enough similar human motives, actions, and situations to justify setting up rules that will apply to all human beings and situations.
2. There are difficulties with this theory.
   (a) As with act utilitarianism, it is difficult to determine what would be good consequences for others.
   (b) It is difficult to see how rule utilitarians can be sure, given the vast differences among human beings and situations, that a rule can really be established to cover such diversity—that

　　　　　they can create a rule that will truly and always bring about
　　　　　the greatest good for all concerned.
　　　(c)　It is difficult to avoid making so many exceptions to rules that
　　　　　the rules cannot really function effectively.
　　D.　Another problem for both forms of utilitarianism is the cost-benefit
　　　analysis, or end-justifies-the-means, approach to morality.
　　　1.　There is danger here of trying to determine the social worth of
　　　　　individuals.
　　　2.　"The greatest good for all concerned" can often be interpreted as
　　　　　"the greatest good for the majority," with possible immoral conse-
　　　　　quences to any individuals in the minority.
　　　3.　Does even a good end justify any means used to attain it, or
　　　　　should we also consider our means and motives?
V.　Problems with consequentialist theories
　　A.　Consequentialist theories demand that we discover and determine all
　　　of the consequences of our actions or rules.
　　B.　This is virtually impossible to accomplish.
　　C.　Are consequences or ends the only possible morality?

Exercises for Review

1. What is the difference between the consequentialist (teleological) and
   nonconsequentialist (deontological) views of morality?

2. Explain the difference between psychological egoism and ethical egoism.

3. What are the two forms of psychological egoism? Why don't they refute
   morality or provide a foundation for ethical egoism?

4. Explain individual and personal ethical egoism. What are the problems
   with these forms?

5. Why do you think universal ethical egoism is the most commonly held
   form of ethical egoism? What difficulties does this form present?

6. Why is the universal ethical egoist's interpretation of "everyone" a questionable one?

7. What are the problems with Jesse Kalin's criticism of the attack on universal ethical egoism?

8. Describe the advantages and disadvantages of ethical egoism.

9. What do act utilitarians believe? How do their beliefs differ from those
   of rule utilitarians?

10. What are the difficulties with act and rule utilitarianism?

11. Describe the cost-benefit analysis, or end-justifies-the-means, approach to morality. Why is this a problem in both forms of utilitarianism?

Discussion Questions

1. Analyze the motivation for some of the decisions you've made and the actions you've taken, and try to determine the extent to which you were motivated by self-interest. Have you ever done what might be called a purely altruistic act? Does this analysis of motivation lead you to believe that psychological egoism is an accurate description of how human beings live their lives? To what extent, and why or why not?

2. On a recent TV show an army surgeon performed an unnecessary operation on a battalion commander merely to remove him from battle during the time he would need to recuperate from the surgery. As a result of overaggressiveness the battalion commander had an abnormally high casualty rate among his men, and the surgeon knew that by performing the operation he would probably save the lives of hundreds of soldiers who would otherwise have been victims of the commander's eagerness. A fellow surgeon counseled him that it was unethical to operate on a healthy body even under those circumstances. But the operating surgeon, feeling that more good than bad would come out of his action, performed the operation anyway. How does this relate to the cost-benefit analysis approach to morality? To what extent do you feel each surgeon was right in his moral position? Do you feel that in this case the good end justified the means the operating surgeon was using? Why or why not? Is there ever a time when a good end justifies *any* means used to attain it? If so, when? If not, why not?

3. To what extent do you feel human beings need rules in order to be moral, and to what extent do you feel they should be free to adapt their behavior to different situations? Be specific, giving examples and illustrations.

4. Read Joseph Fletcher's book *Situation Ethics*, and critically evaluate his act utilitarian position. Keeping in mind that he offers no specific rules for moral behavior, what values and what difficulties do you see in his sole commandment, "Do what is the loving thing to do"? Are there problems with deciding what the loving thing to do is in some situations? If so, what are these problems? If not, why not? Describe a situation in which "the loving thing to do" can be clearly delineated.

5. Read Robert Heinlein's *Stranger in a Strange Land* and critically evaluate the ethical egoism advocated by the author through his main earth-born character. Perform a similar analysis on the protagonists of the

author's other books, *The Moon Is a Harsh Mistress* and *I Will Fear No Evil*.

6. Analyze and critically evaluate U.S. national and foreign policies, attempting to determine whether they are based on egoism in any of its forms or on act or rule utilitarianism. Support your views with examples.

7. To what extent do you feel that Christian ethics is based on egoism or utilitarianism? Give specific examples.

8. Read *The Fountainhead, Atlas Shrugged*, or *The Virtue of Selfishness* by Ayn Rand, and write a critical evaluation of it in relation to ethical egoism.

9. Collect as much information as you can about the Libertarian political party and evaluate what you deem would be the effectiveness or ineffectiveness of its theories if it were the governing party in the United States today.

10. Describe the extent to which you are any form of ethical egoist or an act or rule utilitarian. Show how these theories have or have not worked for you as you have dealt with specific moral issues and problems.

11. To what extent do you believe members of your family or your friends are egoists or utilitarians? Describe how these theories work for them and for those around them.

Notes

1. Both of these essays can be found in William P. Alston and Richard B. Brandt, *The Problems of Philosophy* (Boston: Allyn and Bacon, 1974), 204–19.

2. Ibid., 218.

3. Ibid., 207.

4. For an excellent presentation of this argument, see Kai Nielsen's "Why Should I Be Moral?" in *Problems of Moral Philosophy*, 2nd ed., ed. Paul W. Taylor (Belmont, Calif.: Dickenson, 1972), 497–517.

5. Ayn Rand, *The Virtue of Selfishness* (New York: New American Library, 1964), 57–67.

6. Paul Taylor, *Problems of Moral Philosophy*, 137.

Supplementary Reading

General Readings on Ethical Theories

Baier, Kurt. *The Moral Point of View.* Ithaca, N.Y.: Cornell University Press, 1958.

Brinkley, Luther J. *Contemporary Ethical Theories.* New York: Citadel Press, 1961.

Frankena, William K. *Ethics*, 2nd ed. Englewood Cliffs, N.J.: Prentice-Hall, 1973.

Melden, A.I., ed. *Ethical Theories*, 2nd ed. Englewood Cliffs, N.J.: Prentice-Hall, 1967.

Taylor, Paul W., ed. *Problems of Moral Philosophy*, 2nd ed. Belmont, Calif.: Dickenson, 1972.

Readings on Ethical Egoism

Alston, William P., and Richard B. Brandt. *The Problems of Philosophy*, 2nd ed. Boston: Allyn and Bacon, 1974.

Edel, Abraham. "Two Traditions in the Refutation of Egoism." *Journal of Philosophy* 34 (1937): 617–28.

Fumerton, Richard A. *Reason and Morality: A Defense of the Egocentric Perspective.* Ithaca, N.Y.: Cornell University Press, 1990.

Gautier, David P., ed. *Morality and Rational Self-Interest*. Englewood Cliffs, N.J.: Prentice-Hall, 1970.

Medlin, Brian. "Ultimate Principles and Ethical Egoism." *Australasian Journal of Philosophy* 35 (1957): 111–18.

Olson, Robert G. *The Morality of Self-Interest*. New York: Harcourt Brace Jovanovich, 1965.

Rand, Ayn. *The Virtue of Selfishness*. New York: New American Library, 1964.

Readings on Utilitarianism

Ayer, A. J. "The Principle of Utility." In *Philosophical Essays* by A. J. Ayer. New York: St. Martin's Press, 1955.

Barrow, Robin. *Utilitarianism: A Contemporary Statement*. Brookfield, Vt.: Ashgate Publishing, 1991.

Bentham, Jeremy. *The Principles of Morals and Legislation*. Several editions.

Brandt, Richard B. *Utilitarianism and Rights*. New York: Cambridge University Press, 1992.

Egonsson, Dan. *Interests, Utilitarianism, and Moral Standing*. New York: Chartwell Bratt, 1990.

Fletcher, Joseph. *Situation Ethics: The New Morality*. Philadelphia: The Westminster Press, 1966.

Glover, Jonathan. *Utilitarianism and Its Critics*. Ed. Paul Edwards. New York: Macmillan, 1990.

Iyer, Raghavan. *Utilitarianism and All That*. Santa Barbara, Calif: Concord Grove, 1983.

Kelly, Paul. *Utilitarianism and Distributive Justice: Jeremy Bentham and the Civil Law.* New York: Oxford University Press, 1990.

Mill, John Stuart. *Utilitarianism: With Critical Essays*. Ed. Samuel Gorovitz. Indianapolis: Bobbs-Merrill, 1971.

Narveson, Jan. *Morality and Utility*. Baltimore: Johns Hopkins University Press, 1967.

Ryan, Alan. *Utilitarianism and Other Essays*. New York: Penguin, 1987.

Sen, Amartya, and Bernard Williams, eds. *Utilitarianism and Beyond*. New York: Cambridge University Press, 1982.

Smart, J. J. C. *Outlines of a Utilitarianism System of Ethics*. London: Cambridge University Press, 1961.

Smart, J. J. C., and Bernard Williams, eds. *Utilitarianism For and Against*. New York: Cambridge University Press, 1973.

CHAPTER 3

Nonconsequentialist (Deontological) Theories of Morality and Virtue Ethics

♦────────────────────────────────────

Objectives

After you have read this chapter you should be able to

1. Describe nonconsequentialist and Virtue Ethics theories of morality, showing how they differ from the consequentialist theories.

2. Differentiate between act and rule nonconsequentialism and show how they differ from act and rule utilitarianism.

3. Describe and critically analyze act nonconsequentialism, and the Divine Command theory, Kant's Duty Ethics, and Ross's prima facie duties (the main examples of rule nonconsequentialism) and Virtue Ethics.

4. Define and analyze such important terms and concepts as *universalizability, Categorical Imperative, reversibility, human beings as ends rather than means, prima facie duties, virtue, and the virtues*.

5. Describe Aristotle's Nichomachean Ethics and know what the theory of Virtue Ethics contains and entails.

Nonconsequentialist theories of morality are based on something other than the consequences of a person's actions. We have seen that in both egoism and utilitarianism, moralists are concerned with the consequences or outcomes of human actions. Egoists are concerned that people act in their own self-interest, and utilitarians are concerned that people act in the interests of all concerned. In these two theories, the goodness of an action is measured by how well it serves the interests of someone, whereas the goodness of a human being is measured by the extent to which he or she performs such actions and actually causes good consequences.

The most important thing to remember when discussing the nonconsequentialist theories is that their proponents claim that consequences do not, and in fact should not, enter into judging whether actions or people are moral or immoral. Actions are to be judged solely on whether they are right and people solely on whether they are good, based on some other (many nonconsequentialists would say "higher") standard or standards of morality. That is, acts or people are to be judged moral or immoral regardless of the consequences of actions. The most obvious example of such a theory is the *Divine Command theory*. If one believes that there is a God, goddess or gods and that He/She or they have set up a series of moral commands, then an action is right and people are good if and only if they obey these commands, *regardless* of the consequences that might ensue.

For example, Joan of Arc was acting under the instructions of what she felt to be voices from God. Egoists would probably consider her martyrdom not to have been in her own self-interest; they would be concerned about the consequences of her actions (her torture and death) in refusing to deny the voices. The Divine Command theorist, however, would state that one should obey God and His commandments as relayed to human beings (through voices or any other means) regardless of the consequences *simply* because God is all-good and has told us that is what we should do. What is good and what is right is what God has stated is good and right. That the consequences might involve the loss of life, for example, has nothing to do with the morality or immorality of an act or a person. One must simply accept whatever consequences come about. This is probably the clearest example of a nonconsequentialist theory of morality, but it is not the only one, nor need such a theory be based on the existence of a God or gods.

Act Nonconsequentialist Theories

Just as utilitarianism falls into two categories (act and rule), so do nonconsequentialist theories. Remember, however, that the main difference between act and rule utilitarianism and act and rule nonconsequentialism is that the former are based on consequences, whereas the latter are not. Nevertheless, some of the problems and disadvantages of the theories are similar, as we shall see.

Act nonconsequentialists make the major assumption that there are no general moral rules or theories at all but only particular actions, situations, and people about which we cannot generalize. We must approach each situation individually as one of a kind and somehow decide what is the right action to take in that situation. It is the "how we decide" in this theory that is most interesting. Decisions for the act nonconsequentialist are "intuitionistic." That is, what a person decides in a particular situation, because he or she cannot use any rules or standards, is based on what he or she believes or feels (intuits) to be the right action to take. This type of theory, then, is highly individualistic—individuals must decide what they feel is the right thing to do and then do it. They are not concerned with consequences—and certainly not with consequences for other situations or people not immediately involved in this particular situation—but they must do what they feel is right given this particular situation and the people involved in it.

This theory is characterized by two popular slogans of the 1960s: *If it feels good—do it* and *Do your own thing*. It also has a more traditional basis in intuitionistic, emotive, and noncognitive theories of morality. What these theories seem to stress is that morality in thought, language, and deed is not based on reason. Some of these theories even suggest that morality cannot be rationalized because it isn't based on reason in the same way as scientific experimentation and factual statements about reality are. The "emotive theory," for example, states that ethical words and sentences really do only two things: (1) express people's feelings and attitudes and (2) evoke or generate certain feelings and attitudes in others. This theory will be discussed further in Chapter 4, where we will deal with the meanings of moral propositions. It seems important at this point, however, to discuss the significance of intuition and its relationship to morality.

Intuitionism

Arguments for Intuitionism. In his book *Right and Reason*, Austin Fagothey lists some general reasons for accepting or rejecting intuition as a basis for morality.[1] The general reasons supporting moral intuitionism are (1) any well-meaning person seems to have an immediate sense of right and wrong; (2) human beings had moral ideas and convictions long before philosophers created ethics as a formal study; (3) our reasoning on moral matters usually is used to confirm our more direct perceptions or "intuitions"; and (4) our reasoning can go wrong in relation to moral issues as well as others, and we must then fall back on our moral insights and intuitions.

Arguments Against Intuitionism. There are several arguments against moral intuitionism: (1) First, the word *intuition* has come to mean hunches, wild guesses, irrational inspirations, and clairvoyance, among other meanings lacking in scientific and philosophical respectability. It is, in short, difficult to define "intuition," and it is more difficult still to prove its existence; (2) there is no proof that we have an inborn, or innate, set of moral rules with which we might compare our acts to see whether or not they are moral; (3) intuition is immune to objective criticism because it applies only to its possessor and because intuitions differ from one person to the next; (4) human beings who do not possess moral intuitions either have no ethics or have to establish their ethics on other grounds.

Criticisms of Act Nonconsequentialism

The greatest problem for act nonconsequentialism would seem to be the third argument listed in the foregoing paragraph, for if feelings differ from person to person, how can conflicts between opposing feelings be resolved? All we can say is that we disagree with another person's feelings; we have no logical basis for saying, "Your feeling is wrong, whereas mine is right." Feelings simply cannot be arbitrated as reasons and judgments of evidence can; therefore, any theory of morality based on feelings alone, such as act nonconsequentialism, is highly questionable.

Other criticisms of act nonconsequentialism are

1. How do we know that what we feel—with no other guides—will be morally correct?

2. How do we know when we have sufficient facts to make a moral decision?

3. With morality so highly individualized, how do we know we are doing the best thing for anyone else involved in the situation?

4. Can we really rely on nothing but our momentary feelings to make moral decisions?

5. How will we be able to justify our actions except by saying, "Well, it felt like the right thing for me to do"?

It would seem to be very difficult to establish a morality of any social application here because anyone's feelings can justify any action he or she might take. An angry person might kill the one who made him angry and then justify the murder by saying, "I felt like killing her." But how do we arbitrate the conflict between the killer's feeling and the feelings of the victim's family and friends that the act was wrong? This is moral relativism of the highest degree, and there is absolutely no settlement possible where the only things we have to go on are the feelings of any individual at any particular time.

Another criticism of act nonconsequentialism, similar to the criticism of act utilitarianism, focuses on the questionable assumption that all situations and people are completely different and that none of them have anything in common.

There are, of course, some highly unique situations for which no rules can be set up in advance, but there are many other situations containing enough similarities so that rules, perhaps with exceptions or qualifications, can be stated quite effectively. For example, all situations in which someone is murdered have at least the similarity of a killer and a victim; because human life is generally considered essentially valuable in itself, rules governing when killing is or is not justified are not difficult to set up. Our legal system, with its different degree charges of murder and manslaughter, is a good example of rules with moral import. These generally work quite satisfactorily by condemning immoral acts while at the same time recognizing extenuating circumstances, thereby attaining a significant degree of justice and fairness for all concerned.

These two criticisms—that each act's being completely dissimilar from every other is simply a false empirical statement and the difficulty of relying solely on one's individual feelings—make act nonconsequentialism a questionable ethical system. Even the most active "situationist" of our day, Joseph Fletcher, who wrote *Situation Ethics*, claims that in all ethical actions there should be at least one unifying factor, namely, Christian love. Because of his belief he should probably be classified as an act utilitarian rather than as an act nonconsequentialist.

◆──

Rule Nonconsequentialist Theories

Rule nonconsequentialists believe that there are or can be rules that are the only basis for morality and that consequences do not matter. It is the following of the rules (which are right moral commands) that is moral, and the concept of morality cannot be applied to what happens because one follows the rules. The main way the various rule nonconsequentialist theories differ is in how they establish the rules.

Divine Command Theory

As described earlier, the Divine Command theory states that morality is not based on consequences of actions or rules, nor on self-interest or other-interest-edness but rather on something "higher" than these mere mundane events of the imperfect human or natural worlds. It is based on the existence of an all-good being or beings who are supernatural and who have communicated to human beings what they should do and not do in a moral sense. In order to be moral, then, human beings must follow the commands and prohibitions of such a being or beings to the letter without concerning themselves with consequences, self-interest, or anything else.

Criticisms of the Divine Command Theory. The difficulties of the Divine Command theory are inherent in the lack of rational foundation for the existence of some sort of supernatural being or beings and the further lack of proof that it or they set up the ethical system in question (see Chapter 1).

Even if one could prove conclusively the existence of the supernatural, how could one prove that any supernatural being is morally correct? The rules themselves might be morally valid, but the justification for following them regardless of the consequences is weak indeed. Furthermore, of what validity are the rules if a person does not believe in any kind of supernatural existence? Even if we will accept the existence of this supernatural and its commandments, how are we to interpret them correctly? Interpretations of the Ten Commandments vary and often conflict. Must there not be some clearer and generally more acceptable basis for rules than the existence of a supernatural?

Kant's Duty Ethics

Another famous rule nonconsequentialist theory, often called *Duty Ethics*, was formulated by Immanuel Kant (1724–1804) and contains several ethical principles.

The Good Will. Kant believed that nothing was good in itself except a good will, and he defined "will" as the uniquely human ability to act in accordance with rules, laws, or principles, regardless of interests or consequences.

Establishing Morality by Reasoning Alone. After establishing good will as the most important human attribute, he then argued that reason was the second most important human attribute and that it was therefore possible to set up valid absolute moral rules by reasoning alone, not by reference to any supernatural being or by empirical evidence but by the same kind of logical reasoning that establishes such indisputable truths in mathematics and logic as $2 + 2 = 4$, No circles are squares, and All triangles are three-sided.

Kant's first requirement for an absolute moral truth is that it must be logically consistent; that is, it cannot be self-contradictory, such as the statement "A circle is a square" would be. Second, the truth must be universalizable; that is, it must be able to be stated to apply to everything without exception, not just to some or maybe even most things. This is exemplified in the statement "all triangles are three-sided," for which there are no exceptions. Triangles may be of different sizes and shapes, but they are by definition indisputably and universally three-sided. If moral rules could indeed be established in this same manner, as Kant thought, then they too would be indisputable and therefore logically and morally binding on all human beings. Of course, some people might disobey these rules, but we could clearly brand such people as immoral.

68

In some ways, Kant's ideas were brilliant. For example, he could establish the fact that living parasitically would be immoral because it would also be illogical. He could say that the commandment "Always be a parasite, living off of someone else" is illogical because if all people lived like parasites, then off whom could they live? It is easy to see that it is conflict with the principle of universalizability that causes the inconsistency here. Obviously some people can be parasites, but not all. Now, if one could find such *moral* absolutes, then a completely irrefutable system of ethics could be established, and the obeying of the rules of this system would be what is moral, regardless of the consequences to oneself or to others. The major way Kant established to discover these moral absolutes was his Categorical Imperative.

The Categorical Imperative. The Categorical Imperative can be stated several ways, but basically it asserts that an act is immoral if the rule that would authorize it cannot be made into a rule for all human beings to follow.[2] This means that every time people are about to make a moral decision they must, according to Kant, ask first, What is the rule authorizing this act I am about to perform? and, second, Can it become a universal rule for all human beings to follow? For example, if a lazy person is thinking, Why should I work hard in order to live; why don't I just steal from everyone else? and if this person were aware of Kant's requirement, he or she would have to ask himself what the rule is for this contemplated action. The rule would have to be, I shall never work, but steal what I need from other human beings. If the person then attempts to universalize this statement, it would then read: No human being should ever work, but all human beings should steal what they need from each other. But if no one worked, there would be nothing to steal. How then would human beings live? Who would there be to steal from? It is obvious that some human beings can steal from others but that not all human beings can. According to Kant, stealing must therefore be immoral because it cannot be applied to all human beings.

Another, more crucial example, concerns killing another human being. Kant argued that one could not kill another human being without violating a moral absolute because in order to do so he would have to establish a rule that would be self-contradictory: Everyone must kill everyone else. Because the meaning of *life* is to live, then everyone killing everyone else would contradict that meaning and would therefore violate the Categorical Imperative and also not be universalizable. Killing, then, is immoral, and one should not kill.

The Practical Imperative. Another important principle in Kant's ethical system is that no human being should be thought of or used merely as a means for someone else's end and that each human being is a unique end in himself or herself, morally speaking, at least. This principle is sometimes referred to as Kant's *Practical Imperative.* It certainly seems to be an important principle if we consider fairness and equal treatment to be necessary attributes of any moral system.

Incidentally, this principle can also operate as an antidote to the "cost-benefit analysis," or "end-justifies-the-means," problem I mentioned in connection with both forms of utilitarianism in Chapter 2.

Let's take an example of how this Practical Imperative might work from the field of medical ethics in the area of human experimentation. Kant would oppose using a human being for experimental purposes "for the good of humanity" or for any other reason in which a human being would be considered as merely a "means" to an "end." Thus, in the case I described in Chapter 2 concerning the experimentation on one hundred babies now to save ten million children's lives in the future, Kant would definitely brand such experimentation as immoral. On the other hand, if an experimental procedure were necessary to try to save a child's life and it would also furnish doctors with information that would save lives in the future, Kant probably would allow it because, in this case, a human being would not merely be used as a means to an end but considered an end in him or herself. That is, the experimental procedure would be therapeutic for the human being involved—in this case the child.

Duty Rather than Inclination.   Kant next spoke about obeying such rules out of a sense of duty. He said that each human being is inclined to act in certain ways. That is, each person is inclined to do a variety of things, such as to give to the poor, stay in bed rather than go to work, rape someone, or be gentle to children. Because inclinations, according to Kant, are irrational and emotional and because we seem to operate on whim rather than reason when we follow them, people must force themselves to do what is moral out of a sense of duty. In other words, we have many inclinations of various sorts, some of which are moral and others immoral. If we are to act morally, however, we must rely on our reason and our will and act out of a sense of duty.

Kant even went so far as to say that an act simply is not moral unless duty rather than inclination is the motive behind it. A person who is merely inclined to be kind and generous to others is not to be considered moral in the sense in which Kant uses the word. Only if this person, perhaps because of some unexpected tragedy in his life, no longer is inclined to be kind and generous toward others, but now forces himself to be so out of a sense of duty, only then is he acting in a moral manner. This seems quite a harsh demand to most people, but it does show Kant's emphasis on his concept of duty as it pertains to following clearly established absolute moral rules.

After Kant felt he had established moral absolutes, it seemed obvious to him that to be moral one should obey them out of a sense of duty.

Summary and Illustration of Kant's System.   With the last point established, it appears we finally have an airtight moral system, one that cannot be successfully attacked in any way. We have "proved" that there are absolute moral rules that can be established irrefutably by reason, that one should obey them out of a sense of duty in order to be moral, and that all people must be considered unique individuals who are never to be used for anyone's purposes or ends. But let us continue.

In order to show how Kant carried his theory into practice, it is important to present here one of several "illustrations." First, Kant describes a man who, in despair yet still in possession of his reason, is contemplating suicide. Using Kant's system, the man must discover whether a maxim of his action could be made into a universal law for all human beings, so he frames the maxim as follows: "From self-love I should end my life whenever not ending it is likely to bring more bad than good." Kant then states that this cannot be universalized because it is contradictory to end life by the very feeling (self-love) that impels one to improve it. Therefore, the maxim cannot possibly exist as a universal law for all human beings because it is wholly inconsistent in itself and with the Categorical Imperative.

Second, it also violates Kant's Practical Imperative—that every human being is an end in himself or herself—because if the man destroys himself in order to escape from painful circumstances, he uses a person merely as a means to maintain tolerable conditions up to the end of his life. However, Kant maintains that people are neither things nor means for anyone else's ends but are ends in themselves; therefore, the suicidal man cannot destroy a person (whether it be himself or another) without violating this principle.[3]

Criticisms of Kant's Duty Ethics

Consistency and Conflicts of Duties. As you might suspect, there are several criticisms of Kant's system. He did show that some rules, when made universal, would become inconsistent and, therefore, could be said to be immoral because of their inconsistency. However, this does not tell us which rules are morally valid. Kant promulgated several Ten Commandment–like moral prohibitions based on his moral system, such as "Do not kill," "Do not steal," "Do not break promises."

He argued, for example, that one should not break a promise because it would be inconsistent to state, "I promise that I will repay you in thirty days, but I don't intend to keep my promise." Also, Kant reasoned, you cannot universalize the rule Never break promises except when it is inconvenient for you to keep them because promises would then have no meaning—or at least we wouldn't know when they did or did not. Kant asked what meaning a contractual agreement would have if after having said, "I promise to do 1, 2, 3, and 4," clause 5 read, "but I can break this agreement any time at my convenience."

Suppose, however, that not breaking a promise would result in someone's being seriously injured or even killed. According to Kant, we have to keep the promise, and because consequences do not matter, an innocent person would simply have to be hurt or killed. But which is, in fact, more important—keeping a promise or preventing an innocent person from being injured or killed? One of the problems here is that Kant never tells us how to decide between conflicting duties to obey different but equally absolute rules. We have a duty not to kill and a duty not to break promises, but which takes precedence when the two duties conflict?

Another criticism of universalizability and consistency as criteria of morality is that many rules of questionable moral value can be universalized without inconsistency. For example, is there anything inconsistent or nonuniversalizable about "Never help anyone in need"? If a society were made up of fairly self-sufficient individuals, there would be nothing immoral about not helping anyone. But even if there were people in need, what would establish the necessity of helping them? If one hundred people in a group were self-sufficient and fifteen were in need, would it be inconsistent or nonuniversal for the hundred to keep what they had and survive, allowing the other fifteen to die? It might not be moral under some other kind of rules or principles, but it would not be inconsistent to state such a rule.

The Reversibility Criterion. Kant answered this type of criticism by introducing the criterion of *reversibility*; that is, if an action were reversed, would a person want it to be done to him? This is otherwise known as the Golden Rule concept. For instance, Kant would ask of the rule Never help anyone in need, what would you want done to or for you if you were in need? You would want to be helped; therefore, such a rule, although universalizable, would not be *morally* universalizable because it would not meet the reversibility (would-you-want-this-done-to-you) criterion. This criterion helps to eliminate further what seem to be immoral rules, but isn't it a rather cagey way of smuggling in consequences? Isn't Kant really saying that although Never help anyone in need is universalizable, it isn't morally acceptable because the *consequences* of such a rule might backfire on the person stating it? This, of course, is no problem for the consequentialist (the rule utilitarian who would be the closest to Kant's theory except that the utilitarian considers consequences important), but Kant has said that absolute moral rules, not consequences, are the basis of morality. Isn't it inconsistent of him—especially because he has made such an issue of consistency—to allow consequences to creep into his theory?

Qualifying a Rule Versus Exceptions to It. Another criticism of the concept of absolute rules is that it leaves open to question whether a qualified rule is any less universalizable than one that is unqualified. Kant never distinguished between making an exception to a rule and qualifying that rule. For example, if the rule is stated, "Do not break promises but I feel that *I* can break them any time *I* want to," I would be making an unfair exception of myself to the rule. Kant felt that one should not make an exception to a general rule, and certainly not for one's self alone. However, what if the rule is *qualified* so that it applies to everyone: "Do not break promises *except* when not breaking a promise would seriously harm or kill someone"? Here the exception applies to the rule itself rather than to some individual or individuals. Kant certainly had a strong point to make about not making exceptions; after all, what good is a rule if one can make an exception of one's self any time one wants to? However, "Do not kill except in self-defense" is not any less universalizable than "Do not kill," and the former rule would seem to relate to the history of human values and also to a doctrine of fairness much better than the latter.

Duties Versus Inclinations. There is still another criticism having to do with the inclinations-duties conflict that Kant described, and that is, what happens when your inclinations and duties are the same? For example, what if you are *inclined* not to kill people, a tendency that fits with Kant's rule "Do not kill," which it is your duty to obey. Does this mean that because you are not inclined to kill, you are not a moral person because your duty is not pulling you away from your inclinations? Many moralists disagree with the idea that people are not moral merely because they are inclined to be good rather than always struggling with themselves to be so.

It is true that many times the real test of personal morality comes when human beings go against their inclinations (for example, to steal money when no one can catch them) and act out of a sense of duty (they should not steal because it is wrong or because they would not want someone else to steal from them). But is this any reason to consider people not moral if they lead a good life, do not do harm to others because they do not want to, *and* also think it is their duty not to? Which type of person would you feel safer with, the person who is inclined not to harm or kill others or the person who has strong inclinations to kill others but who restrains himself merely out of a sense of duty? It seems that society has a better chance of being moral if most people in it are inclined to be moral through some sort of moral education.

Ross's Prima Facie Duties

Sir William David Ross (1877–1940) agreed with Kant that morality should not basically rest on consequences, but he disagreed with the unyielding absolutism of Kant's theories. One might place Ross somewhere in between Kant and the rule utilitarians in that he felt that we had certain *prima facie* duties that we must generally always adhere to *unless* serious circumstances or reasons told us to do otherwise. In other words, he did not believe that consequences make an action right or wrong, but he did think that it is necessary to consider consequences in making moral choices.

Prima Facie Duties. The words *prima facie* literally mean "at first glance" or "on the surface of things." A prima facie duty, then, is one that all human beings must do in a general sense before any other considerations enter into the picture. Some of Ross's prima facie duties are

1. Duties of fidelity (or faithfulness): telling the truth, keeping actual and implied promises, and keeping contractual agreements.
2. Duties of reparation: making up for the wrongs we've done to others—in other words, making reparation for wrongful acts.
3. Duties of gratitude: recognizing what others have done for us and extending our gratitude to them.
4. Duties of justice: preventing the improper distribution of good and bad that is not in keeping with what people merit or deserve.
5. Duties of beneficence: helping to improve the condition of others in the area of virtue, intelligence, or happiness.
6. Duties of self-improvement: the obligation we have to improve our own virtue, intelligence, and happiness.
7. Duties of nonmaleficence (noninjury): not injuring others and preventing injury to others.[4]

Thus, Ross, like Kant, had rules that all human beings should adhere to because it was their moral obligation to do so. He also improved on Kant a great deal in the area of what to do when duties (especially prima facie duties) conflict.

Principles to Resolve Conflicting Duties. Ross established two principles to deal with the conflict of prima facie duties: (1) Always do that act that is in accord with the stronger prima facie duty, and (2) always do that act that has the greatest prima facie rightness over prima facie wrongness.[5]

Criticisms of Ross's Theory

There are obviously some "prima facie" problems with Ross's theories.

Selecting Prima Facie Duties. How are we to decide which duties are indeed prima facie? Ross did list some of these duties for us, but on what basis did he do so, and what justification either in evidence or reasoning has he given us? When confronted with questions about how to select prima facie duties, he said that he was

claiming that we *know* them to be true. To me it seems as self-evident as anything could be, that to make a promise, for instance, is to create a moral claim on us in someone else. Many readers will perhaps say that they do *not* know this to be true. If so I certainly cannot prove it to them.

I can only ask them to reflect again, in the hope that they will ultimately agree that they also know it to be true.[6]

What Ross is actually basing this selection of such duties on, then, is intuition; that is, there is no logic or evidence to justify his choices, but we are to accept what he says on the basis of intuition. If we do not have the same intuitions as he, then we are to keep trying until we do! This, of course, is highly speculative and vague in its application with all of the attendant problems we encountered in discussing and evaluating the intuitive basis for act nonconsequentialism.

Deciding Which Prima Facie Duty Takes Precedence. A second problem arises in dealing with the way Ross tries to solve the decision-making difficulty of choosing the correct prima facie duty when it conflicts with another. Both of Ross's principles are difficult to apply. He does not tell us really how we are to determine when one obligation is stronger than the other. Further, he does not give us a clear rule for determining the "balance" of prima facie rightness over wrongness. Therefore, there seem to be no clear criteria for either choosing which duties are prima facie or deciding how to distinguish among them after they have been established.

♦————————————————————————————

General Criticisms of Nonconsequentialist Theories

The criticism of nonconsequentialist theories in general is, can we, and indeed should we, really avoid consequences in trying to set up a moral system? In addition, rule nonconsequentialist theories raise the following problems: (1) Why should we follow rules if the consequences of following them could be bad even for a few, but also, in some cases, for all concerned? (2) How can we resolve conflicts among rules that are all equally and absolutely binding? And (3), is there such a thing as a moral rule with absolutely *no* exceptions, given the complexities of human behavior and experience? If so, what is it?

First, even Kant, who fought against consequences, seems to have smuggled them in with his reversibility doctrine. But even without this doctrine, when you push any ethical system back far enough, asking why one should do the things prescribed, won't your answers have to bring in consequences for yourself, others, or all concerned? For example, in the Divine Command theory, isn't it really possible to justify the more immediately applicable and practical commandments as ethical necessities whether or not you believe God gave them to human beings? One could ask why God is so wise in having stated that human beings should not kill, steal, or commit adultery, and answer that the consequences of not having some rules in those areas would be much worse. If killing were freely allowed, then people's lives would be in danger constantly, human growth would not be able to take place, and there would be no moral systems or cultures, only constant battles to avoid being killed. These commandments and others like them help all human beings to respect the rights of their fellows and bring some stability and order into a social system that would otherwise be in a constant state of chaotic upheaval.

Second, it is true that Kant starts without *officially* using consequences, by beginning with logical inconsistency, but are consequences really very far behind? What is the real point of any moral system if not to do good for oneself or others or both and if not to create a moral society in which people can create and grow peacefully with a minimum of unnecessary conflict? I cannot think of one system of morality that is not concerned with consequences somewhere along the line. Many systems may try to justify their imperatives by stating, "You should do this simply because it is right [or because God said so or because doing otherwise would be logically inconsistent]." But despite these justifications, the moral prescriptions of each system are calculated to bring about some good consequences, usually for most, if not all, human beings.

Third, as I have mentioned before, a quandary arises when there is no clear way of resolving conflicts between moral rules that are equally absolute. Kant did not tell us how to determine what to do when our absolute duties conflict.

Fourth, Ross at least attempted to answer the question of whether there really are any absolute moral rules. However, many people, especially in the twentieth century, when so many of what were formerly considered absolutes have been shown to have exceptions, insist that there are either no absolutes or so few that one can hardly state them. Some moralists—moral relativists—state that everything is relative and that there are no absolutes. Others, like Joseph Fletcher, state that there is but one absolute—love—and that everything else is relative to it. Regardless of whether their arguments are cogent (the problem of absolutes will be discussed more fully in Chapter 4), there is a serious problem with all nonconsequentialist theories in that the selection of moral rules and duties seems to be arbitrary and often destructive of creative argument. One cannot argue that killing may sometimes be justified if a nonconsequentialist has simply stated that in order to be moral one must not kill.

A good example of this type of dead-end reasoning is the antiabortionist argument that under no circumstances may a life be taken and that life begins at conception. How can one argue for the saving of the mother's life or consider the kind of life either mother or baby will live if such absolutes have already been established? On the other side of the coin, how can one argue for the value of the life of a fetus if the prochoice advocate has taken as an absolute the woman's right over her own body regardless of what it contains? What justification can either arguer give for the validity of these absolutes and for why there can be no exceptions to them under any circumstances?

When people are arguing consequences, they might at least be able to show that one action will have more good consequences than another, but when they are merely presenting arbitrary absolutes, there can be no counterarguments to justify exceptions. If we simply adopt an arbitrary, nonconsequentialist, absolute moral rule, then arguments from consequentialists and others are simply excluded. Closing off debate in this fashion is destructive to the search for truth and understanding in other areas, such as science, but it is disastrous in morality, where the need to arrive at right answers is more crucial than in any other area of human experience.

◆————————————————————————————————

Virtue Ethics

Another moral theory that has become significant to many contemporary ethicists is called "Virtue Ethics." It is certainly not a new theory, but finds its beginnings with the Greeks and especially Aristotle in the fourth century B.C. Essentially, this theory differs from all of the previous ones we have discussed in that it does not depend on consequences, feelings, or rules so much as on human beings developing a moral or virtuous character by doing what a good or "virtuous" person would do.

Definition of Terms

The dictionary defines *virtue* as "the quality of moral excellence, righteousness, and responsibility . . . a specific type of moral excellence or other exemplary quality considered meritorious; a worthy practice or ideal."[7] It further lists the "cardinal" or "natural" virtues as "justice, prudence, fortitude, and temperance."[8]

A dictionary of philosophy describes *virtue* in Aristotle's philosophy as "that state of a thing which constitutes its peculiar excellence and enables it to perform its function well . . . in man [it is] the activity of reason and of rationally ordered habits."[9]

As you can see, the emphasis is on the good or virtuous character of human beings themselves, rather than on their acts, the consequences of their acts, or feelings or rules. In other words, it is the development of the good or virtuous person that is important in this moral theory, not abstract rules or consequences of acts or rules except as they derive from a good or virtuous person or cause that person to be good or virtuous.

Aristotle's Nichomachean Ethics

Virtue Ethics derives from Aristotle's *Nichomachean Ethics* (named for his son, Nichomachus), which is teleogical in character (that is, aims toward some end or purpose). As Aristotle put it, "Every art and every inquiry, every action and choice, seems to aim at some good . . . [and] the good has rightly been defined as that at which all things aim."[10] For example, a doctor's art aims at health, seamanship aims at a safe voyage, and economy aims at wealth. He goes on to say that the end of human life is happiness, and the basic activity of human beings is reason—a virtuous activity; therefore, the aim of human beings, according to Aristotle, is to reason well for a whole or complete life.

Emphasis on Goodness of Character

Aristotle is concerned with action, not as right or good in itself, but as it is conducive to human good. In ethics he starts from the actual moral judgments of human beings, and by comparing, contrasting, and sifting them, he says we come to the formulation of general principles. Notice how this differs from the Divine Command theory and the theories of Kant and Ross as to the way principles are established. In the latter three theories, ethical principles are objective to or outside of human beings and are established by the supernatural or abstract reason itself. Aristotle presupposes that there are natural ethical tendencies implanted in human beings and that following them with a general attitude of consistent harmony and proportion constitutes the ethical life.

Development of the Good or Virtuous Human Being

Aristotle describes his ethical system as eminently common sense–based, for the most part, founded as it was on the moral judgments of the ideal human being, who, based on reason, is considered good and virtuous. He states that humans start by having a capacity for goodness which has to be developed by practice. He says we begin by doing acts which are objectively virtuous, without a knowledge that the acts are good and without actively or rationally choosing them ourselves. As we practice these acts, we come to realize that the virtue is good in and of itself. For example, a child is taught to tell the truth (objectively a virtue) by her parents, and then she does so because they have taught her she should. Eventually, she recognizes that truth is a virtue in and of itself and continues to tell the truth because she knows it is virtuous to do so.

This process would seem to be circular except that Aristotle makes a distinction between the acts that create a good disposition (telling the truth without knowing it's a virtue) and the acts that flow from the good disposition once it has been created (telling the truth because a person has come to know it's a virtue). Aristotle states further that virtue itself is a disposition which has been developed out of a capacity by the proper exercise of that capacity.

What Is Virtue and How Does It Relate to Vice?

According to Aristotle, virtue is a mean between two extremes, both of which are vices—either excess or deficiency (or defect). Moral virtue, then, is defined by Aristotle as "a disposition to choose by a rule . . . which a practically wise man would determine" to be the mean between the two extremes of excess or deficiency.[11] And, according to Aristotle, practical wisdom is the ability to see what is the right thing to do in any circumstance. Therefore, a person has to determine what a "practically wise, virtuous man" would choose in any circumstance involving a moral action and then do the right thing. Obviously, Aristotle attaches much more importance to the enlightened conscience than to prior theoretical rules (again unlike the Divine Command theorist, Kant, or Ross).

How to Determine the Proper Mean

What is the mean between excess and deficiency, and how does one determine it? According to Aristotle, the mean in ethics cannot be determined mathematically but rather is a mean "relative to us" or to whoever is trying to determine what the right thing to do is. For example, if ten pounds of food are too much (excess) and two are too little (deficiency or defect), then six pounds, which is the mean between these two extremes, still may be too much for some and too little for others; therefore, one must choose the appropriate mean between the two extremes relative to himself or herself.[12]

Some examples of means between two extremes established by Aristotle and tabulated by Sir William David Ross (who established the ethical theory of *prima facie* duties) are as follows:

Feeling or Action	Excess	Mean	Defect
Confidence	Rashness	Courage	Cowardice
Sensual pleasure	Profligacy	Temperance	Insensibility
Shame	Bashfulness	Modesty	Shamelessness
Giving amusement	Buffoonery	Wittiness	Boorishness
Truth-telling about oneself	Boastfulness	Truthfulness	Self-depreciation
Friendship	Obsequiousness	Friendliness	Sulkiness[13]

This partial list will give you some idea of what Aristotle meant by the mean between two extremes, but it doesn't really show what the mean "relative to us" would actually be. It does, however, give us some general guidelines from which to determine the mean.

Contemporary Analysis of Virtue Ethics

Probably the most significant and prominent contemporary analyst of Virtue Ethics, especially Aristotle's version, is Alasdair MacIntyre in his book, *After Virtue*. In analyzing Aristotle's intentions, MacIntyre stated that virtues are dispositions not only to act in particular ways, but also to *feel* in particular ways, which obviously emphasizes the creation of a virtuous character in oneself, not merely to follow rules or to calculate good consequences. One must create virtuous feelings or inclinations within oneself, not merely act virtuously. He stated further that to act virtuously is not to act against inclination (as Kant thought), but rather to act from inclinations that have been formed by the cultivation of the virtues.[14] The idea, then, is to decide what the practically wise and virtuous human beings would do in any situation involving moral issues, and then do that virtuous act that the virtuous person would do. As MacIntyre says, human beings must know what they are doing when they judge or act virtuously, and then they should do what *is* virtuous merely because it is so.[15]

Advantages of Virtue Ethics

Creating the Good Human Being. Virtue Ethics attempts to create the good or virtuous human being, not just good acts or rules and not just a robot who merely follows preestablished rules or a person who acts on whim or who tries to achieve good consequences. It tries to inculcate virtue by urging human beings to practice virtuous acts in order to create the habitually virtuous or good person who will then continue to act virtuously. Many ethicists see this as one of our major problems today. We have rules and laws and systems of ethics, but we still do not have ethical or virtuous human beings, and these ethicists believe that until we create ethical or virtuous people, our chances of creating a moral society are minimal. After all, they say, we've had rules, laws, and regulations forever and have even more nowadays, but still badness, immorality, viciousness, cruelty, and vice seem to be getting worse rather than better.

An example of this debate is the laws against racial discrimination. When President Harry Truman proposed racially integrating the U.S. military, some argued that "you cannot legislate morality"; that is, you may pass laws that force people to behave certain ways or act differently than they want to or have, but laws cannot change the way people feel inside. Until you change their feelings, they said, you will never really change people's morals. This idea had its point; however, many people's moral views did change when racial integration became the law of the land. Many others' views, of course, didn't and haven't changed, and critics of this view ask, "Isn't it too idealistic to think you can change people's morality to the point where everyone is a virtuous person?" Also, they add that often rules and laws do help to create virtuous people, at least force them to act virtuously, and maybe that is the best we can do.

Unifying Reason and Emotion. Both act nonconsequentialism and Kant's theories attempt to separate reason and emotion or feelings from each other. Virtue Ethics, on the other hand, attempts to unify them by stating that virtues are dispositions not only to act in certain ways but also to feel in certain ways—virtuously in both cases. The purpose again is, through reasoning (practical wisdom), to do what is virtuous, at the same time inculcating that virtuousness within so that not only do humans reason what is virtuous, but also they begin and continue to feel what is virtuous. None of the other theories attempt to do this as well.

Kant eschews acting on inclination almost to the point of absurdity, so that the critical question against his theory is, "What if people are inclined to be virtuous? Shouldn't they act upon those inclinations?" Kant would seem to say they wouldn't be as moral as if they acted virtuously against their inclinations. On the other hand, the act nonconsequentialist stance says we should act only on emotion—that is, what feels right or virtuous at any particular moment or in any particular situation. Aristotle, as Kant, would be aghast at such a theory of morality since he thought that human beings' major activity was to reason well for a complete life; however, he tried much more than Kant to integrate emotion or feelings with reason without excluding the former.

Emphasizes Moderation. Virtue Ethics, at least Aristotle's version, sets up a way to achieve moderation between excess and deficiency. Many ethicists believe, along with the Greeks, that moderation in all things is what human beings ought to strive for. As you will see in Chapters 8 through 15, I often present the moderate point of view, and Humanitarian Ethics often goes along with that view. Aristotle attempts to set up means to achieve moderation by codifying what constitutes excess, defect, and the mean between them, as described in Ross' table shown earlier. He also encourages freedom by allowing individuals to decide the appropriate mean relative to themselves. Again, he seems to encourage an integration between feeling and reason by urging individuals to use both their reason and feelings to decide the appropriate mean for them.

Disadvantages or Problems

Do Human Beings Have an End? One of Aristotle's first assumptions is that all things have a purpose or end at which they aim. He then goes on to say that the end of human life is happiness and that all human beings aim at that. First, is it true or proven that all things have an end or purpose? Many people argue that they do, but many also argue that it is not clear that they do. For example, some argue that the world and everything in it has occurred by chance or randomly and that it is not at all clear that anything in such a universe aims toward any end except its own death or dissolution. Even if we assume that everything has an end toward which it aims, what proves that the end of human life is happiness? Couldn't it just as well be knowledge, spirituality, death, suffering, or other things? Aristotle's assumption is just that—an assumption. Many would also argue that happiness is not an appropriate end for human life but that something more "noble" is appropriate, such as love of God and the hope of being with Him. Furthermore, some argue that "to reason well for a complete life" might be a philosopher's view of what the human aim is, but why couldn't it be other things as well? Again, Aristotle has made another assumption, but religionists might argue that being spiritual is the human aim, and other philosophers might argue that feelings or emotions are the aim.

Are Morals Naturally Implanted? A second major assumption by Aristotle is that the tendency to be moral is naturally implanted in human beings. What evidence is there to support that claim? Many would argue that morality is not some innate characteristic or idea, but rather something that is taught and learned from experience. The only tendency humans have is to be able to reason, and reason in and of itself does not necessarily imply morality, although it is thought by many, Aristotle included, to be its basis. Is it really true, however, that human beings have a natural, innate tendency to be moral? Some argue in the affirmative and some argue the opposite, but there is no clear evidence or proof that Aristotle's assumption is true.

What Is Virtue and What Constitutes the Virtues? One of the most significant problems with this theory, however, centers around the following questions: What is virtue, what are the virtues, and what is the ideal or virtuous human being from whom we are supposed to choose our virtues? Some, including Aristotle, argue that all we need to know and provide is an account of what human flourishing and well-being consist of; then, the virtues can be adequately characterized as those qualities necessary to promote such flourishing and well-being. According to MacIntyre, however, there have been and still are deep conflicts over what is involved in human flourishing and well-being.[16]

He goes on to say that different periods in history and historical figures from those periods present us with several sets of virtues:

1. In ancient Homeric Greece, a man was what he did; that is, a man and his actions were considered identical. Morality and social structure were one in heroic societies; the ideal virtuous man was the warrior, and the virtues were strength and courage.

2. To Aristotle, Aquinas, and the New Testament, virtue is a quality that enables one to move toward the achievement of a specifically human end (natural or supernatural). For Aristotle, this was rationality and the ideal virtuous man was the Athenian gentleman. For Aquinas and the New Testament, the virtues are faith, hope, charity (or love), and humility, and the ideal virtuous man is the saint.

3. To Benjamin Franklin virtue was a quality that has utility in achieving earthly and heavenly success. His concept of virtue was teleological, like Aristotle's, but utilitarian in character. To Franklin the virtues were cleanliness, silence, industry, and chastity, among many.[17]

What Is the Ideal Virtuous Person?

Finally, since Aristotle states that we ought to decide what a virtuous act or person is by modeling ourselves after the ideal virtuous person, how do we determine who and what that paradigmatic person is? I'm sure we could each name an ideal person we ought to emulate, but wouldn't we come up with a lot of different ones, depending on our own backgrounds, experiences, and desires? For example, the Homeric ideal of a virtuous human being would appeal to some people, as would the humble saint to others, or the person of intellect to still others, but wouldn't we all act differently depending on what traits we admired? I'm not saying that we could not agree upon some sort of composite virtuous person, but I argue that it would not be easy. How would we be able to say that we ought to act in connection with such an ideal when it would be just that—an abstract ideal of a human being? Also, how would we know that we had come up with the truly virtuous ideal person?

♦————————————————————————————————

Conclusions

In summary, then, the nonconsequentialist theories of morality have certain advantages. First, they do not necessitate the difficult task of computing consequences for a moral action. Second, they have, in their rule form, a strong set of moral guides—unlike the act moralists of both the consequentialist and nonconsequentialist approaches to morality. Third, nonconsequentialists are able to found their system on something other than consequences, thereby avoiding the pitfall of a cost-benefit analysis approach to morality.

On the other hand, as difficult as computing consequences may be, nonconsequentialists really seem to avoid the whole point of morality—certainly social morality—by trying to ignore the consequences of their rules or acts. Although it is helpful to have a series of strong rules and guides to go by, rule nonconsequentialism makes it difficult to decide which rules these will be and how to rank them in order of importance or otherwise resolve conflicts when absolutes oppose each other. Furthermore, rule nonconsequentialism provides for no open discussion of moral quandaries because it has closed the door by arbitrarily stating what is right and what is wrong, without any possibility of exception. And what is right and wrong is based either on the supposed commands of a supernatural being or beings whom no one is allowed to question or on a theory of logical consistency that can show that human beings should not be inconsistent but can give very few other reasons why one should follow one rule rather than another.

Virtue Ethics has the advantage of trying to develop the moral person from within as well as from without, but it is based on a number of assumptions that are difficult to prove, such as human beings' having an end or purpose and what that purpose is, that morality is innate, and what virtue, the virtues, and the virtuous human being are.

The nonconsequentialist and Virtue Ethics theories do not seem any more satisfying than the consequentialist—to many people, they probably seem even less so. What are we to do, then? Should we retreat to consequentialist theories with their attendant problems or take the nonconsequentialist or the Virtue Ethics approach as the "lesser of two evils"? I believe that there is a value in trying to synthesize the best of these systems while de-emphasizing the worst. We shall examine the possibilities of such a synthesis in Chapter 7. First, however, it is important to tackle three problem areas affecting the setting up of a moral system: absolutism versus relativism, freedom versus determinism, and reward and punishment.

Chapter Summary

I. Nonconsequentialist (deontological) theories of morality
   A. The basic assumption of these theories is that consequences do not, and in fact should not, enter into judging whether actions or people are moral or immoral.
   B. What is moral and immoral is decided on some standard or standards of morality other than consequences.

II. Act nonconsequentialist theories
   A. The act nonconsequentialist's major assumption is that there are no general moral rules or theories but only particular actions, situations, and people about which we cannot generalize.
   B. Decisions are based on "intuitionism"; that is, what is right and wrong in any particular situation is based on what people feel (intuit) is right or wrong—this is, therefore, a highly individualistic theory.
   C. There are several criticisms of act nonconsequentialism.
      1. How can we know, with no other guides, that what we feel will be morally correct?
      2. How will we know when we have sufficient facts to make a moral decision?
      3. With morality so highly individualized, how do we know we are doing the best thing for everyone else involved in a particular situation?
      4. How will we be able to justify our actions except by saying, "Well, it felt like the right thing for me to do"?
      5. Isn't it questionable to assume that all situations and people are completely different and have nothing in common?

III. Rule nonconsequentialist theories
    A. The major assumption here is that there are or can be rules that are the only basis for morality and that consequences do not matter—following the rules, which are right moral commands, is what is moral, not what happens because one follows the rules.
    B. According to the Divine Command theory, an action is right and people are good if, and only if, they obey commands supposedly given to them by a divine being, regardless of consequences. There are some criticisms of this theory.
        1. The theory does not provide a rational foundation for the existence of a supernatural being and therefore not for morality either.
        2. Even if we could prove conclusively the existence of a supernatural being, how could we prove that this being was morally correct?
        3. How are we to interpret these commands even if we accept the existence of a supernatural?
        4. Rules found in the Divine Command theory may be valid, but they need to be justified on some other, more rational basis.
IV. Kant's Duty Ethics
    A. Kant believed that it is possible by reasoning alone to set up valid absolute moral rules that have the same force as indisputable mathematical truths.
        1. Such truths must be logically consistent, not self-contradictory.
        2. They must also be universalizable.
    B. According to the Categorical Imperative, an act is immoral if the rule that would authorize it cannot be made into a rule for all human beings to follow.
    C. The Practical Imperative, another important principle in Kant's moral system, states that no human being should be thought of or used merely as a means for someone else's end, but rather that each human being is a unique end in himself or herself.
    D. Once moral rules are discovered as absolutes, human beings must obey them out of a sense of duty rather than follow their inclinations.
    E. There are criticisms of Kant's system.
        1. Although Kant showed that some rules would become inconsistent when universalized, this does not tell us which rules are morally valid.
        2. Kant never showed us how to resolve conflicts between equally absolute rules, such as Do not break a promise and Do not kill.
        3. Kant did not distinguish between making an exception to a rule and qualifying a rule.
        4. Some rules, such as Do not help anyone in need, can be universalized without inconsistency yet still have questionable moral value.

          (a) Kant answered this criticism with the reversibility criterion, that is, the would-you-want-this-done-to-you, or Golden Rule, idea.

          (b) However, the reversibility criterion suggests a reliance on consequences, which is against everything that Kant set out to do in his system.

    5. Kant seems to have emphasized duties over inclinations too much in stating that we must act from a sense of duty, not from our inclinations. However, he gave no rule for what we should do when our inclinations and duties are the same.

V. Ross's prima facie duties

  A. Ross agreed with Kant on the establishing of morality on other than consequences but disagreed with Kant's overly absolute rules. He falls between Kant and rule utilitarianism in his approach to ethics.

  B. He established prima facie duties that all human beings must adhere to unless there are serious reasons why they should not. Prima facie means "at first glance" or "on the surface."

  C. He listed several prima facie duties.

    1. Duties of fidelity

    2. Duties of reparation

    3. Duties of gratitude

    4. Duties of justice

    5. Duties of beneficence

    6. Duties of self-improvement

    7. Duties of nonmaleficence (noninjury).

  D. He offered two principles to resolve conflicting duties.

    1. Always act in accord with the stronger prima facie duty.

    2. Always act in such a way so as to achieve the greatest prima facie rightness over wrongness.

  E. These are criticisms of Ross's theory.

    1. How are we to decide which duties are *prima facie*?

    2. On what basis are we to decide which ones take precedence over the rest?

    3. How can we determine when there is sufficient reason to override one *prima facie* duty with another?

VI. General criticisms of nonconsequentialist theories

  A. Can we, and indeed should we, avoid consequences in trying to set up a moral system?

  B. Is it entirely possible to exclude consequences in an ethical system?

  C. What is the real point of any moral system if not to do good for oneself, others, or both and if not to create a moral society in which people can create and grow peacefully with a minimum of unnecessary conflict?

D. How do we resolve conflicts among moral rules that are equally absolute? This problem is peculiar to rule nonconsequentialist theories.

E. Any system that operates on such rigid absolutes as does rule nonconsequentialism closes the door on further discussion of moral quandaries.

VII. Virtue Ethics

A. Virtue Ethics is not a new theory, having its beginnings with the Greeks and especially Aristotle in the fourth century BC, but it has become significant to many contemporary ethicists.

B. *Virtue* is defined as "moral excellence, righteousness, responsibility, or other exemplary qualities considered meritorious."

C. Emphasis is on the good or virtuous character of human beings themselves, rather than on their acts, consequences, feelings, or rules.

D. Aristotle's Nichomachean Ethics is based on the following tenets.

  1. It is teleogical in that it aims toward some end or purpose.

  2. The end of human life is happiness, and reason is the basic activity of humans; therefore, the aim of human beings is to reason well for a complete life.

  3. Aristotle starts with the moral judgments of reasonable and virtuous human beings and then formulates general principles, unlike the nonconsequentialists—Divine Command theorists, Kant, and Ross—who start with abstract ethical principles.

  4. Human beings have a capacity for goodness that has to be developed by practice based on what the ideal, virtuous human being would do.

  5. What is virtue and how does it relate to vice?

    a. Virtue is a mean, relative to us, between the two extremes of excess and deficiency (or defect).

    b. In the feeling of shame, for example, modesty is the mean between the excess of bashfulness and the defect of shamelessness.

E. Alasdair MacIntyre gives a contemporary analysis of Virtue Ethics.

  1. The virtues are dispositions both to act and to feel in particular ways, and one must create virtuous feelings within oneself, not merely act virtuously.

  2. One must then decide what the practically wise and virtuous human being would do in any situation and then do the virtuous act that person would do.

F. There are several advantages to Virtue Ethics.

  1. It strives to create the good human being, not merely good acts or rules.

  2. It attempts to unify reason and emotion.

  3. It emphasizes moderation, which is prized by many ethicists.

G. It also has disadvantages.
   1. Do human beings have an end or purpose? If so what is it, and how can we prove any of this?
   2. Are morals naturally implanted, or are they learned from experience?
   3. What is virtue, and what constitutes the virtues? There seems to be a wide variety of opinions on this, so how can we decide what virtue really is and which virtues are really virtues?
   4. What or who is the ideal virtuous human being, and how do we determine and prove this?

Exercises for Review

1. What, essentially, are nonconsequentialist (deontological) theories of morality? How do they differ from consequentialist (teleological) theories?

2. What do act nonconsequentialists believe? How do they differ from act utilitarians?

3. What do rule nonconsequentialists believe? How do they differ from rule utilitarians?

4. Describe and critically analyze the Divine Command theory.

5. Explain and critically analyze Kant's Duty Ethics, responding to the following:
   (a) What are absolute moral truths, according to Kant, and how can they be arrived at?
   (b) Explain the difference between duties and inclinations. Why did Kant think people ought to act out of a sense of duty rather than from inclination?
   (c) Explain the Categorical Imperative.
   (d) What does "universalizability" mean, and why is it important to Kant's moral system?
   (e) What is the reversibility criterion? What are its problems?

6. Explain Kant's Practical Imperative. Do you agree or disagree with this principle? Why?

7. What are prima facie duties? What problems do they raise? Can you think of any moral duties that might be prima facie? What are they?

8. In your opinion, can a moral system really function without regard to consequences? How or how not?

9. Explain the problems that are peculiar to rule nonconsequentialist theories of morality.

10. Comment on the problem of arbitrariness when dealing with moral problems as it relates to creative argument and moral problem solving.

Discussion Questions

1. The act nonconsequentialist theory allows greater freedom in making moral decisions than other theories because it leaves moral decisions completely up to each individual's own feelings. How free do you think individuals should be in moral decision making? To what extent does this theory appeal or not appeal to you, and why?

2. The rule nonconsequentialist theories essentially state that there are certain moral absolutes that should never be violated (for example, rules against killing, mutilating, stealing, and breaking promises). To what extent do you agree or disagree with this idea? Are there certain dos and don'ts to which human beings should always adhere? If so, why should they be adhered to and what are they? If not, why not?

3. One of the advantages of rule nonconsequentialist theories is that they clearly state dos and don'ts, thereby lending a great deal of stability and order to morality. Adherents describe the benefits of this when they say, "We know just where we stand with this type of morality, and it gives us a great deal of security when compared to relativistic morality." To what extent do you feel this advantage is an important one? Why? What are its strong points and its drawbacks?

4. To what extent do you believe that Christians and Jews use the Divine Command theory approach rather than egoism or act or rule utilitarianism as a basis for their ethical systems? For example, do you believe that most Christians follow their religion's moral rules because they believe these rules were established by God or for other reasons? Answer in detail.

5. To what extent do you believe consequences can be eliminated from any moral system?

6. Reread exercise question 2 in Chapter 2. To what extent do you feel that the surgeon is justified in using the battalion commander as a means to what he deems to be a "good" end, that is, saving soldiers' lives? To what extent is the other surgeon justified in his nonconsequentialist rule that doctors should never knowingly perform unnecessary operations?

7. To what extent do you think it is important to rank moral rules in order of importance (for example, Ross's prima facie duties)? Show how you would rank your ethical rules or those of any system of which you are aware.

8. To what extent are emotions or feelings important to any moral system? Be specific, and explain how you think emotions or feelings relate to morality.

9. How much importance do you think duty ought to have in relation to morality? Explain your answer.

10. Rule nonconsequentialist theories stress consistency in their moral systems and codes, whereas the act nonconsequentialist theory seems to imply variety and inconsistency. How important do you think it is for a moral system or code or for a person to be consistent?

Notes

1. Austin Fagothey, *Right and Reason*, 8th ed., rev. Milton A. Gonsalves (St. Louis: C. V. Mosby, 1985), 114–15.

2. Kant's actual formulation can be found in *Problems of Moral Philosophy*, 2nd ed., ed. Paul W. Taylor (Belmont, Calif.: Dickenson, 1972), 219. The version given here is a paraphrase.

3. Immanuel Kant, *Fundamental Principles of the Metaphysics of Morals*, trans. H. J. Paton (New York: Harper & Row, 1957), Sections I, II, and III.

4. William D. Ross, *The Right and the Good* (New York: Oxford University Press, 1930), 21–22.

5. Ibid., 41–42.

6. Ibid., 24.

7. William Morris, ed., *The American Heritage Dictionary of the English Language* (Boston: Houghton Mifflin, 1978), 1432.

8. Ibid., 203.

9. Dagobert D. Runes, *Dictionary of Philosophy* (Totowa, N.J.: Littlefield, Adams and Co., 1968), 332.

10. Richard McKeon, ed., *Introduction to Aristotle* (New York: The Modern Library, 1947), 308.

11. Ibid., 340.

12. Ibid., 339.

13. Sir David Ross, *Aristotle* (London, Methuen and Co., 1964), 203.

14. Alasdair MacIntyre, *After Virtue* (Notre Dame, Ind.: University of Notre Dame Press, 1984), 149.

15. Ibid., 154.

16. Ibid., 162.

17. Ibid., 182–85.

Supplementary Reading

Aune, Bruce. *Kant's Theory of Morals*. Princeton: Princeton University Press, 1980.

Broadie, Sarah, *Ethics and Aristotle*. New York: Oxford University Press, 1991.

Fagothey, Austin. *Right and Reason*, 8th ed., rev. Milton A. Gonsalves. St. Louis: C. V. Mosby, 1985.

Hochberg, Gary M. *Kant: Moral Legislation and Two Senses of "Will."* New York: University Press of America, 1982.

Hospers, John. *Human Conduct*, 2nd ed. New York: Harcourt, Brace, and World, 1982.

Jacobs, Jonathan. *Virtue and Self-Knowledge*. Englewood Cliffs, N.J.: Prentice-Hall, 1989.

Kant, Immanuel. *Fundamental Principles of the Metaphysics of Morals*. Trans. H. J. Paton. New York: Harper & Row, 1957.

———. "The Supreme Principle of Morality." *The Range of Ethics*, eds. Harold H. Titus and Morris Keeton. New York: Van Nostrand, 1966.

Korner, Stephen. *Kant*, rev. ed. New Haven, Conn.: Yale University Press, 1982.

Kupperman, Joel J. *Character*. New York: Oxford University Press, 1991.

MacIntyre, Alasdair. *After Virtue*, 2nd ed. Notre Dame, Ind.: University of Notre Dame Press, 1984.

McKeon, Richard, ed. *Introduction to Aristotle*. New York: The Modern Library, 1947.

Paton, Herbert J. *The Categorical Imperative: A Study in Kant's Moral Philosophy*. Chicago: University of Chicago Press, 1948.

Prior, William J. *Virtue and Knowledge: An Introduction to Ancient Greek Ethics*. New York: Routledge, 1991.

Quinn, Philip L. *Divine Commands and Moral Requirements*. New York: Oxford University Press, 1978.

Reeve, C. D. *Practices of Reason: Aristotle's Nichomachean Ethics*. New York: Oxford University Press, 1992.

Ross, Sir William David. *The Foundations of Ethics*. Oxford: Clarendon Press, 1939.

———. *Kant's Ethical Theory*. New York: Oxford University Press, 1954.

———. *The Right and the Good*. New York: Oxford University Press, 1930.

Scruton, Roger. *Kant*. New York: Oxford University Press, 1982.

Shwayder, D. S. "The Sense of Duty." *Philosophical Quarterly* 7 (1957): 116–25.

Slote, Michael. *From Morality to Virtue*. New York: Oxford University Press, 1992.

Stevens, Rex P. *Kant on Moral Practice: A Study of Moral Success and Failure*. New Orleans: Mercer University Press, 1981.

Sullivan, Roger *Kant's Moral Theory*. New York: Cambridge University Press, 1989.

Taylor, Richard. *Virtue Ethics: An Introduction*. Interlaken, N.Y.: Linden Books, 1991.

Titus, Harold H., and Keeton, Morris. *Ethics for Today*. New York: Van Nostrand, 1973. Chapters 7 and 11.

Walker, Ralph C. *Kant*. New York: Methuen, 1982.

Wood, Allen W. *Kant's Moral Religion*. Ithaca, N.Y.: Cornell University Press, 1970.

Absolutism Versus Relativism

◆————————————————————————————————————

Objectives

After you have read this chapter you should be able to

1. Define the following terms: *absolutism, relativism, proposition, truth, falsity,* and *states of affairs.*
2. Know the so-called anthropological facts about absolutism and relativism and understand the criticisms of these "facts."
3. Describe different types of propositions and show how truth and knowledge relate to them.
4. Understand that absolutes exist and show how human beings can relate them to their moral lives.
5. Understand how basic principles, as "near" absolutes, are important to morality.

Two extremes in ethical reasoning have become very obvious in the twentieth century. One side (usually that of the rule nonconsequentialist moralists) believes that there are absolutes in the world, especially moral absolutes, which once found must be adhered to. That is, they believe that if *Do not kill* is a real absolute that never changes because it is logically irrefutable or because it has come from some absolute being (God), then it applies for all time and to all human beings everywhere. The other side has become cynical about the existence of any absolutes, mainly because modern science has exploded so many former "absolutes" and because there does not seem to be anything that can be *conclusively* proved to be absolute in any area of our experience with the possible exception of logic and mathematics, neither of which can encompass the entirety of human experience.

The moral relativist says that there are no absolutes and that morality (that is, what is moral and what is immoral) is *relative* only to a specific culture, group, or individual. We have all heard sayings such as "What's right for me may not be right for you" or "What's right for Americans may not be right for Asians." Furthermore, anthropological studies prove that cultures do differ. However, such studies also show that there are some similarities. Traditional morality stresses absolutes, whereas the so-called new morality stresses such concepts as "doing your own thing," "if it feels good, do it," or, in a milder form, "as long as you can fulfill the Christian commandment to love, then anything goes."

The Meanings of "Absolute"

In one sense, the word *absolute* means "perfect in quality, and complete"; in another, it means "not limited by restrictions or exceptions"; in still another sense, it means "not to be doubted or questioned—positive, certain, and unconditional."[1] The word has been and is used to describe a supernatural being (e.g., God), "laws" of nature, propositions concerning truth and falsity and law and morality. The question of whether an absolute supernatural being exists and the difficulty of proving its, his, or her existence conclusively have already been discussed in Chapters 1 and 3.

It is also difficult to prove conclusively the assumption that there are certain absolutes ("laws") in nature. One of the problems with so-called scientific natural laws is that although they have held as long as we can remember and as often as we have observed them, they are still only probable (although very strongly probable), rather than certain. For example, the law of gravity would seem to be an absolute "law" of nature, but its validity still depends on our ability to see it verified again and again. In other words, we don't know for certain whether the law of gravity will still hold in the next minute until we have lived through this time and observed it holding. Putting it more specifically, we don't know a ball will fall back down to the ground until we have thrown it up in the air and tested the "law" once again. This doesn't mean, of course, that there are no absolutes in nature, but it does mean—especially because our empirical knowledge of nature and the universe is limited—that we don't know *conclusively* that any exist.

Even harder to prove or discover is the basis for any sort of "natural moral laws." The discussion of the possibility of such laws in Chapter 1 revealed the difficulty of discovering any and brought out the importance of distinguishing between them and descriptive natural laws. It would seem that there is no clear basis or justification for holding that natural moral laws exist.

◆————————————————————————————

The Meaning of "Relative"

Relativism states that there are no absolute values at all and that all values are relative to time, place, persons, and situations. In other words, there are no values that cut across all cultures and peoples that are not relative to the specific place in which they are held, according to the relativist. In its milder forms, relativism merely states that morality varies from culture to culture and from individual to individual and that we ought to respect other people's moral views. In its extreme, relativism means that anything goes, and whatever anyone states as moral is definitely moral and we cannot dispute or refute his morality. This means that if one man thinks it's all right to kill other people and the rest of us don't, we cannot argue with this morality—he is as moral as those of us who don't think killing is moral.

◆————————————————————————————

Cultural Relativism and Cultural Absolutism

Cultural Relativism

Are there any anthropological "facts" that prove conclusively that either cultural relativism or cultural absolutism is true? If so, what are they? The anthropologists who say cultural relativism exists cite the following empirical "facts":

1. In studies of both primitive and modern cultures, there is an extreme variation in customs, manners, taboos, religions, moralities, daily habits, and attitudes from culture to culture.

2. The moral beliefs and attitudes of human beings are learned essentially from their cultural environments, and people tend to internalize—at least a great deal of the time—what is socially accepted or sanctioned in their cultures.

3. People in different cultures tend to believe not only that there is but one true morality but also that the one true morality is the one that they hold to.

Cultural Absolutism

Cultural absolutism, on the other hand, is the view that ultimate moral principles do not vary from culture to culture. This does not mean that all cultures have the same moral rules and standards, which would be an obviously false empirical statement; what it does mean is that ultimate principles underlying all the varying rules and standards are the same. For example, the cultural absolutist might argue that in all cultures there is some principle concerning the value of human life, but that there are many different rules and standards to protect it or authorize its destruction.

With this distinction in mind, cultural absolutists cite the following "facts" to support their theory:

1. Similar moral principles exist in all societies, such as principles concerning the preservation of human life, governing sexual behavior, prohibiting lying, and establishing reciprocal obligations between parents and children.
2. People in all cultures have similar needs, such as survival, food, and sex.
3. There are a great many similarities in situations and relationships in all cultures, such as having two parents of opposite sexes, competing with brothers and sisters, and having in existence the arts, languages, religion, and family.
4. There are a great many intercultural similarities in the areas of sentiments, emotions, and attitudes, such as jealousy, love, respect, and the need for respect.

Evaluation of These Theories

Essentially what do these so-called facts really prove? What are their implications for moral absolutism or relativism?

Evaluation of Moral Relativism. First, just because cultures differ about what is right and wrong does not mean that the belief of any culture is right or wrong. For example, suppose a certain culture believes that the world is flat, whereas another believes that the world is round. It is obvious that what cultures believe has no *necessary* connection with what is true. Second, just because a belief is learned from or accepted by a culture does not mean that it is true or false or that truth is relative only to specific societies.

Evaluation of Moral Absolutism. First, just because moral principles are similar in all societies does not mean that they are valid or absolute. Second, even if people have similar needs, sentiments, emotions, and attitudes, there is still a question of whether these *should* or *should not* be satisfied. And, finally, just because there are similarities in cultural situations and relationships does not mean that these are the only morally correct situations and relationships in existence or that they are morally correct at all.

What this boils down to is that merely because things, situations, and people exist or behave in certain ways, there is no necessary connection between what *is* or what people *do*, and what *should be* or what they *ought to* do. We have returned again to the distinction made in Chapter 1 between descriptive and prescriptive approaches to morality. Anthropologists have given us important information about human and cultural behavior, but they have not proved conclusively that everything is either relative or absolute, nor have they shown what is or is not moral.

How, then, are we to resolve this controversy of absolutism versus relativism? It would seem that if relativism exists, then absolutism cannot, certainly not for all people. An individual can accept or set up for himself a code of morality, but if relativism holds, it will apply only to that person and to no one else unless another individual or group of individuals also chooses the same code. In any case, if moral relativism holds true, there are no absolutes binding any human being to any moral point of view and—to choose an extreme case—we must accept Hitler's value system as well as Jesus', for how can we condemn any human being or culture for doing anything wrong if there are no absolutes by which we can measure their morality? We cannot say, "What they are doing is wrong"; we can only say, "What they are doing is different from what we would do" and then condemn them for the difference and stop them by force or allow them to continue and hope that both sides do not destroy each other.

On the other hand, if we accept certain moral rules as absolutes and another individual or group accepts conflicting rules as absolutes, then there is the great difficulty of trying to resolve the conflicts that arise from two sets of opposing absolutes meeting head-on. How, when two conflicting moral absolutes meet, can we possibly resolve the ensuing controversy? There is no way to do this without declaring one of the absolutes as really not an absolute. This brings up the knotty question of how we know if there are any absolutes or what they might be.

♦————————————————————————————————

Propositions and Truth

Propositions and States of Affairs

As far as morality is concerned, however, the most important way in which the term *absolute* is used is in connection with propositions as they relate to truth and falsity. Propositions are meaningful statements describing states of affairs, and they must be either true or false. A state of affairs is an occurrence, an event, or a happening. It is neither true nor false; it either occurs or it does not occur. A proposition describes a state of affairs, and if it is true, then it describes a state of affairs that did occur (past tense: "It rained yesterday"), that is occurring (present tense: "It is raining right now"), or that will occur (future tense: "It will rain tomorrow"). When a proposition is false, then it describes a state of affairs that did not occur, is not occurring, or will not occur. Only propositions are true or false, never states of affairs.[2]

Are There Any Absolute Truths?

The question that concerns us is, are there any absolute truths or falsities, or are truth and falsity always relative? Let's take an example. Suppose that on January 1, 1995, I state the proposition "It will rain tomorrow, January 2, 1995, in Los Angeles, California." In order to discover whether truth and falsity are relative or absolute, we need to ask what the status of this proposition is on the day I stated it (January 1, 1995). There are a number of possibilities. At the time I state it, is it true until proven false or false until proven true? Is it true to me because I believe it and false to someone else because he or she doesn't believe it? Is it false or true because no one knows on January 1, 1995, whether it actually will rain on the following day? Or is it really neither true nor false because January 2, 1995, isn't here yet?

Let us now suppose that it *is* January 2, 1995, and that it is raining in Los Angeles. Looking back to the proposition stated on January 1, wasn't it actually true when I stated it? On the other hand, if it doesn't rain on January 2 in Los Angeles, then wasn't the proposition false when I stated it on January 1? In other words, the proposition had to be *either* true *or* false when I stated it on January 1; we just didn't *know* at the time which condition applied to it.

The point I am trying to make is that truth does not slip around because of time or because of what anyone believes or even knows. Because I stated the proposition, let us suppose I believe it is true, but that Mary does not. What difference does this make as to whether it is actually true or false? Also, on January 1 neither one of us *knows* it is either true or false, but, again, what difference does that make? None whatsoever—whether the proposition is true or false is based on whether or not the state of affairs actually occurs.

Truth and falsity, then, are indeed absolute. They do not shift around depending on belief, time, feelings, or even knowledge. Propositions, carefully and accurately stated, are not just true or false when they are stated, but are, in fact, true or false for all time. We may not *know* which propositions are true and which are false, but that really has nothing to do with whether propositions really *are* true or false.

Types of Propositions

The real problem with whether or not there are absolute moral truths, however, seems to be centered in the area of knowing. There may be absolute truths, moral or otherwise, but do we know of any for sure? At this point, it is important to distinguish different types of propositions.

Analytic Propositions. First, there are analytic propositions, such as "No circles are squares," "A is A," "Everything is either A or not A," "Nothing can be both A and not A," "All triangles are three-sided," "All bachelors are unmarried," and so on. To deny the truth of this type of proposition would be to contradict oneself; therefore, given the definitions of the words and the meaning of these propositions, they are absolute truths, and we know that they are. For example, given the definitions of a circle and a square, it is not logically possible that one could be the other. Also, assuming that *A* stands for anything, it is a basic and ultimate truth (called a law or principle of logic) that whatever else may or may not be said truly about anything, a thing must by its very definition be what it is (a car is a car, a dog is a dog, a table is a table). Therefore, any analytic proposition is a truth that is known to be absolute.

Internal Sense Propositions. There are also propositions that human beings assert about their own internal senses or states (feelings, moods, emotions), such as "My head hurts," "I feel sick," "I am in a bad mood," "I believe in God," "I am frightened." Such propositions are also always true (assuming that they are honestly spoken) because we alone truly know our own internal states. A doctor can talk all day about there being no reason or cause for you to have a headache, but he or she cannot deny that you have one. Only you know whether you do or not, and when you do have one, merely having it is enough for you to state unequivocally, "I have a headache." You are simply describing what you feel, and you need no further evidence. These two types of propositions, then, state truths that we know are absolute. These propositions can be known to be true in what John Hospers calls the strong sense of knowing, which fulfills the following requirements:

1. I must believe the proposition is true.
2. The proposition must actually *be* true.
3. I must have absolutely conclusive evidence that it is true.[3]

In order to know that the two types of propositions discussed are true, in the first type we need no evidence other than knowing the definitions of words and the meanings of sentences and, in the second type no evidence other than actually experiencing an internal state that we are describing.

Empirical, or External Sense, Propositions. Another type of proposition, an empirical, or external sense, proposition, is different from the first two in that it describes a state of affairs that occurs in the external world, of which we have evidence through our external senses (seeing, touching, hearing, smelling, tasting) or, indirectly, through our reasoning. "Her hair is brown," "There is a table at the front of this room," "There is life on other planets," and "Man has landed on the moon" are examples of empirical propositions. Whether empirical propositions can ever be known to be absolutely true has been the basis of controversy in philosophy through the ages. I happen to agree with Norman Malcolm (b. 1911) and other like-minded philosophers that some empirical propositions can be known to be absolutely true or false. For example, if the light is good, if your eyes are normal, if you understand what the words you are using mean, and if you have carefully examined an object in front of you and have found it to be a table, then the statement "This is a table here before me" would seem to be an absolutely true proposition that you know to be true. So, for the purpose of this book, at least, I will assume that some empirical propositions can be known to be true—and therefore, that there are some empirical propositions that are absolutely true.

Moral Propositions. A fourth type of proposition is a moral proposition, or a proposition that has moral import. Some examples of this type of proposition are "Human beings should never kill other human beings," "You should not treat people so badly," "Martin Luther King was a good man," "Abortion is evil." This type of proposition differs from the other three types we have discussed in that it contains value judgments about the morality of human actions or character. It also contains such key words as *good, evil, wrong, right, bad, should*, and *ought*, among others. The first distinction is the most important because many propositions containing the words just cited have no moral import at all.[4] One example of such a proposition is "You should make a right turn at the next corner." There can be, of course, situations in which making a turn when asked *could* have moral import, but something besides the use of *should* and *right* would have to be involved. In short, making or not making the turn would have to have some moral implication, such as that if you did not make the turn you would run down a child.

The Emotive Theory

Now the question is, are moral propositions ever absolutely true, and, further, can any human being know whether they are or not? As mentioned in Chapter

3, in a discussion of the basis of act nonconsequentialism, some philosophers have stated that moral propositions have only "emotive," or "noncognitive" meanings; that is, they only express feelings or attitudes. For example, when people utter a moral proposition, such as "Tom is a good man" or "One should never steal," they are either voicing their approval or disapproval of an entity, trying to evoke certain feelings or attitudes in others, or perhaps both. Proponents of this theory, called the "emotive theory," maintain that unlike other types of propositions, such as "Tom is six feet tall" or "If you steal my car, I will be unhappy," moral propositions have no real basis in fact.

General Problems with the Emotive Theory. In *Human Conduct*, John Hospers points out some discrepancies inherent in this theory that raise some serious questions about its assumption that moral propositions are only emotive.[5] Hospers does not deny that moral propositions are used emotively; he does, however, question the theory that they have *only* that use or meaning. He sees moral propositions as having three aspects:

1. The purpose or intention of the person who utters them.
2. The effect the propositions have on their hearers.
3. The actual meaning of the propositions.

These three aspects should be carefully distinguished from one another because they all may be present in a particular moral proposition. For example, even though a moral proposition I state may express approval or disapproval or may be intended to evoke certain feelings or attitudes, it may *also* have a meaning that is separate from these other two aspects or functions. Hospers further argues that even though we use moral propositions for emotive purposes we don't *always* use them in this way.[6]

Like other theories we have discussed, such as psychological egoism in its strong form and the theory that there are natural moral laws, the emotive theory exaggerates its claims. For example, if one examines the moral proposition "It was wrong of Brutus to kill Caesar," it becomes clear that there is no way the proposition can be said to evoke a feeling in Brutus that he should not kill Caesar, because the act has already been committed.[7] Even if one tries to translate this proposition into the generalization "Human beings shouldn't kill other human beings," there is a difficulty: One cannot necessarily infer the second proposition from the first. True, one can say that the speaker is expressing his disapproval of Brutus's act, but must the speaker always be doing this when he makes the statement? Might not the speaker simply mean, "Look what followed historically from Brutus's action," a statement that expresses neither approval nor disapproval?

Moore's Naturalistic Fallacy. If we try to state that moral propositions are no different from empirical propositions, then we run into the "naturalistic fallacy" problem (so named by the philosopher G. E. Moore, 1873–1958)—the problem of "getting an *ought* from an *is.*" We discussed this problem in Chapter 1 when we dealt with the difference between the descriptive, or scientific, approach to ethics and the prescriptive, or philosophical-normative, approach. Moore states that a proposition such as "I will be angry if you steal my wife," which can be considered factual (because it describes an actual state of affairs that will take place in the future), has no *necessary* connection to the proposition "You *should* not steal my wife." That is, if the person I am talking to wishes to say, "So you'll be angry; so what? I still think I should steal your wife," how can I logically say, "Therefore, you shouldn't"? However, aren't some moves from the descriptive "is" to the prescriptive "ought" sometimes clear and logical, such as: "AIDS is a sexually transmitted fatal disease; therefore, people ought to practice safe sex if they don't want to get sick and die"? I would agree that you can't get an "ought" from an "is," but I do feel that careful examination of a series of pertinent facts surrounding a moral situation may be able to lead us to some significant moral propositions about good, bad, right, and wrong and also enable us to prescribe what people should do in various situations in which morality is at stake.

Moral Propositions as Types of Empirical Propositions

These assumptions lead me to propose a third alternative that is at least worthy of examination and argument, even though it is not conclusively provable. This alternative is the position that moral statements are indeed propositions of the empirical type, except that they contain either value judgments or moral prescriptions. Let's examine this alternative as objectively as we can.

Normative Moral Statements. Normative moral statements, such as "He is a good man" or "What she did was right," could conceivably be considered propositions much like "That is a green table" and "She cleaned her house." There is a greater problem in establishing what "good" and "right" mean than what "green" and "cleaned her house" mean, but if we can set up some standards for what it means for a person to be good and an act to be right, we ought to be able to say, at least in theory, that these are propositions with moral import.

Prescriptive Moral Statements. However, what about those moral statements that are prescriptive, such as "Human beings should never kill other human beings except in self-defense" and "A woman ought to have an abortion for any reason she thinks necessary"? They certainly assert something about reality, even though they include a value judgment as part of that assertion, but can they

ever be known to be true or false? As I pointed out in Chapter 2, while discussing Jesse Kalin's defense of ethical egoism, there are prescriptive propositions that are nonmoral and yet that could certainly be considered propositions.
That is, they are meaningful statements that assert something about reality and
that are either true or false.

If you remember Kalin's chess game example, John sees that Tom *ought to*
move his bishop in such a way so as to put John's king in check. The proposition
here is simply, "Tom ought to move his bishop to position A." This can also be
stated, "According to the rules for playing chess, Tom's next move ought to be to
move his bishop to position A." This means that within the confines of chess
game rules, to state that "Tom ought to move his bishop to position A" is to state
a true proposition. To say the opposite, that "Tom ought not to move his bishop
to position A," would be a false proposition, again within the structure of chess
game rules. Of course, there could be times when the former proposition might
be false—for example, under the condition that if Tom won the game, his oppo-
nent would kill him, having threatened to do so previously. However, this would
be an extenuating circumstance outside the confines of the chess game itself. In
this case, therefore, the proposition would be based on more than chess game
rules.

Proposition Against Killing Human Beings. Can we now make the same kind of
case as in the foregoing for the proposition "Human beings should never kill
other human beings" because it is similar in structure although moral rather
than nonmoral? It is obvious that we can set up rules for moral behavior as well
as for chess games and that within the framework of that set of rules, we can
state true and false propositions about what human beings or chess players
should or ought to do. But can evidence be brought forth to *really* show that
such a proposition can be known to be true, as in the propositions "All triangles
are three-sided," "This table is green," and "I have a headache"? Let's examine
this type of moral proposition and its implications.

First, by "kill" I mean "taking another human being's life against his will."
Perhaps *murder* would be a more accurate term, because *kill* means "to put to
death, slay, deprive of life, put an end to or extinguish," whereas *murder* means
"the unlawful killing of one human being by another, especially with malice
aforethought."[8] Second, the way this proposition is worded, it applies only to
killing or murdering other human beings, even though there are ethical codes
(pacifism and Jainism to name two) that believe in the sanctity of all life, not just
human life. Now is there any evidence that this proposition can be known to be
true? If we look to our experience of the world and especially of human life, we
must come to the conclusion that life or being alive is the one basic thing we all
have in common. Furthermore, there can be no real morality or immorality in
dealing with a human being who is no longer alive. Even when we are opposed

to mutilation of or cannibalism of dead human bodies, it is either out of respect for the human being that once was or out of respect for the feelings of other human beings still alive.

Because all the qualities we attribute to human beings are based on their being alive, then life or "aliveness" is a fundamental necessity for any moral system. There can be no human beings, moral or immoral, if there is no human life; there can be no discussion of morality, setting up of codes, or even worries about what is or is not moral if there are no live human beings around. We cannot possibly state that "all human beings should kill each other" because (in true Kantian tradition) this would end up being inconsistent and illogical in much the same way as is the statement "Everyone should always be a parasite." There would be no human beings left to follow the rule encompassed by the statement.

All of this, however, merely proves that life or being alive is a necessary condition for morality. Are there any other reasons why human beings ought not to kill one another? First, the social and natural sciences have proved that human beings have a strong drive for survival, and one of the best ways to survive is to "let live," or to not put one's own life in jeopardy by threatening the lives of others. Second, most human beings desire some peace, happiness, and stability in their lives, and they cannot attain any degree of these qualities if human life in general and their lives in particular are constantly being threatened. Third, experience seems to indicate that human beings have a potential for being good and doing right, as well as a potential for being bad and doing wrong, so there is at least a partial urge to be and do good.

When accompanied by the desires for survival, peace, happiness, and stability, however, the urge to do and be good seems to have the greater emphasis. It also seems to be a good thing most of the time that human beings not kill other human beings because if they do, they will deprive those whom they kill of any possible good they might attain while alive. This is in addition to the basic and obvious good of having life itself. Therefore, if life is basic to human beings, their morality, their drive for survival, their desire for peace, happiness, and stability, and their urge to be and do good, then to destroy life is tantamount to destroying the ultimate basis for human being-ness, which includes morality. "Human beings should never kill other human beings" can therefore be seen as a true proposition, and it can be known to be true because the evidence for it can be observed and we can reason consistently from that evidence.

Problems with Moral Propositions. It is generally assumed by reasonable human beings that if we know certain propositions are true, then we should live our lives by them. Following this assumption, human beings who kill other human beings are not living their lives in accordance with a true proposition. They may, of course, not be aware of the proposition, or they may be aware of it but disregard it. We do this many times with other propositions. We know, for instance, that "if you drive too fast and recklessly on a crowded freeway, you will endanger human life" is a true proposition, yet some people drive recklessly anyway. Here we have another moral problem, the matching of propositions that are known to be true with human actions. Many people know that propositions having to do with not killing or not lying or not raping, for example, should be adhered to, but some people still do not act in accordance with such propositions. Of course, that people do not act in accordance with propositions has nothing to do with whether or not they are true. Still another problem arises when propositions conflict—when, for instance, the absolute "Do not kill" conflicts with the absolute "Do not lie." We must have a way of choosing not only between true and false propositions but also between propositions that conflict.

Furthermore, we must distinguish between the term *absolute* as it is used to imply the existence of moral laws outside of human beings (see Chapter 1), and moral absolutes (moral laws), which human beings establish based on reason and evidence. I do not suggest here that these arguments have proved conclusively that there are moral propositions that can be known absolutely to be true or false. I believe I have shown, however, that we can discover and present evidence for the existence of such propositions and, in reasoning from that evidence, perhaps arrive at some *near* absolutes (if there can be such things) and establish basic moral principles similar to Ross's *prima facie* duties. It is also important to recognize that no moral system or code can exist without at least one basic principle (near absolute). Every ethical theory we have examined so far has had one or more basic principles; even total relativism is based on at least one near absolute—that there are no absolutes!

Near Absolutes

The greatest problem raised in the absolutism versus relativism controversy is how to introduce stability, order, and security (absolutism) into morality and moral systems and still allow for individual and group freedom and creativity (relativism). This problem is important because the very crux of a moral system is its ability to match the tremendous complexity of human thoughts, feelings, and actions with absolute moral propositions. The way we can do this is by setting up basic moral principles that are near absolutes. We will try to observe these principles as absolutes in every case we can, but we will realize that there may be some justifiable exceptions to the principles. The term *justifiable* is a key one here, because it means that if we intend to make an exception to a near absolute, then we must fully justify that exception.

I have already argued for the validity of one proposition, that we should never kill other human beings. True pacifists will adhere to this proposition even when their lives are threatened; they will lose their lives rather than take another's. In so doing, they will be acting as consistently as possible with their principles. However, in the complexity and variety of human experience, if life is basic, as the proposition states, then one's own life and the lives of innocent people who are the intended victims of some killer are also basic. Therefore, as many ethical systems state it, one has the right to and should protect one's own life and the lives of other innocent people from someone who is threatening to take them even if it means that a person must take the life of the killer and thus become a killer himself.

The absolute "Human beings should not kill other human beings" thus becomes the basic moral principle "Human beings should not kill other human beings except in self-defense or in the defense of other innocent human beings." Although there is still the problem of defining "self-defense" and "innocent," the absolute has been qualified by the phrases concerning "self-defense" and "defense of the innocent," thus justifying some exceptions to the proposition "Do not kill." There may be other exceptions, but they will also have to be justified very strongly because they are exceptions to an absolute that is basic to all human morality. The arguments necessary for these exceptions, and for other basic principles and their exceptions, will be dealt with in Chapter 7, in the discussion of how a system of morality can be set up. For now, it is enough to say that basic moral principles can indeed be set up to govern most human actions, and that exceptions can be provided for with careful and strong justification.

Conclusion

Relativism

In addition to the argument that just because values differ they are not necessarily right in one culture or another, critics also argue that relativism is really impractical, especially in its extreme form. It is certainly important to allow for cultural and individual freedom in deciding what values people should be allowed to follow, but is anyone really a full-blown relativist in practical living situations? Are any of us willing to say that people should be allowed to do whatever they want to do as long as they think it is right? If we ask ourselves that question, won't we discover that we definitely want to qualify it by saying something like, "as long as they don't harm anyone else" or "as long as they don't interfere with anyone else's rights"?

In stating such a qualification, we may not be setting up absolutes, but neither are we totally accepting the theory that values are completely relative. Doesn't this need to qualify relativism suggest that there must be certain guidelines or limits within which all humans should behave? It would seem, therefore, that the practicality of living will not allow for a totally relativistic point of view.

Absolutism

What about absolutism? It would seem that there are such things as absolutes in both the nonmoral and the moral sphere. Some absolutes, however, are too general for specific situations in which we find ourselves, so they become the basis for establishing basic principles that may have exceptions. Such exceptions must be fully justified because the principles *are* basic; to make unjustified exceptions is to act immorally. These principles, in turn, serve as means to enable human beings to act as closely in accordance with known true propositions as possible. That a proposition is true is no guarantee that people will act in accordance with it, but the proposition remains true whether they do or not.

To repeat, there are absolutes in the sense of absolutely true propositions that we can know. Some of them are analytic, some are internal sense statements, and others are empirical propositions with or without moral import. From these absolutes we derive near absolutes in the form of basic moral principles that form the cornerstone of any human ethical system. All normative moral systems rest on absolutes that are proposed by whoever sets up these systems. This does not mean that morality is relative, for many absolutes are founded on propositions that are known to be true by means of evidence gained through the senses and logical argument supplied through reasoning.

Chapter Summary

  I. Two extremes in ethical reasoning
      A. Absolutism maintains that there are absolute truths and, especially, absolute moral truths to which all human beings must adhere if they are to be moral.
      B. Relativism maintains that there are no absolutes of any kind but that everything, especially morality, is "relative" to specific cultures, groups, or even individuals.
 II. Meaning and application of *absolute* and *relative*
      A. *Absolute* essentially means "perfect in quality; complete; not limited by restriction or exceptions; not to be doubted or questioned—positive, certain, unconditional." We apply this word to supernatural beings (for example, gods); to laws of nature; to propositions; to law and morality; and, most important, to propositions, truth, and falsity.
      B. *Relative* essentially means that there are no values that cut across all cultures and peoples that are not relative to the specific place or person in and by which they are held.

III. Anthropological "facts"
   A. Some anthropological "facts" are cited in support of cultural relativism.
      1. There is extreme variation in customs, manners, taboos, religions, and so on, from culture to culture.
      2. Moral beliefs and attitudes of human beings are learned essentially from their cultural environments.
      3. People in different cultures tend to believe that their morality is the one true morality.
   B. Other such "facts" are cited in support of cultural absolutism.
      1. Similar moral principles exist in all societies.
      2. People in all cultures have similar needs.
      3. There are a great many similarities in situations and relationships existing in all cultures.
      4. There are a great many similarities in sentiments, emotions, and attitudes.
   C. Anthropological "facts" are open to criticism.
      1. Just because cultures differ about what is right and wrong does not mean that one culture is right whereas another is wrong.
      2. Just because a belief is learned from or accepted by a culture does not mean that it is true or false or that truth is relative only to specific societies.
      3. Just because moral principles are similar in all societies does not mean that they are valid or absolute.
      4. Even if people have similar needs, sentiments, emotions, and attitudes, there is still a question of whether these should or should not be satisfied.
      5. Just because there are similarities in cultural situations and relationships does not mean that these are the only morally correct situations and relationships in existence or that they are morally correct at all.
IV. Propositions and truth
   A. Truth applies to propositions that are meaningful statements describing states of affairs (occurrences, events, or happenings). Propositions are either true or false.
      1. A true proposition describes a state of affairs that was, is, or will be occurring.
      2. A false proposition describes a state of affairs that did not occur, is not occurring, or will not occur.
      3. Only propositions are true or false, never states of affairs—they either occur or do not occur.
   B. Truth is absolute and not relative to belief, knowledge, person, place, or time. If propositions are stated accurately, this will always hold.

C. There are several types of propositions.
1. Analytic propositions are truths that are *known* to be absolute ("All triangles are three-sided") because we know the definitions and meaning of words.
2. Internal sense or internal state propositions are propositions we know are true merely because we have the experience—we alone truly know our own internal states ("I have a headache").
3. Empirical, or external sense, propositions describe a state of affairs that occurs in the external world of which we have evidence through our external senses. There is a controversy in philosophy over whether such propositions can be known to be true, but my assumption is that some empirical propositions can be known to be absolutely true ("There is a table at the front of this room").
4. Moral propositions are propositions about morality or those that have moral import ("Human beings should never kill other human beings").
   (a) These are empirical and rational in form.
   (b) They are the larger class of propositions called empirical.
   (c) Some philosophers say moral statements are not propositions at all, maintaining instead that they are merely emotive utterances. Some say moral statements are propositions but that they cannot be known to be true or false because they arc not based on fact. A third alternative, not conclusively provable, is that they are empirical propositions with moral import that can be known to be true or false.
   (d) We still have the problem of matching propositions with the complexity of human thoughts, feelings, and actions, and to do this, we must move from the concept of absolutes to that of "near absolutes," or "basic principles."
   (e) A basic principle, or near absolute, because it is based on an absolute moral proposition, should be adhered to unless strong justification can authorize an exception to it.

Exercises for Review

1. Define and explain the terms *absolutism, relativism, proposition, truth, falsity*, and *state of affairs*.
2. What are the anthropological "facts" cited in support of cultural absolutism and relativism, and what are the problems with basing moral theories on these theories?
3. What are the different types of propositions, and how do they differ?

Give your own example of each type.

4. Is truth absolute, or is it relative to knowledge, belief, people, places, and times? Explain your answer in detail.

5. Can we know for certain (in the "strong" sense of "know"—define this) that any propositions are true? If so, which types can we be sure of? If not, why not?

6. Are there moral absolutes, or is morality strictly relative? What are the implications of your viewpoint on this issue for your own moral attitudes, beliefs, and code?

7. What are the basic principles of each of the ethical theories you have studied? To what extent are they absolutistic or relativistic?

8. What are moral propositions, and how are they similar to and different from other types of propositions? Explain your answer.

9. Basing your answer on your own observations and studies, to what extent do you think cultural absolutists or cultural relativists (in the field of anthropology) are correct in their assumptions? Explain your answer.

10. Are there any absolutes outside of truth and falsity? If so, what are they? If not, why do you believe there are none?

Discussion Questions

1. Under the moral system espoused by Adolf Hitler and the Nazi party, property was stolen and destroyed; countries were invaded, looted, and pillaged; and millions of innocent people were raped, mutilated, experimented upon, tortured, and murdered. Discuss the extent to which you feel such a system is moral or immoral, basing your answer on whether you feel morality is relative or absolute.

2. Read Jean Anouilh's play *Antigone* and evaluate the moral positions of Creon and Antigone from the point of view of the absolutism versus relativism controversy.

3. Analyze any religious code of ethics (for example, Judaism, Christianity, Islam, Buddhism)—preferably one with which you are familiar. Indicate to what extent the code of ethics you choose is absolutistic or relativistic, and discuss the problems created by its position in this controversy.

4. Read Chapter 11 of John Hospers's *Human Conduct* and Chapter 7 of Paul Taylor's *Problems of Moral Philosophy*, then write a paper dealing with the problem of verifying moral reasoning and the relationship between values and facts.

5. Discuss the extent to which you believe the rule "Adults should *never* sexually molest children" is absolute. Do you feel it is ever right to violate this rule? If not, why not? If so, under what conditions? Is this a real absolute moral rule?

6. Discuss the extent to which you think the rule "Rape is always wrong" is an absolute. Can there be any exceptions to this rule? Why or why not?

7. To what extent is it possible to get an *ought* from an *is*? What does this phrase actually mean? Answer in detail. Read Chapter 1 of G. E. Moore's *Principia Ethica* (see supplementary reading).

Notes

1. William Morris, ed., *The American Heritage Dictionary of the English Language* (Boston: Houghton Mifflin, 1975), 5.

2. This is John Hospers's description of truth and propositions, which is the clearest and most meaningful I have read. It appears on pages 114–21 of *Introduction to Philosophical Analysis*, 2nd ed. (Englewood Cliffs, N.J.: Prentice-Hall, 1967).

3. Ibid., 151.

4. Refer to Chapters 1 and 2 and to the chess game example in this chapter, which points out the nonmoral uses of *should* and *ought to*.

5. John Hospers, *Human Conduct* (New York: Harcourt, Brace, and World, 1982), 526–93.

6. Ibid., 559–66.

7. Ibid., 564–65.

8. Morris, 720, 863.

Supplementary Reading

Arrington, Robert L. *Rationalism, Realism, and Relativism.: Perspectives in Contemporary Moral Epistemology*. Ithaca, N.Y.: Cornell University Press, 1989.

Asch, S. E. *Social Psychology*. Englewood Cliffs, N.J.: Prentice-Hall, 1952.

Bayley, James E. *Aspects of Relativism: Moral, Cognitive, and Literary*. Lanham, Md.: University Press of America, 1992.

Gellner, Ernest. *Relativism and the Social Sciences*. New York: Cambridge University Press, 1985.

Ginsberg, M. *Essays in Sociology and Social Philosophy*, Vol. 1. London: Heinemann, 1956.

Hospers, John. *Human Conduct*, 2nd ed. New York: Harcourt, Brace, and World, 1982.

Kluckhorn, Clyde. "Ethical Relativity: Sic et Non." *Journal of American Philosophical Association Fifty-two* (November, 1955).

Linton, Ralph. "The Problem of Universal Values." In *Method and Perspective in Anthropology*, ed. R. F. Spencer. Minneapolis: University of Minnesota Press, 1954.

Marks, Emerson R. *Relativist and Absolutist: The Early Neoclassical Debate in England*. Westport, Conn.: Greenwood Press, 1975.

May, William. *Moral Absolutes, Catholic Traditions, Current Trends, and the Truth*. Shoreview, Minn.: Marquette, 1989.

Meiland, Jack W., and Michael Krausz, eds. *Relativism: Cognitive and Moral*. Notre Dame, Ind.: University of Notre Dame Press, 1982.

Moore, G. E. *Principia Ethica*. New York: Cambridge University Press, 1959.

Siegel, Harvey. *Relativism Refuted*. Norwel, Mass.: Kluwer Academic Publishers, 1987.

Sumner, W. G. *Folkways*. Boston: Ginn, 1934.

Taylor, Paul W. "Social Science and Ethical Relativism." *Journal of Philosophy Fifty-five* (1958): 32–43.

———. *Problems of Moral Philosophy*, 2nd ed. Belmont, Calif.: Dickenson, 1972.

CHAPTER 5

Freedom Versus Determinism

Objectives

After you have read this chapter you should be able to

1. Define the following terms: *freedom, determinism, universal causation, fatalism, predestination*, and *indeterminism*.
2. Understand the differences between hard and soft determinism, fatalism, and indeterminism.
3. Understand the various arguments for and against determinism presented by natural and physical scientists, historians, economists, psychologists, and religionists.
4. Understand the arguments for freedom and free will.
5. Come to some conclusions concerning the freedom versus determinism controversy, and apply those conclusions to moral responsibility.

We have already seen in the previous chapter, how important the controversy concerning absolutism versus relativism is to morality. There is, however, yet another question related to this controversy that affects morality and especially moral responsibility. This question is whether human beings are free to make moral decisions and act on them or whether human beings are "determined" by forces both outside and within them over which they have no control, so that what they think are free decisions and actions really are not.

The problem of freedom and determinism as such is really not a moral problem but, rather, a metaphysical one (having to do with the nature of reality). However, the questions concerning whether human beings are free or not, and to what extent they are or not, have very important implications for whether humans can be held morally responsible or even set up moral systems for themselves.

♦

Meaning of Determinism

What exactly does "determinism" mean? It means the same thing as "universal causation"; that is, for every result, effect, and event that occurs in reality a cause or causes exist. Putting this another way, we can say that there is no such thing as an uncaused result, effect, or event. One example of a moral problem arising from a deterministic point of view was discussed in Chapter 2 in connection with the theory of psychological egoism. To quickly reiterate, how can we tell human beings what they should or should not do if, because they are "determined" by forces they can't control, they can only follow one type of ethical system—egoism? If they must always act in their own self-interest because that is simply the way they are made, then there is no use telling them they should or should not act in their own self-interest. Even ethical egoism is absurd if all human beings are already programmed to always act in their own self-interest.

A related problem inherent in determinism is, What is the point of holding people morally responsible—blaming, praising, rewarding, or punishing them—for what they do and do not do if they cannot help what they do?

As you can see, the freedom versus determinism controversy has powerful implications for morality and moral responsibility, and we will explore these implications in greater detail later.

♦

Types and Theories of Determinism

The various arguments and theories supporting determinism go far back in time and have become increasingly compelling as they have extended into the twentieth century. These arguments and theories come from all aspects of human endeavor and concern: from religion, from the physical and natural sciences, and from history, economics, and psychology. Let's examine the arguments for determinism that have arisen from each of these areas.

Religious Determinism—Predestination

Religious determinism, or predestination, is derived from the attributes assigned, especially in Western religions (Judaism, Christianity, and Islam), to God or Allah. These attributes are omnipotence (being all-powerful) and omniscience (being all-knowing). According to such religions, because God/Allah created the universe and everything in it, including human beings, He has the power to do anything, and He knows everything that has happened, is happening, and will happen. Because of these attributes, then, everything in the world's history—past, present, and future—can be thought to be predestined and foreknown.

If, for example, God has decided that I will lead a good life and "go to heaven," then I will; if, on the other hand, He has decided I will lead a bad life and "go to hell," then I will do that instead. I have absolutely no say over what I or anyone else does because everything has been predestined, programmed, "predetermined" by an almighty supernatural being. This theory, for reasons that will soon become evident, is not generally accepted by the three major Western religions, though it has been held to be true by some theologians. The theory of predestination was most strongly presented by the Protestant minister and theologian John Calvin (1509–64), who said that individuals can do nothing to ensure their own salvation.

There are several problems with this theory. There is the difficulty, which I discussed in Chapter 1, of proving the existence of a supernatural being and, even if we could, of proving that He created the world, that He is indeed all-powerful and all-knowing and, last, that He predestined everything to happen in a certain way. Even if we take all of the preceding on faith, however, the theory of predestination presents some real difficulties in relation to the characteristics of the supreme being, the world, and human beings.

First, if the universe and everything in it was created by God, then He must also have created evil, and this is a definite problem for theologians holding the predestination viewpoint. Most theologians are not willing to assign the responsibility for evil to God, even though the problem of evil's existence, given an all-powerful and all-good God, is a real moral dilemma.[1]

Second, God seems a very strange being indeed—especially in view of the emphasis the three major Western religions place on salvation—if He predetermines that some humans will be good and some will be bad and then punishes and rewards them for something over which they have no control. This characterization of God and His relationship with His creatures certainly does not square with the image of the all-merciful, all-just being that the three religions also accept. Furthermore, the concept of salvation doesn't really mean much if it cannot be assumed that human beings are free to do good rather than evil. None of these problems, of course, actually refutes the theory of religious determinism, but they all indicate why the theory is generally not held, at least in any extreme form, by any of three Western religions. There is, I would add, no conclusive proof or argument that indicates that this theory is anything but one based on very weak assumptions indeed.

Scientific Determinism

Because the physical and natural sciences depend upon experiments, constancy, and prediction in their search for truth, they must accept universal causation. This has led many scientists to presume further that such causation means that there is absolutely no freedom in the universe at all. I stress that not all scientists accept this extreme point of view, but I also hasten to add that the strongest arguments and evidence for determinism have arisen in the twentieth century from the natural and physical sciences, especially as they have affected modern psychology.

Physical Science and Physical Determinism. The greatest exponent of physical determinism was Sir Isaac Newton (1642–1727). He believed that the entire realm of nature and the universe is governed by natural laws (for example, the law of gravity), and that there is, therefore, no such thing as freedom. Because everything observable—even things unobservable to the naked eye, such as atoms and molecules—is physical in nature, then everything that occurs to these things and everything they do is caused by one or another physical law or event. According to Newton, because human beings also are physical in nature, they are subject to physical causes both within and outside them; for them, freedom is simply an illusion. This argument is a very compelling one, for even though, as pointed out in the last chapter, the law of gravity, for example, does not state a certainty but rather a probability, has anyone ever observed any exceptions to what the law states?

Despite the attractiveness of the theory of physical determinism, there is a problem in assuming that because natural physical laws hold, there can be no freedom. Critics of Newton argue that humans are not merely physical, but are also mental (and/or spiritual) beings, and that because they are more than physical, they are able to "transcend" physical laws. Furthermore, the discoveries of modern physics, exemplified most pertinently by Werner Heisenberg's (1901–1976) quantum theory of physics, have raised serious doubts about Newtonian views of nature and the universe. The door has been left open for the possibility of freedom even for nonconscious entities such as atoms and molecules.

Biological and Genetic Determinism. Biological determinism is best exemplified by Charles Darwin's theory of natural selection, which he presented in his most famous work, *The Origin of Species*. Darwin (1809–1882) believed that various species in nature evolve at different stages in the history of the world and that only the fittest survive. For example, even though some prehistoric animals (dinosaurs, for example) were extremely large and powerful, their brain capacity and mental ability were so limited that they did not survive, whereas smaller and more intelligent beings, such as humans, did. Darwin suggested that this process of natural selection essentially has nothing to do with freedom. He believed that it is nature that governs, through its various processes, the makeup, strength, and survival potential of the various species, and that the species that emerge as dominant are determined by the stage along the evolutionary scale at which they appeared.

A more modern and sophisticated version of this theory is concerned with genetic makeup, especially that of human beings. None of us has any say over the identity of our parents, from whom we will inherit our genes; and because our genes determine so much of our makeup—our sex, mental potential, and eye, hair, and skin color—how can we be said to be free in any real sense of the word?

The problem with biological determinism is identical to the problem with physical determinism in that both theories tend to limit human beings strictly to their physical and biological makeup and structure, ignoring the possibility that a mental or spiritual side may exist.

Social-Cultural Determinism

Historical, or Cultural, Determinism. Georg W. F. Hegel (1770–1831) developed a deterministic theory that was based on history. He believed that the various periods of the world's history are manifestations of an "absolute mind" that is trying to realize itself in a state of perfection. He also believed that the basic nature of reality and the world is rational and mental and that the physical is merely a manifestation of the absolute mind's intellectual growth toward perfection. The implications of his theory are that we are neither responsible for nor able to control the period of history or the culture in which we are born. Rather, the character and actions of all individuals are determined by their own culture and all preceding cultures and historical events. Furthermore, because history is a manifestation of an absolute mind that exists in the universe and that is attempting to realize itself, then we, too, are a result, or manifestation, of that absolute mind.

Obvious problems exist with this theory, too. First, it would be difficult at best to prove that any such absolute mind exists and, furthermore, that a mind can exist without a body. Second, even though a rational and evolutionary theory of history has some plausibility, no conclusive proof exists to support it; there are many other theories of history and culture that are equally plausible, if not more so. Third, even though human beings are influenced by their culture and past history, this does not necessarily mean that their development is totally determined or governed by this influence.

Economic or Social Determinism. Karl Marx (1818–1883), following in Hegel's theoretical footsteps, believed that our characters and actions are not so much historically determined as they are economically and socially determined. Marx's theory, called dialectical materialism, states that human beings are determined by an evolutionary economic class struggle. According to Marx, this evolutionary process led from early agrarian economics, through monarchies and feudalism, through the rise of the middle class and industrialism, to capitalism and eventually to socialism. He believed that although people can't control the economic class into which they are born, their natures are determined in every way by this event. He further believed—much like Hegel—that there is an inevitable force in nature (economic rather than historical) that human beings cannot control and that will eventually lead to the ultimate goal, a classless society.

The problems with this theory are similar to those raised by Hegel's theory. First, dialectical materialism is based on unproved assumptions, and there are other theories of economics that are just as plausible yet that do not espouse determinism. Second, even though there is no doubt that people are influenced by their individual economic status and that of their society, there are, as we have seen, many other influences that affect economics as well as human beings. For example, scientific and technological developments have a great deal of influence on the economic status of cultures and their members—probably more than economics itself has on science and technology. Also, economic influence is not the only influence that affects human beings; in fact, one could argue that human beings affect or determine the changes in economics at least to some extent.

Psychological Determinism—Freudianism and Behaviorism. Some of the most convincing of the arguments developed in the twentieth century in support of determinism, especially determinism as it affects human beings, have come from psychology. In the nineteenth century, Sigmund Freud (1856–1939), the founder of psychoanalysis, put forth the theory that human beings are determined, even prior to birth in the womb, by their unconscious minds and by various natural drives which their society's mores and customs required them to repress. For example, one of Freud's theories is that all sons are basically in love with their mothers (Oedipus complex) and all daughters are basically in love with their fathers (Electra complex). Because incest is forbidden in most societies, these unconscious yet natural drives must be repressed, causing human beings to be affected in different ways. Therefore, if mothers or fathers give too much, too little, or the wrong kind of love to their sons or daughters, the entire mental and emotional lives of the children can be affected to the point where they become neurotic or psychotic.

This theory has been used many times in defending criminal killers, when, for example, the defense claims that a certain man who has raped and killed a number of women has done so because they all resembled his mother and that his unconscious hatred of her compelled him to commit the crimes. Just as this man was "determined" by his unconscious drives of love and hate for his parents to perform terrible acts, so, a Freudian would argue, all human beings are determined by inner drives and unconscious motivations to behave the way they do.

The major criticism of Freud's theories is that they are too generalized to have any real basis in fact. That is, he has taken his experiences with a few abnormally disturbed patients as a basis for establishing theories that apply to all human beings. It certainly may be true that some sons are in love with their mothers and that some daughters are in love with their fathers, and further, that these emotions have caused them a great deal of difficulty in their lives. There is, however, little conclusive evidence to show that these problems affect *all* human beings and therefore that their lives can be said to be determined by such influences.

In the twentieth century, psychological determinism has not been most significantly argued from the point of view of the inner psyche, as in Freudianism, but, rather, from the point of view of behaviorism. This approach is best exemplified by the work of B. F. Skinner (1904–1990), who described his theories in two books, *Science and Human Behavior* and *Beyond Freedom and Dignity*, and in his utopian novel, *Walden II*. Skinner based his work on that of Ivan P. Pavlov (1849–1936), the Russian physiologist who first developed the concept of "conditioned reflex." In his experiments with dogs, Pavlov discovered that they would react to the sound of a bell by salivating if he conditioned them to do so by ringing the bell every time he gave them food. Once the dogs were conditioned, Pavlov rang the bell without giving them food, and they began to salivate nonetheless. This led him to posit the theory that all animals, human beings included, could be conditioned to act in certain ways and in fact were and are conditioned by various external forces.

Skinner's theory is more involved and complex than Pavlov's in that he believes that human beings are totally physical beings and that the behavior they exhibit is strictly the result of years of haphazard conditioning from their environments, both physical and social or cultural. Skinner feels that all traditional statements about soul, psyche, self, or mind are merely superstitious, outdated concepts based on a lack of scientific knowledge. He further theorizes that freedom is an illusion and that once this illusion is abandoned human beings will be able to eliminate all the problems (for example, poverty, violence, war, cruelty) that now plague humanity. Even though human beings have been totally and haphazardly conditioned down through the ages, he maintains, now that we have a complete science of human behavior we can create the perfect society.

There are several problems with this theory, the most important of which is that its very basis is a thoroughgoing materialism. That is, Skinner believes that human beings are strictly material, or physical, beings, possessing no mind, self, soul, or ego. This theory reduces mind to brain and body, a reduction that will not work because mental events do differ from physical events in that the former are private and not locatable in space, whereas the latter are public and easily locatable in space.[2] I will discuss the importance of mind and consciousness to human freedom a little later. Another problem with Skinner's theory is that, much like Freud's theories and the concept of psychological egoism, it carries essentially sound premises too far. Skinner is quite right in stating that people can be conditioned by various methods to behave in certain ways or to change certain aspects of their behavior. Weight, smoking, and alcohol control clinics, among others, are perfect examples that this can be done.

That conditioning works under some circumstances does not mean, however, that human beings merely react to external stimuli all the time or that conditioning always works or even that it should be applied in all instances. Many of Skinner's critics are not overly concerned about whether his theories are accurate portrayals of what does and can happen in the realm of human behavior; what truly disturbs them is that he completely denies the existence of human freedom and wants to apply conditioning to everyone in an acculturation process that will alter their behavior. Behavior control techniques probably should be applied in certain instances and to certain people, but—his critics state—not on a total population in an attempt to attain a utopian society of the behaviorist's design. This latter ideal is especially disturbing to his critics, because his theories are based on a questionable, if not totally false, premise (materialism). Further criticisms of Skinner's theories will be discussed in the last section of this chapter, in which we will examine arguments for the existence of human freedom.

Summary. To sum up what has been discussed in the foregoing sections, there are many arguments in favor of determinism, coming from almost all areas of human endeavor—religion, the natural and physical sciences, and the social sciences. But before we accept the arguments for determinism, let's look more deeply into what determinism means and what it implies for morality.

Fatalism and Hard and Soft Determinism

For the sake of clarity, let me redefine determinism. Determinism is the same thing as universal causation. Stated positively, universal causation means that for every result, effect, or occurrence there is a cause or causes; stated negatively, it means that there is no such thing as an uncaused event. Before going on to discuss hard and soft determinism, it is important to make a distinction between fatalism and determinism.

Fatalism

Fatalism is the view that all events are irrevocably fixed and predetermined, that they cannot be altered in any way by human beings, that the future is always beyond our control. In wartime, human beings have expressed this view by saying, "If there's a bullet or bomb with my name on it, then I'll die; if not, then I won't. There's nothing I can do about it." It's certainly true that many events are outside of human control. For example, when people have taken the precaution of getting into a foxhole or bomb shelter, they may still receive a direct hit from the bullet or bomb and die. Are not their chances of being killed increased, however, if they merely stand up in the street or on the battlefield, doing nothing to protect themselves? Therefore, it does not seem to be true—certainly not in all cases—that it makes no difference what a person does; that "whatever will be, will be."

There are very few fatalists (if any at all); otherwise, people would not "be careful" or "take precautions" against getting hurt or killed. True fatalists would never worry about stop signs or hesitate to play Russian roulette; they would never take medications when they were sick or protect themselves when confronted with a dangerous situation. This may not be a total refutation of the theory of fatalism, but it does illustrate the theory's impracticality. It is important to realize that the determinist, especially the soft determinist, is not really saying the same thing as the fatalist, for to say that everything has a cause is not the same as saying that every single thing that happens is completely and irrevocably outside of human control.

Hard Determinism

Hard determinism essentially maintains that if all events are caused, then there can be no such thing as freedom or free will. That is, if you trace causes back far enough in history or in any person's life, you will find that the basic causes are not within human control. Hard determinists are not saying exactly the same thing as the fatalists here: They do not maintain that humans cannot change the future. They are saying, rather, that certain causes that are not within human control have determined both the way human beings are and the way they act. Hard determinists do not maintain that humans can affect nothing; rather, they say that the way humans affect things is caused by their personal makeup and environment and that these, in turn, are caused by factors over which human beings have no control. In presenting their position, hard determinists will use evidence and arguments from every aspect of human existence.

For example, let us say that Mary Smith is born in the 1930s to a middle-class working family, during the Great Depression. Already she has no control over the century or culture into which she is born, the depression her country is in, her economic class, or, most important, the genetic makeup inherited from her parents. She could be born crippled, blind, or quite normal; she has no control over this, either. Let us say that she is born blind and that her father is an alcoholic and her mother a child abuser. Let us also assume that, due to these factors, she endures a miserable childhood that leads to a miserable adult life.

Mary may react, out of anger at her lot, by becoming a criminal, resorting to violence against both men and women in an attempt to avenge herself for the treatment she received from her mother and father. On the other hand, she may lead a blameless life. In this case, freedom advocates would point out that Mary, who had a terrible childhood and was born blind, overcame all of this, whereas her sister Elaine, for example, who was not blind but who also had an unhappy childhood, became a drug addict and prostitute. They would argue that both women had at least some say in determining the outcome of their lives.

Hard determinists would answer, however, that neither Mary nor Elaine was responsible for the way she turned out. There must have been some important differences in the women's genetic makeup or in the way they were treated by their parents, or, hard determinists would argue, some other influence from outside—perhaps a teacher who encouraged Mary, or a prostitute who influenced Elaine's choice of career. The fact that hard determinists cannot trace all of the causes doesn't refute their theory. On the contrary, they would argue, the mere fact that there are causes and that many, if not most of them, are outside the control of Mary and Elaine would indicate that we cannot, and indeed, should not hold the two women morally responsible for the courses their lives take.

What the hard determinist is saying, then, is that if every event, action, result, effect—everything—has a cause, then everything, including human desires, feelings, thoughts, choices, decisions, and actions, is "determined." The hard determinist says further that if human beings are born into a world that has been determined by prior causes over which they have no control, that if their genetic makeup is not theirs to choose freely, and that if their early environment is governed by physical events and human actions over which they have no say, then none of us can be said to be free. He argues that if you keep pushing back far enough in analyzing any human action or choice you will eventually arrive at a cause that is outside the control of the person who is choosing or acting.

Because human beings have no control over their genetic makeup or their early environment, they cannot be responsible for their original character, nor can they control what desires they have. They are, in effect, programmed to choose and act in certain ways because of these earlier forces, as well as the present forces of their environment, which are also determining them at every turn. The heart of the hard determinist's argument is summed up by John Hospers as follows:

"We can act in accordance with our choices or decisions," he will say, "and we can choose in accordance with our desires. But we are not free to *desire*. We can choose as we please, but we can't please as we please. If my biological or psychological nature is such that at a certain moment I desire A, I shall choose A, and if it is such that I desire B, I shall choose B. I am free to choose either A or B, but I am not free to desire either A or B. Moreover, my desires are not themselves the outcomes of choices, for I cannot choose to have them or not to have them."[3]

Soft Determinism

Soft determinists maintain that there is universal causation, but, unlike hard determinists, they believe that some of this causation originates with human beings, thus giving meaning to the phrase "human freedom." If human beings can be said to cause some of their actions by means of their own minds and wills, then they can be said to have some freedom. It is important to note that when we use the word *freedom* here, we mean freedom in a limited sense. No one is completely free. We cannot freely act on all of our desires. We cannot, for example, change ourselves into other beings or live without oxygen or snap our fingers and make people disappear; nor is it necessary that a human being have the freedom to perform such actions in order to be morally free. If there is freedom, we have to recognize that it is by nature limited. That is one reason why the soft determinist can argue that not only within causation but because of it, human beings are free. If human beings can be shown to be the originators of some causes, then—the soft determinist argues—there is human freedom within universal causation, and this is all we can hope to attain and indeed all we really need.

The strongest criticism of soft determinism comes, of course, from the hard determinists. They ask how any causes can be said to originate with human beings when the series of causes leading up to a particular effect can be traced back to factors outside a particular human being's control. The hard determinists do not make the claim that human beings *never* cause anything to happen, but they do maintain that ultimate causes are always beyond an individual's control. Another criticism of soft determinism comes from a group calling themselves "indeterminists," and we will examine their theories before discussing determinism in more detail.

◆————————————————————————

Indeterminism

Indeterminists hold that there is a certain amount of chance and freedom in the world—that not everything is caused and that there is a real pluralism in reality. Furthermore, the indeterminist believes that most of the freedom or chance that exists can be found in the area of human deliberation and choice, especially moral deliberation and decision making. William James (1842–1910), an American psychologist and philosopher, is the most prominent exponent of this view.

James desires that there be novelty and spontaneity in the world, allowing human beings to exercise their faculties of choice and creativity. He suggests that "our first act of freedom, if we are free, ought in all inward propriety to be to affirm that we are free."[4] Our strivings for good and our regrets over bad deeds are, he feels, indications that there is freedom, for if a bad act, for example, were fully predetermined, then there would be no point in feeling regret.[5] James further maintains that because we can't always predict in advance whether a human being is going to take path A or path B, then chance and spontaneity evidently play at least some part in the nature of reality, and that freedom does therefore exist, at least to some extent.

The hard determinists have several strong criticisms of the theory of indeterminism. First, isn't James's theory really based on wishful thinking rather than actual evidence or logic? Wanting to be free or wanting the world to be spontaneous does not make it so, any more than wanting the earth to be the center of the universe makes it so. Evidence and logic, say the hard determinists, point toward the conclusion that universal causation rather than indeterminism accurately describes the way things are. Hard determinists have to admit that there is no absolutely conclusive evidence for determinism, but they maintain, nevertheless, that the evidence points overwhelmingly toward universal causation rather than chance. What would an uncaused event be like, they ask—can we even describe such an event?

One criticism offered by both hard and soft determinists is that indeterminism really will not help solve the problem of human freedom and moral responsibility in any case because if an act is not caused, then it is not caused by anyone, including the moral person. Again, this means that we would have to say that all moral acts are accidents for which we cannot assign responsibility to human beings and for which we cannot give praise, blame, reward, or punishment. Therefore, indeterminism is not only empirically doubtful but also does not support the argument for human freedom in any way. Indeterminism, in short, could only guarantee accident or chance, not human freedom. Let us now return to criticisms of hard determinism to see if we can uncover any support for the concept of human freedom.

Criticisms of Hard Determinism and Arguments for Freedom

We could argue against hard determinists that because morality is not possible with their viewpoint and because we do have morality, hard determinism does not hold. We could also argue that because human beings feel free some of the time they must, therefore, *be* free. However, hard determinists would counter both of these arguments with the "facts" of universal causation; they would state that both morality based on freedom and the feeling that we are free are illusions, not fact.

When we are bad or good, they would argue, it is because we have been determined to be so by forces outside of our control. Even the actions of praising, blaming, rewarding, and punishing are useless unless we can change someone's behavior programming, that is, unless we either strike a "goodness" chord that is already embedded in the person's original character or override some earlier determining factor with a stronger one.

What we are doing, hard determinists would say, is not getting people to freely respond and make moral decisions but merely changing the way in which they are determined. The intimation is that we would not be able to do even this if their characters were not set up to acquiesce to such determinism. Hard determinists might advocate reward and punishment if they felt such means could stop someone from killing people, for example. However, they would feel that it is really impossible to *morally* blame people for the way they act because they are, after all, determined. One can try to change the way a person is determined, but one cannot morally blame someone for acting in a way he or she has been determined to act. From the hard determinist's viewpoint, there is no moral responsibility in the experience of human beings; there is only the illusion of it.

Hospers agrees with the hard determinist that people are very often victims of inner urges and desires that they do not want and cannot escape from, but he argues very effectively in rebuttal that nevertheless, to a very *limited* extent (varying considerably from person to person) and *over a considerable span of time*, we *are* free to desire or not to desire. We can choose to do our best to get rid of certain desires and to encourage other ones; and to a limited extent we may be successful in this endeavor. People who greatly desire alcohol sometimes succeed, by joining Alcoholics Anonymous or by other means, in resisting the temptation to drink until finally they no longer desire it. So, it is not true that we are never free to desire or that we are always the victims of whatever desires we happen to have.[6]

Inaccurate Use of Language

Hospers also argues effectively against the hard determinists' inaccurate use of language, claiming that they tend to push words such as *freedom* out of the context in which they make sense. For example, according to Hospers, the hard determinist maintains the impossible position that if human beings aren't completely free in an unlimited sense, then there can be no freedom at all. The hard determinist argues that in order for human beings to be free, they must have control over their own genetic makeup, their early childhood, and their "original character." This type of argument, says Hospers, pushes language too far away from its meaning. He agrees with the hard determinists that we cannot have caused our original characters but also examines the logical falla-cies they build around this belief. In order to cause our original characters, we would have to already have existed, and how could we exist without an original character? Hospers concludes that this whole argument is in fact self-contradictory.[7]

Human Complexity

I agree fully with Hospers's criticisms of the hard determinists' misuse of lan-guage. I also feel, however, that hard determinism does not account for the com-plexity of the nature of human beings, especially of human minds and con-sciousness but, rather, that it tends to oversimplify and reduce everything to the lowest common denominator. Earlier, we discussed the psychological egoist's belief that all human actions are performed by human beings in their own self-interest, regardless of the altruistic motives they may claim to have. All we need is one case of someone's stating that he or she truly performed an action strictly in someone else's interest to refute this claim. In the same way, we must show that human beings have enough control over causation so that they can be said to originate some causes themselves. Then we can speak of freedom, at least in the limited sense mentioned earlier.

Levels of Differences

Rocks, Plants, and Animals. When talking about universal causation, we must first take into consideration the complexity of the human mind. A rock is depen-dent on outside forces for its movement, change in shape, and change in color. Plant life is subject to forces outside and within it, and a plant grows, changes, and dies in reaction to these forces, which, as far as we can determine, operate at all times on some sort of biological (or botanical) instinct. Animals, too, although closer to human beings in their bodies and minds, are often governed by instinc-tual actions programmed down through the years by hereditary and genetic changes.

As we move along the evolutionary scale from inanimate to animate beings and from vegetative to animalistic beings, we see the element of freedom increase with each step. The rock, which has no freedom at all, is drastically dif-ferent from the plant, which is affected by its own internal workings as well as by outside forces. Animals are much more mobile than plants, have a greater observable consciousness, and can even be said to make some limited choices. For example, if a forest is on fire, the instinct to survive will cause an animal to attempt to escape by running away from the fire. Assuming that the fire is cover-ing the 180 degrees of ground behind the animal, then there are 180 degrees in front of him. Because he has a 180-degree range of directions in which to run, what makes him choose a particular direction? There may be obstacles that narrow the number of possible directions, but even within the narrow range of possibilities, doesn't the animal, in a limited sense at least, "choose" a pathway of escape?

Human Beings. When, on the evolutionary scale, we reach human beings, who have a much more sophisticated consciousness and whose minds and emotions are developed far beyond those of any other observable beings, then the possibility of freedom greatly increases. It is the area of consciousness, or the human mind and reasoning, on which most soft determinists and indeterminists base their arguments for human freedom.

Existentialism and Human Consciousness. One of the best arguments comes from the existentialists, especially the philosopher Jean-Paul Sartre (1905–1980).[8] Sartre believed that there exists a limited determinism in that people cannot help that they are born, how they are born, in what century or to which parents they are born; but he also believed people can help determine how they live. Sartre maintained that human beings have freedom because human perception is open-ended. He agreed with the philosopher Edmund Husserl (1859–1938) that consciousness is directional and creative. (The word Husserl used is *intentional*, in the sense that consciousness "intends" things rather than merely passively receiving them.) In other words, a person may drive along the same route from work every day for a year, yet each trip is different in the sense that the person's mind notices different objects along the way. Naturally, some of the external objects along the route will change from day to day, but even if they did not, the human mind could direct itself in different ways, selecting among the objects and thus, in a sense, *creating* its own experience. If the possibilities are open-ended, there is a myriad to choose from; because the human mind can select and direct itself differently, there are many more possibilities of choice available to the human than to the forest animal with the fire at its back. The level of sophistication of choices is, of course, also much higher.

If the human mind can, even in part, create its own experience, then experience is not just waiting in a deterministic sense to impinge itself on human consciousness. As Sartre pointed out, you may have been born crippled or blind, and you were not free to choose otherwise, but you are free in how you choose to live with your infirmity. You are determined in your physical limitations, you are even determined by the culture, economic level, and family in which you are born, but you are not completely determined—unless you *choose* to be—in how you live out your life, even though it has been influenced, in part, by all of these things. Building on the Hospers example cited earlier, this means that although I may have been born with a physical or psychological lack or urge that causes me to become addicted to alcohol when I drink it, I may become aware of this lack or urge and—with or without help—override this deterministic factor in my life.

One might say that my consciousness is directing itself to a new life experience free from addiction to alcohol and all of its attendant difficulties. I, then, to some extent create that life experience for myself even though I have, by my physical and psychological nature, been formerly determined very strongly toward the completely different life experience of a person who is addicted to alcohol. Almost all the groups that have been successful in the elimination of various drug addictions have stated that all they can really do is try to make people strong enough to make the choice for nonaddiction themselves and then to support them at every point along the way—the choice, however, has to be the addicts'. And until they actively choose the new life experience, their lives will probably not change very much. This argument should convince us that there is such a thing as human freedom. Accepting that it exists, it is logical to assume that it applies to morality as well as to choosing what clothes we will wear or where we will spend this year's vacation.

Conclusion—Soft Determinism

It would seem, then, that the only tenable position in this controversy is soft determinism, which says that universal causation is a strongly supported theory of reality that is compatible with human freedom. At least, that is the position that I support. Our freedom is limited, and there are many times when our actions are not within our control. We may be suffering from a psychological compulsion such as kleptomania and therefore cannot be held morally responsible for stealing because our compulsion for stealing is outside our control. We may be forced at gunpoint to do something that we know to be morally wrong, or we may be constrained so that we cannot do something morally right. We may be powerfully affected by the way we were treated by our family, by our genetic deficiencies, by the century in which we were born, by the culture and economic level into which we were born: All of these things may determine our characters to a great degree. But—paraphrasing Hospers—nevertheless, to some extent (varying considerably from person to person) and over a considerable span of time, we are free to desire or not to desire, to choose or not to choose, and to act or not to act.

With the acceptance of this viewpoint, then, it does make sense to assign moral responsibility to human beings when appropriate, and it also makes sense to praise, blame, reward, and punish them for their actions. We certainly should be careful to ascertain that people are not acting from uncontrollable compulsions or constraints before we assign praise or blame to them. Having ascertained, however, that they have acted in freedom, it does make sense to talk of moral responsibility and its attendant rewards and punishments.

Chapter Summary

I. Freedom versus determinism
   A. *Determinism* means the same thing as "universal causation"; that is, for every effect, event, or occurrence in reality a cause or causes exist. There is no such thing as an uncaused event.
   B. Determinism holds serious implications for morality.
      1. How can we tell people what they should or ought to do if they are programmed or predetermined to act the way they do?
      2. How can we praise, blame, reward, and punish if people can't help acting the way they do?

II. Types and theories of determinism
   A. Religious determinism—predestination—is the theory that if God is all-powerful and all-knowing, then He must have predestined everything that occurs.
      1. There is a problem in proving that there is such a being and, if He does exist, that He is all-powerful and all-knowing and has predestined everything.
      2. Most theories of salvation don't make sense if human beings are not free to make choices between good and evil.
   B. There are several types of scientific determinism.
      1. Physical determinism arose from discoveries in the physical sciences.
         (a) Sir Isaac Newton theorized that everything in reality is basically material, or physical, in nature and is therefore completely determined by natural laws, such as the law of gravity.
         (b) There are problems with this theory.
            (1) Natural laws state probabilities, not certainties.
            (2) Modern physics has raised serious doubts about Newtonian physics.
      2. Advances in the natural sciences gave rise to biological and genetic determinism.
         (a) Charles Darwin's theories—that species evolve through natural selection and that only the fittest survive—led to a belief that nature determines human beings.
         (b) A more sophisticated form of this theory states that human beings are totally determined by their genetic makeup, over which they have no control.
      3. The problem with both forms of scientific determinism is that they limit human beings strictly to the physical, disregarding their mental or spiritual side.
   C. Historical, or cultural, determinism arose from the theories of Georg Hegel.

1. Hegel maintained that there is an absolute mind trying to realize itself in perfection and manifesting itself through the history of the world, and that human beings are therefore completely determined by their past and present history and cultures.
2. There are problems with this theory.
    (a) It is difficult to prove the existence of both an "absolute mind" and a mind that exists without a body.
    (b) Other theories of history are just as plausible, if not more so.
D. Economic or social determinism arose from the theories of Karl Marx.
1. Marx says that human beings are determined by economic class struggles that inevitably will lead to a classless society.
2. The problems with this theory are similar to those raised by Hegel's.
    (a) Marx's theory is based on unproved assumptions, and other theories of economics are equally plausible.
    (b) Even though human beings are influenced by economics, there are other influences, such as science, technology, and human beings themselves, that affect economics.
E. Psychological determinism arose from the work of Freud and the behaviorists.
1. Freudian psychology maintains that human beings are affected by their unconscious drives and their attempts to repress them to the extent that their early childhood determines the course of their adult lives. The main criticism of this theory is that it is too generalized to have any real basis in fact.
2. The type of psychological determinism espoused by the behaviorists, particularly B. F. Skinner, maintains that human beings are completely physical beings whose development is totally determined by external stimuli from their physical and cultural environments.
3. There are problems with this theory.
    (a) It is based on a completely materialistic view of human beings, which does not stand up to evidence or argument.
    (b) It, like Freud's theories, goes too far in its claims, using the validity of operant conditioning in some instances as a basis for claiming its validity in all instances.
III. Fatalism and hard and soft determinism
A. Fatalism is the belief that all events are irrevocably fixed and predetermined so that human beings cannot alter them in any way.
1. Sometimes events are outside of our control, but it does not make sense to act as if all events were outside of human control.
2. This is an impractical theory by which few people, if any, really live.

B. Hard determinism is the theory that if all events are caused, then freedom is incompatible with determinism.

C. Soft determinism is the theory that all events are caused, but that some events and causes originate with human beings. The hard determinist criticizes the soft determinist by questioning how human beings can be said to originate any events when, if you trace causes back far enough, they end up being outside of the control of human beings.

IV. Indeterminism

A. Indeterminists maintain that there is a certain amount of chance and freedom in the world, and that not everything is caused.

    1. William James says that he desires that there be novelty and spontaneity in the world, allowing human beings to be free and creative.

    2. James feels that our strivings for good over bad and regrets over bad deeds mean that we must be free.

B. There are problems with this theory.

    1. This theory seems to be based on wishful thinking rather than on evidence or logical argument.

    2. There is little evidence to suggest that uncaused events exist.

    3. If some events are totally uncaused, then they are not caused by anything or anybody; therefore, indeterminism is no guarantee of human freedom, only of chance.

V. Criticisms of hard determinism and arguments for freedom

A. Hard determinists push language out of context.

B. Their arguments do not account for the complexity of the nature of human beings. Like the psychological egoist, they try to reduce what is really complex to something simple, and this reductionism will not work.

C. Human minds and human perception are open-ended and creative—humans create their experience of the world. They are not passive receivers of sense experience but active seekers and creators.

D. Soft determinism seems to be the only tenable position. Acceptance of this position allows us to assign moral responsibility to human beings and to praise, blame, reward, and punish them when and if it is justifiable to do so.

Exercises for Review

1. Define and explain the terms *determinism, indeterminism, fatalism, predestination, universal causation,* and *freedom.*

2. Differentiate between hard and soft determinism, indeterminism, and fatalism. What are the problems with each theory?

3. Discuss whether you believe human beings are free or determined. If they are free, to what extent are they free? If they are determined, what difficulties does this raise for morality?

4. How does the existentialist view of human consciousness relate to the argument for human freedom?

5. Research any of the following men and their work and explain in full the extent to which you think their theories are valid or invalid where freedom and determinism are concerned: Calvin and predestination, Newton and scientific determinism, Darwin and biological determinism, Hegel and historical determinism, Marx and economic determinism, Freud and psychological determinism, Skinner and behaviorism, William James and indeterminism, Sartre and freedom.

Discussion Questions

1. Analyze any act you have committed for which you have strong feelings (for example, regret or pride), and argue to what extent you feel this act was freely done by you or determined by forces within or outside you. Be specific.

2. Read any of the following literary works and discuss the extent to which the main characters are free or determined: Albert Camus's *The Stranger*, Herman Melville's *Bartleby the Scrivener*, Stephen Crane's *The Open Boat*, Joan Didion's *Play It as It Lays*, Fyodor Dostoyevsky's *Crime and Punishment*, Arthur Miller's *Death of a Salesman*.

3. Research the background of some great men or women (for example, Albert Einstein, Eleanor Roosevelt, John F. Kennedy, Golda Meier, Florence Nightingale, Dwight Eisenhower, Mary Cassatt, Picasso) or some infamous men or women (for example, Charles Manson, Lee Harvey Oswald, Ma Barker, the Boston Strangler, Mata Hari, Lizzie Borden, Adolf Hitler) and discuss the extent to which their goodness or badness was determined by forces over which they had no control (for example, genetic makeup, early childhood, economic or cultural deprivation).

4. Read any of the following books and discuss both how the authors view determinism and freedom and what you think of the societies created in these books: Aldous Huxley's *Brave New World, Brave New World Revisited*, and *The Island*; George Orwell's *1984*; Plato's *The Republic*; B. F. Skinner's *Walden II*; Ray Bradbury's *Fahrenheit 451*; Robert Heinlein's *The Moon Is a Harsh Mistress*; Jean-Paul Sartre's *No Exit* and *Nausea*.

5. In examining the world around you, to what extent do you believe human beings are subject to the same types of determinism as plants and animals? Be specific.

Notes

1. See John Hick, *Philosophy of Religion*, 36–43, and John Hospers, *Introduction to Philosophical Analysis*, 461–76, for a full discussion of this problem.
2. See Hospers, *Introduction to Philosophical Analysis*, 378–91.
3. See John Hospers, *Human Conduct: An Introduction to the Problems of Ethics* (New York: Harcourt Brace Jovanovich, 1961), 508.
4. William James, *The Will to Believe and Other Essays in Popular Philosophy* (New York: Longmans, Green, 1912), 146.
5. Ibid., 161–62.
6. Hospers, *Human Conduct*, 508–9.
7. Ibid., 513–17.
8. Mary Warnock, *Existentialism* (London: Oxford University Press, 1970), 113–24.

Supplementary Reading

Beardsley, Elizabeth L. "Determinism and Moral Perspectives." *Philosophy and Phenomenological Research* 21 (1960): 1–20.

Berofsky, Bernard, ed. *Free Will and Determinism*. New York: Harper & Row, 1966.

Bertocci, Peter A. *Free Will, Responsibility and Grace*. Nashville: Abingdon Press, 1957. This is a discussion of the problem from a Christian perspective.

Brooks, Robert E. *Free Will: An Ultimate Illusion*. Portland, Oreg.: Circa Press, 1987.

Campbell, C. A. *In Defense of Free Will: With Other Philosophical Essays*. New York: Humanities Press, 1967.

Dobzhansky, Theodosius G. *The Biological Basis of Human Freedom*. New York: Columbia University Press, 1960.

Edwards, Jonathan. *Freedom of the Will*. Ed. Paul Ramsey. New Haven: Yale University Press, 1957. This is a good presentation of Calvinistic predestination.

Farrer, Austin. *The Freedom of the Will*. New York: Charles Scribner's Sons, 1958.

Feinberg, Joel *Freedom and Fulfillment: Philosophical Essays*. Princeton: Princeton University Press, 1992.

Hook, Sidney, ed. *Determinism and Freedom in the Age of Modern Science*. New York: Collier Books, 1958.

Hospers, John. *Human Conduct, An Introduction to the Problems of Ethics*, 2nd edition. New York: Harcourt Brace Jovanovich, 1982.

———. *Introduction to Philosophical Analysis*, 2nd ed. Englewood Ciffs, N.J.: Prentice-Hall, 1967.

James, William. *The Will to Believe and Other Popular Essays in Philosophy*. New York: Longmans, Green, 1912. The essay "The Dilemma of Determinism" presents James's theory of indeterminism.

Kane, R. *Free Will and Values*. Albany, N.Y.: State University of New York Press, 1985.

Klein, Martha. *Determinism, Blameworthiness, and Deprivation*. New York: Oxford: University Press, 1990.

Leoni, Bruno, ed. *Freedom and the law*. Indianapolis: Liberty Fund, 1991.

Munn, Allen M. *Free-Will and Determinism*. Toronto: University of Toronto Press, 1960. This book discusses freedom and determinism from the point of view of physics and physical science.

Sartre, Jean-Paul. *Being and Nothingness: An Essay on Phenomenological Ontology*. Trans. Hazel E. Barnes. New York: Washington Square Press, 1964. This book presents Sartre's special point of view on existentialist freedom.

Sellars, Wilfred, and John Hospers, eds. *Readings in Ethical Theory*. New York: Appleton-Century-Crofts, 1952.

Skinner, B. F. *Beyond Freedom and Dignity*. New York: Knopf, 1971.

———. *Science and Human Behavior*. New York: Macmillan, 1953.

Strawson, Galen. *Freedom and Belief*. New York: Oxford University Press, 1991.

Swanton, Christine. *Freedom: A Coherence Theory*. Indianapolis: Hackett Publishing, 1992.

Trusted, Jennifer. *Free Will and Responsibility*. New York: Oxford University Press, 1984.

Warnock, Mary. *Existentialism*. New York: Oxford University Press, 1970.

Werkmeister, William H. *A Philosophy of Science*. Lincoln, Nebr.: University of Nebraska Press, 1965. Chapter 12 contains a discussion of freedom in relation to the laws of nature.

Williams, Clifford. *Free Will and Determinism: A Dialogue*. Indianapolis, Ind.: Hackett Publishing Company, 1980.

Wilson, Gary W. *Free Will*. New York: Oxford University Press, 1982.

Winfield, Richard D. *Freedom and Modernity*. Albany, N.Y.: State University of New York Press, 1991.

CHAPTER 6

Reward and Punishment

Objectives

After you have read this chapter you should be able to

1. Understand the relationship between reward and punishment and justice.
2. Understand the meanings and differences among the three theories of reward and punishment: retribution, utilitarianism, and restitution.
3. Identify and understand the many criteria for rewarding and punishing.
4. Identify and understand the arguments for and against all three theories.

Definition of Key Terms

Retributive Justice

Probably the oldest form of justice, retributive justice, is best expressed in the biblical saying, "an eye for an eye and a tooth for a tooth" (Exodus 21:24–25). This kind of justice means that people should get what they deserve either in reward or punishment regardless of the consequences.

Distributive Justice

Distributive justice concerns itself essentially with the equitable distribution of good and bad to human beings on a just and fair basis.

Reward

Reward is something given or received for worthy behavior, usually on the basis of merit, deserts (what people deserve), or ability.[1]

Punishment

Punishment is the act of penalizing someone for a crime, fault, or misbehavior; a penalty for wrongdoing.[2]

Retribution (Deserts Theory)

Retribution is the act of giving people what they deserve, regardless of the consequences—in punishment sometimes referred to as the "eye for an eye, tooth for a tooth" or "revenge" or "just deserts" theory.

Utilitarianism (Results Theory)

Utilitarianism is the act of rewarding or punishing based on the results of the act and whether or not it brings about the greatest good consequences for everyone involved.

Restitution (Compensation Theory)

Restitution is the act of somehow compensating a victim for harm or wrong done to him; such compensation is usually required to be made to the victim by the perpetrator of the harm or wrong.

Reward and Punishment in Relationship to Justice

Nowhere does the issue of being just or fair arise more powerfully than in the matters of reward and punishment, and especially punishment. One element missing from the ethical theories as I have described them thus far is a discussion of what to do with those who seriously violate one or more of the basic ethical tenets. Should the same principle of justice be applied to grievous wrongdoers as well as to those who follow an ethical system faithfully, or are the transgressors beneath this principle because of their unethical actions and behavior? What I shall attempt to do in this chapter is to discuss reward and punishment as aspects of justice and to present the various theories of distributing reward and punishment to see if we can discover which would be the most just.

Elements of Justice

Several elements of justice in general apply specifically to reward and punishment.

What Justice Involves

Just as ethics or morality involves the "treatment" of human beings by other human beings (see the working definition of ethics in Chapter 1), justice as an aspect of ethics involves the same thing. When we talk about being just or fair, we are talking about being just or fair to other human beings, and reward and punishment have to do with the way one human being treats another. What we are discussing here, then, is the notion of *distributive justice*, or how we can dispense good and bad or reward and punishment on a just and fair basis.

Concern with Past Events

Justice is basically concerned with past rather than future events in that we reward or punish people for what they *have done*, not for what they *will do*. It is certainly unfair and even unrealistic to reward or punish people for what they *might do* even though sometimes incentives are given for future accomplishments and even though—as you will see when discussing the utilitarian theory—to some extent the future can be considered when rewarding or punishing.

Individualistic Rather Than Collectivistic

Justice should be individualistic in application, not collectivistic. Individuals rather than groups deserve reward and punishment. If we punish groups or individuals because they are a part of a group, then our punishment will be collectivistic, or we will be guilty of *mass punishment*, as it is sometimes called. This type of punishment is a source of a good deal of the injustice in our society. It is very closely related to discrimination by race, religion, sex, age, and mental or physical handicap and tends to punish individuals unjustly because they are members of some group against which many people are prejudiced.

The military, among other institutions in our society, is often guilty of collective punishment. If one serviceman does not keep his area clean, his bed made, or his uniform up to snuff, then everyone in his barracks is punished by being denied passes or other privileges. The military's purpose in doing this is to prod the non-wrongdoer into pressuring the wrongdoer to correct his ways, but the punishment as it is meted out to include the innocent is unjust. The offending serviceman should alone be punished, and not his obedient peers.

Comparative Justice

Comparative justice deals with the way a person is treated in relation to another person. For example, if two people have committed murder under similar circumstances and one gets out of prison in ten years but the other is executed, this might be considered as comparative but not collectivistic injustice, depending, of course, on the circumstances, extenuating or otherwise, surrounding each crime.[3]

Reward

Reward is one method of distributing the good we are concerned with on a fair and just basis. There are basically four ways in which the good or rewards can be distributed:

1. As equally among people as possible without regard to their abilities or merits.
2. According to people's abilities.
3. According to what they merit, or deserve.
4. According to their needs.

We will examine these as well as other criteria.

Criteria for Rewarding People

Egalitarian Criterion or Equal Distribution of Goods and Rewards. Wouldn't it be the most just and fair to distribute good things and rewards equally among people regardless of their merits, abilities, needs, or what they produce? An example that shows the significance of distributing good and bad equally among people concerns the scarcity of certain medical resources.

Kidney Dialysis Issue. In 1962 there were not enough kidney machines to dialyze (see Glossary for definition of dialysis) the kidneys of people who were in various stages of kidney failure. When there is not enough of something this important to go around, an ethical question arises—how to make a decision that will be just or fair to everyone concerned. Swedish Hospital in Seattle, Washington, was the first hospital to deal with this problem in connection with kidney patients, and it attempted to solve the problem by establishing two committees— a medical panel to select those people capable of being medically assisted by dialysis and a panel of mostly nonmedical people who would then decide who, out of those medically qualified for dialysis, would actually get the treatment. In 1963, the second panel was composed of a lawyer, a clergyman, a housewife, a banker, a labor leader, and two physicians. The medical panel had narrowed the thirty patients needing dialysis to seventeen, and the nonmedical panel was asked to consider the following factors: age, sex, marital status and number of dependents, income, net worth, emotional stability (especially in the sense of being able to accept treatment), education, occupation, past performance and future potential, and references.

The committee soon realized that making fair decisions was a nearly impossible task. Which factors should be considered seriously and in what order of importance? Whether the person was educated or uneducated? Whether the person was a professional, a laborer, or an office worker? Whether the person was religious or not? Whether the person was male or female? Whether the person had good, mediocre, or only poor references as to his or her character, potential, or past performance? The difficulties were insurmountable, and the decisions were terribly agonizing for this panel of extremely well-meaning people. A much more complete description of the committee and its problems can be found in Paul Ramsey's *The Patient as Person*,[4] but what follows will illustrate a few of the difficulties:

> What happens when we get two men with the same job, the same number of children, the same income, and so forth? Between a man with three children and a man with an older wife and six children we must, for the sake of the children, reckon the surviving widow's opportunity to remarry. In estimating "worth to society," how much chance would an artist or a composer have before this committee in comparison with the needs of a woman with six children? Finally, if a patient is given a place in a kidney dialysis program because he "passed" a comparative evaluation of his worthiness in terms of broad social standards of eligibility, the needs of his dependents, or his potentiality for contribution to humanity, one can ask whether he should be removed from the program when his esteemed character changes. . . . As Dr. George Schreiner said, "You should be logical and say that when a man stops going to church or is divorced or loses his job, he ought to be removed from the programme and somebody else who fulfills these criteria substituted."[5]

Again, the question is how one is to distribute this "good" (dialysis) to people justly and fairly. We can, in this instance at least, rule out need because the patients all "need" the dialysis. If we go by abilities, how are we to distinguish justly between a housewife and mother, a lawyer, a doctor, an executive, a member of the clergy, a teacher, and a laborer, all of whom may be very able in their particular job? If we go by what people deserve or merit, then how are we to distinguish between these people, who may all be deserving of the treatment in the sense that they are productive human beings in their own fields and within their own families and communities? If we are going to rank people by merit, then what are the criteria to be, and how can they be just? For example, will we place a very clever and intelligent lawyer at the top and a rather simple but hardworking laborer at the bottom? These distinctions, of course, can be worked out on a quite arbitrary basis, as indeed they have been in various totalitarian societies, but then we must question whether being arbitrary is just and fair.

The most ideal solution is to gain enough resources so that everyone who needs them can have them, but this will probably never happen in all areas of need because there are so many needs and a definite limitation on available resources. Therefore, how are we to choose justly? Evidently, the "let the better person live" notion that we have just been discussing will not work too well, or at least will fall far short of distributing the resources fairly. We can also consider the alternative "all should die," as Ramsey does, but who would deem it fair to let all seventeen people die when we are certain that ten of them can live—who wants to "throw out the baby with the bathwater"?[6] The other alternative, which is the approach I would argue for, is the "drawing of straws" approach.[7] After having witnessed the agonies undergone by the Swedish Hospital committee, many other committees or dialysis units throughout the country used a lottery method once the medical decisions had been made.

This alternative—that the lives of people must be decided by a lottery—may not be palatable to many people, but how else can you be just and fair toward all seventeen people? Would you, as a kidney patient, rather be denied dialysis because you are not thought to be as worthy, able, or deserving as someone else or because you did not win a fairly conducted lottery? At least, we would have to admit that everyone was treated fairly and justly by the latter means. It seems, then, at least in this situation, that this egalitarian way of determining justice is the most ethical, just, and fair.

Problems with Equality of Distribution. There are problems with the egalitarian method of distribution. By definition, it ignores other criteria that are deemed important by their advocates and by people in general, such as merit, ability, need, productiveness, and effort, in its attempt to be fair and egalitarian in its approach to rewarding. Second, in what ways and to what extent are people equal? Is a doctor with long years of training equal to a janitor who learned the trade in a few weeks or months on the job? Should a beginning pianist and a fully trained concert pianist both be given equal chances to perform at Carnegie Hall? Should students be allowed to depose a fully trained credentialed teacher and conduct class in the teacher's place? As you can see, it doesn't take many examples to point out the inequalities among people, jobs, and professions. So in what sense should they all be rewarded the same?

Perhaps they should all be given equality of consideration *if* they have other attributes or fulfill other qualifications that are necessary to certain jobs or professions, for example. People should certainly not be denied opportunities because of race, sex, religion, age, or handicap, but what if a job requires a great deal of physical strength and stamina? Unless women, senior citizens, or handicapped people can muster these attributes, should they be given equal opportunity for such a job along with those who can?

Finally, can we really ignore all of the other criteria used to determine reward, such as what people produce, effort extended, ability, need, long and expensive training, expensive equipment, physical danger, and unpleasantness of jobs? Shouldn't they at least be considered, and when they are, isn't equality as a basis of reward weakened? It would at least seem that we must examine these other criteria before settling on an egalitarian approach to reward.

Production, or What People Produce. One criteria for rewarding is based on what people produce, achieve, or accomplish through their own efforts regardless of the amount of effort or the time taken. For instance, if a student has done exceptional work in a class, by this criterion she is entitled to a grade of A even if she had to put out very little effort or time because, for example, she has an excellent mathematical imagination and above-average ability. That another member of the class raised himself from failing work to a C by the end of the semester by expending a great deal of time and effort doesn't mean he gets an A, too. He has still produced only C work through his efforts.

This production can be based on quantity or quality or both. For example, fruit or vegetable pickers are paid mostly on a piecework basis; that is, the more potatoes or peaches they pick in a day, the more they get paid. Others are paid basically for the quality of their work: for having creative ideas that improve the quality of a company's product, efficiency, or image. Probably most employers will reward on the basis of both quality and quantity. The worker who can produce a high-quality product in large quantity is more highly paid than one who produces quality goods in small quantity or one who produces a lot of goods of only mediocre or even sometimes poor quality. Therefore, by this criterion, people are rewarded solely on the basis of what they deserve, or merit, in view of what and/or how much they have produced, and little account is taken of effort, ability, or need in determining whom to reward. The problems inherent in this method will be discussed as we proceed.

Effort. Another standard for rewarding, which was hinted at in the previous section, is effort. This criterion would reward effort regardless of the quantity or quality of what is produced, achieved, or accomplished. In a classroom situation, those who put out the greatest effort according to their abilities would be rewarded the most. In a work situation, each employee would be required to put in eight hours of this greatest effort, and each would be paid the same wage.

There are certainly problems with this notion in that, for one thing, those who have contracted to do a job (for example, building contractors) and who are being paid so much for the job are being paid not for how much time and effort they put in but solely for what they produce—a finished job. And how can effort be measured? Some people will work harder if given some incentive to do so, and others will expend only average effort no matter what they are offered. Third, suppose a fairly dull-witted person and a very bright person both work for eight hours at top capacity. Should they both receive the same consideration for wages and promotions? Which one would you want as a foreman or executive, for example, the one who is brighter or the one who is duller, given that they both make a full effort every day? The difficulty in determining effort and the problem that effort alone does not necessarily make a person deserving of reward causes this criterion to be a weak one, at least by itself.

Ability. Some people think that people ought to be rewarded on the basis of their abilities. First, we must distinguish between natural and acquired abilities. Some people, such as the A student I described earlier, have superior natural abilities in certain areas. However, is having natural abilities merely enough? Should people be rewarded merely because they have certain abilities through no fault or responsibility of their own? What if people choose not to put their abilities to use because of laziness or procrastination? If they are more able than others but choose not to employ their abilities, should they be rewarded over people who do not have such abilities but who work hard and produce more and better?

Acquired abilities are different in that people have had to put out time, effort, and money to get them. For example, certain professionals, such as doctors and lawyers, have to spend a great deal of time and money to acquire the abilities of their profession. These abilities, being acquired, would be more significant than natural ones as far as rewarding is concerned. Of course, not using these skills remains as much of a problem as it does with natural abilities. It would seem, then, that abilities, natural or acquired, alone would not be a good criteria for reward—some combination with effort and production would have to be included to measure the use of and achievement attained by such abilities.

Need. Some argue that good things and rewards should be given on the basis of need; that is, people who have the greatest needs should be given the most good things or should be "rewarded" for their need. First, we should distinguish two types of need: private and public.

Private need is concerned with what individuals need as a result of being poor or out of work. Many people argue that we should help the poor and needy among us and that we should give them some of or the same goods as the rest of us. From a humane point of view, of course, helping the needy would seem to be an honorable ideal. However, to what extent do they deserve to be rewarded on the basis of need alone? For example, should we hire only the needy regardless of qualifications or abilities? As John Hospers points out, people who need jobs most are often those who have no employable skills, and should employers load their businesses with unskilled workers and pay them the same as they would skilled workers?[8] What would happen to their businesses if they did, and what incentives would skilled workers have to continue to work for such employers?

The questions pertaining to need often arise in academic situations when financial aid or scholarships are to be awarded. Should they be awarded to the most needy, the brightest, or both? It would seem that the ideal situation would be one in which those who have the highest academic potential and the highest need should be the ones to get these rewards, but often the most needy are not as academically successful as the less needy. And what about the consistently high-scoring student whose need isn't as great as the more needy student's or who has little or no need? Many such students feel that recognition for their outstanding academic achievement is being overshadowed by the needs of those who are average or only slightly above average students. One of the biggest problems with rewarding on the basis of need, both in the academic and the business world, is that it eliminates incentives to make an effort or develop abilities. If students or others are going to be rewarded on the basis of need alone, then why try to do anything other than be needy? Second, this criterion is obviously not just or fair to talented and hardworking people. Helping the needy, then, is admirable, but rewarding them, in the fullest sense of the word, on the basis of need alone would not seem to be just or fair to those who fall into other categories.

Public need is somewhat different than private need in that rewarding is done on the basis of people's contribution to or fulfilling of public needs. For example, doctors are often rewarded because they fulfill a need everyone has—health care. On the other hand, nurses, who fulfill the same need in different but extremely important ways, are not rewarded the same as doctors. In fact, some nurses feel they are penalized rather than rewarded for what they are doing. This points out the difficulty of determining which needs are the most important and how suppliers of those needs should be rewarded. How will we rate farmers, plumbers, jewelers, teachers, police, and entertainers as to importance in supplying public needs? Sometimes people who supply less important needs will get much greater rewards for their efforts than those who supply more important ones. Some entertainers and sports persons, for example, are much more heavily rewarded than police officers, fire fighters, or nurses who risk their lives or deal with protecting human life every day. How we should reward public need, then, is a difficult problem to resolve.

Other Criteria. Several other criteria should be mentioned before discussing the two major theories dealing with reward:

1. Long and expensive training in a profession. For example, it often takes three or four years beyond the bachelor's degree to become a lawyer and more beyond it to become a doctor—shouldn't this be rewarded in some way? On the other hand, teachers who get degrees beyond the B.A., which may take them two to five years, depending on the degree, often aren't paid as much as entry-level skilled laborers who may have never had to finish high school, much less go to college. In other words, rewarding on this basis seems to be uneven to say the least. Also, should incompetent doctors or lawyers be rewarded for the length and cost of their training without regard to ability or effort?

2. Job or profession requiring expensive equipment. Some feel that those who are required to purchase and maintain expensive equipment should also be rewarded. Doctors and dentists, who require very expensive equipment, would be rewarded more than others, according to this criterion. Perhaps this is fair or just, but how much more should they be rewarded than practitioners in professions that don't require expensive equipment but do require a lot of education and training or skills or hazardous duty, and to what extent should their rewards continue after the equipment is essentially paid off? For as long as they practice their professions?

3. Physical danger. Should members of bomb squads and other hazardous duties be paid extra or given higher wages because of the nature of their duties? Often extra pay is allotted to such professions, for example, in the military with its combat, flight, and special duty pay, but very often it is not at all commensurate with the dangers or hazards faced. Again, police officers, fire fighters, and nurses are seldom given any extra pay, and often their regular pay does not really compensate or reward them for all the risks to their and others' lives.

4. Unpleasantness of jobs. Another of the "other" criteria is that of rewarding people for the unpleasantness of their jobs; for example, paying garbage collectors high wages because what they do is necessary, supplies a public need, and few people want to do such jobs. The main difficulties here are how are we to decide which jobs get the greater reward because of their unpleasantness, and how much reward are the people doing them to be given?

5. Seniority. Many institutions and businesses reward on the basis of seniority. The argument here is that those who have indicated loyalty and perseverance by long years of service to a specific organization should be rewarded. Often when people are in jobs for too long a time, however, they may become ineffective or even burned out. If such people are no longer effective workers, should they continue to be promoted and rewarded over those who may be junior to them in seniority but more skillful as workers? Only if qualifications and abilities are equal can seniority be a fair way of rewarding people for their efforts.

Theories of How to Reward

Two major theories dealing with reward also deal with punishment, as you will see in the next section of this chapter. These are the retributivist, or deserts, theory and the utilitarian, or results, theory.

Retributivist or Deserts Theory. The first theory concerns itself strictly with what people deserve, or merit, for what they have done in the past. These theorists feel that people ought to be rewarded for what they have done, not for what the consequences of what they have done will be, or what kind of future good consequences will be derived from rewarding them. Retributivists will generally focus on rewarding people for their efforts. They are not concerned with the utility of rewarding people, such as incentives to do more and better work or what is in the public good, but rather on what effort people have expended, not what they have done as a result of that effort. Therefore, two people who put out their best efforts on the job for eight hours a day would, according to this theory, be rewarded in the same way or paid the same wage because they deserve it regardless of any future consequences.

Obviously, some future consequences might be that a brighter and more productive worker might seek employment elsewhere, where he or she could be rewarded for abilities as well as effort, and then the company might lose its better workers and put out a product of less quality and in less quantity. Also, people would not seek dangerous or unpleasant work because there would be little or no incentive for them to do so. This might not only affect a particular business alone but also, if applied on a widespread basis, an entire economy. The retributivist would argue that at least all people are getting what they deserve and that they should be rewarded on that basis only. The utilitarian would argue that this may be just, but the utility, or "usefulness," of rewarding in this manner would not be in the best interests of everyone.

Utilitarian, or Results, Theory. As we discovered in Chapter 2, utilitarians based their ethical theories on good consequences for everyone affected by acts or rules. Unlike the retributivists they would emphasize the future results of rewarding instead of merely responding to past efforts. The utilitarian would argue that rewards should be given only on the basis of bringing about good consequences for everyone, so that if rewarding a worker in a certain way will give him or her an incentive to do better and work harder or encourage more people to do the same, then the proper reward to accomplish all of this should be given.

The utilitarian would definitely be in favor of paying higher wages or giving extra pay for dangerous or unpleasant jobs because the good consequences that would be derived from doing so would be to attract people to these jobs who might not otherwise be willing to do them. Utilitarians would also believe in rewarding workers who are brighter or who produce more and better results regardless of the effort they put in because in the long run, doing so will bring about the best consequences not only for these particular workers but for the company and the economy in general.

One of the problems with the utilitarian theory is that instead of rewarding hard work and conscientiousness, it essentially rewards production. For example, if a flamboyant, playboy type of employee with little or no effort can bring in more business than a hardworking, conscientious but somewhat dull employee, then the former would be rewarded more than the latter even though the latter might be more deserving. This would be discouraging to the hard worker, who might quit. The retributivist would argue, of course, that the hard worker is not getting what he deserves, whereas the playboy is getting more than he deserves because he has put in much less effort than the hard-working employee.

Another problem with the utilitarian approach is that if good consequences alone are the criteria for reward, then it is possible to reward a totally undeserving person. For example, suppose a boss knows that one of his workers, Tom, is totally incompetent, but extremely well liked by his workers. Thinking of good consequences—the morale and happiness of the workers—and not what Tom deserves, he might give Tom a promotion and a raise. This is possible under a strictly utilitarian results-theory approach to reward.

As you can see, the difficulty of whom and how to reward is a real problem, and before we seek some kind of solution, let's look at the moral issue of punishment, which is even more thorny than reward because it involves doing harm or injury to people, raising the question of whether or not it can be ethically justified at all.

Punishment

Anyone can decide to punish anyone else. For example, when children misbehave, their parents have the authority to punish them, short of child abuse and battering, by grounding them, spanking them, speaking harshly to them, depriving them of fun or social activities, or sending them to their rooms. A husband who cheats on his wife can be punished by her by being thrown out of the house and by not being allowed to see his children easily. There are many ways in which people can be punished by others for real or imagined offenses. However, in discussing punishment in this chapter, we will be talking about that which is meted out for a violation of a duly constituted moral rule or criminal or civil law.

Requirements of Punishment

There are four requirements that punishment should meet:

1. It must involve unpleasantness of some sort. It would hardly be punishment if it did not, and this is one of its dangers in that it usually imposes harm or injury on someone. Therefore, it requires special justification and should only be administered if and when a person has seriously violated the rights of others by injuring or harming them.

2. Punishment must be given or done *for* something. It should not be imposed for no reason at all (what sense would that make?) or because the person doling it out gets pleasure from doing it, for example. This would be unfair to the recipient.

3. It should be imposed by some person or group that has been given "duly constituted" moral or legal authority to punish and should not merely be left up to the whim or caprice of individuals.

4. It must be imposed according to certain rules or laws that have been violated by the offender. This is why it is important for each ethical system to have some theory or rules concerning punishment of violators of that system.[9]

Given these requirements, it would seem that the best context in which punishment should be administered is the legal system because, first of all, individuals are often concerned with vengeance, not justice, whereas the state is concerned (at its best) with the opposite. The state can provide a more objective arena in which to administer punishment than the atmosphere filled with the anger and hurt of the aggrieved victim or victims. In other words, by the authority of the state and its laws, violators should be punished for disobeying the laws within an *institutional* rather than a *vengeful* context.

There are several reasons why punishment by law is more ethical and just than by individual vengeance. First of all, when punishment is done according to law, the matter is ended—that is, once the appropriate punishment is meted out by duly constituted authority, there is no more punishment given for the violation. This is not so with the concept of vengeance—it can go on and on, sometimes decimating whole families, tribes, and societies. For example, in long-standing feuds, if a person of family A is killed, then vengeance requires that a person from family B should be killed to "even the score" or "exact justice," and then, of course, another person from family A must be killed to bring justice to family B, and so on. Punishment is often never-ending when individual vengeance is its context.

Second, as I mentioned previously, law can be more unbiased than individuals. Lawyers, judges, and juries are usually not personally involved with either the offender or the victim and also have to operate within a set of strict rules, procedures, and laws rather than on whim or caprice. The entire situation and the people involved in the crime can be presented and adjudged as fairly as possible, including extenuating circumstances and other special issues. Hurt and angry victims are often incapable of being unbiased and objective—no one really expects them to be. Therefore, despite the failures of our legal system, it is still the more just way to deal with violations of our ethical and legal rules and laws and the punishment of such violations.

◆

Theories of Punishment

Retributive, or Deserts, Theory

The first, and probably the oldest, theory of punishment is the retributive, or deserts (based on what people actually deserve), theory, which states that punishment should be given only when it is deserved and only to the extent that it is deserved. In this sense, the retributivist theory is concerned with the past, not the future. Punishment is not imposed *in order to* do or accomplish anything, such as deter offensive behavior in society. This, as we shall see, is the utilitarian point of view. Rather it should be imposed solely *because of* an offense or crime a person has committed; that is, the punishment must actually be deserved and not be administered to bring about good consequences. F. H. Bradley, a nineteenth century philosopher, stated this point of view succinctly:

> Punishment is punishment, only when it is deserved. We pay the penalty because we owe it, and for no other reason; and if punishment is inflicted for any other reason whatever than because it is merited by wrong, it is a gross immorality, a crying injustice, an abominable crime, and not what it pretends to be.[10]

Why Crime Requires Punishment. Crime requires punishment for two reasons, according to retributivists. First, punishment is required to reestablish the balance of morality, which is disturbed when someone violates laws or moral rules. Such laws and rules are established in order to achieve a balance in a society between individual rights and the common good, and when a crime is committed, the balance is upset and must be restored. According to the retributivist, punishment is the only way to correct this imbalance.

Second, the benefits existing in a society for its members carry with them the burden of self-restraint, and anyone who alleviates himself of this burden acquires an unfair advantage. According to the retributivist, this advantage must be eliminated and the burden of self-restraint restored. For example, in our society two of the benefits that we are all supposed to enjoy are freedom from bodily harm or injury and a noninvasion of privacy. Both require the burden of self-restraint on the part of all of us to see that such benefits are maintained. If a man rapes a woman, however, these benefits are denied her because he did not restrain himself; therefore, the unfair advantage he gained of having power over another and gaining benefits to which he was not entitled needs to be righted in some way. The guilty party must be punished, according to the retributivist, to eliminate the unfair advantage he gained by raping the woman.

Problems with Determining What People Deserve. In many ways, punishing on the basis of what people deserve seems to be the most just—people violate a moral rule or societal law, and they are given punishment for it only because they deserve it for what they did. However, there are several problems with this theory. First of all, what constitutes what people actually deserve? What if a crime deserves punishing by life imprisonment or execution but the person who committed it is old and sick?

For example, in a recent Florida case, a man was convicted of murder for shooting his wife because she had Alzheimer's disease and osteoporosis (softening of the bones). He stated that he felt that she wanted to die, but she was unable to kill herself because of her illnesses. He was seventy-five years old, and in Florida, a person guilty of murder must serve a minimum of twenty-five years before being considered for parole. Many people argued, first of all, that he shouldn't have been tried for murder because what he did was an act of mercy, prompted by love for his wife. Second, they argued that the sentence was not what he deserved because he was old and not well himself and because twenty-five years in prison would probably hasten his death. The sentence would surely mean that he would die in prison—after all, how many people live to be one hundred years old? Many people, including his daughter, begged for mercy for him and asked that he be pardoned or paroled, or that his sentence be commuted (that is, reduced). Whatever one may think about the man's guilt or reasons for doing what he did, critics of retributivism could ask, "Shouldn't his age and state of health be considered?"

Another example points out the problem with punishing on the basis of deserts alone. What if a man had committed a crime several years earlier but was never caught until now and since that time has lived an exemplary life, doing a lot of good for humanity? Should he now be made to pay for that crime? Strictly based on the deserts theory, the answer would be yes. He committed the crime, and he still deserves to be punished for it—the desert theory need not be concerned with any concept of mercy or forgiveness because of what he has done or not done since the crime.

Problem of Mercy. Can mercy play a part in the deserts theory of punishment, and if so, how? To whom and under what conditions should mercy be given to criminals? If retributivists wish to temper punishment with mercy, then how are they to do this? If they give one criminal less punishment for the same crime as another because of mercy, then will their actions be just to victims of the crime or to the other criminal? This problem has caused many retributivists to hold to the idea that retributive justice is enough; a person should be punished only because he or she deserves it, and applying mercy will only dilute justice.

Problem of Determining Seriousness of Offenses and Punishment. The general rule applied by the retributivist to punishment is, "The more serious the crime, the more severe the punishment," but how does one determine which offenses are most serious and which punishments are the most severe? People differ on these two issues. For example, most people feel that the killing of a human being is the most serious of crimes, but a rape victim may wish she had been killed rather than have to live with the physical and emotional injuries she sustained as a result of being raped. In some cultures, stealing is punishable by death, but is theft a serious enough crime for which to be executed?

Even when people generally agree on the seriousness of crimes, which is the proper punishment? Some people advocate life imprisonment or life imprisonment without parole for killing someone; others adamantly urge the death penalty. Which is most deserved? In some Middle Eastern countries, thieves have one hand cut off if they are caught stealing once, and the other if they are caught again. What happens if they are caught a third time? Is this piece-by-piece mutilation just, or would a determinate sentence in prison (as generally prescribed in the West) be more so?

"An Eye for an Eye and a Tooth for a Tooth." The retributivist presents two views based on the retributivistic saying in the Old Testament that reads as follows: "An eye for an eye, and a tooth for a tooth." One is that the punishment should be given in the same degree or severity as the crime, sometimes called the mirror-image theory.[11] In this view, the punishment should mirror the crime exactly in seriousness and severity. For example, if someone kills another, then the killer should also be killed. This is the viewpoint of people who support capital punishment, as we shall see in Chapter 8.

First of all, can one death actually mirror another? Suppose the victim was first tortured or raped and then killed—should the criminal also receive the same treatment? Many people who argue for capital punishment will often feel

150

that the criminal should be put to death painlessly, and, of course, those who are against it do not feel that it is appropriate at all but rather that it is barbaric, outmoded, and inappropriate according to the two-wrongs-don't-make-a-right argument. And what about stealing, rape, or child molestation? Should we set up thieves so that we can also steal from them? Should we rape the rapist or molest the children of the child molester (the latter may have already done so!)? The mirror-image theory, therefore, does not seem to be very feasible.

The second view based on the Old Testament saying is that punishment should be suitable or appropriate to the crime, but this is even more vague than the first view. What is suitable for stealing—six months in jail, one year, three years—and how are we to determine this? Is life imprisonment more suitable than execution or vice versa? When punishment is based solely on what violators actually deserve, determining the appropriate punishment is a real problem that is difficult to solve. Finally, can we ever find an appropriate punishment for crimes such as murder, rape, or child molestation? Can a lengthy prison sentence or even death ever eradicate the scars of the victims and their families or balance the scales? What type of deserved punishment will be sufficient to do any of this?

Utilitarian or Results Theory

The utilitarian theory differs from the retributivist theory in that it is future oriented—that is, it looks forward to results and consequences that might accrue from punishing someone. The utilitarian would not punish *because of* a crime, as in retributivism, but *in order that* something good could result from the punishment. Jeremy Bentham, one of the founders of utilitarianism, stated that punishment should always have as its aim the good of society.

He went on to describe two types of sanctions that are meant to discourage or eliminate criminal behavior: (1) internal sanctions, which are brought about by the development of conscience in children and others in order to mobilize feelings of guilt and shame, and (2) external sanctions, which are usually established by laws providing penalties to be imposed for immoral or criminal behavior.[12] Laws or rules providing penalties and punishment for offenses or crimes could function at both levels to some extent. That is, punishment for certain offenses could provide both forms of sanctions, the penalties helping to form people's consciences while at the same time punishing the actual offenses.

Therefore, in consonance with the utilitarian ideal as described in Chapter 2, that one should try to bring about the best good consequences for everyone by acts or rules, punishment is justified if and only if it brings about better consequences than some other treatment of the offender. There is no point to punishment, according to the utilitarian, if it doesn't produce good consequences or prevent harmful ones. The utilitarian would ask three questions concerning the punishment of any offender: (1) Will the wrongdoer be deterred from future crimes and become a better person or member of society? (2) Will others in the society be deterred from committing crimes because of the wrongdoer's punishment? and (3) Will society be protected from such criminals? If these three questions cannot be answered in the affirmative, then, according to the utilitarian, punishment is not morally justified. To punish people just because they deserve it, unless it brings about the preceding good consequences, would not be moral or just.

Consequences for the Offender. The question of whether or not punishment will bring about good consequences for offenders is a difficult one. According to the utilitarian, the purpose of punishment for offenders is to rehabilitate and reform them so that they are deterred from committing the same offense or any others in the future. Second, punishment should make them better persons and therefore better members of society. It is obvious that capital punishment or executing offenders for a serious offense will certainly deter them from committing future crimes, but it is also obvious that killing them will not rehabilitate or reform them in any way.

What about other types of punishment, short of execution, such as imprisonment for determinate or indeterminate periods of time or for life. Life imprisonment—if it is really life imprisonment, that is, without parole—would deter offenders from committing more crimes in society, not necessarily within prison, but would it rehabilitate or reform them? If it truly did foster reform, then would it be just or fair to keep such offenders in prison? What about lesser sentences? Would the punishment while in prison deter offenders from future crime, and would it rehabilitate and reform them so that they could go back into society as moral members? The answer depends in part on what is to be done with offenders while they are imprisoned. Most experts argue that our whole idea of imprisonment rehabilitating and reforming offenders is at best a bad joke. Very few are rehabilitated by being sent to prison, where they will be associating with habitual criminals who are usually guilty of worse crimes than first offenders ever thought of committing. How can such associations and such an atmosphere rehabilitate or reform?

Utilitarians and others dissatisfied with the prison system have often argued for incarceration not as punishment but for the purposes of psychiatric treatment, hoping that proper psychiatric and psychological techniques and therapies might rehabilitate and reform offenders where imprisonment cannot. However, such an approach of treatment rather than punishment is also often ineffectual for several reasons: (1) prisoners often resent mandatory treatment—they "don't want shrinks messing with their minds," which they often feel are just fine and not in need of adjustment of any kind; (2) therapists all have different standards of what to do and what is to be achieved, and there are no clear general standards of treatment by which to operate or cure; (3) therapists may have too much power over offenders in that often the alternatives to psychiatric

152

or psychological treatment are further penalties within the prison system, such as solitary confinement for those offenders who will not cooperate; (4) therapists also have the power over release dates in that sentences for treatment may be indeterminate, whereas regular sentences are usually determinate. In the play *Nuts*, by Tom Topor, Claudia, a woman who is fighting a legally insane designation so that she can be tried for the crime of first degree manslaughter, states this problem quite well when asked by her attorney what the sanity hearing means to her future:

> If I lose today, I'm committed for a year. . . . Sixty days before the year is up, the hospital can ask to retain me. If I lose again, the hospital can keep me for two years. From then on, the hospital can apply to hold me every two years until two-thirds of the maximum sentence on the highest charge in the indictment. Two-thirds of twenty-five years is seventeen years. . . . But you guys aren't done yet. If the commissioner of the hospital—this is the hospital I've been sitting in for seventeen years—if he decides I'm still mentally ill and need some more treatment, he can apply to get an order of certification. . . . If they do it right, they can lock me up in a hospital for the criminally insane, then they can lock me up in a run-of-the-mill loony bin. And they don't ever have to let me have a trial. That's what it means.[13]

Finally, psychology and psychiatry are such inexact sciences that few therapists can really be certain that one of their patients is cured enough not to commit another crime or endanger anyone in society. One of the most frustrating and discouraging things about societal punishment is that studies have revealed that no matter whether offenders have just been locked up, locked up with punishment, or locked up with treatment, their return to crime and prison (recidivism rate) is the same. No way of punishing offenders seems to work any better than any other. This problem certainly weakens the utilitarian's position of at least trying to find a method of punishment that will actually bring about good consequences for the offender and for society's protection as well.

Consequences for Potential Offenders—Deterrence. Another way that utilitarians have of measuring the future good consequences of punishment is whether or not it deters people from committing crimes or being immoral, that is, to what extent does punishing a criminal or having punishment available deter former criminals or noncriminals from committing offenses? From the utilitarian standpoint, if punishment could do this, it would certainly be worthwhile. The assumption behind this type of deterrence is that if people see or hear of offenders being punished for crimes they have committed, then they themselves will be deterred from committing crimes. In this sense, punishment operates as that external sanction of which Jeremy Bentham wrote.

There are several problems with the deterrence theory, however. First of all, there is no conclusive proof or evidence that punishment of someone deters anyone else from committing crimes. For one thing, not all people know of punishment when it is meted out, but even if they did, there is still no evidence that the knowledge deters. In early England, thieves used to be hanged publicly, and pickpockets worked their way through the crowds while the hangings were taking place. Also, none of our capital punishment executions are seen by the public; they only hear or read about it on radio, television, or in the newspapers, so how or why should they be deterred?

Moreover, to punish for deterrence is to use a person as a means to an end, which is unjust according to many. For example, remember that Kant in his Practical Imperative (see Chapter 3) stated that no person should be used merely as a means to an end but should be considered as a unique end in him- or herself. This is one of the retributivist's strongest criticisms of the utilitarian theory—that people may be punished, not because they deserve it, but rather because they should be "made an example of" or because their punishment will deter others. The retributivist argues that offenders should be punished if and only if they deserve it, not for some other future-good-consequences reason.

This problem worsens when we realize that if deterrence works or is thought to work, then it could be accomplished as well by punishing the wrong or innocent person. Many tyrants in history have used this technique to cause fear in their subjects, and people who are punished do not need to be guilty of anything. Suppose that a particular heinous crime has been committed—such as the rape, torture, and murder of a little girl—and that the public is highly outraged by this crime. The public's cry for justice could be satisfied by punishing the wrong person as well as the right one, as long as someone is caught and punished for the crime. If we thought it was unjust to use real criminals as means to the end of deterrence, then what of using the wrong or innocent person and the harm it would do to that person and his or her family?

We can see, then, there are some serious problems with the deterrence argument for punishment. John Hospers states that a legal system that is strong and pervasive and relatively free from corruption—where "at all times the police, the courts, and the jails are in operation, and there is always a good chance that they will catch violators of the law"—probably deters most people from committing crimes rather than a particular criminal or even criminals being punished.[14]

Effect on Society at Large—Protection. The last area from which good consequences may derive is the protection of society in general by punishing criminals. Almost everyone will agree that probably the major reason for punishing criminals, particularly imprisoning or executing them, is to protect society in general from their actions, which may be dangerous, harmful, and even fatal to its members. There is no doubt that executing criminals or keeping them out of the mainstream of society by imprisonment certainly counts as good consequences, but even this has its problems. First of all, as has been mentioned, when should we let them back into society, and what will they be like after being subjected to the deeply criminal atmosphere of most of our prisons? Will they be worse or better members of society after they come out? Nobody can tell, not psychiatrists, psychologists, sociologists, parole board members, wardens, not even the prisoners themselves.

For example, I know of two cases where exconvicts should have been able to work their way back into society perfectly, and indeed they did—for a while. One exconvict I knew of was a good writer and even had a job waiting for him on the outside at a newspaper. He was allowed to leave prison to take college courses in journalism and generally did well during this period, writing articles (which were considered quite good) for the school and local newspapers. When he got out, he continued to do well for a while, and then he was involved in a fight that resulted in a murder and was sent back to prison.

In the second case, a man who had served eight years for dealing and using drugs was released, returned to college, learned a skilled trade, and even did well enough to own his own business and become bonded. When he had marital problems, however, he again resorted to drugs, lost his business, attempted to kill someone, and very nearly lost his life. This does not mean that some exconvicts don't make it on the outside and no longer threaten society in any way, but it does raise the question of how effective punishment is in protecting society, at least in the long run.

Another criticism of this theory of punishment is that some crimes are crimes of passion, and the persons who commit them will probably never commit them again. For example, a husband who comes home and catches his wife with a lover and in a fit of passion kills them both is not any more dangerous to society after the murder than someone who has not committed a crime, according to many psychologists. The retributivist would say that he should be punished because he deserves it, but from a utilitarian point of view if his punishment would not protect society in that he is no longer a danger, should he be punished? Many would argue that because he demonstrated the inability to stop himself from committing such a heinous crime, then isn't that at least some evidence that society should be protected from him? Further, how can we know for certain that he won't kill again if he is put into another similar stressful and emotional situation?

Problem with Justice. The last and major criticism leveled against the utilitarian theory of punishment is that it doesn't concern itself with the *justice* of punishment, as retributivism attempts to, but rather only with its utility. Utilitarians are accused of being interested in social engineering rather than justice. Some utilitarians agree to the accusation of social engineering but would argue that justice is really an old-fashioned concept and that social engineering for the common good is more useful.

This problem with justice was first discussed in Chapter 2 in the danger of utilitarianism degenerating into a cost-benefit analysis, or end-justifies-the-means, approach to morality so that it is not surprising that it again rears its ugly head in the matter of punishment.

We have seen that the utilitarian theory of punishment avoids some of the problems of the retributivist theory, but the utilitarian theory has problems that raise issues of the justness of punishment from the point of view of utility. Before discussing any possible synthesis between the two theories and their problems, one other and newer theory should be presented.

Restitution or Compensation for Victims Theory

This restitution or compensation for victims theory holds that justice is served only if victims are given restitution for crimes against them. For example, if someone steals from a man, then what is stolen should be paid back in some way, either by returning his property in its original form or furnishing him with some sort of compensation for what he has lost.

Crime Against the State, Not the Individual. The crimes-against-the-state theory has come about because of a change in the views about whom a crime is really against. Prior to the American Revolution, crimes were considered violations committed against individuals, but in contemporary society, crimes are considered as violations committed against the state; therefore, restitution has not been a major concern until recently. If someone murders another, the murderer has legally committed a crime against the state; therefore, the state through its judicial system will seek to bring the murderer to trial and punish him or her for the crime if found guilty. Of course, the perpetrator has in actuality murdered a person, not the state, and the survivors of the victim are made to suffer because of the crime.

Given this view, perhaps it is easier to understand why so many survivors demand the death penalty for killers. They feel that it is a crime against them and the person they lost and that taking the criminal's life is the only way to attain justice. The state, on the other hand, sees this as a crime against the state that may or may not require the death penalty.

The restitution theory, then, has been established in order to counteract the emphasis on crimes being committed against the state, which has tended to ignore compensation or restitution to the victims of the crime. Whatever other kind of punishment is being considered for the criminal, this theory requires that some sort of compensation or restitution to the victim or the victim's family be included. For example, if a woman kills the husband and father of a family, part or all of her punishment may be to work most or all of her life to support that family because she has eliminated—in this case, for instance—its major source of financial support. She can also be ordered to pay medical and hospital bills where injury or harm has ensued and to give some sort of compensation for injuries sustained as determined by a court of law.

It is important that restitution not be decided by the victims themselves because they are often too emotionally involved to be fair in their demand for compensation; therefore, it must be decided through the judicial process. In this way criminals can either compensate victims with money or be put to work for the victims' advantage, either at their home or place of business. If not, then criminals can be forced to work in some state-supervised job from which all money earned will go to their victims.

Restitution's Relationship to the Retributivist and Utilitarian Theories. Restitution fits in well with the retributivist theory in that it not only takes into consideration the deserts of the criminal but also those of the victims. It provides a more meaningful punishment to satisfy these two types of deserts, and the retributivist can avoid criticisms of punishment for punishment's sake.

Utilitarians, on the other hand, may be happier with this type of punishment because they will see it as more useful and bringing about more good consequences than, say, locking up criminals to do nothing for the rest of their lives or killing them. Utilitarians may feel that good, honest work for criminals will be rehabilitative, whereas some good consequences will also accrue to the victims of the crime in that they will be compensated to some degree for the crimes against them.

Problems with Restitution. Although the idea of compensation and restitution for victims sounds good, there are several problems with this approach to punishment. To begin with, there is really no restitution possible for the crime of murder. How much money will compensate for the taking of a human life? Because each life is unique and basically irreplaceable, then how can one put a price on it? Further, such heinous crimes as rape and child molestation are not much more easily compensated. How can you give people back their privacy once you've invaded it or their dignity once you've taken it away? How can you ever make restitution to children for taking away their childhood and affecting them adversely forever?

If restitution is made in monetary form, which it mostly is, such punishment or restitution will be uneven; that is, the richer criminals will be able to afford it, whereas the poorer will not. How can punishment under such circumstances be just? Would you make the rich pay more and the poor pay less? If so, victims will not be compensated evenly, and rich criminals will still get off with less punishment than poor ones.

Further, if criminals are old or sick, how can they compensate by their labor or in any other way? We cannot expect a man who is seriously ill or dying, for example, to hold down a job or even come up with money. And what if he becomes too old or sick to work after the restitution has been made for a while?

Can we expect him to continue somehow? And won't the victim be denied restitution if any of this happens?

Finally, the most serious problem is that restitution does not distinguish between intentional and unintentional injury or harm. What if, for example, an accident in which someone is seriously injured or killed occurs because a car's brakes fail and the driver didn't know they were faulty? Should she be required to make restitution to the same degree as one who intentionally robbed, raped, molested, or murdered his or her victim? There is still a victim, and the victim is still due restitution or compensation under this theory, but would this be fair to the unintentional perpetrator of the injury or harm?

As a matter of fact, this kind of case where harm occurs but the people causing it are really without fault presents problems for all three theories of punishment. For example, people who are unknown carriers of injurious or fatal diseases certainly can be the cause of injury, harm, or death, but to what degree should they be punished? Are there really any criminal deserts from the retributivist's point of view? It would certainly seem not; therefore, why should carriers be punished? And yet quarantining or isolating is after all a form of punishment, isn't it? The strict view of the retributivist that punishment should be deserved, then, presents a problem in such cases. As far as the utilitarian is concerned, perhaps quarantining or isolating the person is good for society in general, but it certainly would not bring about good consequences for the carrier—in other words, not to everyone concerned. And, as I mentioned earlier, why should such people have to make restitution to or compensate victims when they are not essentially at fault?

The AIDS (acquired immune deficiency syndrome) crisis is a good example of this problem. There has been so much bumbling and confusion in the handling of the crisis at so many levels and for such a long time that many people who had the virus, but not the overt disease, could infect others with the virus long before they knew they had it. Most of these carriers engaged in activities (sexual intercourse, drug use, and intravenous blood donation) that transmitted it to others. Some who were warned that what they were doing was dangerous did change their life-styles, but some paid no attention to the warnings and continued to engage in activities that would infect others. Should all AIDS carriers be punished in some way, or only the latter group who disregarded warnings? Is it even fair to punish the latter group because we didn't know for sure that people were carriers unless they had full-blown AIDS or until a test had been developed to detect the AIDS virus in the bloodstream (not until 1985—the infection has been thought to have begun as early as 1976)?

There were a few carriers who seemed intentionally set on transmitting the disease, and scientists and doctors were quite upset with them for being so careless in their life-styles, but the attempt to stop them forcefully was really impossible. The so-called Patient Zero, Gaetan Dugas, described in Randy Shilts's fascinating book on the AIDS crisis, *And the Band Played On*, was one of these people.[15] He was thought to have been the first person to bring AIDS into the United States, and because of his multiple sexual contacts he may have infected as many as 2,000 people! When told of this problem, he refused to accept any responsibility or change his life-style in any way. Should he have been punished in some way? How? No matter how angry we are with such people, imposing punishment under any of the three theories would be extremely difficult.

♦——

Is a Synthesis Possible?

Because all three theories have disadvantages and because difficulties exist if we try to apply them singly to the problems of reward and punishment, perhaps a compromise or a reasonable synthesis might work.

From Retributivism. From the retributivist theory we could certainly consider what people deserve or merit before rewarding them, at the same time recognizing we don't have to settle on this criterion alone. In relationship to punishment, we could use the idea that no one who is innocent should be convicted or punished no matter how many good consequences might come from doing so (general deterrence, for example). We would have as a basic principle that in order for people to be punished, they must truly deserve punishment and that the punishment must "fit the crime" and not be excessive. We could also adopt from the retributivist the principle that in general more serious crimes would require more severe punishment and vice versa.

From Utilitarianism. After we have adopted these preceding basic principles, we could then modify or moderate the distribution of rewards and punishments or suspend sentences based on what would be useful, especially in cases where retributivism might seem to border on the unjust or unfair. In other words, we could insert the idea of utility into our deliberations on rewarding or punishing. We could say, for example, "This man deserves to be punished because he has committed a serious crime," but then we must ask ourselves what useful purpose will severely punishing a sick 80-year-old man accomplish? In this way we could temper what is at times deemed to be too severe or unfair punishment with what usefulness it would serve—if it would not bring about the best good consequences or at least do more good than not punishing or punishing less, then retribution could be tempered by the utilitarian approach to reward and punishment.

From Restitution. Actually, the theory of restitution can fit nicely into the utilitarian theory of reward and punishment because it can certainly bring about good consequences for the victim of a crime, while at the same time helping the criminal to a more worthwhile and noncriminal life.

159

From the point of view of the retributivist, not only would criminals get what they deserve, but compensating victims might be seen as a more just type of desert for the criminals than many of the useless types of punishment, such as putting them in solitary confinement or executing them. Further, the innocent and most deserving victims of crimes would also be rewarded to the best extent possible by being compensated at least in part for the harm done to them.

Some Other Possibilities for the Distribution of Good or Rewards

In addition to synthesizing the preceding three theories, we could also try to synthesize the four major ways and other criteria for distributing good or rewarding people (mentioned earlier in this chapter). We could start with a basis of distributing as equitably as possible and with respect to need, then we could temper these considerations where applicable with what people deserve, or merit, as a result of their abilities or other factors, such as their productivity, effort, and the stress, danger, or unpleasantness of their jobs. A synthetic approach, then, might be the best one to use. Whether the problems inherent in all three theories could be resolved enough to make such an approach work remains to be seen.

Another important variable in deciding how and to whom to distribute good and bad would have to be the situation or context in which the distribution is to take place. For example, in the kidney dialysis situation previously described, need was a given in that all patients with kidney failure need dialysis or they will die. Also, the committee had determined that they all basically deserved to be dialyzed. The problem arose when the committee tried to determine the individual and comparative worth of their lives. In this case, then, a system that distributed good *and* bad equally without regard to desert or merit or ability seemed to be the most just approach to this problem, and so the lottery or chance method of distribution was used.

It is quite possible that a situation could arise where an exception could be made to this egalitarian approach. Suppose, for example, that one of the patients needing dialysis was a world-renowned doctor, a *nephrologist* (a specialist in kidney diseases) working to expand the availability of dialysis machines and kidneys for transplantation. Might it not be advantageous to the other and future patients with kidney failure to allow him to be dialyzed even if he didn't win the lottery? Further, if the president of the United States were in need of dialysis, shouldn't he be given preferential consideration considering that what happens to him affects everyone under his jurisdiction? Other issues have arisen since these decisions were made. Some nephrologists have required that patients who are to receive dialysis must stay on their required regimen (a very strict one for kidney patients) in order to receive dialysis, the idea being that if the patients are not going to do what is necessary to help themselves, then dialysis is

160

essentially wasted on them and would be better utilized with patients who will cooperate with their own health care.

In some cases, we would not use the egalitarian method of distribution at all. For example, it is not required that in order to be fair, all of us should have the same security and protection as the president. Because of his ability, the dangers of his exposure, and the good of all people for whom he is responsible, he deserves and merits such protection, whereas the rest of us don't unless our situation is such to require it (for example, threats to our lives by an escaped criminal at whose trial we were key witnesses).

In conclusion, it would seem that some type of synthetic approach could be brought to bear in both reward and punishment, utilizing those principles from the three major theories—retributivism, utilitarianism, and restitution—and taking into consideration the situations and contexts in which distribution of good and bad is to take place, but never losing sight of the significance of need and an egalitarian method of distribution wherever possible. In the next chapter, the principle of justice or fairness will be presented, justified, and discussed, and this issue of fair and just distribution will again arise. Further, in Chapter 8, the moral issue of capital punishment will be presented and discussed, to which this chapter will be applied in a more specific way.

Chapter Summary

I. Key Terms
   A. Retributive justice: People should get what they deserve either in reward or punishment, regardless of the consequences.
   B. Distributive justice: The distribution of good and bad on a just and fair basis.
   C. Reward: Something given or received for worthy behavior.
   D. Punishment: The act of penalizing someone for a crime, fault, or misbehavior—a penalty for wrongdoing.
   E. Retributivism (deserts theory): The act of giving people what they deserve, regardless of the consequences.
   F. Utilitarianism (results theory): The act of rewarding or punishing based on its consequences.
   G. Restitution (compensation theory): The act of compensating victims for harm or wrong done to them.
II. Reward and punishment in relationship to justice
   A. Reward and punishment are both aspects of distributive justice.
   B. Elements of justice are defined.
      1. Justice, as ethics in general, involves the treatment of human beings by other human beings.

2. It is concerned basically with past rather than future events.

3. It should be individualistic rather than collectivistic in application.

4. Comparative justice is different from collectivistic injustice in that the former has to do with the way a person is treated in relation to another person.

III. Reward

    A. Four basic ways in which good and bad can be distributed:

        1. As equally among people as possible.

        2. According to people's abilities.

        3. According to what they deserve or merit.

        4. According to their needs.

    B. Equal distribution of goods and rewards.

        1. Scarce medical resources problem (kidney dialysis issue is a good example of this). The lottery or chance method of distribution would distribute good and bad equally.

        2. Problems with this theory:

            (a) It ignores other criteria that are deemed important.

            (b) It is difficult to determine in what ways and to what extent people are equal.

            (c) Can we really ignore all of the other criteria?

    C. Production, or what people produce or achieve, is often used but ignores effort, ability, or need.

    D. Effort is also used but also has several problems:

        1. Those who have contracted to do a job are not paid for time and effort but for the finished job.

        2. It is difficult to measure effort.

        3. How does one distinguish between bright and dull-witted people if they are being rewarded only for effort?

    E. Ability.

        1. Natural ability. People can't help the abilities they come by naturally: Should they be rewarded for these?

        2. Acquired ability. This type may be more significant where reward is concerned because often a great deal of money, time, and effort goes into acquiring skills.

        3. One problem with both of these is the possibility that people may not use their abilities or may not use them well.

    F. Need. There are two types of need:

        1. Private need is used to describe the personal, material needs of individuals who are poor or out of work. Should such people be rewarded regardless of their abilities or qualifications? These people are often the most unskilled in our society.

        2. Public need refers to the system by which people are rewarded for contributing to needs of the general public; but which needs—

individual or collective—are the most important, and how are we to decide?

G. Other criteria:

1. Long and expensive training in a profession. Trying to reward on this basis would be uneven, and what if the professionals are incompetent? Should they still be rewarded for this?

2. Job or profession requiring expensive equipment. How much more should such people be rewarded in this case, and should they continue being rewarded for it even after the equipment is paid for?

3. Physical danger. It would seem people who are in such professions should be rewarded, but how much and for what dangers?

4. Job unpleasantness. How do we decide which jobs get the greater reward because of their unpleasantness, and how much should be given?

IV. Two major theories of how to reward

A. Retributivist, or deserts, theory states that people should be rewarded strictly on what they deserve or merit for what they have done in the past.

1. This theory is not concerned with the future good consequences that might come out of what people do.

2. It also tends to reward efforts rather than achievement, productivity, or consequences.

B. Utilitarian, or results, theory would reward on the future good consequences of rewarding.

1. This theory would definitely be in favor of paying higher wages or giving extra pay for dangerous or unpleasant jobs.

2. It would reward production and achievement rather than hard work or effort.

3. Another problem is that if consequences are the only criteria, then it is possible to reward a totally undeserving person.

V. Punishment

A. Four requirements of punishment:

1. It must involve unpleasantness of some sort.

2. It must be given or done for some reason.

3. It should be imposed by some person or group that has "duly constituted" moral or legal authority.

4. It must be imposed according to certain rules or laws.

B. Given these requirements, punishment should be administered from within a duly constituted legal system for several reasons:

1. Under law, once punishment is done or given, the matter is ended, as opposed to vengeance or whim, which can go on indefinitely.

2. Law can be more unbiased and objective than individuals.

VI. Theories of punishment

   A. Retributive or deserts theory, which states that punishment should be given only when it is deserved and only to the extent that it is deserved, is concerned with the past rather than the future.

   B. Why crime requires punishment:

     1. To reestablish the balance of morality that has been disturbed when someone has violated laws or moral rules.

     2. Benefits carry with them the burden of self-restraint, and anyone who alleviates himself or herself of this burden acquires an unfair advantage, and, according to the retributivist, this must be eliminated and the burden of self-restraint restored.

   C. Problems with this theory:

     1. It is difficult to determine what people deserve.

     2. It is difficult to utilize mercy in this theory.

     3. It is also difficult to determine the seriousness of offenses and punishment.

     4. What is meant by "an eye for an eye"?

       (a) The mirror-image view says that the punishment should mirror the crime exactly, but how can we do this with exactness without arriving at absurdity (e.g., should we steal from the thief?).

       (b) The second view states that the punishment must be suitable or appropriate to the crime, but this is also difficult to calculate.

       (c) Can we ever find appropriate punishment for murder, rape, or child molestation?

   D. Utilitarian, or results, theory is future oriented and given *in order that* . . . rather than *because of* . . . , as in retributivism.

     1. Bentham stated that punishment should always have as its aim the good of society.

     2. Two types of sanctions are meant to discourage or eliminate criminal behavior:

       (a) Internal sanctions, which are brought about by the development of conscience in children and others.

       (b) External sanctions, which are established by laws providing penalties to be imposed for criminal behavior.

       (c) Laws or rules providing penalties and punishment for offenses or crimes could function at both levels.

     3. Three questions the utilitarian would ask of the punishment of any offender:

       (a) Will the wrongdoer be deterred from future crimes and become a better person or member of society?

      (b) Will others in society be deterred from committing crimes because of the criminal's punishment?

      (c) Will society be protected from such criminals?

E. Consequences for the offender bring up the problems of rehabilitation and reform.

    1. Imprisonment, in which first-time offenders are usually lumped with habitual criminals, is not conducive to rehabilitation and reform.

    2. Psychiatric or psychological treatment instead of punishment is also ineffectual for the following reasons:

      (a) Prisoners often resent and resist mandatory treatment.

      (b) There are no general standards of treatment.

      (c) Therapists may have too much power over offenders because of alternatives to treatment (e.g., solitary confinement).

      (d) Therapists also have power over release dates for offenders.

      (e) Psychology and psychiatry are inexact sciences; therefore, therapists can never be certain that patients have been cured.

F. Consequences for potential offenders or deterrence also has several problems:

    1. No conclusive proof or evidence that punishment of one person deters anyone else from committing crimes.

    2. To punish for deterrence is to use a person as a means to an end, which is considered unjust by many moralists.

    3. It is even worse when we see it is possible to punish the wrong person for deterrence reasons.

G. Its effect on society at large or protection is probably the major reason for punishing criminals, particularly by imprisonment or execution, but this reason has its problems also:

    1. When should we allow criminals back into mainstream society?

    2. Some crimes are crimes of passion, and the perpetrators may never commit them again, so from a utilitarian point of view, why punish them?

H. The last major criticism of the utilitarian theory is that it doesn't concern itself with the justice of punishment, as retributivism attempts to do, but rather only with its utility and with social engineering.

I. The restitution, or compensation for victims, theory holds that justice is served only if victims are given restitution for crimes against them.

    1. This theory has come about because the older attitude that a crime is committed against the individual has given way to the newer attitude that all crimes are committed against the state. The restitution theory has been established to counteract this point of view and to give compensation to victims.

    2. Restitution should not be decided by victims but through the judicial process.

3. Restitution can fit in well with both the retributivist and utilitarian theories.

    (a) For the retributivist, it considers both the deserts of the criminal and the victim and may provide a more meaningful punishment, helping the retributivist avoid the criticism of "punishment for punishment's sake."

    (b) The utilitarian may see restitution as more useful and bringing about more good consequences both to the criminal and victim as well.

4. Problems with restitution:

    (a) There is really no restitution for such crimes as murder, rape, or child molestation.

    (b) Restitution in monetary form will be uneven for rich and poor criminals and for their victims as well.

    (c) If criminals are old or sick, how can they compensate victims?

    (d) The most serious problem is that restitution does not distinguish between intentional and unintentional injury or harm—this is actually a problem with all three theories.

VII. Synthesis

  A. With retributivism we could consider what people deserve or merit before rewarding them, at the same time realizing that we don't have to use this criterion alone.

    1. No one who is innocent should be convicted or punished despite any good consequences that might be derived from the punishment.

    2. People must truly deserve any punishment they get, and the punishment should fit the crime and not be excessive.

    3. More serious crimes would require more severe punishment.

  B. With utilitarianism we could modify or moderate the distribution of rewards and punishments or suspend sentences based on what would be useful.

  C. Because restitution could fit in with both retributivism and utilitarianism, it could function to modify their excesses and problems while providing the additional reward or punishment of compensating victims of crimes.

  D. We could also try to synthesize the four major ways and other criteria for distributing good and bad.

    1. We could start with a basis of distributing as equitably as possible and with respect to need.

    2. We could then temper these with what people deserve or merit through their abilities, productivity, effort, and other criteria, such as stress, danger, and unpleasantness of their jobs.

    3. The situation or context would be another important variable; for

example, the egalitarian method of distributing good and bad would work well in the kidney dialysis situation but not in others.

E.   In conclusion, a synthesis might work out if it is organized carefully.

Exercises for Review

1.   Describe and explain the relationship between reward and punishment and justice.

2.   What are the elements of justice, and to what extent do you agree with them?

3.   What are the four major ways of distributing good, and which of them do you think is or are the most fair and just?

4.   What do you think of the other criteria for distributing good: production, effort, ability, need (both private and public), long and expensive training, expensive equipment, physical danger, unpleasantness of jobs? Which ones do you think are the most important and which least important? Why?

5.   Describe and explain retributivism and utilitarianism as theories of reward or distributing good. Which do you think is most valid? Why?

6.   Do you agree with the requirements of punishment? Why or why not? To what extent do you agree that punishment should be meted out within the legal system?

7.   Describe and explain the three theories of punishment. Which do you think is most valid? Why?

8.   Which is the more important principle in punishing—giving people what they deserve or punishing only if you can bring about good consequences? Why?

9.   What should be emphasized in punishment—the deterrence and rehabilitation of the offender, the deterrence of others, or the protection of society? Why?

10. To what extent should restitution to or compensation of victims be a part of any system of punishment? Answer in detail.

Discussion Questions

1.   Whenever you have had occasion to reward or punish someone, which of the three theories have you used, and why?

2.   How do we in America generally reward, punish, or distribute good or

bad, and which theories do you think we basically follow? Give specific examples and illustrations to support your main points.

3. How effective do you feel our judicial and penal systems are in punishing or rehabilitating criminals? Why? Again, give specific examples and illustrations.

4. To what extent do you feel that the purpose of punishment is to (1) protect society, (2) punish criminals, or (3) rehabilitate and reform criminals? Why? Answer in detail.

5. When you have had occasion to distribute good or bad to others, which of the many ways described have you used? Why? Have you found yourself using different ways for different situations and people? Which and why? Answer in detail.

6. What method of reward and punishment is used in your family, and how does it fit in with the three theories? Does it work? Be specific.

7. Analyze any group or institution of which you are or have been a member (e.g., church, school, the military, sports team, honorary club or society in school or out of it), and describe what theories are or have been used in distributing good and bad and in rewarding and punishing. Do you believe that the methods are fair and just? Why or why not?

8. To what extent do you feel that as a country and a people we should take care of our less fortunate and "needy" members and why? How should this be done—through private donations, government support, or both? If private donations are not sufficient, should we through government taxation ensure that these people are cared for? Why or why not?

Notes

1. William Morris, ed., *The American Heritage Dictionary of the English Language* (Boston: Houghton-Mifflin, 1978), 113.

2. Ibid., 1060.

3. I am heavily indebted to John Hospers, *Human Conduct*, 2nd ed. (New York: Harcourt Brace Jovanovich, 1982) 306–8, for these elements.

4. Paul Ramsey, *The Patient as Person* (New Haven: Yale University Press, 1970), 239–52.

5. Ibid., 246–47.

6. Ibid., 259–66.

7. Ibid., 252–59.

8. Hospers, 321–22.

9. Ibid., 328–30.

10. Francis H. Bradley, *Ethical Studies* (London: Oxford University Press, 1876), 26–27.

11. Hospers, *Human Conduct*, 341.

12. Ibid., 331.

13. Tom Topor, *Nuts* (New York: Samuel French, 1981), 66–67.

14. Hospers, *Human Conduct*, 334.

15. Randy Shilts, *And the Band Played On* (New York: St. Martin's Press, 1987), Chapter 13.

Supplementary Reading

Barnett, Randy. "Restitution: A New Paradigm of Criminal Justice." In *Assessing the Criminal*, ed. Randy Barnett and John Hagel. Boston: Ballinger, 1978.

Barry, Brian. *The Liberal Theory of Justice*. London: Oxford University Press, 1973.

Bentham, Jeremy. *Principles of Morals and Legislation*. Many Editions (1789).

Bradley, Francis H. *Ethical Studies*. London: Oxford University Press, 1876.

Broad, R. A. *Punishment Under Pressure: The Probation Service in the Inner City*. Bristol, Pa.: Taylor and Francis, 1991.

Cederblom, Jerry, and William Blizek, eds. *Justice and Punishment*. Cambridge, Mass.: Ballinger, 1977.

Cohen, Marshall, et al., eds. *Equality and Preferential Treatment*. Princeton, N.J.: Princeton University Press, 1977.

Feinberg, Joel. *Doing and Deserving*. Princeton, N.J.: Princeton University Press, 1970.

Feinberg, Joel, and Hyman Gross, eds. *Philosophy of Law*, 3rd ed. Belmont, Calif.: Wadsworth, 1986.

Garland, David. *Punishment in Modern Society: A Study in Social Theory*. Chicago: University of Chicago Press, 1990.

Gray, Ian, and Moira Stanley. *Punishment in Search of a Crime: Americans Speak Out Against the Death Sentence*. New York: Avon Books, 1989.

Gross, Hyman. *A Theory of Criminal Justice*. New York: Oxford University Press, 1979.

Grupp, Stanley E., ed. *Theories of Punishment*. Bloomington, Ind.: Indiana University Press, 1971.

Harding, Christopher, and Richard W. Ireland. *Punishment: Rhetoric, Rule, and Practice*. New York: Routledge, 1989.

Hospers, John. *Human Conduct*, 2nd ed. New York: Harcourt Brace Jovanovich, 1982.

McDonald, Douglas C. *Punishment without Walls: Community Service Sentences in New York City*. New Brunswick, N.J.: Rutgers University Press, 1989.

Morris, Herbert. "Persons and Punishment." In *Understanding Moral Philosophy*, ed. James Rachels. Belmont, Calif.: Dickenson, 1976.

Rawls, John. *A Theory of Justice*. Cambridge: Harvard University Press, 1971.

Rescher, Nicholas. *Distributive Justice*. Indianapolis: Bobbs-Merrill, 1966.

Sterba, James. *The Demands of Justice*. Notre Dame, Ind.: University of Notre Dame Press, 1980.

Szasz, Thomas. *The Manufacture of Madness*. New York: Harper & Row, 1977.

Vlastos, Gregory. "Justice and Equality." In *Moral Concepts*, ed. Joel Feinberg. New York: Oxford University Press, 1970.

Von Hirsch, Andrew. *Doing Justice: The Choice of Punishment*. New York: Farrar, Straus, and Giroux, 1976.

Waelder, Robert. "Psychiatry and the Problem of Criminal Responsibility." In *Criminal Law*, ed. Richard Donnelly, et al. New York: Free Press, 1961.

Williams, Bernard. "The Idea of Equality." In *Moral Concepts*, ed. Joel Feinberg. New York: Oxford University Press, 1970.

CHAPTER 7

Setting Up a
Moral System:
Basic Assumptions
and Basic Principles

◆————————————————————————————————

Objectives

After you have read this chapter you should be able to

1. Identify, define, and explain the major conflicting general moral issues in setting up a moral system.

2. Present, describe, and discuss basic assumptions about what characteristics or attributes any meaningful, livable, and workable moral system or theory should contain.

3. Try to resolve the central problem areas of morality, which are how to attain stability, unity, and order without eliminating individual freedom by the establishment of basic ethical principles.

4. Establish and justify the priority in which the five basic principles should be applied.

At this point in a course in ethics or in most texts on ethics, students usually throw up their hands in frustration, saying, "If all of the ethical theories and systems are so full of problems, then perhaps there is no such thing as a workable and meaningful moral system. Perhaps morality *is* relative to whoever sets it up and to no one else." Too often teachers of ethics courses and authors of ethics books do very little to alleviate these frustrations, except to say that maybe students ought to take another course or simply try to do the best they can with the "broken" theories or systems to which they have been exposed. I believe, however, that we can attempt to show the way toward building a moral system that is workable not only for many individuals but for most, if not all, human beings.

In order to do this, we need to point toward the reasonable synthesis mentioned in Chapter 1. We must try to combine what is best in all of the ethical systems and theories we have examined—religious, nonreligious, consequentialist, nonconsequentialist, individualistic, and altruistic—to arrive at a common moral ground, while at the same time dealing with or eliminating their problems and difficulties. We must search for a larger meeting ground in which the best of all these theories and systems can operate meaningfully and with a minimum of conflict and opposition.

Conflicting General Moral Issues

In dealing with those traditional ethical theories in Chapters 2 and 3, we have discovered several general moral issues that must be resolved or synthesized in some way before beginning to set up a moral system of our own. They are the issues of consequentialism versus nonconsequentialism, self- versus other-interestedness, act versus rule, and emotions versus reason.

Consequentialism Versus Nonconsequentialism

First, in order to set up a moral system, it is important to decide to what extent a moral system will be based on consequences and to what extent it will be nonconsequentialist. In presenting the criticisms at the end of Chapter 3, I arrived at the conclusions that I simply could not be moral without taking into consideration the consequences of moral decisions, acts, or rules. At the same time, I was definitely made aware of the difficulty of considering only consequences or ends without regard to means or motives. The cost-benefit analysis, or end-justifies-the-means, problems brought this home to me, and Kant's Practical Imperative pointed to a way out of this problem. My own synthesis of this conflict is to basically be concerned with consequences in my moral system and yet be aware that the end, even a good end, does not always justify the means or motives leading to it. How this is to be synthesized will be shown later in the chapter, after I have presented my own moral system.

Self- Versus Other-Interestedness

Although I feel that people are certainly justified in considering themselves in any moral system they establish, I do not feel, for the reasons I stated in Chapter 2, that ethical egoism, or self-interest, will provide a workable basis for a valid moral system because of its many disadvantages. Therefore, I feel I must go along with the utilitarian viewpoint of always striving for the best good consequences for everyone, which, of course, includes myself. With some modifications, I feel that there is a greater chance of maximizing good consequences and attaining justice and fairness with this approach.

Act Versus Rule

Another problem in establishing a moral system is how to allow for the most individual freedom and yet incorporate stability, security, and order. The act approach allows for the most freedom, whereas the rule approach imposes certain constraints on freedom and yet provides for greater stability. As you will see, I attempt to bring in the best of both approaches by establishing rules that nevertheless include a strong element of freedom within them.

Emotion Versus Reason

Emotion versus reason will be discussed largely in the justification for the first assumption which follows, but the synthesis here will be to base my moral system on reason without excluding emotions, which are a definite part of morality; that is, it is natural to feel very strong about most moral issues, and these feelings should contribute to the formation of a moral system. However, it is my contention that a viable moral system should ultimately be based on reason.

◆───────────────────────────────

Basic Assumptions

First, it is important to clearly delineate several basic assumptions concerning what constitutes a workable set of standards for morality. I will list these assumptions and then try to argue why they should be a part of any moral system.

In order for a moral system to be tenable and viable, I believe it ought to have the following characteristics:

1. It should be rationally based and yet not be devoid of emotion—this was implied in my criticism of a religiously based morality and of an intuitionally based act nonconsequentialism.

2. It should be as logically consistent as possible, but not rigid and inflexible—this was implied in my criticisms of egoism, especially universal ethical egoism, and of the rule nonconsequentialist theories.

3. It must have universality or general application to all humanity and yet be applicable (in a practical sense) to particular individuals and situations—this I implied in my criticisms of both act consequentialist and act nonconsequentialist theories, as well as individual and personal ethical egoism (for their highly individualistic approach to morality) and rule nonconsequentialist theories (for their failure to be applicable in a practical way to practical situations).

4. It should be able to be taught and promulgated—this was implied in my criticisms of all forms of ethical egoism and all types of act theories of morality.

5. It must have the ability to resolve conflicts among human beings, duties, and obligations—this was implied in my criticisms of both universal ethical egoism and Kant's Duty Ethics.

Including the Rational and Emotional Aspects

Human Nature—Rational and Emotional. It is an obvious empirical fact that human beings are both feeling (emotional or affective) and reasoning (rational or cognitive) beings and that in order to establish any sort of system that might apply to everyone, we have to take these two human aspects into consideration. However, if we rely only on our emotions for moral decisions, we can run into severe problems in resolving conflicts that may arise from the very different and individual feelings we have. Also, if we are thrown back solely on feelings for moral decisions, then there is no real basis for arbitration between what A feels is right and what B feels is right, for anyone's feelings are as good as anyone else's. How can we argue against the way I feel or the way you feel if feelings are the sole basis for what is right and wrong?

Emotion. Just because feelings are difficult to work with in making moral decisions does not mean that morality should be completely cold, calculating, and unemotional. After all, moral issues are some of the most emotional ones we face; therefore, it is too much to expect that we would not feel strongly about them. However, as a sole basis for making moral decisions, feelings are too unreliable and individualistic, and some other basis that is fairer and more objective is needed. That basis is reason.

Reason. The word *reason* implies giving "reasons" for a decision or an action, and this activity already involves more than merely expressing feelings. Further, "reason," which is an ability, should be differentiated from "reasoning," which is an activity; reason is something human beings *have*, whereas reasoning is something they *do*. All humans have the ability to reason in varying degrees, but there are formal rules for reasoning that can be taught in common and can thereby form the basis for our understanding each other and for supporting any decisions or actions we make or perform.

Reasoning implies several things:

1. Logical argument, which includes supplying empirical evidence to support one's position.

2. Logical consistency, which involves avoiding fallacies and making sure one's argument follows smoothly from one point to the next until it arrives at a logical conclusion.

3. A certain detachment from feelings because of reasoning's formality, which forces one to consider the truth and validity of what the individual and others are thinking and saying.

4. A common means by which differences in feelings, opinions, and thoughts can be arbitrated.

At this point, let me briefly cite an example from the controversy over abortion, which is covered in much more detail in a later chapter. Suppose Tom says that he "feels" abortion is always wrong, and Barbara says she "feels" abortion is always right. We have two sets of opposing feelings; and if feelings are the only basis for what is right and wrong, where can we go from here? True, Tom can attempt to refuse to let his wife have an abortion or he can lobby for legislation to prevent any woman from getting one, whereas Barbara can have an abortion herself or encourage other women to have one or lobby for legislation opposed to Tom's. However, how will any of us, including Barbara and Tom, know whose position is the correct one? All we can know is how the two of them feel and that their feelings differ radically. If Barbara and Tom were the only two people involved, then perhaps we could live with their conflicting feelings; however, the lives of fetuses and of other people affected by the results of their feelings, decisions, and legislation are also involved.

If we ask Barbara and Tom why they feel the way they do, the process of reasoning has already begun. Tom might give the following "reasons":

1. All human life is very precious, including that which is yet unborn, and only God has the right to decide which life should begin or end.

2. Human life begins at conception.

3. Women do not have absolute rights over their own bodies when they contain another life.

4. Once a woman becomes pregnant, she has a moral obligation to carry the fetus to term regardless of any reasons to the contrary.

On the other hand, Barbara might give the following reasons:

1. A person who is already born has a greater right to life than one who is yet unborn.

2. Only a woman can decide whether she ought or ought not to bear a child because she has absolute rights over her body.

3. Human life does not begin until viability (about the twenty-eighth week of pregnancy) or until the child is actually born.

Once we are given reasons to work with, we can begin to examine the basis for Barbara's and Tom's feelings, bring evidence and facts to bear on their reasons, and test these bases with rational and logical arguments. We can, for example, examine all of the biological, sociological, and psychological evidence that is available concerning when human life can actually be said to begin. We can also examine all of the arguments and evidence for the existence or nonexistence of God and we can consider, if He exists, whether He is the lord of life or whether He has delegated the authority for life and death decisions to human beings. Next, we can examine the reasons for terminating a pregnancy and see if any evidence can be shown to justify any such termination. Then we can look into how we might compare the worth of an already existent human being with one yet unborn. The main point here is that whereas before Barbara and Tom were merely spouting their strong feelings, they are now in a position to critically evaluate and analyze those feelings by bringing evidence and reasoning to bear on them. In this way, we have a broader and less arbitrary basis on which to decide the difficulties with either position on abortion.

Logical Consistency with Flexibility

It is important that any ethical system be logically consistent so that there is some stability to the moral decision making we have to do. A moral system that says that in situation A we should kill a person but in similar situation B we should not gives us neither a guide nor stability, only capricious whim. On the other hand, if a moral system says that we can *never* in *any* situation kill anyone and still be moral, then all of the complexity and diversity that comprise human being-ness has become rigidly boxed in, with no possibility of justification for the extenuating situations we often face. We must, instead, strive to be as logically consistent as we can in our morality and yet allow enough flexibility so that our system can remain truly applicable to the complexity and variety of human living.

Including Universality and Particularity

Universality. Any morality that attempts to help all human beings relate to each other meaningfully must strive for a universal applicability; if, like individual or personal ethical egoism, a moral system applies only to one person, then all remaining human beings are essentially excluded from it. Also, if it depends on a belief in a certain God or gods and a set of dogmatic "truths" that have no conclusive evidential or rational basis, then those who do not believe at all or who believe only in part are also excluded. Therefore, it is very important that any moral system apply to human beings in general, which means it must be broadly enough based not to exclude anyone who is striving to be good, and to include as many meaningful and workable moral systems as possible.

Particularity. In its universality, one's moral system should not become so generalized and abstract that it cannot apply to particular situations and individuals. Morality, after all, always takes place at particular times, in particular places, in particular situations, and between or among particular individuals; it never takes place in the abstract.

Morality may be theorized about or discussed in the abstract, but decisions, actions, or failures to act always occur in concrete, everyday situations. That is why, for example, universal pronouncements, such as "Abortions are never justified," sound highly moral and certainly apply to all people at all times but do not take into consideration the many serious implications for all the people involved in the situation surrounding an abortion. Such pronouncements never give any real criteria for weighing one human life (the mother's) against another (the fetus's) when one is definitely threatened by the other. The particular situation may be that the expectant mother has a family of little children and a young husband who all need her very badly. Yet because of the abstract absolutism of the abortion pronouncement thus cited, she is almost forbidden to consider that one life has to be sacrificed, either hers or that of her unborn child. In short, the particular situation is often much more complicated than the abstract generalization allows for; therefore, in such cases the generalization is unusable.

Ability to Be Taught and Promulgated

If any moral system is to apply to more than one person, it must be able to be promulgated, that is, laid out for people to see and understand; it should also be teachable so that others can learn about it regardless of whether they wish to accept or reject it. If, as in egoism, teaching or promulgating one's moral theory violates the very basis of that theory, then it must be kept secret and therefore can have no real applicability to anyone other than the individual who holds it. Furthermore, if there is really nothing to teach except, for example, the concept that one should act on what feels right without considering what right feelings might be, then the moral system is questionable because it cannot be passed on to anyone in a meaningful way. These problems are very serious because the greatest emphasis for morality is the social emphasis. If a moral theory is not teachable or cannot be promulgated, then how can it be applicable to society or any part of it beyond the one person who holds it?

Ability to Resolve Conflicts

A final consideration is that a workable moral system must be able to resolve conflicts among duties and obligations, and even among its participants. In universal ethical egoism, for example, if it is not possible to decide whose self-interest should be served when self-interests conflict, then the entire theory is thrown into doubt because, on the one hand, it states that everyone's self-interest should be served, and yet, on the other hand, it does not say how that can be done when there is a conflict of interests.

Further, if any moral theory or system proposes a series of duties or obligations that human beings ought to perform or be responsible for yet does not show what to do when they conflict, then again the system is not workable. For example, if a system proposes that it is wrong to lie and also wrong to break promises, and yet does not tell its adherents which of the two wrongs takes precedence when they conflict, then how does one know what to do if one has promised to protect the lives of some friends but must tell a lie to a killer who is in search of them? Simply to say that both actions are wrong or right will not help in making an actual moral decision. People must know, when clashes between or among moral commandments occur, how they can choose the action that will be most moral. Any system that does not provide for the resolution of such conflicts may be abstractly or theoretically meaningful, but, again, in the concrete moral situation, it will be of very little use to human beings who are striving to do the right thing.

With these assumptions in mind, then, the most important question we have to face is how to go about setting up a moral system that is rationally based and yet not unemotional; that is logically consistent but not rigid or inflexible; that is universal and yet practically applicable to particular individuals and situations; that can be taught and promulgated; and that can effectively resolve conflicts among human beings, duties, and obligations.

In Chapters 4 and 5, I examined the problems having to do with absolutes and freedom and arrived at two conclusions: (1) there are moral absolutes that can be known and (2) although freedom is limited, human beings can be said to be free in a very real sense. I also concluded that because of the variety, diversity,

178

and complexity of human beings, we must move from absolutes to "near" absolutes, which I labeled basic principles. It now seems that the problems of morality center essentially in these two areas: that of working with basic principles to avoid the chaos of situationism and intuitionism, while at the same time allowing for the freedom that is necessary for individual human beings and groups to work with such basic principles in a meaningful, practical, and creative fashion. The way this can best be accomplished is to find those principles that are indeed truly basic and necessary to almost any moral system or theory and to incorporate individual freedom as one of them. I intend to show how this can be done in the remainder of this chapter.

◆————————————————————————————

Basic Principles, Individual Freedom, and Their Justification

What we need first is a basic principle or basic principles. If we remember the ethical systems described so far, we will note that each of them has at least one basic principle and that some have more. In ethical egoism, the basic principle is self-interest; in utilitarianism, it is the interest of all concerned; in Kant's system it is the Categorical Imperative, the emphasis on duty rather than inclination, the reversibility criterion, and the principle that each human being is an end and not a means. Even the ethical system that advocates rules the least and stresses particular situations the most—situation ethics—still has one basic principle, which is love.

Is there any way that we can cut across all of these ethical systems to arrive at basic principles with which they all might agree? I am not referring here to agreement in the sense of how these basic principles are carried out or acted on; rather, I am concerned with agreement as to the ultimacy of principles necessary to the formation of any ethical system that will successfully apply to human morality.

Choosing Principles

Number of Principles. One must first decide on how many principles the system will have. One principle does not seem to be enough, and yet in the interest of simplicity, neither does one want too many. In my experience, one principle will not cover everything that is needed in a system. For example, Michael Scriven states that the equality principle ("Everyone has equal rights with you in moral matters until they prove otherwise") is the only one needed in his moral system. This principle is certainly admirable in that it sets up individual freedom, but it doesn't state any other values (freedom from what, to do what?), not does it specify exactly what "until they prove otherwise" means.

The Golden Rule. One of the most popular rules or principles people put forth when asked what they base their ethics on is the Golden Rule, or what Kant called "the reversibility criterion." It can be stated many ways, but the usual way is, "Do unto others as you would have them do unto you." In other words, if you want to find out what the moral thing to do is in any situation, you should ask yourself what you would like done to or for you if you were going to be the recipient of your own moral action. There is nothing basically wrong in putting oneself in the other person's shoes, as the saying goes, but as a primary and especially *only* principle on which to base a moral system, it is not very adequate.

First of all, in applying the Golden Rule, we are assuming that what the other person will want or need is the same as what we will want or need, and this is not always true. For example, some people thrive on physical contact that may cause minor and sometimes major injury. There are some people who feel their weekend is not complete until they have had at least one fistfight. Such people going only by the Golden Rule may figure that that's what they would want done to them, and therefore that's what they should do to others. Perhaps this example is somewhat exaggerated, but it does point out at least one problem with using the Golden Rule as the only principle.

Second, the Golden Rule does not really tell us what we should do: It only gives a method for testing what we have chosen to do against how it would affect us if we were to be the recipients of a certain act. That we would consider what we think to be the wishes of others in any act we are about to do is in itself admirable, but it does not tell us what we actually should do, thereby failing to provide a realistic basis for choosing among acts that will affect others.

Too often, such principles as the Golden Rule are chosen solely on the basis of custom or tradition. But reflection will reveal that we need to ask ourselves, "What are the important things in life, and which principles will protect and enhance them?" in order to construct a significant basis for morality. In attempting to do just that, I will first suggest certain principles and show how almost all ethical systems adhere to them, either explicitly or implicitly. Next, I will provide evidence and rational argument in an attempt to prove that these principles are absolutely necessary to any meaningful, workable, and livable system of human ethics.

The Value of Life Principle

The first principle we shall discuss is the Value of Life principle. This principle can be stated in several ways, but I prefer to state it as follows: "Human beings should revere life and accept death." As I argued in Chapter 4, no ethical system can function or persist without some statement, positive or negative or both, that reflects a concern for the preservation and protection of human life. It is perhaps the most basic and necessary principle of ethics because, empirically speaking, there can be no ethics whatsoever without living human beings.

180

This does not necessarily mean that no one may ever be killed or that people should never be allowed to die or that no one can ever commit suicide or have an abortion. Each ethical system might differ in many of these areas for logical reasons, but there must be some sort of concern for human life for pragmatic reasons alone.

However, I think more justification than the practical necessity of "no human life, no ethical system" can and should be given. Most ethical systems have some sort of prohibition against killing—the "Thou shalt not kill" of Judeo-Christian ethics; the "Never kill" of Kant; the prohibitions against killing in Buddhism, Hinduism, and humanism, to name but a few—in fact, even the most primitive society has had something to say about killing in general. All of these systems do allow killing under some circumstances, but they usually contain very strong commandments against the destruction of human life in general. Many systems extend the not-killing ideal beyond human life to all living things, but all concern themselves with some sort of preservation of human life. Even the least ethical systems, such as Hitler's, concern themselves with the value of *some* life (for example, its leaders' or Aryans' lives only).

Justification of the Value of Life Principle

It is my assumption, as stated earlier in this chapter, that morality should be based on reason and empirical evidence, but it remains to be shown whether the principles proposed here can be so supported. I believe that I have already given sufficient evidence and argument to support the Value of Life principle at the end of Chapter 4. This principle is empirically prior to any other because without human life there can be no goodness or badness, justice or injustice, honesty or dishonesty, freedom or lack of it. Life is a basic possession, the main possession of each individual human being. It is the one thing that all living human beings have in common, yet each individual experiences life uniquely—no one else can truly share or live another's life.

Therefore, individuals (as Kant correctly maintained) should never be treated merely as means, but rather, as unique and individual ends in themselves. This does not mean that the ending of a human life is never justified. In fact, it is precisely because such an occurrence is sometimes justified that I formulated the Value of Life principle as "Humans should revere life and accept death." This means that although we recognize life as basic and important, we also realize that no human life has been everlasting and that none probably ever will be. All of us must die sometime; therefore, "life at all costs" is not what the principle stands for, nor does it stand for the quantity of life over its quality. It merely proposes that no life should be ended without very strong justification.

One of the important adjuncts of this last statement and the statement about the uniqueness of an individual's life is that an individual's right to his own life *and* death is a basic concept; that is, decisions about whether a person should or should not live should not be made without the person's informed consent unless the justification is very great. This means that it is morally wrong to take people's lives against their will unless great justification can be brought forward; it also means that it is morally wrong to interfere with their death or dying against their will without similar justification. The four other principles enforce the value of life here. I see these principles as mutually supporting at various points, as flexibly able to act and react with each other to form the unity that a universal ethical system needs. But before discussing their justification, let me reiterate that the Value of Life principle is justified as a near absolute because life is held both in common and uniquely by all human beings, and it has to be that empirical starting point for any morality or humanity whatsoever.

The Principle of Goodness or Rightness

The second principle implied in every ethical system I have ever heard of is the Principle of Goodness or Rightness. This principle is sometimes presented as two separate principles (see Ross's prima facie duties in Chapter 3 for example): (1) The Principle of Beneficence, which states that one should always do good, and (2) the Principle of Nonmaleficence, which states that one should always try to prevent and avoid doing badness or harm. We shall see how these relate to each other when we list what the Principle of Goodness or Rightness demands of us. If morality means what is "good" or what is "right," then every system of morality must clearly imply, whether it is stated or not, the Principle of Goodness or Rightness. That is, all ethical systems are based on the idea that we should strive to be "good" human beings and attempt to perform "right" actions; and, conversely, that we should both try *not* to be "bad" human beings and avoid performing "wrong" actions. By the very definition of the terms *morality* and *immorality* we are concerned with being good and doing right. In actuality, the Principle of Goodness or Rightness demands that human beings attempt to do three things:

1. Promote goodness over badness and do good (beneficence).
2. Cause no harm or badness (nonmaleficence).
3. Prevent badness or harm (nonmaleficence).

Ethicists may differ over what they actually consider good and bad or right and wrong, but they all demand that human beings strive for the good and the right and avoid and prevent the bad and the wrong. Ethical systems embody this principle by implying, "If human beings are to be good (moral), then they should do so-and-so" (for example, act in their own self-interest).

Justification of the Principle of Goodness

Unless one wants to argue the question "Why be moral?" (see Chapter 1 for references to this), when one accepts morality, one also accepts goodness, because that is essentially what the first term means. In Chapter 1, I defined "morality" as goodness or rightness and "immorality" as badness or wrongness. When we speak of a moral person, life, or action, we mean a good person, a good life, and a right action; when we speak of an immoral person, life, or action, we mean a bad person, a bad life, and a wrong action. I also defined "good" and "right" as involving happiness, pleasure, excellence, harmony, and creativity and "bad" and "wrong" as involving unhappiness, pain, lack of excellence, disharmony, and lack of creativity. How these characteristics are to be defined by individuals, however, is not so clear because they are subject to the same truths and facts as the Principle of Individual Freedom—that is, they will mean different things to some extent because each individual is by nature different from every other one.

Despite all of these differences, however, it is possible to discover some "goods" that human beings have generally been able to agree upon. These include life, consciousness, pleasure, happiness, truth, knowledge, beauty, love, friendship, self-expression, self-realization, freedom, honor, peace, and security. There is no doubt that people rank these "goods" differently or even omit one or two from their list of "good things," but most people, after careful discussion, will probably include many of these. Some moralists hold that there is only one thing (for instance, happiness) that is intrinsically good (good in itself); this view is called *monism*. However, as you might guess, because I have stressed freedom and individuality and uniqueness so much and have also stressed a synthesis of ethical approaches, my view would be that there are many "goods"; this view is called *pluralism*.

Having defined "good" and "right," and having shown that all of these must be manifested in human experience and in human interpersonal relationships, the question is whether we can justify the Principle of Goodness—that human beings should always do good and avoid or prevent what is bad.

There is not one ethical system that advocates that a person do what is bad and avoid what is good. But this in itself is not justification; it is merely an empirical fact. If a person thinks that human beings ought to be moral, then he or she thinks that they ought to do good and avoid or prevent bad. If, however, a person thinks that people need not strive for the good and avoid or prevent bad, then his or her concern lies outside of morality, and the question "Why should I be moral at all?" has to be answered. Because this question is nonmoral and cannot be answered within morality, the Principle of Goodness is simply an ultimate principle for morality of any kind and cannot be justified any further than was done in Chapter 1. The Principle of Goodness is *logically* prior to all other principles, just as the Value of Life principle is *empirically* prior. This distinction will be clarified at the end of this chapter.

The Principle of Justice or Fairness

The third principle is the Principle of Justice or Fairness and concerns itself essentially with the distribution of good and bad on a just and fair basis. It says that human beings should treat other human beings fairly and justly in distributing goodness and badness among them. It is not enough that people should try to be good and to do what is right; there must also be some attempt made to distribute the benefits from being good and doing right. Ways in which "distributive" justice can be considered have been discussed fully in Chapter 6 and should be referred to at this point.

It is difficult to find an ethical system that does not include some concern for justice. Even ethical egoism, which one might think would have no concern for justice because its major aim is self-interest, does in its most accepted form—universal ethical egoism—want everyone to act in his or her own self-interest. Isn't this asking, in essence, that everyone be treated justly? Egoists would be strongly opposed to some versions of distributive justice, but they at least advocate that *everyone* should act in his or her own self-interest. Kant's Duty Ethics—with its universal applicability, the Categorical Imperative, reversibility criterion, and regard for all human beings as ends rather than means—has justice at its core. Utilitarianism, whether it be act or rule, advocates a general concern for justice because it attempts to deal with the happiness of all concerned, not just self and not even just other people. Judaism and Christianity, in their Ten Commandments—which stress not killing, not stealing, not committing adultery, and not coveting—are concerned with justice, and the urgings of Jesus to "love thy neighbor as thyself" and "love even your enemies" emphasize justice and fairness, among other things.

Justification of the Principle of Justice

I would argue that it is another empirical truth that there are many human beings in the world and that very few, if any, live in complete isolation; in fact, most of our actions and lives are performed and lived in the company of others. In such a situation, should one bring goodness only to oneself and do absolutely nothing for others? Very few strong egoists would accept such behavior as being in one's self-interest, and it certainly would not be in the interest of others or of all concerned.

If one accepts the concept that good should be shared, the next issue to be considered is who should get the benefits resulting from good human actions and how should they be distributed. Because there are very few occasions when an individual's moral action would not affect anyone besides her- or himself, the good or bad resulting from this action must inevitably fall on other people. One could, of course, merely let the consequences fall where they may, but we are attempting to work with a rationally based morality, and reason dictates that there should be some order to any distribution of good or bad.

All human beings have common characteristics, as we have said, and yet they are each unique, so how do we distribute goodness and badness with these truths in mind? What does it mean when we say we should try to distribute goodness and badness fairly and equally among all human beings? If, for example, we return to the dialysis case described in the previous chapter, it means that everyone gets an equal chance at both the good and the bad in the situation. Presuming that for people with kidney failure getting kidney dialysis is a good and not getting it is a bad, then by the lottery method, we make it possible to distribute this good and this bad equally among the seventeen patients. Some will have to receive the bad, but all will have an equal chance at obtaining the good.

Does this mean that we must share each other's property, families, jobs, or money? Not necessarily. There are, for example, exceptions to the equal distribution ideal in a *triage*, a medical emergency situation in which the patients greatly outnumber the medical personnel and facilities. Choices have to be made, and the lottery method may not and probably will not be the fairest way of dealing with the situation. Because so many need medical attention and so few are able to give it, then, under the circumstances, medical personnel who can be put back into service after receiving medical attention should have first priority, and the patients who can with some certainty be saved should be next.

These emergency situations are rare exceptions for the most part, but what about using the lottery method to determine who gets money, property, and jobs? This view of justice, of course, would be absurd; however, everyone must have an equal opportunity to *acquire* these things if they desire them. Not everyone has the persistence or intelligence to become a doctor or lawyer, for example, but everyone who has the necessary qualifications ought to have an equal opportunity to apply and to be accepted at medical and law schools.

It is almost too obvious to state that no one should be denied this opportunity because of his or her skin color, sex, religious belief, age, or beauty or lack thereof, nor should anyone be denied the opportunity to earn as much money as anyone else for these or other reasons that have nothing to do with fair qualifications for obtaining a position. In this way, we recognize the common equality of human beings as human beings and yet allow for individual differences in attempting to distribute goodness and badness fairly. We must have the Principle of Justice, then, in order to be moral toward other people because they are inevitably affected by our actions.

The Principle of Truth Telling or Honesty

The fourth basic principle is almost a corollary to the Principle of Justice or Fairness; however, I think that it is important enough in its own right to be a separate principle of equal status with the other four described in this chapter. This is the Principle of Truth Telling or Honesty. It is extremely important, if for no other reason than to provide for meaningful communication, which is an absolute necessity in any moral system or in any moral relationship between two or more human beings. How, indeed, can any moral system function if its participants can never know whether anyone is telling the truth? How, with the stress placed on teaching and promulgating, can moral theories be communicated if no one can be sure whether the communicators are lying or telling the truth? One of the basic criticisms I leveled at individual and personal ethical egoism was that such egoists would undoubtedly have to lie or be dishonest in order to satisfy their own self-interests; that is, they would believe in one ethical theory but would have to pretend they actually believed in another. If they did not do this, they would probably not be operating in their own self-interests.

Further, all of morality depends on agreements between human beings, and how can agreements be made or maintained without some assurance that people are entering into them honestly and truthfully? Therefore, it would seem that truth telling and honesty are important and basic cornerstones of morality. Most ethical systems have some prohibition against lying. In Judeo-Christian ethics, the commandment "Thou shalt not bear false witness" makes it clear that lying is wrong. Kant states that lying cannot be made into a maxim for all humanity without being inconsistent, and most other ethical systems have at least a general prohibition against lying even if they allow many exceptions where lying would be "the lesser of two evils." Lying will be discussed in more detail in Chapter 11.

Justification of the Principle of Truth Telling or Honesty

I have already argued that a basic agreement to be truthful is necessary to the communication of a moral theory or system, but such an agreement is also extremely important in establishing and maintaining vital and meaningful human relationships of any kind, moral or nonmoral. Human beings need to enter into relationships with each other with a sense of mutual trust, believing that whatever they say or do to one another will be as honest and open an expression of their thoughts and feelings as possible. This principle may be the most difficult of all the principles to try to live with because human beings are essentially very vulnerable in the area of human relationships, and to protect this vulnerability may have built defenses against exposing themselves to others. This is especially true in a modern, crowded, and complex civilization such as ours.

Because of such obvious vulnerability, this very demanding principle is open to many carefully justified exceptions. Basically, however, it must still be adhered to wherever possible. It is not true that people will never lie to one another and not even true that lying or dishonesty might not be justified; however, it is true that a strong *attempt* must be made to be truthful and honest in human relationships because morality, in the final analysis, depends on what people say and do.

For example, suppose that A borrows money from B and agrees to pay it back, but then does not. When B asks A for the money, A says that he does not intend to pay it back and never did. Now, when the money was borrowed and loaned, there was a mutual sense of trust involved in that B was going to help A out by loaning him money, and A was going to pay her back in gratitude for the help. When B discovers that A has not only defaulted but also never intended to pay back the money, the sense of mutual trust is broken, not only for this one transaction and relationship but also, perhaps, for any future relationships that B might have with A or with other people.

The problem is that the basis of human relationships is communication, and when communication is eroded by lying or dishonesty, that basis is destroyed, and meaningful human relationships—especially those in the moral sphere—become impossible. Therefore, because all human relationships are based on communication and because—to my way of thinking—morality is the most important of all human relationships, it is absolutely necessary that truth telling and honesty be considered fundamental and basic to any theory or system of morality.

The Principle of Individual Freedom

The fifth and last basic principle is the Principle of Individual Freedom, or the Equality principle, sometimes referred to as the Principle of Autonomy. For Michael Scriven, this is the ultimate moral principle; in fact, he defines "morality" as "equal consideration, from which all other moral principles (justice, and so on) can be developed" and as the recognition that "people have equal rights with you in moral matters until they prove otherwise."[1] He goes on to stress that this does not mean that they are equal in height or weight or intelligence but rather that they are equal in moral matters. This principle means that people, being individuals with individual differences, must have the freedom to choose their own ways and means of being moral *within the framework of the first four basic principles*. This last stipulation is, of course, mine and not Scriven's since I do not believe that the equality principle in itself is enough of a basis on which to develop an ethical system. In fact, I have presented this principle last so that it is understood that individual moral freedom is limited by the other four principles: the necessity of preserving and protecting human life, the necessity of doing good and preventing and avoiding bad, the necessity of treating human beings justly in distributing goodness and badness, and, finally, the necessity of telling the truth and being honest.

It seems to be a powerful necessity, if one considers the tremendous variety of human desires, needs, and concerns, that people be allowed to follow the dictates of their own intelligence and conscience as much as possible. Most people will agree with this statement, especially in a definitely pluralistic society such as ours; but they will also want to stipulate that this principle is valid only as long as it does not interfere with someone else in some serious way.

Because no person is exactly like another and no situation is exactly like another, there must be some leeway for people to deal with these differences in the manner best suited to them. However, neither freedom itself nor moral freedom is absolute. For example, just because one man wants the freedom to rape and kill all the women he desires, does not mean he ought to have the freedom to do so, nor should he have the freedom to steal someone's new car just because he has the freedom to wish he could have it. The limitations of one's freedom, then, should be established by the other four principles.

It is important to distinguish between this principle and the second one in that the second principle has to do with the equal *distribution* of goodness and badness, whereas the Principle of Individual Freedom has to do with the equality of human beings *themselves* when it comes to moral matters. When Kant stated that each human being ought to be considered an end in himself or herself and not a means for anyone's else's end, he implied the equality principle. The Golden Rule says that one ought to consider other people in the same way that one considers oneself—that is, as one's equals insofar as moral choices and treatment are concerned. When Jesus was asked, "But who is my neighbor?" in relation to His commandment "Love thy neighbor as thyself," He answered with the parable of the Good Samaritan, indicating that all people are to be considered as moral equals despite any belief that they might not be one's social, religious, or economic equal. One person should not condemn another for the way he or she lives, no matter how great are the differences in life-style, as long as both people adhere to the principles of goodness, justice, value of life, and honesty.

Justification of the Principle of Individual Freedom

I have already argued, in Chapter 5, that human beings have freedom in a limited but real sense to make decisions and choices, including, of course, moral decisions and choices. The important question is to what degree they should be allowed such freedom in their dealings with other human beings. The Principle of Individual Freedom resolves the problem of instilling flexibility within a moral system—a flexibility it needs because of the very real diversity that exists among human beings.

I justify the Principle of Individual Freedom on the basis that there are many human beings to be considered in establishing a human morality, and although they have common characteristics (bodies, minds, feelings, and so forth), each person is, nevertheless, unique. Human beings are at different stages of development, have different talents and abilities, and possess different feelings, wants, and needs, and if we are not to completely obliterate these differences we must recognize and allow for them. The only way to allow for them is to let individuals live out their lives in whatever unique and different ways they choose.

What I am saying is that there is no possible way that one human life can be lived by anyone other than the person who is living it; therefore, we must accept each human being as he or she is. This acceptance amounts to granting to all individuals the freedom to live their lives in ways best suited to them, thereby recognizing what is actually a natural and empirical truth about human beings—that they are in fact different and unique. Freedom, like life, then, is "built into" the human structure both empirically and rationally.

Nowhere is freedom more important or significant than in morality. As stated in Chapter 5, morality could not exist if human beings were not to some extent free to make moral choices and decisions. There is no point to assigning moral responsibility, to praising or blaming, or to rewarding or punishing if human beings are not somehow free to be responsible, praiseworthy, or blameworthy. Therefore, it seems that freedom must be built into any moral system for such a system to function properly.

It is even more important, however, if a system is to work for all human beings who are trying to be moral that they be allowed the greatest latitude possible in making moral choices and decisions. It is important not only because of the obvious diversity among human beings, which has already been recognized, but also because the basic principles are only *near* absolutes, and every opportunity must be given human beings to follow these principles in the way that best suits their individuality, their lives and life situations, and their relationships with other human beings. The Principle of Individual Freedom, then, is extremely important to any moral system in that it can encourage the widest expression of moral preferences, choices, and decisions within the structure of the other four principles, thus allowing for the combination of flexibility and stability that all livable and workable moral systems need.

◆————————————————————————————————

Priority of the Basic Principles

One of the problems with any set of basic principles is the priority in which they should be used. For example, is the Value of Life Principle always inviolable even though it may bring badness rather than goodness? Must we be concerned about the distribution of goodness and badness even where such distribution seriously violates someone's freedom? Further, must we always tell the truth even if it will bring badness, not goodness? As I have already said, our five basic principles—the value of life, goodness or rightness, justice or fairness, truth telling or honesty, and individual freedom—are not absolutes, but near absolutes, and they can be violated as long as there is sufficient justification to do so. But what, for example, constitutes sufficient justification to violate the Value of Life principle?

Even though, as the reader might suspect, I have presented and have attempted to support these principles in the order in which I feel they should be followed, that order and any other considerations of priority that are to be made remain to be justified. First, there are two important ways in which the priority of the basic principles may be determined:

1. A general way, in which the five principles are classified into two major categories based on logical and empirical priority.

2. A particular way, in which priority is determined by the actual situation or context in which moral actions and decisions occur and in which all basic principles must inevitably function.

A General Way of Determining Priority—Two Categories

The Primary Category. Under the general way of classifying the five basic principles, the first two are logically and empirically prior to the other three and, therefore, fall into the first major category. *Logical priority* means the way logic determines in which order the principles must occur, or in which order logical thinking forces us to place them. *Empirical priority* means that priority which is established by evidence gained from observation through the senses. Logical reasoning plays a part here, too, but the emphasis is on evidence derived through the senses.

Logically speaking, the Principle of Goodness comes first. What this means is that in establishing any moral system, one immediately has to assume the ultimate moral principle: goodness. After all, "morality," as I have already said means the same thing as "goodness," so in speaking of morality, one can assume that this ultimate moral principle is *logically* prior to any other.

As I have also argued, however, in an empirical sense one cannot have human morality unless one first has human life. If there are no human beings, then there can be no human morality—this is an obvious empirical fact. These two principles, then, are logically and empirically necessary to morality, and because of this necessity they take precedence over the other three principles and must be placed in the first, or primary, category.

The Secondary Category. The other three principles fall into the secondary category in the following order: the third principle is that of justice or fairness, because in most human actions more than one person is involved, and some kind of distribution must be established. The fourth principle is that of truth telling or honesty, because it follows from the need to be fair and just in dealings with others. This principle is also very important, as we have seen, because it is basic to human communication and human relationships, which underlie all morality. Last, but certainly not least, is the fifth principle, that of individual freedom, which is important because each individual is unique and in many cases is the only one able to successfully determine what is good for himself.

By putting five principles into these two major categories, I do not mean to imply that principles from the secondary category will not, under certain circumstances, take precedence over those in the primary. For example, many times in history, human beings have willingly given up their lives for their freedom and the freedom of others. The two categories merely give human beings a priority to follow in a *general* sense; in general, we would observe the Value of Life principle and the Principle of Goodness as being more important than the other three principles because the former are absolutely essential to any moral system or theory.

Another justification for placing the five principles in categories is that principles one and two are often interchangeable with each other in terms of priority, whereas principles three through five are also interchangeable among themselves. For example, it is wrong or bad to take a person's life against his or her will, but if this person is violating the first two principles by aggressively seeking to take the lives of innocent people, one's own included, then one might have the right to attempt to stop the person from doing bad by any means one can, including killing him if no lesser means can be used. In this case, the Principle of Goodness may take precedence over the Value of Life principle.

As an example of the fact that the second three principles are at times interchangeable, consider the following. If any decision involves freely consenting individuals but does not seriously affect others, then the Principle of Individual Freedom may override the Principle of Justice. The implication is that people ought to be able to do what they want as long as it does not interfere with others in any serious manner. This is why most sexual activity between freely consenting adults may not be governed by the Principle of Justice so much as by the Principle of Individual Freedom. Here, the former may take precedence over the latter.

Rape, child molestation, and sadistic acts performed on unwilling victims are, of course, violations of the Principle of Justice, but sexual activity agreed upon by consenting adults may not be. Offense to others' taste may not be a sufficient reason to invoke the Principle of Justice unless other people are being forced into such acts. For example, just because I may feel that group sex would be wrong for and distasteful to me does not mean I can impose my own feelings on other freely consenting adults. (These issues and others will be discussed in much more detail in Chapter 12.) To sum up, the principles may overlap, depending on the particular situation, but basically and generally the first two principles should be stressed and should be seen as interchangeable in terms of priority, whereas the last three should be given lesser status and should also be seen as interchangeable among themselves in terms of priority.

The Particular Way of Determining Priority—Situation or Context

In discussing the second, and particular, way in which priority is determined, it is important to note that morality and moral decision making do not occur in the abstract but in concrete, everyday-life situations. Because morality or immorality occurs in *particular* situations or contexts, such situations and contexts must be observed and analyzed carefully. Any theories or rules or ethical principles that cannot be applied to actual human situations in a meaningful manner should definitely be questioned and should probably be discarded as worthless.

This does not mean that one cannot generalize from these particular situations, especially where they are sufficiently similar; on the contrary, it means that generalizations must be made from the particular whenever possible so that the generalizations will be supported with as much real and actual evidence as one can muster. It is for this reason that I am opposed to a strictly nonconsequentialist approach to ethics—because I believe that all actions have consequences and that moral or immoral actions have the most serious of all consequences for human beings. This is also why I am opposed to a strictly "rules" approach to ethics; too often rules are so broad and general that there can be no disputing them until one tries unsuccessfully to apply them to a particular situation. It is at this point that people discover that rules may sound and even be moral, but they do not tell people how to act in particular situations A and B.

Nevertheless, because I advocate five basic principles that I have stated should not be violated without strong justification, I obviously do not feel that simply waiting to see what happens in each situation is the most meaningful way to go about being moral. I feel that we must start from some broad yet humanly applicable basic principles so that we will have some foundation for acting morally and avoiding immorality and so that the profusion of different situations we face in life will not confuse our thinking when it comes to making moral decisions. For these reasons, my approach to ethics is eclectic (that is, made up from what I consider the best of many systems). It can also be called "mixed deontological," or what I would describe as a combined consequentialist-nonconsequentialist and rules-act approach to ethics—in other words, another reasonable synthesis.

This means that one enters all situations with a reverence for human life and an acceptance of human death, with the idea of doing good and avoiding and preventing bad, with the hope of justly distributing the good and bad that result from the situations, with the desire to be truthful and honest, and with the idea of granting individual freedom and equality to everyone involved in the situations as long as it does not violate the other four principles.

Then each situation will help human beings determine how these principles will be adhered to or carried out. The particular situation will help them determine whether a life should be taken or not, how much freedom should be allowed or denied, what is the right or wrong act to perform, and what is the fairest way to act toward everyone. In this way, the unity that human beings need will be provided by the basic principles of morality, whereas the diversity that is also required will be provided by the individual interpretation and carrying out of these principles in particular situations involving moral decisions.

For example, it is quite easy to state that one should not steal from another person under the principles of goodness, justice, honesty, and individual freedom. That is, *generally*, it is not right to steal from another because stealing violates a person's freedom to earn and own property; it does not bring satisfaction to the person stolen from (although it might bring satisfaction to the thief); it is not an action with any excellence in it (although one might be a clever and "excellent" thief); it does not create harmony because one should, if one is able, earn one's own property; and it would not be fair to the other person, who has worked hard for what she or he owns.

We could say, then, that people who steal merely because they like to or because they would rather not work are performing a dishonest and immoral action. However, let us suppose that your sister is searching diligently for her gun in order to kill someone who has made her angry. You would certainly be justified in stealing your sister's gun so that she would not be able to violate all five of the principles by doing something bad, by taking a life, by encroaching on someone else's freedom, and by not being fair or honest to the person who made her angry. Because the value of life and the goodness principles are more crucial to morality than the other three, you are justified in stealing in this situation because you would save a life and prevent badness by doing so.

Another example actually occurred when a plane with missionaries aboard crashed in the Amazon jungle of South America. The only survivor was the missionaries' daughter, who attempted to make her way to a village or city to save herself. At one point in her wanderings, she arrived at a river where she found a boat. Following to the letter the Judeo-Christian commandment against stealing, she refused to take the boat and went on wandering through the jungle. She adhered to a moral rule very strictly, but would she have been immoral if she had not? Under the system I have proposed, she would not have. She might have waited to see if the boat was abandoned, but after awhile, when she was fairly sure that it was and that no one was around to use it or help her, she would have been justified under the Value of Life principle to violate the rule against stealing.

Let us also note, however, that she was not *obligated* to take the boat; in her own individual freedom, she could choose—as she did—not to steal at the risk of losing her life. She could have reasoned further that whoever might have left the boat would know the jungle much better than she and would therefore be better able to survive. She could also have marked the spot where she took it, and as soon as she arrived at the first village, she could have sent some villagers back to find the boat's owner, thus being as fair as she could under the circumstances. Therefore, the situation or context in which we have to act does, indeed, have a bearing on how we interpret and use the five basic principles to make moral decisions; however, the principles remain the basis for deciding or acting at all.

How the System of Humanitarian Ethics Works

Before concluding this chapter, it seems important to try out two human events involving moral issues and run them through the five principles to see how the system works. The two events I will apply the principles to are (1) two young adults living together without benefit of marriage, and (2) rape.

Living Together Without Marriage

Let's say that a young man and woman, age eighteen, want to live together, enjoying the full benefits of a live-in relationship. Both sets of parents object strenuously to their doing so. Is what they are doing immoral? Let's apply the five principles.

Value of Life Principle. There doesn't seem to be a violation of the Value of Life principle in that no one's life is threatened by this action. If the woman becomes pregnant, the problem of abortion could arise, but we can presume that the couple will utilize contraception or will have something moral set up in the event of pregnancy.

Principle of Goodness. It's difficult to see any significant violation of the Principle of Goodness unless one applies specific standards of a particular religion, for example, which says such a relationship is immoral. If, however, the couple does not adhere to this religion, even though their parents might, then such a standard cannot be forced on them. The couple evidently feels that living together will bring about goodness for them, whereas their parents feel it will not. The parents also may feel that this will not bring about goodness for them; that is, it will make them worry, embarrass them in front of family and friends, and generally upset them.

Principle of Justice. The Principle of Justice really seems to be the only principle that would affect the parents. That is, is the distribution of goodness fair if the parents are not made happy by this arrangement? In other words, the man and woman feel that they are being fair to each other and their parents, but the parents feel that their children are not being fair to their families. What their children are doing is offensive to them—to their taste and to their beliefs in the sanctity of marriage.

Two questions arise: "Is this sufficient reason for not allowing the couple's living together and branding their actions as immoral?" and "How long must children conform to their parents' life-style or values?" Is not eighteen an age at which young people should have the right to live their own lives and take the responsibility for what they do?

Principle of Honesty and Truth Telling. There seems to be no violation of the Principle of Honesty and Truth Telling because the young people are quite open about their intentions.

Principle of Individual Freedom. The question really centers in the Principle of Individual Freedom. If there is no serious violation of the other four principles, according to this ethical system, then individual freedom should be allowed. I do not feel that any of the principles can be clearly shown to have been seriously violated; therefore, though what the couple is doing may be offensive to some people's (obviously their parents') tastes, this in itself should not deny these young consenting adults the right to live together if they want to as long as they are moral toward each other. This, of course, is another area where the principles should be applied, and that would be a different issue. We presume that the young people have agreed to be moral toward one another. Serious breaches of morality in their relationship toward one another would, of course, alter the conclusion concerning the morality of their living together. On the face of it, however, there would seem to be no reason not to allow them to live together.

Rape

Suppose a man wants to rape a woman; would this ever be a moral act?

Value of Life Principle. The Value of Life principle would certainly be violated whether or not the woman were killed because her life and its quality would be threatened by the act of rape. She would be sexually violated and also violated in other ways, both physically and psychologically.

Principle of Goodness. Obviously, there is nothing good for the woman in the act of rape. The only possible good in the act would be the pleasure the rapist might get, but that pleasure is certainly to be classed as malicious because it totally disregards the pain and unhappiness of his victim.

Principle of Justice. There is no way the rapist's act could be considered just or fair to the woman because he would be forcing himself on her against her wishes and without her permission, committing the greatest invasion of her privacy and her life.

Principle of Honesty and Truth Telling. The Principle of Honesty and Truth Telling may or may not come into the picture depending on whether or not the rapist lies to the woman to get her into a situation where the rape can take place.

Principle of Individual Freedom. Because rape violates all of the first four principles, it can never be considered as moral, and therefore no man or woman should ever have the freedom to rape another.

♦

Conclusion

We now have five fairly well-established principles under which any ethical system can operate. These principles are broad enough to take cognizance of all human beings and their moral treatment, and, as such, they are near absolutes in that exceptions to these principles can be made only if they can be completely justified through empirical evidence and reasoning. Generally, however, these principles will take precedence over all other ethical concerns.

My contention, then, is that if we recognize the value of human life, always attempt to do good and avoid or prevent bad, attempt to distribute good and bad fairly and justly, try to be honest and tell the truth, and yet allow for the fullest individual freedom and for equal consideration within the limits of the other four principles, we will have an ethical base from which many varied individual and group ethical systems can function without serious conflict or the need to eliminate one system because it conflicts with another.

I maintain that the five principles described here are extremely essential to a morality that will relate effectively to all human beings everywhere and yet will allow them the individual freedom to manifest these basic principles in their own individual ways, suitable to their cultural, social, and personal situations. What I envision as the ideal universal moral system, out of which many individual moral systems can be successfully formulated without serious conflict, is one that stresses "unity in diversity." The unity is provided by the first four basic principles, which are not absolutes but near absolutes, and which, therefore, should not be violated without careful and well-documented justification. The diversity is provided by the fifth principle, which not only allows but also encourages all human beings to seek out the best ways to carry out the other four principles. This means that as long as the five principles are adhered to—with the exceptions being fully justified—whether people are religious or nonreligious, consequentialist or nonconsequentialist, rule or act in their approach to ethics, they should be able to pursue their own lives within the limitations of the principles without hindrance.

For example, religious and nonreligious ethical systems can easily flourish side by side if the five basic principles are adhered to by both. A particular religion may wish to make certain other moral demands on its members, such as having them worship a god and requiring their participation in its religious activities, but it cannot in any way impose such demands on any human beings outside of the religion itself. Similarly, it cannot take any immoral action against nonreligious persons that would violate the five principles, such as harming or killing them because they do not accept its religious tenets. On the other hand, nonreligious ethicists must allow for the free religious worship of others as long as those others observe the five basic principles. By the same token, nonreligious ethicists cannot violate any of the principles because they do not like what the particular religion believes in or does.

It is even acceptable that a particular religion demand greater moral requirements of its members than those set down in the five principles. For example, Jainists and Quakers have greater requirements against taking human life and, indeed, all life than those encompassed in the Value of Life principle.

This system, which I call *Humanitarian Ethics*, allows for the greatest amount of diversity and variety, at the same time providing enough stability and order to protect all human beings while they explore their diverse ethical possibilities.

In the search for the greatest and widest possible morality, I also wish to stress that the views of all ethical systems should be allowed to be set forth and openly, honestly, and freely discussed and argued. It is not wrong for one ethical system to attempt to convince others to accept its views as long as this is done by reasonable argument, not force, and as long as the five principles are carefully observed in the process. The principles, then, provide the framework for all ethical systems.

Chapter Summary

I. Conflicting general moral issues
   A. Consequences versus nonconsequences. We must consider consequences of our decisions, acts, and rules but at the same time be aware of and avoid the end-justifies-the-means problem.
   B. Self- versus other-interestedness. There are problems with a totally self-interested basis for morality; therefore, I agree with the utilitarian approach to doing what is in the best interest of everyone.
   C. Act versus rule. In a moral system, we need freedom (act) and yet stability and order (rule).
   D. Emotions versus reason. A moral system should be based on reason without excluding emotion.

II. Basic assumptions concerning what constitutes a workable and livable moral system
   A. It should be rationally based and yet not devoid of emotion.
   B. It should be as logically consistent as possible but not rigid and inflexible.
   C. It must have universality or general application to all humanity and yet be applicable in a practical way to particular individuals and situations.
   D. It should be able to be taught and promulgated.
   E. It must have the ability to resolve conflicts among human beings, duties, and obligations.

III. Basic principles, individual freedom, and their justification
   A. The problems of morality center essentially in two areas.
      1. How to attain unity and order by working with basic principles to avoid the chaos of situationism and intuitionism.
      2. Allowing for individual and group freedom to work with such principles meaningfully.
   B. The Value of Life principle states that human beings should revere life and accept death.
   C. The Principle of Goodness or Rightness is ultimate to any moral system, and it requires that human beings attempt three things: to promote goodness over badness and do good, to cause no harm or badness, and to prevent badness or harm.
   D. The Principle of Justice or Fairness
      1. The type of justice referred to here is distributive, meaning human beings should treat other human beings justly and fairly in distributing goodness and badness among them.
      2. Theories about and ways of distributing good and bad have been fully described in Chapter 6.
   E. The Principle of Truth Telling or Honesty provides for meaningful communication.
   F. The Principle of Individual Freedom states that people, being individuals with individual differences, must have the freedom to choose their own ways and means of being moral within the framework of the first four basic principles.
IV. Two ways of establishing the priority of the five moral principles
   A. In the first, or general, way, the principles are classified into two major categories based on logical and empirical priority.
      1. The Value of Life principle (because without life there is no other aspect of morality) and the Principle of Goodness (because it is the ultimate principle of any moral system) form the first category because they are logically and empirically prior to the other three principles.
      2. The other three principles fall into the second category: the Principle of Justice or Fairness (because in most human actions more than just one person is involved and some form of distribution of goodness and badness must be established), the Principle of Truth Telling or Honesty (because it follows from the need to be fair and just in dealing with others), and the Principle of Individual Freedom (because each individual is the only one truly able to decide what is good for himself).
   B. In the second, or particular, way, priority is determined by the actual situation or context in which moral actions and decisions occur.

V. Importance of the situation and context of moral problems and basic principles.

    A. The situation or context is important because morality always occurs in particular situations to particular people, never in the abstract.

    B. We must start from a broad yet humanly applicable, near-absolute principle so that there will be some basis for acting morally and avoiding immorality.

    C. Humanitarian Ethics is an eclectic approach, a "mixed deontological," or combined consequentialist-nonconsequentialist and act-rule, approach to morality.

Exercises for Review

1. Explain and analyze the five attributes that the author says must be present for any moral system to be livable and workable. With which ones do you agree, and why? With which do you disagree, and why? Can you suggest any others?

2. Do you agree that the central problem of morality is how to attain unity and order in a moral system without denying individual freedom? Why or why not? If you think another problem is more important, explain and discuss it.

3. Explain in detail the five basic principles presented by the author.

4. Would you eliminate any of these five principles as not really basic? If so, which ones and why? If not, why not?

5. Are there any other principles you think are important enough to be added to or to replace any of the five given in this chapter? If so, present them in detail and support your contention with as much argument and evidence as you can.

6. In what order of priority should the five basic moral principles be applied? Distinguish between the general and particular ways of establishing such priority.

7. What is the respective importance of (a) considering the situation or context in which moral problems occur and (b) establishing moral principles, rules, or guidelines?

8. How many of the basic principles does the moral system you believe in ascribe to? Which ones are they, and why?

9. How have you chosen to resolve the four general moral issues, and why?

Discussion Questions

1. Examine a system of ethics or moral code with which you are quite familiar (for example, your religion's code of ethics, your family's code of ethics, or your desired profession's code of ethics) and describe the extent to which any or all of the five basic principles described in this chapter are found in that system or code. What other principles are found there? Is the addition of these principles an improvement on Humanitarian Ethics? Explain your answer.

2. To what extent do you believe that the United States as a nation follows the five basic principles? Does it follow any other principles? Is the addition of these other principles (if there are others) an improvement on Humanitarian Ethics? Why or why not? Answer all parts of this question in detail.

3. What is your personal moral system or code of ethics? On what principle or principles is it based? Justify that principle or those principles in detail. How does your system make allowances for individual freedom and yet maintain order and stability? Develop your answer fully.

Note

1. Michael Scriven, speech on "Rational Moral Education" and also *Primary Philosophy* (New York: McGraw-Hill, 1966), 232.

Supplementary Reading

Amato, Joseph A. *Ethics: Living or Dead? Themes in Contemporary Values.* Tuscaloosa, Ala.: Portals Press, 1982.

Beauchamp, Tom. *Philosophical Ethics: An Introduction to Moral Philosophy.* New York: McGraw-Hill, 1982.

Bond, E. J. *Reason and Value.* New York: Cambridge University Press, 1983.

Finnis, John. *Fundamentals of Ethics.* Washington, D.C.: Georgetown University Press, 1983.

Frankena, William K. *Ethics*, 3rd ed. Englewood Cliffs, N.J.: Prentice-Hall, 1974.

Hospers, John. *Human Conduct*, 2nd ed. New York: Harcourt Brace Jovanovich, 1982.

Kirkendall, Lester A. *Premarital Intercourse and Interpersonal Relationships*. New York: Julian Press, 1961.

Nielsen, Kai. "Why Should I Be Moral?" In *Problems of Moral Philosophy*, 2nd ed. Ed. Paul W. Taylor. Belmont, Calif.: Dickenson, 1972.

Ramsey, Paul. *The Patient as Person*. New Haven, Conn.: Yale University Press, 1970.

Rawls, John. *A Theory of Justice*. Cambridge: Harvard University Press, 1971.

Scriven, Michael. *Primary Philosophy*. New York: McGraw-Hill, 1966.

The Taking of Human Life

Objectives

After you have read this chapter you should be able to

1. Understand further the importance of having basic principles, rules, or guidelines on which to base an approach to dealing with moral issues.
2. Show how basic principles can be applied to the general and significant problem of the taking of human life.
3. Show how basic principles are used to deal with the specific moral problems of suicide, defense of the innocent, war, and capital punishment, and know the arguments for and against these issues.

Some of the basic arguments for and against the taking of human life in certain instances (for example, suicide and war) will be examined in this chapter and the next two, and some cases will be laid out for readers to try to solve through their own ethical systems, considering the problems and issues that must be faced. Also, if instructors and students are interested, there is a special appendix for each chapter that explains how Humanitarian Ethics (the system I have proposed in Chapter 7) would attempt to solve the problems being presented. In this way readers are not subjected, unless they want to be, to my system of dealing with moral issues but will still have the moral issues presented to them as such. If they wish, however, they may use the Humanitarian Ethics solutions for critical discussion and evaluation. The Humanitarian Ethics discussion for this chapter may be found in Appendix 1, for the next chapter in Appendix 2, and so on.

The Taking of Human Life

One of the worst possible moral offenses that human beings can commit is the taking of human life. As I stated earlier, the Value of Life principle is empirically the most important of the five, inasmuch as morality itself depends on it; therefore, one must revere life and accept death. Does this mean that human life may never be taken? We will examine different types of situations involving the taking of human life, and will see how basic principles can be applied to them.

Suicide

Definitions of Suicide

In Chapter 4, I presented definitions of killing and murder. To reiterate, *killing* means "to put to death, slay or deprive of life," whereas *murder* means "the unlawful killing of one person by another, especially with malice aforethought." *Suicide* is defined in the same dictionary as "an intentional taking of one's own life."[1] Under this definition, the act of suicide certainly involves both killing and the taking of a human life, but it is extremely difficult to justify the argument that it involves murder. Furthermore, suicide is not generally considered civilly or criminally unlawful in most states and countries because it involves the taking of one's own life, not the life of another; it is a decision made by people about their own lives based on their own thoughts and feelings.

Arguments Against the Morality of Suicide

The Irrationality of Suicide. One of the most common arguments against the morality of suicide is the one that suggests that *all* people who attempt or commit suicide are irrational or mentally or emotionally disturbed, a viewpoint characterized by the statement "No one in his right mind would commit suicide." This argument states further that because suicide is *never* a rational act, it can never be considered anything but immoral. The problem with this assumption is that it is too all-encompassing, as are the theories of psychological egoism (see Chapter 2) and hard determinism (see Chapter 5). How can a person who maintains this point of view prove that *all* people who attempt or commit suicide are irrational when they perform these acts? It would certainly be empirically true to say that *some* people have been driven by a mental imbalance to attempt or commit suicide; evidence for this exists both in suicide notes and in the explanations of those who have failed in their attempts. However, there is also some evidence to suggest that many suicide attempts and suicides are carefully thought out and rationally decided upon.

For example, Socrates, who was condemned to death by his peers, was urged to escape and had every opportunity to do so. Instead, he chose to drink hemlock, a poison. Before he committed this act, he rationally discussed his decision with his students and friends, a conversation that is dramatized in Plato's dialogue *Crito*. Anyone who reads this dialogue will be hard put to say that Socrates was irrational in any sense of the word. One may not agree with Socrates' arguments or with his final decision, but it would be difficult to question the soundness of his mind.

Parenthetically, it is interesting that if people commit suicide in order to save someone else's life— for example, falling on a grenade during wartime or stepping in front of a bullet to save someone else from being shot—they are never considered irrational, but if they decide that their own lives are not worth living, they are. In any case, the argument that suicide is an irrational act, though sometimes valid, cannot be used to declare all suicides as immoral because it cannot be proven to be true in all cases.

The Religious Argument. Various religions are opposed to suicide because they believe that only God has the authority to give and take away life and that human beings are only loaned their lives to live as well, morally, and religiously as they can. Religions are certainly entitled to this belief, and they may require that their members adhere to it by not committing suicide, but in no way can this view be imposed on nonmembers, religious or nonreligious, without some violation of the principles of Freedom and Justice. Furthermore, there are real problems with this view of God and life, whether one is religious or not, and they are carefully pointed out by Daniel Callahan in his book *Abortion: Law, Choice and Morality*:

> [This view] presupposes that God intervenes directly in natural and human affairs as the primary causative agent of life and death. Not only is this theologically dubious, it also has the effect of obscuring the necessity that human beings define terms, make decisions and take responsibility for the direct care of human life. Moreover, to say that God is the ultimate source of the "right to life," which is less objectionable theologically, still does not solve the problem of *how* human beings ought to respect that right or how they are to balance a conflict of rights.[2]

This theological problem applies to all aspects of the taking of human life, not just suicide; and therefore, it would be good to keep this problem in mind as we deal with the other issues in this area.

The Domino Argument. People who hold to the domino argument believe that if you allow human life to be taken in some instances you will open the door to its being taken in other instances and, eventually, in all instances. Like the religious argument, the domino argument also applies to areas of the taking of human life other than suicide. Furthermore, it is a good argument to be aware of when we are discussing any moral issue, because it forces us to be concerned about the effects of our moral decisions or laws. For example, if we argue that suicide is moral, then we should be concerned with where this will lead us: Will murder be made moral next? Or, if suicide is all right, then why not mercy killing and abortion?

Even though it is important for us to try to gauge the effects of our rules and actions, where there is no definite or conclusive proof that one thing necessarily leads to another, we cannot use this argument as the *sole* reason for not allowing an act or person to be declared moral or immoral. And, there is no conclusive proof that if suicide is allowed, murder will soon be allowed as well. As I have said, most states and countries have laws against capital punishment, abortion, mercy killing, and, of course, murder.

The Justice Argument. Probably the most effective case against the morality of suicide is made by those who argue that the people who survive a person who commits suicide pay an unjust penalty. A husband or wife may leave behind a despondent and destitute spouse and grief-stricken children; sons and daughters may leave guilt-ridden parents; society may be denied the important contributions that could have been made by the person who killed himself. This is an argument that must be carefully considered, for it involves the Principle of Justice, which, in the matter of suicide, conflicts with the Principle of Individual Freedom. This is a conflict that must be dealt with when deciding whether suicide is moral.

Argument for the Morality of Suicide

The basic argument in favor of suicide as a moral act involves a person's rights over his or her own body and life and is also concerned with the freedom of a person to make decisions affecting his or her own body and life. Life is important, but to whom? Mostly to the person to whom it belongs, of course. Because suicide is an individual decision made by a person about his or her own life, it cannot be described as taking a life against a person's will. Therefore it does not fully violate the Value of Life principle except in the sense that one ought to think carefully about the importance of life before one commits the act. When individuals decide that they would rather die than live, however, no one else, according to this argument, should have the right to tell them otherwise.

The Principle of Individual Freedom is important here, of course, and so is the Principle of Goodness. Suicide is such a private act that only the person who is considering it can know to any degree whether continuing to live would bring her more satisfaction, excellence, or harmony than ending her life. This argument stresses that individuals are unique and that only they know whether or not their lives are worth living; therefore, only they should be able to make decisions concerning whether they live or die. According to this argument, a decision to commit suicide may be considered rational provided that a person's reasoning faculties are not impaired by severe mental or emotional disturbances. Even when they are in perfect mental health, however, people who successfully commit suicide should not be blamed for being immoral, nor should people who attempt suicide be blamed or punished in any way.

The main criticism of this argument, other than those presented in the arguments against suicide we have already discussed, is that it tends to imply that people have absolute rights over their own bodies and lives. In other words, it suggests that the Principle of Individual Freedom has no limitations, an implication that can raise some difficult problems.

For example, if a man has a highly contagious disease and doesn't want to be placed in quarantine because it will limit his freedom over his own body and life, his freedom must nevertheless be restricted; otherwise, he could be responsible for the sickness and death of many other innocent people. That is, because of the priority of the first four basic principles, his freedom to do what he wants with his body and his life must be curtailed. In a similar manner, when a person's contemplated suicide will definitely affect the lives and welfare of others (for example, his dependents), then questions must at least be raised concerning the possible limits of the person's freedom over his own body and life.

Generally speaking, neither the arguments for nor the arguments against the morality of suicide advocate the taking of one's own life, and most people on either side would probably urge the use of all possible means to prevent people from killing themselves. The side supporting the morality of suicide, however, would probably allow for greater freedom for individual decision making. For example, those who feel suicide is always immoral might advocate the use of physical and legal restraints of people who are known to be suicidal, whereas people who believe that suicide can be a moral act will try to prevent people from committing suicide but will not use force in attempting to deny them the freedom to make their own rational decisions.

◆

Cases for Study and Discussion

Read the following cases and decide to what extent suicide is moral or immoral in each. Use any of the five basic principles you feel are involved and any other principles or guides that you feel to be relevant to the cases.

CASE ◆ 1

In Vietnam, four GIs are sitting in a bar when a hand grenade is tossed through the window. Joe, twenty-two, decides on the spur of the moment to give up his own life to save the lives of his buddies. He falls on the grenade and is killed. At the time of his death, he is married and has a two-year-old daughter; he also has two brothers, and his parents are living.

CASE ◆ 2

William, sixty, has had inoperable cancer for several months, and it is now in the terminal stages. Unwilling to go to a hospital or a hospice, he lives unhappily at home. Everything about living has lost its savor: he no longer enjoys eating, drinking, smoking, or any of his other former pleasures. He has made a will and taken care of all unfinished business. Finally he confronts his wife and two teenage children with his wish to commit suicide—to die with dignity, as he expresses it, rather than linger on and become increasingly ill. His wife and children don't like the idea, but they agree with him that the choice is his. He shoots himself and dies.

CASE ◆ 3

Joan, eighteen, has lived in one foster home after another since she was born. She has been in and out of mental institutions, having been treated for extreme depression. She has used drugs but is not using them now. Having twice become pregnant, she has had two abortions. She feels she has no real friends, she has no parents to relate to, and she can't concentrate on school or work. Although she has talked to several psychiatrists and psychologists, she does not feel any better about herself or her life. She finally decides, calmly, that she is tired of living, takes an overdose of barbiturates without leaving a suicide note or telling anybody what she is going to do, and dies.

◆

Defense of the Innocent (the Self Included)

Argument Against Killing in Defense of the Innocent

There is really only one argument against killing in defense of the innocent, and that is based on the assumption—held by the adherents of a few ethical systems (Pacifists, Jainists, Kantian Duty Ethicists)—that the taking of human life is always wrong. This position is the most consistent one possible in terms of the Value of Life principle because it respects human life at all costs. According to this argument, all human life is to be revered and no one may ever be killed for any reason, even if one's life is threatened by another. In such a case, one who is being threatened may try everything short of violence or killing to prevent being killed, but he or she may not kill another, even in self-defense or in defense of other innocent people.

Not killing any humans is, of course, an admirable ideal, and it is one to which most people are able to adhere throughout their lives. The main criticism of this point of view is that it does not take into consideration all the complexities of human existence, especially the fact that some humans—fortunately a relatively small number—do not respect the lives of others. If all humans would respect human life completely, then maybe everyone could completely adhere to the ideal of not killing other humans under any circumstances. This ideal is certainly put forth in Christianity in Jesus' teachings "Love thy enemies" and "Turn the other cheek." However, very few Christians or other human beings are willing to adhere to such an ideal; they simply do not feel that it is good, fair, or just for innocent people to lose their lives to killers who violate this ideal, and who often cannot be stopped in any other way than by being killed themselves.

Argument for Killing in Defense of the Innocent

The argument for killing in defense of the innocent generally rests on two assumptions: First, even though the Value of Life principle advocates a reverence for all human life, people have a right and, indeed, a moral obligation to protect any innocent lives, their own included, when it becomes clear that another human being no longer recognizes the value of other people's lives. Second, the good of defending the innocent far outweighs the bad of killing a person who is threatening to kill or who actually kills innocent people. The essence of this argument is that by threatening to kill or by killing others, killers in a sense forfeit their rights to have their lives considered as valuable, especially when their acts cannot be stopped unless they themselves are killed. This argument qualifies the Value of Life principle by stating that one should never kill other humans *except* when defending innocent people, including oneself.

The main criticism of this argument is that violence tends to breed more violence, and that once the killing of humans is allowed, even in defense of the innocent, no one knows where the violence will end (the domino argument again). The religious argument also applies here, adding the criticism that only God can create or take away life, and that, in His infinite wisdom, He will duly punish the killer in some way. Killing, in any case, is not the right of other humans under any circumstances. The religious argument is open to the same criticism presented in the discussion of suicide.

◆

Cases for Study and Discussion

C A S E ♦ 1

Hearing a noise at the back of his house one afternoon, Ed picks up his loaded automatic pistol from a drawer in his desk and goes to investigate. He surprises an eighteen-year-old man in the act of going through his dresser drawers. The man has no weapons in his hands or in view. Ed asks what he is doing there, and the young man runs for the back door. Ed points the gun at his retreating back, fires three shots, and kills him. Is Ed morally justified in killing the young man?

C A S E ♦ 2

Mary, twenty-two, returns home fairly late one evening from a party, and as she enters her bedroom, a man jumps at her from behind the door, pins her down with one arm, and covers her mouth with the other. He wrestles her to her bed, and as she attempts to scream, he hits her several times in the face and on other parts of her body. She somehow manages to push him off the bed and onto the floor, and while he is recovering his equilibrium, she gets a loaded pistol out of the bedside table drawer. As the man stands up again, ready to lunge at Mary, she fires several shots and kills him. Is Mary's action justifiable?

C A S E ♦ 3

The scene is a crowded outdoor shopping mall that has a clock tower at its center. Rifle shots ring out from the tower and several people, including children, drop to the ground—three are seriously injured and three are killed. Police try for several hours to get the sniper to throw down his weapon and come out, but he continues to fire his rifle into store windows, into a nearby parking lot, and into a nearby street. One of the officers, a sharpshooter with a high-powered rifle, manages to maneuver himself into a position where he can get a perfect shot, but only at the sniper's head. He does so, killing the sniper instantly. Was the officer justified in killing the sniper?

War

Arguments Against the Morality of War

The Standard College Dictionary defines *war* as "an armed conflict openly carried on between nations or states, or between different parties in the same state." The dictionary could have added, "and in which people, many of them completely innocent, are usually violently killed." Because of the wholesale killing that almost inevitably accompanies any type of war except a so-called *cold* one, war is a powerful threat to the Value of Life principle and should be avoided by every human effort possible. The arguments against war have increased during the twentieth century because of our advanced military technology, especially the nuclear capability of various nations, which could lead to world destruction. The chances of a world war occurring seem to have diminished, and at least the larger nations have begun to see the futility of a nuclear war that would destroy everything and everybody. However, small wars would seem to have increased in various parts of the world, and even though they do not involve nuclear weaponry, their destructiveness to life and the environment in each respective location is still unacceptable to peace-loving people and nations. Further, such small wars inevitably attract involvement from larger nations with nuclear capability, which makes any war a danger to world peace.

The main argument against the morality of war is that it is a direct and massive violation of the Value of Life principle. War doesn't just involve the killing of one human being by another; rather, it involves a mass killing of up to millions, depending on the scale of the war. Furthermore, especially because of modern military techniques, war necessitates the useless killing of a great number of innocent noncombatants, many of them children. Those who take an antiwar stance maintain that, in the long run, so little is gained by war and yet so much is lost in terms of human life and human possessions that it has to be considered an immoral act—in fact, the most immoral act human beings can perform.

This point of view was widely held during the Vietnam War era, when there was a tremendous rise in the number of conscientious objectors and outspoken pacifists. Pacifists have argued that war in all its aspects should be banned worldwide and that violence and aggression should never be met with similar force but, rather, with nonviolence and nonaggression. They would argue, for example, that every peaceful effort must be exerted to avert war, but that even if a country is invaded, its citizens should try to pacify their violent invaders rather than resort to violence. This extreme form of the antiwar argument is held by a minority of the world's peoples, even though it has grown in popularity because of the many destructive wars that have occurred since 1900. Many more people hold a more moderate view—a general policy of nonaggression toward other people or countries.

Arguments for the Morality of War

Even though I believe few people advocate war openly as a general solution to human problems, there are some traditional arguments in favor of war that should be examined.

War as the Best Controller of Overpopulation. War as the best controller of over-population is based on the fact that the population of the world is increasing at too rapid a rate and that therefore war, which effectively decreases the population, helps to solve this problem very efficiently. The argument is, of course, morally weak because alternate solutions are available, especially in our scientifically and technologically oriented society. In addition, one could argue effectively that the quality of population control achieved by war is very poor because it is the youth, the best hope of all societies, that usually suffers the greatest casualty rate. In any case, many countries have found alternate methods for reducing their populations without resorting to the destruction and decimation of war.

War as the Mother of Invention. The argument has been advanced that war is the only way in which societies can develop and experiment with advanced technology. There is no doubt that many technological advances that were developed for military purposes have also been used in a peaceful way. Some of these advances are directly dependent on war, for example, the development of advanced surgical techniques, prosthetic devices, and plastic surgery techniques that occurred during the Korean War. These certainly could have been developed without war, but perhaps it would have taken much longer to do so. Obviously, one has to consider the price for such "invention." Furthermore, it is certainly true that technological development can occur without war (for example, the space development program) even though peacetime development may be slower or more expensive.

War as a Boon to Economic Gain and National Unity. Many argue that nothing unifies a people more than to work together to achieve a national goal, such as winning a war. Furthermore, it is argued, such unification, which often involves the production of war machines and matériel, creates an upsurge in economic well-being and prosperity. This argument became particularly popular during and after World War II, especially in the United States. Nothing had ever unified the nation to the extent that the "war effort" did, and, despite wartime shortages, the nation achieved an economic prosperity that continued even after the war was over. The country mass-produced planes, tanks, weapons, and other matériel on a greater scale than ever before, and after the war, factories produced great numbers of peacetime goods—cars, homes, appliances—which the entire population desired after four years of deprivation. After two more wars, however, the divisive aspects of war became obvious, and people began to recognize that the cost of achieving economic prosperity through war was too high. Since World War II, countries have been able to unify and to achieve economic well-being without wartime production, and this fact encourages most people to seek alternative means to attain these national goals.

War as a "Necessary Evil"—The Just War Argument. Probably the most morally significant argument for war is that although war is generally immoral, there is such a thing as a morally just war under certain conditions. One example of such an argument can be found in Roman Catholic teachings. Before discussing this argument, I would like to stress that it applied essentially to nonnuclear warfare; also, it would be incorrect to assume that this is the position presently held by the Roman Catholic church. With these disclaimers in mind, the following conditions might be considered to describe a morally just war:

> . . . that it shall be undertaken by the lawful authority; that it shall be undertaken for the vindication of an undoubted and proportionate right that has certainly been infringed; that it shall be a last resort, all peaceful means of settlement having been tried in vain; that the good to be achieved shall outweigh the evils that war will involve; that there shall be a reasonable hope of victory for justice (a war undertaken in face of certain failure is, however heroic, irrational, and therefore indefensible); there must be a right intention, that is, to right the wrong and not simply to maintain national prestige and influence or to enlarge territory (territory is not a just cause of war), nor may war be waged as part of a scheme for converting the heathen to Christianity; and the methods of warfare must be legitimate, i.e., in accordance with international agreements, with our nature as rational beings and with the moral teachings of Christianity.[3]

The Catholic Encyclopedia, from which this was taken, goes on to remark that there may be vagueness and uncertainty concerning any case of war being considered, and of course there is a great deal of vagueness and ambiguity in the above quotation itself. It does, however, give some guidelines that have a moral basis: that the reason for war must be serious enough to outweigh its evils; that it cannot be carried on for prestige, for territory, or to increase the influence of the nation waging it; that all peaceful means of settlement must have been exhausted; and that a nation's methods, once war is declared, must be legitimate. Even such justifications, however, would seem to apply only to limited, nonnuclear wars, because there is probably no political situation important enough to justify the possibility of setting off World War III and risking the total destruction of the human race and the world.

The Indefensibility of Nuclear War. Even the arguments in support of a just war pale when one stops to consider the total devastation possible in a nuclear war. This carries over to any defense of even limited wars because there would always be a possibility that one of these could set off a large-scale nuclear holocaust. Given the tendency toward violence of the human species in general (*Homo sapiens* is the only species that destroys itself), it is probably too much to hope for that wars of all kinds could be totally eliminated, although every effort should be made to do so now and in the future. Barring the success of such an effort, however, any small wars should be contained and not allowed to mushroom into the use of nuclear weapons, especially by those countries that have large arsenals of such weapons. None of the arguments in support of war, including the just war argument, can morally justify a nuclear holocaust.

◆

Cases for Study and Discussion

C A S E ◆ 1

A small nation located on a seacoast has both the commercial ports and the natural resources that a larger neighboring inland nation needs. The larger nation negotiates for use of the ports and purchase of the resources, and an agreement is reached between the two nations that lasts for several years. Eventually, however, a new government that has come to power in the larger nation decides that it should not have to pay for natural resources so close to its own borders and that it should have complete control of the seaports it now uses. After a breakdown of new negotiations, the larger nation invades its smaller neighbor, and the smaller nation aggressively defends itself. Is the larger nation justified in starting a war, and is the smaller nation justified in defending itself?

C A S E ◆ 2

In the 1940s, a large nation on the European continent consistently states its intention to become the dominant world power. Using a tremendously effective army, navy, and air force, all magnificently equipped with the latest war machines and weapons, this nation attacks several smaller countries. Its methods of attacking its victims are ruthless, and even after an invaded nation has been subdued, the torture and mass killings continue. The aggressor nation seems to be practicing a planned program of genocide in every country it attacks, sparing only healthy, young, and strong Caucasian men and women. Other large nations not on the continent form an alliance and negotiate with the aggressor nation in an attempt to get it to stop its ruthless invasions, but to no avail. Finally, this alliance declares war on the aggressor nation and enters into a nonnuclear war against it. Is the aggressor nation justified in its actions? Is the alliance justified in declaring war?

C A S E ♦ 3

A small Far Eastern country that is rich in natural resources has suffered an ideological split. One-half of the populace advocates communism as a form of government, while the other half advocates a democratic form. Two larger powers outside the country develop an interest in the struggle: Country A supports the communist faction, while country B supports the democratic faction. Both of the larger countries have vested interests in the Far Eastern country in the form of mines, factories, land, and financial investments. When the two factions in the small country declare war on each other over their differing ideologies in a struggle for control over the entire land, the two larger countries begin supporting their respective sides by sending money, arms, supplies, and military advisers. As the democratic faction weakens and begins to lose the war, country B steps up its support by sending in elements of its own army, navy, and air force, committing itself to helping the democratic side by any means other than nuclear warfare. To what extent are the two factions in the Far Eastern country justified in entering into warfare against each other, and to what extent are the larger powers justified in supporting their respective sides with actual military aid?

♦——

Capital Punishment

A Definition

As most dictionaries define it, *capital punishment* means "the infliction of death for certain crimes." These crimes are often called "capital crimes," and depending on the society in question, they have varied from stealing to murder. For the most part, especially in the United States, capital punishment is usually applied for murder—especially premeditated murder—or kidnapping with intent to do bodily harm or kill, and sometimes for instances of treason that endanger the lives of the people living in a country.

Theories of Punishment

It would behoove readers to review Chapter 6 on reward and punishment, because there are three major theories as to when and why punishment should be meted out. As a quick reiteration, however, the theories are as follows.

Retributive (Deserts Theory). Punishment should be given only when it is *deserved* and only to the extent it is deserved. It should have no other goal than punishing people who deserve the punishment *because of* some immoral act that they have done, and the punishment should fit the crime.

Utilitarian (Results Theory). Punishment should always have as its aim the good of society. If punishment will bring about good consequences for people, then it should be given, but if it won't, then it shouldn't. It should always be *in order that* some good can be done, for example, the deterrence of future crime, the protection of society, or the rehabilitation of the criminal.

Restitution (Compensation Theory). Justice is served only if the victims of a crime or offense are given restitution or compensation for the harm done to them.

Capital punishment could conceivably be acceptable in all of the preceding theories at least in some cases but not in others. For example, it would certainly fit the retributive theory but only if the person to be punished truly deserved the punishment. Utilitarians might also approve of such punishment but only if the greatest good consequences would come about because of it. If the only compensation for murder, for example, was considered by restitutionists to be the execution of the murderer to satisfy and compensate the victim, then capital punishment might be acceptable by them too. However, most restitutionists would probably consider that such punishment would actually thwart proper compensation of the victim because the criminal or offender would no longer be alive to work for the victim's benefit, for example.

Arguments Against the Morality of Capital Punishment

Violation of the Value of Life Principle. Many argue against capital punishment on the grounds that it is a direct violation of the Value of Life principle. They maintain that capital punishment amounts to murder—social murder—directed by society against one of its members. The argument further says that if taking human life is wrong in other instances, then it is also wrong in this instance. True, the argument continues, capital punishment can function as a form of societal revenge, but in a civilized society, revenge should not be a sufficient motive for taking a human life.

Effect on the Criminal's Victims or on Society. Because killing a criminal will not bring back his or her victims or in any way recompense the survivors of the victims, there is really no purpose in taking the criminal's life except to satisfy the society's need for revenge or the victims' need for satisfaction. This, according to the opponents of capital punishment, is not a civilized emotion. They feel that capital punishment encourages violence, acts of revenge, and murder in society at large because it leads to the rationale that if society can kill its members, then individuals can also take revenge into their own hands.

Ineffectiveness as a Deterrent. One of the most common arguments for capital punishment, as we shall see, is that it deters crimes throughout the society; its opponents, however, argue that there is no conclusive evidence to support this claim. They point to history in support of their argument, stating that when capital punishment was used against thieves in England, pickpockets were operating throughout the crowds of watchers who gathered to see a thief hanged. They also question why, if this punishment works so well as a deterrent, executions by hangings and firing squads and in gas chambers are not shown on television or performed in the streets instead of being accomplished in the relative privacy of our prisons. They argue further that killings even occur in prison, right outside the execution chamber. Therefore, they state, capital punishment does not effectively act as a deterrent.

Inequality of Capital Punishment. Sometimes people accused of capital crimes are convicted mainly on circumstantial evidence, and it is therefore quite possible to execute an innocent person. If even one innocent person is executed, this argument continues, then capital punishment is a moral wrong. Furthermore, because rich people who are charged with capital crimes can afford better attorneys, the people most often convicted of capital crimes are poor people, often members of minority races—for example, African Americans, Hispanics, Native Americans. This means that punishment by killing may be applied unequally to people who commit similar crimes.

Denial of the Chance for Rehabilitation. The denial of the chance for rehabilitation argument states that nothing is accomplished by capital punishment except the compounding of the badness already caused by the original crime: Instead of one human life being taken, capital punishment causes two to be taken. Wouldn't it be more valuable, opponents of capital punishment ask, for society to eliminate killing by reforming killers through education and other methods of rehabilitation? They argue further that most killers have been shaped by a corrupt society or a poor early environment (child-abusing parents, for example), and that if we could only reeducate them they could become useful members of society.

Arguments for Capital Punishment

The Effective Deterrent Argument. People who argue for capital punishment strongly disagree with those who state that it is not an effective deterrent. They argue, with irrefutable logic, that capital punishment deters the killer from killing again by terminating his life. They admit that the evidence for general deterrence may not be conclusive, but they strongly believe that many people are prevented from killing, or at least think twice about it, when they know that they might have to face the death penalty for their crime. According to capital punishment's supporters, the reason it isn't always an effective deterrent is that it isn't used enough. Many of its supporters are also in favor of making everyone watch the execution of legally convicted killers so that deterrence would be more effectively reinforced.

The Economic Argument. There is no proof that murderers can be successfully rehabilitated, and sentences of life imprisonment seldom really mean life because many murderers are released from prison after seven or ten years. Some have been released and have killed again. With these facts in mind, supporters of capital punishment feel that it is much too costly for innocent taxpayers to support killers in prison for long sentences or for life. Why, they ask, should innocent people pay for the continued support of criminals who have proved themselves unfit to live in society? The crimes they have committed are so terrible that there is no reason why they should be allowed to live while innocent people pay for their upkeep.

One criticism of this argument is that it costs more to give a criminal capital punishment than it does to give him or her life imprisonment without parole because of all the appeals and court action often gone through for a criminal who has been sentenced to death. The main criticism of this argument, however, holds that when human life, even reprehensible human life, is at stake, a civilized society and humanity should not be concerned with monetary costs. Even though it costs a great deal to keep criminals in prison, and even more when rehabilitation programs are implemented, critics of the economic argument believe that it is more moral to try to make a human life useful than to terminate it even though it is cheaper to execute prisoners than to rehabilitate them. Isn't it extremely dehumanizing, they ask, to argue that the maintenance and possible rehabilitation of human life is less important than mere financial cost? This issue will surface again when we discuss the cost of maintaining the lives of innocent people who are in terminal stages of illness.

The Effect on Society's Laws. By having the option of applying the death penalty, some argue, we give strong sanction to the entire criminal law enforcement system—we "put teeth" into that system. For example, suppose a criminal is convicted of armed robbery, serves a term in prison, and then is released. The very existence of capital punishment reminds this person that if he or she returns to armed robbery and later kills someone while committing this second crime, the death penalty may be applied.

The sanction argument suggests that criminals will be deterred from escalating the nature of their crimes because of the death penalty threat, and that this in turn gives the entire criminal justice system strength. The threat of the death penalty may even encourage criminals to leave the "armed" out of armed robbery, thus minimizing the chance that an innocent person will be killed.

The main criticism of this argument is that there are other, more humane ways of giving a system of law enforcement sanction. Highly effective legal systems have existed without capital punishment (England's, for example), and there is no conclusive evidence that the existence of capital punishment has any deterrent effect on the thieves, embezzlers, rapists, and other criminals to whom the death penalty cannot usually be applied. Effective prosecution and just punishment would seem to be as effective in preventing crime as maintaining the death penalty as a part of the system.

The Forfeiture of Killers' Rights. Another argument for capital punishment in answer to the violation of the value of life argument is that killers, having violated both morality and the law, have forfeited their right to be treated ethically: Just as you would kill a rabid dog or a wild animal who threatened the lives of innocent members of society, you should punish these killers. Some argue further that capital punishment is merely another form of self-defense, one that applies to the entire society. Just as individual people have the right to protect themselves against killers who threaten their lives, so society has the right to protect itself against anyone who has killed once by ensuring that he or she does not kill again. Prison, they argue, is not an adequate means of ensuring this because killers can be paroled or can escape; therefore, the argument continues, capital punishment is moral.

It would certainly seem to be the case that people who have killed should forfeit some of their rights. The question is whether this forfeiture should include their very lives. Certainly killers have proved themselves dangerous enough to forfeit their right to live freely among other innocent people, but does this mean that they must be killed? Furthermore, there are some cases in which killers have been paroled and have lived normal lives from that time on, even contributing something positive to society in the process. There are even cases in which criminals have contributed something good to society while in prison.

The Uselessness of Rehabilitation Argument. In answer to the argument against capital punishment based on the inability to rehabilitate those who have been executed is the argument that rehabilitation, especially in the case of murderers, is useless and often impossible. How can serial or mutilating killers be rehabilitated? In the first place, no one can know for sure whether someone is rehabilitated. Psychology and sociology are inexact sciences when it comes to this issue. Second, how is it possible to rehabilitate a Charles Manson, Ted Bundy, or Jeffrey Dahmer? These heinous killers are no better than societal "mad dogs" and should be executed, according to proponents of capital punishment.

219

Revenge. A final, classic argument for capital punishment is based on the idea of revenge, or the "eye for an eye" concept of justice. This argument says that if people kill, they must forfeit their lives in order to "balance the scales." This is an ancient concept, dating back at least to the Old Testament times, and it has often been the basis for long-lasting feuds and vendettas between families, gangs, tribes, or other groups. For example, if the son of a chief of tribe A is killed by a member of tribe B, then the son of the chief of tribe B must be killed and so on.

This concept has been pretty much (although not completely) discarded in more civilized societies because it leads to continuing killing and bloodshed—an unnecessary loss of many lives. Another criticism is that this concept conflicts with the moral and legal view that two wrongs don't make a right. Most societies now feel that people who kill can be justly punished without being executed. Besides, as stated earlier, some convicted killers have in fact made positive contributions to society, either while in prison or on parole.

◆

Cases for Study and Discussion

CASE ◆ 1

As an intellectual game, two male college students, ages eighteen and nineteen, attempt to commit the "perfect crime" by kidnapping a young boy and demanding ransom from his parents. They receive the ransom money but kill the boy anyway. Later, they are caught, tried, and convicted of murder and kidnapping with intent to do bodily harm. Their defense attorney, a brilliant lawyer, successfully argues against the death penalty and both men are sent to prison for life. After about five years one of the men is killed in a fight, but the other completes his college education while still in prison and teaches other convicts English. He also volunteers for medical experiments, allowing himself to be injected with malaria germs in order to test new drugs. A model prisoner, he causes no trouble throughout his entire prison term. After about thirty years, he is paroled, whereupon he goes to a different country and continues to teach English. Two years later he dies of natural causes. Should this man have been given capital punishment or not?

CASE ◆ 2

A young man of twenty is guilty of killing both his grandparents and his mother. He is judged to be legally insane and is sent to a mental hospital for the criminally insane. After three years, he is judged to be cured of his mental illness and is released as sane. Six months later, however, he goes berserk and kills six young people in the mountain area where he now lives. What treatment or punishment should he receive?

CASE ◆ 3

A twenty-seven-year-old man who has been a criminal most of his life is charged with attacking several young couples in a deserted area. Specifically, he is charged with beating the men and then raping the women after having transported them to a different area (thus technically kidnapping them). The man is convicted mainly on circumstantial evidence and continually denies that he is guilty. Although he is given the death penalty, he manages to stave off execution for ten years. While in prison he studies psychology and law and learns a great deal about both. He analyzes how and why he turned to crime and writes and publishes several books about his life. He does not express remorse for his criminal activity, yet he continues to deny that he is guilty of the last crime with which he was charged. After ten years, he exhausts all his appeals and again is up for execution in the gas chamber. Should he be given the death penalty?

CASE ◆ 4

A man of thirty was discovered to have enticed boys and men to his apartment to have sex with them. In fifteen of these encounters, he killed them, had sex with their corpses, ate their flesh, and dismembered their bodies, keeping some body parts in the freezer and disposing of others in a vat of acid. When caught, he admitted to all of these actions. Though obviously bizarre and perverted, he was nevertheless considered legally sane—that is, as knowing right from wrong. What should be done with such a person? Explain in detail, giving reasons for your answer. Should he be executed? Why or why not?

Chapter Summary

I. Applying the five basic moral principles to the taking of human life
   A. It is questionable whether suicide, which is defined as "an intentional taking of one's life," is moral or immoral.
      1. There are several arguments against the morality of suicide.
         (a) Some argue that suicide is always irrational; there is evidence, however, that although it is an irrational act in some cases, in others it is not.

      (b) The religious argument states that only God can create or end life.
- (1) This applies only to members of a specific religion that states this as its belief.
- (2) It is theologically questionable.
- (3) It removes human responsibility in protecting, preserving, or ending life.

      (c) The domino argument states that if suicide is allowed, then other forms of murder will follow.
- (1) This argument is worth consideration.
- (2) There is, however, no conclusive evidence to support it.

      (d) The justice argument questions whether suicide is fair to survivors of the victim.

  2. There are also arguments for the morality of suicide.
- (a) A person has rights over his or her own body and life.
- (b) A person should have the freedom to make decisions concerning his or her own body and life.
- (c) Individual human beings are solely responsible for deciding whether their own lives are worth living.
- (d) The main criticism of this argument is that no one has absolute rights over his or her own body or life.

B. It is questionable whether killing someone in defense of the innocent (one's self included) is moral or immoral.

  1. There is one main argument against the morality of such an act.
- (a) The taking of human life is always wrong.
- (b) The main criticism of this argument is that it doesn't recognize the complexities of human existence or that some humans are capable of violating all five basic principles.

  2. There are arguments for the morality of killing in defense of the innocent.
- (a) People have rights and obligations to protect innocent lives (their own included).
- (b) The good of defending the innocent far outweighs the bad of killing a murderer of innocent people.
- (c) The main criticism of these arguments is that violence breeds violence (the domino argument again).

C. It is questionable if war is moral or immoral.

  1. There are arguments against the morality of war.
- (a) It is a direct and massive violation of Value of Life principle, especially when nuclear weapons are used.
- (b) It causes a great deal of useless killing, especially of innocent noncombatants.
- (c) The destruction caused by war far outweighs the gain.

   (d) The solution is to deal with aggression and violence through peaceful means—to pacify one's enemy through nonviolence.

  2. There are arguments for the morality of war.

   (a) War is the best controller of overpopulation.

   (b) It is the "mother of invention."

   (c) It is a great unifying factor and economic boon for individual nations.

   (d) War is sometimes a "necessary evil"—the morally just war does exist.

    (1) Early Catholic doctrine describes the possibility of just wars.

    (2) War is a more encompassing form of defense of the innocent.

  3. Given the devastation possible in a nuclear war, most arguments, including the just war argument, cannot support a nuclear holocaust: Such a war is indefensible.

 D. It is questionable whether capital punishment is moral or immoral.

  1. Capital punishment is defined as punishment, usually by death, for certain "capital crimes" such as murder, kidnapping, rape, or torture.

  2. Theories of punishment are as follows.

   (a) Retributive or Deserts Theory: Punishment should be given only when it is deserved and to the extent it is deserved.

   (b) Utilitarian or Results Theory: Punishment is justified only if it will bring about good consequences for everyone.

   (c) Restitution or Compensation Theory: Justice is served only if the victim of a crime or offense is given restitution or compensation for the harm done to him or her.

   (d) Capital punishment could conceivably be acceptable in all of the preceding theories in some cases but not in others.

  3. There are arguments against the morality of capital punishment.

   (a) It is a direct violation of the Value of Life principle—a "murder" planned and executed by society.

   (b) It doesn't bring back the killer's dead victims or in any way, other than vengeance, recompense the survivors of the victim.

   (c) There is no conclusive proof that it really acts as a deterrent, especially when executions are performed in relative privacy.

   (d) There is a certain inequality of justice inherent in capital punishment: first, because it is possible to wrongly execute an innocent person; and second, because rich people who can afford good lawyers are less frequently subject to capital punishment than are the poor and members of minority races.

(e) Capital punishment eliminates any possibility for rehabilitation and adds the cost of the killer's life to that of his or her victim.

4. There are arguments for the morality of capital punishment.

   (a) It is obviously a deterrent for the killer, who is put to death, but it also deters others who are contemplating murder.

   (b) It is less costly than imprisonment (critics question this), and there is no reason to make innocent, hard-working taxpayers pay for a guilty killer.

   (c) It puts real teeth into laws, giving them force and sanction and strongly encouraging everyone to obey them.

   (d) A person who has killed has forfeited his or her right to be treated ethically; therefore, taking such a person's life is not immoral.

   (e) Rehabilitation is often infeasible if not impossible, especially when dealing with serial and mutilitating killers.

   (f) It is only fair that killers pay with their own lives for having taken the lives of others.

Exercises for Review

1. What does it mean for something to be "logically and empirically prior" to something else?

2. Describe the type of approach to moral problems found in Humanitarian Ethics.

3. What are your general views on suicide, and why? Do you agree or disagree with the conclusions of the author in Appendix 1? Why?

4. What are your general views on taking a human life in defense of the innocent (the self included)? Be specific in explaining how and why your views agree or disagree with the author's as expressed in Appendix 1.

5. Do you consider war moral or immoral? Why? (If you think it is always immoral, state your reasons; if you think it may be moral sometimes or under certain conditions, describe the conditions and give reasons that could morally justify war.)

6. Is a nuclear war ever justifiable?

7. Do you think that capital punishment is morally justified? Why or why not? If you believe it is *sometimes* justified, when and when not?

8. Analyze and critically evaluate the author's alternatives, cited in Appendix 1, for dealing with people who have killed other people. Be specific in your criticisms and/or support of these alternatives.

9. What possible alternatives to capital punishment would you put forth for dealing with convicted killers?

Notes

1. William Morris, ed., *The American Heritage Dictionary of the English Language* (Boston: Houghton Mifflin, 1975), 1287.

2. Daniel Callahan, *Abortion: Law, Choice and Morality* (New York: Macmillan, 1970), 417–18. See also Chapter 9.

3. John P. O'Connell, ed., *The Catholic Encyclopedia*, Holy Bible (Chicago: The Catholic Press, 1954), 278–79.

Supplementary Reading

Suicide

Alvarez, A. *The Savage God: A Study of Suicide*. New York: Random House, 1972.

Battin, M. Pabst. *Ethical Issues in Suicide*. Englewood Cliffs, NJ: Prentice-Hall, 1982.

Battin, M. Pabst, and David J. Mayo, eds. *Suicide: The Philosophical Issues*. New York: St. Martin's, 1980.

Battin, Margaret P., and Ronald Maris. *Suicide and Ethics: A Special Issue of Suicide and Life Threatening Behavior*. New York: Human Science Press, 1984.

Brody, Baruch, ed. *Suicide and Euthanasia*. Norwell, Mass.: Kluwer Academic Publications, 1989.

Choron, Jacques. *Suicide*. New York: The Free Press, 1951.

DeSpelder, Lynne A., and Albert L. Strickland. *The Last Dance*, 2nd ed. Palo Alto, Calif.: Mayfield, 1987. Chapter 12.

Donnelly, John, ed. *Suicide: Right or Wrong*. Buffalo, N.Y.: Prometheus Books, 1989.

Durkheim, E. *Suicide*. New York: The Free Press, 1951.

Farberow, Norman L., and Edwin S. Schneidman. *Clues to Suicide*. New York: McGraw-Hill, 1959.

Opposing Viewpoints Series. *Suicide: Opposing Viewpoints*. San Diego, Calif.: Greenhaven, 1992.

Szasz, Thomas S. "The Ethics of Suicide." *The Antioch Review* (Spring 1971): 7–17.

War

Arendt, Hannah. *On Violence*. New York: Harcourt Brace Jovanovich, 1969.

Beck, Robert N., and John B. Orr. *Ethical Choice: A Case Study Approach*. New York: The Free Press, 1970. (See Part II, Section 8.)

Holmes, Arthur F., ed. *War and Christian Ethics: Classic Readings on the Morality of War*. Grand Rapids, Mich.: Baker Books, 1991.

O'Brien, William V. *War and/or Survival*. Garden City, N.Y.: Doubleday, 1969.

O'Connell, John P., ed. *The Catholic Encyclopedia*, Holy Bible. Chicago: The Catholic Press, 1954.

Ramsey, Paul. *The Just War: Force and Political Responsibility*. New York: Charles Scribner's Sons, 1968.

Somerville, John. "Democracy and the Problem of War." In *Moral Problems in Contemporary Society*, ed. Paul Kurtz. Englewood Cliffs, N.J.: Prentice-Hall, 1969.

Taylor, Telford. *Nuremberg and Vietnam: An American Tragedy*. Chicago: Quadrangle Books, 1970.

Wasserstrom, Richard A. *War and Morality*. Belmont, Calif.: Wadsworth, 1970.

Capital Punishment

Beck, Robert N., and John B. Orr. *Ethical Choice: A Case Study Approach*. New York: The Free Press, 1970. (See Part II, Section 7.)

Bedau, Hugo, ed. *The Death Penalty in America*, 3rd ed. New York: Oxford University Press, 1982.

Ewing, Alfred C. *The Morality of Punishment*. London: Routledge and Kegan Paul, 1929.

Gray, Ian, and Moira Stanley. *Punishment in Search of a Crime: Americans Speak Out Against the Death Sentence*. New York: Avon Books, 1989.

Guernsey, JoAnn B. *Capital Punishment*. Minneapolis: Lerner Publications, 1991.

Hart, H. L. A. *Punishment and Responsibility*. New York: Oxford University Press, 1968.

Hospers, John. *Human Conduct*, 2nd ed. New York: Harcourt Brace Jovanovich, 1982.

MacLagan, W. G. "Punishment and Retribution." *Philosophy* 14 (1939): 281–98.

Menninger, Karl. "The Crime of Punishment." In *Taking Sides*, ed. Stephen Satris. Guilford, Conn.: Dushkin Publishing Group, 1988.

Murphy, Jeffrie G., ed. *Punishment and Rehabilitation*, 2nd ed. Belmont, Calif.: Wadsworth, 1985.

Vanden Haag, Ernest, and John P. Conrad. *The Death Penalty: A Debate*. New York: Plenum, 1983.

Williams, Glanville. *The Sanctity of Life and the Criminal Law*. New York: Knopf, 1957.

C H A P T E R

9

Allowing Someone to Die, Mercy Death, and Mercy Killing

◆───

Objectives

After you have read this chapter you should be able to

1. Define and make distinctions among the following terms: *euthanasia, allowing someone to die, mercy death, mercy killing, ordinary* and *extraordinary means* for keeping people alive, *persistent vegetative state* (PVS), and *brain death.*

2. Explain why allowing someone to die has become an issue in the light of advanced medical technology and discuss a dying person's right to refuse treatment, "living wills," natural death declarations, and durable powers of attorney for health care.

3. Critically analyze and evaluate the moral aspects of allowing someone to die, mercy death, and mercy killing in light of the hospice approach to care for the dying.

4. Evaluate the question "Is allowing someone to die morally justified?"
5. Evaluate the question "Is mercy death morally justified?"
6. Evaluate the question "Is mercy killing morally justified?"

◆
Definition of Terms

The word *euthanasia* comes from the Greek and originally meant "a good or happy death." However, it has also been interpreted, especially in the twentieth century, to mean "mercy killing," legally a form of murder in most countries of the world. Dr. Richard Lamerton, former director of St. Joseph's Hospice Home Care Service in London, has stated that in using the term "euthanasia" to stand for both mercy killing and allowing someone to die, we seriously blur a very necessary and important distinction between an act of murder and what is merely good medical practice (allowing people to die of natural causes, without using any extraordinary or heroic measures to keep them alive).

Dr. Lamerton stated further that even though "euthanasia" once meant "happy death," it no longer has that meaning, but rather means mercy killing or murder.[1] Therefore, because of this and the confusion and ambiguity of the meaning of "euthanasia," I will not use this term but will substitute three other phrases: allowing someone to die, mercy death, and mercy killing. Each of these phrases has a different meaning, and they must be clearly defined and distinguished before one can deal with the important moral issues surrounding them.

Allowing Someone to Die

The phrase "allowing someone to die" implies an essential recognition that there is some point in any terminal illness when further curative treatment has no purpose and that a patient in this situation should be allowed to die a natural death in comfort, peace, and dignity. In no way does this involve an active termination of someone's life. Rather, it involves a refusal to start curative treatment when no cure is possible and the willingness to halt curative treatment when it can no longer help a dying patient.

What it means, in short, is allowing a terminally ill patient to die his or her own natural death without interference or intrusion from medical science and technology. It does not mean that there is nothing that can be done for the patient or that the patient should be abandoned to die in pain and misery. It does mean, however, that medical science will not initiate heroic efforts to save a dying patient and that it will stop any such efforts that have already been started when it becomes clear that they cannot serve any useful purpose for the patient and his or her family.

228

Mercy Death

I have coined the phrase "mercy death" to mean taking a direct action to terminate a patient's life because the patient has requested it—in short, mercy death is really an assisted suicide. Terminally ill patients are often unable to commit suicide and therefore ask someone to "put them out of their misery." These patients not only give their permission to end their lives but also, in most cases, request or even demand that their lives be terminated.

Mercy Killing

The phrase "mercy killing" refers to someone's taking a direct action to terminate a patient's life without the patient's permission. The decision to take such an action is often made on the assumption that the patient's life is no longer "meaningful" or that if the patient were able to say so, he or she would express a desire to die. The important distinction between mercy killing and mercy death is that mercy killing is involuntary, or does not involve the patient's permission or request, whereas mercy death is done with the permission of the patient, and usually at his or her request.

It should be noted here that neither mercy death nor mercy killing is legal in the United States or in most countries throughout the world, whereas allowing someone to die a natural death is generally legally sanctioned. Of course, legality is not our main concern in dealing with these problems; we are concerned with whether any of these three options is moral and, if so, under what conditions. Therefore, we will now discuss each of these options in more depth, examining the arguments for and against each of them and exploring the full implications of each. Before doing this, however, it is important to define one more phrase.

Brain Death

The advanced medical technology and sophisticated procedures available in the twentieth century have created new moral dilemmas, one of which involves irreversible brain damage, popularly known as "brain death." Before medical technology became so sophisticated, when patients' hearts or lungs failed, their brains also soon failed, and when their brains failed, heart or lung failure soon followed. In our time, however, we have discovered ways (for example, respirators and heart pumps) to bypass the brain, thus avoiding heart or lung failure.

If a patient is brought in with a head injury from a motorcycle accident, for example, the emergency crew may get the person's heart and lungs restarted and may stabilize these two organ systems. Later, doctors may discover that the head injury was so serious that the patient's brain is *irreversibly* damaged; in

229

other words, the brain is permanently dead, not just temporarily injured or even partly injured. Without brain activity, the patient is reduced to a body with a beating heart and breathing lungs. After a number of such instances had occurred, the medical community began to recognize the possibility that a person could be pronounced dead in a medical sense if his brain were irreversibly damaged—even if the patient's body could be considered to be alive in all other respects.

In 1968 an *ad hoc* committee was formed at Harvard Medical School to decide upon criteria for determining brain death. The *ad hoc* committee's final report cited four criteria: (1) unreceptivity and unresponsiveness, (2) no spontaneous movements or breathing, (3) no reflexes, and (4) a flat electroencephalogram (EEG).[2] What this means, then, is that people can be declared medically dead even though their hearts and lungs are still functioning. Many people have confused the problem of brain death with allowing someone to die and mercy killing; they maintain that if a doctor or nurse disconnects the respirator or heart machine aiding a patient who has suffered brain death, then this person is guilty of allowing the patient to die or of mercy killing. This, however, is not the case; if patients are declared dead in an official medical sense, then any equipment can be disconnected and any procedure can be stopped without there being any implication of wrongdoing. After all, how can a patient who is already medically dead be allowed to die or undergo a mercy killing?

I believe that the confusion that arises in such cases comes from our distaste for disconnecting patients with breathing lungs and beating hearts from machines that would keep these organs functioning. Suffice it to say that brain death has nothing to do with allowing someone to die, mercy death, or mercy killing. Some states (California, for example) have even included brain death in their legal definition of death. There is still a problem, however, in dealing with people who have not suffered brain death but who are severely brain damaged. Some injuries do not kill the brain; rather, they leave it badly damaged so that when and if patients awake from a coma, their lives may be radically changed. Furthermore, such patients may remain in a coma for an indefinite period yet not meet the criteria cited above for brain death. The issues of allowing someone to die and mercy killing may definitely arise in relation to this last type of case, but they should not be considered in any way related to a clear-cut case of total brain death.

Persistent Vegetative State (PVS) or Irreversible Coma

Brain death should be carefully distinguished from persistent vegetative state (PVS). PVS results from damage to the cerebral cortex, or neocortex, which controls the cognitive functions. For this reason, it might be called cortical or cerebral death. The body, however, is not dead because the functions of the brain stem continue in whole or in part. In PVS there may still be, and usually is, spontaneous breathing and heartbeat. Persons in this state are often awake, but they are not aware of what is going on around them. There is no conscious interaction with the environment and no awareness of self or the environment. A person in this state lacks and will permanently lack even the minimum that makes life human life. They are, in short, incapable of any human interaction. The very famous cases of Karen Ann Quinlan and Nancy Cruzan are examples of PVS, as you will see later.

◆———————————————————————————————

Allowing Someone to Die

As we have already defined it, "allowing someone to die" means allowing a terminally ill patient to die a natural death without interference from medical science. The problems surrounding this issue, along with those surrounding mercy death and mercy killing, have arisen much more frequently in the twentieth century than at any other period in time. The reason for this, as we have already mentioned, is that advancing medical technology has made it possible for more people to live longer than ever before. As recently as a few years ago, when the heart or lungs failed, a person would be dead in a short period of time. Nowadays, however, a person can be kept alive almost indefinitely by respirators, heart pumps and pacers, miracle drugs, organ transplants, kidney dialysis machines, and so on.

With these advances, which are certainly a blessing for many, we have also incurred problems as to the quality of the lives we are extending. For example, people with kidney failure, who would have died prior to 1960, can now be saved. Many of them adjust beautifully to their situations, but others feel that if they have to live hooked up to a kidney machine for the rest of their lives, they would rather be dead.

Medical science is also working very hard on a cure for cancer, frequently a long, drawn-out disease that causes patients to slowly deteriorate and eventually lose their sense of dignity. It is ironic that as these patients' lives are extended through advanced medical technology, so, too, are their pain, suffering, and misery—sometimes in the hope that a cure will be found and sometimes simply because the doctors don't want to give up on any of their patients.

Similarly, because most people live longer than ever before, they sometimes become senile and infirm. We tend to relegate such people to hospitals or nursing homes, where, in many instances, they live out a tiresome, dreary, and despairing existence, often in pain and suffering. Therefore, literally thousands upon thousands of people, of various ages and in various stages of dying, face what many would describe as lives of low quality. If we add to this the extremely well-documented fact that people of the Western world, and especially people of the United States, generally do not have the ability to face aging or death well, we have a serious problem that we must try to solve in the most ethical way possible.

Very few of us want to see other human beings suffer or live lives from which they are begging to be released. For this reason, it seems to many people that what we need to do is accept as moral, and then legalize, some methods of allowing patients to die, mercy death, or mercy killing, preferably in some painless form to be administered by doctors or by patients with the help of doctors so that "miserable, meaningless" lives can be ended with dignity.

It is difficult to question the validity of the motives behind the desire to end the misery and pain of others. Furthermore, we can justify these motives within the five basic principles. Because we revere life and yet *accept death;* because we can bring happiness and eliminate pain, both for patients and their families, creating harmony where there was disharmony, and ending lives lacking excellence while enhancing other lives with excellence; because we can be just and fair, not only to patients and their families but also to the rest of society on whom sick and dying patients are often a burden; and because we can grant individual freedom to terminally ill patients to die and be allowed to die, as well as the freedom to decide how and when to die, it seems obvious to many that allowing someone to die, mercy death, and mercy killing can be morally justified.

Let us now examine the arguments for and against allowing someone to die.

Arguments Against Allowing Someone to Die

It is a common assumption that human life is always to be protected and preserved, regardless of its quality, by every means we have at our disposal. This assumption has given rise to a number of arguments against allowing someone to die.

Abandonment of Patients. Some people argue that not using or discontinuing any means that might keep dying people alive even a little longer is tantamount to refusing them proper medical care. They feel that if health care professionals (doctors, nurses, etc.) refuse to apply curative treatments, they are abandoning patients and their families to suffering and misery.

It is certainly true that health care professionals could conceivably abandon patients for whom "nothing more can be done." This probably has happened in the past, and, indeed, it may be happening in some cases today. However, there is no reason why this should occur. Abandonment arises from an overemphasis on the aspect of medicine involving curing and healing patients and a deemphasis of the aspect involving comforting and caring for them. As we shall see a little later, the hospice approach to care for the dying makes this distinction clear and completely eliminates the abandonment problem.

The Possibility of Finding Cures. Another argument frequently offered is that if we are too quick to let people die, we may be denying them the opportunity to be cured of their illness. New cures for disease are constantly being discovered, and there are also so-called miracle cures; that is, cures that occur in seeming defiance of all medical knowledge. Therefore, it is argued, if we continue every effort to keep dying patients alive, a miracle cure might occur or a scientific cure (a new drug or surgical procedure) might be discovered that would lengthen patients' lives or even cure them completely.

Not all doctors are willing to accept the existence of miracle cures, however, and many of them also argue that the time to be concerned with cures is when the disease is first diagnosed, not when the patient is completely debilitated by it. They would argue, for example, that the time to perform radical surgery, radiation therapy, and chemotherapy on cancer patients is not when the cancer has completely *metastasized* (spread) throughout the patients' bodies, but when such treatment can do some good, either in slowing cancer growth or in stopping it completely. Using "aggressive" medicine to treat completely metastasized cancer patients, they would argue, is closer to torturing patients than to healing them.

The Impossibility of Opting for Death. Many doctors, as well as others not in the medical profession, will argue that by virtue of the nature of medicine, we can never opt for death; we must always choose life. After all, the reason medicine exists is to save lives, not end them, and the minute we start making choices for death rather than life the very basis for medicine will be nullified. This will result not only in discouragement of doctors but also in an elimination of patients' trust in doctors, often a necessary adjunct to the healing process.

One of the arguments brought against this view is that there is a great difference between "choosing" death and "accepting" death when it is inevitable. A second argument is that many dying patients do not agree that "everything must be done" to save them, and they strongly object to doctors' overriding their decisions about their own bodies and lives. The doctors, of course, argue that they know best and that they must be the ones to make all decisions about a patient's treatment. The patients, however, feel that they ought to have the right to refuse treatment as well as to accept it.

Interference with God's Divine Plan. The final argument against allowing someone to die states that only God can create and take away life, and that mere human beings should not be permitted to allow people to die, much less take their lives in an active way. According to this argument, we must use all our ability and every method at our command to save, protect, preserve, and extend human life until the Creator has decided that it is time for a terminally ill patient to die. We have, of course, heard this argument before in the last chapter, and we have already discussed some of the problems surrounding it.

However, in this situation it becomes a two-edged sword—that is, the concept of God's divine plan can be used to argue for or against allowing someone to die. The argument against such an action has already been stated. The argument for allowing someone to die begins with the assumption that God meant for all humans to die, and that the development of medicine has interfered to a great extent with God's original plan. That is, God did not mean for human beings to live forever, and when medicine prolongs life it interferes with His plan.

The problem with both sides of the argument, of course, is that it is not at all clear what God's specific plan is in relation to allowing someone to die. Furthermore, deciding when to start or stop medical treatment is not a decision made by God. Rather, people—doctors or patients—make these decisions. People who believe in God can certainly say that God has given them the choices in this issue, but they cannot abdicate their responsibility by saying that God is doing the deciding.

Arguments for Allowing Someone to Die

Most arguments for allowing someone to die are based on the Principle of Individual Freedom—specifically, on the rights of individual dying patients to make decisions about their own bodies and lives.

Individual Rights over Bodies and Lives. Much as it applied to the arguments for suicide, the idea that people have the right to decide about their own lives or deaths applies to allowing someone to die, and also—as we shall see later—to requesting mercy death. This right also includes the right of rational patients to refuse treatment when they so desire.

There is, of course, a difference between taking a direct action to end one's own life and merely allowing a disease, deemed to be a part of the natural process, to follow its course without interference. And the process of allowing someone to die does not involve suicide or killing of any kind. In "A Patient's Bill of Rights," which was drawn up by the American Hospital Association, patients are accorded, among other rights, "the right to refuse treatment to the extent permitted by law and to be informed of the medical consequences" of their actions.[3]

The main criticism of the individual rights argument was discussed in Chapter 8; to recapitulate, no one has absolute rights over his or her own life and death. This belief is reflected in the phrase "to the extent permitted by law" in the Patient's Bill of Rights—a phrase that obviously limits people's rights over their own bodies and lives. The general view, however, is that mentally competent people (and mental incompetence is very difficult to prove legally) should have the right to refuse treatment in most cases. This point of view is most strongly held when the treatment is as bad if not worse than the disease—which is often the case. For example, many treatments for cancer result in constant nausea, loss of hair, destruction of healthy as well as diseased tissue, and disfigurement. The individual rights argument offers patients the option of simply letting the disease follow its course rather than being subjected to the sometimes horrible effects of the various treatments offered to them.

Shortening of the Period of Suffering. Another argument for allowing someone to die is that it shortens the time during which a dying patient must endure suffering, pain, and misery. Often our highly advanced medical technology is used to prolong the death—rather than the life—of patients so that they can "enjoy" a few more hours, days, weeks, or months, of pain. For example, if a cancer patient has about eight hours left to live and goes into kidney failure, then prolonging his or her dying by starting dialysis would be considered an extension of pain and suffering, not of meaningful life. It is much more humane, according to this argument, to alleviate the person's misery by allowing him or her to die of uremic poisoning.

The main criticism of this argument attacks its very basis. Yes, critics may say, allowing someone to die will shorten a patient's suffering, but it will also shorten his or her life, and shortening a person's life is immoral. Furthermore, if the policy of allowing people to die becomes general practice, it might be applied to those whose pain could be controlled and who therefore might have led relatively happy, significant lives.

The Right to Die with Dignity. Another argument for allowing someone to die is that people have the right to die with dignity rather than waste away and suffer until there is little left of their original character. This argument is especially forceful in relation to long-term debilitating and degenerative diseases, such as cancer. The idea at the basis of this argument is that if nothing is done in the way of extensive medical treatment, then patients will die without enduring the indignities of being operated on, fed intravenously, or hooked up to machines. The argument states further that "dignity" is also achieved when patients are given choices concerning the kind of living and dying they will do.

The main criticism of this argument is that the phrase "death with dignity" can mask everything from medical abandonment to mercy death and mercy killing and, furthermore, that no dignity will be lost as the result of a heroic attempt to save people's lives or to keep them alive as long as we can.

Ordinary and Extraordinary Means

There is an important distinction to be made in dealing with the problem of allowing someone to die, and it has to do with what means doctors are justified in using to keep people alive. In a speech to anesthesiologists in 1957, Pope Pius XII described two types of means that may be applied in medicine to keep people alive, calling them ordinary means and extraordinary means. What he said, essentially, was that doctors are justified in using extraordinary means up to a point to keep people from dying but that they are not obligated to use such means indefinitely. In hopeless cases, doctors are obligated only to use ordinary means, and they are given the option either to not start or to discontinue extraordinary means. The distinction inherent in these two phrases sounds promising, but unfortunately the terms are often quite difficult to define clearly. Let us examine more closely what Pius XII said and then see if we can make some clear distinctions ourselves.

Extraordinary, or Heroic, Means. The pope defined *extraordinary means* as those that, "according to circumstances of persons, places, times, and cultures . . . involve a grave burden for oneself or another."[4] This is, of course, a rather vague definition, and because persons, places, times, and cultures vary a great deal, it is not easy to come up with a stock list of extraordinary means. I believe that the situation I described earlier in this chapter of the completely metastasized cancer patient who went into kidney failure is a clear example of this. To apply dialysis in this case would be to employ extraordinary means to save this person's life; on the other hand, to merely try to control pain and keep the patient comfortable would be to use ordinary means of treatment.

If a patient is in a coma as a result of a drug overdose, then perhaps using dialysis to purify his or her blood of the toxic substances would be more justified than it would be in the cancer case, but one might still question whether kidney dialysis is not always to some extent extraordinary treatment. Nevertheless, there is certainly a difference between keeping a patient comfortable and well cared for and doing radical surgery or giving radiation therapy.

Ordinary Means. The phrase "ordinary means" is almost as hard to define as extraordinary means, again because of the great variation in people, places, times, and cultures. We could make the distinction that once a patient's disease has been diagnosed as terminal, then continuing with chemical and radiation therapy or doing radical surgery would be extraordinary means, whereas controlling pain and other symptoms would be ordinary. This example may offer a fairly clear distinction, but there are other cases that are much more problematic.

For example, when kidney dialysis machines were in scarce supply and when individual patients had to pay the expenses (about $30,000 per year then), the use of these machines would have been considered extraordinary even though they were necessary to keep people with kidney failure alive. Now, however, when there seem to be enough machines to dialyze all kidney failure patients and when about 85 percent of the cost is paid by the government, perhaps dialysis can be considered ordinary means. It is interesting, though, that this treatment has placed heavy enough financial, physical, and emotional burdens on a few kidney failure patients and their families that they considered it "extraordinary" means to the extent that they discontinued it.

At any rate, when discussing the problems inherent in allowing someone to die, the distinction between these two types of means usually comes into play. Generally speaking, when we are considering allowing someone to die we are talking about not starting or about discontinuing extraordinary means (for example, respirators, heart machines, radical surgery, organ transplants). However, we also may be considering the not starting or discontinuing of ordinary means. For example, feeding patients is certainly considered ordinary means in most circumstances I can think of, but doctors can switch from high-nutrient feedings to minimal-nutrient feedings that will not effectively prolong patients' lives.

There was a case several years ago concerning a man in his eighties who told his family he didn't want to live any longer. From that moment on he refused to eat anything, and he begged his two grandsons not to let anyone force-feed him in any way. They honored his request, and he was allowed to die the death he had chosen.

Similarly, a woman in advanced stages of metastasized cancer had a large growth blocking the tube that passes food to the stomach. The doctor and her family did not use any extraordinary means, such as surgery, to remove the growth, nor did they try to force-feed her in any way. They merely kept her comfortable, letting her taste homemade food even though she couldn't swallow it and letting her suck on ice chips to quench her thirst. Literally, they were allowing her to die of starvation. As these two cases illustrate, there are times when even the refusal to use ordinary means may also be involved in allowing someone to die.

Appropriate or Inappropriate Care. Perhaps with the confusion abounding over the terms "ordinary" and "extraordinary," better terminology might be "appropriate" and "inappropriate" care. Although these terms may initially seem as vague as the others, they allow doctors, nurses, patients, families, and other caregivers to decide how to treat a patient based on what is *appropriate* to the particular patient. Rather than trying to decide what would constitute ordinary or extraordinary means, caregivers and patients could base their decisions on what would seem to suit the particular situation of the patient.

Patient Self-Determination Act (PSDA)

In 1990 the U.S. Congress passed the Patient Self-Determination Act (PSDA) as a part of the Omnibus Reconciliation Act (OBRA 1990). The PSDA requires that health care providers inform patients of their rights to make health care decisions and to execute advance directives. It also requires health care providers to educate their staff and community regarding these rights. The following are some of these rights:

1. The right of patients to considerate and respectful care.

2. The right of patients, in collaboration with their physicians, to make decisions involving their health care, including the following:

(a) The right of patients to accept medical care or refuse treatment to the extent permitted by law and to be informed of the medical consequences of such refusal.

(b) The right of patients to formulate advance directives and appoint a surrogate to make health care decisions on their behalf to the extent permitted by law.

3. The right of patients to acquire information necessary to enable them to make treatment decisions that reflect their wishes.

In connection with item 2b, even though advance directives had existed long before, until the effective date of the PSDA (December 1991), there was no requirement that patients be informed that they could execute an advance directive. This directive would eliminate the confusion surrounding persistent vegetative state patients, especially when family and caregivers are trying to decide on appropriate treatment.

Two extremely famous cases concerning patients in a persistent vegetative state have focused the attention of millions of people in the United States on the importance of executing advance directives. They are the cases of Karen Ann Quinlan of New Jersey and Nancy Cruzan of Missouri.

Karen Ann Quinlan. Karen Ann Quinlan was twenty years old when she stopped breathing long enough for a part of her brain to be destroyed; she then lapsed into a persistent vegetative state. She was put on a respirator, but her parents wanted her to be in a natural state without any artificial means of life support; therefore, they petitioned the hospital and doctors to remove the respirator, which the latter refused to do. After a lengthy court trial that eventually went to the New Jersey State Supreme Court, Quinlan was taken off the respirator and allowed to exist with just simple bed and body care and food and water.

She continued in this persistent vegetative state for another ten years, finally succumbing to pneumonia while residing in a skilled nursing facility. It should be made clear that at no time was Karen ever brain dead. She would sit up, thrash about in her bed, react to sound, light, and touch, but at no time was she conscious or aware of her surroundings or the people in them.

Nancy Cruzan. Another woman in her thirties, Nancy Cruzan, lay in a persistent vegetative state for seven years following a serious automobile accident. She was fed through an abdominal tube, and her parents asked that the tube be removed and that Nancy be allowed to die her own natural death. This case was litigated up to the Missouri State Supreme Court and finally to the U.S. Supreme Court. Since Nancy had not executed any sort of advance directive, the U.S. Supreme Court ruled that "clear and convincing evidence" that Nancy desired to refuse treatment was lacking, and therefore that it could not and would not rule that her parents had the right to act as her proxies in such a decision.

When her case was returned to Missouri, after hearing further testimony from several of her friends and acquaintances that Nancy had made clear that she would not want to continue in such a state, a Superior Court judge ruled this additional testimony provided "clear and convincing evidence" of her desire to refuse treatment and ruled that the feeding tube could be removed. It was, and she died several weeks later.

The Quinlan and Cruzan cases and others like them have created an urgency concerning the rights of people to determine their own treatments and deaths and have led to the creation of the previously mentioned PSDA and the encouragement of people to execute advance directives, three of which I will describe now.

Advance Directives

Because being allowed to die seems to have become a significant moral issue of our time, and because this issue involves individual freedom and patients' rights over their own bodies, treatments, and lives, certain documents or directives have been created to allow people to inform others of the kind of treatment they wish to receive if and when they become seriously ill. Through such documents, people hope to ensure that they receive the kind of treatment they want even if they become too ill later to communicate effectively to others how they wish to be treated. Further, by such documents, these people hope to relieve their families, doctors, nurses, and hospitals of the burdens (economic, emotional, moral) of making decisions that would allow them, as patients, to die their own natural deaths "with peace and dignity." Let's look at three such documents.

Living Will. The living will is a document established by an institution in New York called Choice in Dying, Inc. The legal status of a living will depends totally on state laws regarding it or a document like it. It is signed by individuals (see Figure 9–1).

California Natural Death Act Declaration. The second type of advance directive, established by the California Natural Death Act in 1976 and broadened by legislation in 1992, is the Declaration Pursuant to the Natural Death Act of California. It is the first formally legalized directive in the nation (see Figure 9–2). Cali-

---

ADVANCE DIRECTIVE
Living Will and Health Care Proxy

*D*eath *is a part of life. It is a reality like birth, growth and aging. I am using this advance directive to convey my wishes about medical care to my doctors and other people looking after me at the end of my life. It is called an advance directive because it gives instructions in advance about what I want to happen to me in the future. It expresses my wishes about medical treatment that might keep me alive. I want this to be legally binding.*

If I cannot make or communicate decisions about my medical care, those around me should rely on this document for instructions about measures that could keep me alive.

I do not want medical treatment (including feeding and water by tube) that will keep me alive if:

* I am unconscious and there is no reasonable prospect that I will ever be conscious again (even if I am not going to die soon in my medical condition), *or*
* I am near death from an illness or injury with no reasonable prospect of recovery.

I do want medicine and other care to make me more comfortable and to take care of pain and suffering. I want this even if the pain medicine makes me die sooner.

I want to give some extra instructions: *[Here list any special instructions, e.g., some people fear being kept alive after a debilitating stroke. If you have wishes about this, or any other conditions, please write them here.]*

**The legal language in the box that follows is a health care proxy.
It gives another person the power to make medical decisions for me.**

I name _____, who lives at _____
_____, phone number _____,
to make medical decisions for me if I cannot make them for myself. This person is called a health care "surrogate," "agent," "proxy," or "attorney in fact." This power of attorney shall become effective when I become incapable of making or communicating descisions about my medical care. This means that this document stays legal when and if I lose the power to speak for myself, for instance, if I am in a coma or have Alzheimer's disease.

My health care proxy has power to tell others what my advance directive means. This person also has power to make decisions for me, based either on what I would have wanted, or, if this is not known, on what he or she thinks is best for me.

If my first choice health care proxy cannot or decides not to act for me, I name _____, address _____,
phone number _____, as my second choice.

(over, please)

Figure 9–1

I have discussed my wishes with my health care proxy, and with my second choice if I have chosen to appoint a second person. My proxy(ies) has(have) agreed to act for me.

I have thought about this advance directive carefully. I know what it means and want to sign it. I have chosen two witnesses, neither of whom is a member of my family, nor will inherit from me when I die. My witnesses are not the same people as those I named as my health care proxies. I understand that this form should be notarized if I use the box to name (a) health care proxy(ies).

Signature _____

Date _____

Address _____

Witness' signature _____

Witness' printed name _____

Address _____

Witness' signature _____

Witness' printed name _____

Address _____

Notary [to be used if proxy is appointed] _____

Drafted and Distributed by Choice In Dying, Inc.—the National Council for the right to Die. Choice In Dying is a National not-for-profit organization which works for the rights of patients at the end of life. In addition to this generic advance directive, Choice In Dying distributes advance directives that conform to each state's specific legal requirements and maintains a national Living Will Registry for completed documents.

CHOICE IN DYING INC.—
the national council for the right to die
(formerly Concern for Dying/Society for the Right to Die)
200 Varick Street, New York, NY 10014 (212) 366-5540

Figure 9–1

fornia residents who legally execute such a directive in accordance with the Act are guaranteed the same legal power as they have with estate wills in determining the type of care they would receive. Presumably such a document could be challenged in court, just as other wills are challenged, but as far as I know, no such court cases have yet arisen.

People can execute this declaration at any time, and it is valid for an indefinite period unless revoked by them. A declaration becomes effective when (1) it is communicated to the attending physician and (2) the declarant is diagnosed and certified in writing by the attending physician and a second physician (who has personally examined the declarant) to be terminally ill or permanently unconscious and no longer able to make decisions regarding the provision of life-sustaining treatment. A physician must either honor a legally executed declaration or ensure that the declarant is transferred to another physician who will honor it.

Durable Power of Attorney for Health Care (DPAHC). The Durable Power of Attorney for Health Care has been devised for patients in order that they may appoint someone to act for them in health care matters in the event that they become incapacitated or incompetent. A sample Durable Power of Attorney for Health Care is shown in Figure 9–3. This document allows someone else—family member or otherwise—to make significant health care decisions for a patient who cannot make such decisions for him- or herself. It has the advantage over the living will of being fully legal and much more thorough in designating an attorney-in-fact or agent for the patient, and it has the advantage over the Declaration Pursuant to the Natural Death Act of being able to legally designate an agent to act in the patient's behalf when she or he no longer can communicate her or his own wishes. A California resident may execute both documents, but the Durable Power of Attorney for Health Care will take precedence unless the patient states otherwise. It is my opinion that the Durable Power of Attorney for Health Care is the best of these three advance directives.

Regardless of how one feels about such documents, they are evidence of a growing concern on the part of human beings about the encroachment of medicine and medical technology on their freedom, lives, and dignity. These documents are also further evidence that people wish to have a strong voice in determining the nature of the medical treatment they receive and to exert individual control over their living and dying. Finally, it is important to note that none of these documents in any way authorizes either mercy death or mercy killing; they pertain only to allowing someone to die.

The Hospice Approach to Care for the Dying

Before discussing mercy death and mercy killing, it is important to present a different approach to care for the dying than that generally practiced in this

DECLARATION

PURSUANT TO THE NATURAL DEATH ACT OF CALIFORNIA

(formerly referred to as "A Living Will")

If I should have an incurable and irreversible condition that has been diagnosed by two physicians and that will result in my death within a relatively short time without the administration of life-sustaining treatment or has produced an irreversible coma or persistent vegetative state, and I am no longer able to make decisions regarding my medical treatment, I direct my attending physician, pursuant to the Natural Death Act of California, to withold or withdraw treatment, including artificially administered nutrition and hydration, that only prolongs the process of dying or the irreversible coma or persistent vegetative state and is not necessary for my comfort or to alleviate pain.

If I have been diagnosed as pregnant, and that diagnosis is known to my physician, this declaration shall have no force or effect during my pregnancy.

Other instructions:

Signed this _____ day of _____

Signature _____

Address _____

The declarant voluntarily signed this writing in my presence. I am not a health care provider, an employee of a health care provider, the operator of a community care facility, an employee of an operator of a community care facility, the operator of a residential care facility for the elderly, or an employee of an operator of a residential care facility for the elderly.

Witness _____

Witness _____

The declarant voluntarily signed this writing in my presence. I am not entitled to any portion of the estate of the declarant upon his or her death under any will or codicil thereto of the declarant now existing or by operation of law. I am not a health care provider, an employee of a health care provider, the operator of a community care facility, an employee of an operator of a community care facility, the operator of a residential care facility for the elderly, or an employee of an operator of a residential care facility for the elderly.

Witness _____

Witness _____

Figure 9–2

California Medical Association
DURABLE POWER OF ATTORNEY FOR HEALTH CARE DECISIONS
(California Civil Code Sections 2410-2444)

WARNING TO PERSON EXECUTING THIS DOCUMENT

This is an importatant legal document. Before executing this document, you should know these important facts:

This document gives the person you designate as your agent (the attorney-in-fact) the power to make health care decisions for you. Your agent must act consistently with your desires as stated in this document or otherwise made known.

Except as you otherwise specify in this document, this document gives your agent power to consent to your doctor not giving treatment or stopping treatment necessary to keep you alive.

Notwithstanding this document, you have the right to make medical and other health care decisions for yourself as long as you can give informed consent with respect to the particular decision. In addition, no treatment may be given to you over your objection, and health care necessary to keep you alive may not be stopped or withheld if you object at the time.

This document gives your agent authority to consent, to refuse to consent, or to withdraw consent to any care, treatment, service, or procedure to maintain, diagnose, or treat a physical or mental condition. This power is subject to any statement of your desires and any limitations that you include in this docu-

ment. You may state in this document any types of treatment that you do not desire. In addition, a court can take away the power of your agent to make health care decisions for you if your agent (1) authorizes anything that is illegal, (2) acts contrary to your known desires or (3) where your desires are not known, does anything that is clearly contrary to your best interests.

This power will exist for an indefinite period of time unless you limit its duration in this document.

You have the right to revoke the authority of your agent by notifying your agent or your treating doctor, hospital, or other health care provider orally or in writing of the revocation.

Your agent has the right to examine your medical records and to consent to their disclosure unless you limit this right in this document.

Unless you otherwise specify in this document, this document gives your agent the power after you die to (1) authorize an autopsy, (2) donate your body or parts thereof for transplant or therapeutic or educational or scientific purposes, and (3) direct the disposition of your remains.

If there is anything in this document that you do not understand, you should ask a lawyer to explain it to you.

---

1. CREATION OF DURABLE POWER OF ATTORNEY FOR HEALTH CARE

By this document I intend to create a durable power of attorney by appointing the person designated below to make health care decisions for me as allowed by Sections 2410 to 2444, inclusive, of the California Civil Code. This power of attorney shall not be affected by my subsequent incapacity. I hereby revoke any prior durable power of attorney for health care. I am a California resident who is at least 18 years old, of sound mind, and acting of my own free will.

2. APPOINTMENT OF HEALTH CARE AGENT

(Fill in below the name, address and telephone number of the person you wish to make health care decisions for you if you become incapacitated. You should make sure that this person agrees to accept this responsibility. The following may not serve as your agent: (1) your treating health care provider; (2) an operator of a commnity care facility or residential care facility for the elderly; or (3) an employee of your treating health care provider, a community care facility, or residential care facility for the elderly, unless that employee is related to you by blood, marriage or adoption. If you are a conservatee under the Lanterman-Petris-Short Act (the law governing involuntary commitment to a mental health facility) and you wish to appoint your conservator as your agent, you must consult a lawyer, who must sign and attach a special declaration for this document to be valid.)

I, _____, hereby appoint:
(insert you name)

Name _____

Address _____

Work Telephone (_____) _____ Home Telephone (_____) _____

as my agent (attorney-in-fact) to make health care decisions for me as authorized in this document. I understand that this power of attorney will be effective for an indefinite period of time unless I revoke it or limit its duration below.

(Optional) This power of attorney shall expire on the following date: _____

Figure 9–3

3. AUTHORITY OF AGENT

If I become incapable of giving informed consent to health care decisions, I grant my agent full power and authority to make those decisions for me, subject to any statements of desires or limitations set forth below. Unless I have limited my agent's authority in this document, that authority shall include the right to consent, refuse consent, or withdraw consent to any medical care, treatment, service, or procedure; receive and to consent to the release of medical information; to authorize an autopsy to determine the cause of my death; to make a gift of or part of my body; and to direct the disposition of my remains, subject to any instructions I have given in a written contract for funeral services, my will or by some other method. I understand that, by law, my agent may <u>not</u> consent to any of the following: commitment to a mental health treatment facility, convulsive treatment, psychosurgery, sterilization or abortion.

4. MEDICAL TREATMENT DESIRES AND LIMITATIONS (OPTIONAL)

(Your agent must make health care decisions that are consistent with your known desires. You can, but are not required to, state your desires about the kinds of medical care you do or do not want, including your desires concerning life-sustaining treatment. If you do not want your agent to have the authority to make certain decisions, you must write a statement to that effect in the space provided below; otherwise, your agent will have the broad powers to make health care decisions for you that are outlined in paragraph 3 above. In either case, it is important that you discuss your health care desires with the person you appoint as your agent.

(Following are three general statements about withholding and removal of life-sustaining treatment. If, after carefully reading all of these statements, you agree with one of them, you may initial that statement. If you wish to add to one of the printed statements, or to write your own instead, you may do so in the space provided.)

> I do **not** want efforts made to prolong my life and I do not want life-sustaining treatment to be provided or continued: (1) if I am in an irreverisible coma or persistent vegetative state; or (2) if I am terminally ill and the application of life-sustaining procedures would serve only to artificially delay the moment of my death; or (3) under any other circumstances where the burdens of the treatment outweigh the expected benefits. I want my agent to consider the relief of suffering and the quality as well as the extent of the possible extension of my life in making decisions concerning life-sustaining treatment.
>
> *If this statement reflects your desires, initial here:* _____

> I want efforts made to prolong my life and I want life-sustaining treatment to be provided unless I am in a coma or persistent vegetative state which my doctor reasonably believes to be irreversible. Once my doctor has concluded that I will remain unconscious for the rest of my life, I do not want life-sustaining treatment to be provided or continued.
>
> *If this statement reflects your desires, initial here:* _____

> I want efforts made to prolong my life and I want life-sustaining treatments to be provided even if I am in an irreversible coma or persistent vegetative state.
>
> *If this statement reflects your desires, initial here:* _____

Other or additional statements of medical treatment desires and limitations: _____
_____
_____

(You may attach additional pages if you need more space to complete your statements. Each additional page must be dated and signed at the same time you date and sign this document.)

5. APPOINTMENT OF ALTERNATE AGENTS (OPTIONAL)

(You may appoint alternate agents to make health care decisions for you in case the person you appointed in Paragraph 2 is unable or unwilling to do so.)

If the person named as my agent in Paragraph 2 is not available or willing to make health care decisions for me as authorized in this document, I appoint the following persons to do so, listed in the order they should be asked:

First Alternate Agent: Name: _____ Telephone: (_____) _____
                        Address: _____

Second Alternate Agent: Name: _____ Telephone: (_____) _____
                        Address: _____

Figure 9–3 (continued)

6. USE OF COPIES

I hereby authorize that photocopies of this document can be relied upon by my agent and others as though they were originals.

DATE AND SIGNATURE OF PRINCIPAL

(You must date and sign this power of attorney)

I sign my name to this Durable Power of Attorney for Health Care at _____, _____

(City)   (State)

on _____, _____

(Date)   (Signature of Principal)

STATEMENT OF WITNESSES

(This power of attorney will not be valid for making health care decisions unless it is either (1) signed by two qualified adult witnesses who are personally known to you (or to whom you present evidence of your identity) and who are present when you sign or acknowledge your signature or (2) acknowledged before a notary public in California. If you elect to use witnesses rather than a notary public, the law provides that none of the following may be used: (1) the persons you have appointed as your agent and alternate agents, (2) a health care provider or an employee of a health care provider, or (3) an operator or employee of a community care facility or residential care facility for the elderly. Additionally, at least one of the witnesses cannot be related to you by blood, marriage or adoption, or be named in your will. IF YOU ARE A PATIENT IN A SKILLED NURSING FACILITY, ONE OF THE WITNESSES MUST BE A PATIENT ADVOCATE OR OMBUDSMAN.)

I declare under penalty of perjury under the laws of California that the person who signed or acknowledged this document is personally known to me to be the principal, or that the identity of the principal was proved to me by convincing evidence,* that the principal signed or acknowledged this durable power of attorney in my presence, that the principal appears to be of sound mind and under no duress, fraud, or undue influence, that I am not the person appointed as attorney in fact by this document, and that I am not a health care provider, an employee of a health care provider, the operator of a community care facility or a residential care facility for the elderly, nor an employee of an operator of a community care facility or residential care facility for the elderly.

Signature _____ Signature _____

Print name _____ Print name _____

Date _____ Date _____

Residence Address _____ Residence Address _____

(AT LEAST ONE OF THE ABOVE WITNESSES MUST ALSO SIGN THE FOLLOWING DECLARATION)

I further declare under penalty of perjury under the laws of California that I am not related to the principal by blood, marriage, or adoption, and, to the best of my knowledge I am not entitled to any part of the estate of the principal upon the death of the principal under a will now existing or by operation of law.

Signature: _____

---

*The law allows one or more of the following forms of identification as convincing evidence of identity: a California driver's license or identification card or U.S. passport that is current or has been issued within five years, or any of the following if the document is current or has been issued within five years, contains a photograph and description of the person named on it, is signed by the person, and bears a serial or other identifying number: a foreign passport that has been stamped by the U.S. Immigration and Naturalization Service; a driver's license issued by another state or by an authorized Canadian or Mexican agency; or an identification card issued by another state or by any branch of the U.S. armed forces. If the principal is a patient in a skilled nursing facility, a patient advocate or ombudsman may rely on the representations of family members or the administrator or staff of the facility as convincing evidence of identity if the patient advocate or ombudsman believes that the representations provide a reasonable basis for determining the identity of the principal.

Figure 9–3 (continued)

SPECIAL REQUIREMENT: STATEMENT OF PATIENT ADVOCATE OR OMBUDSMAN

(If you are a patient in a skilled nursing facility, one of your witnesses must be a patient advocate or ombudsman, who must sign the statement of witnesses above <u>and</u> must also sign the following declaration.)

I further declare under penalty of perjury under the laws of California that I am a patient advocate or ombudsman as designated by the State Department of Aging and am serving as a witness as required by subdivision (f) of Civil Code Secton 2432.

Signature: _____   Address:_____

Print Name: _____   _____

Date: _____   _____

CERTIFICATE OF ACKNOWLEDGMENT OF NOTARY PUBLIC

(Acknowledgment before a notary public is <u>not</u> required if you have elected to have two qualified witnesses sign above. Do not use a notary public if you are a patient in a skilled nursing facility.)

State of California   )

)ss.

County of _____)

On this _____ day of _____ , in the year _____ ,

before me _____ ,
(here insert name of notary public)

personally appeared _____
(here insert name of principal)

personally known to me (or proved to me on the basis of satisfactory evidence) to be the person whose name is subscribed to this instrument, and acknowledged that he or she executed it. I declare under penalty of perjury that the person whose name is subscribed to this instrument appears to be of sound mind and under no duress, fraud, or undue influence.

NOTARY SEAL

_____
(Signature of Notary Public)

COPIES

YOUR AGENT MAY NEED THIS DOCUMENT IMMEDIATELY IN CASE OF AN EMERGENCY. YOU SHOULD KEEP THE COMPLETED ORIGINAL AND GIVE PHOTOCOPIES OF THE COMPLETED ORIGINAL TO (1) YOUR AGENT AND ALTERNATE AGENTS, (2) YOUR PERSONAL PHYSICIAN, AND (3) MEMBERS OF YOUR FAMILY AND ANY OTHER PERSONS WHO MIGHT BE CALLED IN THE EVENT OF A MEDICAL EMERGENCY. THE LAW PERMITS THAT PHOTOCOPIES OF THE COMPLETED DOCUMENT CAN BE RELIED UPON AS THOUGH THEY WERE ORIGINALS.

Additional forms can be purchased from: Sutter Publications, P.O. Box 7690, San Francisco, CA 94120-7690

Figure 9–3

country: I call this "the hospice approach to care for the dying." The word *hospice* formerly meant a refuge for wayfaring strangers. Now, however, it refers to a place where tired, sick, and dying people can be cared for and comforted. The modern hospice does not deal with acute cases or with emergency medical care; rather, it seeks to help terminally ill patients live as comfortably and meaningfully as they can until they die. The hospice approach involves seven different aspects of patient care. A close examination of these will help to clarify how hospices differ from hospitals and other medical facilities.

Comforting and Caring for Patients. First of all, the hospice approach emphasizes "comforting and caring" for patients rather than "curing and healing" them. As I mentioned earlier, there comes a time in every terminal illness when the possibility of curing patients of their diseases no longer exists. At this point, medical care should not be discontinued, nor should patients and their families be abandoned; rather, the medical care should shift from curing and healing to comforting and caring for the patients. The emphasis here is on *appropriate* medical treatment, which involves pain and symptom control and assistance at all levels to patients and their families until the patients die; it also means continued assistance, when needed, to the patients' families after they have died.

A Team Approach. Recognizing that human beings have dimensions beyond the physical, which is the basic focus of medicine, the hospice approach utilizes a team concept in its care for the dying. The team includes patients, their family and friends, other patients, doctors, nurses, clergy, social workers, physical and occupational therapists, psychologists or psychiatrists, and volunteers. Because sickness, dying, and death involve all dimensions of people, their mental, emotional, social, and religious needs must be met along with the physical needs. The assumption is that dying patients and their families must have total care to get through what often is a difficult time.

Pain and Symptom Control. The hospice approach recognizes that there is a difference between "acute pain" and "chronic pain." Acute pain is that which will eventually disappear—for example, the pain one feels after surgery. Chronic pain, on the other hand, is pain that not only will remain, but which will also probably get worse. Obviously, a completely different approach to controlling pain must be used in dealing with the chronic type. Second, the hospice approach recognizes that pain, especially chronic pain, is a complex phenomenon that involves the mental or emotional, the social or sociological, and the spiritual or religious aspects of patients as well as the physical. This is another reason why the hospice approach utilizes a team; there is a basic recognition that social pain can be helped by social workers, mental and emotional pain can be alleviated by psychologists or psychiatrists, and spiritual pain can be eased by clergy.

248

Once chronic pain is understood for what it is, a "preventive" rather than a "reactive" approach to pain control should be used. For example, once a terminal cancer patient begins to suffer pain, the method of pain control should not be to wait until the moment the pain returns, thus "reacting" to the pain symptoms; rather, the patient's pain should be prevented from occurring. Pain medication should be given to patients orally wherever possible so as not to further aggravate already existing pain with hypodermic needles, and the method of pain control must be examined daily to ensure that it fits each patient's individual needs. A more detailed description of the hospice approach to pain control can be found in Sandol Stoddard's *The Hospice Movement*.[5]

Outpatient and Home Care. Because dying patients do not as a rule need extraordinary medical care, they can often be treated at home. Whenever possible, the hospice approach encourages dying patients to remain at home, offering both patients and their families total care and support from the entire team whenever it is needed. This brings greater "comfort" to the patients by allowing them to stay in familiar surroundings with their families and their own favorite belongings around them. The key to this type of care, of course, is that complete support and care must be available from the team. One of the reasons more people have not chosen to die at home, especially in our country, is that there has been no support available to patients and their families, and families are not always able to cope alone with all of the problems surrounding the dying of a loved one. If the support is there, however, then the home is often the place where patients receive the best care and are the most comfortable.

Humanized Inpatient Care. When home care coupled with outpatient care is not feasible—and many times it is not—humanized, homelike, comfortable inpatient facilities should be available. Patients should be placed in wards so that they can relate to others in similar situations. The rooms should be warmly decorated and should have large floor-to-ceiling, curtained windows and at least partial carpeting. Patients should be allowed to have their own familiar belongings around them (easy chairs, plants—even pets, where feasible), and visiting hours should be liberal, with no restrictions on age so that children can visit their parents and grandparents. Food and drink of the patients' choice (including alcoholic beverages if desired) ought to be available. And, finally, patients should be kept pain- and symptom-free and be given loving care, but they should be spared the intrusion of extraordinary or inappropriate medical technology, such as intravenous lines, respirators, and so on.

Freedom from Financial Worry. All hospice care, in- or outpatient, should be performed on a nonprofit basis. Where available, existing medical insurance, private or government, should pay for as much as possible, but no hospice patient should be refused treatment because of lack of finances. Nor should patients be dunned for money. Many hospices will tell patients and their families how much their care costs and ask them if they can contribute anything toward their care, but they are usually asked only once and never refused treatment because they have no money. Hospices mainly operate on fund-raising activities, grants, and donations or memorial gifts for their financial support. Also, it has been proved that keeping dying patients at home on an outpatient basis or even in hospice facilities is far less expensive than keeping them in convalescent homes or acute care hospitals. This is not the main reason we should consider the hospice approach, however; rather, we should be concerned with the humane and compassionate care it provides for dying patients and their families.

Bereavement Counseling and Assistance. Helping dying patients and their families adjust to the fact of death before, during, and after its occurrence is an important part of the hospice approach. This is yet another reason that the team approach is used—so that social workers, clergy, trained volunteers, and other nonmedical members of the team can aid medical personnel in caring for the entire family unit. Too often in our society the patient is cared for and the family is forgotten. When the patient dies, however, the grieving family remains, and its members often experience tremendous difficulty in dealing with the death of their loved one. If the family *and* the patient can be treated as a unit during the dying period, then much of the difficulty that might occur after the patient dies can be averted—that is, family members can go through at least some of their mourning while the patient is still with them.

Some Concluding Comments. The hospice approach allows patients to die their own natural deaths in peace and dignity with support from their families, friends, the medical community, and society in general. Because two of the main reasons for mercy death and mercy killing are to "put people out of their pain, suffering, misery" and to end lives that allegedly have no meaning, the hospice approach obviates the need for such measures in most instances. If patients can die in peace and dignity, free from pain and suffering, they will have no need to commit suicide, assisted or otherwise, or have their "lives of despair" terminated for them. The reasons for mercy death and mercy killing have not been completely eliminated, but a humane alternative does exist in many cases that might call for such drastic measures.

◆

Cases for Study and Discussion

Cases 1 and 2 should be studied together because they have a number of elements in common. Some discussion questions related to the two cases are presented after the second case description.

C A S E ◆ 1

A thirty-eight-year-old nurse gave birth to a baby girl who had both Down's syndrome (a disease that involves mental retardation) and an intestinal blockage. This type of birth often occurs in women over age thirty-five. The nurse and her husband agreed that the child's existence would be poor in quality because of her mental retardation, and, knowing that she would die if the intestinal blockage weren't removed, they refused to sign a permit for surgery to remove the blockage and told the doctors to do nothing to save their daughter. The doctors and the hospital agreed that the parents had the right to make this decision, so the child was left in the nursery to die. After eleven days, she died of starvation.

C A S E ◆ 2

Another woman, age forty-two, was rushed to the hospital to have her baby, but the little girl was born in the car on the way to the hospital. The child was born with Down's syndrome, intestinal blockage, and a hole in her heart that made it very difficult for her to breathe. The woman and her husband already had three children and had not planned for this one. Because of these problems, they also had both financial and marital difficulties. They refused to sign the permission form the doctors needed to remove the intestinal blockage, saying that even if the little girl survived this surgery, she would still have to have extremely complicated heart surgery later. Furthermore, they said, if she managed to survive the heart surgery, she would still be severely mentally retarded. The doctors disagreed with the parents, and after obtaining a court injunction allowing them to operate, they removed the blockage. The parents did not even name their daughter, and they refused to take her home until the pressure put upon their other children by their peers forced them to do so. A year later the little girl was still alive, but because of her heart defect she often had to gasp for breath. The parents were so unhappy with the situation that the mother even contemplated smothering the infant with a pillow, but she could not bring herself to do it. The family's financial situation was deteriorating, and the mother was concerned because the longer they kept the baby, the more everyone in the family was becoming attached to her and the harder it would be for them all if the baby were to die. The parents blamed the doctors and the judge who handed down the injunction for creating this nearly unbearable situation.

Some questions for study and discussion:

1. Both of these cases are quite similar except that the second baby has an additional serious defect, the hole in her heart. Should this make a difference?

2. Which set of medical personnel do you feel did the "right thing"? Explain your answer, giving specific reasons.

3. How do you resolve the conflicts among the following rights involved in these two cases?

(a) The right of the babies, regardless of their problems, to medical care that could save their lives.

(b) The right of parents to decide whether their defective or deformed babies should be allowed to live, when, in the past, they would not have lived because our medical technology was less advanced.

(c) The doctors' and hospitals' right to save lives when they know they can.

(d) The conflicting rights of society to (1) protect its members (in this case, the babies) and allow them to live and (2) not be burdened with defective and deformed children when the omission of extraordinary care would allow the children to die of natural causes.

4. In Case 1, how do you feel about the fact that the baby was left for eleven days to die of starvation? Do you feel she should have been immediately and painlessly killed instead, or do you feel she should have been operated on regardless of the parents' wishes?

5. If parents do not wish to take the responsibility of raising children who have defects and deformities, do you feel society as a whole has an obligation to give such parents extensive financial and social aid in raising the children, or to assume responsibility for raising such children itself?

6. If society or the parents have to institutionalize such children in places where bare maintenance is all the children receive, do you think it would be better to allow the children to die, as in Case 1?

7. To what extent do you think that not performing what is a relatively simple and safe surgery on a deformed or defective child is discriminating unfairly against handicapped children?

C A S E ◆ 3

Louise, fifty, was diagnosed as having leukemia. She was divorced and had a five-year-old daughter and a thirty-year-old son who was married, with two children. Louise was sent away to a large medical center and kept in protective isolation while undergoing extensive chemotherapy treatments. These left her very nauseated and made her hair fall out, and the protective isolation meant that anyone visiting her would have to be completely gowned, masked, and gloved because her body could not fight off infection. After a while, she went into temporary remission and was sent home to be with her family.

About three months later, she was taken to a local hospital and was again placed in protective isolation and given chemotherapy. By this time, she knew that she had leukemia and that the chemotherapy—given the advanced stage of the disease—would at most give her a few more months of life. She wanted very much to be with her family but could see only their eyes when they visited her; she could not see her young daughter at all.

Although she had been a somewhat passive person all of her life, she finally got up enough courage to ask the doctor to release her from the hospital, even though she knew that this course of action might result in her dying much sooner than if she remained there. The doctor, who was very compassionate, wanted to keep treating her to extend the length of her life as much as possible, but he also realized how important it was for her to be with her family. One of the nurses on the case volunteered to help Louise at home during her off-duty hours whenever she could, but the doctor knew this would not be as good as hospital treatment. Needless to say, he had mixed feelings about what he should do. What would you do if you were he?

♦————————————————————————————————————

Mercy Death

As stated at the beginning of this chapter, the phrase "mercy death" means a *direct* action taken to terminate someone's life at his or her request—it amounts to an assisted suicide. I want to stress that although allowing someone to die may also require some direct actions (unplugging respirators, removing IVs, and so on), it is not the same as mercy death. In the case of mercy death, patients, often because they are in pain or because they just do not want to live longer, ask to have their lives ended immediately, usually by some painless means. The motives for such a request vary. Often such patients do not feel they will have the courage to commit suicide and want someone to help them, whereas at other times patients are not able to end their own lives because they are either paralyzed or too weak to do it themselves. In any case, however, these patients want to be mercifully put to death, not just allowed to die.

Arguments Against Mercy Death

Many of the same arguments used against suicide are applicable to mercy death, at least to some extent, but the issues surrounding mercy death are further complicated by the fact that someone else has to do the killing. Let us examine the arguments used against suicide as they apply to mercy death.

The Irrationality of Mercy Death. This argument may have less force here than when it is applied to suicide because people are more likely to accept as rational a decision to die when the person making the decision is to die soon anyhow and when his or her life at the time of the decision is full of pain, suffering, and misery. Furthermore, even when people who request mercy death are not in imminent danger of dying, their lives may now be so radically different that they would rather not live any more (for example, a physically active person who will be paralyzed permanently from the neck down because of a serious accident). Despite these mitigating factors, however, the argument against mercy death goes on to say that people who are suffering and in pain are in such a state of fear and depression that they simply cannot make rational decisions. If these people will patiently wait to see what therapy and medical science can do for them, the argument continues, maybe they will adjust to their situation and change their minds about dying.

The criticism of this argument is that many requests for mercy death have come from people who have tried for some time to live with their tragic situation and who have still decided that death is preferable to a limited life. Also, it is difficult to argue that because a person is suffering he or she cannot make a rational decision for death.

The Religious Argument. The religious argument applies to mercy death in much the same way as it does to suicide. Indeed, it gains force in this case from the fact that a second person must do the killing, which, in religious terms, is even worse than suicide. The religious argument maintains that killing is killing regardless of the motive and states that no one has the right to take innocent people's lives, even at their request.

This argument is further supported by many of our laws. It is true that most states and countries have repealed laws designating suicide as illegal, but many of them still have laws against helping others to commit suicide. People who do this can, in fact, be charged as accessories to murder. Mercy death does fit our earlier definition of "murder" except that the phrase "especially with malice aforethought" does not apply. Furthermore, it differs from murder in that it is not done against the will of the "victim."

In addition to the criticisms already presented in rebuttal to the religious argument against suicide, there is another criticism we can consider: that it is precisely the difference in motive that makes mercy death morally acceptable, especially because the person to be put to death agrees to his or her own death and may even request it. Most killings are committed from motives of greed, revenge, anger, hate, or viciousness; mercy death, on the other hand, is done out of love and mercy for a person who is suffering.

The Domino Argument. Both the domino argument and the criticisms of it apply here in much the same way as they do to suicide, war, and capital punishment. Those who argue against mercy death, however, believe that the domino effect that results from permitting mercy death can be much more pernicious than in other cases. It is obvious, they say, that if mercy death, which is performed at a person's request, is authorized or given moral sanction, the next step will be mercy killing—that is, decisions for death will be made by others for those unable to request death for themselves. Once we open the door for one, they say, it is open for the other. As I have mentioned before, this is a possibility that should concern us. It is also possible, however, to legally allow mercy deaths and not mercy killings, just as it is legally possible to permit allowing someone to die (as does the California Natural Death Act described earlier) without condoning either mercy death or mercy killing.

The Justice Argument. Here again many of the same arguments that apply to suicide also apply to mercy death. There are some additional problems, however. For example, is it just for people to ask others to kill them? Doesn't this place a terrific burden of guilt and depression on the person who has to perform the act? And what about the feelings of guilt and loss on the part of the family members? Won't they always wonder whether something more should have been done, perhaps on their part, to help the person live? There is no doubt that mercy death places a greater burden on others than suicide does.

The Possibility of Finding Cures. The arguments here are much like those presented in the discussion of allowing someone to die, and they are best characterized by the cliché "Where there's life, there's hope." The counterarguments are also the same, with the additional criticism that many patients who request mercy death either feel that they have no chance of being cured or find the wait for a cure too painful to bear.

The Hospice Alternative. In his article "Euthanasia," Dr. Richard Lamerton said, "If anyone really wants euthanasia, he must have pretty poor doctors and nurses."[6] He might just as easily have said that the patient must be receiving pretty poor medical care from the entire society. According to the hospice argument, because we already know that the hospice approach will work, we should exert our efforts in that direction rather than in trying to discover how we can morally and legally justify mercy death or mercy killing. Under the five principles, the hospice approach reveres, preserves, and protects human life; it promotes goodness by giving pleasure and avoiding pain, by creating harmony, by making lives as excellent as they can be, and by allowing and encouraging creativity at whatever level is possible; it provides for honesty and truth telling by dealing with the patients where and as they are and relating to them as real and whole human beings, not merely as diseased bodies; and it gives patients and their families the freedom to enjoy life and each other for whatever time is left, while at the same time allowing them the freedom of a truly dignified death, not by killing, but by compassionate treatment.

It seems obvious, then, that if all of these things can be done to alleviate pain and misery and meaningless in people's lives, and if the hospice approach can be made the rule rather than the exception, then the need for mercy death or mercy killing should be decreased a great deal, if not eliminated entirely.

The only criticism of this argument is that there may be some patients who do not want any further treatment of any kind, in a hospice or elsewhere, and who choose death rather than limited life. Furthermore, there are those to whom the hospice approach does not really apply—for example, paraplegics, quadriplegics, victims of paralysis, and other patients who suffer from extremely debilitating chronic, but not necessarily terminal, diseases. In the opinion of such patients, the alternative of mercy death is still viable.

Arguments for Mercy Death

Individual Freedom and Rights. The main argument for individual freedom and rights, as in the suicide issue, is the argument that people ought to have the right to decide when their lives should end. If they choose not to live any longer and request to die, we should oblige them, recognizing that they have made a free, rational choice. All we are doing is carrying out their decisions out of love, compassion, and mercy.

The difference between mercy death and suicide, however, is that in mercy death we are asked to end their lives for them, and this can certainly be seen as an infringement on our rights and freedom. I remember hearing a doctor expressing this point of view on a television show called "Right to Die." The doctor said, "You have the right to choose death for yourself, but you do not have the right to involve *me* in your choice."

Human Rights Versus Animal Rights. Another argument states that just as we are generally willing to put animals out of their misery when they suffer, so we should accord our fellow humans, who are certainly of higher worth to us, the same consideration. Furthermore, because they have asked us for death, we should have no compunction about ending their lives mercifully.

The main criticism of this argument is that the rights of human beings to live or die are not in any way the same as those of animals. No matter what science may say, no human being is merely an animal. Western religions, of course, maintain that human beings have immortal souls, but even nonreligious humanists talk about the "human spirit," or personality, stating that it should be accorded a greater respect than the mere physical self.

Legal Status and Ramifications of Mercy Death

Active Advocates for Mercy Death. Presently mercy death is illegal in all the 50 states and in most countries of the world, but there is a strong advocacy for not only allowing people to die their own natural deaths, but also for allowing people to be assisted by doctors in committing suicide when they no longer feel that their lives are worth living (mostly, but not always, when their illnesses are terminal). Two men—Derek Humphry and Dr. Jack Kevorkian—have been active in furthering the cause of mercy death, or assisted suicide.

Derek Humphry is probably the more famous of the two. He is an Englishman, now residing in the United States, who, in 1975, assisted his first wife, Jean, in committing suicide in England when she was dying of cancer. This was perhaps a somewhat strange action because both of them resided in the country where modern day hospice was brought to life. Humphry wrote a book about it, called *Jean's Way*. In 1980 in California, Humphry founded the Hemlock Society, which is famous for two things: (1) working to change laws so that doctors can legally help terminally ill patients commit suicide and (2) giving advice to people who have decided to die on their own when doctors cannot or will not help.

The Hemlock Society attempted to introduce legislation in both California and Washington that would legalize assisted suicide, but both measures failed. After these failures, Humphry and his second wife wrote *The Right to Die: Understanding Euthanasia* in 1986. He then wrote his most famous and best-selling book, *Final Exit,* in 1991, which, as *Playboy* described it in its interview with Humphry, "is nothing short of the last self-help book you'll ever need."[7] A fourth book, *Dying With Dignity: Understanding Euthanasia,* will be published soon. Humphry is currently assisting a group called "Californians Against Human Suffering" with their initiative, which was on the ballot in California in November 1992 and did not pass.

Dr. Jack Kevorkian from Detroit, Michigan, is probably the more controversial of the two men. A retired pathologist, he has helped more than twenty people commit suicide, few of whom, interestingly enough, could have been classified as terminally ill. He has, as of this writing, been brought to trial and acquitted of assisting suicide. It should be noted that in all of these cases, Dr. Kevorkian provided the means, but the people administered their own suicides.

◆

Cases for Study and Discussion

CASE ◆ 1

A truck overturns on one of our major highways, and the engine catches on fire, engulfing the cab, where the driver is trapped. A highway patrol officer arrives on the scene and realizes that no one can get near enough to the cab to get the driver out. The driver sees the patrolman and begs the officer to shoot him so that he won't have to suffer the horror of burning to death. The officer is close enough to kill him instantly. What should he or she do?

CASE ◆ 2

A twenty-four-year-old man named Robert who has a wife and child is paralyzed from the neck down in a motorcycle accident. He has always been very active and hates the idea of being paralyzed. He is also in a great deal of pain, and he has asked his doctors and other members of his family to "put him out of his misery." After several days of such pleading, his brother comes into Robert's hospital ward and asks him if he is sure he still wants to be put out of his misery. Robert says yes and pleads with his brother to kill him. The brother kisses and blesses Robert, then takes out a gun and shoots him, killing him instantly. The brother is later tried for murder and acquitted by reason of temporary insanity. Was what Robert's brother did moral? Do you think he should have been brought to trial at all? Do you think he should have been acquitted? Would you do the same for a loved one if you were asked?

CASE ◆ 3

A sixty-seven-year-old woman has been sick for the last ten years with heart, lung, and kidney problems that have given her a great deal of pain and discomfort. In her own words, her life is "a misery" and "not worth living." Her children are all grown, and she lives alone with her husband, who is sixty-eight. She has talked with him on several occasions during the past two years, begging him to help her to die. She has told him that she is tired of living and that she gets no pleasure from her life any more. On this particular morning, they discuss her life and death for four hours, and again and again she begs him to help her to die. He finally gives in to her wishes and takes her out to the garage, puts her in their car, turns on the engine with the garage door closed, and goes back into the house for about an hour. At the end of the hour, he takes her out of the car and then calls the police and tells them what he has done. They arrive on the scene and arrest him for murder. Did the husband do the right thing? Did the wife have the right to request this action of her husband? Did he have an obligation to satisfy her request? Should he have been arrested?

CASE ◆ 4

As previously discussed, Dr. Kevorkian originally invented a suicide machine that he can hook up to an intravenous line that can be inserted into a person's arm, so that the person can push a button or release a clamp and administer a fatal but painless dose of chemicals. More recently, he has used carbon dioxide that the people can inhale until they die. Few of the people who used his machine or the carbon dioxide were terminally ill. For example, one forty-five year old woman had just been diagnosed as having Alzheimer's disease, one had severe pelvic pain, and another had multiple sclerosis. Do you think that what he is doing is moral or immoral? Why? Would it make any difference to your decision if the people had been terminally ill? Should anything be done to the doctor legally? If so, what? If not, why not? If you were asked by someone you loved to help him or her die, and you had the means, like Dr. Kevorkian, to do so, what would you do? Why? Would you like doctors to have the right to assist people in committing suicide? Why or why not? Would the people have to be terminally ill, in your opinion, or not? Why?

♦————————————————————————————————————

Mercy Killing

Mercy killing is similar to mercy death in the sense that it involves a direct action to end someone's life; the difference is that mercy killing is not done at the person's request. People who perform mercy killing may assume that the person they are going to kill wants this act to be done, but they don't know for sure, nor do they have the person's explicit request or permission to perform the act. Very often the decision for mercy killing is based on a belief that the "victim's" life is no longer worth living because he or she is just merely existing as a mindless organism, not as a full human being.

Therefore, mercy killing can be defined as the termination of someone's life without that person's explicit consent by a direct means from a motive of mercy—that is, in an attempt to end suffering and/or a "meaningless existence." Obviously, the greatest moral problem with mercy killing is that, unlike allowing someone to die and mercy death, in this case the patient's consent cannot be obtained, nor can his or her desires be known for sure. "Mercy killers" must make a decision about someone else's life without the person's permission or acquiescence.

Arguments Against Mercy Killing

Many of the arguments that have been used in relation to mercy death and allowing someone to die also apply to mercy killing. I will not repeat all of these arguments here but will try to emphasize the main aspect that distinguishes mercy killing from the other two categories—that is, the lack of consent on the part of the "victim."

Direct Violation of the Value of Life Principle. Mercy killing is a direct violation of the Value of Life principle, especially because, unlike defense of the innocent, war, and capital punishment, it usually involves taking the life of an innocent person. As in the mercy death situation, the argument here is that murder is murder regardless of motive; therefore, mercy killing is nothing less than premeditated murder. This argument is even more convincing here than in the case of mercy death because in this case people either haven't or can't give their consent to the termination of their lives.

The Domino Argument. Because the consent of patients cannot be obtained, an outside decision about the worth, value, or meaning of their lives has to be made, and according to this argument against mercy killing, this sets a dangerous precedent. In the first place, who has the right to decide whether any person's life is worthy, has value, or is meaningful? What standards are to be used in making such a decision? Won't the sanctioning of such an action set a dangerous precedent for eliminating old, senile people, for example, because they may be considered "useless" to a youth-oriented society? Can we allow such decisions to be made? If so, by whom should they be made? This is certainly one of the more serious problems related to mercy killing, and it is one that does not affect either allowing someone to die or mercy death to such a great extent. In both of the latter cases, the individual decides what the worth of his own life is, whereas in mercy killing one person decides for another.

The Possibility of Finding Cures. Both this argument, which states that mercy killing should not be authorized because cures may be found, and the criticism of this argument are the same as those for allowing someone to die and mercy death.

Arguments for Mercy Killing

Mercy for the "Living Dead." The main argument for mercy killing is that it is not a violation of the life principle because in most cases the people killed are not fully alive as human beings; rather, they are merely existing as organisms—a network of organs and cells. It is an act of mercy, a proponent of mercy killing might argue, to end the life of those people, who, although not "brain dead," have suffered 80 percent brain damage. Even if such people recover from their comas, the damage to their brains is so extensive that their lives will never be normal again. They will have a plantlike existence, exhibiting no personality or real human consciousness whatsoever; therefore, it is an act of mercy to end their existence.

The main criticism of this argument is that one is actually murdering such people. Because they cannot be declared dead under any acceptable medical or legal criteria, a dangerous precedent is set when someone is sanctioned to directly end their lives. It is one thing to allow them to die by refusing to use any extraordinary means to save them if they are attacked by pneumonia or kidney or heart failure; it is quite another, however, to directly murder them, even out of a motive of mercy.

Financial and Emotional Burdens. People with extensive brain damage, along with many other sick and injured people, are financial and emotional burdens on their families and on society. Such burdens are often tremendous, and, some argue, they serve no significant purpose because patients in such situations gain absolutely nothing from their maintenance except the continuation of what is assumed to be a minimal and worthless existence.

The main criticism of this argument is that finances should not be a determining factor where human life is concerned. It is true that the emotional burden is often difficult to bear, but here again we should not sanction the sacrifice of one human life just to ease the emotional burden on another.

The Patient's Desire to Die. Another argument for mercy killing is that if patients with brain damage could communicate with us, they would say that they would rather be killed than to linger on as burdens to their families and society or to exist as organisms without consciousness.

The main criticism here, however, is that we cannot *know* any of this for certain because the patients cannot communicate. It is possible that living wills or directives to physicians could be revised to include mercy death and mercy killing as well as allowing someone to die, but it would be very difficult to get such documents legalized. Faced with such a directive, the state would probably feel that it had the obligation to preserve and protect human life rather than authorize the execution of innocent people, regardless of the status of their existence.

The Possibility of Establishing Legal Safeguards. One of the strongest arguments against both mercy death and mercy killing is that if such actions were sanctioned they would undoubtedly be abused. For example, if it were legal to perform mercy killing on people who had reached a certain point in their illness or a certain age, wouldn't such a law invite abuse by people who wanted such things as organs to transplant, inheritances, or elimination of personal financial burdens, and couldn't it become an instrument of revenge or other motives usually connected with killing that is not "mercy" oriented? O. Ruth Russell, who advocates a comprehensive euthanasia law that would include mercy killing, has stated that legal safeguards can be established to avoid abuses and yet allow people a right to "death with dignity." She lists no fewer than fifteen carefully stated provisions or safeguards. Briefly, some of these are as follows: the law would be permissive rather than mandatory or compulsory; there could be no secrecy; there would have to be a written, notarized request; an advisory panel would be used; several doctors must be involved; a waiting period would be required; and it would be a criminal offense to falsify any documents, coerce patients or next of kin, or perform any malpractice involving any act of euthanasia.[8]

The main criticism of this argument is that most of these safeguards provide for mercy death, but few of them would help to protect people against mercy killing against their wills. Any legislation that would give power to the state or to certain individuals to take the lives of those who were too "unworthy" or "useless" to live would be extremely hard to control, and there would be little protection for helpless, innocent human lives.

◆

Cases for Study and Discussion

CASE ◆ 1

A doctor who was performing a legal abortion on a woman five months pregnant noticed that the "aborted fetus" was actually alive, so he held the fetus's head inside the woman's vaginal canal until the fetus suffocated. The doctor's thinking was that the fetus was intended to have been killed or born dead during the abortion, and that its being born alive was an error that could result in an unwanted or deformed child. Therefore, he felt that he had performed an act of mercy. What do you feel about the doctor's action?

CASE ◆ 2

Laura, a nineteen-year-old woman, fell into a coma because of an overdose of drugs and alcohol. She was given emergency treatment at a hospital and was placed on a respirator, which stabilized her breathing. She remained in a deep coma, and when she was tested by neurologists and neurosurgeons it was discovered that about 70 percent of her brain was irretrievably damaged. She was not brain dead, however: She reacted to pain, her eyes would sometimes open and her pupils would contract, she would at times thrash about, and her EEG showed some brain activity. She was in a persistent vegetative state. Because she could not be pronounced dead in any medical or legal sense, the hospital and doctors refused to take her off the respirator or stop any other treatments they were giving her. At one point Laura's sister was alone in the room with her, and thinking that Laura wouldn't want to live this way, she disconnected the respirator and caused her sister's death. Discuss in detail your reactions to the sister's decision.

CASE ◆ 3

Before much was known about Tay-Sachs disease, Betty and Irv, a young Jewish couple, gave birth to a son who had this disease. They were told by their doctor that the boy would become very sick and slowly degenerate over a period of about a year and that he would become blind and suffer convulsions. They were also told that there is absolutely no cure for the disease and that their son was sure to die. After watching the child for about six months Irv was not able to stand it any longer, and he put a pillow over his son's face and suffocated him.

Under these circumstances, do you feel that Irv was justified in performing a mercy killing?

CASE ♦ 4

A seventy-five-year-old man in Florida, a state with many retired and sick senior citizens, shot his wife twice in a mercy killing. The wife was suffering from Alzheimer's disease and osteoporosis (a degenerative bone disease). The couple was well off because the husband was a retired engineer. He had hired several women to care for his wife, who often was disoriented, irritable, and confused. The wife did not deal well with these women and was constantly embarrassing her husband by showing up in public, sometimes half-dressed and confused. One day she sought him out at a condominium owners' meeting and was particularly confused and troublesome. He took her back to their condominium and sat her down on a couch. He then picked up a pistol he owned and shot her in the back of the head once and then a second time because he thought she might still be alive. The man was arrested for murder in the first degree, tried, convicted, and sentenced to a minimum of twenty-five years in prison (Florida law for a first degree murder conviction).

Several points about this case should be noted: (1) There was no evidence that his wife had asked for death, nor that he had asked her if that was what she had wanted. (2) He showed very little remorse in court, stating that he believed he had acted morally. (3) The prosecuting attorney stated that the husband's sentencing was correct because allowing him to go unpunished would set a dangerous precedent in Florida, that any time confused or sick old people became hard to care for or deal with, someone could mercy kill them with impunity. (4) Despite being well off, at no time did the husband look into or attempt to place his wife in one of the many facilities established to care for Alzheimer's patients.

Since the husband was seventy-five and not well, many people, including his daughter, thought his sentence should be commuted or that he should be pardoned since he would probably die in prison. His case was referred to a commission appointed by the governor to make recommendations concerning the husband's situation, but the commission ruled that he should remain in prison. Several years later the governor commuted his sentence, and he is now out of prison. Do you think that what the husband did was moral or immoral? Why? Do you think this case was handled correctly? Why or why not? Do you feel that the husband should've been prosecuted at all? Why or why not? Do you feel that he tried all available alternatives before killing his wife? If not, what should he have done? Do you think his sentence should have been commuted or not? Why? How is this case different from the preceding cases under the mercy death section of this chapter? Are the other cases more justifiable than this one? Why or why not?

Chapter Summary

I. Definition of terms
   A. *Euthanasia* is a confusing and ambiguous term because it is subject to emotionalism. The word originally meant a "good or happy death." More recently it has come to mean mercy killing.
   B. Because this term is so confusing, it is replaced in this book by three phrases: "allowing someone to die," "mercy death," and "mercy killing."
   C. Allowing someone to die involves both not starting curative treatment when no cure is possible and stopping treatment when it is no longer able to cure a dying patient. It means allowing a dying patient to die a natural death without interference from medical science and technology.
   D. Mercy death is the taking of a direct action to terminate a patient's life because the patient has voluntarily requested it—essentially an assisted suicide.
   E. Mercy killing is the taking of a direct action to terminate a patient's life without his or her permission.
   F. It should be noted that neither mercy death nor mercy killing is legal in the United States or in most countries throughout the world.
   G. Brain death occurs when a patient has a normal heartbeat and normal respiration but has suffered irreversible and total brain damage.
      1. The criteria for "brain death" are unreceptivity and unresponsiveness, no spontaneous movements or breathing, no reflexes, and a flat EEG.
      2. When patients are declared "brain dead," removing life-support equipment or stopping treatment obviously cannot be the cause of their death, so this does not constitute allowing someone to die, mercy death, *or* mercy killing.
   H. Persistent Vegetative State (PVS) results from damage to the cerebral cortex, or neocortex, which controls the cognitive functions. A PVS patient is not brain dead, but lacks and will permanently lack even the minimum that makes life human life.
II. Allowing someone to die
   A. This problem has become more crucial in the twentieth century because of the availability of advanced lifesaving and life-supporting technology and procedures.
   B. There are a number of arguments against allowing someone to die.
      1. Some say it is tantamount to abandoning a dying person, though this need not be the case if we distinguish carefully between the "curing and healing" and "comforting and caring for" aspects of medicine.

2. Cures may be found or miracle cures may occur.

3. We can never choose death over life—we can never opt for death. Medicine must save lives, not end them. There is a difference, however, between accepting death as inevitable and choosing it.

4. Some argue that allowing someone to die interferes with God's divine plan. One can also ask, however, which constitutes interference with God's plan: allowing someone to die when his or her time has come or prolonging the person's death? The argument can be used to support either side.

C. There are a number of arguments for allowing someone to die.

1. Individuals have rights over their own bodies, lives, and deaths. One can also argue, however, that their freedom is not unlimited.

2. Patients have the right to refuse treatment, and we should not overrule this right—treatment often will not cure a particular patient, and it is sometimes worse than the disease.

3. Allowing someone to die will shorten suffering; however, it will also shorten the person's life.

4. Patients have the right to die with dignity. The phrase "dying with dignity," however, can cover up abandonment, mercy death, and mercy killing.

D. Extraordinary means to keep people alive are those that involve a grave burden for oneself or another, and they vary according to circumstances involving persons, places, times, and cultures. Such measures as radical surgery, radiation therapy, respirators, and heart machines probably fall into this category when they are used merely to prolong dying.

E. Ordinary means are also difficult to define, but for terminally ill patients they would include controlling pain and other symptoms as opposed to performing radical surgery or using respirators or heart machines.

F. "Appropriate" or "inappropriate" care might be better terms than "ordinary" and "extraordinary" because of the confusion surrounding the latter terms. Thus, people could decide what would be appropriate or inappropriate care depending on the particular situation of a patient.

G. The Patient Self-Determination Act (PSDA), effective December 1991, was passed to give patients a number of rights:

1. The right to considerate and respectful care.

2. The right to make decisions involving their health care, including the following:

(a) The right to accept or refuse treatment.

(b) The right to formulate advance directives and appoint a surrogate to make health care decisions on their behalf.

3. The right to information necessary to make treatment decisions.

H. Advance directives take three forms.

1. Two cases, the Quinlan and Cruzan cases, were instrumental in raising the consciousness of many people concerning the need for advance directives.

2. The Living will, established by the organization called Choice in Dying, was the first such documented suggested. It is not a legal document unless a particular state makes it so.

3. The California Natural Death Act Declaration was signed into law in 1976 and was broadened by further legislation in 1992. It does not provide for the designation of a surrogate to act on a patient's behalf when the patient can no longer do so.

4. The Durable Power of Attorney for Health Care (DPAHC) is the best of the three documents because it is fully legal, at least in California, and also provides for the designation of a surrogate for the patient.

I. The hospice approach to care for the dying can solve most of the problems surrounding allowing someone to die, and it can often eliminate the necessity for mercy death and mercy killing.

1. There is an emphasis on comforting and caring for patients rather than on curing and healing them.

2. The team approach is utilized to provide support for patients and their families.

3. Hospices take a unique approach to pain and symptom control.

   (a) They recognize the difference between acute and chronic pain.

   (b) They recognize that pain has four levels—physical, mental or emotional, sociological, and spiritual—and they treat all four levels.

   (c) They utilize the preventive rather than the reactive approach to pain control.

4. They utilize outpatient and home care wherever possible, using the team approach to provide all levels of support.

5. Where this is not possible, hospices provide homelike, humanized inpatient care in comfortable surroundings.

6. They attempt to provide freedom from financial worry for patients and their families.

7. They provide bereavement counseling before, during, and after a patient's death.

8. This approach allows patients a natural death in peace and dignity with support from their families, friends, the medical community, and society in general.

9. This approach also obviates most of the necessity for mercy death and mercy killing, at least where it concerns suffering, terminally ill patients.

III. Mercy death (voluntary dying or assisted suicide)

A. The arguments against mercy death are much like those used against suicide except that in mercy death the issue is further complicated by the fact that someone else has to do the killing.

1. The argument of irrationality has less force here than in the case of suicide because of the patients' pain and suffering and because they are going to die soon anyway. However, one can question whether patients in extreme pain and suffering can ever be rational about wanting death.

2. The religious argument remains the same except that the situation is further complicated by the fact that someone else has to do the killing—the mercy motive, it is argued, does not justify murder.

3. The domino argument has additional force in that if mercy death is allowed, mercy killing may soon follow.

4. The justice argument in this case involves the guilt and other negative feelings of the person who has to do the killing, and it also involves the burden of guilt placed on family members because they couldn't do anything to prevent their loved one from wanting to die.

5. That a cure may be found is another argument presented here.

6. One can argue that the hospice alternative has eliminated the need for mercy death; however, some patients may not want any treatment, hospice treatment included, and it can therefore be argued that they should be allowed to make a choice for death.

B. The arguments for mercy death are much like those for suicide.

1. Patients should have the freedom to decide about their own deaths, and the person who performs the act merely carries out the patient's wishes.

2. We do the same for dumb animals, and we owe our fellow humans at least as much consideration and mercy.

C. The legal status and ramifications of mercy death.

1. Two active advocates for mercy death are Derek Humphry and Dr. Jack Kevorkian.

2. Mercy death is currently illegal in all of the 50 states and in most countries of the world. Both California and Washington attempted to pass legislation making it legal, but both attempts failed.

IV. Mercy killing

A. Mercy killing is the termination of someone's life without that person's explicit consent by a direct means out of a motive of mercy.

B. There are several arguments against mercy killing.
   1. It is a direct violation of the Value of Life principle—murder is murder, regardless of motive.
   2. Since the consent of patients cannot be obtained, mercy killing involves an outside decision about the worth of their lives and sets a dangerous precedent for eliminating others who may be considered "useless" to society. Who should be entrusted with decisions concerning the worth of people's lives?
   3. Cures may be found or patients may come out of deep comas; if we kill them, we eliminate these possibilities.
C. There are several arguments for mercy killing.
   1. We are not violating the Value of Life principle because most of those who undergo mercy killing are not fully alive human beings; rather, they are mindless organisms.
   2. The longer people continue to "merely exist," the greater the financial and emotional burdens on the family and on society.
   3. If patients in such situations could make their wishes known, they would say that they wanted to die. The only trouble with this argument is that we cannot *know* this for sure since the patients cannot communicate with us.
   4. Legal safeguards can be clearly established to prevent abuses of legalized mercy 9killing.

Exercises for Review

1. Define the following terms, showing the distinctions among them: *allowing someone to die, mercy death, mercy killing, brain death, persistent vegetative state, ordinary and extraordinary means and appropriate and inappropriate care.*

2. How do mercy death and mercy killing in general differ from other types of killing? Do you agree that there is a real difference here? Why or why not?

3. Why have dramatic advances in medicine forced us to take an increasingly harder look at allowing someone to die, mercy death, and mercy killing?

4. Explain the hospice approach to care for the dying. Do you think this eliminates the necessity for mercy killing and mercy death? Why or why not?

5. What are the living will, California Natural Death Act Declaration, and the Durable Power of Attorney for Health Care (DPAHC), and how do they differ? Do you think such advance directives are important? Why or why not? Which do you think is or are more useful, and why?

6. Select the advance directive you like the best, and complete it for yourself (if you strongly object to doing this, carefully explain why).

7. What kinds of safeguards, if any, are necessary in any consideration of allowing someone to die, mercy death, and mercy killing?

8. To what extent do you think the following are moral or immoral: allowing someone to die, mercy death, and mercy killing? Be specific, and support your answer with evidence whenever possible.

9. Assuming that such acts were legal, could you yourself ever allow someone to die or perform the acts of mercy death or mercy killing? If not, why not? If so, under what circumstances? Describe the circumstances fully, and explain the reasoning behind your answers.

10. If mercy death and/or mercy killing were legalized, should doctors terminate patients' lives? Why or why not? If not, who should terminate them? Why? Could you do this for members of your family or friends? Why or why not?

Notes

1. From a presentation given by Dr. Richard Lamerton, M.D., at Bakersfield College, April 10, 1975.

2. Henry K. Beecher, et al., "A Definition of Irreversible Coma," *Journal of the American Medical Association* 205 (August, 1968). 85–88.

3. John A. Behnke and Sissela Bok, *The Dilemmas of Euthanasia* (Garden City, N.Y.: Anchor Books, 1975), 157–59.

4. Pope Pius XII, "The Prolongation of Life," *Pope Speaks* 4 (1958): 393–98.

5. Sandol Stoddard, *The Hospice Movement: A Better Way of Caring for the Dying* (Briarcliff Manor, N.Y.: Stein and Day, 1978), 221–29.

6. Richard Lamerton, "Euthanasia," *Nursing Times* (London), February 21, 1974.

7. David Sheff, "Playboy Interview with Derek Humphry," *Playboy* (August 1992): 49–144.

8. O. Ruth Russell, "Moral and Legal Aspects of Euthanasia," *The Humanist* 34 (July-August 1974): 22–27. See also Russell's *Freedom to Die: Moral and Legal Aspects of Euthanasia* (New York: Human Sciences Press, 1975).

Supplementary Reading

Beecher, Henry K., et al. "A Definition of Irreversible Coma." *Journal of the American Medical Association* 205 (August 1968): 85–88.

Behnke, John A., and Sissela Bok. *The Dilemmas of Euthanasia.* Garden City, N.Y.: Anchor Books, 1975.

Brody, Baruch, ed. *Suicide and Euthanasia.* Norwel, Mass.: Kluwer Academic Publications, 1989.

Cundiff, David. *Euthanasia Is Not the Answer: A Hospice Physician's View.* Totowa, N.J.: Humana, 1992.

Dobihal, Edward F., Jr. "Talk or Terminal Care," *Connecticut Medicine* 38 (July 1974): 364–67.

Dumont, Richard G., and Dennis C. Foss. *The American View of Death: Acceptance or Denial?* Cambridge, Mass.: Schenkman, 1972.

Feifel, Herman, ed. *The Meaning of Death.* New York: McGraw-Hill, 1959.

Glaser, Barney G., and Anselm L. Strauss. *Awareness of Dying.* Chicago: Aldine, 1965.

Glover, Jonathan. *Causing Death and Saving Lives.* Harmondsworth, Middlesex, England: Penguin Books, 1977.

Horan, Dennis J., and David Mall, eds. *Death, Dying and Euthanasia.* New York: University Publications of America, 1980.

Humphry, Derek. *Final Exit.* Secaucus, N.J.: Carol Publishing, 1991.

———. *Jean's Way.* New York: HarperCollins, 1986.

———, and Ann Wickett. *The Right to Die: Understanding Euthanasia.* New York: Harper and Row, 1986.

Kohl, Marvin, ed. *Beneficent Euthanasia.* Buffalo, N.Y.: Prometheus Books, 1975.

Lack, Sylvia, and Richard Lamerton, eds. *The Hour of Our Death.* London: Geoffrey Chapman, 1975.

Lamerton, Richard. *Care of the Dying.* Westport, Conn.: Technomic Press, 1976.

Mappes, Thomas A., and Jane S. Zembaty, eds. *Biomedical Ethics,* 2nd ed. New York: McGraw-Hill, 1986.

President's Commission for the Study of Ethical Problems in Biomedical and Behavioral Research. *Deciding to Forego Life Sustaining Treatment.* Washington, D.C.: Government Printing Office, 1983.

Rachels, James. *The End of Life: Euthanasia and Morality.* New York: Oxford University Press, 1986.

Robitscher, Jonas B. "The Right to Die." *The Hastings Center Report* 2 (September 1972): 11–14.

Ross, Elisabeth K. *On Death and Dying.* New York: Macmillan, 1969.

———. *Questions and Answers on Death and Dying.* New York: Collier Books, 1974.

Rossman, Parker. *Hospice.* New York: Association Press, 1977.

Russell, O. Ruth. *Freedom to Die: Moral and Legal Aspects of Euthanasia.* New York: Human Sciences Press, 1975.

———. "Moral and Legal Aspects of Euthanasia." *The Humanist* 34 (July-August, 1974): 22–27.

Saunders, Cicely. "St. Christopher's Hospice." *Death: Current Perspectives.* Ed. Edwin S. Schneidman. Palo Alto: Mayfield, 1976.

Sheff, David. "Playboy Interview with Derek Humphry." *Playboy* (August 1992): 49–144.

Steinbock, Bonnie, ed. *Killing and Letting Die.* Englewood Cliffs, N.J.: Prentice-Hall, 1980.

Stoddard, Sandol. *The Hospice Movement: A Better Way of Caring for the Dying.* Briarcliff Manor, N.Y.: Stein and Day, 1978.

Thomasma, David C., and Glenn C. Graber. *Euthanasia: Toward an Ethical Social Policy.* New York: Continuum, 1990.

Veatch, Robert, with Edward Wakin. "Death and Dying." *U.S. Catholic* (April 1972): 7–13.

Wertenbaker, Lael Tucker. *Death of a Man.* New York: Random House, 1957.

Williamson, William P. "Prolongation of Life or Prolonging the Act of Dying." *The Journal of the American Medical Association* 202 (October 1967): 162–63.

CHAPTER 10

Abortion

Objectives

After you have read this chapter you should be able to

1. Define the following terms: *conceptus, zygote, embryo, fetus, child, viability, amniocentesis,* and *chorionic villus sampling (CVS).*

2. Understand the present legal status of abortion in the United States.

3. Understand that abortion involves the conflict of two basic principles: the Value of Life principle and the Principle of Individual Freedom.

4. Understand that, along with a moderate position, it involves a conflict of two "absolute right" positions: the strong antiabortion (prolife) position and the strong abortion-on-request (prochoice) position.

5. Discuss when human life begins, and present the stages in the development of the conceptus.

6. Distinguish between potential and actual human life and define and differentiate among life, human life, and human person.

7. Discuss who should make abortion or no-abortion decisions and why.

8. Present and discuss alternatives to abortion.

Introduction to the Abortion Issue

Definition of Terms

Many moral issues involve special terms or phrases that need defining, and the abortion issue is one of these. Before going on to discuss abortion, therefore, we shall briefly examine a few terms that relate to this issue.

Abortion. An *abortion* is the premature termination of a pregnancy—that is, termination prior to birth. A *spontaneous abortion* is the same thing as a miscarriage, whereas an *induced abortion* is caused by the woman herself or by another, usually a medical doctor.

Zygote. A *zygote* is the cell or group of cells that results from the union of the sperm and egg cells.

Embryo. The term *embryo* refers to the developing human individual from the second through the seventh weeks of gestation, or pregnancy.

Fetus. The term *fetus* refers to the developing human individual from the eighth week until birth.

Child. The term *child* is normally used after the fetus is born. However, as you shall see, it is also often used by strong prolife advocates to refer to the developing human individual from shortly after conception onward.

Conceptus. The very useful term *conceptus,* coined by Daniel Callahan, means "that which has been conceived."[1] It is useful because it is a neutral term that can be used to refer to the developing human individual from conception until birth, thus avoiding the many emotional overtones given to the other terms by both sides of the abortion issue.

Viability. Viability occurs somewhere between the twenty-sixth and twenty-eighth weeks of gestation when the conceptus is considered *viable,*—that is, able to survive outside of the mother's womb. Birth usually occurs between the thirty-ninth and fortieth weeks of pregnancy.

Amniocentesis. In *amniocentesis,* which can be performed after the sixteenth week of pregnancy, a needle is inserted into the amniotic sac, where the conceptus is gestating, and some of the amniotic fluid is withdrawn. When this fluid is tested, a great deal of information about the conceptus—its sex and the presence or absence of certain abnormalities—can be determined.

Chorionic Villus Sampling (CVS). CVS is another tool that can be used to diagnose genetic defects in the fetus as early as the ninth week of pregnancy. In CVS, a flexible catheter, inserted vaginally, is guided by ultrasound along uterine walls. Suction allows the catheter to extract fetal cells from the threadlike projections (villi) on the chorion, the outermost embryonic layer. The advantage of this procedure over amniocentesis is obviously the fact that results and diagnoses can be acquired much earlier, allowing for early abortion, if the woman desires. The disadvantages are that some studies have revealed that CVS might be the cause of limb deformities in children born to mothers who had the CVS procedure.[2]

General Statement of the Abortion Problem

Two basic principles come into conflict in the abortion issue: the Value of Life principle (basically in relation to unborn life, but also in relation to the life of the mother) and the Principle of Individual Freedom, that is, the mother's right over her own body, procreativity, and life.

Another basic question that comes into play in this issue is when human life begins and, perhaps more importantly, at what point it is to be valued and protected to the same extent as the lives of human beings who already have been born.

Yet another conflict between the positions for and against abortion centers on so-called *absolute rights.* According to the strong antiabortion (prolife) position, the conceptus has an absolute right to life from the moment of conception onward. According to the strong abortion-on-request (prochoice) position, however, women have absolute rights over their own bodies and lives. Both of these positions and the arguments used to support them will be discussed in detail later in the chapter.

Abortion in American History. From colonial times to the nineteenth century, the choice of continuing pregnancy or having an abortion was the woman's until "quickening" (when she is first able to feel the fetus move). An abortion in the first or even second trimester was at worst a misdemeanor. In 1800, there was not a single statute in the United States concerning abortion, but by 1900, it had been banned at any time in pregnancy by every state. According to Carl Sagan, this was due mostly to the change from an agrarian to an urban-industrial society and to the lowering of birthrates in the United States. Sagan also states that the newly formed American Medical Association (AMA), in trying to enhance its status and the status and influence of physicians, put a great deal of force behind the laws so that the choice concerning abortion was taken totally out of the hands of women. Finally, in the 1960s, a coalition of individuals and organizations, including the AMA, sought to overturn laws against abortion and reinstate the previous values, which were later embodied in *Roe* versus *Wade* in 1973.[3]

The Legal Status of Abortion in the United States. At the present time, abortion is legal in the United States and in many other countries. In the famous *Roe* v. *Wade* decision of the U.S. Supreme Court in 1973, which continues to be upheld, most individual state laws making abortion illegal were ruled unconstitutional. The Supreme Court stated that an abortion is permitted at the request of the woman without restriction in the first trimester (12 weeks) and with some restrictions, to protect a woman's health, in the second trimester. It allows states to forbid abortion in the third trimester except when there is a serious threat to the life or health of the woman.

On July 3, 1989, however, the Supreme Court heard another case, *Webster* v. *Reproductive Health Services,* in which it ruled that states had the constitutional right to legislate against using public funds, lands, institutions, and employees to perform abortions except when the mother's life is in danger. Further, in essence, the Court did away with the trimester decision-making process, accepting the importance of protecting potential human life from conception onward, and stating that the provision of the *Webster* v. *Reproductive Health Services* case that required the doctor to run several tests to determine the viability of 20-week fetuses was also constitutional. If such fetuses are determined to be viable, then an abortion cannot be performed. What the Court did, in effect, was to dilute *Roe* v. *Wade* to the extent that allowed at least some abortion decisions to be restricted by state law. The Court also agreed to hear three more cases in October 1989, the beginning of its next session, which could further change the original *Roe* v. *Wade* decision.

In July 1992, the Supreme Court heard another case, from Pennsylvania, *Planned Parenthood* versus *Casey,* in which it upheld a woman's right to choice (for example, it ruled against a woman's having to get her husband's permission). However, the Court also allowed Pennsylvania to institute a "gag rule" in any clinic receiving state or federal funds, meaning that no staff member of a clinic, except physicians, could counsel a woman on abortion. Also, there was a waiting period before any woman could have an abortion. Even though the Supreme Court did not throw *Roe* versus *Wade* out, it did allow states to restrict abortion counseling and the availability of abortion.

These changes, if enacted by states into laws, could strongly affect the rights of women from lower economic classes to secure abortions because most of them depend on public funding and assistance. The viability requirement, if enacted by states into laws, could vitally affect late abortions for fetal reasons—that is, when the woman has discovered through amniocentesis or CVS that her fetus will, if carried to term, be born with deformities of some kind. Presumably, if the fetus were determined to be viable by a doctor, then a late abortion for fetal reasons could not be performed. To what extent such laws will be enacted by other states remains to be seen, but restrictions on abortion rights are a probability for the future. Essentially, then, abortion is legal in the United States. Of course, that abortion is legal does not necessarily make it moral, and it is the moral question that we will be most concerned with in relation to this issue. In fact, the major questions we will deal with in this chapter are "Is abortion moral? If so, under what conditions? If not, why not?"

When Does Human Life Begin?

The first question in any discussion of the morality of abortion must be "Is abortion the taking of a human life?" In Chapters 10 and 11 of his book *Abortion: Law, Choice and Morality* (a book I urge those on both sides of the abortion issue to read because of the extensive evidence, rational arguments, objectivity, and compassion it offers), Daniel Callahan outlines several arguments for determining when life exists. He finally settles on the developmental view as the best approach to understanding the "conceptus." According to this view, one recognizes that *life* is present from conception but allows for the possibility that there may be a later different point at which such a life can be considered *human*.

It would seem to be obvious that human life *in potentiality* is existent in various stages of development during the nine months of gestation. I want to clarify here that when I use the word *potentiality* I am referring to the stage of zygote and to nothing previous; although some potentiality exists in both the sperm of the male and unfertilized ova of the female, they must be brought together under the appropriate conditions for there to be the beginnings of a new life. Once an ovum is fertilized, a process is begun that, barring accidents (miscarriage, or spontaneous abortion) or intentional actions (induced abortion), will eventually result in the birth of a human being.

Therefore, if we wish to make decisions consistent with the Value of Life principle, revering life and accepting death, we must recognize that human life *in potentiality* exists from conception. The conceptus passes through various key stages of development:

1. All human life starts from a fertilized egg the size of a period at the end of a sentence; then one cell becomes two and then four, and by the sixth day the egg implants itself on the walls of the uterus.

2. By the third week, the forming embryo is about two millimeters long and is developing various parts, but it looks a little like a segmented worm.

3. By the end of the fourth week it has grown to five millimeters (about 1/5 of an inch). Its tube-shaped heart is beginning to beat; it has gill-like arches and a pronounced tail; and it looks something like a newt or a tadpole.

4. By the fifth week, gross divisions of the brain can be distinguished, and developing eyes and limb buds appear.

5. By the sixth week, it is thirteen millimeters (about 1/2 an inch long); its eyes are still on the side of the head, as in most animals, and its reptilian face has connected slits where the mouth and nose will eventually be.

6. By the end of the seventh week, the tail is almost gone, sexual characteristics can be discerned, and the face is mammalian but somewhat piglike.

7. By the end of the eight week, the face resembles a primate's but is still not quite human; some lower brain anatomy is well-developed, and the fetus shows some reflex response to delicate stimulation.

8. By the tenth week, the face has an unmistakable human look, and it begins to be possible to distinguish male and female fetuses.

9. By the fourth month (sixteen weeks), one can distinguish faces of fetuses from one another; the mother can feel the fetus move by the fifth month; the lungs don't begin to develop until the sixth month; and recognizably human brain activity begins intermittently around the middle of the seventh month.

10. Brain waves with regular patterns typical of adult human brains do not appear in the fetus until about the thirtieth week of pregnancy—near the beginning of the third trimester. Fetuses younger than this, however alive and active they may be, lack the necessary brain architecture—they cannot yet think.[4]

At which of these stages can we say that the conceptus is a human life? Every stage is vital, but the closer the conceptus gets to viability, the more human qualities are present (at least biologically and genetically). This is why most people who advocate or even "suffer" an abortion to be performed argue that it should be done as soon as possible after pregnancy is discovered. There is, of course, some validity to this argument. Obviously, less human potential has been realized at earlier stages of development, but at any of these stages potential human life does exist.

Many antiabortionists argue that human life is an actuality at any stage after conception. Although it is certainly true that with abortion actual life is being taken or prevented from continuing, it is very difficult to positively state, in some of the earlier stages, at least, that the life is fully human. On the other hand, it is equally difficult to argue that the fetus is not an actual human life *in the womb* after the twelfth week, when "the brain structure is essentially complete and a fetal electrocardiograph through the pregnant woman can pick up heart activity."[5] The arguments that viability or actual birth, when the child can breathe on its own, are the only points at which human life begins, rely too heavily on humans' being able to survive without life support of some kind. Many human beings are dependent on some person or some machine in order to stay alive, and it is difficult to argue that if they cannot breathe for themselves or eat and drink on their own they are not actual human beings. The length of time that a child, once born, is heavily dependent on both of his or her parents is in itself almost a refutation of the viability argument or the argument "once born, now human."

What the available data essentially illustrate is that there is human life either in potentiality or in actuality from the moment of conception. This means that the Value of Life Principle is definitely involved in any consideration of abortion. We cannot say with any validity that the conceptus is nothing more than—as I heard one woman phrase it—"an intrusion upon the woman's body," like some unnecessary tumor or invading virus. It is not even like any of her organs, which, of course, may be removed for various reasons. It is, rather, a very special organism, which develops slowly but surely into a human life, and one must recognize this fact when discussing what is to be done with or to it, either for its own good or for the good of someone else (usually the woman who is carrying it).

The biological, genetic, and physical data remain the same regardless of the position we take concerning when human life begins; and they do not in themselves answer the important question "At what point in development is the conceptus to be valued to the extent that terminating its life would be equivalent to terminating the life of people who are already born?" This determination, as we shall see, is not made solely on biological or genetic data; rather, it is made on some sort of moral bias or assumption.

The strong prolife position takes the genetic view that human life is to be valued from conception onward. The strong prochoice position, on the other hand, takes the view that human life does not have value until birth. There are, of course, various positions between these two extremes, such as, for example, the view that human life is to be valued only from viability onward.

◆————————————————————————————————

Arguments Against Abortion

The Genetic View of the Beginning of Human Life

The strong prolife position, as I have mentioned, accepts the genetic view of when human life begins and when it is to be valued as such. According to this view, human life starts at conception; that is, as soon as the chromosomes from the sperm of the father and the ovum of the mother are united, then a human being exists that must be valued in the same way as if "he or she" were already born. The basis for this argument is that because a person's genetic makeup is established at conception, and because, once established it "programs" the creation of a unique individual, then the human being exists from the point of conception onward and must be valued as a human life. If we are truly concerned about protecting and preserving human life, the argument continues, then the safest position for us to hold is this one. Because people cannot agree on when human life actually begins—or, in a religious sense, when the human "soul" is present—then by valuing a conceptus as human from conception onward we are ensuring that we do not act immorally or irreverently toward human life, especially innocent, unborn human life.

The Sanctity or Value of Life Argument

We have already discussed the arguments concerning the sanctity or value of life in the two previous chapters, but this factor becomes even more crucial in relation to the issue of abortion precisely because the conceptus is innocent and cannot defend itself from being killed. The sanctity or value of life argument states that every unborn, innocent *child* (and this term, or the term *person,* is used by the strong prolife advocates instead of the terms *embryo, fetus,* or *conceptus*) must be regarded as a human person with all the rights of a human person from the moment of conception onward. The word *innocent* is a key one here: Some strong prolife advocates may accept killing in self-defense, capital punishment, or war as moral because the lives involved are often not "innocent." This argument holds that the conceptus not only has a right to life, but also that his or her right is absolute. This means that it overrides all other rights that might come into conflict with it, such as a woman's right to determine the course of her own procreative life or even her right to decide between her own life and the life of her conceptus if her pregnancy is complicated in some way.

The Domino Argument

This argument has been discussed in detail in the two previous chapters, but according to prolife proponents it is most forceful when applied to the abortion issue. They argue that recent history offers proof of the validity of the domino argument, stating that the individual killings, mass tortures, and genocide committed by the Nazis under Adolf Hitler began with the legalization of abortion. They feel that abortion is more vulnerable to starting the domino effect than any other type of act because it is not as visible or blatant as the murdering of already born children or adults. Because women never see their conceptuses, it is easier for them to disregard the human life involved; however, the argument continues, the minute we display a disregard for any form of innocent human life, born or unborn, we will start the domino effect, which can end only in a complete disregard for human life in all of its aspects.

The Dangers of Abortion to the Mother's Life

Another argument against abortion states that abortion procedures are dangerous to the mother's well-being, life, and future procreativity. These dangers have two aspects: the medical and the psychological.

Medical dangers. The medical dangers argument is that abortion involves an intrusion into the woman's vagina and womb that involves some danger to her body, especially these two parts of it. In order to understand specifically what these dangers are, we will briefly examine the abortion methods used at various stages of pregnancy.

1. *Uterine aspiration.* In this method a suction machine (aspirator), which consists of a plastic instrument at the end of a hose, is used to "aspirate," or suction off, the conceptus and related material. This method is generally used prior to the twelfth week of pregnancy, but it is an improvement on the D & C in that it does not require the use of a sharp curette. There are still possibilities of infection, however, but there's much less chance of uterine perforation. This method has come to replace the D & C in most early abortion situations.

2. *Saline abortion.* This procedure, like the hysterotomy, is usually performed during later pregnancies (after the twelfth week), and it is usually preferred to the hysterotomy (see item 3). In this procedure, a needle is inserted through the abdominal wall into the amniotic sac, where the conceptus is floating. Some of the amniotic fluid is drawn off and replaced by a glucose, saline, or prostaglandin solution. In about twenty hours, the woman goes into labor and usually delivers a dead fetus. There is some danger inherent in the injection of such substances into the amniotic sac. Also, even though the doctor performs the abortion procedure, he or she is not usually present during delivery, which causes problems when complications arise. This method can also cause some psychological problems because the woman involved has to go through labor just as if she were having a baby, yet the result is a dead fetus.

3. *Hysterotomy.* After the twelfth week of pregnancy, a miniature caesarean section can be performed. An incision is made in the abdominal wall and the conceptus and related material are removed, after which the incision is closed. There is always a danger involved in major surgery, and once a caesarean operation has been performed on a woman, any babies she may have in the future may also have to be delivered by caesarean section.

4. *Self-induced abortion.* Almost all of the experts agree that self-induced abortions are probably the most dangerous of all abortions because they are not done under proper medical supervision. They can easily result in infections and hemorrhaging, complications that can kill both the fetus and the woman. No one that I know of supports or promotes such abortions; in fact, one of the strongest arguments for allowing abortions to be legalized has been to discourage women from performing self-induced abortions.

Aside from the potential dangers of abortion methods in general, abortion increases a woman's chances of having miscarriages in later pregnancies; this is especially true for young girls who have had an abortion. Also, repeated abortions increase the level of danger. All of this leads prolife proponents to conclude that pregnancy and childbirth are normal functions of a woman's body and that artificial interruption of these functions can cause medical problems that make such procedures hazardous to women.[6]

Psychological Dangers. The psychological dangers argument is that it is psychologically very destructive to a woman to authorize the "killing of her baby." A woman who has committed such a terrible act, prolife supporters argue, has to live with a great deal of guilt. In fact, the emotional scars will never be eradicated from her psyche, whereas if she had gone through with her pregnancy, even though it might have required a psychological adjustment, it would never compare with having to adjust to the guilt resulting from an abortion.

The Relative Safety of Pregnancy

One of the strongest arguments put forth for abortion is that pregnancy can endanger a woman's health and even her life. The prolife people, however, maintain that these dangers have been virtually eradicated by advances in medicine. We are at the point now, they argue, where with only a very few exceptions a woman can be brought safely through a pregnancy. In the case of those few exceptions, as Father Josef Fuch, a Jesuit theologian, puts it, "There is in fact no commandment to save the mother at all costs. There is only an obligation to save her in a morally permissible way.... Consequently only one obligation remains: to save the mother without attempting to kill the child."[7] Father Fuch seems to be suggesting here that if the mother cannot be saved, then her life may have to be sacrificed to allow her child to be born, an action not morally acceptable to many if not most people.

The Existence of Viable Alternatives to Abortion

If a child is unwanted or if it is to be born deformed in some serious way, viable alternatives to abortion do exist. There are literally millions of childless couples who would love to adopt a child and raise it as their own. As a matter of fact, the number of babies now available for adoption (especially Caucasian babies) has dropped tremendously ever since abortions became legal in the United States. There are many fine, reputable agencies who can place children unwanted by their natural parents in homes where they will be cared for and loved. And even if such homes cannot be found, there are governmental institutions in which unwanted or deformed children can be placed and cared for by trained personnel. Certainly the fact that a conceptus is unwanted or handicapped cannot be a moral justification for "murdering" it, according to the prolife people.

The Irrelevance of Economic Considerations

Many women desire an abortion because they feel that they cannot financially afford to go through a pregnancy or to raise a child. The prolife proponents argue, however, that where innocent, unborn human life is involved, economic considerations cannot come first. If a woman becomes pregnant, she must accept the financial responsibility, along with the conceptus's father, for the birth and raising of their child. There are agencies in society—welfare, Medicaid, and private charitable organizations—that can give financial assistance to pregnant women whether they are married or not. According to this argument, families that are financially overburdened should be judicious about having more children, but if the woman does become pregnant, she cannot use financial problems as a reason to "take the lives of unborn children."

Responsibility for Sexual Activities

The responsibility for sexual activities argument states that whenever women engage in sexual acts with men, whether contraceptives are used or not, they must realize that pregnancy may ensue. Furthermore, they must accept the responsibility for their actions, whether or not the men shoulder the responsibility with them, and they cannot sacrifice an innocent human life because of their carelessness or indiscretion or because of the failure of a contraceptive device. A woman is responsible for not getting pregnant in the first place, according to the argument, and there are many methods she can use to avoid pregnancy. However, if it does occur, it is her responsibility to go through with it and give birth to her child.

Rape and Incest

Pregnancies resulting from rape are fairly rare, and those resulting from incest are rarer still. If rapes are reported in time, contraceptive procedures can be used effectively. If, however, women do become pregnant after rape or incest, this argument maintains that the destruction of innocent unborn human life is still not justified. Women must go through with the pregnancies, and, if they do not want the children because of the circumstances of their conception, they should put them up for adoption or place them in government-run institutions. In any case, according to this argument, innocent, unborn conceptuses should not have to pay with their lives for the sins or crimes of others.

◆

Arguments for Abortion

The argument for abortion essentially states that a woman ought to be allowed to have an abortion, regardless of the reason, if she requests it. Furthermore, she ought to be able to have her abortion without suffering recrimination, guilt, or restrictions, legal or otherwise. This position is based on several arguments.

Absolute Rights of Women Over Their Own Bodies

The central argument for absolute rights of women over their own bodies is that women, like men, should have absolute rights over their own bodies, including procreative rights. In the past, women, because of an "accident of nature"—the fact that they are the ones who get pregnant—have not shared in these equal rights, but now that birth control is possible, they can. These rights must also include abortion, which is, according to this argument, just another method of birth control that is used when other methods fail or have not been used. To carry this argument one step further, any conceptus is a part of a women's body until it is born; therefore, she has absolute say over whether it should continue to live in that body or whether it will be allowed to be born.

There are several corollaries to this major argument. First, there is the assumption that enforced maternities should not take place. No woman should be forced or even urged to go through her pregnancy against her will; she, and she alone, must decide her future. Second, it is male domination that is responsible for strict abortion laws. Because men do not know what it is like to be pregnant they can afford to be "highly moral" about the lives of conceptuses. Third, female freedom is ultimately dependent on full and free control of procreative life, and this includes abortion as well as other methods of birth control.

For example, let us say that a woman wants to pursue a career in medicine, which requires a long and arduous period of study. If she gets pregnant for one reason or another, unless she has complete control over her procreativity her life desires may never in fact be realized. The implication is that a woman shouldn't have to go through pregnancy, giving birth, and raising a child if this could completely destroy her life plans. How many men are required to make such a sacrifice? The answer is virtually none, and, according to the absolute rights argument, this is unfair to women. A man always has complete control over his sex life, except for forced sexuality, such as rape or child molestation, and a woman is entitled to the same freedom and rights. True, both she and the man can share the responsibility for contraception, but abortion must also be available when these methods fail or are not used for one reason or another.

Birth as the Beginning of Human Life

The prochoice point of view assumes that until a child is actually born, human life does not exist, at least not to the extent that the conceptus should have the same rights as people who have already been born. As mentioned earlier, as long as the conceptus is within the woman's body it is a part of her body and is subject to her decision about whether it is to be carried to term or not. Most prochoice women would probably argue that abortions should be performed as early as possible both because the conceptus is less developed and because this is safer for the woman. However, abortions should also be allowed later in pregnancy if, for example, a woman discovers that the conceptus will be born seriously deformed, which can't be determined until around four months after conception. In any case, because, according to this argument, an unborn conceptus at any stage of development cannot be considered a full human being, then its right to life is not absolute; rather, it must be subordinated to the woman's right over her own body and life, which is absolute, just as men's right are.

The Problem of Unwanted or Deformed Children

Since the arrival of significant birth control methods, including abortion, it has been possible to ensure that every child born into the world is thoroughly wanted. And now that people can limit the size of their families, they can better control the quality of their lives and the lives of their children. This argument states that given present-day conditions—overpopulation, pollution problems, economic difficulties—only children who are planned for and really wanted should be born, and abortion makes this possible. If a woman becomes pregnant, she must bear the responsibility of her pregnancy and should not pass this burden on to society. If she is willing to bear the child and raise it, she should be allowed to do so, but if she does not intend to take responsibility for it, she should have it aborted rather than put it up for adoption or have it institutionalized and allow it to become a burden on others.

There are two additional assumptions that contribute to the prochoice position on unwanted or deformed children.

Adoption as a Poor Solution. According to prochoice advocates, adoption is not as viable an alternative as the prolife forces describe. First, even if a woman agrees to put her child up for adoption after it is born, she still has to go through nine months of pregnancy, which will hamper her freedom and life a great deal. Second, it is much more difficult, both physically and psychologically, to go through pregnancy and give a child up for adoption than it is to have a conceptus aborted before it is born. Third, adoptive children don't always have as pleasant an existence as prolifers like to have us think. Adoptive children often feel rejected when they discover that their natural mothers gave them up. Often they go in search of their natural parents regardless of the love and quality of their adoptive parents and homes. Also, some of these children end up moving from foster home to foster home, enduring a poor quality of life.

Lack of Humane Institutions. One of the arguments of the prolife people is that orphaned and handicapped children can be maintained in institutions established by society for this purpose. The prochoice people answer, however, that life these days is difficult enough for children who are wanted or "normal," and they question why women would want to give birth to children who are not wanted or who will be handicapped, especially those with serious handicaps. Furthermore, the quality of the institutional or even private care available for deformed children is below minimum and sometimes inhumane; therefore, bringing children into such situations is much worse than terminating their lives before they are born. It goes without saying, according to prochoice people, that no woman, with or without a family, should be required to give birth to or raise a deformed child unless she wants to. With the availability of the amniocentesis and CVS procedures that I described earlier, women can, in many cases, know between the fourth and fifth month of pregnancy whether or not their child will be deformed, and they can choose whether to abort the deformed conceptus or to give birth to it.

The Relative Safety of Abortion

The argument of the prolife people that states that abortion is dangerous to women's medical and psychological well-being is flatly opposed by the prochoice people.

The Medical Aspect. First, according to the prochoice position, the only dangerous abortions are either self-induced abortions or those performed by unqualified personnel in unsanitary conditions at the time when abortions were not legal. Many more women lost their lives from these procedures than have since abortions have been legalized. As long as abortions are performed by qualified medical personnel in qualified medical settings, the risk for all of the procedures, according to the prochoice argument, is minimal. Essentially, abortion in the first twelve weeks is a minor procedure that carries with it almost no risk. Later abortions are, of course, more complicated, but even in such cases, with appropriate medical care and facilities, women can be brought through abortions quite safely.

As a matter of fact, prochoice people would argue, abortions are much safer—especially in the early stages of pregnancy, when they are most often performed—than going through nine months of pregnancy. This is particularly the case when the woman has some sort of debilitating illness (for example, diabetes, hypertension, or a diseased heart). They maintain that the drain on a woman's strength, health, and body caused by going through pregnancy leaves marks that can far outlast the short-term effects of an abortion procedure, especially when abortion is performed early in the pregnancy.

The Psychological Aspect. Some women who decide to have an abortion may, of course, feel guilt, but many women do not experience any such feelings because they do not consider the conceptus a human being in any respect. Furthermore, if guilt feelings do exist, they can be overcome either by the women themselves or with counseling. The prochoice people go on to say that most of these guilt feelings, if they do exist, will be temporary, and that they are nothing compared to the psychological damage of going through nine months of pregnancy and then bearing an unwanted and/or deformed child.

Also, if a woman has to spend eighteen or more years raising a child when she really doesn't want to, the psychological damage she suffers may be longer lasting and much more detrimental than a few hours, days, weeks, or even months of guilt over having to abort an unwanted conceptus. Moreover, going through a pregnancy and having to give a child up for adoption will cause greater psychological damage than having an early or even a late abortion. The prochoice people also believe that this psychological damage extends to the child itself once it is born. What psychological damage will be wreaked upon children who grow up unwanted and unloved by mothers who were forced to have them against their will? Physical and emotional deprivation extending to child abuse and even death is far worse, the argument states, than not letting the child be born at all.

Refutation of the Domino Argument

As far as the domino argument is concerned, prochoice people argue that there is no hard evidence showing that legalizing abortion will necessarily result in a loss of reverence for human life in any other areas. They point to the many laws against capital punishment in existence around the world; the laws against mercy death and mercy killing; and to other laws against murder in all forms. They also argue that the Hitler example is not valid evidence for the prolife position. They maintain that Hitler's motives were *never* beneficent in any sense of the word—that he was out to destroy any enemies of the Third Reich, innocent or not.

The prochoice people argue further that they are not favoring mandatory abortion in any way, shape, or form; rather, all they want is free choice for women who do not want to go through pregnancies. Making abortion legal does not mean that eventually all Jewish women, for example, would be forced to abort because they and their offspring would be considered unfit or subhuman as in the Third Reich; it only means that women of all races and religions would have a choice in terms of abortion. They argue further that the availability of abortion has not made women more callous toward human life, but that it has, in fact, made them more loving of the children that they really wanted and planned for.

The Danger of Pregnancy to the Mother's Life

Another argument of the prochoice advocates is that pregnancy does pose dangers to the health and life of women. Furthermore, they believe that if human lives have to be traded off, the life of someone already born, in this case the pregnant woman, should obviously take precedence over the life of an unborn conceptus. They would disagree strongly with Josef Fuch, maintaining that abortion is a permissible way to save a woman's life when it is threatened by a complicated pregnancy. In fact, they believe that even if there is only *some* risk to the woman, she still has the right to decide for her life over that of the unborn conceptus.

Rape and Incest

The prochoice people would argue that rape and incest are two of the most serious crimes committed against a woman and that under no circumstances should she be forced to endure an unwanted pregnancy resulting from either of these actions. There is no argument, they feel, other than the woman's own desire to go through with the pregnancy, that would justify putting her through the torment of pregnancy and childbirth under these circumstances.

Responsibility for Sexual Activities

The prochoice advocates would agree with their prolife opponents that women must accept responsibility for their sexual activities, but, as I stated earlier, they believe that this responsibility definitely includes the right to terminate a pregnancy. They are particularly disturbed by the notion that "if a woman is stupid enough to get pregnant despite the availability of contraceptive devices and the ability to abstain from sex, then it's her fault, and she must go through with the pregnancy." To them, this attitude reflects society's desire to punish women for their carelessness or indiscretions. They feel that no matter how pregnancy occurred, the woman does not deserve punishment any more than does the man who is also responsible for the pregnancy; in no way should a woman be abused or discriminated against for exercising her free choice in dealing with her problem.

Abortion as the Woman's Choice

The final argument for the prochoice position is that abortion is purely a medical problem and, therefore, women should be legally free to make a private decision about their bodies and their lives that should not be intruded upon by others. No one else has to go through the pregnancy; no one else has to go through the childbirth; and no one else has to then devote eighteen years or more to raising the child; therefore, the final decision to abort or to go through with pregnancy must be the woman's, and hers alone, with no interference from anyone else or any part of society.

♦————————————————————————————

The More Moderate Positions on Abortion

As I have mentioned before, the strong prolife and the strong prochoice positions embody the extreme approaches to the abortion issue. As I have also mentioned, there are more moderate positions that can be found all along the spectrum between these extremes. It is difficult to characterize all the moderate positions on abortion, for some may allow abortion in cases of rape or incest or when the mother's life is in danger but not for other reasons. Some may allow abortion up to viability but not after, whereas others may allow it up to twelve weeks but not after. Some may allow abortion for psychological reasons or in cases of fetal deformity, whereas others may not. Because of this diversity, what I will present in this section is a set of basic assumptions that the more moderate positions might hold and that will also embody criticisms of the two extreme positions.

An Unresolvable Conflict of Absolutes

One aspect of the abortion issue that most moderates would agree on is that neither of the extreme positions is workable: They are both based on unresolvable and conflicting "absolutes" that, in turn, are based on questionable premises. The first approach to this problem generally taken by moderates is that there are no absolute rights—there are strong rights, but there are no rights that supersede all other human rights. In Chapter 4, I showed that there are such things as absolute *truths;* I never said, however, that there were absolute *rights*.

No Absolute Right to Life. The Value of Life principle is important, but it is not the only value there is—that's why there are other principles. As I have mentioned before, many people have sacrificed their lives for ideals that the other principles embody: goodness, justice, freedom, and honesty. It is also true that the Value of Life principle involves other aspects besides the mere right to existence—even the right to existence of innocent, unborn life.

One of these other aspects of the life principle is the survival and integrity of the human species. This aspect includes the problem of overpopulation and the burden placed on society when children are born with deformities. A second aspect is the right of families to procreate and reproduce their own kind without hindrance. Obviously, this aspect comes into conflict with the first aspect in cases where families exhibit a high risk of passing on genetic deficiencies that may cause burdens on society as a whole. A third aspect is the integrity of bodily life, which involves the protection of human beings from life-threatening situations such as war, capital punishment, poverty, mercy death and mercy killing, suicide, and abortion. Finally, a fourth aspect is the freedom to live life the way we want to—an aspect that affects both the pregnant woman and the conceptus.[8]

As we can readily see, then, the Value of Life principle involves a great deal more than just the right to life of the unborn (although this is definitely included), and that is why we cannot say that anyone has an *absolute* right to live.

No Absolute Rights over One's Body. I have already described in several chapters situations in which people do not have absolute rights over their bodies. Generally we view the rights of individual people over their bodies as strong, but we do not, for example, allow people ridden with plague or other contagious diseases to refuse treatment or quarantine, because if we did so, they could harm or even cause the death of others. We also feel that people should be prevented from mutilating or killing themselves whenever this can be done without destructive or excessive force.

However, in earlier chapters on suicide and mercy death, I described the position that individual human beings should have the basic freedom to decide about their own living or dying, and this, of course, includes a complete decision over what is done to their bodies. That is, all individuals can refuse treatment for themselves and die rather than live because it is their bodies and lives that are at stake. Our courts have generally upheld individuals' refusals of treatments as long as these refusals were for themselves and not someone else. Patients with kidney failure have refused dialysis because they did not want to live what they felt was the undignified life of a dialysis patient and preferred to die instead; other patients have refused surgery and radiation and chemical therapy because of what it would do to their bodies and lives. All these situations come under the heading of individual rights, and no one has the right to interfere with these decisions as long as severe harm is not being done to anyone else.

This argument, however, falters somewhat when we begin to talk about a pregnant woman's rights over her own body. The problem here, of course, is that her body and her life now contain another body and life in some stage of development. For this reason, the argument of individual rights over one's body does not hold in an absolute sense, because now what affects this woman's body and life will also affect the body and life of another potential human being. In her moral considerations, which involve her life and the life of the conceptus, the woman should observe the Value of Life principle.

Much less moral justification can be given for the taking of a human life if that life could be a normal one, with the possibility of its also being good and meaningful. This does not mean that the woman's individual rights over her life and her body should not be considered—they definitely should, and the final decision to abort or not abort still must rest with her—but it does mean that there is also another potential or actual human life and body at stake in her decision. Therefore, the pregnant woman does not have *absolute* rights over her body, but neither does the conceptus have an absolute right to life.[9]

The Problem of When Life Begins—A Synthesis

Generally those who hold a moderate position feel that the genetic or strong prolife view of when human life begins draws the line too early, even though this provides for the safest and most consistent means of protecting human life from its earliest stages onward. It is difficult for moderates to accept the idea that a group of cells—regardless of their potentiality—can be considered a human being with full personhood and all the rights accorded to human beings who are already born.

On the other hand, waiting until birth to assign value to developing human life seems wrong because it disregards the significance of the increasing potentiality toward actual human life that occurs throughout the entire gestation period. The attempt to determine when a conceptus becomes human has caused people to draw some rather ridiculously fine lines. For example, what essentially is the difference between a fetus in the thirty-eighth week and one that is newly born? Is this difference significant enough to allow one fetus to be valued as human, whereas the other is not?

The moderate position essentially takes what Daniel Callahan calls "the developmental view of when human life begins." What this view essentially maintains is that although conception does establish the genetic basis for an individual human being, some degree of development is required before one can legitimately speak of the conceptus as an "individual human being."

Furthermore, this view suggests that because the human individual develops biologically in a continuous fashion, it might be worthwhile to consider the possibility that human rights develop in the same way. Callahan goes on to say that the simplest and most satisfactory position on abortion is to avoid ascribing any legal or theological status to the embryo during the first two weeks of development. Beyond this time, however, the embryo becomes increasingly important and at viability the fetus should have almost the same rights as a newborn child.[10]

In her brilliant essay "Ethical Problems of Abortion," Sissela Bok essentially holds, like Callahan, to the developmental viewpoint. She also argues well for the difficulty of defining the term "human being" and lists instead some cogent reasons for protecting life:

1. Killing is seen as the greatest danger for victims because the knowledge of it causes "intense anguish and apprehension" and the actual taking of life can cause great suffering. Furthermore, once life has begun, its continued experience is so unique and valuable that no one should be deprived of it.

2. "Killing is brutalizing and criminalizing *for the killer.*"

3. Killing affects the family and friends of the victim, causing them great grief and loss.

4. Therefore all of society "has a stake in the protection of life" because killing "sets patterns for victims, killers, and survivors that are threatening and ultimately harmful to all."[11]

Bok goes on to say that these criteria do not lead her to the conclusion that early human life is unimportant; on the contrary, she believes that the conceptus definitely should be considered, along with the mother, as having value. However, she is led by these criteria to suggest that abortion on request should be allowed up to the end of the first trimester (the first twelve weeks, or three months). Between the thirteenth week and the twenty-sixth to twenty-eighth weeks (when viability occurs), special reason, such as severe malformation of the conceptus, should be required to justify an abortion; and from viability onward, abortions should not be allowed except to save the life of the mother, which must be truly endangered by a continuation of the pregnancy.

These guidelines, Bok adds, do not in any way suggest that abortion can be morally justified for everyone. Doctors, nurses, and prospective parents who feel that participation in an abortion would adversely affect their lives and their feelings are perfectly justified in refusing to have or perform an abortion at any stage in pregnancy.[12] Generally, then, Bok's position (which, as I have said, coincides with Callahan's) could accurately be described as the "moderate" position as to when human life begins and, more importantly, when it has sufficient value to cause it to receive the same protection as already born life.

♦

Cases for Study and Discussion

CASE ♦ 1

Janice, fifteen, and Bob, sixteen, have had sexual intercourse several times, and now Janice has discovered that she is two months' pregnant. Janice's mother was raised a Roman Catholic and does not want her daughter to have an abortion. Neither, however, does she wish to raise or help Janice raise the child. Instead, she wants Janice to go through with the pregnancy and give the child up for adoption. Janice's father is an agnostic, and he wants her to have an abortion because he knows that Janice is a good student and is interested in a law career—he is a practicing lawyer himself. Bob, who wants to be an engineer, also wishes Janice to have an abortion, and he is willing to see that all of her expenses are paid. Janice herself is quite confused about what she wants. She has been raised a Roman Catholic and shares some of her mother's misgivings about abortion, although she is not as committed to her faith as her mother is. She has talked to a young, sympathetic priest at her church, but he has told her she must not have an abortion as this would be a mortal sin. She has also gone to an abortion clinic to discuss the abortion procedure and its cost. What should Janice do, and why? Support your statements.

C A S E ◆ 2

Mary, thirty-eight, is married and has three children, ages ten, fifteen, and eighteen. Her husband manages a service station, and Mary has been working part-time as a bank teller. They are having a difficult time financially because their eighteen-year-old has just started college and they bought a new house a year ago. Although Mary was using a contraceptive, she now discovers that she is one month pregnant. She and her husband do not want any more children—indeed, they had thought they were finished bearing and raising them. Added to their other reasons for not wanting any more children, they are also worried by the knowledge that women who have pregnancies late in life have a greater chance of bearing a child with Down's syndrome. They finally decide that Mary should have an abortion. Were they right in making this decision? Should Mary wait until the fourth month and have an amniocentesis performed to see if the baby has Down's syndrome? If the baby does, then what should they do, and why?

C A S E ◆ 3

Leonard, twenty-five, and Rachel, twenty-three, discover that they are Tay-Sachs carriers after Rachel has become pregnant, and the doctor informs them that they have a one-in-four chance of bearing a Tay-Sachs child. Tay-Sachs is a fatal disease that is both degenerative and particularly horrible. They decide to wait until the fourth month of Rachel's pregnancy to have an amniocentesis performed. The results, which they receive in Rachel's fifth month of pregnancy, show that she will indeed give birth to a child with Tay-Sachs. What should they do?

C A S E ◆ 4

Lupe and Robert, both in their early twenties, are having their first child. Because Lupe had some problems early in her pregnancy, her doctor recommends that an amniocentesis be performed. At four months of pregnancy she undergoes the procedure, and the results six weeks later show that Lupe will give birth to a child with Down's syndrome. The results do not indicate how severe the mental retardation will be or if there are any other deformities. Lupe and Robert want children very badly, but they would rather not have to raise a mentally retarded child, especially since they are young enough to try again for a normal child. What should they do?

C A S E ◆ 5

Bill, thirty-seven, and Isabel, thirty-five, are married and have three daughters. One night when they had sexual intercourse Isabel forgot to wear her diaphragm, and she became pregnant as a result. After adjusting to the idea, Bill and Isabel decide it would be nice if they could have a son, since they already have three daughters. Since Isabel is thirty-five, she decides to have an amniocentesis performed to see if her fetus has Down's syndrome. After the procedure is done, the genetic counselor informs Bill and Isabel that the child will be normal as far as the test can determine, and also that the child will be a girl. Because Bill and Isabel do not want another girl, Isabel has an abortion, after which she has herself sterilized so that she can have no more children. Do you feel that she did the right thing?

Chapter Summary

I. Introduction to the abortion issue
   A. A number of terms related to the abortion issue must be defined.
      1. *Abortion* is the premature termination of a pregnancy.
         (a) A *spontaneous abortion* is a miscarriage.
         (b) An *induced abortion* is caused by the woman herself or by another, usually a doctor.
      2. *Zygote* is a cell or group of cells that results from the union of the sperm and egg cells.
      3. *Embryo* is a term to describe the conceptus between the second and eighth weeks of gestation.
      4. *Fetus* is the term used to describe the conceptus from the eighth week onward until birth.
      5. *Child* is the term normally used after the conceptus is born.
      6. *Conceptus* is a neutral term, coined by Daniel Callahan, which means "that which has been conceived."
      7. *Viability* is that period of pregnancy somewhere between the twenty-sixth and twenty-eighth weeks when the conceptus is considered *viable*—that is, able to survive outside of the mother's womb.

8. *Amniocentesis* is a procedure that can be performed after the sixteenth week of pregnancy and that reveals a great deal of information about the conceptus, including its sex and possible deformities.

9. *Chorionic Villus Sampling (CVS)* is another tool that can be used to diagnose genetic defects in the fetus as early as the ninth week of pregnancy.

B. The abortion issue is highly complex, involving a great number of factors.

1. Two basic principles come into conflict in relation to abortion: the Value of Life principle and the Principle of Individual Freedom.

2. Another basic question is, When does human life begin and at what point is it to be valued and protected?

3. Abortion also involves two conflicting "absolutes."

   (a) According to the prolife position, the conceptus has an absolute right to life.

   (b) According to the prochoice position, a woman has absolute rights over her body and life.

4. Abortion has gone through various stages of acceptance and rejection in American history:

   (a) From colonial times to the nineteenth century, the choice was the woman's until "quickening."

   (b) By 1900, it had been banned at any time in pregnancy by every state.

   (c) In 1973, *Roe versus Wade*, in effect, made abortion legal in all of the fifty states.

5. The legal status of abortion in the United States has also seen changes.

   (a) In 1973, the Supreme Court essentially made abortion legal in the first two trimesters of a woman's pregnancy, but allowed states to forbid abortion in the third trimester except in the case of a serious threat to the life of the mother.

   (b) In July 1989, in *Webster versus Reproductive Health Services*, the Court allowed states to put some restrictions on abortions when federal and state funds were used and did away with the trimester system.

   (c) In July 1992, in *Planned Parenthood versus Casey*, the Court allowed further restrictions while at the same time upholding a woman's right to choice.

II. When human life begins

A. *Life* is present from conception, and from this point on it develops.

B. There are certain key stages in the conceptus's development.

1. All human life starts from an egg the size of a period at the end of a sentence.
2. By the third week the embryo is developing various parts.
3. By the end of the fourth week, its heart begins to beat.
4. By the fifth week divisions of the brain occur, and developing eyes and limb buds appear.
5. By the sixth week it is about 1/2 inch long, its eyes are still on the sides of the head, and it is developing slits where its mouth and nose will be.
6. By the end of the seventh week, sexual characteristics can be discerned, and the face is mammalian but somewhat piglike.
7. By the end of the eighth week, the face resembles a primate's, there is some lower brain anatomy, and the fetus has reflex reactions.
8. By the fifth month, the mother can feel the fetus move. Lungs begin to develop during the sixth month, and human brain activity begins at about the seventh month.
9. Brain waves with regular patterns typical of adult humans begin only at about the thirtieth week of pregnancy.

C. There is *human life* either in potentiality or in actuality from the moment of conception. (Many consider that actual human life begins after the third month of life in the womb.)

III. Antiabortion (prolife) arguments
A. The prolife group believes in the genetic view of the beginning of human life—that human life begins at conception.
B. One prolife argument is based on the sanctity or value of life.
  1. The right to life is absolute, especially the right of innocent, unborn life.
  2. Every unborn "child" must be regarded as a human person with all the rights of a person from the moment of conception onward.
C. The domino argument applies to this issue much as it does to others. One proof of its validity cited by the prolife group is that Hitler started his history of atrocities by legalizing abortion.
D. Abortion is both medically and psychologically harmful to women.
E. The danger of pregnancy to a mother's life is almost nonexistent because of medical and technological advances.
F. There are viable alternatives to abortion.
  1. Unwanted babies can be put up for adoption.
  2. There are institutions and agencies to care for unwanted and/or deformed children.
  G. Economics cannot be a consideration when human life is concerned.

H. Women must accept full responsibility for their sexual activities, and when these activities result in pregnancy, innocent life cannot be sacrificed because of women's carelessness or indiscretion.

I. Rape or incest usually doesn't present problems because contraceptives can often be used in time; when they can't, however, even such means of conception do not justify the taking of innocent lives.

IV. Abortion-on-request (prochoice) arguments

A. Women have absolute rights over their bodies, and the conceptus is part of a woman's body until birth.

B. A conceptus cannot be considered a human life until birth.

C. Unwanted or deformed children should not be brought into the world.

1. It is more responsible to have an abortion than to burden society with an unwanted or deformed child.

2. Adoption is not always a solution.

D. Abortion is a no-risk medical procedure. Medical and psychological problems are much greater for women who go through pregnancies than for those who have abortions.

E. The domino argument used by prolife groups is not supported by hard evidence. Hitler's overall motives for permitting abortions were not at all the same as the motives of today's women.

F. Pregnancies resulting from rape and incest should never have to be gone through by any woman because of the horror of the circumstances of the conception.

G. Women do have responsibilities for their sexual activities, and having abortions when necessary is a part of these responsibilities.

H. Abortion is and must be totally a matter of the woman's choice—no one else should be able to interfere.

V. The more moderate positions on abortion

A. The strong prolife and prochoice positions present an unresolvable conflict of absolutes.

1. There is no absolute right to life, even though the Value of Life principle is important.

2. There is also no absolute right over one's body and life, even though it is a strong right.

B. The problem of when life begins may be considered through a synthesis.

1. The prolife position draws the line (for when life begins) too early.

2. The prochoice position draws it too late.

C. The moderate favors the developmental view of when life begins, which states that life does indeed begin at conception but gains value as it develops through the gestation period.

Exercises for Review

1. When, in your opinion, does human life begin? Substantiate your answer with as much evidence and reasoned argument as you can.

2. How would you distinguish among the following: life, human life, human person, potential life, actual life?

3. Briefly describe the five major stages of the development of the conceptus.

4. Do you agree or disagree with the position that the mother must be the one to make the final decision on whether to have an abortion? Why? Should anyone else be involved in the decision? If so, who, and if not, why not?

5. What workable alternatives to abortion would you recommend, and why?

6. Under what conditions do you feel it is moral to have an abortion? Under what conditions do you feel it is immoral? Be specific in giving reasons for your answers.

7. Would you classify abortion as murder, mercy killing, self-defense, or merely as the elimination of an organism? Explain.

8. What are the problems with the concepts that a woman has absolute rights over her own body and that a conceptus has an absolute right to life? Be specific.

9. Do you agree that if we are going to take a strong stand against abortion, we must do much more in the way of counseling and giving other kinds of assistance to the prospective mother? Why or why not? What kinds of assistance and counseling do you feel are necessary? (See Appendix 3, pp. 495–506.)

10. What do you think of the moderate position on abortion? Do you feel that it successfully resolves the conflict between the two extreme positions or not? Why?

Notes

1. Daniel Callahan, *Abortion: Law, Choice and Morality* (New York: Macmillan, 1970), 44.

2. Jean Seligman et al., "Is My Baby All Right," *Newsweek* (22 June 1992): 62–63.

3. Carl Sagan and Ann Druyan, "Is It Possible to Be Pro-Life and Pro-Choice," *Parade Magazine* (22 April 1990): 2.

4. Ibid., 6.

5. Callahan, *Abortion*, 373.

6. See Callahan, *Abortion,* 31–43, for a fuller discussion of abortion hazards.

7. Callahan, *Abortion,* 425.

8. Ibid., 328–33.

9. Callahan argues that either of these extremes—absolute right over one's body and absolute right to life—are one-dimensional and too simplistic for such a complex moral issue. See Chapters 12, 13, and 14 for a discussion of both extremes and synthesis of their conflicting views.

10. See Chapter 11 in Callahan for a full discussion of the various views concerning when human life begins, and especially pp. 384–90 for a description of the developmental viewpoint.

11. Sissela Bok, "Ethical Problems of Abortion," *The Hastings Center Studies* II, No. 1 (January, 1974): 42.

12. Ibid., 42–52.

Supplementary Reading

Bok, Sissela. "Ethical Problems of Abortion." *The Hastings Center Studies* 2(1) (January 1974): 33–52.

Brodie, Janine. *Abortion Politics.* New York: Oxford University Press, 1992.

Callahan, Daniel. *Abortion: Law, Choice and Morality.* New York: Macmillan, 1970.

Callahan, Daniel, and Sidney Callahan, eds. *Abortion: Understanding Differences.* New York: Plenum, 1984.

Carnana, Claudia M. *Abortion Debate.* Brookfield, Conn.: Millbrook Press, 1992.

Chandrasekhar, S. *Abortion in a Crowded World.* Seattle: University of Washington Press, 1974.

Cohen, Marshall et al., eds. *The Rights and Wrongs of Abortion.* Princeteon, N.J.: Princeton University Press, 1974.

Colker, Ruth. *Abortion and Dialogue: Pro-Choice, Pro-Life, and American Law.* Bloomington, Indiana.: Indiana University Press, 1992.

Cozic, Charles, and Stacy Tipp. *Abortion: Opposing Viewpoints.* San Diego: Greenhaven, 1991.

Feinberg, Joel. *The Problem of Abortion,* 2nd ed. Belmont, Calif.: Wadsworth, 1984.

Gardner, R. F. R. *Abortion: The Personal Dilemma.* New York: Pyramid Books, 1974.

Goldman, A. "Abortion and the Right to Die." *Personalist* 60 (1979).

Grisez, Germain G. *Abortion: The Myths, the Realities, and the Arguments.* New York: Corpus Publishing Division of World Publishing Company, 1970.

Hall, Robert E., ed. *Abortion in a Changing World.* 2 vols. New York: Columbia University Press, 1970.

Labby, Daniel H., ed. *Life or Death: Ethics and Options*. Seattle: University of Washington Press, 1968.

Luker, Kristin. *Abortion and the Politics of Motherhood*. Berkeley, Calif.: University of California Press, 1984.

Lunneborg, Patricia. *Abortion: A Positive Decision*. Westport, Conn.: Greenwood, 1992.

Noonan, John T. Jr., ed. *The Morality of Abortion: Legal and Historical Perspectives*. Cambridge: Harvard University Press, 1970.

Olasky, Marvin N. *Abortion Rites: A Social History of Abortion in America*. Wheaton, Ill: Good News, 1992.

Petchesky, Rosalind P. *Abortion and Woman's Choice: The State, Sexuality, and Reproductive Freedom*. Brookfield, Conn.: Northeastern University Press, 1990.

Rodman, Hyman, et al., eds. *The Abortion Question*. New York: Columbia University Press, 1987.

Rubin, Eva R. *Abortion, Politics, and the Courts: Roe vs. Wade and Its Aftermath*. Westport, Conn.: Greenwood, 1982.

Sagan, Carl, and Ann Druyan. "Is It Possible to Be Pro-Life and Pro-Choice," *Parade Magazine* (22 April 1990): 2–8.

Sumner, L. *Abortion and Moral Theory*. Princeton, N.J.: Princeton University Press, 1981.

Tooley, Michael. *Abortion and Infanticide*. New York: Oxford University Press, 1983.

Tribe, Laurence, ed. *Abortion: The Clash of Absolutes*. New York: Norton, 1992.

Zaitchik, Alan. "Viability and the Morality of Abortion," *Philosophy and Public Affairs* 10(1) (1981):18–24.

Lying, Cheating, Breaking Promises, and Stealing

◆───

Objectives

After you have read this chapter you should be able to

1. Know the definitions of lying, cheating, breaking promises, and stealing.
2. Understand why these moral issues are significant.
3. Know the arguments for and against lying, cheating, breaking promises, and stealing.
4. Be able to analyze and critically evaluate specific cases involving all of the above moral issues.

◆───

Introduction

Other than the taking of human life, the moral issues of lying, cheating, breaking promises, and stealing are usually considered the most important and the least acceptable moral violations humans can perform. These actions are not usually in direct violation of the Value of Life principle, as are the moral issues in Chapters 8, 9, and 10, but are definitely violations of the Principles of Truth Telling and Honesty, Justice and Fairness, and Goodness or Rightness. They can also be considered violations of the Principle of Individual Freedom in that they tend to give unjustified freedom to the perpetrators but deny freedom to the victims of such violations.

I have chosen to place this chapter right after the chapters on taking human life and before the chapters on human sexuality, bioethics, and business ethics because many of the issues in the following three chapters are really specific or applied instances of violations of telling the truth, being honest, keeping promises and agreements, and respecting the belongings of others. For example, adultery in the moral area of human sexuality usually involves telling lies by the adulterers to their spouses. It certainly involves breaking promises usually stated in the marriage vows concerning fidelity. *Adultery* is also sometimes referred to as "cheating on your wife (or husband)." And finally, some adulterers are often considered as having stolen another person's spouse.

In the area of medical ethics or bioethics, lying can be involved in whether or not to tell the patients about the seriousness of their illnesses. Cheating takes place when patients are given treatment they don't need and are charged for it. A promise may be broken when doctors assure patients that they will not abandon the patients but then do. And stealing is seen in the overcharging or in the robbing of a patient's dignity or right to make choices about his or her own treatment.

In business ethics, false or misleading advertising is lying. Cheating is involved when a product is made with inferior materials. Breaking promises is the issue when employers or employees don't keep agreements that have been negotiated. And stealing is the proper term to describe what happens when employees pilfer or embezzle from their companies or when companies steal ideas from each other.

The significance of the moral issues in this chapter cannot be overemphasized because violations and nonviolations affect every level and activity of our daily lives. I have pointed out how they generally affect certain areas of our lives, but they come into play in all human relationships and therefore require careful scrutiny. In this chapter, I will state the issues as fully as I can, giving arguments for and against lying, for example, and citing cases for the application of these arguments. Further, I hope that both instructors and students will apply the arguments in these issues to their own experience, bringing out their own applicable cases for discussion and striving for some kind of resolution whenever possible.

♦——

Definition of Key Terms

Lying

General Definition. Lying, according to Sissela Bok in her book *Lying,* is "an intentionally deceptive message in the form of a statement."[1] The dictionary defines a lie as a "piece of information deliberately presented as being true; anything meant to deceive or give a wrong impression."[2]

White Lie. According to Bok, a white lie is "a falsehood not meant to injure anyone, and of little moral import."[3] Bok presents this definition as how she understands most people to define a "white lie," but does not herself feel that white lies have little or no moral import.

Commission or Omission. I would like to add a further distinction to the definition of lying, which is that some lies are lies of commission or are direct statements that are outright lies. Other lies are lies of omission, which involve the not stating of certain information that is vital to a decision, relationship, or other important human activity. For example, to tell someone you are no longer taking drugs or drinking when you actually are would be a lie of commission; on the other hand, to allow them to go on believing you have quit when you haven't, especially when the issue is vitally important to your relationship, would be a lie of omission.

Cheating

To cheat is "to deceive by trickery; swindle; to mislead; to act dishonestly or practice fraud."[4] As you can see by this definition, cheating and lying both fall under deception.

Promise

According to the dictionary, a promise is "a declaration assuring that one will or will not do something; a vow." Breaking a promise, then, would be to fail to conform to or to act contrary to or to violate the promise.[5]

Stealing

Again according to the dictionary, stealing is taking something without right or permission, generally in a surreptitious way.[6] In a legal sense, larceny is the felonious taking and removing of another's personal property with the intent of permanently depriving the owner.[7] This is further broken down into degrees, such as "grand larceny" and "petit (or petty) larceny," which are based on some arbitrary standard.[8] For example, stealing apples from a grocery store is usually considered petty larceny, but stealing a car is grand larceny.

Nonconsequentialist and Consequentialist Views

It is of some value to return to the basic approaches to morality described in Chapters 2 and 3 because their basic positions on these issues are almost diametrically opposed, with the exception that the act nonconsequentialist in these issues would probably be closer to consequentialist theories than to the nonconsequentialist.

Rule Nonconsequentialist Views

As we might expect, the rule nonconsequentialist views, most typified by Kantian Duty Ethics, would be opposed to any of the four acts. Kant would argue that we cannot universalize lying, cheating, breaking promises, or stealing because they would all be contradictory if we did. For example, if we said everyone should always lie, then we would contradict the meaning of truth telling; if we said everyone should break promises, then promises would no longer have any meaning. He would also state that we would be treating human beings as means rather than ends if we lied to them, cheated them, broke our promises to them, and stole from them. Although Sir William David Ross might allow any of these if serious matters warranted, his basic position, like Kant's, is that we generally should not lie, and so forth. This same position is held by St. Augustine (A.D. 354–430) and John Wesley (1703–1791), the British founder of Methodism.

This traditional view that lying, cheating, breaking promises, and stealing are always wrong, then, is fairly strong in our history. Sometimes these actions are viewed as the next worst immoralities to taking human life, and in some cultures and their moral codes they *are* worse than killing and death. Very often, for example, a culture will punish such immoral acts by death, whereas in others, the violation of these important moral codes will bring such disgrace on the perpetrator and even his family, that he will be seriously ostracized from the group and may even commit suicide, seeing death as more honorable than living under such circumstances.

Consequentialist and Act Nonconsequentialist Views

Act Nonconsequentialism. The reason I have not included act nonconsequentialism with rule nonconsequentialism is that even though act nonconsequentialists do not use consequences in their decision making or consider them important, in their approach to morality, based on feelings or intuition alone, they would not necessarily take a stand for or against these issues unless they *felt* like it. It seems quite possible that they might feel like lying or breaking promises at one time and not feel like it at others; therefore, although they might establish a permanent position against doing these acts on the basis of their feelings in general, they would not have to opt either for or against and could change their positions on these matters from situation to situation based on how they felt at any particular time.

Consequentialism. Consequentialist theories would bring ends, results, or consequences into the picture when lying, cheating, breaking promises, or stealing is contemplated. Obviously, if consequences would warrant it, then any of the preceding could be acceptable. Consequentialists, even rule utilitarians, could not, based on this theory, say that we should *never* lie, cheat, break promises, or steal. They would state instead that these should or should not be done based on whether or not what you did brought about the best consequences.

Ethical egoists would allow for doing any of these, provided that they could be reasonably sure it would be in their best interests to do them. They could, of course, not ever do any of them or do some of them only sometimes, but there certainly would be no absolute prohibition against doing any of them because it might be in their self-interest to do them.

Act utilitarians might do or not do any of them if they thought the action would bring about the best consequences for everyone affected by the act. If they thought lying would bring about the best consequences for everyone, for example, they would certainly lie.

Rule utilitarians might have rules against all four actions if they thought that bad consequences would generally ensue if people didn't basically adhere to rules prohibiting the four actions. They would have to make exceptions, of course, to those rules in circumstances where violating the rules would definitely bring about the best consequences for everyone.

Although people may fall into any of these different categories—given that there are ethical egoists, Kantians, and act and rule utilitarians—I believe that most feel such acts are wrong in general because they tend to destroy the trust that is so essential to vital human relationships. People like to think, for example, that others will not lie to them, cheat them, break promises they make to them, or steal from them. Yet many are realistic enough to realize that one may do these things and they therefore must be on their guard.

The recipients of lies, cheating, broken promises, and theft often feel disappointed, resentful, angry, and upset, reactions that do not engender contentment or happiness. In addition, their ability to trust the offenders is diminished and may lead to a general distrust of all human relationships. In my estimation, most people will not hold to principles of "never" or "always" where lying, cheating, breaking promises, or stealing are involved; though generally against them, they will permit them in certain circumstances. Of course, as we learned in Chapter 1, what the majority does has nothing to do with what it ought to do, but in a practical sense we should be aware of the impact of these actions on our daily lives. I intend to present each action with what I feel are the major arguments pro and con, and each of you can decide for yourselves which arguments are the most compelling.

Lying

Arguments Against Lying

Dupes and Deprives Others. A major argument against lying is that it misinforms the people lied to and thus may frustrate their own objectives. For example, suppose a wife and mother of two children wants to stay home with her children, but her husband says he is going to school and wants her to take a job so that he can continue. After a month, he decides not to stay in school and drops out but tells his wife he is still attending. By so lying, he has thwarted her wish to stay home and raise their children. His lying has not only blocked his wife's objective but has also deprived his children of their mother's care.

In another example, Jane thinks she has a chance for a promotion at the company where she works because the present manager tells her so, though he has actually selected David for the job. Thus Jane may decide not to seek a better job elsewhere or may turn one down, hoping she will be promoted where she is. The manager, first of all, has led Jane to believe she has more alternatives than she really has, which is a violation of the Justice Principle—it's unfair to her. Second, though she would much rather stay with her present firm if she could move up, the manager's duplicity has caused her to lose confidence in what, for her, may have been the best alternative.

Causes Distrust in Human Relationships. Another major argument against lying is that it causes a breakdown in human relationships. If you think about it, human relationships are at their best when people can trust each other. Was Jane mistaken in trusting her boss? Most ethicists who do not support lying feel that we should be able to proceed on the positive assumption that we can trust, not on the negative one that we cannot. An entirely different atmosphere exists when human relationships are approached negatively rather than positively.

Lying not only causes distrust but also resentment, disappointment, and suspicion in the deceived. For example, if a woman has been continuously lied to by her husband and the marriage relationship therefore collapses, she may continue to distrust all future relationships with others, especially men. Thus, lying has not only ruined this relationship for her, it has affected all future relationships as well. This may explain why some people who have been lied to say, "It's not so much what you did (for example, had an adulterous affair), but that you lied to me about it."

Human relationships generally depend on the communication of thoughts, feelings, and information. Because lying essentially amounts to a lack of honest communication, human relationships are very hard to establish or maintain when their main foundation—honesty—is undermined or destroyed.

The Domino Argument. The domino argument has been discussed in previous chapters but bears looking at again in connection with lying. I have said that the domino argument in itself without further evidence will not influence people not to perform certain acts. Nevertheless, we should always be aware that what we do can affect us and others by causing additional problems or reverberations beyond the initial action.

Those who are against lying feel that one lie tends to beget others in order to maintain the first one. As Sissela Bok states,

> It is easy, a wit observed, to tell a lie, but hard to tell only one. The first lie "must be thatched with another or it will rain through." More and more lies may come to be needed; the liar always has more mending to do. And the strains on him become greater each time—many have noted that it takes an excellent memory to keep one's untruths in good repair and disentangled. The sheer energy the liar has to devote to shoring them up is energy the honest man can dispose of freely.[9]

For example, in refusing to tell dying patients the truth about their condition, a situation is set up in which many other lies must follow to back up the first. It might be argued that lying will make the patients try harder to recover (even though recovery may not be possible) and that knowing their true condition will only depress them and make communication with them harder and their last days terrible. The initial lie will seem reasonable in this setting. However, if the patients ask any serious questions about their condition, then more lies may have to be told. Precautions must be taken to prevent any information or even hints from leaking through to disrupt the growing web of lies that began innocently enough as a "protection" for the dying patient.

Added to the difficulties of maintaining the initial lie (which was one of omission, not commission) is the fact that many people are involved in the care of such a patient, and as the patient's situation worsens and more procedures (or fewer, where a doctor deems there is nothing more to be done) have to be done, the patient may ask questions of all these people, causing more lies to be told: "I don't know; you must ask your doctor. You're going to get better. There's no need to worry." The irony of all this, according to Dr. Elisabeth Kübler-Ross, who has worked with dying patients for many years, is that all those she dealt with knew the seriousness of their illnesses whether or not they had been told, and many even knew when they were going to die.[10] This means that the deception was not only painful and blocked communication, but it was also not really necessary because the truth was generally known to everyone involved—even those whom the lies were supposed to protect.

Additionally, once a lie is told, further lying in other situations becomes easier, often to the point where liars no longer can distinguish between what is or is not the truth as they know it. And if a liar gets away with one lie to "save his neck," in no matter how trivial a situation, then future lies become easier and sometimes almost a way of life. Habitual lying, of course, increases the chance of discovery, leading to the breakdown of trust and the dilution if not destruction of vital human relationships. Therefore, although the domino argument may not in itself prohibit one from doing an act, in the case of lying, it is especially pertinent and should be carefully considered.

Unfair Advantage or Power for Liars. Another argument against lying is that because most liars do not themselves wish to be deceived, then to deceive others gives liars an unfair advantage. This is of course a violation of the Principle of Justice. A perfect example of the power one person can have over another occurs in Shakespeare's play *Othello.* Iago, Othello's aide, weaves one of the most insidious webs of lies ever seen in drama and literature. By the end of the play, Iago has not only controlled Othello's every move but caused the death of Othello's wife, Desdemona, about whom most of the lies are concocted, and the injury and death of several others, including Othello himself. The power Iago has over most of the people in the play is almost unbelievable, and all of it is attained through the diabolical cleverness of his many deceptions.

Self-destructiveness of Lying. A major disadvantage in lying is that once liars are found out, their word is no longer trusted, their deceptions fall apart, and their power is decreased or lost. The Watergate affair during President Nixon's administration exemplifies this loss of power. Few people are as powerful as the President of the United States, and Nixon evidently maintained some of that power through various deceptions. As long as the public generally did not know this, he retained and even increased his power; but once his lying and dishonesty were discovered, he definitely lost prestige and was forced to resign rather than be impeached.

Another effect on the liars themselves, according to proponents of this argument, is that lying undermines one's own self-image. In other words, liars lose self-esteem because of their deceptions, and the more they occur, the greater the loss.

Effect of Lying on Society. Bok states the general overall effect of lying on society as follows: "The veneer of social trust is often thin. As lies spread . . . trust is damaged. . . . When it is damaged, the community as a whole suffers; and when it is destroyed, societies falter and collapse."[11] Many people in the United States and the world were shocked by the President's lying in the Watergate affair. Trust in politicians and lawyers, shaky to begin with, fell to a new low. Some faith was renewed through the efforts of Archibald Cox and Leon Jaworski, chief prosecutors, and Senator Sam Ervin, who was in charge of the investigative committee; but the American public certainly experienced a loss of morale and faith in its leaders that hadn't occurred before to such an extent in the nation's history. Most people feel that a person's word is his or her bond and that it should be possible to trust everyone. Therefore, every breach of honesty destroys that belief, causes cynicism, condones lying, and destroys the thin "veneer of social trust." If the holder of the highest office in the land can and does lie, then why should not anyone else at any level of human relationships? Let's hope that most people won't let a bad example influence them in this way, but the temptation is certainly always there.

Arguments for Lying

Most ethicists and others would not argue for lying all the time, although some people might. Inveterate liars usually will *not* lie all the time because they can then be more strategically effective when they do. If one lies all of the time, one has a greater chance of being found out and of losing at least the semblance of trustworthiness, something a "good" liar needs to maintain.

Most arguments for lying suggest there are sometimes good reasons for telling lies. Therefore, to state unequivocally, as do Kant and others, that lying is never moral and should never be allowed, would be impractical and in some situations perhaps immoral. In some cases, they say, lying should be encouraged. For example, people ought to be able to lie when they need to or when lying could prevent the occurrence of a more serious moral infraction, such as killing.

Defense of the Innocent, Including Self-defense. According to Bok, "Deceit and violence . . . are the two forms of deliberate assault on human beings. Both can coerce people into acting against their will."[12] In most instances, however, ethicists deem lying less harmful to human life than violence, especially when the latter terminates human life. With some exceptions, if killing or allowing innocent lives to be lost is wrong, and if one can save such lives by lying, most ethicists allow for lying in such instances. For example, if an extremely angry man is looking for his gun to kill someone, and if you know where it is, these ethicists will state you are justified in lying and not telling him where it is in order to save the lives of his intended victims. He may indeed find a gun somewhere else, but you at least have done all you can, by lying, to protect the potential victims.

Another example would be a wartime situation in which a member of the underground knows where other members are hiding. He would be justified in lying about their whereabouts rather than risking their capture and death.

One problem arising in such a case is what constitutes defense of the innocent or self-defense. In the preceding two examples, the situation is clear, and in either case one can see that lives would be protected by lying. However, what about the president of a major corporation vital to national defense who is accused of embezzling funds and lies about it? When found out, she might argue that even though she was not protecting herself by her lie, as president of the company she felt a responsibility to lie to protect shareholders, workers, and also the "innocent public" for whom her corporation manufactures defense products. Are her contentions justified? First, it might be seriously argued that for her crime to be covered up only to surface at a later date would cause even more problems in the future. Second, it's unlikely that her being found out and removed from the presidency would seriously affect the lives she is presumed to be "protecting" by lying, because someone else could function as president.

National Security. Many ethicists argue for lying in order to maintain national security, an act that may certainly protect many innocent people. For example, if a woman spying for her country is caught, then she may lie about information she has in order to protect her country's security. Presidents and other members of the government sometimes state that they cannot reveal certain important information to the press or public because "it would endanger national security." Such people should certainly have some discretion in revealing information that would seriously affect national security, but they must be very careful not to abuse this right in order to protect their own self-interest.

For example, President Nixon often claimed that the reason he lied about the Watergate affair, the tapes, and everything else was that telling the truth would have endangered national security. Obviously, national security was affected very little, although morale may have been. One could argue for national security in this instance only on the broadest basis, as, for example, that other world powers might condemn the United States because of its president's actions. It would be Nixon who would lose prestige, however, not the nation as a whole, which cannot take the responsibility for its president's actions. National security could be used as a valid reason for lying in certain circumstances only as long as it is not abused by members of the government or the military.

Trade Secrets in Business. Ethicists favoring lying might argue that business people may lie justifiably, either by omission or commission, rather than reveal vital trade secrets to their competitors. They aver that no business person has an obligation to tell competitors of his or her inventions or patents, which would give competitors unfair advantage. This permission to lie can also be extended to anything that would be in the business's self-interest, such as false and misleading advertising and lying for unfair advantage over other people or companies. Very often arguments sanctioning lying in business try to separate actions

310

in the business world from those in life outside it, on the principle that in business anything goes, whereas one should never lie to loved ones or friends.

"Little White Lies." Many people, including ethicists, allow for unimportant or harmless "little white lies," which are told to avoid hurting people's feelings or to protect those lying from embarrassment. The arguments for these lies are that people need to have leeway in social intercourse and daily activities to keep things running smoothly. For example, if one woman asks another how an expensive new dress looks on her, the other woman might answer that the dress looks fine even if she doesn't think so because she doesn't want to hurt the asker's feelings. In another case, a young man might ask a young woman for a date, but she doesn't want to go out with him because she dislikes his looks and personality. Rather than hurt his feelings and to save herself from the embarrassment of telling him the real reasons for not going out with him, she will lie and state that she already has a date when she really doesn't.

In all of these instances the liars usually feel that what they are lying about is unimportant and is a tactful way to avoid hurting people's feelings and save the liars some embarrassment. Further, they argue, in getting along in the world, lying sometimes can maintain the "social veneer" rather than crack it, as is advocated by the people who argue against lying. In other words, rather than hurting someone or suffering embarrassment, as long as no serious harm is done, it's all right to lie to prevent either from happening.

Moderate Position

As with other topics in this book, a moderate rather than a strict pro or con attitude toward lying is the one most people probably favor. It advocates that, generally, one should avoid lying if possible and lie only as a last resort or clearly to save a life. This viewpoint is generally expressed in the old saying "Honesty is the best policy." Moderates feel that lying is a serious matter, however little or white the lie. Moderates agree with those opposed to lying that the domino argument makes sense—that the more you lie, the easier it is to do so, and that one lie leads to another and another and another. They also agree that lying tends to break down the "social veneer," brings harm to those deceived, and destroys the integrity and human dignity of the liar whether or not he or she is caught.

Further, they believe that it's important to consider the consequences of *any* lie, however trivial. For instance, the woman who lied to her friend about her dress may lose a friend if her lie is found out. Moreover, if by lying she encourages her friend to wear an unbecoming dress, then her lie has hurt, not helped, her friend. In the example about the man rejected for a date, if he happens to learn that the woman didn't have another date, then his feelings will be hurt much more than if she had told him the truth. Thus, moderates argue, the consequences of even white lies may be worse than if one had told the truth.

One point moderates stress is that lying is not the only other alternative to giving someone truthful information that might hurt. As Elisabeth Kübler-Ross has stated, the important question is not whether I should tell the truth but *how* I should tell the truth, or how I should share information, important or not, with others who are asking me questions or who need to know what the truth is.[13] In other words, one does not have to be brutally frank. One can tell the truth, however terrible, but gently and with an intent to support and to give hope wherever possible. In the case of the women and the dress, for example, the friend could tell the one who asked, "Actually, I don't think that dress especially suits you, and I suggest you take it back and buy another. Since you thought enough of me to ask my opinion, may I help you return the dress and look for one that would be more flattering to you?" By replying this way, the woman would not be lying and would be giving her friend some hope and encouragement about purchasing another dress that would be more becoming.

Even in situations where the truth is frightening to both hearer and deliverer, it can still be stated without materially harming another. Take the situation where a family has been in a serious car accident in which a wife/mother was killed, the husband/father is very critical, and the son is basically all right, what do you tell the man who asks about the others in his family? Do you lie and say that they are all right, or do you tell the truth? First you should stress that his son is doing well. Because of his critical condition, you would merely say about his wife that she was also injured in the accident (the truth) without saying anything further until he becomes stronger. However, if he asks you point-blank "Is she dead?" or states "She's dead, isn't she?" Dr. Kübler-Ross says that you should be truthful but try to stress that his son is alive to give him a reason to try to recover.[14]

The basic thrust of the moderate position, then, is that one should generally try to tell the truth because telling lies often causes more problems than not doing so. Moderates also feel that

1. If one does choose to lie, he or she must try to make the consequences of his or her lying as harmless as possible.
2. One should try to avoid habitual lying and be aware of the risks of telling even one lie or a white lie.
3. One should also be aware that lying may have a deleterious effect not only on the deceived but also on the liar.
4. One should never lie about important matters that may affect the recipient of the lie significantly.
5. Lying is allowed when there is no other recourse and when innocent life

is really at stake, such as in the cases cited earlier, concerning the enraged killer in search of his gun, the member of the underground during wartime, and the captured spy. Every other type of situation must be fully justified and the consequences carefully weighed. One should favor telling the truth, however, remembering that *how* one tells it is as important as the telling.

◆

Cases for Study and Discussion

C A S E ◆ 1

Jesusita, eighty years old and with a bad heart, is living in a convalescent hospital where she is visited regularly by her fifty-year-old son, along with other members of the family. Her son dies suddenly one night of a heart attack. The remaining members of the family feel that she shouldn't be told of this because of her own weak heart, and in collusion with the hospital staff, no one tells her. After a week, Jesusita asks why her son hasn't visited her, and the family tells her he is on a business trip, hoping she will forget about him. But the next week she asks where he is and when he will return. She also wants to know why he hasn't called her or written a letter or postcard from where he is. The family tells her he is very busy but should be back soon. Another week passes and Jesusita becomes very restless and upset about her son not visiting her; she becomes harder and harder to care for, and she cries a lot. The staff and family gather to discuss what to do about the situation. They wonder whether they should tell her the truth now or think up some more excuses.

1. Did they do the right thing in the beginning by lying to Jesusita?
2. If she were your mother or grandmother and your brother or uncle had died, what do you think she should be told? Why or why not?
3. If you had done what they did or if you were staff dealing with this situation, what would you advise? Do you feel she should be told the truth now? If so, how would you do the telling? If not, how would you suggest this situation be handled?
4. Do you think it would have been better to tell her the truth in the beginning or not? Why or why not? Do you think not telling her in the beginning has made the situation better or worse? Why or why not? If so, in what ways?

C A S E ◆ 2

Mike and Barbara Barnes live next door to you with their two children—Casey, a boy, and Shelley, a girl. Mike often comes home drunk and usually acts violently

313

toward Barbara and the children, giving them black eyes, bruises, and even broken bones. One night after a particularly severe beating of all of them, Barbara visits after Mike has passed out and tells you she is going to a shelter for battered wives and children and asks you not to reveal to Mike where they've gone. Having always prided yourself on your truth telling, what do you tell Mike the next morning when he asks you to tell him where Barbara and the children have gone, expressing remorse for what he has done? Do you adhere to your past principles and tell him the truth, or do you lie to him? Why or why not? What exactly would you tell or not tell him and why?

CASE ♦ 3

Tom has been having an affair with his secretary, Francine, for about a year now but both decide to end it, and Francine leaves the company and gets a job in another state. Tom doesn't think that his wife, Carol, knows about the affair, but he feels very guilty and wonders whether he ought to be honest about it and tell her. He doesn't intend to have another affair and feels that he does love his wife and their three children. Yet, he has strong guilt feelings and an urge to confess his adultery to Carol. He asks one of his friends, Doug, who knows of the affair, what he should do, and Doug tells him to leave well enough alone: "What she doesn't know won't hurt her," Doug says. Tom goes to confession and tells the priest what he's done. This particular priest (some might not say this) advises him to tell Carol, express his remorse, and promise never to do it again. Carol notices how preoccupied Tom is and asks him if there is anything wrong. What should Tom do? Should he tell Carol the truth or not? Why? Suppose, if he tells Carol about the affair, she asks for a separation and maybe even a divorce? And if he chooses not to tell her the truth, how can he alleviate his strong guilt feelings? Would it be better or not in this case to tell the truth? Why?

Cheating

Cheating, like lying, involves deception and dishonesty, except that lying is basically verbal, whereas cheating is generally nonverbal. Lying, as Bok defines it, is a statement of deception. Cheating, on the other hand, is an action meant to deceive. For example, if students copy the answers from your test, for which you've studied hard, that's cheating. If you tell them to stop cheating, and they deny it, then that's lying.

Cheating can take many forms. As stated earlier, adultery usually encompasses both "cheating on one's spouse" and lying to cover up the action. People can cheat on their income tax, on forms used in their businesses (for example, deduction for expenses), in games played with others (whether simple games or serious gambling, such as poker) on insurance claims, on tests in school as already mentioned, on applications for employment or unemployment, and in sports.

Cheating, like lying, is a serious infraction of most moral systems because, like lying, it shatters the trust needed for the continuance and survival of human relationships. For example, if you buy a used car that is supposed to have 40,000 miles on it but the dealer turned the odometer back and it really has 140,000, then you have been cheated. You will probably never buy a car from that dealer again and may be wary of even honest business people. If you are playing poker with presumed friends whom you think you can trust, and you discover that one of them has been playing with marked cards, you will probably never trust that person again—certainly not in a card game where you stand to lose a good deal of money.

Arguments Against Cheating

Unfair and Unjust to Others. Obviously, cheating is unfair and unjust to those who are dedicated to "fair play." It's as if everyone, including the cheater, is playing by rules understood by all, but the cheater then abrogates the rules and deceives everyone else. For example, if other students are trying to get good grades and you cheat and get them, then your getting grades unfairly may deny the other students what they have earned and truly deserve. In addition to demeaning the importance of their careful studying, you may also skew the grading scale so that some students who might have gotten better grades through honest studying get worse ones because your cheating has affected the entire grading scale.

In the same way, people playing in a game with a cheater may lose the game unfairly. This of course is a violation of the Principle of Justice and Fairness and also of a general code that most people observe when playing games or gambling. Game players generally agree to abide by the rules. If it's a trivial game, and someone cheats, we won't want to play any further, because the game has lost its value. In a gambling game like poker, some deception is accepted, as when you fool your opponents into thinking you have a good hand when you don't. But one does not mark cards, deal from the bottom of the deck, or bring high cards into the game in a dishonest manner. In casino gambling, cheaters when caught are often ostracized, and in illegal gambling they have sometimes been beaten or even killed. Players in such games are expected to follow the basic rules and take them very seriously.

Falsified Qualifications. Another argument against cheating is the serious effect it has on others in regard to professional qualifications or licensing. If, for example, medical or law students cheat on crucial facts they must know in their intended professions, then their not learning them could cause loss of life or other kinds of harm to others. The cheating is even worse when it results in obtaining a license on the basis of presumed qualifications falsely attained. To some people cheating on an exam or two doesn't seem very serious. "After all," the student might say, "when am I ever going to use this dull and ancient anatomy information?" If such a student, however, becomes a surgeon and neglects to perform an important procedure because he or she missed really learning something about anatomy in medical school, then someone's life could be in danger.

Effects on the Cheater. I have mentioned the harm that can be done to others by not being properly qualified or being falsely licensed because of cheating, but the effect on the cheater is also significant. People who cheat hurt themselves in the long run, which is another argument against cheating. If something bad occurs as a result of people's cheating, then they can be held responsible and subject to the law, both criminal and civil, and perhaps even lose their license to practice their profession.

And cheating, like lying, can become a habit. It's easier to do than studying or other hard or necessary work. Successful cheaters may become lazy and will generally cheat again at an opportune time. This weakens their moral fiber and can affect their whole lives adversely, especially if they get caught. If people know you cheat, the needed trust for vital human relationships, as in lying, will be broken, and you won't be able to maintain strong relationships. As in the gambling example, no one wants to play poker with a known cheater because the basic code and rules of the game are then destroyed. Further, if business people become known as cheaters in their dealings with others—for example, in the manufacture of their products—their credibility is weakened as much and maybe more so than if they had lied.

Arguments for Cheating

Surviving and Winning. Many people who condone cheating regard the world and society as a "dog-eat-dog" jungle of corruption where one can survive only by using corrupt means such as cheating. They believe that "all's fair in love and war" and anything else and that people should cheat if necessary to get what they want and need. Such people see the world as so competitive and ruthless that in order to survive, one may have to break all the moral dos and don'ts and lie, cheat, break promises, and even steal if it will get them ahead.

Along with this viewpoint is the idea that winning is the most important thing in life, so if you can't win fairly, then win any way you can. In our moral teachings, good sportsmanship and fair play are supposedly held in high esteem, but in specific cases and instances, winning sometimes takes precedence over moral teachings. Often we see this in sports involving children. In many of

316

children's competitive sports, such as baseball, the main goal in teaching is to have the children enjoy playing a game. To fulfill this goal, good, mediocre, and poor players are distributed evenly among the competing teams and the rules decree that everyone must play at least one inning. Often, however, if it's a close game, the manager will not use the lesser players, or play them so little that they learn nothing. This may win games, but it does not fulfill the stated goal, nor is it fair to the lesser players on the winning manager's team or to the other managers and their team members.

Everybody Does It.   Right along with the "dog-eat-dog" theory is the "everybody does it" argument. This assumes that because most people probably cheat sometime in their lives, everyone is justified in also doing so if necessary. The argument further says that it's commonly known that all people cheat on their income taxes, on insurance claims by including other earlier damages, on expense vouchers, in golf games, and on their wives or husbands. One problem with this attitude is that it is questionable whether *most* people do these things. Another problem is that even if some or most people do these things, this does not mean that people *ought* to do them, as discussed in Chapter 1 in the difference between descriptive and prescriptive approaches to morality. History reveals that even the majority can be morally wrong, so "everybody does it" is not a very supportable or justifiable argument for doing something.

As Long as You Don't Get Caught.   Many argue that cheating is all right if you can get away with it. Being caught is what's bad, not cheating. And the less chance you have of being caught, the more justified your cheating will be. This attitude could work with consequentialist but never with nonconsequentialist theories. And even with consequentialist theories, being caught or not has nothing to do with whether an action is right or wrong. Only if you can show that greater good consequences can come from cheating could you justify it in any way.

◆

Cases for Study and Discussion

CASE ◆ 1

Mike has an average between a C+ and a B- in his history class, and the last exam he is taking could make all the difference. He studied, but he didn't finish one section on World War II. When he starts the test, he discovers many more questions than he expected on that section. He needs a B in this class to get into graduate school. He notices that Renee, sitting next to him, seems to know the answers to the questions he needs. She likes him a lot and has not minded his looking at her tests before. A student stops to talk to the teacher on his way out of the testing room, and Mike sees that the teacher's vision will be blocked long enough for him to get the correct answers from Renee. Should Mike cheat or not? Consider the following questions in your deliberations:

1. Would it make any difference to your answer if the test grade were not as crucial as it could be to Mike's career? Why?
2. Considering that Mike has a good chance of not being caught, why shouldn't he cheat?
3. What arguments would you give to justify Mike's cheating or not cheating? Be specific.

CASE ♦ 2

Dick and Lorraine have been insured with Farmer's Mutual for their automobiles and house for ten years. During this time they have only filed a claim for $500, and the costs of premiums have risen 100 percent. One day while backing out of the garage, Lorraine badly damages the right fender, but she and Dick delay having it fixed. After several weeks, someone hits the right side of the car, while parked, damaging everything but the right front fender. In attempting to get the car repaired, they try to decide whether or not to include the fender, which is much more than their deductible allowance, in their estimate of the damage. Should they? They feel that the insurance company has made literally thousands of dollars from their premiums alone, not to mention those of other clients. They argue that the big corporations have made millions from their subscribers; they wouldn't miss a few hundred or even a thousand dollars. Many of their friends have done the same thing on occasion, saving themselves hundreds of dollars. Because the fender could easily have been damaged in the same accident, it's unlikely their cheating would be discovered. What do you think they should do, and why? How would you answer all of their arguments for including the fender in the claim if you believe they shouldn't? If you believe they should include it, explain why, and what arguments you would add to justify their action.

CASE ♦ 3

Mark, an ethics professor, has completed a manuscript for a new book entitled *Being Moral*. Before submitting it to a publisher, he writes a phony letter of recommendation from a well-known ethicist and sends it with his manuscript, reasoning that because there are so many ethics books on the market, his manuscript won't have a chance without something special to recommend it. The publisher accepts the book for publication. Just as he begins distributing it, he discovers the letter is a fake. At first, the publisher thinks he might publish the book anyway, but decides not to, given the fact that the author is an ethicist and the book is about ethics. Was what Mark did wrong? Why or why not? Do you think the publisher was wrong to pull the book off the market for the reasons given? Why or why not? Does what Mark did seem worse to you because he is a teacher of ethics? Why or why not? How would you feel about using such a text knowing what the author had done? Be specific.

Breaking Promises

As stated earlier, a promise is a declaration, a vow, or an agreement into which a person enters freely. To the extent that a person is forcefully or subtly coerced into making a promise, he or she should not be expected to keep it as if it were made freely.

Implied Agreements

There are many *implied* agreements that allow us to live safely and meaningfully with each other in various groups in our societies. Some of these are

1. Not to do harm to one another.
2. Not to lie or cheat.
3. To obey laws for the general good.
4. To stop at red lights and stop signs.
5. To treat each other with respect and dignity.
6. To keep promises we make.

This chapter, however, will deal only with direct promises such as "I promise not to tell anyone what you have just told me since you have asked me not to."

A Form of Dishonesty

Breaking promises, like cheating, is a form of dishonesty and is also outright lying when the person making the promise has no intention of keeping it. An example is if you say to someone, "I promise I won't tell anyone what you told me," but then think to yourself, "Wait until Maureen hears this!" Not intending to keep the promise you just made violates the same bases of trust abused by lying and cheating and is therefore considered an important moral issue to most people.

A Person's Word

In earlier times, a person's promise or "word" was an integral part of his or her reputation, and many promises and agreements were made verbally or by just shaking hands. Some promises—usually personal ones—are still made in this fashion, but many are now written down, witnessed, notarized, and otherwise elaborately executed. One reason for this is the complexity of many contracts and agreements (sets of formal promises). But also such written and carefully executed agreements are necessary because in modern society fewer people actually honor their agreements or promises.

For example, when my wife and I moved two houses into one, we sold some appliances, furniture, and clothes to three individuals. They made small down payments and agreed to pay the rest later. Not *one* of the three kept his promise! We haven't been able to locate them, and we've just written off the losses. On the other hand, some people I know, including myself, *would* keep such promises. All things considered, it's important to get a written agreement on such matters so that people can be sued if necessary.

However, even written agreements and promises (contracts or policies) do not guarantee that promises will be kept. Some people who violate them think they won't be caught or that no one will take the time or trouble to sue them. There are many aspects involved in keeping or breaking promises and it's an important issue in all types of human relationships and activities.

Arguments Against Breaking Promises

Destruction of Personal Relationships. Next to lying, no action has a greater effect on relationships than breaking promises. One of the most emotional statements a person can make to another is, "But you promised!" When we are asked to promise something, or when we promise on our own to do something, most people tend to believe our word. If we break our word, it weakens our relationship with that person. For example, a superintendent of a school district urged many of the older faculty in the district who were close to retirement to leave by July 1. One of the incentives promised was that they could keep their almost full-coverage health plan although the active faculty was having to change to a health plan with less coverage because of financial difficulties within the district. However, on July 1, the superintendent moved everyone—retirees and active faculty—into the new, lesser-coverage plan. Breaking his promise aroused tremendous protest in the district among both retirees and active faculty. After much discussion and concern on the part of both faculty and retirees, the situation finally was rectified and the superintendent had to make good on his promise. However, the lack of trust that existed between him and the active faculty and retirees made it difficult to form agreements on other matters.

Domino Theory. As in lying and cheating, the domino theory is relevant here. Once a person breaks a promise and gets away with it, it's easier to break other promises, especially when convenient. For example, if a spouse should commit

320

adultery, it's easier to continue doing it with the same person or with others. In other words, it can become a way of life, as with lying or cheating. Of course, a person may break a promise for a serious reason, but one must be on guard to prevent breaking promises from becoming a habit.

Effects on People's Life Choices. Because people depend on the promises made to them and the implied and direct agreements they have with others, breaking them can seriously affect their lives. For example, in the health-plan situation described earlier, most if not all of the older faculty retired earlier than they wished mainly because of the health plan. Many would have worked another year or two to gain more retirement benefits if they were not to benefit from their previous good health plan. So the superintendent's keeping or breaking his promise had a most important effect on their lives. In another example, if a woman promises to marry a man within a year and he works hard toward that marriage and sacrifices to build a nest egg, if she breaks her promise because she's found someone else, whom she's been seeing for six months, she will significantly hurt the man to whom she made the promise.

Destruction of General Social Trust. There is no doubt that breaking promises also effects society in general. Kant's position is that if we were to establish a rule that promises should always be broken, then the word *promise* would be totally contradicted and lose its meaning. It amounts to saying, "I promise . . . but I have absolutely no intention of keeping my promise." Promises sometimes must be broken for good and serious reasons, but intentionally breaking promises must seriously concern society in general. As I stated earlier, much of what we do is based on promises or agreements, so when these start to break down, the "thin veneer" of social trust begins to warp and crack. This loss of trust is very evident in regard to promises in political campaigns. Voters generally are somewhat cynical about politicians, many of whom seem to promise the moon, but when elected show more concern for helping special-interest groups or for gaining money or power for themselves. Indeed, some politicians who do try to keep their promises, especially on controversial issues (abortion, for example), sometimes fail to achieve reelection. As a result, many candidates for office tend to dodge important issues and promise nothing really significant during their campaigns. This further weakens the trust people have in their elected representatives.

Loss of Personal Integrity. A final argument against promise breaking centers around the loss of personal integrity for the person who fails to keep promises. As with lying and cheating, promise breaking involves not only loss of reputation for honesty with other people but also loss of one's own self-esteem. We may have a difficult time living with ourselves after having "gone back on our word" and having let someone down. Even those who behave as if they don't feel any guilt may do so within. For example, many spouses who break their marriage vows (promises) experience tremendous guilt feelings whether or not they are found out. When they are, the guilt feelings are multiplied not only because of the injury to their spouses but also because of the effects on their children and the entire family unit. Most people have some moral sense and cannot escape their promise breaking totally unscathed.

Arguments for Breaking Promises

Changed Circumstances. One argument favoring promise breaking is that an individual who has made a promise should have the right to break it when circumstances under which it was made change. An example would be of marriage vows made when the spouses were in love. If they "fall out of love," then the situation has changed and the vows should no longer apply. Suppose, for instance, that the sexual relationship of a married couple is no longer vital, because one spouse has become indifferent to that aspect of their relationship. Proponents for breaking promises might feel therefore that the other spouse has no obligation to remain faithful.

Another example might be if a person borrows some money from a friend and promises to pay it back at a certain time. Later, however, he loses his job and decides to forget his promise and not repay the loan because the situation has changed so drastically. It could be argued that despite this the borrower still has an obligation to pay *sometime* and ought to make arrangements to do so. But defenders of his action would dispute this on the basis that individuals must have the right to break such a promise when it interferes with their own interests and welfare.

When There Are Moral Conflicts. Those who defend promise breaking also believe that promises can be broken when important moral conflicts are involved. For example, suppose Bruce tells his good friend Louise that he is secretly going to a cabin in the mountains they both know about because he is having financial difficulties and although he wants her to be able to contact him, he doesn't want anyone else to know where he is. He asks her to promise to tell no one of his whereabouts and she agrees. Later she is visited by police, who reveal that Bruce's partner has been violently murdered and that Bruce is their prime suspect. Is she still obligated to keep her promise to Bruce, or should she break it to aid the police? Proponents of promise breaking would argue for the latter in that protecting human life takes precedence over keeping one's word.

When It's a Trivial Issue. Promise breaking proponents also feel that promises may be broken when doing so will not harm or when they seem trivial. Suppose, for example, a family has a rule that their children have only one piece of candy a day but Freddie takes three pieces and makes his sister Marie promise not to tell on him. She agrees, but when their mother arrives home, Marie immediately tells what Freddie has done, and he's punished for breaking the rule. When he asks Marie why she broke her promise, she explains she had her fingers crossed, so the promise didn't count. To defenders of promise breaking, the situation is trivial and has caused no real harm. Of course, Freddie *was* punished but the counter-arguers would point out that Freddie *did* indeed break the rule, and in any case it is still a minor issue.

Another example is when someone makes a small bet, let's say a dime, and then when he loses refuses to pay (a form of promise breaking) because he thinks the bet too trivial to honor. Is there any serious harm done here? Some would argue that breaking promises even in such small matters still tends to destroy the social trust that exists in all human relationships and therefore is never minor. As was pointed out in Sissela Bok's discussion of little white lies, the whole social fabric is injured by breaking even the smallest promises. Could Freddie ever trust Marie again to keep her promises? Did the person who won the dime but was not paid learn something about this so-called friend that would lead that person never to trust him again in either small or large issues? This argument should be scrutinized closely, not for the triviality of a situation or the little harm done within it, but for what it can mean in a larger sense.

Where Unusual Situations Justify It. Another argument for promise breaking centers on situations in which promises are made that later may and perhaps should (in the view of the promise maker) be broken. Suppose, for example, a friend on his deathbed reveals that he has made you an heir to his estate because he wants you to use the money to care for his cats and dogs, leaving out of his will his two devoted children. He begs you to promise to execute his wishes so that he can die in peace. You do so, but after his death, feeling that his children should inherit most of the estate rather than the animals and that what he has done is morally wrong, you break your promise so that his estate will go to his rightful heirs. Your action in this unusual situation would be defended by proponents of promise breaking in that what you do after your friend's death will not be known by him, and also the children deserve the inheritance more than the animals.

No Promise Is Sacred. The Latin phrase *caveat emptor*—"let the buyer beware"— is used by some to sanction promise breaking. The implication is that it is foolish and naive to believe that a promise will be kept simply because it was made and more realistic to accept that it probably will be broken. In a way, this shifts the responsibility onto the recipient rather than the promise maker and entirely reverses the concept of social trust under which we live. It certainly promotes an atmosphere of wariness and distrust in human relationships.

◆

Cases for Study and Discussion

C A S E ◆ 1

Bernard and Janice are considering marriage, but Bernard smokes and Janice can't stand smoking. She will marry Bernie only if he quits. Before they are married, he promises to do so and presumably does. He is a psychiatric nurse and works in an atmosphere where almost all patients and staff members smoke. After several years of marriage, Janice discovers that Bernie never gave it up but just hasn't smoked at home. He evidently brushed his teeth and used breath mints before he came home, and the smell of smoke on his clothes was attributed to the atmosphere in which he worked. Very upset, she feels that he has broken an important promise to her. Do you feel that this promise was a trivial one and that Janice is being unreasonable? Why or why not? Does the fact that this promise was made in connection with their marriage have more significance than it otherwise might? Why? Their marriage later ended after a series of other broken promises, not the least of which was an affair of Bernie's that constituted a negation of his marriage promises or vows. In your experience, to what extent do people who break a promise on one occasion continue to do so on other occasions? Give examples.

C A S E ◆ 2

Harold and David, in their mid-twenties, are avid mountain climbers. David has been dating Harold's sister, Doris. During a mountain-climbing expedition by just the two men Harold is seriously injured and is dying. He begs David to promise to marry Doris, who, as Harold knows, is very much in love with David. Moreover, Harold is worried about what will happen to her when he dies. Because Harold is David's best friend, David promises he will marry Doris. After Harold dies, David tells no one about the promise. He enjoys Doris's company, but he doesn't love her and breaks his promise to marry her. Did David do the right thing? If no one knows about a promise, does it have to be kept? Why or why not? Under what conditions, if any?

C A S E ◆ 3

Wanda is divorced from her husband and lives alone with her ten-year-old daughter, Sandy. She has told Sandy that she will always tell her the truth about anything she asks, and if she doesn't know what the truth is, she will find it out for her. After about a year without dating, Wanda meets Howard and they begin seeing each other. After awhile, they discreetly engage in sex, usually when

Sandy is with her father on weekends. Sandy suspects this and finally gets up enough courage to ask her mother about their relationship. Embarrassed and concerned about her image with Sandy, and feeling that Sandy is too young to understand, Wanda tells her they are not having sex. One weekend Sandy comes home unexpectedly and finds Wanda and Howard in bed together. Sandy is very angry with her mother and asks how long this has been going on. Not wanting to lie to her anymore, Wanda tells Sandy, "For a couple of months." Sandy yells, "You lied to me!" and "You promised you would always tell me the truth!" Wanda also becomes angry and tells Sandy she is too young to understand what's going on, and when she gets older she *will*. She also tells her that what she does when Sandy is not around is none of Sandy's business. Should more leeway be allowed in keeping or breaking promises where children are involved since they may be too young to understand? Why or why not? Does Sandy have a right to know the truth about her mother's life outside of their immediate relationship? Why or why not? Are Wanda's reasons for not telling Sandy and her reactions to Sandy's anger justified? Why or why not? How do you think Wanda should have dealt with this whole situation if you don't like the way she did deal with it? Why? Be specific.

♦———————————————————————————————————

Stealing

A basic assumption in most societies and cultures is that stealing is an immoral act. If the victim of theft needs what is stolen from him to survive, then the theft is even more reprehensible. Stealing applies not only to the taking of material things but also to the stealing of ideas (for example, plagiarizing), inventions, and other creations by an individual.

Arguments Against Stealing

Property Rights. Stealing involves taking someone else's property without that person's permission. This is a violation of property rights, which are often considered as important or even more important than life itself. Many people feel strongly, for example, about governments taking private property or forcing people to sell their property for the "public good." Often when people won't willingly sell their property, they can be forced by the state to do so. In one way or another, it will condemn the property so that a freeway, public building, or even a private building can be built on it. Property rights, especially in a democracy, are considered important, and stealing is therefore strongly condemned. Even in societies where property is owned by the state rather than private individuals, stealing is forbidden because it is stealing from the state, which actually means stealing from all the people of the state.

Breakdown of Trust. Like lying, cheating, and breaking promises, stealing severely breaks down trust among people. People who have earned their possessions feel that they have an inalienable right to them. When a theft occurs and the thief is known, any relationship with that person will be difficult to maintain because of the loss of trust. If you've ever been the victim of theft, and you suspect someone you know such as a friend or even a relative, you can never truly trust that person again. Moreover, if you were to actually catch that person stealing, then your relationship with him or her will usually be destroyed.

For example, most of us feel we can leave money or jewelry around our homes without locking them up, but once such things are stolen, we will probably take more precautions against everyone, including family and friends. Once stealing has taken place, trust is abrogated.

Invasion of Privacy. Another argument against stealing is that it is an invasion of privacy. The thief violates the privacy of the victim's person, home, car, or office. A further assault on privacy takes place when a thief steals a wallet or a purse and then has access to the person's identity and credit cards. This can interfere with the victim's daily life until matters can be straightened out and new cards obtained.

The Domino Argument. Some people, of course, are habitual thieves and steal for a living. They had to start somewhere, which recalls the domino theory. Once people steal and get away with it, they might tend to steal again, especially if they discover that they can get what they want easier and faster than if they have to work at a steady job. Stealing becomes a pattern, a way of attaining what the thief aspires to—"if you want or need something, just steal it" can become the motto by which they live. Consider the number of thieves who spend time in prison and return to stealing after their terms are up and they are back in society.

Material Losses to Victims. In addition to the invasion of privacy, victims of theft also suffer the loss of hard-earned or cherished items. When people's cars are stolen, for example, they may get them back and the insurance may pay for damages, but the loss has been a terrible inconvenience, and their cars are not the same after thieves have used and abused them. When ideas, inventions, or other aspects of creativity are stolen, the victims suffer even greater loss, for it involves the products of their own thinking. An example would be if someone discovers or invents something that revolutionizes an industry or our lives and a big corporation steals it from the inventor so that she gets no recognition, reimbursement, or reward for her own ideas.

Effect on the Thief. In addition to the punishments of fines and imprisonment, proponents of arguments against stealing point out that stealing also affects a thief's self-image. When thieves are caught, they generally lose the trust and respect of others. But even if they are not caught, and if they continue to steal, it's likely that their precarious existence and the guilt they feel can seriously affect their self-respect. Of course, some thieves enjoy stealing (see the "Thrills and Adventure" section later in this chapter) and find it exciting and more interesting than working at a steady job.

Overall Effect on Society. Opponents of stealing see it as a threat beyond the loss of personal possessions. In a neighborhood where many thefts have occurred, for example, people may be constantly worried that they and their homes will be victimized at any time. Additionally, because many thieves are armed with dangerous weapons, injury or possible death can occur. But even if they don't, the victims still suffer in that their trust in their fellow human beings must be lessened.

Like the other moral issues discussed in this chapter, stealing and the fear that it engenders cause a breakdown in human relationships that are based on mutual trust. If theft has not occurred and is not threatened, people tend not to be afraid or generally concerned about the possible loss of their possessions; but when it is definitely indicated that it might occur because it has happened to someone else nearby, then people's attitudes are changed from trust and security to distrust, fear, and insecurity. Therefore, stealing has enormous effects on the entire social fabric.

Arguments for Stealing

Corrupt Economic System. One argument for stealing rests on the assumption that we live in a corrupt social and economic system in which the rich get richer and the poor get poorer. The only way to balance these inequities is by sometimes stealing what you need and want. Everyone needs to have basic necessities and even some luxuries, and if the entire system prevents this, then people are entitled to steal when they get the chance.

Sometimes people attempt to balance what they deem to be inequities by stealing, in small ways or large, from the companies where they work, on insurance claims, in taxes to the government, and from other human beings, especially those who are better off than they are. A good example of this attitude is given in Case 2 of Chapter 14 on business ethics, where Steve's union can get him an 8 percent raise when he had hoped for 15 percent. To make up the difference, Steve steals tools and materials from the plant where he works to remodel his house, which is what he intended to do with the expected raise.

Many people justify padding their expense accounts because they consider themselves underpaid by their companies. They cheat on their income taxes because they feel the government wastes tax money anyway and they ought to get some good out of what they give to the government. Or they misrepresent their losses to insurance companies because of large sums they have paid in premiums over the years and because they feel that the insurance companies won't miss it while they never have enough money to live on.

Crucial Emergency Situations. Many people who do not condone stealing in general would allow it in crucial emergency situations, such as if a family is poor, the parents cannot get work, and there is no food for the family to eat. If the husband steals food so that his wife and children won't starve, then stealing is justified in this case. Another example is if a man is chased by killers and finds a car with keys in it, to save his life, he may steal the car. Human life is more important, according to this argument, than property rights, and stealing, when more important issues like preserving human life are at stake, is morally justified.

Thrills and Adventure. To some, stealing provides a life of excitement, thrills, and adventure not obtainable in ordinary life and is therefore worth the risks involved. The notorious bank robber Willie Sutton, who spent most of his life in prison for theft, felt that his life out of prison was more exciting when he could steal than it was leading a mundane existence in a nine-to-five job. How many thieves would take this position is uncertain, but whether such an exciting regimen would be worth all the time spent in prison or suffering other hardships can be decided only by the thieves themselves.

From Institutions and Organizatons. Many people think that stealing from fellow humans is not justified but that stealing from big institutions and organizatons is. Because most large organizations and institutions make huge profits at the expense of us "little guys," they argue, then we have a right to recoup some of what they get from us by stealing from them in various ways. I mentioned earlier that stealing small or large items from companies where we work, padding our expense accounts, cheating on income taxes, and making false claims against insurance companies are all ways of "getting even" with big business and big government for acquiring more than they deserve. Stealing from large organizations and institutions is morally justified, according to this argument, in that it helps to rectify the imbalance in goods and services received.

As Long as You Don't Get Caught. As with cheating, some argue that it's not stealing that is wrong but rather getting caught. Therefore, they would probably argue, you shouldn't steal if there's a good chance you will be caught and therefore punished. They sanction stealing if it can be done safely. This argument is not concerned with a moral issue in stealing but rather with the consequences of it if caught. It would be rejected by nonconsequentialists and at least some consequentialists (unless more good consequences came from stealing than not) as in the matter of cheating and not getting caught.

328

Military and Government Secrets. Many feel that stealing military or government secrets in wartime and also peacetime is justified in the interests of national security. Therefore, if the United States knew that one of its enemies had a secret weapon that it had recently developed, our undercover agents would be perfectly justified in stealing the plans for it if it would enable our nation to keep ahead of its enemy in military preparedness.

An interesting reversal of this argument is the justification of stealing one's own country's secret documents to expose injustice. The Pentagon Papers, for example, were stolen and given to the press to reveal improper practices of the government and the military in conducting the Vietnam War. The justification for this theft and the relevation of the contents of the stolen documents was that the immorality should be exposed and not allowed to continue. It's interesting to speculate whether the same people would justify stealing secrets from foreign powers for national security as they would from our own government to reveal immorality and corruption.

Similar to these two instances is the stealing of trade secrets in business activities. To exceed or stay abreast of one's competitors, one needs to know what plans they have that might give them control over the entire market, including oneself. Some support such theft (it's called industrial espionage) as a necessity in the competitive business world we live in. Others see and abhor it as just simply stealing.

◆

Cases for Study and Discussion

CASE ◆ 1

Seven years ago, Victor published what has become a popular ethics textbook called *Ethics with Applications*. The book is now in its third edition. Looking through flyers for new ethics texts, he sees one with the exact same title as his. Dismayed, he immediately contacts his editor, who tells him that titles, unfortunately, cannot be copyrighted but are fair game for anyone who wants to use them. Victor angrily writes both the publisher and the authors of the other text, complaining they have stolen his title. They never answer him, and he remains extremely upset. He would never knowingly steal someone's title and can't understand their action. Even though what they did is legal, are they morally obligated not to use Victor's title? Why or why not? Should they at least apologize for doing so? Is there anything else they could do to make things right, or do they need to? Why or why not? If titles cannot be copyrighted, then can this be considered stealing? Why or why not? Is this an important or trivial issue, to your way of thinking? Why or why not?

C A S E ♦ 2

During wartime, Katia and her family have been starving because their town has been bombed and under siege. She breaks into someone's house, finds food in the kitchen, and steals it for her family. Is she justified in stealing in this instance? Why or why not? Be specific. Would it may any difference it it were during peacetime but times were hard and Katia couldn't get a job and earn money to buy food? Why or why not?

C A S E ♦ 3

During riots in various cities throughout the United States, many poor people looted TV and appliance stores for items they said they were denied by a corrupt society that segregated and oppressed them. Some of them said that such items were not really luxuries because most Americans had them. Do you believe that this stealing was justified or not? Why? If not, how does it differ from stealing food? Is there anything to the poor people's arguments? Why or why not? Are there any times when you would justify stealing? If not, why not? If so, when? Be specific.

C A S E ♦ 4

Leroy died suddenly, leaving Margaret, his wife, who was suffering from atherosclerosis (hardening of the arteries) of the brain, for whom he had cared devotedly because she was practically an invalid. In his will he left his substantial estate to her, to go upon her death to his side of the family. He had actually earned all the money because Margaret had never gone to work. Margaret's sister, Anne, and her husband, Eric, an attorney, agreed to take care of her, putting her into a skilled nursing facility near their home for which all expenses were paid from Leroy's estate. While she was still alive, they changed Margaret's will, splitting the estate 40/60 in favor of her side of the family. They had a doctor certify that she was mentally competent to make such a change, but Leroy's family, who had visited her, noticed that she was capable of very little in the way of decision making. As longtime friends of Anne and Eric, they had trusted them not to do anything improper. When they learned that Anne and Eric had changed Leroy's will under what they felt to be very shady circumstances, they accused them of stealing. Do you believe that what Anne and Eric did was theft? Why or why not? Do you feel they had a right to change Leroy's will? Why or why not? If they felt their side of the family had been wronged, was there anything that Anne and Eric could have done differently to rectify the problem? What and why? This action ended a friendship of many years' standing and caused hard feelings on both sides. Are such effects worth considering in such a situation? Why or why not?

Chapter Summary

I. Definitions of key terms
- A. Lying is an intentionally deceptive message in the form of a statement or piece of information deliberately presented as being true—anything meant to deceive or give a wrong impression.
    1. A white lie is a falsehood not meant to injure anyone and often considered as having little moral import.
    2. Lies of commission are direct statements that are outright lies. Lies of omission involve not stating certain information that is vital to an important human activity.
- B. Cheating is deceiving by trickery, swindling, misleading, and acting dishonestly or practicing fraud.
- C. A promise is a declaration or vow that one will or will not do something, and breaking a promise is to fail to conform to or to act contrary to or to violate the promise.
- D. Stealing is taking something without right or permission, generally in a surreptitious way.

II. Nonconsequentialist and consequentialist views
- A. Rule nonconsequentialist views are opposed to any of the four acts at any time.
- B. Consequentialist and act nonconsequentialist views.
    1. Consequentialist theories would accept any of the four actions if the greatest good consequences would result.
    2. Act nonconsequentialists would not necessarily take a stand for or against these issues unless they felt like doing so.

III. Lying
- A. Arguments against lying are as follows:
    1. Lying may obscure objectives of those lied to.
    2. It may also obscure relevant alternatives.
    3. It causes distrust in human relationships.
    4. The domino argument seems to have more relevance here than with other moral issues because very often one lie of necessity leads to another to protect the first, and so on.
    5. Lying gives an unfair advantage or power to the liar.
    6. Lying has a deleterious effect on society in general.
- B. Arguments for lying also exist.
    1. Lying is justified in defense of the innocent, including self-defense.
    2. Lying is justified for reasons of national security provided this reason is not abused.
    3. Lying is moral to protect trade secrets in business.

       4. Little white lies should be allowed as a way of getting along with others in our daily lives.

  C. The Moderate position has the following aspects.

       1. This position would generally accept the attitude that "honesty is the best policy."

       2. One must be very careful of the consequences of any lie, even white lies.

       3. Lying is not the only alternative to giving hurtful truth—one may give this truth gently, compassionately, and with hope wherever possible.

       4. If one has to lie, then he or she must try to make the consequences of the lying as harmless as possible.

       5. One should try to avoid habitual lying.

       6. One should be aware that lying can also have a bad effect on the liar as well as the person lied to.

       7. One should never lie about important matters that may affect the recipient of the lie adversely.

       8. Lying can be allowed when there is no other recourse and when innocent life is really at stake.

IV. Cheating

  A. Cheating is related to lying in that deception and dishonesty are both being practiced except that lying is generally verbal, whereas cheating is basically nonverbal.

  B. There are arguments against cheating.

       1. It is unfair and unjust to others.

       2. Falsified qualifications for professions, for example, will have a serious effect on everyone.

       3. Effects on cheaters may also be destructive if they are caught in a lack-of-qualifications situation and also because it can become a habit affecting the cheater's relationship with others.

  C. Arguments for cheating are as follows.

       1. The world is a dog-eat-dog jungle in which you must often cheat to survive and get ahead. Also, winning is everything no matter how you do it.

       2. Everybody does it; therefore, why not cheat?

       3. It's all right to cheat as long as you don't get caught.

V. Breaking promises

  A. Implied agreements allow us to live safely and meaningfully with each other in society:

       1. Not to do harm to one another.

       2. Not to lie or cheat.

       3. To obey laws for the general good.

       4. To stop at red lights and stop signs.

     5. To treat each other with respect and dignity.

     6. To keep promises we make.

  B. Breaking promises is a form of dishonesty, as is cheating.

  C. In earlier days a person's promise or word was an integral part of his or her reputation, but now many promises or agreements have to be written down for two reasons:

     1. Because they are much more complex than they used to be.

     2. Fewer people actually honor their agreements these days.

  D. Arguments against breaking promises.

     1. Breaking promises destroys human relationships.

     2. Again the domino argument applies here.

     3. Breaking promises seriously affects people's life choices.

     4. Breaking promises destroys general social trust.

     5. Loss of personal integrity may result if people continually break their promises.

  E. Arguments for breaking promises.

     1. One should have the individual freedom to decide which promises to keep and which to break. Any rules against breaking promises are a denial of such freedom.

     2. Breaking promises should be allowed when more important moral issues are involved, such as protecting and saving human life.

     3. It should also be allowed when no harm is done to anyone through breaking the promise.

     4. Just as we often say, "buyer beware," recipients of promises should also beware—they shouldn't count on promises to be kept.

     5. Promises made in unusual situations, as for example to satisfy someone on his or her deathbed, can justifiably be broken later, especially for good reasons.

VI. Stealing

  A. A basic assumption in most societies is that people are entitled to what they have inherited, invented, created, and earned; therefore, stealing is generally considered immoral.

  B. There are many arguments against stealing.

     1. People have property rights, which are often considered as important or even more important than life itself.

     2. Like the other three moral issues discussed in this chapter, stealing breaks down the trust people have in one another.

     3. Stealing constitutes a serious invasion of privacy.

     4. The domino argument applies here as well as in the other three issues.

     5. Stealing has both physical and psychological effects on victims that are destructive.

     6. Thieves themselves can be seriously affected through loss of integrity and through punishment if they are caught.

7. As in the other three issues, stealing also has a bad effect on society in general.

C. Arguments for stealing are as follows.

1. We live in a corrupt economic system in which the rich get richer and the poor get poorer, and sometimes the only way to achieve some sort of balance between these inequities is to steal.

2. Stealing should be allowed in crucial emergency situations, such as to prevent the starvation of children.

3. Stealing is a way out for those who crave a life of thrills, adventure, and excitement.

4. It is allowable from institutions and organizations because they can afford it and end up with most of our money anyway.

5. As in cheating, one ought to be allowed to steal as long as one doesn't get caught.

6. It can be condoned when it involves stealing government and military secrets from potential or real enemies to protect one's own national security.

Exercises for Review

1. In your own words, define lying, cheating, breaking promises, stealing, white lies, and acts of commission and omission. Give a clear example of each.

2. What is the "domino argument," and how does it apply to the four moral issues described in this chapter? Do you think it's an important consideration or not? Why?

3. Take each of the four issues and show how an egoist, act utilitarian, rule utilitarian, act nonconsequentialist, divine command advocate, Kantian, and a Sir William David Ross advocate would, in your opinion, deal with them. Review Chapters 2 and 3 before answering this question.

4. What are the arguments *against* lying, cheating, breaking promises, and stealing, and to what extent do you agree or disagree with them? Be specific. Present any other arguments you can think of and justify them as fully as you can.

5. What are the arguments *for* lying, cheating, breaking promises, and stealing, and to what extent do you agree or disagree with *them*? Again be specific, and present any others you can think of.

6. To what extent do you feel that lying, cheating, breaking promises, and stealing really have an effect on society in general? Give specific examples or illustrations.

7. To what extent do you feel that doing these things really has an effect on the one who does them? Again give examples and illustrations to show how they do or do not have an effect.

8. Defend or attack the position that "little white lies" are not important or serious in any way and are really needed in our everyday human relationships.

9. Discuss fully the idea that it's all right to lie, cheat, break promises, or steal "as long as you don't get caught." To what extent do you support this contention and why? Be specific.

10. To what extent do you agree or disagree with the statement that promises and agreements need to be written down more today than in the past because fewer people actually honor their promises and agreements? Why? Give examples to support your position.

Notes

1. Sissella Bok, *Lying: Moral Choice in Public and Private Life* (New York: Vintage, 1979), 16.

2. William Morris, ed., *The American Heritage Dictionary of the English Language* (Boston: Houghton-Mifflin, 1978), 754.

3. Bok, *Lying,* 61.

4. Morris, *American Heritage Dictionary,* 229.

5. Ibid., 1047, 162.

6. Ibid., 1261.

7. Ibid., 738.

8. Ibid., 573, 981, respectively.

9. Bok, *Lying,* 26–27.

10. Elisabeth Kübler-Ross, *On Death and Dying* (New York: Macmillan, 1969), 262.

11. Bok, *Lying,* 28.

12. Ibid., 19.

13. Kübler-Ross, *On Death and Dying,* 28.

14. Elisabeth Kübler-Ross, *Coping with Death and Dying,* a set of audio tapes, date and publisher unknown.

Supplementary Reading

Adler, Mortimer J. *The Time of Our Lives: The Ethics of Common Sense.* New York: Holt, Rinehart and Winston, 1970.

Atiyah, Patrick S. *Promises, Morals, and Law.* New York: Oxford University Press, 1981.

Atkinson, Ronald et al. *Sexual Latitude: For and Against.* New York: Hart, 1971.

Barnsley, John H. *The Social Reality of Ethics: The Comparative Analysis of Moral Codes.* London: Routledge and Kegan Paul, 1972.

Bell, J. Bowyer, and Barton Whaley. *Cheating and Deception.* New Brunswick, N.J.: Transaction Publications, 1991.

Bok, Sissela. *Lying: Moral Choice in Public and Private Life.* New York: Random House, 1989.

————. *Secrets: On the Ethics of Concealment and Revelation.* New York: Pantheon Books, 1982.

Cowell, Frank A. *Cheating the Government: The Economics of Evasion.* Cambridge, Mass.: MIT Press, 1990.

Cunningham, Robert L., ed. *Situationism and the New Morality.* New York: Appleton-Century-Crofts, 1970.

Fletcher, Joseph. *Moral Responsibility: Situation Ethics at Work.* Philadelphia: Westminster, 1967.

————. *Morals and Medicine: The Moral Problem of the Patient's Right to Know the Truth.* Princeton: Princeton University Press, 1979.

Girvetz, Harry K., ed. *Contemporary Moral Issues*, 2nd ed. Belmont, Calif.: Wadsworth, 1968.

Gonsalves, Milton A. *Fagothey's Right and Reason: Ethics in Theory and Practice*, 8th ed. St. Louis: Times/Mirror Mosby, 1985.

Hare, R. M. *Applications of Moral Philosophy.* Berkeley: University of California Press, 1972.

Kübler-Ross, Elisabeth. *On Death and Dying.* New York: Macmillan, 1969.

Miller, Nathan. *Stealing from America: A History of Corruption from Jamestown to Reagan.* New York: Paragon House Publishers, 1992.

Ousterhoudt, Robert G., ed. *The Philosophy of Sport: A Collection of Original Essays.* Springfield, Ill.: Charles C. Thomas, 1973.

Robins, Michael H. *Promising, Intending, and Moral Autonomy.* New York: Cambridge University Press, 1984.

CHAPTER 12

Morality and Human Sexuality

Objectives

After you have read this chapter you should be able to

1. Distinguish between public, or societal, and private aspects of human sexuality.
2. Discuss the purposes of human sexual activity.
3. Discuss the following moral issues in sexuality: premarital sex, sex in marriage-type relationships (including the issues of homosexuality and adultery), prostitution, masturbation, pornography, and perversion, or unnatural sexual relations.

Major Aspects of Human Sexuality

The first distinction we must make when discussing morality and human sexuality is that which exists between its public, or societal, aspect and its private aspect. First of all, the public aspect is concerned with the way matters of sex *overtly* affect others, and the basic governing principles of morality here are life, goodness, and justice. The private aspect, on the other hand, is concerned with sexual relations between or among consenting adults, and the basic governing principles in this case are those of goodness, justice, freedom, and honesty.

In other words, it is important to distinguish between two kinds of actions involving human sexuality: those that have such an adverse effect on people other than the participants that they should be forbidden by moral commandment or by law, and those that affect only the participants and should therefore be left up to the private moral deliberations of the people concerned. Needless to say, one of the main issues surrounding human sexual activity is whether we should greatly restrict such activities on the one hand, or allow a great deal of sexual freedom on the other. Before dealing with arguments concerning restriction or liberalization of sexual activity, it would probably be of value to examine what the meaning and purposes of human sexuality are deemed to be.

The Meaning and Purposes of Human Sexuality

The meaning and purposes of human sexual activity appear to be four-dimensional, involving (not necessarily in order of importance) procreation, pleasure, an expression of love for other people, and an expression of friendship and liking. These, of course, need not be mutually exclusive, and often they are not; however, sexual activity may also be limited to only one of these purposes. Although procreation is a rather obvious purpose of sexuality, sexuality is also—in the opinion of many—the deepest and most intimate expression of the love of human beings for one another. This does not mean that one cannot love others without sexual activity—for example, that one could never love his or her children, brothers, sisters, parents, or grandparents without being incestuous. What it does mean is that when a love involving meaningful sex occurs, it is deeper than any other kind. For instance, two people need not have sex to love each other, but deep and loving sex between two persons can add a rich new dimension to any love.

It is, many feel, a terrible oversight on the part of society in general that the loving aspect of sex has been considered relatively unimportant when compared to its procreative aspect or to other areas of human relationships. Our society has, at least until recently, often emphasized that sex is somehow a necessary evil. This approach to human sexuality implies either that its primary purpose is to produce children or that sexuality is not a very important aspect of human relationships and human life. This is an attitude reflected in many of our laws, which are throwbacks to nineteenth-century Victorianism. In the Victorian era, all kinds of private sex acts between or among consenting adults were forbidden, to the extent that if a husband and wife wished to practice oral sex, for example, they would, under the law, be guilty of a felony.

Many of these archaic and unfair laws (unfair, that is, when applied to all human beings) have been repealed in many states and revised in accordance with the American Bar Association's suggestions. The reason for this change in attitude is that these laws reflected a view of human sexual activity that does not square with studies made in the nineteenth and twentieth centuries, including those of Freud, Kinsey, and Masters and Johnson.[1]

Almost all the research conducted by twentieth-century psychologists (see the bibliography at the end of this chapter) reveals, first of all, that sexuality as it is practiced did not and does not adhere to the general societal moral pronouncements and laws. Second, it reveals that human sexuality for many people is very limited and that sexual relations are often unsatisfying because of these people's upbringing, which has been strongly influenced by the taboos against meaningful sexual relations set up and generally sanctioned by their society. Third, this research reveals that psychologically, sexuality is extremely important to human living and especially to human relationships. In view of such strong evidence, it seems that the expression-of-love, friendship-and-liking aspects of human sexual activity should be emphasized more than they have been—in fact, that they should be emphasized at least as much as procreation and pleasure.

The conservative, or restrictive, view toward sexual activity often emphasizes either the procreation aspect of sex or the view that sex is a "necessary evil"— that is, a biological urge felt by men (but not, it is implied, by women) which must be satisfied. Advocates of complete freedom in sexual matters, on the other hand, usually emphasize the pleasure aspect and the rights of individuals to enjoy such pleasure. There is also a more moderate position, whose proponents tend to accept both the procreative and pleasure aspects while also including— and often emphasizing more strongly—the expression-of-love, friendship-and-liking aspects. I do not want to suggest that the lines are always drawn this clearly; a proponent of sexual freedom may, for example, strongly emphasize the expression-of-love aspect—as may a supporter of the conservative view. However, the general tendency is for each group to emphasize the aspects in the way I have described.

Moral Issues and the Public Aspect of Human Sexuality

Those sexual acts that immediately affect the public or individuals in such a way as to bring them possible harm, that are generally considered immoral, and that are usually controlled by laws are rape, child molestation, and sadism performed on unwilling victims. The possible harmful effects that can ensue from these three types of acts are bodily harm and/or death and the general perniciousness of forced sexual activity. No matter what set of ethical principles they follow, most people generally agree that these acts are immoral and that there should be laws and/or moral taboos forbidding them.

Other activities considered by many to be against the public interest are pornography, homosexuality, sex outside of marriage (including premarital and extramarital sex and adultery), prostitution, masturbation, nonmonogamous marriages, and "unnatural," or "perverted," sexual activity. Agreement about the immorality of these activities is not, however, as general or as clear as is agreement about the first three activities. I will present specific arguments for and against these issues later in the chapter, but first it is worthwhile to examine some arguments for and against sexual freedom in general.

Arguments Against Sexual Freedom

Violation of Tradition. The first argument against sexual freedom is that such freedom is a violation of the traditional moral "absolutes" embodied in our Judeo-Christian heritage. According to this tradition, heterosexual sex is the only morally permissible sexuality. Furthermore, sexual acts should be performed as "God and nature intended" (that is, generally in the "missionary position," with the man on top and the woman on the bottom). Finally, sexual activity must take place only within a legally and, preferably, a religiously sanctioned marriage between one man and one woman who are joined mainly for the purpose of bringing children into the world. Outside of marriage the only acceptable approach to sexuality is abstinence. Of course, pornography, homosexuality, sex outside of marriage, prostitution, masturbation, nonmonogamous marriages, and "unnatural," "perverted," sexual activity are considered violations of these traditional moral teachings, either because they tend to undermine our family and societal structure, or because they will eventually lead to the destruction of these institutions.

The Domino Argument. The domino argument applies here, as it does to so many moral issues, this time in two ways. First, allowing sexual freedom in any of the areas named previously will eventually lead to violations in more dangerous areas. It is argued that if, for example, we allow people the freedom to read, view, and acquire pornography openly, eventually there will be an increase in rapes, child molestation, and sadism performed on unwilling victims, all of which may lead to sexual murders. According to this argument, pornography so inflames the sexual appetites and desires of people that they will have to find outlets for these appetites and will resort to these unacceptable means. Second, it is argued that allowing more sexual freedom in these areas will undermine our society and all the good and decent things it stands for, such as the family, respect for marriage, love rather than lust, respect for the human body, respect for women and men, and respect for children.

Offensiveness to Public Taste. This argument presumes a certain general agreement concerning what is acceptable and what is offensive to the public taste.

Heterosexual relationships are acceptable whereas homosexual ones are not. Monogamous marriages are acceptable, whereas polygamous (more than one wife) or polyandrous (more than one husband) ones are not. Sexual activity within a marriage is acceptable, whereas outside of marriage it is not, and so on.

Social Diseases and AIDS. The social-diseases argument cites the probability of getting certain social diseases, such as syphilis, gonorrhea, herpes, and the dreaded and fatal acquired immune deficiency syndrome (AIDS), through sexual promiscuity and sexual freedom. The proponents of this argument state that all of the so-called sexual freedom of the 1960s, 1970s, and 1980s has led to an increase in such diseases, which are not only painful, destructive, and contagious, but also in many cases (especially with AIDS) fatal. A return to and reemphasis of traditional sexual morality would be the best way to eliminate such terrible diseases, according to proponents of this argument.

Arguments for Sexual Freedom

Individual Freedom. The main argument presented by the proponents of this position is that people ought to have the freedom to do what they want to do as long as they are consenting adults and are not materially or directly harming other members of society by their actions. Obviously, people should not be free to rape, to molest children, or to perform sadistic acts on unwilling victims; however, they ought to be completely free to have any kind of sex they wish with other consenting adults or by themselves, in or outside of marriage, as long as they do not harm others.

Traditions as Irrelevant. Even though the prosexual freedom advocates recognize that there are Judeo-Christian or other traditions that have, in the past, served as guides for sexual morality, they do not consider such traditions "absolute." In fact, they argue that such traditions are based on archaic views of the biological and psychological makeup of human beings—views that twentieth-century advances in the sciences and social sciences have revealed to be inaccurate. Now that we know more about human sexuality, the prosexual freedom forces argue, we should allow a wider and more open expression of one of the most important human drives in existence.

They also argue that there is no clear-cut indication of what "God and nature intended" in sexuality except what is condoned or prohibited in certain religious teachings, which one may or may not believe. They state that the marriage contract is merely a piece of paper, and that there is evidence that sex that takes place outside of marriage can be just as meaningful as that which takes place within it. Furthermore, sex between homosexuals and in polygamous or polyandrous relationships or marriages can be as meaningful as sex between heterosexuals in monogamous marriages. Because human beings are so varied and unique in their feelings and desires, sexual-freedom proponents argue, they ought to be allowed the greatest freedom of sexual expression possible as long as they do not harm others.

Refutation of the Domino Argument. The sexual-freedom proponents would argue that there is no hard evidence to suggest that allowing greater sexual freedom in the six "questionable" areas will lead to violations in the areas of rape, incest, and forced sadism. They argue further that some evidence exists that in countries such as Denmark, where pornography has been made totally legal and freely available, the rate of sexual crimes, such as child molestation, has dropped. Sexual-freedom supporters see pornography as a force that relieves sexual repressions and eliminates the need for these more harmful types of sexual activities.

Even if, however, there are abuses of freedom in relation to pornography—for example, sexual murder or so-called kiddie porn—laws can be passed restricting and punishing people involved in those activities without restricting people's general freedom of access to pornography. Second, this argument states that rather than undermining our society, greater sexual freedom will enhance it by allowing for fuller sexual expression. This in turn will deepen the love, respect, and intensity of human relationships, which can only improve marriage, family life, and society in general.

Offensiveness to Public Taste. According to the sexual-freedom proponents, offensiveness to public taste is not in itself a reason to halt the activities of others, and therefore it should be considered more of a violation of customs and manners than a violation of morality. Bodily harm and/or death are immoral under most ethical principles, but offensiveness to public taste is not unless it can be shown that the Principle of Justice has been seriously violated. This does not mean that the rights and feelings of others in matters of taste should not be considered; what it does mean is that the excuse that something is offensive to others, even though they are not required to participate in any way, is not sufficient to bar someone, either by moral censure or by law, from engaging in certain activities.

Discretion certainly should be employed in the public display of pornography and other sexual activities offered for those who wish to participate (topless or nude shows, films, and so on), and there should be control of indecent exposure, overt solicitation, or coercion to participate in any sexual activities. However, this is not to say that an open display of affection that does not involve indecent exposure or overt solicitation or coercion is immoral even though—especially between or among homosexuals—it may offend some people's tastes. Therefore, if sexual activity does not violate any of the preceding criteria, and it often does not, it then becomes largely a private matter to be dealt with between or among consenting adults, according to the sexual-freedom proponents.

There are many ways in which the problem of offensiveness to public taste can be handled. For example, if people want to sunbathe or swim in the nude, then special locations can be purchased or set aside for them to do so. Those who do not wish to do so need never go near these locations. If some adults want to view pornographic films, buy books, or see live nude people, then as long as those who do not want to do such things are not forced to do so, and as long as these theaters, bookstores, and nude shows are obviously marked and advertised to show what they are, then how can there be an overt offense to taste?

Furthermore, there is no conclusive evidence that participation in any of these activities has caused harm to society in general; that is, that people who read pornographic books, for example, go out and molest children or rape others. In fact, as mentioned earlier, some studies have shown that in countries where laws against pornographic shows, films, and books have been relaxed, overt sexual crimes have tended to decrease. The proof for this is not conclusive either, but if there is no conclusive proof either way, then such activities should not be considered immoral or illegal merely for the above reasons.

Social Diseases and AIDS. Proponents of sexual freedom certainly recognize the dangers of social diseases and especially AIDS; however, proper precautions can certainly be taken to avoid or minimize the contracting of such diseases, such as abstinence (if a person desires), the use of condoms and other devices and chemicals, and the careful choosing of one's sexual partners. Such choices, however, should be free ones, and no one's freedom should be curtailed because such diseases might be contracted. After all, smokers may get cancer and drinkers may get cirrhosis of the liver, but this does not mean we have the right to restrict their freedom to indulge in these activities.

◆——

Premarital Sex

Premarital sex refers to those sexual relations that occur prior to marriage; it is referred to in the Bible as "fornication."

Arguments Against Premarital Sex

The Undermining of Traditional Morality. As I have mentioned, the conservative position toward liberalizing sexuality states that one of the greatest problems created by encouraging or even allowing premarital sex is that it tends to undermine traditional Western morality. According to this view, as we have said, sexuality should be something that is reserved for a heterosexual, monogamous marriage and that should be used mainly, but not necessarily exclusively, for procreation. Allowing premarital sex discourages the special and unique rela-

343

tionship that exists between one man and one woman in a lifetime of marriage, it undermines marriage itself as an institution, and it encourages sexual activity that is separate from "true" love and from having children. According to this argument, the only acceptable form of sexuality for boys and girls and men and women is no sexuality or abstinence until marriage.

The argument continues that if marriage breaks down, then the traditional family unit breaks down, and the family unit is the basic building block of traditional Western society. Premarital sex also encourages an inflated view of sex as the most important aspect of marriage, thereby further eroding one of our most important social institutions. According to this view, sexuality is considered such an intimate part of the relationship between a man and a woman that it must have the stability and security of the marriage relationship to foster and support it.

The Encouragement of Promiscuity. Another argument that supports the conservative point of view is that premarital sex fosters promiscuity and encourages transitory rather than lasting human relationships. If sex is allowed outside of marriage it becomes separated from its "true" purposes, which are to enhance marriage relationships and produce children. Instead, according to this argument, the only purpose of premarital sex is to achieve selfish individual pleasures without accepting the responsibility for one's own actions or the lives of others involved. Premarital sex also encourages promiscuity in that without marriage the societal restrictions are loosened, and one can virtually have sex with anyone at any time. Therefore, the lasting, meaningful relationships between men and women that are established and developed through marriage are replaced with "one-night stands," which reduce human relationships to an animal level.

Social Diseases and AIDS. One of the most powerful arguments against premarital sex is the possibility of spreading social diseases and especially AIDS. People who argue against premarital sex state that abstinence is the best way to avoid contracting these diseases. Therefore, as traditional values have always taught, one should abstain from sexual intercourse or other sexual activity until one gets married. Before men and women get married they should voluntarily be tested for the AIDS virus to ensure that neither partner will infect the other. Obviously, however, premarital sex puts one in danger of contracting such diseases and passing them on to other sexual partners or future wives or husbands.

The Fostering of Guilt and Ostracism. Because premarital sex is frowned upon by our culture and our society, it can result in various degrees of guilt and ostracism for those who engage in it. Whatever is initially felt by individuals who want to engage in premarital sex, most of the people around them—especially their parents, other relatives, and sometimes their friends—are generally opposed to their actions, and because of this they may experience guilt and be ostracized from accepted society.

Having Children. Within the accepted marital relationship, children who are brought into the world can be protected and raised with some security. They will also legally have a family name. There is always the possibility within the premarital relationship that children will be born, and if they are, they may be raised out of wedlock. If a couple decides on an abortion, then the premarital relationship has fostered yet another moral wrong—the murder of an innocent fetus. If children are raised in such a relationship, what will they think once they discover that their parents are not married and everyone else's parents are?

The Compatibility and Experience Fallacy. One argument often given for premarital sex is that it allows people to gain sexual experience so that when they enter into marriage they will know what they are doing. Another aspect of this argument is that people who have sex or live together are able to find out whether they are really sexually compatible, thus avoiding the misfortune of finding out after they are married that they aren't and perhaps never will be.

According to the conservative view, this argument provides no excuse for premarital sex. After all, classes in marriage and the family and in sex hygiene are now offered in school, and there are many good scientific books available on the subject. The compatibility argument, furthermore, places the sole emphasis for a relationship on sexual attraction, and a marriage is much more than that. Besides, any advantages gained in the way of experience or knowledge about compatibility are far outweighed by the violation of the sacredness of marriage, the inevitable loss of respect that occurs when two people become mere sex objects in each other's eyes, and the instability of the relationship. For if there is no marriage, people who live together can leave any time they want to, experiencing no sense of concern for the other person or for any children who may have resulted from their relationship. Also, it is argued, there is something unique in the marriage of two people who come to each other as virgins because sex then becomes a very special offering of love from one person to the other. For this reason, as well as the others cited, premarital sex, therefore, should not be encouraged or allowed.

Arguments for Premarital Sex

The Obsolescence of the Old Traditions. Certainly the prevalence of premarital sex may change the society's life-style, but, according to the liberal viewpoint, the old traditions have already been undermined because they are simply no longer applicable in an advanced, technological, and rapidly changing world such as ours. The family unit has already become more mobile and flexible in reaction to the complexity of our modern culture. Some of the changes that have taken place in society are for the better and some are not, but, according to the liberal view, what we need is a number of alternative life-styles that will allow us to enjoy the freedom and individuality that are encouraged these days.

Besides, the sexual-freedom proponents argue, what is so great about the old style of marriage in which the father is a dictator and the mother a slave to her housework and her children? Furthermore, what is good about hypocritical marriages in which unhappy couples stay together just because they are married or "because of the children"? Many adulterous relationships are spawned by these "sacred" but unsatisfying marriages, and how is that any better than premarital sex? At least the two people involved in a premarital relationship can have some prior agreement that if it doesn't work, they will try something else.

Social Diseases and AIDS. It is unreasonable in our modern day and age to advocate abstinence from sexuality. The proponents of premarital sex state that abstinence is unnatural and an elimination of one of humanity's greatest pleasures. All one needs to do is take the proper precautions, such as using a condom and eliminating certain sexual acts that perpetuate the spread of AIDS, for example. Further, one can enter into a relatively monogamous premarital sexual relationship or limit one's partners to those who are known to be free from these diseases. Social diseases in themselves, then, are not a sufficient reason for not engaging in premarital sex.

The Promiscuity Fallacy. First of all, many premarital sex arrangements do not condone promiscuity. Many of these affairs are long-lasting—sometimes as long-lasting as a marriage—and such relationships may even develop into marriages. Second, sexual-freedom proponents ask, is the promiscuity in premarital relationships any greater than that in marriages? Does being married preclude the fact that one or both spouses will be promiscuous? Third, even if unmarried people are promiscuous, as long as they are freely consenting adults, whose business is it but theirs?

The Guilt and Ostracism Fallacy. People's views of premarital sex have changed a great deal, and few people who engage in premarital sex nowadays are ostracized from society; this also applies to children born out of wedlock. People are just not as concerned about these matters as they used to be. Guilt, furthermore, is a matter of private conscience, and as long as the consciences of the people who enjoy premarital sex are not disturbed, then why should anyone else's be? People who do not approve don't have to condone or engage in premarital sex themselves, and they shouldn't concern themselves with other people's behavior as long as it doesn't intrude into their lives. Parents of people involved in premarital sex certainly don't have to condone these activities in their own homes, but what their children do on their own is their business as long as they are consenting adults.

Contraception and Responsibility. People who engage in premarital sex can, of course, use contraceptive devices, and they probably do use them more often than not. Often, proponents would state, the children resulting from such relationships are cared for as well as or even better than they would be if they were born into a marriage. Furthermore, when such couples plan for or discover they are going to have a child, they will often get married out of respect for the child's position in their relationship and in society in general. And, if an accidental or unplanned pregnancy occurs, then abortion exists as a viable alternative. This alternative is often used even within marriages when children are not wanted, so why can't it be used here also?

Sexual Experience and Compatibility. Sexual experience and compatibility, according to those who would allow premarital sex, is one of its greatest advantages. They feel that learning through experience what sexuality is all about and relating to different people sexually will enable people to discover what type of relationship they want and what type of person they want to share it with.

One of the myths of our culture is that sexual activity is a natural ability which one can easily utilize after one is married. As a matter of fact, a sexual relationship, not mere biological coupling, is terribly complex and requires a great deal of knowledge and ability. Sexuality does not "come naturally," and is particularly hard to acquire in a culture that has repressed it for so long. A good sexual relationship also requires awareness of and being comfortable with one's body and the bodies of others so that greater freedom can be attained. Premarital sex is the best means of achieving sexual experience and knowledge, especially if two people are considering a long-lasting relationship. If they live together from day to day, they will find out over a period of time whether they will be compatible in a marriage. Even if they discover that they are not compatible, they will probably have learned something about themselves that will not only help them to avoid making the serious mistake of entering into marriage but will also help them to discover what kind of partner they really do want.

Sexual Pleasure. Another advantage of premarital sex is that sexual activity is pleasurable in itself, whether or not it leads to marriage or even a lasting relationship. By allowing premarital sex, sexual pleasure can be enjoyed freely to the extent any individual wishes without permanent commitment. This kind of relationship may not be suitable for some people, but those who find it morally acceptable ought to be free to indulge in it without regard to society's standards or the wishes of others who are not involved in their relationship or relationships.

A Private, Not a Public, Matter. Despite what the critics of premarital sex say about the undermining of Western traditions and so on, premarital sex is one of those private sexual matters that should be left to the discretion of free, consenting adults. As the liberal arguments presented at the beginning of this chapter illustrate, this is a matter for individuals to decide, and just because some or even the majority of people living in our society do not approve of premarital sex, as long as it is not forced on them or their children it should both be allowed and be considered moral.

Sex in Marriage-Type (Including Nonlegal) Relationships

A marriage-type relationship is one that is continuous and lasting (or intended to be) rather than temporary or transitory. There is, or course, some overlap between this type of relationship and a premarital one. For example, some premarital sex relationships that begin as transitory or temporary may become permanent or lasting. Also, many people classify any sexual relationship occurring between two never-married people as premarital or *extramarital* (occurring *outside* of marriage). The latter term is also often used to mean adultery, which will be dealt with later. However, I am using the phrase "marriage-type" to refer to any relationship that is intended by the two or more people involved to be permanent or lasting and in which sex is a deeper part of a more involved human relationship than is the case in many premarital relationships.

The purpose of sex in a marriage-type relationship appears to be twofold. First, it provides a deep and intimate expression of love between or among persons, including the giving and receiving of pleasure. Second, it provides the means for procreating, or having children. These purposes are not *necessarily* compatible *or* incompatible. That is, people may have a permanent or lasting sexual relationship without ever having children; or, in expressing their love for each other, a man and a woman might have children as a part of that expression.

Obviously, the description of a deep expression of love as the main purpose of sex does not square with some societal and religious views. Nevertheless, I do not believe that merely because the main way children can be created is through sexual intercourse between a man and woman (at least at the present time, with the exception of artificial insemination, although life created in the laboratory is a distinct future possibility especially since the recent successes in producing test-tube babies) that procreation must *necessarily* be the only valid reason or purpose for the sex act. To take this stand reduces human beings to the level of animals who mate instinctively and infrequently for purposes of procreating their species and relegates sex to a merely biological function.

The overwhelming evidence produced by psychology in the nineteenth and twentieth centuries strongly suggests that human beings are not merely instinctive animals, mating only at certain times of the year for procreation, nor is human sexual intercourse merely a biological function; rather, it is a deep and personal expression and communication of oneself to others that brings forth one of the greatest human pleasures and in which a great deal of oneself is involved.

This may also include the desire to join together in the creation of a child, but it need not—the expressing of love and the giving and receiving of pleasure are both extremely valid reasons for engaging in sexual activity. That even animals express some love and affection before, during, and after sexual intercourse would seem to be supported by observation, but the type of expression they indulge in pales alongside that which human beings are capable of. Furthermore, because the need and desire for sexual love among human beings does not diminish after children are created and because even childless couples have such desires and needs, then it becomes more questionable to classify human sexuality solely as a means of procreation.

Various Types of Marriage Relationships

In using the phrase "types of marriage relationships," I am referring to nonlegal marriages as well as those that have been legalized by certificate or sanctioned by a particular religion. What I mean by "marriage" is an agreement, legal or nonlegal, between people to live together and share each other's lives in a deep, meaningful, and (intentionally) lasting way. Such a relationship usually includes sexual expression, but it need not (even some legal marriages—the so-called brother and sister marriages—are for convenience, and the people involved have agreed not to have sex as a part of their relationship). Given this definition, then, many different types of "marriage" relationships are possible.

Monogamy. The most common type of marriage relationship in the Western world is monogamy, which involves one man and one woman. There are advantages, both legal and otherwise, in having a monogamous marriage relationship:

1. The love relationship can be so intimate and involved that most people would find it very difficult to have more than one such relationship.
2. Financially, it is usually much easier for two people to support each other.
3. Legally, in our present societal structure, it is nearly impossible for a husband to have more than one wife or for a wife to have more than one husband.
4. As has been argued earlier, such a relationship, if kept monogamous, will avoid the contracting of social diseases and AIDS.

Despite these advantages, there are no evident *rational* moral reasons why monogamy need be the only valid marriage-type relationship. The Bible decrees that monogamy is the most accepted form of marriage, but unless one feels morally obligated to follow that particular set of teachings, there seems to be no reason why other forms of marriage should be either illegal or immoral as long as ethical principles are adhered to. (It would be terribly unfair, for example, for a person to have more than one spouse if the two spouses did not know about it and had not agreed to such an arrangement.) From experience, then, it appears that monogamy relates best to Western culture, but that does not mean that other forms cannot coexist.

Polygamy (Including Polyandry and Bigamy). Strictly speaking, *polygamy* means having more than one husband or wife, *polyandry* means having more than one husband, and *bigamy* means having two wives or two husbands. However, I shall refer to all of these types of situations as polygamy. As long as all of the people involved are informed about the situation and agree to be involved in it, no form of polygamy need be considered immoral in and of itself.

Many cultures (including the ancient Hebrew culture depicted in the Bible) have accepted various forms of polygamy, and they have worked with varying degrees of success. Quite often men have had more than one wife and kept them subordinate and submissive; *this* is considered by many to be immoral—unless the wife knowingly prefers it this way—under principles involving justice and freedom. However, especially where there has been a shortage of men or women, some form of polygamy has often saved from extinction the culture in which it was practiced, protecting it by ensuring procreation and also by making it possible for men or women who did not want to live without a mate of the opposite sex not to have to live alone. The Islamic and early Mormon cultures are good examples of polygamy's success. There may have been violations of ethical principles in these cultures, but one would be hard put to blame them *necessarily* on the fact that polygamy rather than monogamy was being practiced.

Group Marriage (With and Without "Free Love"). A great deal of experimentation with marriage-type relationships has occurred during the last half of the twentieth century. One example of this is the "group marriage," with or without "free love." This approach to marriage grew out of the desire in the 1960s to return to a communal and cooperative kind of living in which various people, sometimes already married (legally or nonlegally) and sometimes not, chose to live together in a community—sometimes small (as in one house) sometimes large—usually partially or completely outside of the larger society from which they originally came. In most of these types of marriages, the children are raised in common and all of the adult members are parents; however, some of these groups retain the small family unit.

Some groups indulge in "free love"; that is, any two or more people in the group may have sexual relations as they so desire on a "free" basis as long as no force or coercion is used and without regard to any previous monogamous arrangements. Other groups keep a monogamous autonomy, merely choosing to live more closely together with other couples or single people than our society generally encourages or makes possible. Again, the children may either be raised in common by all of the people or be kept within the usual monogamous relationships while at the same time having a closer relationship with other children and adults than our society usually makes possible.

It is very difficult to assess the results or effects on the human beings concerned in such relationships because this kind of experimentation has not been going on for very long; also, few scientific studies are being made of these groups because of the members' desire for privacy. One of the advantages of group marriage cited by members or former members is that the children (when all the adults were considered their parents) received a great deal of attention from all kinds of adults and were never without supervision or diversified companionship. A second advantage often cited is that when members of such groups are compatible, very meaningful communities often develop, thus avoiding much of the isolation and alienation often found in our dehumanized technological society.

Most reports indicate that those group marriages in which free love is not accepted tend to have less friction and upheaval than those in which it is accepted. This may indicate that sexuality is so intimate, intense, and personal it is difficult to diffuse it among several adults without engendering strong feelings of jealousy, guilt, and sadness from being separated from a loved one who goes off with someone else. It also may indicate that because our culture has been so steeped in monogamy, it is extremely difficult to adjust to free-love relationships. Another advantage to the non-free-love approach is that any chance of contracting or passing on social diseases or AIDS would be minimized.

Arguments Against Nonmonogamous Marriages

The conservative view accepts monogamy as the exclusive marital relationship for the reasons I have already described. To summarize them: First, marriage is prescribed in the Bible, which is the great moral book of the Western tradition. Second, whether one believes in the Bible or not, marriage is part of our society's tradition. Third, the love relationship is too intimate to involve more than one man and one woman. Fourth, such a relationship will eliminate any problems connected with social diseases or AIDS provided spouses keep their marriage vows. And, finally, children are better off when they are raised in the traditional family structure. This does not mean that groups of families cannot live in some kind of communal situation, but in this conservative view, the immediate family structure, the nuclear family unit, should remain autonomous.

Arguments for Nonmonogamous Marriages

The liberal view does not prescribe a specific type of marriage; instead, it encourages alternative family life-styles as ways of adapting to our changing culture. Proponents of liberalization would also remove all laws forbidding nonmonogamous marriages on the grounds that they constitute an interference in private sexual and family matters. The emphasis, if this group had its way, would be on the freedom of consenting adults to experiment with or adopt any type of freely chosen marriage or family life-style as long as people were not directly harmed (for example, children were not abused or neglected).

They would not accept offenses to taste or to tradition as valid excuses for legislating against or otherwise forbidding these alternative life-styles, but they would insist that everyone involved in a relationship fully understand and accept it. For example if a man wanted to have two separate wives and families, then each wife and family unit should know about the situation and agree to it. This is merely a matter of dealing honestly and truthfully with people.

Homosexual Marriage

Homosexuality means sexual attraction or love for a man by a man, or sexual attraction or love for a woman by a woman; the latter is also called lesbianism. Homosexuality is, for the most part, frowned upon in our culture, although it is accepted in some areas of the world. In some nations and states it is illegal, and it is often considered immoral. The Bible, especially the New Testament, is firmly opposed to it, a fact that concerns people who adhere to the Bible, but it need not be a concern for those who do not. Furthermore, if the main purpose of sexuality is a deep and intimate expression of love, and if procreation is only secondary, as I have argued, then one cannot attack homosexuality as unnatural merely because it can never result in the creation of children as can heterosexual relationships (that is, sex between or among members of the opposite sex). It is an obvious empirical fact that some men prefer sex with and can truly love only other men and that some women feel the same way toward other women.

Psychologists are not agreed on whether homosexuality is "abnormal," or, in some cases, "normal," but it should be noted that the American Psychological Association has taken homosexuality off its list of mental illnesses. Some experimentation has been done to try to determine whether homosexuality in males is caused by a chemical imbalance (mainly of the male hormone testosterone), but the results have not been conclusive. Some have argued that homosexuality is environmentally induced (for example, in young boys who have cruel or indifferent fathers and doting mothers), but there is no conclusive evidence for this, either. Many homosexuals themselves argue that they are not at all abnormal; rather, they feel that they have freely chosen a sexual life-style that is just as valid as heterosexual relationships, and they argue that it is society's problem if it is too narrow-minded to accept their chosen life-style. Let us now take a look at arguments against and for the morality of homosexuality.

Arguments Against Homosexuality. The basic argument against the morality of homosexuality is that it is unnatural and perverse; that is, it is against the laws of God and the moral laws of Nature. As I have pointed out, there are sections of both the Old and New Testaments of the Bible that call homosexuality "an abomination" and prohibit it as an acceptable sexual activity. In fact, many, if not most, of the world's major religions are opposed to it, branding it immoral. An argument also used by nonreligious people is that homosexuality is unnatural—that is, against the moral laws of Nature. The main evidence for this conclusion is that the primary purpose of sexuality is to procreate, and because homosexuals obviously cannot do this, they are perverting the true meaning of sexuality.

Second, it is argued that homosexuality sets a bad example for children and that it attempts to proselytize (that is, gain followers or adherents for its cause), thereby undermining our traditional cultural values. In this proselytizing process, the argument continues, young boys and girls are often molested by homosexuals, and this of course is a terrible crime. Furthermore, if their proselytizing is greatly successful, what will become of the human race when procreation is no longer feasible because most, if not all, people are homosexual? Our tradition under God's law and in accordance with nature is heterosexual, and we owe it to our children to see both that they are informed of this and that they are protected against homosexuals' teaching or preaching their immoral beliefs to them.

Third, those who argue against homosexuality feel that the homosexuals are totally responsible for the AIDS crisis because they are in a high-risk group (along with drug abusers) and because many of the first AIDS victims in the United States were homosexuals. Many, especially religious people, feel that AIDS is a manifestation of God's displeasure with homosexuality; but religious or not, many feel that homosexuality and bisexuality are the major causes of the spread of AIDS and that therefore homosexuality should be banned. They also feel that the AIDS crisis weakens any argument supporting homosexuality as a private type of sexuality that doesn't affect or harm others.

Finally, homosexuals and homosexuality are offensive to our taste in our basically heterosexual society. Therefore, we have absolutely no obligation to condone or legalize homosexuality in any way; as a matter of fact, we have, instead, the obligation to legislate against and otherwise prohibit it in order to protect our children and the moral future and physical survival of our society.

Arguments for a Homosexual Alternative. First of all, there is no conclusive evidence that because most people are heterosexual in our society homosexuality is therefore immoral or unnatural. As we saw in Chapter 1, it cannot be proved that natural moral laws do indeed exist. As for religious laws, they have force if one is a member of a particular religion, but they have little effect on those who aren't. Furthermore, many members of various religions interpret religious teachings differently. For example, Christians who favor homosexuality or who are homosexual themselves argue that Jesus' "commandment" to love one another is much more important than minor references to sexuality between members of the same sex.

Second, the main issue involved in homosexuality is the right of freely consenting adults to engage in private sexuality in any way they see fit as long as it does not directly harm others. This is, after all, a private, not a public, sexual matter, and even if it offends some people's tastes, that is no reason for branding it as immoral. As long as no other laws are broken and people are not harmed or killed as a result of homosexuality, then freedom in this sexual matter ought to be allowed. Furthermore, as far as the AIDS crisis is concerned, as soon as it became clear what types of sexual activity caused AIDS, homosexuals as a group have lowered the rates of infection and contagion tremendously through more careful behavior—much more so than drug abusers who are now probably the largest group of AIDS victims because they use and share infected needles. Therefore, people who believe homosexuality is moral argue that we don't discriminate against heterosexuals when they contract the other social diseases or even AIDS, so why do so with homosexuals?

Third, the condoning of homosexuality does not mean that child abuse or molestation is also condoned—it isn't, and it should continue to be branded as immoral. Most child molestations, in fact, are probably more heterosexual than homosexual in nature, usually involving men and young girls. Sadism performed on unwilling victims, child molestations, and forced sexuality of all kinds have no direct connection with homosexuality as a life-style, and laws against such activities should remain in force. That some homosexuals, like some heterosexuals, are guilty of such crimes doesn't mean that homosexuality itself is immoral. There are already laws, the argument continues, that forbid proselytizing for any type of overt sexuality in schools, and there are also laws protecting children against pornographic sexual materials (films, books, live shows). Furthermore, it is difficult to prove that homosexuals proselytize any more than heterosexuals do.

The last appeal made by those who believe that homosexuality is moral is that although homosexuals might have different sexual preferences, they are still human beings; therefore, they should not be discriminated against in any way by society.

Adultery

Before leaving the topic of marriage-type relationships, it is important to discuss the matter of adultery, sometimes also referred to as *extramarital sexual relations* (sexual relations outside of a marriage contract, agreement, or relationship). Adultery actually means the voluntary engaging in sexual intercourse with someone other than one's marriage partner. It involves infidelity or unfaithfulness in the marriage relationship, especially in its sexual aspects, and is generally considered immoral by our society. Our question, however, is not what society in general thinks but what grounds we can give for describing adultery as moral or immoral.

It would be foolish, of course, not to recognize that many marriages are not ideal, that one (or both) of the partners may not relate well to the other at any level, including the sexual. This means that dissatisfied partners often look for other human relationships that will fulfill them in ways their own marriage relationship will not, and when their marriage relationship is an unhappy one, people are often tempted to engage in adultery with a person they feel will make them happy or give them pleasure, if only for a brief period of time. (Occasionally, this time lengthens and leads to some form of permanence.)

What usually happens when people are tempted to engage in adultery is that they simply begin the adulterous relationship and worry about the consequences later. The problem with this approach, however, is that the damage is done before any attempt is made to solve the marital problems with any degree of honesty or justice. Once an innocent spouse is betrayed in this way, it is very difficult to resolve marital problems and to maintain the unity of the marriage relationship.

Arguments Against Adultery. The main argument against the morality of adultery is that adultery is a direct violation of the most personal and intimate human contract into which two people can enter. When people get married, they usually contract to live together as husband and wife and to be faithful to each other—this especially means sexually faithful. Committing adultery involves lying, cheating, and infidelity on the part of one marriage partner or another, and these actions are morally reprehensible in most ethical systems.

Adultery is also destructive of the marriage relationship; it can lead to separation or divorce and to the injuring of innocent children. Even when both spouses agree to adultery (for example in so-called wife swapping or swinging), they are making a mockery of marriage, which is our greatest traditional human institution. If they want to have this much freedom, why do they marry at all? The only virtue of such activities as wife swapping and swinging, as opposed to most other forms of adultery, is that at least the spouses know and have agreed to what they are doing, so lying and dishonesty are not issues. There is again the problem of social diseases and AIDS, which an adulterous spouse can contract and then, even worse, pass on to his or her spouse. Hence, this is another important reason not to indulge in adultery.

Arguments for the Morality of Adultery. The basic argument for the morality of adultery is that individuals ought to be free to do what they want to do in terms of their own private sex lives, and whether they lie, cheat, or are unfaithful to their spouses is their business and no one else's—certainly not society's. Some people who condone adultery would say that the basic ethical assumption here is that "what they don't know won't hurt them"; bad results only occur when adultery is discovered. If adulterers are discreet and can avoid breaking up their families, then what's wrong with adultery? One of the problems is certainly the contracting of social diseases or AIDS, but if the adulterer will practice safe sex, then whose business is it what he or she does?

Furthermore, some argue that families should not be broken up under any circumstances because of the children involved and for economic and social reasons, and, according to this argument, adultery provides a means by which unsatisfied spouses and their families "can have their cake and eat it, too." That is, wives, husbands, and children continue to have economic security and social status while the adulterous spouse or spouses additionally enjoy a satisfying sex life. As long as these affairs can be conducted smoothly and discreetly, then what's wrong with adultery? Finally, wife swapping and swinging are no more than sexual life-styles, and as long as adult couples freely consent to such arrangements, no harm is done. These are, after all, private sexual matters, and society should not interfere in any way.

Masturbation

Masturbation is a sex act that people usually perform with and by themselves.

Arguments Against Masturbation

In earlier times, all kinds of superstitious arguments were applied against masturbation—for example, the notion that people who performed this act too often would go insane or deplete their physical strength. However, there are basically only two arguments used against it today. First, there is the religious argument that it is an abuse of one's sexuality, which is a gift given by God. The second argument is that it causes people to become preoccupied with sex and can lead them to other sexual "violations" of morality (fornication, pornography, adultery, and so on). Another argument that serves as a corollary to both of these is that masturbation constitutes a failure in self-control.

Arguments for Masturbation

All the information revealed by modern science indicates that masturbation is a perfectly normal act, both biologically and psychologically, and that it causes no ill effects whatsoever. As a matter of fact, the argument continues, it is probably one of the earliest and best ways that human beings can become familiar with, knowledgeable about, and at ease with their own bodies and their own sexuality.

For example, until recently women in our culture were taught that it is wrong to masturbate and, further, that it is not even necessary that they attain orgasm. Many women, in fact, are not sure what orgasm is and have never experienced it. Through masturbation, they can learn what about their bodies causes orgasm and gives them the greatest pleasure, and this could aid them in finding more meaningful sexual relations with others. At any rate, sexual liberals can see no disadvantages in masturbation, and because it can harm no one else because it is usually a private act performed by one person alone, they argue that it cannot be considered immoral. It can also be considered the safest sexual act in an age of AIDS and sexually transmitted diseases.

◆——

Pornography

Pornography is a vague term, difficult to define. It usually refers to obscene literature, art, film, or live display. The word *obscene* usually means morally offensive according to the general and prevailing standards of morality in any particular culture, society, or group. The Supreme Court of the United States has tried to use the standard definition that pornography is that which appeals to the prurient interest (lust and desire for the impure in thought and deed) and which has no redeeming social, literary, or artistic value. However, within the last fifty years, legal attempts to permit or ban so-called pornographic works or activities have run into problems because it is extremely difficult to decide what is or is not pornographic and to whom.

Pornography seems to involve a definite matter of taste on the part of most people, and tastes differ tremendously. Such things as formalized instruction in sex hygiene are labeled obscene by some, and any kind of nudity (for example, even in a classical Greek sculpture) or any work that contains four-letter words is labeled obscene by others. Some people, on the other hand, can view the most explicit scenes involving bestiality or sadism and find nothing obscene about them. With such differing tastes and opinions about "obscenity" and "pornography," how do we determine whether or not pornography is moral? Let's look at the arguments against and for its morality.

Arguments Against Pornography

First of all, those who would argue against pornography consider it degrading to humans. A preoccupation with pornography, they maintain, will lower the viewer's, listener's, or reader's humanity to the animal level, and as such preoccupation becomes more widespread it will destroy the moral fabric of our civilization.

Second, because some restrictions on pornography have been lifted, it has escalated to an even greater level of criminality, including the filming of actual sadistic sexual murders and the use of children in pornography (child molestation and kiddie porn). This would not have occurred if pornography had continued to be restricted by law.

Third, pornography is degrading to human sexuality in general and to the sexuality of women in particular. It emphasizes lust rather than love and exploitation and domination rather than tenderness, respect, and reciprocation.

Finally, pornography encourages trafficking in sex, rape, homosexuality, child molestation, sadism, prostitution, exhibitionism, voyeurism, and all kinds of other sexual "perversions," and for this reason it cannot do anything but lower and destroy human dignity. For all of these reasons, sexual conservatives argue, pornography should not be considered moral in any way and, in fact, should be considered perniciously immoral and be severely restricted or completely banned.

Arguments for Pornography

The basic argument for the morality of pornography is that because tastes and opinions in this area differ so widely, the use of pornographic materials is obviously a matter of individual discretion. As long as people are not coerced into reading, listening to, or viewing it, it should be available to consenting adults.

Second, there is no proof that pornography is degrading (it is, after all, a matter of opinion and taste) or that it will destroy our moral fabric. In fact, as mentioned earlier, there is evidence to indicate that it helps to eliminate sexual repression, relieve sexual tensions, and actually lower sex crime rates rather than raising them. In one study done after 11 years of having no restrictions on pornography in Denmark, child molestation was down 56 percent, indecent exposure was down 58 percent, and voyeurism was down 80 percent. Rape, however, was on the increase "but only by a small fraction relative to the rising rates of robbery and vandalism."[2] In fact, the study further maintains that after restrictions have been lifted for a while, the interest in pornography begins to drop off and sales go down as people begin "to take it in stride."[3]

Third, although it is true that pornography can involve actual sexual crimes, our laws against murder and against child abuse and molestation can be enforced to stop this type of criminality.

Finally, that pornography is "degrading and exploitative" is again a matter of personal opinion, taste, and definition. Some might find pornography exciting, pleasurable, and fantasy fulfilling. Furthermore, because the men and women who perform in pornographic movies, for example, generally do so willingly, how can they be considered to be degraded or used? Pornography may not present the loving and tender aspects of sex, but no one can deny that lustful and aggressive aspects of sex also exist, and their depiction therefore has its own validity. For these reasons proponents state that pornography should be considered a moral activity when indulged in by free and consenting adults. It should also be considered a private sexual matter that should not be legally controlled unless it causes harm to others.

◆―――――――――――――――――――――――――――――――――――――――

Prostitution

Sometimes referred to as the "world's oldest profession," prostitution is, like pornography, a confused issue in morality. Some regard it as a "victimless" crime, whereas others brand it as a terribly immoral act. What prostitution essentially means is that people will pay others (prostitutes—male or female) to have sex with them.

Arguments Against Prostitution

Extramarital and Commercialized Sex Is Immoral. The conservative position is, of course, opposed to sex prior to or outside of marriage and doubly opposed to the commercialization of sex where pleasure is the only reason for it. It may be the world's oldest profession, but it is also the world's most immoral one, according to this argument. Prostitution fosters a lack of respect for the prostitute (usually a woman) and for human sexual activity itself, which is supposed to enhance the intimacy of a relationship between partners and also contribute to the creation of children. Prostitution instead lowers human sexuality to an animalistic act of lust.

Causes Crime. Prostitution is a big business and is usually managed and run by the criminal element in the United States. Prostitutes are often treated like animals by their pimps and customers; many are beaten, and some are ultimately killed. In addition, many prostitutes have been addicted to drugs by their pimps to keep them dependent on them and always in need of money. According to the critics, because of all this, prostitution is the most degrading and immoral of activities and should be eliminated from our culture.

Social Diseases and AIDS. There is no faster or more certain way of transmitting social diseases and AIDS than prostitution, for in addition to its being transmitted sexually, prostitutes may also become infected by needles as drug abusers. Because prostitutes and their customers, or "johns," generally don't know each other, there is no clear way of knowing who might or might not have these diseases. Further, because prostitutes and their clients may have many partners, the chances of spreading these diseases are multiplied.

Arguments for Prostitution

Safe Sexual Release. Prostitution is the world's oldest profession because human beings have sexual needs that are not always able to be satisfied by dating and marriage, partially because of all our taboos against sex as pleasure giving and against sex outside of marriage. With prostitution, people can have the pleasure of sex by paying for it and not having to become involved with their partners—sex can be enjoyed for pleasure only, without any commitments and with no strings attached. It is also a safe sexual release, which may eliminate the desire to rape or molest children (not in all cases, of course, but in general).

A Victimless Crime. Proponents of prostitution as moral argue that it should not be considered either immoral or illegal because there really are no victims. Presumably, prostitutes have chosen at some point to do what they are doing and so have their clients. It is only a crime because society has legislated against it, but there shouldn't be such laws. People should be free to be prostitutes or to go to them, and such freedom shouldn't be interfered with.

Social Acceptance and Governmental Control. The solution to any problems arising out of prostitution, such as crime, abuse of prostitutes, and social diseases, would be solved by social acceptance or at least social permissiveness and proper government regulation and control. "Houses of ill repute" could then be privately run but regulated by city, county, state, or federal governments so that sanitary conditions could be established and testing for social diseases could be done. In addition, the criminal element could be eliminated by such control and policing. All of these problems, according to the proponents of prostitution as moral, could be eliminated if society would just accept that people have sexual needs and allow them to satisfy them in an acceptable yet regulated manner.

Sexual Perversion or "Unnatural" Sexual Activity

Sexual perversion is often as difficult to define as pornography. Some people think that any sexual activity other than sexual intercourse between a man and a woman in the traditional "missionary" position described earlier is perverted or unnatural. Others feel that any type of regular sexual intercourse between a man and a woman, but nothing else, is all right, and still others allow that "anything goes" as long as pleasure is given and received.

As I mentioned at the beginning of the chapter, many sexual activities, such as oral sex, anal sex, sadism, masochism, homosexuality, group sex, and bestiality (sex acts between human beings and animals) have been listed as "unnatural" or "perverted." The conservative viewpoint is that all of these except for traditional sexual intercourse between a man and a women are perverted. The liberal viewpoint varies, but essentially it states that as long as a sex act is performed between or among freely consenting adults it is a matter of individual freedom and should not be legislated against or forbidden in any way.

Bestiality presents a special problem. Although it is probably rare (though perhaps less rare in rural areas), it does not fit the description of sexuality "between or among consenting adults." One partner to the sex act, that is, the animal, cannot consent; therefore, one could say that bestiality is immoral because the animal is not a consenting adult human being. However, when we consider that we kill animals for food without their consent, we can ask if it is worse to have sex with them and to let them live than to kill and eat them. Some people also feel that sex between a human being and an animal is even a greater crime against natural laws than are sex acts between human beings of the same sex. The extreme liberal, I suppose, would condone bestiality, whereas the "moderate" liberal might or might not condone it; the conservative, of course, would vehemently condemn it.

♦

Cases for Study and Discussion

CASE ♦ 1

Two college students, Tom, nineteen, and Barbara, eighteen, have decided to live together both for sexual reasons and because they enjoy each other's company. Barbara intends to take birth control pills, they intend to share expenses, and they have an agreement to be honest with and faithful to each other throughout the entire relationship. They have also agreed that if either one of them wants to break off the relationship, he or she has only to say so and the relationship will end with no recriminations. Is what they are doing moral? Why or why not?

CASE ♦ 2

You have been working with Richard for about a year and have always found him witty, intelligent, compassionate, and friendly. One night he invites you to have dinner with him and his friend Walter at their apartment. You discover that the two men are homosexuals and that they have been living together for about three or four years. You are surprised to find that they are not effeminate in any way; in fact, except that they prefer homosexuality to heterosexuality, they are in no way different from a lot of other nice people you know. They do not molest children, nor do they attempt to impose their values on anyone else; all they want is to live together happily and in peace. Is what Richard and Walter are doing moral? Why or why not?

CASE ♦ 3

Sarah and Ben, both in their seventies and widowed, have fallen in love and feel a strong need for each other's companionship. Because Sarah would lose her social security pension if she remarried, they have moved into an apartment together without getting married and are enjoying a full sex life. Their grown children for the most part are very upset by this and constantly tell Sarah and Ben how they feel about their domestic arrangement. Some of the children even refuse to call or visit them because they are living together. Despite this situation, Ben and Sarah seem to be happy. Is what they are doing moral? Why or why not?

CASE ♦ 4

Eric, forty-five, is married to Joanne, forty-three, and they have three teenage children. Generally speaking, they have a pretty good marriage, except for their sex life. Although they both know it is poor, they don't discuss it very often. Over a period of several months Joanne notices a change in Eric, and she finally asks him if there's anything wrong. Eric blurts out that he is in love with another woman with whom he's had an affair for several months. Joanne is so angry and hurt that she immediately demands that he leave the house and states that she wants a divorce. They both refuse to seek help from marriage counselors, and eventually the divorce ensues at a great emotional cost to Eric, Joanne, and their three children. Was what Eric did moral? Why or why not? Do you feel Joanne handled his adultery well or not? Why or why not? Should Eric have told her? Why or why not?

CASE ♦ 5

One street in a small town has several stores that sell pornographic materials and a theater that shows pornographic films. Various parents and religious groups in town want the licenses for these place of business revoked because, as they put it, these places are a "blight on the community" and a bad influence on everyone, particularly the young people of the town. The managers of the stores, however, carefully check identification cards to make sure that no one who is underage can enter, and there are no pornographic displays in the windows or anywhere outside the buildings. The owners of the stores and the theater feel that those who enter their businesses want to be there and seem to enjoy themselves. Should their licenses be revoked, and should pornography in the town be further restricted because what these proprietors are doing is immoral? Why or why not? If you think there should be further restrictions then what should they be?

Chapter Summary

I. Major aspects of human sexuality
   A. The public, or societal, aspect is concerned with how matters of sex overtly affect others, and the governing principles of morality here are life, goodness, and justice.

B. The private aspect is concerned with sexual relations between or among consenting adults, and the governing principles here are goodness, justice, freedom, and honesty.

II. Moral issues and the private aspect of human sexuality

    A. The meaning and the private aspect of human sexuality is not one-dimensional but includes the following:

        1. Procreation.

        2. Pleasure.

        3. An expression of love for another.

        4. An expression of friendship and liking.

    B. The conservative, or restrictive, position concerning sexual activity often puts the most emphasis on the procreation aspect or the view that sex is "a necessary evil."

    C. The position advocating complete freedom in sexual matters usually emphasizes the pleasure aspect and rights of individuals to enjoy such pleasure.

    D. The more moderate position tends to accept both the procreation and pleasure aspects while also including—and often emphasizing more strongly—the expression-of-love aspect.

III. Moral issues and the public aspect of human sexuality

    A. Sexual activities that affect the public or others in such a way as to bring them possible harm include the following:

        1. Rape.

        2. Child molestation.

        3. Unwilling sadism.

        4. Less clearly, pornography, homosexuality, prostitution, "unnatural" sexual activities, sex outside of marriage, masturbation, and nonmonogamous marriages.

    B. Most ethical systems are agreed that the first three types of activity under point A are immoral, but there is less agreement on the seven activities listed in part 4.

    C. There are a number of arguments against allowing people the sexual freedom to engage in the last seven activities:

        1. These activities are a violation of traditional morality.

        2. According to the domino argument, allowing these seven activities will eventually lead to a general acceptance of the first three immoral activities.

        3. These activities are offensive to public taste.

        4. Probability of getting social diseases, including AIDS.

    D. There are several arguments for allowing people the sexual freedom to perform these activities.

        1. Individual rights and individual freedom should take precedence because these activities cause no direct harm to others.

2. Traditional values, which oppose such activities, are not absolute.

3. There is no hard evidence to support the domino argument; furthermore, laws can be passed to prohibit these activities from escalating toward the first three.

4. Offensiveness to public taste is not in itself sufficient cause to deny individual rights in these matters, and if discretion is used, the offensiveness to others can be minimized.

5. Proper precautions can be taken to guard against social diseases and AIDS; therefore, this is no reason to deny one's freedom in sexuality.

IV. Premarital sex

A. The term *premarital sex* refers to sex relations that occur prior to marriage; it is called *fornication* in the Bible.

B. There are several arguments against premarital sex.

1. It undermines traditional morality.

2. It fosters promiscuity.

3. It fosters social diseases and AIDS.

4. It fosters guilt and ostracism.

5. It can be detrimental to children born of such a relationship.

6. The opportunities provided by premarital sex to test compatibility and gain sexual experience are no excuse for such activity, and any advantages obtained in these areas are outweighed by the violation of the sacredness of marriage and the loss of respect that inevitably ensues.

C. There are several arguments for premarital sex.

1. Old moral traditions are no longer applicable in our changing society.

2. Abstinence is not acceptable, and proper precautions can eliminate most concerns about social diseases and AIDS.

3. Promiscuity is not a necessary adjunct of premarital sex, but even if promiscuity occurs, as long as the people involved are freely consenting adults, what difference does it make?

4. Not as much guilt or ostracism occurs these days because of our changing mores (for example, the recognition and acceptance of illegitimate children). Furthermore, as long as those involved can handle the guilt or ostracism that may occur, that is their choice.

5. Contraception and sexual responsibility can eliminate any problems concerned with the children that result from such a union. Contraception can prevent pregnancy, and if a child is born, sexual responsibility ensures that the couple will marry or otherwise provide for its care.

6. The opportunity provided by premarital sex to gain sexual experience and test compatibility is one of its greatest advantages.
7. That sex gives great pleasure is also an advantage.
8. Premarital sex is a private, not a public, matter, and legislation should not enter into it.

V. Sex in marriage-type (including nonlegal) relationships
  A. Marriage-type relationships are continuous and lasting rather than temporary.
  B. Their main purpose is to provide a deep and intimate expression of love between or among persons, including the giving of pleasure.
  C. A secondary but not unimportant purpose is to procreate.
  D. The purposes noted in points B and C are not *necessarily* compatible *or* incompatible.

VI. Various types of marriage relationships
  A. Monogamy, the marriage relationship involving one man and one woman, is the most common type in the Western world.
  B. Polygamy, including bigamy and polyandry, means having more than one husband or wife.
  C. Group marriage, with and without "free love," involves a communal or cooperative kind of living arrangement and may include already married and/or single people.
  D. There are several arguments against nonmonogamous types of marriage.
    1. Only monogamy is prescribed in the Bible.
    2. Monogamy is an essential part of our society's tradition.
    3. Love relationships are too intimate to involve more than one man and one woman, and children are better off raised in the traditional monogamous family structure.
    4. Such a relationship will eliminate any problems connected with social diseases or AIDS, provided spouses keep their vows.
  E. There are several arguments for allowing nonmonogamous marriages.
    1. It is not up to society to prescribe a specific type of marriage, and our changing culture encourages experimentation with alternative types of marriage.
    2. All laws prohibiting nonmonogamous marriages should be removed because they encroach on private sexual matters.
    3. Consenting adults should be free to experiment with alternative types of marriage.
    4. As long as there is honesty in a relationship, any type of marriage that does not directly harm others should be acceptable.
  F. Homosexual marriage is a married relationship between two men or two women.

1. There are several arguments against the morality of homosexuality.
   (a) It is unnatural and perverse sexuality.
   (b) It is against the laws of God.
   (c) It sets a bad example for children, and it is dangerous because its adherents attempt to proselytize for its cause.
   (d) It is totally responsible for the AIDS crisis, which makes it a public rather than private act.
   (e) It is offensive to the taste of most people in our society and to our basically heterosexual traditions.
2. There are several arguments for the morality of homosexuality.
   (a) There is no conclusive evidence that homosexuality is unnatural or immoral.
   (b) It is the right of freely consenting adults to engage in private sexuality in any way they see fit.
   (c) Homosexuals as a group have lowered rates of infection and contagion tremendously through careful behavior and shouldn't be discriminated against any more than heterosexuals are.
   (d) The acceptance of homosexuality doesn't mean that child abuse or molestation is condoned; in fact, more of these crimes are probably committed by heterosexuals than by homosexuals.
   (e) Homosexuals are human beings, and for this reason they should not be discriminated against in any way by society.

VII. Adultery
   A. Adultery is the voluntary engaging in sexual intercourse with someone other than one's marriage partner.
   B. There are several arguments against the morality of adultery.
      1. It is a violation of the most personal and intimate contract into which two people can enter.
      2. It involves lying, cheating, and infidelity, all of which are morally reprehensible.
      3. It is destructive of the marriage relationship and can lead to separation or divorce and to the emotional injuring of innocent children.
      4. Even when both spouses agree to adultery, it makes a mockery of marriage.
      5. There is again the problem of social diseases, with the additional problem of transmitting such diseases to one's spouse.
   C. There are several arguments for the morality of adultery.
      1. Individuals ought to be free to do what they want with their own private sex lives.

2. What spouses don't know won't hurt them—getting caught is the only thing that can cause harm.

3. As far as social diseases and AIDS are concerned, if an adulterer practices safe sex, then whose business is it what he or she does?

4. Marriages generally should not be broken up if doing so threatens financial security and the security of the children; adultery provides a means whereby adulterers and their families can "have their cake and eat it, too."

5. "Wife swapping" and "swinging" are just other sexual life-styles, and if couples agree to such practices there is no reason why they should not be allowed.

VIII. Masturbation

    A. Masturbation is a sex act that people usually perform with and by themselves.

    B. Arguments can be made against the morality of masturbation.

        1. In a religious sense, it is an abuse of one's sexuality, which is a gift from God.

        2. It causes people to become preoccupied with sex and can lead them to other sexual violations of morality (fornication, pornography, adultery, and so on).

    C. Arguments can be made for the morality of masturbation.

        1. It is perfectly normal both biologically and psychologically, and it causes no ill effects.

        2. It is the best way of learning about sex and getting in touch with our own bodies.

        3. It can be considered the safest form of sexual activity.

IX. Pornography

    A. Pornography is difficult to define, but it generally has been defined by the U.S. Supreme Court as that which appeals to the prurient interest and which has no redeeming social, literary, or artistic value.

    B. There are several arguments against the morality of pornography.

        1. It is humanly degrading, and as it becomes more widespread it will destroy the moral fabric of our civilization.

        2. It can involve actual sex crimes such as sexual murders, child molestation, and kiddie porn, which have, in fact, occurred.

        3. It degrades human sexuality in general and women in particular.

        4. It encourages trafficking in sex, rape, child molestation, sadism, prostitution, exhibitionism, voyeurism, and other types of sexual "perversions."

    C. There are several arguments for the morality of pornography.

        1. Consenting adults have the right to view, read, or listen to anything they wish.

2. There is no proof that pornography is degrading or that it will destroy our moral fabric.

3. It can involve actual crimes, but we have strong enough laws to stop such crimes if they are committed.

4. That it is "degrading and exploitative" is a matter of taste and opinion; to many it is exciting and pleasurable.

X. Prostitution

A. Prostitution, like pornography, is a confusing issue in morality. It essentially means people paying others (prostitutes) to have sex with them.

B. There are several arguments against prostitution.

1. Extramarital and commercialized sex is immoral from the conservative point of view.

2. Prostitution causes crime and degradation.

3. There is no faster or surer way of spreading social diseases and AIDS.

C. Arguments for prostitution also exist.

1. It is a safe sexual release in a sexually repressive society.

2. It is a victimless crime in that both prostitutes and their customers enter into sexual activity freely.

3. If there were social acceptance and governmental control, then the criminal and social disease aspects of prostitution could be eliminated.

XI. Sexual perversion

A. Sexual perversion, or "unnatural" sexual activity, is as difficult to define as "pornography."

B. The conservative viewpoint is that activities such as oral sex, anal sex, sadism, masochism, homosexuality, group sex, and bestiality are perverted. The only sex activity that isn't perverted is sexual intercourse between a man and a woman, generally in the "missionary" position.

C. The liberal viewpoint varies, but in general it states that as long as a sex act is performed between or among freely consenting adults it is a matter of private discretion and should be considered moral.

D. Bestiality (sex between human beings and animals) presents a special problem in that it extends beyond the category of "freely consenting adults." For this reason, some would say this type of sex involves "animal molestation" and is therefore wrong. Yet we kill animals for food and eat them; is this any more respectable than having sex with them and letting them live?

1. The extreme liberal would condone such activity.

2. The moderate liberal might or might not condone it.

3. The conservative would vehemently condemn it.

Exercises for Review

1. Distinguish between the public and private aspects of human sexuality. Do you think the distinction is a valid one? Why or why not?

2. Do you agree or disagree with the description given of the meaning and purpose of human sexuality, especially the prime importance given to sexuality as a deep and intimate expression of love for another? Why or why not?

3. How can the five basic ethical principles be applied to the area of human sexuality?

4. What are some of the advantages and disadvantages of engaging in pre-marital sex?

5. How does a marriage-type relationship differ from other relationships, and what are two of its purposes?

6. In your own words, briefly define monogamy, polygamy, group marriage, and homosexual marriage. What positions do you take in reference to the morality of each of these relationships? Why?

7. What are your personal views on the moral issue of adultery? Consider the arguments presented for and against adultery in answering this question.

8. Explain why masturbation is or is not an immoral sexual act.

9. How would you define pornography? Give examples of the type of literature and activities you consider pornographic, and explain why you place them in this category. Do you think pornography is moral or immoral? Why?

10. How would you define "unnatural sex," or "sexual perversion"? When is it moral and when is it immoral, if ever?

11. To what extent do you think prostitution is moral? What effect does the argument that social acceptance and governmental control would eliminate the crime and social-disease problems have on your views of this activity? Answer in detail.

Notes

1. See Sigmund Freud, *Collected Papers of Sigmund Freud,* Volume 8, *Sexuality and the Psychology of Love* (New York: Collier Books, n.d.); and Virginia E. Johnson and William H. Masters, *Human Sexual Response* (Boston: Little, Brown, 1966).

2. Lloyd Shearer, "Porno and Crime," *The Bakersfield Californian* "Parade," (December 10, 1978): 17.

3. Ibid.

Supplementary Reading

General Readings on Sexuality and Sexual Morality

Baker, Robert, and Frederick Elliston, eds. *Philosophy and Sex,* rev. ed. Buffalo, N.Y.: Prometheus Books, 1984.

Bayles, Michael. *Reproductive Ethics.* Englewood Cliffs, N.J.: Prentice-Hall, 1984.

Bell, Alan P., et al. *Sexual Preference: Its Development in Men and Women.* Bloomington, Ind.: Indiana University Press, 1981.

Bertocci, Peter A. *Sex, Love, and the Person.* New York: Sheed and Ward, 1967.

Crosby, John F. *Sexual Autonomy: Toward a Humanistic Ethic.* Springfield, Ill.: Charles C. Thomas, Publisher, 1981.

Ellis, Albert. *The Art and Science of Love.* New York: Lyle Stuart, 1965.

Freud, Sigmund. *Collected Papers of Sigmund Freud. Sexuality and the Psychology of Love,* vol. 8. New York: Collier Books, n.d.

Fromer, Margot J. *Ethical Issues in Sexuality and Reproduction.* St. Louis: C.V. Mosby, 1983.

Grummon, Donald L., and Andrew M. Barclay, eds. *Sexuality: A Search for Perspective.* New York: Van Nostrand, 1971.

Hanigan, James. *What Are They Saying About Sexual Morality?* Ramsey, N.J.: Paulist Press, 1982.

Johnson, Virginia E., and William H. Masters. *Human Sexual Response.* Boston: Little, Brown, 1966.

Klassen, Albert D., et al. *Sex and Morality in the U.S.: An Empirical Enquiry Under the Auspices of the Kinsey Institute.* Hanover, N.H.: University Press of New England, 1989.

Leiser, Burton. *Liberty, Justice and Morals,* 3rd ed. New York: Macmillan, 1979.

Levy, Donald. "Perversion and the Unnatural as Moral Categories." In *The Philosophy of Sex,* ed. Alan Soble. Totowa, N.J.: Littlefield, Adams, 1980.

McCary, James L. *Human Sexuality: Physiological and Psychological Factors of Sexual Behavior.* New York: Van Nostrand, 1967.

Pierce, Christine, and Donald VanDeVeer, eds. *AIDS: Ethics and Public Policy.* Belmont, Calif.: Wadsworth, 1987.

Taylor, Richard. *Having Love Affairs.* Buffalo, N.Y.: Prometheus, 1982.

Vannoy, Russell. *Sex Without Love: A Philosophical Exploration.* Buffalo, N.Y.: Prometheus, 1980.

Homosexuality

Batchelor, Edward, Jr., ed. *Homosexuality and Ethics,* rev. ed. New York: Pilgrim Press, 1982.

Bayer, Ronald. *Homosexuality and American Psychiatry: The Politics of Diagnosis.* New York: Basic Books, 1980.

Cameron, Paul. "A Case Against Homosexuality." *Human Life Review* 4 (Summer, 1978): 17–49.

Dannecker, Martin. *Theories of Homosexuality.* New York: Gay Men's Press, 1981.

Dynes, Wayne R. *Homosexuality: Discrimination, Criminology, and the Law.* New York: Garland, 1992.

———. *Homosexuality and Religion and Philosophy.* New York: Garland, 1992.

Dynes, Wayne R., and Stephen Donaldson, eds. *Homosexuality and Government, Politics, and Prisons.* New York: Garland, 1992.

McWhirter, David P., ct al. *Homosexuality—Heterosexuality: Concepts of Sexual Orientation.* New York: Oxford University Press, 1990.

Opposing Viewpoints Series. *Homosexuality: Opposing Viewpoints.* San Diego, Calif.: Greenhaven Press, 1993.

Pollard, Patrick. *André Gide: The Homosexual Moralist.* New Haven, Conn: Yale University Press, 1992.

Shilts, Randy. *And the Band Played On.* New York: St. Martin's Press, 1987.

Premarital Sex and Sexuality in Marriage

Barnhart, J. E., and Mary Ann Barnhart. "Marital Faithfulness and Unfaithfulness." *Journal of Social Philosophy* 4 (10–15) (April, 1973).

Bartell, Gilbert D. *Group Sex: A Scientist's Eyewitness Report on Swinging in the Suburbs.* New York: Peter H. Wyden, 1970.

Bell, Robert R. *Premarital Sex in a Changing Society.* Englewood Cliffs, N.J.: Prentice-Hall, 1966.

Duval, Evelyn Ruth, and Reuben Hill. *Why Wait till Marriage?* New York: Association Press, 1965.

Neubeck, Gerhard, ed. *Extra-Marital Relations.* Englewood Cliffs, N.J.: Prentice-Hall, 1969.

O'Neill, George, and Nena O'Neill. *Open Marriage: New Life Style for Couples.* New York: M. Evans, 1972.

Pornography and Prostitution

Assiter, Alison. *Pornography, Feminism, and the Individual*. Concord, Mass.: Paul and Co., Publishers, 1991.

Baird, Robert M., and Stuart E. Rosenbaum, eds. *Pornography: Private Right or Public Menace*. Buffalo, N.Y.: Prometheus Books, 1991.

Christensen, F. M. *Pornography: The Other Side*. Westport, Conn.: Greenwood Press, 1990.

Decker, John F. *Prostitution: Regulation and Control*. Littleton, Colo.: Rothman, 1979.

Dworkin, Andrea. *Pornography: Men Possessing Women*. New York: NAL-Dutton, 1991.

Hawkins, Gordon, and Franklin Zimring. *Pornography in a Free Society*. New York: Cambridge University Press, 1991.

Itzin, Catherine, ed. *Pornography: Women, Violence, and Civil Liberties: A Radical View*. New York: Oxford University Press, 1992.

Randall, Richard S. *Freedom and Taboo: Pornography and the Politics of a Self Divided*. Berkeley, Calif.: University of California Press, 1989.

Reed, Robert D., and Danek S. Kaus. *Pornography: How and Where To Find Facts and Get Help*. Ed. Diane Parker. Saratoga, Calif.: R and E Publications, 1993.

Shearer, Lloyd. "Porno and Crime." *The Bakersfield Californian*, "Parade" (December 10, 1978): 17.

CHAPTER 13

Bioethics—Ethical Issues in Medicine

Objectives

After you have read this chapter you should be able to

1. Know how ethics can be applied to specific areas of human life, such as bioethics.

2. Know what the term *bioethics* means and describe the areas and issues it covers.

3. Understand the rights and obligations of health care professionals and patients and their families as they are defined according to three different views: paternalism, radical individualism, reciprocity, and collegiality.

4. Understand the importance of truth telling, confidentiality, and informed consent to significant relationships between professionals and patients.

5. Understand what some of the ethical issues are in the areas of allocation of scarce medical resources, behavior control, human experimentation, and genetics.

◆

Introduction and Definition of Terms

The last chapters in this book—this chapter, which is concerned with bioethics, Chapter 14, which is concerned with business ethics, and Chapter 15 on environmental ethics—are included here to show how ethics is applied in specific aspects of society and human life and how ethical problems and issues affect human beings at all levels and in all areas of life. As a matter of fact, ethical problems arising in areas such as medicine and business have caused a revival of interest in ethics, not only as theory or as an aspect of religion but also as something that must be applied to human affairs in a practical way. I believe that the issues that have arisen in medicine have served as the greatest catalyst in our century for the renewed interest in applied ethics.

Bioethics means "life ethics," or ethics in medicine. It covers a larger area of concern than the phrase "medical ethics," which is often used to refer strictly to the doctor-patient relationship or to such issues as whether doctors should advertise, split fees, or report incompetence within their ranks. Bioethics covers the following areas in medicine: treatment of dying patients, allowing someone to die, mercy death, and mercy killing (see Chapter 9); behavior control; human experimentation and informed consent; genetics, fertilization, and birth; health care delivery and its costs; population and birth control, abortion (see Chapter 10), and sterilization; allotment of scarce medical resources, organ transplantation, and hemodialysis; and truth telling and confidentiality in medicine.

In short, what bioethics is really concerned with is the establishment and maintenance of vital and moral human relationships between the sick and the dying on the one hand, and the healthy and medical professionals on the other. It is concerned with "treatment" in the broadest sense; that is, it deals not only with how we treat patients in a medical sense, but also how we relate to, or deal with, our fellow human beings, especially in matters of illness, injury, dying, and death. If you will refer to my working definition of "morality" in Chapter 1, you will find that except for the reference to sickness, injury, and dying, the idea of significant human relationships is the same, only more specifically applied.

◆

Health Care Professionals and Patients and Their Families—Rights and Obligations

Health care professionals are doctors, nurses, and attendants or aides, therapists, technicians, and all others involved in medical aid. There are three views of what the relationship between health care professionals and patients and their families should be.

Paternalism

Paternalism, as the name suggests, is the position that health care professionals should take a parental role toward patients and their families. According to this position, professionals have a superior knowledge of medicine; therefore, they and they alone are privileged because of their long and specialized training to decide what is best for patients and their families. This attitude is characterized by the old cliché "The doctor always knows best."

A number of arguments are put forth to support this viewpoint. First of all, lay people lack the professional knowledge of medicine to deal with both physical and mental illness and injury; therefore, they have no way of knowing what is best for them. Second, because of their long, hard professional education and because of their experience, professionals (especially doctors) know the characteristics of diseases and injuries; therefore, patients should place themselves totally in the professionals' hands. Finally, any and all decisions about patients' care and treatment, including the information that should be given them and decisions concerning hospitalization, tests, and so on, should be completely in the hands of the doctors and their professional assistants. Patients must trust them and not interfere with the treatment suggested.

Radical Individualism

Radical individualism is the position that patients have absolute rights over their own bodies and lives and therefore may reject all recommendations of health care personnel (especially doctors). There are a number of arguments supporting this position. First, doctors are human like everybody else, and they are capable of errors in judgment, diagnosis, prognosis, and treatment. They are even at times guilty of malpractice, negligence, or maltreatment. Second, patients (or their families when patients are totally incapacitated) are best qualified to decide if, how, when, and what treatment is to be given; after all, their bodies and lives are at stake, not those of the professionals. Third, many issues having to do with treatment are not strictly medical, and professionals sometimes are not qualified to make appropriate decisions concerning such issues (for example, at what point debilitating, painful treatment should be stopped because its negative effects outweigh any curative powers it may have.) Fourth, these days lay people are better educated about their bodies and minds and about the illnesses and injuries that affect them. They are also able to understand their medical condition, diagnoses, and prognoses if professionals will only have the kindness and courtesy to explain things to them clearly and in plain language. Because they can understand these things, they are qualified to make decisions about how they should or should not be treated. Finally, paternalism has often led to total patient dependence and sometimes to complete dehumanization, when a patient is regarded merely as a living body to be investigated, analyzed, medicated, or operated on without recognition that a *person* still resides within it.

The Reciprocal, or Collegial, View

The reciprocal, or collegial, position involves a team approach to treatment much like that described in the hospice approach to care for the dying (see Chapter 9). In this view, patients and their families are key members of the team, and doctors, nurses, and other health care professionals work together to do what's best for patients and their families. This position is supported by a number of arguments, some of which are similar to those for individualism.

First, professionals, particularly doctors, are neither gods nor valid father figures; rather, they are human beings with specialized education, training, and experience, which makes them an important element in the care of patients and their families.

Second, many of the decisions concerning the treatment of patients and their families are not strictly medical in nature and therefore should not be made solely by medical professionals. Doctors need to rely on other health care personnel, such as nurses; psychiatric, physical, and occupational therapists; and nurses' aides. They also need the support of nonmedical personnel such as clergy, social workers, and trained volunteers if they are to properly treat patients and their families as whole human beings rather than medical specimens.

Third, it is important to recognize the rights of individual patients to make free choices concerning their treatment because it is their bodies and lives that are at stake. As I have already discussed, these rights are not "absolute," but they are and should be given high priority. The recognition of these rights is exemplified by the creation and dissemination of a list of patients' rights (see the section on Patient Self-Determination Act in Chapter 9). In addition to the right to participate actively in decisions regarding medical care, including the right to refuse treatment, patients also have the right to considerate and respectful care; information about their diagnosis, treatment, and prognosis; the information they need to give informed consent to any procedure; full knowledge about human experimentation, and the right to refuse it.[1]

All of this means that neither patients nor professionals alone "know best" but that decisions involving care and treatment are to be reciprocal (that is, involving give and take) and collegial (that is, involving a group or team approach in which each member has equal input) rather than dictatorial, paternalistic, or anarchistic. Obviously professionals do "know best" in certain areas, but they should share their information and expertise with patients and their families. In this way, proper recommendations can be made as to alternatives in care and treatment, and proper decision making can be accomplished. Furthermore, patients and their families are entitled to more than one professional opinion.

Patients must realize, however, that no matter how well informed they are, they can't know everything about medicine, and they must defer to professionals in some areas. However, once they are well informed (and they have a right to be), they are certainly qualified to make decisions about their care and treatment. In some areas, they definitely "know best." In other words, patients and their families are entitled to be apprised of all the expertise that can be brought to bear on their cases so that they can make important decisions. According to this position, in short, all decisions should be arrived at through a free exchange of ideas and a full discussion of alternative methods of care and treatment, with final decisions being made jointly by patients or their families (when patients are incapacitated) and their doctors.

In other words, collegial care calls for proper, intelligent, and informed communication between patients and their doctors. Doctors can facilitate such communication, as one family practice doctor in Seattle did, by furnishing their patients with a list of questions to ask: (1) What is wrong with me? (2) What caused it? (3) What should be done about it? (4) What will it cost? (5) How long will it take? (6) What tests should be done and why? (7) What is my prognosis? (8) What will you do next? (9) Is it necessary? (10) Is it dangerous? (11) Do I have any alternatives? If so what are they? (12) If I must go into the hospital, how long will I be there? (13) How long will be laid up, and when can I go back to school or work?[2] Such a list of questions can really help to stimulate communication between doctors and patients and also enhance the doctor-patient relationship.

◆————————————————————————————————

Truth Telling and Informed Consent

The issue involving truth telling is to what extent patients and their families should be told the truth about their illnesses, injuries, and/or dying. The term *informed consent* refers to a formalized procedure whereby patients (or family members, when patients are incapacitated) "consent," usually in writing, to some sort of medical treatment, procedure, or surgery that may have questionable side effects, affect patients' future lives, or even involve the risk of death. Somewhat like the discussion of patients' and professionals' rights and obligations, there are two views of truth telling in medicine: the paternalistic view and that of the patients' right to know.

The Paternalistic View of Truth Telling

There are several arguments put forth to support the paternalistic viewpoint. First, because patients are not medically trained, they cannot understand what doctors tell them; therefore, they do not need to know more than the fact that professionals are doing their very best for them. Second, it is best both for patients' morale and for their will to get better or will to live if they are not told the truth, especially if it is bad news, because full knowledge of their situation might cause them to "lose heart" and not fight to survive. Third, it would serve no purpose to give them bad news, because if the prognosis is that they are going to die, for example, they will die anyway; therefore, one should let them live out the time they have left as happily as they can. Fourth, it is all right to tell the families but not the patients—patients should be protected from bad news. Finally, it is important for the doctor, nurses, and other professionals as well as the family members to avoid "being morbid" and discussing the seriousness of patients' illnesses, injuries, or dying with them. Everyone connected with patients should try to cheer them up and deny bad news whenever possible.

The Patients' Right to Know

There are a number of arguments supporting the patients' right to know, many of them criticisms of the paternalistic arguments. First, because it is the patients' bodies and lives that are involved, not those of the professionals or even other family members, patients have a right to know everything and should be told all. Second, it is much easier to treat and deal with patients if they are aware of what is going on and if professionals and family members don't have to constantly pretend that patients' illnesses or injuries are not serious or that patients are not dying.[3] Third, patients are often angry if they don't know about side effects or other painful or disturbing aspects of treatment. (For example, a woman whose radiation therapy made her arm swell and become very painful became angry because she was never told she would have this problem.)

One negative aspect of the patients' rights position is that some professionals adopt this view so fervently that they are brutally frank with their patients, often leaving them without any hope or frightening them unnecessarily. As I pointed out in Chapter 11, it is a false dilemma to assume that either you have to give people terrible news or lie to them.

The Moderate Position

A third view, which lies between paternalism and brutal frankness, is a sharing of appropriate information with patients when they want to know it and to the extent they want to know it. This view lets patients be the guide in determining the information they will receive. It involves the following aspects:

1. Listening to patients carefully and hearing what they are really asking or trying to ask.

2. Not avoiding persistent, roundabout, or direct questions but rather answering them truthfully, yet not brutally.

3. Not forcing information on patients when they are not ready just because the professional is ready to discuss the matter or is too busy to wait until patients are ready.

4. Not avoiding the truth by using medical and technical language or jargon, but trying instead to explain everything patients want to know in lay terms.

5. Being aware that explanations or answers may have to be given in gradual doses or more than once because human beings will often defend themselves against the shock of bad news by not really "hearing" what is being said.

6. Always telling the truth clearly, gently, and humanely, never brutally, coldly, hopelessly, or cruelly.

7. Never leaving patients and their families without some hope, even if it is only that professionals will keep trying to do the very best they can to cure patients and to keep them comfortable and out of pain.

Informed Consent

As I mentioned earlier, *informed consent* is a more formalized approach to truth telling and to involving patients in decisions concerning their treatment. This approach is necessary in our time because of the many complex technological tests, procedures, and surgeries required, not only for individual therapeutic reasons, but also for experiments that can help science benefit others (by testing reactions to new drugs, for example). I shall discuss the problems of human experimentation later in this chapter.

In our country, the Department of Health and Welfare, with the agreement of the American Medical Association (AMA) and most hospitals, mandates that patients on whom complex, painful, risky, or dangerous procedures need to be performed, either for their own good or for the good of others, should be fully "informed" of what is to be done, why it is to be done, when it is to be done, and what to expect in the way of pain, discomfort, or risk. For example, except in emergency situations—in which saving a life requires immediate action—patients or their closest next of kin (wife, husband, parents) must authorize any procedure of a serious nature, such as surgeries, laboratory tests of certain kinds, and certain types of therapy, such as chemotherapy or radiation therapy.

The assumption behind the "informed consent" approach is that in order to intelligently "consent" to a procedure, patients must be fully "informed"; furthermore, they must agree in writing to undergo the procedure in order to avoid any later confusions and legal complications that may arise from such procedures. In order to facilitate the informed consent procedure, many hospitals and laboratory groups have printed informed consent forms for patients to read and sign. These forms should do the following: explain the procedure and its purpose clearly and in ordinary language; explain what kinds of discomfort or pain the procedure will cause patients to feel before, during, and after its completion; explain any and all complications that may arise because of the procedure; state how long the procedure will take; include a statement that the patient's doctors have judged that the procedure should be performed, for the patient's best interests and welfare and despite any discomforts or risks. Figure 13–1 provides an example of an informed consent document.

Permit for Percutaneous Trans-Hepatic Cholangiography

The term "percutaneous trans-hepatic cholangiography" means a study of the bile ducts (part of the drainage system of the liver) which is performed by entering a bile duct in the liver with a catheter (tube) which is passed through the skin to reach the proper position. Your doctor has requested that we perform a trans-hepatic cholangiogram on you to help him in his care of you. Since this type of examination is probably new to you, this note is intended to explain what you should expect.

Trans-hepatic cholangiography is performed by introducing a small catheter into a bile duct in the liver. The catheter is introduced in combination with a sharp stylet (special needle). It will be passed through the skin under your right ribs. More than one attempt may be needed to position the catheter. It is unusual to make more than four complete attempts. Once the catheter is positioned, an "x-ray dye" will be injected and films will be taken in several projections to help to identify your problem.

What will you feel? You will be sedated before the procedure, and, if needed, more sedation can be given during the procedure. We will use a local anesthetic where the catheter is introduced. This will sting and burn for about 30 to 40 seconds. Insertion of the catheter is done with a rapid motion and often causes a sharp pain which is generally short-lived. The major source of discomfort is leakage of bile or blood around the catheter into the abdomen. This is painful but can be treated with pain medication. This leakage is unpredictable, but probably occurs in 10–20% of patients.

What are the complications? The two most common complications have already been mentioned—bile leak and bleeding. Bleeding always occurs but is generally minor. Bile leakage into the abdomen often occurs when a dilated bile duct is entered and may be painful. This problem is the reason why the examination is performed only when surgery is planned to follow. There are a series of other complications related to catheter positioning which are unusual, but we will discuss them with you if you wish. The "x-ray dye" occasionally causes an "allergic" type reaction which cannot be predicted in advance. This generally consists of hives or nausea, but rarely is the reaction life-threatening or fatal (less than 0.0025% or 2 in 100,000 cases). This type of reaction is carefully watched for, and treatment can be instituted promptly should this occur. Occasionally infection of bile ducts can be spread into other parts of the body during the procedure.

The study will take 30 to 60 minutes. We should point out that a negative study—failure to enter a bile duct—provides important clinical information and may be the anticipated result of the study. If this occurs you may be returned to your room.

It is the judgment of your doctor that the potential benefits of this procedure as far as diagnosis of your condition far outweigh any of the above possible complications.

I have read and understand the above statements and have discussed them to my satisfaction and I consent to the performance of the above procedure by a qualified physician assigned by the above medical corporation upon

_____ (Name) _____ (Unit No.) _____ (Date)

_____ (Signature) _____ (Witness)

Figure 13–1   An informed consent document

The best approach in getting informed consent is for the physician who is requiring or performing the procedure to explain it in some detail in addition to having the patients read the form. Patients and their families should also be encouraged to ask any questions they wish, and should be given honest and clear answers. The idea behind such verbal explanations is that when patients sign these forms it is important that they have truly been fully informed; merely reading a paper is often not enough, especially when patients are confused, worried, or even scared about the procedure.

Doctors' Reactions to Truth Telling and Informed Consent

Some doctors are generally opposed to full disclosure of truth to the patients and are also opposed to informed consent, except as a mere formality. First of all, such doctors feel that patients don't need to be fully informed because doctors know what they are doing and explanations of complicated medical procedures will only confuse patients and break down the relationship of faith and trust that should exist between doctor and patient (paternalism).

Second, patients often don't want to hear explanations, and forcing them to against their wills is an invasion of their rights; furthermore, making them face facts about their physical or mental status or well-being that they aren't ready to accept is a highly questionable, perhaps even dangerous, course of action.

Third, every procedure has its risks, but there is no reason to frighten patients unnecessarily when chances are only, for example, two in one hundred thousand that a particular allergy or side effect will occur.

Fourth, such explanations may unnecessarily frighten patients to the extent that they will refuse to undergo a procedure that may be necessary to their health or well-being.

Finally, doctors sometimes feel that by describing certain side effects, such as headaches, for example, they can induce such problems through the power of suggestion; that is, patients may worry so much about getting a headache that their worry may actually bring one on. Doctors sometimes feel that if patients don't know they "are supposed to" have some sort of reaction, they won't get it, at least not psychosomatically.

The other extreme in truth telling is, of course, to go overboard and "tell all." Some doctors feel that it is important that patients know every "sordid" detail of what's going to happen to them, whether they want to or not. For example, a woman in her mid-seventies who had broken her hip and was to undergo orthopedic surgery was told by the anesthetist that he was going to use curare, a paralyzing drug, to anesthetize her. He explained in detail how her heart would stop beating for a short while, but assured her that he would be able to "bring her back from the dead." The woman told the anesthesist—and I believe rightly so—not to give her so many details; to just do his work and not discuss it with her. It would seem that giving information to such an extent really serves no purpose unless the patient insists on knowing *every* last detail, which very few would. Except in such cases, overly detailed explanations merely cause unnecessary anxiety.

Patients' and Families' Reactions to Truth Telling

As we have already mentioned, some doctors base decisions concerning what information to give on a sensitivity to what patients and their families want to know. It is certainly true that many patients and families don't want to know the truth; they prefer to deny that "terrible things" are happening to them. However, most patients want to know what is happening to them because it is their bodies and lives that are at risk. Perhaps they don't want or need to know all the details, but they do want to know the crucial facts.

Furthermore, just because patients and their families sometimes want to deny the existence of serious illness, injury, dying, and death, doesn't necessarily mean they don't really want to know the truth. After all, there is often "unfinished business" that can be accomplished if the truth is faced: dealing with inheritance and wills, settling family feuds, resolving other relationship problems, and doing things families have always wanted to do but have put off. If patients and their families are not told the truth, they can miss an important opportunity to put their lives in order.

A great deal of sensitivity is required on the part of the whole health care team, especially doctors, to know what to tell and when to tell it, and to be able to gauge possible reactions of patients and their families to different types of information. The team members must let patients guide them as much as possible in determining what information to give. Needless to say, it is difficult to deal well with the issue of truth telling, and health care professionals—especially doctors—should have extensive training in this area of patient-professional relationships.

Generally speaking, according to this point of view, patients and their families should be kept as fully informed as possible about their situation, especially when it is clear that they really want to know. Such openness and honesty helps to prevent the often painful game playing that goes on when people aren't honest with each other. Patients and their families should be dealt with truthfully, honestly, and compassionately but without cruelty, coldness, or brutal frankness. If, however, they consistently indicate that they don't want to be told about a specific situation, and if leaving them in ignorance would do no harm to them or their families, then one can avoid telling them until they indicate that they are ready to know. Finally, if patients want to know the truth about their illness but families don't want them to, the patients' wishes should come first—family members should be counseled to let patients be given the knowledge that they want and need.

◆——

Confidentiality

Confidentiality in patient-doctor relationships would on the surface seem to be fairly clear—that is, whatever a doctor and patient discuss and whatever the patient reveals in this relationship is to be held in strictest confidence, just as in other professions like the lawyer-client or priest/minister-parishioner relationships. And, generally, that clarity holds true, but confidentiality isn't always a clear-cut issue in the doctor-patient one. For example, what happens when a doctor tests a patient for a sexually transmitted disease (STD), including AIDS? The law is clear that STDs will have to be reported, but it is also clear that test results showing that a patient is HIV positive or has AIDS generally are not to be revealed. Other infectious diseases, such as leprosy, tuberculosis, or plagues must be reported by individuals' names, but not HIV positive or AIDS results, which can only be reported anonymously as numbers of such cases. Why?

Positive HIV Tests and AIDS

Spouses and Partners. Because of tremendous misunderstandings concerning the AIDS epidemic, and the stigma connected with people who are HIV positive or who have AIDS, laws have protected such people from being singled out since they could lose their jobs, societal status, and even friends if these results were revealed. However, problems have arisen in matters of justice or fairness, especially with sexual partners or drug-using partners. For example, should this information be revealed to such partners or spouses so that they can protect themselves from infection, especially since AIDS is a fatal disease without cure as yet?

For example, if a man goes on a trip, has sexual contact with an HIV-positive man or woman, and then tests HIV positive himself, should his wife or other sexual partners be told about his infection, or should his confidentiality be protected as it would be under most other medical circumstances? One solution, of course, is to urge the man to tell his wife or partners or to get his permission to let the physician do so, but what if he refuses?

The Centers for Disease Control (CDC) recommends that if HIV-infected persons are unwilling to notify partners, then physicians should use confidential procedures to ensure that partners are notified. Unfortunately, what is meant by "confidential procedures" is not clear. A California law now permits disclosure by a physician to a spouse or needle-sharing partner if attempts to obtain the patient's voluntary consent have failed. The physician, however, is not required to make or not make such disclosure and is protected from liability whichever approach he or she uses. Both the American Psychological Association (APA) and the American Medical Association (AMA) agree that it is ethically permissible for physicians to notify an identifiable person in danger of contracting the virus from a partner if they have good reason to believe the infected person has failed to or is unwilling to do so. Another way of resolving this dilemma is to warn infected persons of the limitations of confidentiality before counseling them.

Health Care Givers with HIV/AIDS. Another problem has arisen with health care givers who are HIV positive or who have AIDS. If this information is revealed, then most such people will be out of a job, and yet, is it fair to their patients not to know that their health care givers have this problem? Recently a young woman died as a result of having been infected with the AIDS virus from her dentist, who has also since died from AIDS.

Some health care givers feel that there would be a double standard if care givers had to reveal their problems, since their livelihoods would be at stake, but patients did not. As health care givers, they should, of course, take the responsibility for their infectiousness and remove themselves from any part of their work that would involve the possibility of passing on their body fluids to patients. For example, a surgeon should stop doing surgery and retrain or go into a different area of the medical field for which he or she is already trained. But, again, what if such doctors choose not to take that responsibility? What should be done? Shouldn't care givers have the same protection as anyone else who tests HIV positive or has AIDS?

As one can see, the matter of confidentiality is not always so simple and straightforward. It would seem that, as a general rule, confidentiality should be maintained to the utmost degree. At the same time, however, everything must also be done to protect the innocent from any kind of contagion. In these difficult times, every effort must be put into both of these areas of medicine, and people who are capable of infecting others must bear the responsibility of warning others. If they refuse, then confidential action must be taken to protect the innocent. Each case or situation must be dealt with on an individual basis.

◆───

Guilt and Innocence in Treating Patients

Another general medical ethical issue that sometimes arises is the effect on the treatment of patients by health care professionals who have judged them to be either "guilty" or "innocent" (that is, the degree to which a patient is deemed to be the cause of or contributor to the illness for which he or she is being treated). For example, it is often difficult for a health practitioner to be objective when dealing with alcoholics or drug abusers if any members of his or her family have used alcohol or drugs or, worse yet, died from either form of abuse. Similarly, it must be hard for a parent of a small child to treat a child abuser for an injury or a disease.

The inability to suspend personal feelings that can cloud professional judgment has to some extent always been a problem in medicine, especially when medical personnel are obliged to keep treating patients who continuously abuse themselves and thereby give rise to their own injuries or disease. Allowing personal attitudes to compromise patient care has become a more prevalent dilemma since the increase in the number of AIDS patients. Will a doctor or nurse treat an AIDS patient differently if he or she became infected from tainted blood from a transfusion as opposed to having acquired the disease as a result of homosexual activity or drug abuse? Should this difference in treatment or attitude in giving treatment be allowed or not? Perhaps the answer to this question is centered in what a health professional's purpose is. Most will agree that it is not the job of such a professional to try, judge, or convict any patient of crimes, no matter how heinous. It is, rather, the task of such professionals to treat a sick or injured patient to the best of their knowledge and ability regardless of the patient's religion, race, lifestyle, or alleged or known involvement in criminal activity. Of course, this is often easier said than done, but just as a court reporter must report testimony accurately and without judgment of the guilt or innocence of a defendant, so must health care professionals treat sick and injured patients as well as they can regardless of their background. Such professionals need not like these patients or in any way condone what they have done or are doing, but neither must they allow their own preconceptions or feelings to enter into the quality of treatment they give such patients.

---◆

Ethical Issues in Medicine

We have already dealt with two major bioethical issues: the questions surrounding allowing someone to die, mercy death, and mercy killing, in Chapter 9, and those surrounding abortion, in Chapter 10. Because this is merely an introduction to bioethics, there is only space to present problems in three other areas—behavior control, human experimentation, and genetics. For a more complete discussion of bioethics, you may want to read some of the texts listed in the Supplementary Reading section at the end of this chapter.

Ethics and Behavior Control

Behavior control is the aspect of bioethics that deals with general questions concerning the extent to which the behavior of human beings should be controlled by the various technologies available to us in our century. In particular, the following specific questions arise: How do we determine what constitutes undesirable or socially unacceptable behavior, who defines such behavior, and to what extent should we control or eliminate it? Which methods of controlling behavior are considered ethical, and which are not? Who should determine how and to whom behavior control is to be applied—the individuals suffering psychological problems, their families, others living around them, the government, their doctors, medicine in general? These issues are particularly crucial in cases involving mentally ill patients, prisoners, children, or antisocial human beings.

Before going any further, it is important that we understand precisely what "behavior control" is. It has been defined as the modification, or changing, of individuals' behavior by means of various technologies with or without their permission and with or without coercion. Some means used in behavior control are drugs, psychotherapy, behavior modification techniques (reward or aversive conditioning), electrical brain stimulation (EBS), hypnotism, biofeedback, surgery, and incarceration.

The major ethical issue that arises in terms of behavior control is that such control involves an encroachment upon or even an elimination of individual freedom: the question, then, is to what extent this should be allowed. Our recent past and present history are rife with situations that give rise to these issues. Recently, for example, it was discovered that about two hundred male sex offenders in California had been given a choice of prison or castration. In another case, which occurred in the South, two mentally retarded young black girls were told they were getting birth control medication but instead were sterilized by the government without their knowledge or permission. Mental patients who are subject to episodes of violence have been either kept totally sedated on drugs or subjected to brain surgery, both of which eliminate their violent episodes but also transform them into virtual zombies. Hyperkinetic children in some cities have not been allowed to go to school unless their parents agree to give them a drug that slows their level of activity—but which also may have questionable side effects.

Some prisoners and mental patients are kept sedated so that they can be controlled more easily in understaffed institutions. People who are subject to depression are sometimes given electroshock therapy or have electrodes implanted in their brains, which, when stimulated, eliminate the depression, again with possible questionable side effects. Many people have sought to eliminate "bad habits" such as drinking alcohol, taking drugs, and overeating by going to clinics where they are aversively conditioned (that is, made to suffer physical or mental discomfort) for continuing the habit and rewarded for stopping it. These are just a few of the many situations in which ethical issues in behavior control arise. Implied in all of them are various problems and concerns that I will now attempt to clarify.

Ethical Issues and Problems with Behavior Control. Because much behavior control is subtle, we must question whether we have the right to change people's behavior whether they know it or not or whether they consent or not. Ardent probehaviorists would say yes for several reasons. They would insist that we have a good idea of what "normal behavior" is, and that when people don't conform to it, their behavior should be changed for their own good and the good of others. The farther away from the norm the behavior is, they would argue, the more drastic the control must be (for example, a scolding might be sufficient for a child who swears, but brain surgery might be considered for an adult given to episodes of uncontrollable violence).

Strong antibehaviorists, or individualists, however, would disagree. They believe that we *don't* know what the standard for normal behavior is and that setting one arbitrarily is dangerous. Individual freedom, uniqueness, and creativity arc to be encouraged and prized, and for these to exist we must allow some deviation from the norm. True, they say, some behaviors should be discouraged and some encouraged, but proper ethical procedures must be employed at all times. For example, just because a person in a mental hospital wants brain surgery to curb his or her violence does not necessarily mean that the doctors should comply. According to the antibehaviorists, we must ask several important questions concerning the protection of such people's rights as individuals. For example, can they really know, if they are so mentally disturbed that they must be institutionalized, what they are consenting to? Are they competent to judge what's best for them in these situations?

Another question that comes up in relation to changing behavior is how far can we carry the use of rewards, bonuses, or punishment. Isn't it rather strong coercion to give a man a choice between three to six years in prison and castration, or to give an impoverished man in India a bonus for having himself sterilized? Can people be considered to "freely" consent when they are being forcibly or even subtly coerced by financial rewards or promises of freedom?

Yet another problem that arises involves the therapist or controller as well as the patient. First of all, who should such controllers be, and to whom should they be responsible? To the society in which they live? The institutions at which they work? Their government? Their patients? For example, if a homosexual who lives in a militantly heterosexual society comes to a therapist for help, what is the therapist's duty? Should he or she help the homosexual to adjust to this type of sexuality and to the possibility of ostracism by some segments of society or should the therapist help the homosexual learn to embrace heterosexuality? Therapists' decisions about their responsibilities affect their patients and, more indirectly, the rest of society.

Human Experimentation

Human experimentation is the use of human beings for experimental purposes for their own therapy, for the good of humanity in general, or for the purpose of advancing scientific knowledge. Why is the question of human experimentation even raised? First of all, medical knowledge concerning human beings can only be advanced so far by experimenting on animals; sooner or later a drug, procedure, or technology must be used on human beings if medicine is to discover whether it is effective or ineffective. Also, experimentation is sometimes done in areas that apply only to human beings, not to any other animal species; in such cases, experimentation on animals simply will not yield the necessary knowledge.

This problem becomes even more crucial in relation to pediatric medicine (medicine pertaining to children). Children are physically and mentally different from adults, so even if adults can be safely and ethically used for experimentation, the data is often not very useful in the treatment of children. Experimentation on children, however, raises even more serious ethical problems because they are rarely thought of as competent to freely consent to experimentation. One can even raise the issue of whether parents or guardians can really decide for their children, without their consent, whether they will undergo experimentation which may cause pain, discomfort, or even a life-threatening situation. The main question here, then, is to what extent can human beings be experimented on and under what conditions, and also to what degree must they be informed about and freely consent to such experimentation.

The Proexperimentation Argument. Those who take a strong proexperiment stance believe that as long as a specific experiment can advance scientific knowledge or aid humanity in some way, human experimentation is justified. People who are to be experimented on should be informed just enough so that they know something about what's being done to them but not enough to interfere with the outcome of the experiment.

People in prison or in mental institutions who are willing to participate should be allowed to volunteer to aid humanity; in this way, they can make up for their previous crimes or their present uselessness. As an incentive, such people can be offered rewards (for example, parole, release, or a better living situation). It is, further, even justifiable to experiment on institutionalized children or on children whose parents have given consent, in order to cure them when nothing else has worked or in order to benefit future children with similar problems.

The Antiexperimentation Argument. According to this point of view, human beings should generally not be used for experimentation. If science can't advance its knowledge by using lesser animals, it simply cannot be advanced. No experimental drug or procedure should be used on any human being unless the following criteria are met: It is a last resort; it is meant to cure the person on whom it is used; the patient has given fully informed consent; and science has gone as far as it can with animal experimentation. Opponents of human experimentation point to the terrible experiments performed by doctors of the Third Reich during World War II. Never again, these people argue, can science be given carte blanche to perform experiments on humans.

Furthermore, experimentation must never be done on human beings who are not mentally competent to consent, including people in mental institutions and all children, whether or not their parents are willing to consent. Experiments must also never be performed on people who are not really free to consent, such as those incarcerated in prisons or other institutions. Finally, any human experimentation that is done, after all of these criteria are satisfied, must also be extremely safe; it must not involve serious risk of illness, injury or loss of life.

Immanuel Kant's Practical Imperative (see Chapter 3) can be very useful here. Remember that the principle states that each human being must be considered as a unique end in himself or herself and never used merely as a means to someone else's end. In human experimentation this would mean that no human being could be used for experimentation unless it would be therapeutic for that human being and would not be any more harmful or risky than other treatments that generally would be used for such patients. This would mean that no experimentation only for "the good of humanity or others" could be done. If this "good" were an indirect result of the experimentation, then it would be allowed, but the experimental procedure must be for the primary benefit of the patient on which it is to be performed.

Many medical ethicists will follow this imperative as a guideline, but they may also allow experimentation when the person to be experimented on can give fully free and informed consent, realizing that the experiment may not be therapeutic for him or her but for the good of humanity or the advancement of science. Where there is any doubt, however, the Practical Imperative forms a useful ethical criterion for human experimentation.

Genetics

Genetics is the area of medicine and science that is concerned with the manipulation and control of the human genetic makeup. Research in genetics includes everything from discovering the causes of genetic problems and correcting such problems to creating human life in the laboratory. The main problem created by genetics is in determining how to use the technology we have acquired for gaining genetic information and manipulating genes. It is obvious that this problem is very important, especially when we consider the potentially enormous effect of genetic manipulation on individuals, families, and the overall gene pool as well.

There are, first of all, such procedures as amniocentesis and chorionic villus sampling that have been discussed earlier, and other investigative and diagnostic procedures that can bring us important information about genetic defects or abnormalities. This information can, in turn, enable us to correct such deficiencies—if and when we can perfect the corrective procedures—or to avoid them altogether by means of either abortion or birth control, including sterilization. Genetic counseling is, therefore, intimately tied to important ethical questions.

Second, even more crucial ethical problems will arise as we approach the point where we can correct and avoid genetic defects or create life in the laboratory. Someday, we may even be in a position to decide what male and female types would best ensure the survival of the race and then reproduce them artificially. We could go even further and decide, as in Aldous Huxley's *Brave New World,* how many intellectuals, laborers, white-collar workers, and other types of people a "balanced, well-functioning society" needs and then create such a society in the laboratory.

At this point in scientific development these are somewhat exotic problems, but there is no reason to think that we will not be able to do these things in the future. Frogs and other animals have been cloned with some success. Also, scientists have already declared a moratorium on various types of experimentation having to do with changing and creating life in the laboratory. As does human experimentation, the issue of genetic experimentation and development arouses strong opinions.

The Argument for Genetic Experimentation and Development. According to this argument, nothing and no one should stand in the way of advances in scientific knowledge and the chance to perfect the human race. The more we know about genetics, the more we can improve the human race and condition, and the better things will be. This betterment should be our primary goal; we should not worry about such trivial matters as the effects of experimentation on the gene pool or whether our information and abilities will result in abortion, sterilization, the elimination of defects, or the ability to create life in the laboratory. Self-imposed moratoriums and laws that prevent scientific advancement cannot be justified.

The Argument Against Genetic Experimentation and Development. According to this argument, in the case of anything that tampers with the natural life process or interferes with God's or nature's plan, no scientific experimentation in this area, especially the artificial creation of life, should be allowed. Nature or God had a purpose in allowing some imperfections to exist in the human species, and tampering with this purpose could be disastrous, not only to the natural development and progress of humanity, but also to its moral and spiritual development. Nature or God has given us human beings with handicaps and genetic problems to help us recognize that human imperfections do exist, and also to encourage us to love and care for less fortunate human beings. If we create completely perfect human beings and eliminate all those with imperfections, we will lose our humanity, from both a biological-physical and a moral-spiritual point of view.

◆

Cases for Study and Discussion

CASE ◆ 1

Richard is a sixty-seven-year-old man with terminal cancer. He has just had a liver scan and is told to visit his doctor, an oncologist (that is, a cancer specialist whose work focuses on tumors), and get the results. When Richard arrives, the doctor says that there is no change in his condition, which is, nevertheless, not good. Richard asks the doctor what can be done, and he replies that there is no remedy for this kind of cancer. Becoming somewhat agitated, Richard asks the doctor what he would advise him to do, but the doctor merely repeats his opinion that there is nothing to be done. By this time Richard is both frustrated and upset, and he asks the doctor why he won't care for him and doesn't care about him. In response the doctor gives Richard a prescription, but he makes it clear that the drug is only being prescribed as a psychological crutch—that it will not improve Richard's health. When he finally leaves the doctor's office, Richard feels totally depressed, abandoned, and dehumanized. Do you feel the doctor handled Richard's case well? If so, why; if not, why not? How would you have handled the situation or advised the doctor to handle it? Discuss both the truth telling aspect of what the doctor said and his methods of giving out information and relating to his patient.

C A S E ◆ 2

In Chapter 10, which dealt with abortion, I described a case in which a middle-aged wife became pregnant and underwent amniocentesis testing to see if the baby would have Down's syndrome. When the procedure was over, the genetic counselor was happy to inform the prospective parents that their baby would be quite healthy. She also told them, however, that the sex of the child was female. The husband and wife then decided to have an abortion because they already had several daughters, and the genetic counselor was beside herself with shock and concern. She felt that she might have done the wrong thing by revealing the sex of the child to the parents—that if she had merely told them about the Down's syndrome results they would not have decided on an abortion. Should the counselor have withheld the information about the sex of the child? Do the parents have the right to know all of the information disclosed by amniocentesis, only the information that is crucial to the health of the child, or only the information for which they ask? In short, what are counselors' obligations in revealing the results of such tests?

C A S E ◆ 3

A psychologist wants to videotape some of his patients during their therapy sessions, partly for a study he is doing and partly as a teaching device for advanced psychology students. He feels that if the patients know they are being taped they won't act naturally, which will both taint his study and diminish the film's value as a teaching device. For this reason, he feels that the patients should not know that they are being taped even though what they do or say on the tape may reveal certain aspects of their private feelings and lives. What should the psychologist do? Should he tell the patients he is taping them, or should he just go ahead and tape without their permission, assuming that he is just going to use the tapes for his own research and as a teaching device? Are there any other alternatives you can think of for the psychologist to follow?

C A S E ◆ 4

A doctor-researcher in residence at a private institution for mentally retarded children discovers that the children in one of the dormitories have dysentery, whereas those in the other dormitories do not. She decides to experiment with the children both to see what has caused this particular phenomenon and to study the effects of dysentery and its various cures on children in general. She sets up a scientific study with control groups (in which some students receive medication and some do not), and part of her experiment involves infecting healthy children with dysentery germs. The institution for which she works has a long waiting list, and the doctor takes advantage of this, admitting only those children whose parents will sign a release allowing her to conduct experiments on them. What are the ethical implications of what the doctor is doing? Should such experimentation be allowed? Why or why not?

C A S E ◆ 5

John, twenty-five, comes to a psychiatrist very depressed about his homosexuality. He has had two heterosexual relationships, neither of which was satisfactory, and numerous homosexual ones, some of which were satisfactory and some of which were not. He has also used his homosexuality as a means of getting jobs, money, and other benefits. John is not quite sure what he wants to do about his homosexuality, but he does know that he is not very happy the way he is. What should the psychiatrist do? Should he try to help John become a heterosexual? Should he try to get him to adjust to his homosexuality? Discuss both of these alternatives, and describe the psychiatrist's responsibilities to himself, to John, and to society in general.

C A S E ◆ 6

Mary, forty-five, is in a mental institution, on a ward for violent people. She is given to episodes of extreme violence during which she loses all control and becomes very dangerous. Between such episodes, she remembers at least some of what she has done, but when one of these episodes comes on, she just can't seem to stop or control it. There does not seem to be anything physiologically wrong with her brain, but a doctor suggests to her that she have surgery performed that will eliminate her violence.

The doctor explains that this operation may cause extreme loss of memory—to the extent that Mary could read a newspaper and immediately forget everything she has read. Furthermore, the operation will make Mary so passive that she probably will not want to do very much with the rest of her life; however, after undergoing such an operation, she probably could be released from the institution. Mary is so deeply distressed by her violent episodes that she signs a release to have the surgery performed.

Describe the implications of informed consent in this case, and discuss Mary's ability to give it freely as an inmate of a mental institution. Also discuss the extent to which coercion exists in the doctor's promise that Mary's violent episodes will end and in the suggestion that she may be released from the institution. Can Mary fully understand what she is agreeing to? And even if she does not fully understand, because she hasn't been cured by other methods, should she be allowed the brain surgery as a viable alternative or not?

Chapter Summary

I. Introduction and definition of terms
    A. *Bioethics* literally means "life ethics," or ethics in medicine.
    B. Bioethics covers the areas of caring for the dying: allowing someone to die, mercy death, and mercy killing: human experimentation and informed consent; genetics, fertilization, and birth; health care and its costs; population and birth control, abortion, and sterilization; allocation of scarce medical resources; and truth telling and confidentiality in medicine.
    C. It is essentially concerned with the establishment and maintenance of vital and human relationships between the sick and dying and the well and the professional.
II. Health care personnel and patients and their families—rights and obligations
    A. Paternalism is the position that professionals should take a parental role toward patients and their families.
        1. Lay people don't know what's best for them; therefore, they should place themselves totally in the hands of professionals because they and they alone have the proper medical background.
        2. Patients and their families are essentially like children when it comes to medical problems, so the professionals should serve as father figures.
    B. Radical individualism is the position that patients should have absolute rights over their bodies and lives and may therefore reject doctors' recommendations.
        1. Doctors are nothing more than humans with special training, who are, nevertheless, capable of making errors.
        2. Patients and their families are better qualified than anyone else to make decisions concerning their treatment because their bodies and lives are at stake.

3. Many issues having to do with treatment are not strictly medical, and professionals are not qualified to make decisions about them.

4. Many lay people these days are quite knowledgeable about their bodies and about medicine, and even when they are not, they can be made to understand the nature of their medical problems when explained clearly and in plain language.

5. Paternalism has often led to total patient dependence on doctors and has sometimes resulted in dehumanization.

C. The reciprocal or collegial position utilizes the team approach, in which patients and their families work with health care personnel to do what is best for patients.

1. Professionals are not gods or even father figures; they are merely human begins with specialized training.

2. Many decisions are not strictly medical; therefore, they should not be made strictly by professionals. Doctors need to rely on other support personnel (nurses, therapists, etc.) as well as nonmedical personnel, such as social workers, clergy, and trained volunteers in order to properly care for patients and their families as whole persons.

3. This view recognizes the importance of individual patients' rights in all medical areas.

4. It accepts that neither patients nor professionals alone "know best" but that decisions should be both reciprocal (involving give and take) and collegial (involving a team approach) rather than dictatorial, paternalistic, or anarchistic.

5. Patients are entitled to know what is happening to them, and decisions should be arrived at through a free exchange of ideas and should be made jointly by everyone on the team.

III. Truth telling and informed consent

A. The main issue here is to what extent patients and their families should be told the truth about their medical situations and to what extent they should not.

B. *Informed consent* is a formalized procedure in which patients or their families consent in writing to medical procedures involving some degree of risk to their health or lives.

C. The paternalistic view holds that because patients are not medically trained, they cannot understand what doctors tell them; therefore, they do not need to know more than that professionals are doing their very best for them.

1. It is best for patient's morale and their will to get better or will to live that they aren't told bad news.

2. Keeping patients in the dark allows them to live the remainder of their lives without worry, concern, or depression: Telling them bad news will not keep them from dying.

      3. It is all right to tell the bad news to the families but not to the patients.

      4. Professionals and patients' families should avoid being morbid and should try to cheer up patients.

D. There are several arguments supporting the position that patients have a right to know about their condition.

      1. They have a right to know because it is their bodies and lives that are at stake.

      2. It is much easier to deal with patients who are aware of what is going on, so that pretense is unnecessary.

      3. Patients are often angry and feel dehumanized if they don't know what is going on or what to expect.

      4. This approach, however, may lead some professionals to be frank to the point of being brutal or even cruel in telling patients the truth.

      5. It is a false dilemma to assume that either you have to give people terrible news or lie to them.

      6. A third view, the moderate position, which lies between paternalism and brutal frankness, is sharing of appropriate information when patients want and/or need to know, letting the patients be the guide as to how much information should be revealed. This involves the following:

        (a) Listening to and really hearing patients.

        (b) Answering patients' questions truthfully and compassionately.

        (c) Not forcing information on patients but letting them decide what should be told and when it is to be told.

        (d) Not avoiding questions or issues by using medical technical language or jargon.

        (e) Recognizing that explanations may have to be given in parts or more than once because of the shock of the news and resultant patient denial.

        (f) Always giving information clearly, gently, and humanely, never coldly, brutally, or cruelly.

        (g) Never leaving patients and their families without some hope, even if it is only that the patients will be cared for and kept free of pain.

E. Informed consent is necessitated in our times by the increase in complex technological tests, procedures, and surgeries, not only for therapeutic reasons but also for experimental purposes.

      1. In the United States patients must be informed of the risks involved in any procedures that are to be performed on them.

      2. The assumption behind this approach is that in order to intelligently consent to any procedure, patients must be fully informed;

they should also consent in writing to avoid future confusions or legal problems.

3. Most informed consent forms do the following:

    (a) Explain the procedure and its purpose clearly and in ordinary language.

    (b) Explain what the procedure will cause the patient to feel in the way of discomfort or pain before, during, and after the procedure.

    (c) Explain any and all complications that may arise because of the procedure.

    (d) State how long the procedure will take.

    (e) Include a statement that the patient's doctors have judged the procedure so important to the patient's well-being that the risks involved are justified.

4. Often the best approach is for the physician to provide information in person as well as having a consent form for the patient to read and sign; this will help to ensure full understanding and truly informed consent.

F. Doctors vary greatly in their reactions to truth telling and informed consent.

1. Doctors who are generally against both full disclosure of the truth and informed consent support their position with a number of arguments.

    (a) Doctors know what they are doing, and having to explain complicated medical procedures to patients will only confuse the patients and break down the relationship of faith and trust between doctor and patient.

    (b) Patients often really don't want to know the truth, and forcing it on them against their wills both invades their privacy and is bad for their morale.

    (c) Every procedure has its risks, but there is no reason to frighten patients unnecessarily, especially when risks are very low.

    (d) Patients may be unnecessarily frightened to the point where they will refuse to have necessary procedures performed.

    (e) Unnecessary side effects may also be caused by the power of suggestion.

2. Some doctors, on the other hand, have gone overboard in giving information whether or not the patients want to hear it, thus causing unnecessary anxiety.

G. The reactions of patients and their families to truth telling and informed consent also vary.

1. Some patients, and their families, don't want to know the truth

because they wish to continue denying their problems. However, most patients want to know what's happening to them; perhaps they don't need to know everything, but they certainly want to know the crucial facts.

    2.   That patients and their families want to deny their problems doesn't necessarily mean they don't want to know the truth. After all, there may be unfinished business to take care of, and knowing the truth may help all of them take care of it.

    3.   A great deal of sensitivity is necessary on the part of the whole health care team to know how, what, when, and where to tell the truth.

H.   There are a number of guides to truth telling and informed consent.

    1.   Generally, patients and their families should be kept as fully informed as possible, especially when they clearly want to know the truth.

    2.   They should be dealt with truthfully, honestly, and compassionately and without cruelty, coldness, or brutal frankness.

    3.   If they consistently indicate that they don't want to know the truth, and if ignorance will do no harm to them or their families, then one can avoid telling them until they do want to know.

    4.   If patients want to know the truth but their families don't want them to, then the patient's desire should come first.

IV. Confidentiality

A.   Generally the matter of confidentiality seems fairly clear in that what goes on between doctors and patients should always be confidential. This is usually the case.

B.   The problems with HIV testing and AIDS have, however, made the matter of confidentiality a difficult issue in the following cases:

    1.   Spouses and partners deserve to be protected.

    2.   Patients deserve to be protected from health care givers infected with HIV or AIDS.

C.   As a general rule, confidentiality should be maintained, but at the same time everything must be done to protect the innocent from any kind of contagion.

    1.   People who are capable of infecting must take the responsibility for warning others.

    2.   Where they won't or can't, confidential action must be taken to protect the innocent.

V. Guilt and innocence in treating patients

A.   It is often difficult for health care professionals to be objective in treating patients who have certain problems that have also been personal problems for the professionals in some way (e.g., a child abuser who needs treatment and a doctor or nurse who is a parent of a small child).

    B. Another aspect of this issue is when professionals have to keep treating patients who continuously abuse their own health (e.g., alcoholics).

    C. This issue has become even more of a problem since the advent of AIDS.

    D. It is not the job of health professionals to try, judge, or convict any patient of crimes, no matter how heinous. It is their job, rather, to treat sick or injured patients no matter what their background or lifestyle.

    E. Professionals need not like such patients or condone what they have done or how they live, but neither must they let their own preconceptions or feelings enter into the quality of their treatment.

VI. Ethical issues in medicine

    A. Ethics and behavior control is that aspect of bioethics that deals with general questions concerning the extent to which the behavior of human beings should be controlled by the various technologies available to us.

       1. Several specific questions arise in relation to this issue.

          (a) How do we determine what constitutes undesirable or socially unacceptable behavior?

          (b) Which means of behavior control should be considered ethical and which should not?

          (c) Who should determine when behavior control is to be used?

       2. Behavior control is the modification or changing of human behavior—with or without permission and with or without forcible or subtle coercion—by means of various technologies: drugs, psychotherapy, behavior modification techniques (reward or aversive conditioning), electrical brain stimulation (EBS), hypnotism, biofeedback, brain surgery, and incarceration.

       3. The major problem here is that any control of behavior involves an encroachment on or even an elimination of individual freedom: the question, then, is to what extent this should be allowed.

       4. There are many ethical issues and problems concerned with behavior control.

          (a) Because much behavior control is subtle, we must question whether we have the right to change people's behavior whether they know it or not or whether they consent to it or not.

          (b) Probehaviorists would say that we have this right because we know what normal behavior is, and those in society who can't conform to these norms ought to have their behavior changed.

          (c) Antibehaviorists would say that we do not have this right because we don't know what the norm is, and setting one arbitrarily is dangerous. Individual freedom, uniqueness, and creativity should be prized and protected at all costs.

    (d) There are also questions concerning how far we can carry rewards, bonuses, or punishments in changing or controlling behavior.

    (e) We must ask ourselves to whom controllers should be responsible.

B. Human experimentation is the use of human beings for experimental purposes either for their own therapy, for the good of humanity, or to advance scientific knowledge.

    1. Experimentation must eventually be done on human beings because science can only go so far with animal experimentation.

    2. The main question concerns the extent to which human beings can be experimented on and under what conditions. Another important question concerns the extent to which people should be informed and freely consent to such experimentation.

    3. There are two highly divergent viewpoints on this issue:

        (a) Proponents of experimentation believe that as long as an experiment can advance scientific knowledge or aid humanity in some way, human experimentation is justified.

        (b) Opponents of human experimentation believe that human beings should never be used for experimentation unless protective criteria are met because of the ease of abusing the rights of people whose freedoms are limited (prisoners, mental patients, and children).

    4. Immanuel Kant's Practical Imperative—that each human being must be considered as a unique end in himself or herself and never used merely as a means to someone else's end—can be useful here.

        (a) A person should generally not be experimented on unless the experimental procedure is therapeutic and not harmful.

        (b) A person may be experimented on provided he or she is fully informed and can freely consent to such experimentation, realizing it may not be therapeutic to himself or herself but good for humanity.

C. Genetics is the area of bioethics that is concerned with the manipulation and control of the human genetic makeup.

    1. The main problem created by genetics is in determining how to use the technology we have acquired for gaining genetic information and manipulating genes, especially when we consider the effect of genetic manipulation on individuals, families, and the overall gene pool.

    2. Procedures such as amniocentesis and chorionic villus sampling

give us information that force us to make decisions concerning birth control, abortion, and sterilization.

3. As our technology increases we can correct genetic deficiencies, create life in the laboratory, and clone ideal human beings. This raises questions as to whether we should do any of these things and, if so, to what extent? Also, what effect will this technology have on the human species?

4. There are two highly divergent viewpoints on genetic experimentation and development.

   (a) Supporters of genetic experimentation and development believe that nothing and no one should stand in the way of scientific advancement and the chance to perfect the human race because the world can only benefit from such improvements.

   (b) Opponents of genetic experimentation and development believe that anything that tampers with the natural life process, interfering with nature's or God's plan, should be prohibited. This includes scientific experimentation in the area of genetics, especially the artificial creation of life.

Exercises for Review

1. Investigate and research one of the areas of bioethics not covered in this chapter (for example, organ transplantation), and write or give an oral report on your research following your instructor's guidelines.

2. Outline in detail what you feel are the rights and obligations of doctors, nurses, patients, families, chaplains, and hospitals, and discuss whether these relationships should be paternalistic, radically individualistic, or reciprocal and collegial.

3. To what extent do you think the truth about terminal illness should be told to patients and their families? Why?

4. Describe the difference between "informed consent" and general truth telling, and design an informed consent form for some procedure, experiment, interview, or task you might want people to participate in. Explain in detail what you expect them to do. Then describe the methods you would use to help them understand the project so that they could give their informed consent to it, and explain how you would protect them from exposing their private lives or endangering themselves or their reputation.

5. To what extent and under what circumstances do you feel that people's behavior should be controlled? Do you feel that it is acceptable to con-

trol people in such a way that they don't know they are being controlled? Why or why not?

6. To what extent do you feel that reward, punishment, or other types of forcible or subtle coercion should be used to get people to behave in certain ways?

7. If someone is in a position to control behavior (for example a teacher or a psychotherapist), to whom should he or she be responsible, and to what degree?

8. To what degree do you believe human beings can or should be experimented on? Under what conditions would you allow such experimentation? What safeguards or guidelines would you establish and enforce to protect both the subjects being experimented on and the experimenters? Why?

9. Discuss at length the extent to which you would allow behavior control and experimentation to be performed on children with or without their parents' permission. Support your position in detail.

10. To what extent do you feel that genetic experimentation and development should be allowed, especially experiments that involve the creation of human life in the laboratory and the cloning of human beings? Answer in detail, giving evidence and supporting arguments for your position.

11. How do you feel about guilt and innocence in treating patients? How do you suggest health care professionals treat patients they consider guilty of terrible crimes or immoralities? What types of patients would you find it difficult to treat and why? How would you overcome your distaste or hatred of them? Do you think that all patients deserve the best treatment health professionals can give them, regardless of what they've done or who they are? Why or why not? Explain in detail.

Notes

1. John A. Behnke and Sissela Bok, *The Dilemmas of Euthanasia* (Garden City, N.Y.: Anchor Books, 1975), 157–59, and PSDA, 1990.

2. Some of these questions are mine, and some were taken from an Ann Landers column in *The Bakersfield Californian*, Bakersfield, Calif. (29 October 1987): E8.

3. See Barney G. Glaser and Anselm L. Strauss, *Awareness of Dying* (Chicago: Aldine, 1965), for the best presentation of the difficulty of maintaining the various types of pretense between the healthy and the professional and the sick and the dying.

Supplementary Reading

Bioethics in General

Beauchamp, Tom L., and Walters, LeRoy, eds. *Contemporary Issues in Bioethics.* Encino, Calif.: Dickenson, 1978.

Bier, William C., ed. *Human Life: Problems of Birth, of Living and of Dying.* New York: Fordham University Press, 1977.

Caplan, Arthur L. et al., eds. *Concepts of Health and Disease.* Reading, Mass.: Addison, Wesley, 1981.

Coppenger, Mark. *Bioethics: A Casebook.* Englewood Cliffs, N.J.: Prentice-Hall, 1985.

Culver, Charles M., and Bernard Gert. *Philosophy in Medicine.* New York: Oxford University Press, 1982.

Dedek, John F. *Contemporary Medical Ethics.* Mission, Kan.: Sheed, Andrews, and McMeel, 1975.

Edwards, Rem B., and Glenn C. Grober. *Bioethics.* New York: Harcourt Brace Jovanovich, 1988.

Fletcher, Joseph. *Morals and Medicine.* Boston: Beacon Press, 1954.

Furrow, Barry R., et al. *Bioethics: Health Care, Law, and Ethics.* Anaheim, Calif.: West Publishers, 1991.

Mappes, Thomas A., and Jane S. Zembaty. *Biomedical Ethics,* 2nd ed. New York: McGraw-Hill, 1986.

Ramsey, Paul. *The Patient as Person.* New Haven: Yale University Press, 1970.

Regan, Tom, ed. *Matters of Life and Death.* New York: Random House, 1980.

Shannon, Thomas A. *Bioethics,* 3rd ed. Mahwah, N.J.: Paulist Press, 1987.

Vaux, Kenneth. *Biomedical Ethics: Morality for the New Medicine.* New York: Harper & Row, 1974.

Warner, Richard. *Morality in Medicine.* Sherman Oaks, Calif.: Alfred, 1980.

Weiss, Ann E. *Bioethics: Dilemmas in Modern Medicine.* Hillside, N.J.: Enslow, 1985.

Truth Telling and Informed Consent

Annas, George, J., et al. *Informed Consent to Human Experimentation: The Subject's Dilemma.* Cambridge, Mass.: Ballinger, 1977.

Applebaum, Paul, et al. *Informed Consent: Legal Theory and Clinical Practice.* New York: Oxford University Press, 1987.

Bok, Sissela. *Lying: Moral Choices in Public and Private Life*. New York: Pantheon Books, 1978.

Cowles, Jane. *Informed Consent*. New York: Coward, McCann, and Geoghegan, 1976.

Eck, Marcel. *Lies and Truth*. New York: Macmillan, 1970.

Klawans, Harold L. *Informed Consent*. New York: New American Library, 1988.

Ravin, Neil. *Informed Consent*. New York: Putnam, 1983.

Rosoff, Arnold J. *Informed Consent: A Guide for Health Care Providers*. Rockville, Md., 1981.

Behavior Control

Ayd, Frank J., Jr., ed. *Medical, Moral and Legal Issues in Mental Health Care*. Baltimore: Williams and Wilkins, 1974.

Bandura, A. *Principles of Behavior Modification*. New York: Holt, Rinehart and Winston, 1969.

Birk, Lee, et al. *Behavior Therapy in Psychiatry: A Report of the American Psychiatric Association Task Force on Behavior Therapy*. New York: Jason Aronson, 1974.

Bosco, James J., and Stanley S. Robin, eds. *The Hyperactive Child and Stimulant Drugs*. Chicago: University of Chicago Press, 1977.

Brecher, Edwards, ed. *The Consumers Union Report: Licit and Illicit Drugs*. Boston: Little, Brown, 1972.

Delgado, José M. R. *Physical Control of the Mind: Toward a Psychocivilized Society*. New York: Harper & Row, 1969.

Duster, Troy. *The Legislation of Morality: Law, Drugs and Moral Judgment*. New York: The Free Press, 1970.

Ennis, Bruce, and Loren Siegel. *The Rights of Mental Patients*. New York: Avon Books, 1973.

London, Perry. *Behavior Control*, 2nd ed. New York: New American Library, 1977.

Pines, Maya. *The Brain Changers: Scientists and the New Mind Control*. New York: Harcourt Brace Jovanovich, 1973.

Rudovsky, David. *The Rights of Prisoners*. New York: Avon Books, 1973.

Schrag, Peter. *Mind Control*. New York: Pantheon Books, 1978.

Shuman, Samuel I. *Psychosurgery and the Medical Control of Violence: Autonomy and Deviance*. Detroit: Wayne State University Press, 1977.

Skinner, B. F. *Beyond Freedom and Dignity*. New York: Alfred A. Knopf, 1971.

————. *Science and Human Behavior.* New York: Macmillan, 1973.

Stolz, Stephanie et al., eds. *Ethical Issues in Behavior Modification.* San Francisco: Jossey-Bass, 1978.

Uhr, Leonard M., and James G. Miller. *Drugs and Behavior.* New York: Wiley, 1960.

Human Experimentation

Barber, Bernard et al. *Research on Human Subjects: Problems of Social Control in Medical Experimentation.* New York: Russell Sage Foundation, 1973.

Beecher, Henry K. *Experimentation in Man.* Springfield, Ill.: Charles C. Thomas, 1959.

————. *Research and the Individual: Human Studies.* Boston: Little, Brown, 1970.

Bogomolny, Robert L., ed. *Human Experimentation.* Dallas: Southern Methodist University Press, 1976.

Greenwald, Robert A., et al. *Human Subjects Research: A Handbook for Institutional Review Boards.* New York: Plenum, 1982.

Milgrim, Stanley. *Obedience to Authority.* New York: Harper & Row, 1974.

Sjoberg, Gideon, ed. *Ethics, Politics, and Social Research.* Cambridge, Mass.: Schenkman, 1967.

Genetics

Bayles, Michael D. *Reproductive Ethics.* Englewood Cliffs, N.J.: Prentice-Hall, 1984.

Ellison, Craig, ed. *Modifying Man: Implications and Ethics.* Washington, D.C.: University Press of America, 1977.

Fletcher, Joseph. *The Ethics of Genetic Control: Ending Reproductive Roulette.* New York: Prometheus, 1988.

Hamilton, Michael, ed. *The New Genetics and the Future of Man.* Grand Rapids, Mich.: William B. Eerdmans, 1972.

Hilton, Bruce et al., eds. *Ethical Issues in Human Genetics.* New York: Plenum, 1973.

Holmes, Helen B., et al., eds. *The Custom-Made Child? Women Centered Perspectives.* Clifton, N.J.: Humana, 1981.

Karp, L. E. *Genetic Engineering: Threat or Promise?* Chicago: Nelson-Hall, 1976.

Lebacqz, Karen. *Genetics, Ethics, and Parenthood.* New York: Pilgrim, 1983.

Lubs, Herbert A., and Felix de la Cruz. *Genetic Counseling*. New York: Raven Press, 1977.

Milunsky, Aubrey. *The Prevention of Genetic Disease and Mental Retardation*. Philadelphia: W.B. Saunders, 1975.

Ramsey, Paul. *Fabricated Man: The Ethics of Genetic Control*. New Haven: Yale University Press, 1970.

Smith, George P. III. *Genetics, Ethics, and the Law*. New York: Associated Faculty Press, 1981.

CHAPTER 14

Business Ethics

Objectives

After you have read this chapter you should be able to

1. Understand what business ethics is and why there is a need for education and training in this area.
2. Understand how rights, obligations, justice, truth telling, and honesty apply specifically to business ethics.
3. Understand the rights and obligations that exist between employers and employees and between businesses and consumers.
4. Understand some of the ethical issues in the areas of advertising, business and the environment, affirmative action, reverse discrimination, and sexual harassment.

Introduction

Business ethics, like bioethics, is a specialized area in which an awareness of ethical issues and a systematic approach to solving them are particularly important. Like other areas of ethics, business ethics has to do with the establishment and maintenance of vital and significant relationships among human beings—specifically, in this case, among employers, employees, businesses, and consumers. As in other areas, ethical principles, such as the five I have argued for—the valuing of life, the striving for goodness and avoiding of badness, the just and fair distributing of good and bad, honesty and truth telling, and individual freedom—apply to business ethics.

The main difference between business ethics and bioethics is that the specific issues, problems, and situations that arise often require a different application of the principles, although the general applications are roughly the same. There is a difference, for example, between a patient signing an informed consent and a builder signing a contract to build a house for a client. In the first situation, the doctor needs the patient's consent so that the patient can undergo some sort of procedure necessary for his or her health and well-being. In the second situation, a business person with specialized knowledge and abilities agrees to provide a client with something he or she wants, and the client, in turn, agrees to pay the builder a certain amount for doing this. The two situations are similar in that the "contracts" in both cases are an expression of trust, honesty, and mutual agreement executed for the benefit of both parties, but they differ in the specific ways in which ethics is applied.

Rights and Obligations in Business

First of all, by "rights" I mean those things to which human beings are entitled by law, morality, or tradition, such as "the right to life" or "the right to be free." By "obligations" I mean some sort of responsibility or duty that people have toward one another—also accorded by law, morality, or tradition—to see that their rights are protected and accorded them. I have discussed rights before in dealing with other areas of morality, such as allowing someone to die, suicide, and abortion. I also expressed my conclusion that no rights are absolute—that is, no right is so important that it *always* supersedes all others. All human beings, for example, have a right to life, rights over their own bodies and lives, and also rights to be free, but none of these rights is ever absolute; indeed, they often conflict with one another. Conflicts of rights are not ethically resolved, however, by declaring certain rights to be absolute; rather, these conflicts are resolved by trying to establish some sort of priority system, some prima facie rights, and adjusting those rights to each other with reasonable justification and with regard to the attendant circumstances.

Just as the basic rights—the rights to life, justice, honesty and truth telling, and freedom—apply to life in general, so they apply in business. However, there are also specific rights or specific applications of the general rights listed above. These rights are the right to have one's own life protected whether one is an employer, an employee, or a consumer; the right to have the opportunity to pursue and qualify oneself for employment without hindrance; the right to establish a business, own property, employ whom you want, and make a profit; the right to expect agreements and contracts to be executed fairly, whether between employers and employees, businesses and other businesses, business and government, or business and consumers; the right to fairness, honesty, and truth telling at all levels of business dealings; the right to employment security; the right of businesses to try to get consumers to use their products and services and the right of consumers to choose which products and services they wish to buy.

As far as obligations in business are concerned, participants in business activities are obligated to be honest and tell the truth; be fair and just in dealing with others; be honest and trustworthy in executing and carrying out agreements and contracts; pay off debts, including interest on money loaned, in a manner agreeable to all parties; create a safe atmosphere for employees to work in; give the effort and perform the work for which wages are being paid; and, finally, be loyal to employers, employees, and customers within reasonable and ethical limits.

◆————————————————————————————————————

Two Ways of Approaching Rights and Obligations in Business

There are two highly divergent ways to approach the issues of rights and obligations in business, one of which emphasizes competition, and the other of which emphasizes government control.

The Competitive Approach

The aggressively competitive approach is referred to by a number of names: free enterprise, laissez-faire, survival of the fittest, and, by some, the "dog-eat-dog" approach. Supporters of this approach believe that the main obligation in business and in life in general is to "make a buck," that is, to establish and maintain a business without hindrance from the government at any level. The point—whether we are talking about management, labor, or consumers—is to get as large a share as possible of the profits to be made in business, using any method one can. According to this position, the best approach for a local or national economy to take is that of laissez-faire (meaning "let people do what they want"), free enterprise, and competition. The theory behind this approach is that existing economic problems will be solved if all participants in business are completely free to compete as aggressively as they can. If there's a demand for certain goods, then businesses that can convince consumers that they can supply those goods at the best quality and the lowest prices should be free to compete with other businesses. In this way, everyone who can survive will profit—successful businesses, governments, and consumers.

If small businesses or new businesses can't survive the competition, then they will be eliminated from it, just as the weaker animals in the jungle are killed by those that are stronger. On the other hand, if businesses can make themselves larger and more secure by subsuming or destroying smaller businesses, this is an acceptable part of the competition process. The goal of any state or nation, from this viewpoint, is to allow individuals to compete aggressively with each other for wealth and power because consumers can only benefit from this process, receiving the best products and services at the lowest cost.

Proponents of this position see this as the most meaningful and, in some cases, the only possible position for a free, democratic society to hold. They feel that whenever state and government controls are levied, power becomes centered in government, which tends to feed itself at the expense of individuals, both in business and in society in general.

The Government Control Approach

This approach argues for state or government ownership and control of all business enterprises in the name of and for the good of the people. Laissez-faire may sound good, proponents of this position state, but it often puts power and affluence in the hands of a few aggressive people at the expense of the many. Furthermore, wealth is kept in the same hands as families that own big businesses continue to pass them on to their children and grandchildren.

The competitive approach also brings out the most animalistic aspects of human beings, dehumanizing them both because it glorifies the "might makes right—survival of the fittest" jungle ethic, and also because it consigns the have-nots to poverty and hopelessness. It's all well and good to speak of seeing everyone profit from free enterprise, but in fact only a few do. These people use their control of the supply of goods to control the demand for the goods or to satisfy the demand at higher profit to themselves—often offering less quality in the bargain. Furthermore, if small, independent businesses can't and don't survive, then everyone who isn't in control of power becomes a slave to those who are. In other words, what all of this adds up to, according to this view, is that good and bad are distributed unjustly in a laissez-faire society, with the haves getting all of the good while the have-nots get all of the bad.

The only ethical and fair way for business to be conducted, according to this view, is to put it in the hands of the government, which will then operate it for the good of all concerned. In this way, no one individual or group of individuals has control over power and affluence to the detriment of others. Everyone in such a system works for the good of all, and a just distribution of good and bad is made by a central governing body representing all of the people.

Some of the good is distributed equally; some according to merit; and some by need and ability (see the discussion of these and other methods in Chapters 6 and 7). In this view, everyone will share—at least with some equality—both the bad and the good emanating from the society's business dealings. For example, if the main business of a country is agriculture and agriculture has a good year, then everyone shares equally in the food distribution and the profits. On the other hand, if it has a bad year, then everyone shares equally in the lack of food and the losses. This is the only fair way. Furthermore, by not stressing aggressiveness and competition and by giving everyone a fair and equitable living that is free from poverty and hardship, more time can be spent on civilizing and humanizing the people.

◆————————————————————————————————————

The Moderate Position

The Moderate Position on Business Ethics

It is difficult to characterize accurately a "moderate position" because unlike extreme positions, moderate ones are spread all along the spectrum between the two extremes. Nevertheless, I will present some generalities that I feel are somewhat characteristic of a moderate view. Both extreme positions have strong points to make and, of course, imply or put forth criticisms of each other. It is important to remember, however, that the system that will work best for a society depends on a great number of factors; it is not just a theoretical matter.

Both extreme positions, and variations or combinations thereof, have had failures and successes in many different societies throughout history. If, for example, a government and its leaders are benevolent and ethical, government control of business activities may work well. There is always a problem, of course, of corruption in government, and there is also a problem when governments change and the new one is not benevolent or ethical enough to make a government control system work.

On the other hand, if individuals in business are fair, honest, and otherwise ethical toward one another and toward their employees and consumers, then free enterprise can work also. The danger here, as supporters of government control are quick to point out, is that power and affluence can land in the hands of the few, and they, too, can be uncaring and corrupt in their treatment of others. If profit becomes the main or only goal for business, then it becomes easy to leave humaneness behind.

Generally, however, the moderate position would encourage free enterprise and honest competition, with some controls exerted by employee groups (for example, unions), by consumer groups, and by government where necessary. For example, there might be laws regulating the absorbing of small businesses

411

into larger ones or the merging of larger ones to prevent the accumulation of too much power in the hands of a few to the detriment of society in general.

On the other hand, government should not establish controls on private businesses except to protect society from dangers that businesses themselves refuse to prevent. In short, freedom should be allowed, but not unlimited freedom. This position would also encourage the development of employee groups to protect workers' rights in employer-employee relationships and the establishment of consumer groups to protect customers from false advertising, risky or dangerous products, and unfair business practices.

What the moderate position advocates is a system of checks and balances to ensure that people have as much freedom in their business dealings as possible while remaining protected from corrupt, unethical, and destructive practices. It goes without saying that the more that businesses, employee groups, and consumer groups monitor and control their own activities from an ethical standpoint, the less government control will be needed.

The moderate position also maintains that both extremes are based on false assumptions. It is not true, for example, that a democratic society can exist only if completely free enterprise is allowed; there are many societies that are largely democratic but that nevertheless maintain some government and private control of business activities. Neither is it true, however, that the only way to achieve equality and protection for everyone is to allow the government to control business "for the good of everyone." The moderate position tends to try to combine the advantages of both of these extremes while eliminating their disadvantages.

---◆

Justice, Truth Telling, and Honesty in Business

Justice

Justice has already been discussed generally in Chapters 6 and 7; however, it is important to examine exactly how this principle applies to business activities. Three types of justice are of concern in business.

Exchange Justice. Exchange justice[1] involves reimbursement for services rendered or products made or sold. For example, if an object costs ten dollars and I agree to purchase it for that price, then I owe the business person from whom I bought it ten dollars. In another example, if I agree to erect a satisfactory carport for eighteen hundred dollars and I keep my end of the bargain, then I'm entitled to eighteen hundred dollars. Similarly, if I agree to pay employees ten dollars an hour each for doing a particular job and they do it for eight hours, then I owe them eighty dollars each. All of these examples demonstrate an exact and just "exchange" of goods or services for some kind of payment.

Distributive Justice. This type of justice has also already been defined, described, and discussed in a general way in Chapters 6 and 7. When applied specifically to business, however, it has to do with the distribution of profit among owners, managers, employees, and shareholders. Distributive justice raises questions concerning what portion of the gross profit made in any business endeavor should be distributed among all concerned (by means, for example, of higher wages, bonuses, and fringe benefits for employees and managers; greater dividends to shareholders; greater profits to owners).

Social Justice. Social justice is concerned with how businesses and their members should treat consumers and members of society in general. For example, the extent to which business should be willing to protect the public against pollution and other dangers to their property, well-being, and lives is a question of social justice.

Truth Telling

Truth telling, which has been discussed in general in Chapters 7 and 11 and in relation to bioethics in Chapter 13, applies to business in a number of ways. These are telling the truth in agreeing to render and pay for services and products; not lying in employer-employee relations; not lying to shareholders about the status of the business; and telling the truth in advertising.

Truth in advertising is a large area of concern in the business world because it involves consumers and, by extension, society as a whole. It is business's obligation to consumers not to lie to them and also not to mislead them through the omission of important facts. For example, car manufacturers may advertise that you only need to change oil every six thousand miles, but they neglect to tell you that you will have greater need of repairs than if you changed it every two thousand miles. Although this is not a direct lie, it does mislead consumers through the omission of important facts.

Honesty

Honesty applies to business in the following ways: keeping agreements and contracts, whether oral or written; admitting errors that have been made in creating products, especially when safety is involved, and correcting those errors wherever possible; giving an honest day's work for pay received; giving appropriate wages for work performed; setting honest prices that allow for a reasonable but not exorbitant profit; giving the best quality for the price that one can, especially when people's health and lives could be endangered; and, finally, constantly inspecting business practices at all levels to ensure that dishonesty and corruption are both discovered and eliminated.

———————————————————————————————◆

Ethical Issues in Business

As in the area of bioethics, there are many moral issues in business ethics that might be discussed; however, I will concentrate on three areas: advertising; business and the environment; affirmative action, reverse discrimination, and sexual harassment.

Advertising

A large and important part of any business is advertising, for this is the means by which products, services, employees, and the business itself are presented to the public as favorably as possible. As mentioned earlier, advertising is an important area for the application of truth telling and honesty because advertising plays such a large part in our lives at all levels. Surely there is hardly any aspect of our society that does not use advertising to some degree. The government, charities, and even races and religions advertise to try to get the public "to buy the product." There are two major approaches to advertising: one states that anything goes as a means to sell products and services, and the other states that advertising should always be honestly presented and properly supported by facts and evidence.

The Anything-Goes Approach. The anything-goes view, which is held by many businesses, states that because advertising does not force anyone to do anything, it is the responsibility of consumers and competitors to be on their guard about the claims made for specific products and services. It is assumed by those who hold this approach that most people will not check claims made in advertising, such as that one serving of a breakfast cereal will provide you with all the vitamins you need for the day.

One argument used in support of this approach is that in most advertising, very little harm is done by making somewhat extravagant claims for a product. False advertising endangers no one; it's just part of the "business game," and the stimulation of the economy provided by advertising is good for business, the economy, and, in the long run, for society in general. In a highly competitive society, the important thing is to out-advertise one's competitors to create a more successful business by inducing consumers to buy one's product whether they need to or not. Consumers have minds of their own, the argument runs, and it is their responsibility to choose wisely among the products and services that are offered.

The Truthful Approach. The other view of advertising held by some business people, as well as by consumers, consumer groups, and the government, is that any claims made by any business concerning its products or services ought to be supported or backed up by facts and evidence. According to this approach, businesses have a right to advertise freely but not to lie to the public about their products or services. The argument given by the anything-goes view that there's no harm done as long as life isn't threatened is highly questionable because any constant lying or dishonesty breaks down significant communication, erodes the trust and faith humans have in one another, and breaks down human relationships. Because lying and misrepresentation in advertising contribute to this breakdown, they harm business specifically and society in general.

Some questions raised by this approach are what actually constitutes lying and misrepresentation, and what guidelines can be presented for establishing ethically proper advertising. First, no unsafe product or service should be advertised as safe. Of course, products or services that purport to be safe but aren't should not even be put on the market until they are made safe, especially because some consumers will assume in good faith that they are. This is not to say that no product or service that might be dangerous can't be advertised and sold. For example, most people know that knives, guns, and scuba-diving gear are potentially dangerous; this doesn't mean, however, that they shouldn't be advertised.

Sometimes, in the case of some products and services, warnings about their use or misuse can be given. People certainly know that all automobiles can be dangerous if they are misused, but there is a difference between this kind of danger and the kind generated by an automobile whose brakes are likely to fail or whose gas tank might explode in any collision. Such products or services should not be advertised or sold as safe until they are made so. There can, of course, be safety problems that were not foreseen by businesses; in such cases, it is the obligation of the business concerned to warn the public immediately and recall the product or service for repairs or changes that will make it safe.

Second, businesses should not, according to this view, make claims about their products and services that are not true or that are exaggerated or only half true. It's all right to claim that a beauty soap softens and moisturizes skin and even that it enhances skin beauty if indeed it does these things, but it would be dishonest to say that it removes wrinkles if it doesn't. It is also dishonest to make the claim that a product is used or endorsed by medical doctors or scientists, for example, if it really isn't. In fact, it's even questionable to have people in white coats acting as if they are laboratory scientists or doctors when they are not.

Third, all claims and guarantees about a product's or service's nature, effects, and uses should be completely true and should be supported by evidence. This evidence, furthermore, ought to be readily available to the public. Finally, no one who works in advertising or public relations should be required to make untrue claims about products or services.

Business and the Environment

One of the most compelling problems that has arisen in business ethics in our century concerns the depleting of natural resources through careless overuse and the destruction of the environment. Although people in business should not have to bear total responsibility for these problems, they must certainly accept a large share of it. In fact, now that these problems are so serious, businesses are truly blameworthy if they fight against viable solutions and don't do what they can to alleviate problems that are either already present or that soon will be. As in other problem situations we have discussed, this one provokes two extreme views.

The Primacy of Business. According to this position, it is not business's fault that there are environmental problems; business has always striven simply to give consumers what they want. The ethical responsibility of business begins and ends with business dealings, and it cannot be held responsible for the problems that occur in nature and society. This view also holds that the interference of "nature-loving do-gooders" and government will destroy business, our economy, and finally society itself. If not interfered with, science and business will find a way to solve the environmental problems in time.

Business has always operated in good faith, and those bad results suffered by employees, the public, and the environment were not intended or foreseen. Moreover, now that they have occurred, business shouldn't have to bear the total responsibility for these health and environmental problems. The solutions to environmental problems that have been proposed by nature groups and the government are extremely expensive, and businesses should not have to pay for them out of their profits; furthermore, they should have as long a time as they need to make necessary changes, if indeed they must be made at all.

The Primacy of the Environment. According to the primacy of the environment view, we have been on such a rampage of rape, gluttony, and waste where natural resources and the environment are concerned that the only solution is to immediately stop any business practices and activities that are adversely affecting health and the environment. Business, according to the environmentalists, must take the major blame for environmental waste and destruction; therefore, it must use its profits to reverse the damage it has wrought. Furthermore, business—through advertising—has helped to foster the consume-at-all-costs mentality that has been a major factor in creating these problems in the environment. Therefore, it must now attempt to reeducate the public in any way possible, even if this means some loss of profit.

Because business has ignored its responsibilities, government should immediately step into the breach, using fines, imprisonment, withholding of govern-

416

ment contracts, and even business shutdowns to force business to repair the damage it has done. A massive reeducation of business people and the public must be conducted by the government in order to save our environment. Even if businesses are destroyed and the economy is hurt, these actions must be forced on business in order to change our present situation before it becomes irreversible.

The Moderate Position on Business and the Environment. Business isn't totally to blame, say the moderates, for the destruction of the environment; rather, both the government and society in general share the blame for waste and destruction. However, none of us—business included—can now afford to ignore the situation; we must all work toward turning it around and conserving what remains of the environment. Business must change its advertising techniques—which encourage a consumer society—stop all sorts of pollution, and adjust its methods so that it works in harmony with the environment.

All of this must be accomplished within a period of time considered reasonable by both business and the environmentalists, and business must pay its fair share of the financial burden out of its profits. Consumers—through both taxes and higher prices, as businesses pass *some* of the share of the cost for environmental protection on to the public—must also pay a fair share of the costs.

Neither side should try to profit financially from the situation or to escape from paying its fair share. Constant vigilance concerning environmental protection should be maintained by businesses themselves, by the government, and by consumer groups. All of us—business included—must recognize that we have an ethical obligation to protect human beings and the environment, both of which are more important in the long run than power or affluence.

Affirmative Action and Reverse Discrimination

Another serious problem in our society that relates to business practices is discrimination in the hiring, promotion, and firing of employees. Those generally discriminated against in these areas have been ethnic and religious minorities, women, the handicapped, and the aged. It's common knowledge that prejudice and discrimination against Jews, African Americans, Hispanics, Asian Americans, Native Americans, other minority groups, and women have been going on for hundreds of years. For this reason, I don't feel it is necessary to describe the problems in detail. Instead, I would like to deal with the methods that have been used to solve these problems and also some of the negative effects caused by these methods.

Definition of Terms. Literally, *prejudice* means the prejudgment of someone or something without ever having encountered this person or thing. Prejudice is often based on biased opinions one has been taught, has heard, or has read.

417

Discrimination, as the term will be used here, means to differentiate among people in a prejudiced way in hiring, promoting, or firing them. This does not mean that there is anything wrong with "discriminating" among people in choosing your friends. Nor is there anything wrong with "discriminating" between two well-qualified applicants in an attempt to choose the best person for the job. There is, however, a problem when that discrimination is based on people's race, religion, sex, sexual preference, or age rather than on their qualifications for a job or promotion.

Affirmative action is a term that describes the process of trying to avoid future discrimination in employment practices and of actively trying to correct the problems arising from hundreds of years of past discrimination. *Reverse discrimination* is a term that describes the plight of some, primarily white men, who have in turn been discriminated against when affirmative action programs have been instituted. Reverse discrimination would occur, for example, if a company hired an African American man or woman who was less qualified than a white person mainly because of the person's race or sex. Here again, as in other problem areas, there are two extreme points of view.

The Argument for Discrimination. According to the argument for discrimination, a business's employment practices are its own affair. If employers want to hire white men, then they have a right to do so without interference because they own these businesses. Furthermore, even if one accepts that there has been discrimination in the past, this is seldom the fault of present employers; therefore, they should not have to correct deficiencies they didn't cause. And even if the employers themselves were guilty of past discrimination, they shouldn't be forced to hire those discriminated against to rectify their former errors. In any case, employers definitely should not have to hire less qualified people just to "integrate" their businesses, nor should they be responsible for giving additional training to people who are unqualified because of past discrimination.

Also, the argument continues, discriminatory practices did not occur only in business; they occurred everywhere. Therefore, there is no reason why businesses should have to make reparations for a practice that was generally accepted only a few years ago. Now that discrimination in general has been alleviated, people who were formerly discriminated against will have the opportunity to become more qualified. At this point, business can begin to hire them. But it's not fair to prevent employers from hiring the employees they prefer just because these people are not minority group members. And it's not fair to ask white or male employees to pay for a problem they never participated in or caused.

The Argument Against Discrimination. Discrimination in employment practices is one of the most insidious kind because those who have been discriminated against need better jobs and a steady income if they are to advance themselves. Our own generation may not have practiced discrimination—although it's highly questionable that we haven't—but our forebears did; therefore, we, as fellow human beings and good citizens, owe the victims of discrimination some sort of recompense for the immoral actions committed against them. Every effort must be made immediately to put affirmative action into effect. When employees retire, resign, or are fired, they should be replaced—at all levels, including management—by members of those groups that have been discriminated against.

According to this view, quotas, goals, and timetables for affirmative action must be established and adhered to. Training programs must be established for employees who have been discriminated against in the past, and in some cases less qualified applicants may have to be hired or promoted in order to accomplish affirmative action. Reverse discrimination may result from such actions— and this is deplorable—but it is necessary in order to right the wrongs of all of the past years. The government should mandate affirmative action employment practices and enforce them fully in all businesses by withholding government contracts and funding, and imposing fines and prison sentences where necessary.

The Moderate Position on Discrimination. According to the moderate position, discrimination is a complex, controversial problem that must be resolved as equitably as possible. Both extreme positions have strong and valid points to make, but they do go too far. There is no doubt, for example, that affirmative action must be taken at all levels of business in order to right the long-standing wrongs that have been caused by terrible discriminatory practices over the past several hundred years. Employers should have the freedom to hire and promote the best-qualified employees; however, they also have a moral obligation at all levels of society to halt the immoral discriminatory employment practices of the past. They should try to do this equitably, avoiding reverse discrimination wherever they can, but this shouldn't mean that they have to hire or promote unqualified or less qualified people.

Government, as a representative of all members of society, certainly has an obligation to mandate affirmative action and to attempt to enforce it. It should, however, encourage businesses to set up their own viable programs on a voluntary basis. Government has the right to make fair employment practices a qualification for receiving government contracts or funding. However, some of the more stringent measures for obtaining business's compliance—for example, fines and imprisonments—should be used only as a last resort.

No one person has an inalienable right to a job in any business, nor does any employer have the obligation to hire or promote any and all persons who apply for employment or who desire promotion. However, employers are obligated to see that equal opportunities exist for all people, regardless of race, religion, sex, handicaps, or age (within reason—one need not hire a ten-year-old, for example), to apply and be seriously considered for jobs in their businesses.

Reverse discrimination can be avoided for the most part if less qualified people belonging to groups that have been discriminated against are not hired over more qualified people from the majority group. Reverse discrimination can also be avoided by setting up training programs for people from minority groups that can also include white men who lack qualifications. All trainees should be informed that the training must be accomplished satisfactorily, after which full consideration for employment will be given. Sustaining salaries for trainees should be financed partly by businesses and partly by government through public taxation; in this way, everyone pays his or her fair share.

In cases where reverse discrimination is difficult to avoid, each case must be decided on an individual basis to achieve as fair a decision as is possible. However, when applicants or employees are equally well qualified for jobs and promotions, efforts must be made to hire or promote people from groups that have been discriminated against in the past.

Sexual Harassment

One of the most significant and controversial topics today is sexual harassment, a problem that has existed for a long time but which only recently has come to light as being unethical. A recent survey conducted by Louis Harris and Associates for the American Association of University Women (AAUW) revealed that sexual harassment at school is an experience common to the vast majority of public school students in the eighth to eleventh grades. The survey discovered that four in five students (81%) have been sexually harassed at some time in their school life and that the majority of both boys (76%) and girls (85%) have been harassed at school.[2] My main emphasis in this chapter is to discuss sexual harassment in the workplace, but if it goes on as early as junior high school for most boys and girls and has for the most part been ignored by school officials, one can only imagine what happens when these same children, both harassers and harassed, grow up and enter the workplace.

Definition of Terms

According to federal law—Equal Employment Opportunity Commission (EEOC)—and, for example, California's Departments of Fair Employment and Housing, sexual harassment is defined as "unwanted sexual advances, or visual, verbal, or physical conduct of a sexual nature." This includes many forms of offensive behavior and includes gender-based harassment of a person of the same sex as the harasser. The following is a partial list of actions deemed as sexual harassment: unwanted sexual advances; offering employment benefits in exchange for sexual favors; making or threatening reprisals after a negative response to sexual advances; visual conduct such as leering, making sexual gestures, displaying of sexually suggestive objects or pictures, cartoons or posters; verbal conduct such as making or using derogatory comments, epithets, slurs, and jokes; verbal sexual advances or propositions; verbal abuse of a sexual nature; graphic verbal commentaries about an individual's body; sexually degrading words used to describe an individual; suggestive or obscene letters, notes, or invitations; and physical conduct such as touching, assaulting, impeding, or blocking movements.[3]

What Constitutes Sexual Harassment Under Federal Law

Under federal law, unwelcome sexual advances, requests for sexual favors, and other verbal or physical conduct of a sexual nature constitute sexual harassment in any of the following circumstances:

1. When submission to such conduct is made either explicitly or implicitly a term or condition of an individual's employment.

2. When submission to or rejection of such conduct by an individual is used as the basis for employment decisions affecting such individual.

3. When such conduct has the purpose or effect of unreasonably interfering with an individual's work performance or creating an intimidating, hostile, or offensive working environment.[4]

Arguments That Sexual Harassment Is Not Immoral

Sexual harassment has gone on so long that many people think that it's just the way things are—the "boys will be boys" attitude. This attitude also implies a double standard for men and women, even though sexual harassment also applies to women who harass men and same sex harassment in the workplace. Many employers and employees, mainly men, see nothing wrong with the kinds of actions and language that sexual harassment includes and would present several arguments to allow them.

Enlivening the Workplace. Many sexual harassers feel that jokes, comments, sexual "compliments," and other actions or language are ways of enlivening an otherwise boring work situation and atmosphere. Such comments or actions are nothing more than clever repartee or ways of "having fun at the office." No one should get upset at such activities but should instead take them with a grain of salt because they are all in fun. After all, men (mostly) and women have done or said these things for years now. Why should anyone get so worked up over them now?

Women and Men Are Naturally Sexually Attracted to One Another. It's simply natural that men and women are sexually attracted to one another (the same may be true for attractions to the same sex), and so it's also natural that this sexual attraction would not cease merely because people are together at work as well as

421

outside of working hours. Therefore, it should be acceptable for people to express this sexual or romantic attraction at work as well as other places. The recipients of such expression should take it as a compliment, not as harassment, and should not feel threatened by it.

Positions of Power Imply Certain Rights. People who have power in the workplace ought to be free to use that power any way they see fit, especially when dealing with employees, as long as the latter make good salaries and have good jobs. Such employees ought to be willing to acquiesce gratefully when their bosses or others in power request dates, make sexual advances, or even initiate romantic or sexual affairs. Certainly a positive response is not a condition of employment; rather, these advances are like expense accounts—everyone pads expense accounts and everyone who wants to stay employed and get ahead participates in romantic interludes. If people don't want to accept the conditions of people who have power over them, then they should look for employment elsewhere or not expect to be promoted or retained where they are.

Those Being Harassed Often Ask for or Cause Harassment. People in the workplace, especially women, often ask for flirtatious jokes and sexual advances by their attitudes (flirtatious and sexy), the clothes they wear, and their desire to please employers and supervisors and get ahead in the business.

The conclusion of all of these arguments is that employees, especially women employees, make way too much out of common, everyday acts of humor and fun, and that laws governing sexual harassment are ridiculous and put employers and supervisors in unnecessarily delicate and litigious situations for actions and words that are trivial and harmless.

Arguments That Sexual Harassment Is Immoral

The bases for all the arguments that sexual harassment is immoral are that all people deserve to be treated with respect, dignity, and humaneness everywhere, which definitely includes the workplace. Sexual harassment denies individuals all of these rights and often makes their lives in and out of the workplace difficult, humiliating, and terrifying.

Unfairness of Treatment. Basically it is unfair to hire, promote, retain, or fire people on the basis of their willingness to give or receive sexual favors. People should be judged on their intelligence, abilities, conscientiousness, and cooperation, not on whether they are sexually attractive or well endowed or willing to get involved romantically or sexually with their supervisors. Because these latter attributes or attitudes are not and should not be requirements for doing a good job, people should not be judged on them or discriminated against because they do or do not display them.

Creation of a Hostile or Offensive Working Environment. Rather than enlivening the workplace, sexual harassment can create a very hostile, unpleasant, and offensive environment in which it can be extremely difficult for people to get their work done. If people are constantly worried about being bumped, squeezed, or pinched or receiving other unwanted physical or verbal advances, then valuable time and effort that could be spent doing their jobs is wasted in fending off such advances. Such words and actions also are both physically and emotionally upsetting and destructive to those who are forced to endure them. This destructiveness does not occur only while people are at work but also when they are not working; it may adversely affect their personal life as well as their public life.

Positions of Authority Do Not Imply Power over Personal Lives. It is certainly true that people in positions of authority in a business have supervisory and management control over what goes on in the business and therefore over what the people working for them do and how they do it. However, in no way does this control extend to employees' personal lives when they are not at work, especially not to requiring them to accept dates or sexual advances. This latter type of control is an abuse of power and authority and is therefore unacceptable according to all principles of business ethics. Managers or supervisors engaging in these activities are misusing their authority and should be removed from their positions.

Attraction Does Not Imply Involvement. It is true that people are often romantically and sexually attracted to each other, but such attraction does not imply coercion of or involvement with others, especially when those others do not wish to be involved. If people who work together are attracted to each other, then they must do everything to keep such activities that result from the attraction out of the workplace entirely, and people should be very careful about getting involved with anyone with whom they work. Sometimes such involvements work well, but other times after a breakup occurs, life on the job can be miserable. The best advice is probably to avoid getting involved with anyone at work. At any rate, even if people are attracted to others with whom they work, they should not use this attraction in any way to sexually harass those others.

Harassees Often "Ask for It." This argument is often used by rapists when denying they have done anything wrong to their victims. Even if people wear sexually attractive clothing or flirt and laugh at dirty jokes, they are not asking to be sexually harassed. For example, just because a woman wears low-cut dresses or short skirts or is physically well endowed or attractive does not mean that anyone has the right to sexually harass her, especially when she makes it clear that she resents the harassment. One may not assume anything from her appearance and certainly must not manifest any sexual harassment in the workplace. If people feel that they would like to ask others for a date, then they should contact them off duty, but keep all of this outside the workplace. And, of course, if the person contacted does not wish to date, that should be the end of it and not a matter for pressure or coercion at work.

◆

Cases for Study and Discussion

C A S E ◆ 1

Susan, a design engineer in a major auto company, receives two reports concerning engine fires and explosions that occurred in hot weather in the company's popular economy car. At the time the engine of this model had been approved and released for production, she had advised the plant that she felt the carburetor and gas lines were constructed so that under excessive heat conditions there could be a gas leak. At that time, she had argued for a modification that would have added about fifty dollars to the cost of producing each engine, but her proposal had been turned down. She had continued to argue for the modification and for special testing, but the standard tests performed on the car did not indicate any danger, and she was told to drop the issue.

Upon receiving the two reports, however, Susan again presses for special testing under excessive heat conditions and urges the company to warn the public and immediately recall all of the cars of this model. By this time, however, such a recall will probably cost the company between $500,000 and $1 million, and Susan is again told to mind her own business or she will be fired.

In the meantime, four more reports of engine fires come in from a desert area in the southwest. The engineer is now convinced she is right. What should she do? To what extent does she owe loyalty to the company, where she has worked for fifteen years and has been promoted several times, and to what extent is she obligated to let the public know the truth? Because the company is taking the responsibility off the engineer, should she do something about what she knows, or should she just drop the problem? Considering that the company may lose up to $1 million, what are its obligations? What do you think of the way it has handled the entire situation?

C A S E ◆ 2

The cost of living in Alderdale, California, has gone up 10 percent during the year, and Steve's union has been negotiating with the management of the plant where he works for a 15 percent raise to cover the present cost of living plus an additional expected increase. The plant, however, has not had a good year, and management and the union decide on an 8 percent raise, which a majority of the members, not including Steve, agrees to. Steve decides that because he has been shorted 2 to 7 percent of his raise money, he will try to make up for it by taking some expensive tools, small pieces of equipment, and supplies home from the plant in order to remodel his workshop at home. He was planning to do this remodeling with some of the raise money anyway, and he feels he was cheated out of this money unfairly because he didn't vote for the raise that was accepted by the union.

Is Steve justified in his actions? Why or why not? Does management have any obligation to meet the cost of living? Because Steve voted against the smaller raise, is he under any obligation to accept it? Why or why not? Is he justified in making up the difference between the raise he got and the cost of living by taking things from the plant? Why or why not?

CASE ♦ 3

Mike, who is very knowledgeable about stereo components, knows that there are two models made by the Ozato Company: the OC 4000, which sells for two thousand dollars, and the OC 5000, which sells for three thousand. The difference between the two models is that the OC 5000 has a larger, more powerful amplifier-receiver and larger speakers. Because of this difference, Mike buys the more expensive model. A few weeks later, a loose connection causes him to examine the left speaker, and when he takes it apart he discovers that while the right speaker is the one designated for the OC 5000, the left speaker is the one designated for the OC 4000. Several of his friends also have the more expensive model, and when he examines those speakers he finds the same situation. To save money, the company has evidently put one more expensive and one less expensive speaker together in each of the expensive models, figuring that the difference in sound might not be very noticeable.

Given that the less expensive speaker was almost the same quality as the more expensive one, was the company right or wrong in making the substitution? Why? What should the company now do about customers who have already bought the OC 5000? Why? Suppose the difference between the two speakers was so minimal that no one ever discovered the switch—would the company then be justified in having made the switch? Why or why not? Suppose the company offers to replace the less expensive speakers of Mike and his friends with OC 5000s and also offers Mike an additional thousand dollars' worth of stereo equipment if he promises not to say anything more about the switch? What should Mike do in these circumstances? Why?

CASE ♦ 4

Myra, thirty, is an up-and-coming executive in a large public relations and advertising firm, and she is very close to a big promotion. She is given the assignment by her boss of creating an advertising campaign for the popular economy car described in Case 1. Her assignment is to try to make up for some of the bad press the company has been getting because of the six engine explosions that have occurred. Because she is a well-informed person, she knows about the explosions and tells her boss that she doesn't think their firm ought to take the account, and, in any case, she can't in good conscience handle the account unless the car company makes the car safe.

Her boss argues that this is the single biggest account that their firm has ever had, and what the auto manufacturer does or doesn't do is not their firm's responsibility; their job is strictly to advertise and promote products and services. He also tells her that if she refuses the account, the promotion she is up for will go to someone else, and he further implies that she may lose her job. What should Myra do, and why? Do you believe her boss's description of his firm's responsibilities is right or wrong? Why? Do you think he is right in denying Myra her promotion and/or firing her for refusing to handle the account? Why or why not? In this instance, to whom should Myra be loyal—the public? her firm and clients? herself? Explain your answer.

C A S E ◆ 5

Denise, twenty-two, an African American woman, and Bonnie, twenty-three, a Caucasian woman, are the two top applicants for a computer technician job in a major data-processing center. The center has about 10 percent minority employees and about 30 percent female employees. Both women seem to be equally well qualified except that Bonnie is both prettier and more outgoing than Denise. This particular job doesn't require the person who fills it to meet the public very much, but it is a large office in which almost everyone is Caucasian and in which relations among employees are particularly important because of the constant pressures of the job. If you were the personnel manager, whom would you pick for the job? Why? What should this person's criteria for employee selection be, and in what order of importance should these criteria be placed? Why? To what extent should the personnel manager be concerned about affirmative action or reverse discrimination in this situation?

C A S E ◆ 6

The town of Farling, Texas, was almost a ghost town when the Kem Chemical Company decided to establish one of its plants there ten years ago. Because it moved in, the town has grown tremendously, and most people in the town now work at the plant. The only problem is that the chemical waste that the plant emits is gradually polluting the air, the earth, and the water near the town. The company and the town's mayor have both been informed by the government that this pollution must be eliminated as soon as possible. The plant manager tells the mayor that in order to satisfy the government requirements, the company will have to spend about $1.5 million. If this has to be done right away, he says, the company has decided to close this particular plant rather than sink that much money into making the changes. The plant manager also tells the mayor that they can probably stall the government for two years by paying relatively small fines, which the company is willing to do. This will allow the company to spread out the expenses for converting the plant over a longer period and will permit the company to keep the plant open. During this period, of course, the pollution would continue, endangering—according to the government report— the land, water, air, and, of course, animals, plants, and human beings.

If the mayor works with the company, he can help them avoid making immediate changes. If he doesn't, Farling will again become a ghost town and most of its people will lose their jobs. What should the mayor do and why? Was the government right in investigating and reporting as it did? Why or why not? Do you feel that the company is doing the right thing in relation to the government, the town, and its mayor? Why or why not? Is the company obligated to spend some of its profits in order to save its plant and the town? Explore the alternatives and suggest some possible compromises. Assuming that no compromises will work and the mayor has to make his choice, what should he do?

C A S E ♦ 7

In an actual case in the Long Beach, California, Police Department, two female police officers were treated so badly that they sued the City of Long Beach and were awarded over one million dollars each for sexual harassment. In the first case, one of the women was having an affair with a higher ranking male police officer (a sergeant) after he told her he was divorcing his wife. When she found out he was lying about his divorce and many other things, she broke off the affair and embarrassed him every time he later made advances. Not only did he use his rank to see that she was treated badly by the whole department, but when she called for backup on a call involving a violent suspect, none of the officers available (and there were several) responded to her call because they sided with him rather than her, thus placing her life at risk. Several times he made it quite clear that he wanted to continue the affair, and when she refused, he told her her job and life would be miserable because she wouldn't cooperate.

C A S E ♦ 8

In the second case, a female police officer whose husband was also a police officer was trained and joined the K9 section of the police department, the first and only woman to crack this formerly all-male section of the police department. The other police officers constantly verbally humiliated and harassed her and even sent their dogs to attack her when she was acting as decoy. The dogs were supposed to find her and stand guard, but instead, the officers involved in the training ordered their dogs to attack. Despite protective padding, she was badly bitten and suffered bruises and contusions.

Both women required psychotherapy and psychological leaves because of the harassment they received. The K9 officer's life was threatened by phone calls, her marriage broke up (she also had a small child), and both women left the police department because they could no longer function due to the severe sexual harassment they had received. Even though they were both awarded the large sums of money two years after they initiated their suits, they have not yet received any money because the City of Long Beach is appealing the jury's decision. Both women lost their careers and have found it exceedingly difficult, because of the psychological and emotional trauma brought about by the harassment, to enter any other careers with the exception of low-paying jobs, such as part-time waitressing. None of the other police officers involved has been reprimanded or punished in any way; they still have their jobs. Both officers had complained to the Chief of Police several times, but he did nothing substantive about their complaints—both he and the department psychologist (a female sergeant) told the women that they should expect hazing and that if the job was too tough for them, they should get out and get into another line of work.

Describe your feelings and thoughts about what actually happened to these two women, who, by the way, were evidently exemplary police officers before harassment drove them out of the department. Do you think the first officer asked for what she got by having an affair with a married police officer? Do you think that one case has more merit than the other? Which, and why? What do you think should happen to resolve this case? What should happen to the other police officers and anyone else found guilty of such harassment? Should the women be offered their jobs back? Should they receive retroactive compensation as well as the award of the court? How serious do you think this harassment was? Does this somehow support the feelings of many that women should not be allowed in such high-stress and formerly all-male jobs? Why or why not? Describe any cases or situations where you think sexual harassment has taken place. What was done about it? How do you feel about what happened, and why?

Chapter Summary

I. Introduction
   A. Business is a specialized area in which ethics can be applied.
   B. Ethics in business has to do with establishing and maintaining relationships among employers, employees, businesses, and consumers.
II. Rights and obligations in business
   A. *Rights* are those things to which human beings are entitled by law, morality, or tradition.
   B. An *obligation* is a responsibility or duty that people have toward one another to see that their rights are protected.

C. As I have discussed in other chapters, no rights are absolute; conflicts are solved by establishing a priority of rights.

D. There are a number of rights that relate to business.

1. There are general rights to life, justice, honesty, truth telling, and freedom.

2. There is the right to have one's life protected as an employer, an employee, or a consumer.

3. There is the right to pursue and qualify oneself for employment without unfair hindrance.

4. There is the right to expect agreements and contracts to be executed fairly.

5. There is the right to establish a business, own property, employ whomever you want, and make a profit.

6. There is the right to fairness, honesty, and truth telling at all levels of business dealings.

7. There is the right to employment security.

8. There is the right to try to get consumers to use products and the right of consumers to choose which product they wish to buy.

E. There are a number of obligations related to business.

1. Participants in business activities are obligated to be honest and tell the truth.

2. They must be fair and just in dealing with others.

3. They must be sincere and trustworthy in honoring agreements and contracts.

4. They must pay off debts in a fashion agreeable to all parties.

5. They must create a safe atmosphere for employees to work in.

6. They must give effort and perform work for which wages are being paid.

7. They must be loyal to employers, employees, and customers within reasonable and ethical limits.

F. There are two highly divergent approaches to fulfilling rights and obligations in business.

1. The first is the competitive approach, also called free enterprise, survival of the fittest, or the dog-eat-dog approach.

   (a) The main objective is to make money in any way one can.

   (b) Laissez-faire is the best approach for a local or national economy to take because it eventually solves all economic problems.

   (c) This is the only approach a free democracy can take.

2. The second approach advocates government control of business.

   (a) Free enterprise puts power in the hands of a few to the detriment of the many.

   (b) Aggression and competition bring out the worst in human beings.

(c) The only ethical way to conduct business is to put it in the hands of the government, which operates for the good of everyone.

(d) This system allows everyone to share equally in the good and the bad, eliminating the uneven distribution that exists under free enterprise.

(e) This approach lessens aggressiveness and competition, allowing more time to be spent on the civilizing of human beings.

G. The moderate position would encourage free enterprise with some controls exerted by employee groups, consumer groups, and government to provide a system of checks and balances.

III. Justice, honesty, and truth telling in business

A. There are a number of different types of justice that are of concern in business.

1. Exchange justice involves reimbursement for services rendered or products made or sold.

2. Distributive justice involves the distribution of profit among owners, managers, employees, and shareholders.

3. Social justice is concerned with how businesses and their members treat consumers and members of society in general.

B. Truth telling applies to business in a number of ways.

1. Business people must tell the truth in agreeing to render and pay for services and products.

2. They must not lie in employer-employee relations.

3. They must not lie to shareholders about the status of the business.

4. They must tell the truth in advertising.

C. Honesty applies to business in a number of ways.

1. Business people must keep agreements and contracts, whether oral or written.

2. They must admit errors that have been made in creating products, especially where safety is involved, and they must correct those errors wherever possible.

3. They must give an honest day's work for pay received.

4. They must give appropriate wages for work performed.

5. They must set honest prices that allow for a reasonable but not inflationary profit.

6. They must give the best quality for the price that they can.

7. They must constantly inspect business practices at all levels to ensure that dishonesty and corruption are discovered and eliminated.

IV. Ethical approaches to advertising

A. Advertising is a big part of any business.

B. There are two highly divergent approaches to advertising.

1. The anything-goes approach argues that advertising does little harm to anyone and is good for business, the economy, and society as a whole.

2. The approach based on truth telling decrees that businesses have the right to advertise freely but not to lie to the public about their products or services.

   (a) Harm is done by not telling the truth in advertising because lying or dishonesty that is continued over a period of time tends to break down faith and trust in human relations.

   (b) Advertising must neither lie nor misrepresent products or services by omitting important facts.

3. Some questions raised by the issue of truth in advertising are what actually constitutes lying and misrepresentation, and what guidelines can be presented for ethically proper advertising?

   (a) No unsafe product should be advertised as safe.

   (b) Businesses should not make claims about their products and services that are not true or that are exaggerated.

   (c) They should not make false claims about medical endorsement of their products or services.

   (d) All claims and guarantees should be supported by evidence that is readily available to the public.

   (e) No one who works in advertising should have to make claims about products or services that aren't true.

V. Business and the environment

   A. Business should not take total blame for environmental problems, but it bears a large share of the blame.

   B. There are two extreme positions related to this issue.

      1. Some people hold that business should always come first.

         (a) It is not business's fault that environmental problems exist; business has always striven to give consumers what they want.

         (b) Interference by nature-loving do-gooders will ruin business, our economy, and our society.

         (c) If they are not interfered with, business and science will eventually find answers to environmental problems.

         (d) Business has always operated in good faith and could not have foreseen these problems; therefore, why should it shoulder any blame?

         (e) Changes required to solve environmental problems are too expensive, and business should not have to suffer this burden.

      2. Some people hold that the environment should always come first.

         (a) We have been ruining the environment, and the only solution now is to stop all destructive activities before it is too late.

(b) Business must take the major blame for our environmental problems.

(c) Business, through its use of advertising, has caused the consume-at-all-costs syndrome, which has led to environmental depletion.

(d) Government should immediately pass legislation to ensure a clean environment.

(e) Government must conduct a massive reeducation of everyone in society, including business people.

(f) If businesses are destroyed in the process, then so be it—the environment must be saved at all costs.

C. There is also a moderate view on business and the environment.

1. Business isn't totally to blame for the destruction of the environment.

2. The government and society in general share the blame.

3. Business, government, and society must work together to stop this destruction, recognizing that we all have an ethical obligation to protect human beings and the environment.

VI. Affirmative action and reverse discrimination

A. There are a number of terms related to this issue.

1. *Prejudice* means the prejudgment of someone or something from a biased point of view.

2. To *discriminate* means to differentiate among people in a prejudiced way in hiring, promoting, or firing them.

3. *Affirmative action* describes the process of trying to avoid present and future discrimination and trying to make up for past discrimination.

4. *Reverse discrimination* is discrimination practiced against white men in the course of implementing affirmative action.

B. There are two extreme arguments related to this issue.

1. Some people argue for discrimination.

(a) A business's employment practices are its own affair because it is privately owned.

(b) Even if discrimination has been practiced in the past, this is not the fault of present employers; therefore, they should not be held responsible and be forced to pay for errors that weren't theirs.

(c) Even if some present employers were guilty of discrimination, they should not be forced to pay for old mistakes.

(d) Employers should definitely not have to hire less qualified people to make up for past errors.

(e) They should not have to be responsible for training unqualified employees to make them qualified.

        (f)   Business is not responsible for discrimination—it exists on all levels of society—therefore, there is no reason why business should have to bear the burden alone.

        (g)   If employers are left alone, things will eventually work themselves out in a fair manner.

        (h)   Forced hiring of minorities and women will result in reverse discrimination and be unfair to whites.

  2. Some people argue against discrimination.

        (a)   Discrimination in business is the most insidious kind of discrimination and must be stopped immediately.

        (b)   Even though we might not have discriminated in the past (which is difficult to believe), we still owe these wronged people something, as their fellow human beings and as good citizens.

        (c)   Every effort must be made immediately to put affirmative action into effect.

            (1)   When employees retire, resign, or are fired, they should be replaced with minority-group members.

            (2)   Quotas, goals, and timetables for affirmative action must be established and adhered to.

            (3)   Training programs must be established for these people immediately.

        (d)   Unfortunately, reverse discrimination may take place, but it has to exist in order to right past wrongs.

        (e)   Government at all levels should mandate affirmative action and enforce it fully by any legal means available.

  C. There is a moderate position related to this issue.

    1. Business has an obligation to halt immoral discriminatory practices as equitably as it can, but employers shouldn't have to hire or promote unqualified or less qualified people.

    2. Government has an obligation to mandate affirmative action and nondiscriminatory practices and to enforce them.

    3. Society as a whole must also halt its discriminatory practices wherein they affect human rights.

    4. Reverse discrimination should also be avoided wherever possible.

VII. Sexual harassment

  A. *Sexual harassment* is defined as "unwanted sexual advances, or visual, verbal, or physical conduct of a sexual nature."

  B. Some people argue that sexual harassment is not immoral.

    1. Actions now deemed sexual harassment enliven the workplace and are just ways of having fun at the office.

    2. Women and men are naturally sexually attracted to each other.

    3. Positions of power imply certain rights.

    4. Those being harassed often ask for or cause harassment.

C. Others argue that sexual harassment is immoral.
1. Sexual harassment constitutes unfairness of treatment.
2. It creates a hostile or offensive working environment.
3. Positions of authority do not imply power over personal lives.
4. Attraction does not imply involvement.
5. No one has the right to assume that people are asking to be harassed, especially when they clearly reject harassment, regardless of the types of clothing people wear or the comments they make.

Exercises for Review

1. If you have a job, analyze the affirmative action needs and/or program at the place where you work. If you don't work, set up a detailed affirmative action program that might work in any business.

2. How does business ethics differ from bioethics and other specific ethical areas?

3. List in detail what you feel are the rights and obligations in business activities for each of the following groups: business people in general, employers, employees, consumers, and government. Give reasons for your answer.

4. Analyze in detail several advertisements in any of the communications media (newspapers, magazines, radio, TV) and show the degree to which they tell the truth, misrepresent a product or service, warn the public of dangers, omit important information, or make unsupported and unsupportable claims.

5. Write an essay discussing the value or lack of value of competition in business and in other specific areas of society—for example sports. Do you feel that our society places too heavy an emphasis on competition? Why or why not?

6. To what extent do you feel that government controls and regulations of business are necessary? Describe in detail some situations in which government should intervene and some in which it shouldn't, explaining why you feel as you do.

7. To what extent should business take precedence over the environment, and to what extent should the environment come first? Explain in detail, giving reasons for your answers.

8. Focus on a specific situation relevant to the business versus environment issue and analyze what has or hasn't been done to correct the problems involved. Do you agree with what has been done? Why or why not? What's your general blueprint for how to deal with environmental problems in business?

9. To what extent do you feel it is important for our society to encourage and protect small, independent businesses? How should this be done, and to what degree?

10. To what extent do you believe women should get the same jobs, pay, benefits, promotions, and considerations as men? Why? Discuss the following sayings or phrases: "A woman's place is in the home"; "Women are the weaker sex"; "Women don't need jobs as badly as men do."

Notes

1. Herbert Johnston, *Business Ethics,* 2nd ed. (New York: Pitman, 1961), 64–65.

2. *Hostile Hallways: The AAUW Survey on Sexual Harassment in America's Schools* (Washington, D.C: AAUW, June 1993).

3. State of California. *Sexual Harassment Is Forbidden by Law* (Sacramento, Calif: Department of Fair Employment and Housing, December 1992).

4. California Chamber of Commerce. *No Sexual Harassment Allowed* (1993).

Supplementary Reading

Attfield, Robin. *The Ethics of Environmental Concern.* New York: Columbia University Press, 1983.

Barry, Vincent, and William Shaw. *Moral Issues in Business,* 4th ed. Belmont, Calif.: Wadsworth, 1989.

Beauchamp, Tom L. *Case Studies in Business, Society, and Ethics.* Englewood Cliffs, N.J.: Prentice-Hall, 1983.

Bok, Sissela. *Secrets.* New York: Vintage, 1983.

DesJardins, Joseph R., and John J. McCall, eds. *Contemporary Issues in Business Ethics.* Belmont, Calif.: Wadsworth, 1985.

Donaldson, Thomas, and Patricia H. Werhane, eds. *Ethical Issues in Business.* Englewood Cliffs, N.J.: Prentice-Hall, 1979.

Ezorsky, Gertrude, ed. *Moral Rights in the Workplace.* Albany: State University of New York, 1987.

Frankena, William K. "Ethics and the Environment." *Ethics and Problems of the 21st Century,* ed. Kenneth Goodpaster and K. M. Sayre. Notre Dame, Ind.: University of Notre Dame Press, 1979.

Gibson, Mary. *Workers' Rights.* Totowa, N.J.: Roman and Allanheld, 1983.

Gross, Barry R., ed. *Reverse Discrimination.* Buffalo, N.Y.: Prometheus, 1977.

Hay, Robert D., et al., eds. *Business and Society.* Cincinnati: South-Western, 1976.

Hoffman, W. Michael, and Jennifer Mills Moore, eds. *Business Ethics.* New York: McGraw-Hill, 1984.

Hoffman, W. Michael, et al. *Business, Ethics, and the Environment: The Public Policy Debate.* Westport, Conn.: Quorum Books, 1990.

Hook, Sidney, ed. *Human Values and Economic Policy.* New York: New York University Press, 1967.

Johnston, Herbert. *Business Ethics,* 2nd ed. New York: Pitman, 1961.

McGee, Robert W., ed. *Business Ethics and Common Sense.* Westport, Conn.: Greenwood, 1992.

May, William W. *Business Ethics and the Law: Beyond Compliance.* Iowa Falls, Iowa: P. Lang Publishers, 1992.

Pettit, Phillip. *Judging Justice.* London: Routledge and Kegan Paul, 1980.

Rawls, John. *A Theory of Justice.* Cambridge: Harvard University Press, 1971.

Regan, Tom, ed. *Earthbound: New Introductory Essays in Environmental Ethics.* New York: Random House, 1984.

―――, ed. *New Introductory Essays in Business Ethics.* New York: Random House, 1984.

Scherer, Donald, and Thomas Attig. *Ethics and the Environment.* Englewood Cliffs, N.J.: Prentice-Hall, 1983.

Shaw, William H. *Business Ethics.* Belmont, Calif.: Wadsworth, 1991.

Silk, L., and D. Vogel, eds. *Ethics and Profits.* New York: Simon and Schuster, 1976.

Singer, Peter. "Is Racial Discrimination Arbitrary?" In *Moral Issues,* ed. Jan Narveson. New York: Oxford University Press, 1983.

Snoeyenbos, Milton et al., eds. *Business Ethics.* Buffalo, N.Y.: Prometheus, 1983.

Stewart, Robert M., ed. *Readings in Social and Political Philosophy.* New York: Oxford University Press, 1986.

Taylor, Bron R. *Affirmative Action at Work: Law, Politics, and Ethics.* Pittsburgh: University of Pittsburgh Press, 1991.

Velasquez, Manuel G. *Business Ethics.* Englewood Cliffs, N.J.: Prentice-Hall, 1982.

Wasserstrom, Richard, ed. *Today's Moral Problems,* 3rd ed. New York: Macmillan, 1985.

White, Thomas J. *Business Ethics: A Philosophical Reader.* New York: Macmillan, 1993.

Wilson, Lascelles A. *Ethics: Its Impact in Real Estate.* New York: Vantage, 1992.

Zwerdling, Daniel. *Workplace Democracy.* New York, Harper & Row, 1979.

CHAPTER 15

Environmental Ethics

Objectives

After you have read this chapter you should be able to

1. Recognize environmental ethical issues.
2. Understand what lies behind our attitudes toward the natural environment and everything in it (plants, trees, animals.)
3. Discern whether we have a moral obligation to preserve and protect nature.
4. Understand and deal with the question, "To what extent do animals and plants have rights?"
5. Know and understand the arguments for and against the use and exploitation of the natural environment and everything in it.

Key Terms

1. Speciesism: A prejudice for one's own species and against other species.
2. Sentientism: The theory that only those beings with mental states should be the subject of moral concern.

3. Wholism: A conception of nature wherein humans and nature together form a moral community.

4. Vegetarianism: The refusal to eat the flesh of animals and the favoring of a diet of vegetables.

5. Endangered species: A species of animals in danger of becoming extinct because of encroachment of civilization upon the natural environment and careless exploitation by human beings.

Nature and Morality

In recent years, people have come to realize that natural resources and animals, plants, and trees are not boundless, but are subject to diminishment, destruction, and loss through careless exploitation, pollution, and the general encroachment of civilization. In the past, despite inklings of this realization in cases such as the near extinction of the American buffalo by white people in the old West through whole-sale slaughter, people assumed that natural resources would last forever and were there merely to be used and exploited. Water, air, forests, animals, plants, and minerals were considered to exist in abundance and without end. In recent years, however, with the rise of industrialized, technological, producing, and consuming societies, people have discovered that this is just not so. There indeed are limits to the natural resources of the world, and it is possible to eliminate whole species of animals through lack of concern for their survival and willful exploitation.

I refer you to my discussion of the four aspects of morality in Chapter 1, and especially to the second aspect, "Nature and Morality," which has to do with human beings and their relationship to nature. In that discussion, I said that for most modern, "civilized" people, this was a new category, but that in reality it was an ancient idea among primitive human beings who tended to see themselves much more closely allied with nature than we do. Even our modern-day concerns are often centered around nature's destruction affecting our own lives rather than nature having value in and for itself. In this sense, human relations with nature could be subsumed under the social aspect having to do with people in relationship to other people.

However, I also said that many people do consider nature as valuable in itself and insist that we have specific moral obligations toward it and all it contains, especially animals that are closer to us in nature's order. In this chapter, we will look at both aspects but will concentrate on nature and morality.

Environmental Ethical Issues

Several environmental ethical issues will be discussed throughout this chapter, and it is important to describe them briefly now.

Waste and Destruction of Natural Resources

As I pointed out, we have assumed that our natural resources would last forever, that our water, air, oil, minerals, earth, plants, and trees would always be there for us to use and would never be depleted. However, in recent times we have discovered that there is a limit to everything, including our natural resources. As we willy-nilly cut down trees for use in wood and paper products, for example, we began to realize that our forests were disappearing. When we had an oil shortage in 1973 and were held hostage by the Arab nations, we began to realize that there was only so much oil in the ground and the sea and that our pumps would not bring up oil forever. As our rainfall diminished along with our water supply, we began to realize that there was a limit to our water as well, and we simply could not overwater our lawns or let water flow down the drains of our sinks, bathtubs, and toilets or we would actually run out of it.

As each of these realizations hit us, we were shocked that the earth's bounty would not last unless we stopped destroying without rebuilding or replanting and unless we began to conserve our precious natural resources. We simply could not continue cutting down trees without planting new ones to take their places. We also had to recycle paper so that not as many trees would be used up to make it. We had to be careful not to merely let water flow, but to restrict our use of it. We couldn't just use and misuse our land by destroying it in digging for oil, coal, and other minerals, and we had to be careful not to exhaust its fertility by continuing to plant in the same soil without protecting it and letting it lie fallow.

Exploiting, Misusing, and Polluting the Environment

We also discovered, probably with what first happened to the air in Los Angeles, California, that heavy industrialization and a tremendous proliferation of automobiles polluted the environment so badly that we found it difficult to breathe, grow things, or even see on particularly smoggy days. We further discovered that such heavy pollution also destroyed the ozone layer that protects the earth against excessive rays of the sun.

We found further that we could not continue dumping our waste in the ground and in the rivers, lakes, and oceans without dire effects on those bodies of water and their inhabitants. If we drilled for oil in the ocean and sprung a leak or had a spill, we could adversely affect the natural and recreational environments surrounding them, including the plants, animals, or fish within them. As our industrialization and technology increased, so did the toxicity of the waste, and we found ourselves burying in the land or dumping in bodies of water very dangerous and poisonous materials, such as strong chemicals, atomic waste, and other dangerous materials that seriously affected our whole environment and us, its inhabitants.

Exploiting, Abusing, and Destroying Animals

One of the most controversial ethical issues concerning the environment is the question of animal rights and whether we have moral obligations toward animals. These issues encompass destroying animals for food, parts of their bodies (for example, furs, skins, or tusks); hunting them for sport; and using them for scientific and other experimentation.

Hunting and Destroying Animals for Food and Body Parts. Since human beings are basically carnivores—that is, meat eaters—and have been throughout history, destroying animals for food has been and is quite common. In the past, we hunted animals for food and often used their skins or other parts of their bodies for clothes. Primitive people seemed, however, to use only what they needed and did not destroy whole herds of animals just for the sake of killing them. Hunting for food and other necessities is an ancient activity. Hunting and acquiring food and other items were combined, but early human beings seemed to have more respect for animals and the environment than modern ones do.

Several changes have occurred, however, which some people see as eliminating the necessity of using animals for these purposes. First, we have created wonderful synthetic materials—even furs—which eliminate the need for killing animals for their skins. We no longer need whale blubber in order to operate oil lamps because we now have electricity. We no longer need to hunt animals for food because we now raise animals specifically for food that we eat (creating another ethical issue that we will discuss later). Killing wild animals, then, has become a sport that many enjoy and many others decry because they feel it amounts to murdering animals for excitement and also threatens to make certain wild animals become extinct.

Raising Animals for Food. Ethical issues have also arisen in the raising, slaughtering, and eating of animals for food. Demands of modern humans for tastier meats and other animal products, such as eggs, butter, and milk, have caused the food industry to resort to different ways of raising animals for food, some of which cause animals to suffer until they are slaughtered. For example, in the past, animals were raised in the open plains and were allowed to graze, roam, and live in the open air until such time as they were to be slaughtered for food. Nowadays, many animals are raised inside, cooped up in narrow pens, and are never allowed outside to graze normally. Some animals never see the sun or breathe the open air, and they are fed food and chemicals that will make them the fattest the soonest without regard for their own likes or dislikes or any concern for their comfort or the pain such conditions or diets may bring.

Some people argue that with what we know about the way animals are raised and about what foods really are good for us, we should stop eating meat at all, thus making the need to raise and slaughter animals for food obsolete. Such people state further that even if we continue to eat meat, we ought to do so sparingly, and, at any rate, we should not use cruel and inhumane methods to raise animals for this purpose.

Using Animals for Scientific Experimentation. One of the oldest controversies concerning our moral obligations toward animals is whether they should be experimented on for scientific or medical advancement. Since the antivivisection movement of the nineteenth century protested the cutting into live animals for scientific research, these protests have expanded to include any experimentation on animals "for the good of humanity." There are strong laws concerning experimenting on human beings, and thus animals must be used, according to science, to test drugs and scientific or medical procedures. Without the use of animals, many of our greatest scientific advancements and cures for diseases (such as heart disease, kidney disease, and diabetes) would never have been made. Opponents of animal experimentation argue that it is often totally unnecessary as well as harmful and fatal to the animals being experimented on. They argue that research should be conducted without the use of either humans or animals.

Endangerment, Decimation, and Extinction of Animal Species. Because of the encroachment of civilization, as when forests are cut down and towns are built, the natural habitats of animals have shrunk significantly or been destroyed. In addition, because of the continuing demand for animal skins, parts, and trophies, whole species have been slaughtered to the point of extreme endangerment or extinction. Animal rights supporters deplore such activities and have called for an end of the hunting of all animals, especially endangered species, and also for the restriction of any activities that will destroy the environments in which animals live and thrive. They argue that every effort must be made to stop all activities that threaten any animal species, and that attempts should be made to restore such environments to their natural states.

Many issues have arisen in our century that deal with the proper stance people should be taking toward the natural environment and all of its inhabitants. The first important question we should address concerning these issues is what lies behind the attitudes that brought the issues to a head. What caused us to see nature as something to be controlled and manipulated for our own use, regardless of the effects on it and all it contains? Why have we arrived at such a state where we have to be concerned about our relationship with the environment and animals?

◆

Our Attitude Toward Nature and What Lies Behind It

Attitudes toward nature have not developed overnight; however, we cannot say that they have always been nor that they are always present in every culture. In the Native American culture, for example, there exists a kind of monistic (oneness) or wholistic view of nature and human beings as one, not as separate from each other. Native Americans historically and currently see themselves as a part of nature, as closely related to everything natural rather than as something or someone separate from it. They believe that spirit inhabit everything, not just them, and they relate to nature and animals as if they were family. They take only what they need and have a deep respect for all of aspects of nature and animals.

Eastern religions, such as Hinduism, Buddhism, and Taoism, also see nature and human beings as one unified whole instead of seeing nature as subordinate to humans or as something to be manipulated and controlled by them. Here again, unlike Western religions, if spirituality is accepted by the religion, it tends to permeate everyone and everything, not just human beings. The whole universe is spiritual, not just humans and God. The Western view, however, has tended to see humans and nature in a dualistic relationship that is sometimes almost adversarial. There are two major sources in Western culture from which this dualism emerged.

Platonic Dualism—The Beginnings of Western Philosophy

Socrates and then Plato both tended to see the external world as the shadow copy of a real world that exists somewhere else in what Plato called the "world of ideas." With these two men, philosophy moved away from the external world, which had been the focus of the pre-Socratic philosophers (the first scientists), to a focus on human beings and their reason, which enabled them to attain the real world of ideas, a world that Plato felt exists outside of or beyond this world. Both Socrates and Plato, then, tended to deemphasize the importance of this world as opposed to the world of ideas where they felt that ultimate truths could be found, but only through human reason. Plato felt that if human beings concentrated on the external world and everything that was in it, they would only be seeing shadow copies of the real world that exists beyond this world. For example, when Socrates asked a question of his students, such as "What is justice?" and they answered, "Justice is how Zeus treated Achilles in a certain situation," he then said, "No. I mean what is justice, 'itself by itself'?" In other words, he felt that somewhere there exists the ultimate true idea of justice from which all just acts are mere manifestations. This dualism enabled the Greeks to think abstractly for the first time in their history, but it also tended to split them away from nature in that they, as reasoning beings, saw themselves as different from and more important than nature and the external world, since they and no other beings in nature could attain the "real" world of ideas that Plato thought actually existed.

Judeo-Christian Teachings in the Bible

The second dualistic view emerges from the early Judeo-Christian tradition, which taught that God is a supernatural, spiritual being who shares His spirituality with human beings. No other being in nature, according to the teachings in both traditions, has any spirituality. Again, this world is viewed as God's creation and significant, but not the real world that lies beyond in the supernatural world (according to Christianity). In Genesis, Adam is told by God that he has "dominion over the animals of the earth, the birds of the air, and the fish of the sea" and that nature is essentially there for his purposes. Adam was told to "go forth and multiply" and have dominion over everything. This again makes nature and everything in it subservient to human beings and their wishes, implying that nature exists strictly for their use and has little or no value in itself. This may not be the way many worshippers in Judaism and Christianity feel today, but there is no doubt that these teachings have had a definite influence on the attitudes people in the Western world have toward nature.

The Rise of Science and Scientific Progress

It is ironic that the influences just mentioned, although giving rise to an exploitative attitude toward nature, also made science and scientific progress possible. It is no accident that science has progressed by leaps and bounds in the Western world while being almost nonexistent in the Eastern world. And why not? If nature, and all it contains, is subservient to us or if we can make it so, harnessing its powers and using it for our own best interest, then why not do so?

As science and technology advanced, nature became more and more subservient to human needs and desires, and the environment and animals were used and exploited without regard to any inherent value they might have. After all, so the attitude went, we are the only beings with intrinsic value; nature had only instrumental value, that is, was only valuable as it helped us attain whatever goals we believed were important to us.

Industrialization

With the tremendous advancement of science and technology (100% or more in the past 100 years than in the whole previous 2,000), most nations in the West and many in the East have become highly industrialized, requiring a greater use of natural resources and also causing a greater deleterious effect on the environment because of the need for more land, and air, and a greater disposal of waste. For example, with our civilization's need for certain chemicals or chemical products, a chemical plant may be situated in a natural setting on a river, which requires trees to be cut and hills to be leveled, while the plant pours its poisonous waste into that body of water and pollutes the air by belching chemical-laden smoke into it.

Encroachment of Nature by Civilization

As I have suggested, with industrialization, civilization has encroached upon nature. This encroachment has also taken many forms. As we have moved out of crowded cities into the countryside nearby and created suburbs, we have eliminated more and more of the natural environment and replaced it with our own. As we have leveled trees and hills to put in housing developments, shopping centers, and other "civilized" creations, we have shrunk the natural environment and pushed species of plant growth and animals back into narrower areas where they often have not been able to survive because of the elimination of their space, air, water, and food supplies.

All of the preceding have contributed to our attitudes toward the natural environment and all it contains. It remains to be seen whether these attitudes should prevail, or whether they should undergo radical or moderate changes. An examination and analysis of the arguments for and against the use and exploitation of nature will help us to look at both sides of environmental ethical issues.

Arguments for Use and Exploitation of the Natural Environment

Dominion-Over-Nature Arguments

A strong set of arguments states that human beings are the highest form of natural creation and, therefore, should have complete dominion over nature and everything that it contains. Nature exists strictly for the use of human beings and has no other purpose for its existence. These arguments come from two sources: religion and science.

Religious Basis for Dominion. As pointed out, Western religions seem to support the stance that people, although related to nature, are yet other and higher than nature by virtue of the spirituality that has been conferred upon them by God. No other beings in nature have such high status as humans; therefore, they do not deserve the same ethical considerations as humans do. It is strictly up to human beings to decide what the value of nature is, since it has no value in and of itself.

Natural Order and Evolution Argument. The other argument that supports humans' dominion over nature is that which comes from the evolutionary scale and natural order of things, which places human beings at the top of everything. Humans, by virtue of their fantastic brains that are considered (by them) to be the highest achievement of nature and evolution, should obviously have dominion over everything else in the natural world. Humans have shown through their ability to reason and invent that, even though nature towers over them in size, they are capable of harnessing it and all of its aspects by flying, traveling on and staying under water, controlling rivers, streams, and seas, leveling tallest mountains, cutting down nature's biggest trees, and overcoming nature's most ferocious species of animals. And even though nature does in some respects have more control over humans (such as in earthquakes, tornadoes, floods, and tidal waves), it is just a matter of time until humans will be able to control these aspects of nature too by being able to predict them and then by either averting them or diminishing their destructive powers.

Human Reasoning Versus Nature as Blind and Nonreasoning

The main reason that human beings are at the top of the natural order of things is that they have the capacity for reasoning that the rest of nature does not. Inanimate objects and plants have no reasoning ability, and animals have it to only a minor degree, if at all. Because nature is blind and nonreasoning, it is obvious that human beings should have complete dominion and control over it.

Civilization More Important Than Nature

Because the human brain and its reasoning capacity is the highest form in the natural order, then civilization, including its institutions, technology, science, industry, and systems of all kinds, should take precedence over nature. Neither nature nor any of its inhabitants except for human beings is capable of reasoning, analyzing, organizing, using a language, or creating. Therefore, if nature must be destroyed to allow human civilization to expand and progress, then it simply must as it is less important in all of its aspects.

Moral Rights and Obligations

Because humans are at the top of the religious and natural orders, then humans and only humans are deserving of moral rights and obligations; therefore, we have moral obligations only to ourselves and other human beings and not to nature in any of its aspects. Morality does not exist as far as the rest of nature is concerned, but either comes from God or is established by humans for humans; therefore, humans have no moral obligations toward any part of nature, nor does any part of nature have any moral rights. Nature, then, can be used and exploited in any way that humans see fit, for it is merely there for their purposes.

♦

Arguments Against the Use and Exploitation of Nature

Monistic Wholism Versus Dominion and Domination

Critics of the dualistic arguments that human beings and nature are separate and that the former have been given dominion over the latter state that, first, religious arguments have either been misinterpreted or are irrelevant. Since nature is part of God's creation, say some religionists, then it should also be treated with respect. Just because there are no souls in nonhumans doesn't mean they have no value whatsoever. Second, having dominion, as given by God, means that humans should treat nature as God treats humans, with respect, mercy, and love. If humans are rulers over the world, then they should be benevolent and care for those beings under their rule who do not have the great human capacity for reason.

Also, some passages in the King James version of the Bible could be interpreted as supporting acting morally rather than destructively or dominatingly toward nature.

The Old Testament. First, in the Old Testament in Genesis, chapter 9, verses 12 and 15, it would seem that God made His covenant with Noah to include not only human beings but also animals:

> *Verse 12:* And God said, "This is the token of the covenant which I make between me and you and every living creature that is with you for perpetual generations."

> *Verse 15:* "And I will remember my covenant, which is between me and you and every living creature of all flesh; and the waters shall no more become a flood to destroy all flesh."

The New Testament. Second, in the New Testament, in Revelations, chapters 7 and 9, God again seems to express some concern for the nature He created:

> *Chapter 7, verses 2 and 3:* And I saw another angel ascending from the east, having the seal of the living God, and he cried with a loud voice to the four angels, to whom it was given to hurt earth and sea, saying, "Hurt not the earth, neither the sea, nor the trees, till we have sealed a hundred and forty and four thousand of all the tribes of the children of Israel."

446

Chapter 9, verses 3 and 4: And there came out of the smoke locusts upon the earth; and unto them was given power, as the scorpions of the earth have power. And it was commanded them that they should not hurt the grass of the earth, neither any green thing, neither any tree; but only those men which have not the seal of God in their foreheads.

Nonreligionists argue that, first, just because people have evolved as higher beings because of their brains doesn't mean that someday they won't be replaced by a yet higher species. Second, this argument does not mean that nature is inferior to but rather that it is equal to them in every respect. The proper relationship between humans and nature is not dualistic, but wholistic; that is, human beings are an integral part of nature and nature is an integral part of them. Therefore, instead of being a relationship of "survival of the fittest" or domination of one species over all the rest, this relationship should be reciprocal and wholistic in which all aspects are a part of the whole of nature, to be preserved and protected and to coexist in harmony.

Reasoning Should Not Separate Humans from Nature

Because humans can reason, they should realize that nature is intrinsically valuable and must be nurtured and related to in a meaningful manner. Reason should not cause humans to reject nature, but to prize it; as a matter of fact, having reason endows humans with much more responsibility toward nature and all it contains than other beings in nature who do not have it. Where animals are concerned, the importance of reasoning should be expanded to include sentientism (having mental states) so that animals can be respected even though they cannot reason. There are also certain criteria put forth by some ethicists that clearly can be used to give rights to animals and require human obligations toward them (see the following section on criteria for animal rights).

Civilization Versus Nature. Nature, which contains most human needs and which relates to humans in a vital way, should never be made subordinate to civilization, which is human-constructed. Civilization has its value and importance, but nature should never be seriously endangered or destroyed at the expense of expanding civilization. For example, when builders are contemplating putting up a housing development or other buildings, they should never destroy any part of the natural environment in which they are working. Plant and animal life must be preserved and not destroyed as designing and building take place. Frank Lloyd Wright (1869–1959), the great American architect and advocate of organic architecture, felt that buildings should be designed to fit into the natural environment and should emerge from the environment in an organic way. His famous cantilevered house at Willow Run is a perfect example of this attitude.

Moderate Position

Both of the preceding sets of arguments take extreme positions either for or against the use and exploitation of nature. The arguments for such use and exploitation advocate the total subordination of nature to humans and the free use and exploitation of nature for whatever reasons humans deem acceptable. On the other hand, the arguments against these suggest that nature must be considered on an equal footing with humans and should never be used as a means to human ends (see Chapter 3 and Kant's Practical Imperative). A more moderate position exists between these two extremes, however, in which nature is generally regarded as important and significant, but not necessarily on the same footing with humans, and in which it may be used for human means, with some care so as not to seriously endanger or destroy it.

This position generally agrees with the wholistic position, seeing nature and human beings as intimately related and requiring that humans treat nature with respect; however, it is not against using nature for the good of humans, but insists that this be done carefully, allowing for the preservation and protection of the environment and animals in the process and being careful not to overuse either of these. Perhaps these three positions dealing with humans and their relationship to nature can be best exemplified through a discussion of animal rights and human moral obligations toward animals.

Criteria for Animal Rights
Life and Being Alive

Some might argue that as long as something has life or is alive, then it deserves moral consideration, and people have a moral obligation to protect and preserve life wherever it is found. Critics of this position say that it is much too vague and unrealistic and that it would seem to violate the way nature itself works. A food chain exists in nature in which plants feed on other plants, animals feed on plants, and animals feed on other animals. Nature is able to achieve a balance in this process in which species survive but do not necessarily become extinct because they are not destroyed through overhunting, overeating, or overkilling.

Human beings also make distinctions concerning whether just life and being alive are enough criteria to preserve life. They have and do follow nature in that they eat plants and animals for their own survival just as the latter do for theirs. Further, humans even allow killing of their own species in certain instances.

Even though these are controversial areas, humans allow the termination of life in their own species in abortion, defense of the innocent, capital punishment, just wars, mercy death, and mercy killing (see Chapters 8, 9, 10). If humans allow this in their own species, why not in others as well, especially if it is clearly for the good of the human species? Therefore, the fact that something or someone merely is alive or has life does not in itself seem to be a strong criterion for not having that life terminated for good reason.

Having Interests

Joel Feinberg states that "to have a right is to have a claim *to* something and *against* someone," and goes on to say that only beings who can be said to have interests are capable of claiming such rights.[1] He considers that animals, even though they can't express them verbally, do have interests, especially the interest not to suffer pain, and therefore he would argue that animals do indeed have rights.

Attributes of Soul, Mind, and Feelings

Some would argue that rights for moral treatment are based on whether a being has a soul, a mind, or feelings. The difficulty of proving the existence or nonexistence of a soul creates problems with such a criterion. Furthermore, even if we could prove a soul's existence, why should that be the only claim to moral rights?

As far as mind and feelings are concerned, animals, being sentient beings like humans, have to be described as having both of these merely through our observation of them. It seems obvious that they have sense experiences, although often different from humans, and they seem to be able to express sadness, happiness, and anger as well as other emotions and states of consciousness (for example, conscious awareness and response to stimuli).

Reason

Although limited, animals seem to also have an ability to reason, even if only on a rudimentary level. Current language experiments with chimpanzees and gorillas would seem to indicate this. Furthermore, human beings with severe mental impairment can reason no higher than animals, and we generally give them rights and feel we have moral obligations toward them; therefore, why do we not also have such obligations toward animals? It would seem that being sentient (having mental states) in itself would require at least the obligation to not inflict pain and suffering on one who is so.

Ways of Dealing with Animal Rights

Vegetarianism

One way of ensuring animal rights is to avoid using animals for food at all, but to eat only vegetables. In this way hunting or slaughtering animals for food would no longer be necessary. There are many kinds of vegetarians—some who will not eat any meat at all, some who will only eat poultry and fish, and some who will not even eat animal products, such as eggs. Some extremists, such as the Jainists, will not even eat vegetables from plants that have to be killed to yield the fruit or vegetable, such as potatoes. They will themselves not kill plants to eat their food but will wait until food drops from plants or trees or accept food donations from others who will pick them. One vegetarian I know felt comfortable eating only vegetables until he discovered that the pinto bean was actually an embryo for the bean plant!

I am not describing all of this to ridicule vegetarians and their ideals, but only to show how difficult it is to attain some consistency in trying to preserve the lives of plants and animals. For example, what is the difference, except for health reasons, between eating red meat and eating poultry or fish? Is it any more moral to kill and eat a chicken or a fish than it is to kill and eat a cow or sheep?

Arguments Against Vegetarianism

Some argue that even though animals have interests and rights, their interests and rights are less than those of humans, and therefore, we have a right to use them for food, just as animals in nature use other animals and vegetables for food. The moderate view states that with these rights go certain responsibilities to not make animals suffer or feel pain or to not slaughter whole species and make them extinct, but humans are still entitled within these moral limitations to kill animals for food.

Sentientism

A second way of dealing with animal rights is to respect the fact that they have mental states to some extent like those of humans and are therefore deserving of rights. The critics of this argument ask, "What about plants and trees?" Sentientism is too restrictive and ignores the livingness of nonanimals. Don't our forests and fields deserve the same kind of consideration as any other living being? These people generally argue for wholism.

Wholism

Every living thing is deserving of respect in this view because humans, animals, and plants are part of a natural whole and must learn to live in harmony with one another. This attitude relies heavily on human beings and their reasoning, especially moral reasoning. The critics of this view argue against the blurring of important distinctions between humans, animals, and plants and state that there is indeed a hierarchy of beings that allows for the rights of certain beings to be more important than others. For example, animal rights activists are more concerned about animals than they are about plants and feel that animals should be given more consideration than wholism would allow.

◆————————————————————————————————

Use of Animals for Food

One of the most important issues because of its prevalency is the raising and slaughtering of animals for food. Is it moral to kill sentient beings, with all of the attributes described previously, and use them for human consumption? There are people who stand on both sides of the issue and some who are in the middle. What's involved in both the raising and slaughtering of animals for this purpose?

Ways of Raising Animals for Food

In the past, wild animals were hunted and their flesh was used for food while their skins or other body parts were used for clothes and other items. When humans became more civilized, they began domesticating animals, such as cows, pigs, sheep, and chickens, and raising them for food. Animals were raised in the open air on farms or ranches alongside one or both of their parents, allowed to graze in pastures, or fed corn or other grains or foods while sometimes being penned in the open air. This is called the "free range" system of raising animals for food. When the time came for slaughter, the animals were generally put to death as quickly and as painlessly as possible.

However, as the demand for more and better meat and other animal products increased, something called "factory farming" came into use. Animals are raised in very close pens, often in the dark, and few of them ever see their mothers or the light of day. Even though killing animals for food is considered immoral by some, in the old system, animals were at least treated more or less humanely prior to the time of slaughter. An example of what goes on in factory farming can be seen in a description of how calves are raised for the veal that humans eat.

In order to make their flesh pale and tender, these calves are given special treatment. They are put in narrow stalls and tethered with a chain so that they cannot turn around, lie down comfortably, or groom themselves. They are fed a totally liquid diet to promote rapid weight gain. This diet is deficient in iron and, as a result, the calves lick the sides of the stall, which are impregnated with urine containing iron. They are given no water because thirsty animals eat more than those who drink water. Is this cruel treatment morally justified? Should we do this to animals just because we enjoy eating their flesh?[2]

A similar description could be given for the raising of chickens, lambs, or pigs and also for using animals for their products, such as eggs, milk, and cream. Is this moral?

The Vegetarian Position

Because vegetarians oppose using animals for food in any way, shape, or form, such people would be totally against the factory farming way of raising animals, calling it even more decadent and corrupt than raising animals on the open farms as before. To raise and kill animals strictly for our needs is to use living, sentient beings merely as a means to our own ends without even the kindness of letting them have a relatively happy and good life before we kill them.

The Carnivore Position

The carnivore or meat-eating position accepts this approach as a modernized and much more efficient way of giving humans the best quality food possible. Because animals are here basically for our use and have no intrinsic value, then we have no moral obligations toward them, and their suffering has no meaning, since they are less than human. Therefore, any method that brings humans the best quality of meat possible is morally acceptable regardless of how it affects the animals involved.

The Moderate Position

The moderate position might condone using animals for food, but might decry the factory farming method as cruel. It would state that animals may be used by humans for food, but might insist on the free-range method of raising them and their painless slaughter as basic requirements for dealing morally with them. It would not, of course, deny the rights of vegetarians, but it would not brand as immoral the eating of meat aside from the cruelty to animals in the process of raising or slaughtering them.

◆——

Use of Animals for Experimentation

The use of animals for experimentation has gone on for many years and has resulted in the development of many of the greatest scientific and medical discoveries that have helped people rid themselves of all kinds of chronic and fatal diseases.

Arguments for Animal Experimentation

Scientists would argue that without the ability to use animals for experimentation, humans would have to be used, to their harm and sometimes fatality. Cures simply would not be found for diseases, nor would training in certain procedures, such as surgeries, be possible. Because by law, humans cannot be used for experimentation without their informed consent and without tremendous safeguards being imposed, progress in science and medicine would simply have to come to a standstill if animals could not be used.

They would argue further that animals have much less value than human beings, so it is morally correct to use them for experimentation because what will be discovered will benefit many people and sometimes the whole of mankind. Many of the animals scientists use are merely put to death because no one wants them and they cannot be kept in pounds or animal shelters indefinitely; therefore, why not get some use out of them rather than just killing them? The mere fact that nobody wants them or will take care of them should make it all right to use them to benefit humans.

Arguments Against Using Animals for Experimentation

In the view of animal rights activists, animals are thinking, feeling beings that suffer pain to the same extent and degree as humans. Just because they cannot talk about how much what is being done to them hurts doesn't mean they don't feel the pain. Therefore, it is immoral to put animals through suffering, torture, and painful death just so humans can make progress in science and medicine. Even though Kant's Practical Imperative was stated to apply to rational human beings, animal rights activists would apply it to animals, giving them the same rights and status as human beings.

Many experiments are absolutely unnecessary to the health and well-being of human beings, and yet experiments continue to put animals through terrible tortures and death to satisfy scientific curiosity. For example:

At the Lovelace Foundation in New Mexico, experimenters forced sixty-four beagles to inhale radioactive strontium 90. Twenty-five of the dogs

453

died; initially most of them were feverish and anemic and had hemor-
rhages and bloody diarrhea. One of the deaths occurred during an
epileptic seizure, and another resulted from a brain hemorrhage. In a
similar experiment, beagles were injected with enough strontium 90 to
produce early death in fifty percent of the group. . . . It was already
known that strontium 90 was unhealthy, and that the dogs would suffer
and die. Furthermore, these experiments did not save any human lives or
have any important benefits for humans.[3]

Animal rights activists see absolutely no redeeming moral value in such
experiments and in fact deem them terribly immoral. Even when the outcome
of experiments may be such as to help scientists fight human diseases, other
methods besides using animals merely as a means to our own ends must be
found, or scientific progress simply should not be made. It is immoral, in these
activists' eyes, to use animals for such purposes regardless of how much it may
help mankind.

Moderate Position

The moderate position would not be against using animals for experimentation
but would insist that, first of all, experiments must be absolutely necessary to the
health and well-being of human beings. Animals should never be experimented
on merely to satisfy human curiosity, nor should they ever be used for unnecessary experiments such as that described with the beagles.

Second, every care must be taken to avoid giving animals more pain and suffering during the experiment than is actually needed. Every effort must be
made to keep animals out of pain while experiments are going on, and they
should be given almost the same amount of respect that would be tendered
toward our fellow humans. With these safeguards in mind, necessary animal
experimentation may be done.

♦

Killing Animals for Sport

It Should Be Allowed

An Ancient Activity of Man. Several arguments exist for killing animals for
sport. Hunting animals is an ancient activity of men in many of the tribes and
cultures of the past and also in cultures of the present. Some would argue that it
is a part of manhood to engage in hunting and killing animals for food, skins,
trophies, or just for the thrill of the hunt.

Controlling Animal Population. Protagonists of this position would argue that killing animals at will is the only way of keeping the animal population under control. As humans have built ranches and farms further into the natural environment, wild animals have often attacked their crops or their domestic animals which are raised for food or for commercial reasons. Such animals must be trapped and killed to preserve civilization. If hunting of wild animals is not allowed, even the least ferocious of them will destroy crops and domestic animals. Further, they will overrun our farms, ranches, and even our towns and cities, especially where there are suburbs. Therefore, in order to keep the animal population under control, hunting should not merely be allowed, but encouraged.

Need for Animal Meat and Other Body Parts. First, despite the fact that we have all the domestic meat we may wish, many people like to eat wild game, such as duck, venison (deer meat), quail, and pheasant, and they should be allowed to indulge their tastes.

Second, many people like to use the skins of animals of all kinds to make clothes, shoes, boots, handbags, floor coverings, and wall hangings. Even though all of these items can be made from synthetic materials or from domestic animals' skins, the more exotic wild skins are often prettier, rarer, and valued more highly. It is one thing, for example, to own a pair of cowboy boots made of cowhide, but another to own a pair made from lizard, crocodile, porcupine, or rattlesnake hides. The higher prices for boots made from these skins attest to their higher value.

Third, it is exciting to be able to have the heads of animals one has hunted and killed in the jungles and forests hanging on one's walls to indicate prowess and bravery as a hunter. And it is fun and different to have a wastebasket made of an elephant's foot, carved ivory figures made from its tusks, and coats and capes made from the beautiful skins and furs of real wild animals. Some people play tennis, swim, or ski for sport, why shouldn't the hunter or fisherman be allowed to pursue his or her own preferred sport?

It Should Not Be Allowed

An Ancient Activity No Longer Required. The very fact that hunting is an ancient activity should indicate that it is not necessarily needed in modern times. We no longer have the need for the meat, skins, or body parts of wild animals. Furthermore, modern civilized males should not need to prove their masculinity at the expense of innocent and often beautiful animals who do nothing to harm them and who should be allowed to roam free as they once did.

The Animal Population Will Control Itself. The major cause of the increase in the animal population is that humans have hunted and killed carnivores such as mountain lions, wolves, and bobcats. These predators used to hunt and eat animals such as deer and rabbits, thereby keeping the animal population under control naturally. If hunting these animals were no longer allowed, then the animals that they hunt would no longer be a menace. If this natural control system cannot be, then there must be more humane ways of controlling animal populations other than shooting them for sport.

No Further Need for Wild Game or Body Parts. It is a decadent civilization, antagonists to hunting as a sport would say, that needs to hunt animals for their meat when perfectly good domestic meat exists for human consumption. In addition, to use animals' body parts, such as their skins, when we have perfectly good synthetic, man-made materials for these purposes is indefensible. We can make synthetic fur coats that look as if they are made of real furs and that do not require killing animals for them. The days of using wild animal skins and hides are over or should be, and there is absolutely no need to kill fifty lizards, for example, to make a pair of cowboy boots or club to death hundreds of baby harp seals in order to make fur coats for women. It is the height of decadence that members of a civilized world have to continue to hunt and kill beautiful wild animals for these purposes.

The Moderate Position

Killing for Sport Can Be Allowed on a Limited Basis. We must recognize that other sports, such as skiing and swimming, do not involve the killing of innocent animals. This position recognizes the enjoyment some people get from the hunt and will allow hunting for sport on a limited basis as long as animals, especially endangered species, are generally protected and that there are limits on the type, age, and sex of the animal to be hunted. The hunt must be a fair one, allowing animals to try to save themselves. "Shooting fish in a barrel," as the saying goes, should not be allowed, and poachers should be fined or otherwise penalized heavily.

There should be specific seasons set aside by forest rangers and other officials, and rules protecting animals from extinction should be strictly enforced. Also, until the predator population can be expanded, hunting should coincide with the need for control of populations of "huntable" animals. Here again, strict limits must be enforced to ensure that there is no extinction of any species.

No Reason to Kill Wild Animals for Meat. Except where hunting is allowed, as described, no hunting outside of established limits should take place for meat or body parts unless done by primitive tribes for meat for their villages where no other meat can be acquired.

No Killing Animals for Body Parts and Skins. Again, except where allowed within the limits described, no hunting should take place to acquire animal body parts, such as heads for trophies, skins or furs for clothes and footwear, feet for wastebaskets, or tusks for ivory. In order to help ensure that this type of hunting stops, civilized people should not demand such items and should make a strong effort not to order or purchase them; they should openly declare their opposition to such wasteful and useless hunting. In other words, every effort should be made to restrict hunting to a minimum.

♦
Protection of Endangered Species

People who are not particularly concerned about the extinction of species of animals, especially exotic species, cannot see what all the fuss is about. Why worry about such things? Nature has always allowed various species to become extinct; perhaps it is now occurring through the advancement of human beings and their civilization. Why, for example, should people try to preserve the California condor? It is one of the ugliest birds in existence and is basically a carrion or vulture-like bird feeding off the carcasses of dead animals. Why does it matter whether we save such species or even those that are prettier to look at? There are several arguments that animal protectionists bring up regarding endangered species:

1. An irreverence for even a small segment of life affects one's reverence for all life. If one has no consideration for even one species, then he or she is likely not to have consideration for any others, including his own. Protectionists argue that human beings should protect and preserve all viable life in all of its forms, not just human life, as best as they can.

2. Most species of animals are beautiful or at least interesting to see and know about, especially in their natural habitats, so they should be available not only for us, but also for our children, grandchildren, and great-grandchildren. If we are not careful about encroaching upon animals habitats and destroying them in all the ways we can and do, then there will be fewer and fewer species around for us and our kin to experience.

3. All animals seem to contribute in some way to the balance of nature and to the natural food chain. We may not clearly know how everything fits into the overall plan of nature, but we should be careful not to upset the balance any more than we have to. It's one thing for nature to take its course and to make certain species extinct, but whenever it is obvious that humans, not nature, are the cause of destruction or extinction, we should cease what we're doing or do what we're doing less so as not to affect nature and its inhabitants adversely.

These are the reasons animal protectionists give for doing our utmost to protect and preserve all species of animals, and especially those that are becoming endangered. Obviously such people would be totally against hunting any of these species and also would tend to want to curtail the progress and encroachment of civilization upon nature wherever it tends to threaten the existence of such species.

Conclusion

As in most moral issues I have presented in this book, I have tried to present as fairly as I can the extreme pro and con positions. In some cases I have also presented a moderate position. Perhaps the most important question we are left with after contemplating the moral issues connected with the natural environment is to what extent is it possible for a balance to be achieved between civilization and its progress and the natural environment and all it contains. Civilization in and of itself is not a bad thing. Human beings have had magnificent achievements through their civilization; at times they have even worked ingeniously to preserve what is best in nature. People who argue for such preservation feel that human beings must never forget that they come from and are a part of nature and that they must always treat it with respect. To the extent that they do not, they will eventually only hurt themselves as well as all the living beings around them.

◆

Cases for Study and Discussion

C A S E ◆ 1

Every year in order to satisfy the demands for seal fur coats, hundreds, even thousands, of baby harp seals are bashed to death on the ice by groups of villagers for whom the sale of such animal skins is the major industry of their village. What occurs is a bloody massacre of a large part of the seal community. Animal rights activists decry this wholesale slaughter of an animal species that is quite innocent and that does not endanger anyone's life. Such slaughter takes place for the sole purpose of satisfying female vanity throughout the "civilized" world when perfectly good synthetic furs could serve the same purpose. The villagers, on the other hand, make their living basically by killing the baby seals and would probably live in poverty if they didn't have this particular business activity. This issue could be extended to include many other animals as well. If you know of other species involved in such "harvesting," present the problem and answer the following questions for that issue also. Do you think that what the villagers are doing is morally right? Why or why not? Can the needs of the villagers be balanced against the lives of the seals? How? What solution to this problem would you suggest?

C A S E ♦ 2

In a recent Ann Landers column, an upset woman wrote in because someone had criticized her for wearing a rabbit fur coat. She had been asked, "I wonder how many beautiful rabbits died so you could have that coat?" The woman noticed that her questioner was wearing a down coat and retorted, "Do you think the geese they got the down from which to make your coat are still alive?" Ann Landers stated that most of the fur produced in North America is raised on family farms and added that in her opinion it is no more cruel to kill animals for their fur than it is to kill them for food or their hides. She wondered further whether critics of killing animals for fur would be willing to give up their shoes, belts, handbags, saddles, and luggage and any meat they might eat at meals.[4] What do you think of these statements and questions? Is the killing of animals any more justified for food, hides, or feathers than it is for furs? Why or why not? Support your answers in detail. Does it make any difference whether animals are raised on family farms or trapped in the wild? Why or why not? Is there any way to be consistent or to justify inconsistencies when it comes to the use of animals for food, hides, feathers, or furs? For example, someone recently wrote a letter to the editor of a newspaper stating that the setting on fire by the Animal Liberation Front of a store that sold animal furs is no more justified than setting a restaurant on fire for killing and cooking chickens. How would you sort out and differentiate these issues? Explain in detail.

C A S E ♦ 3

A major oil corporation constantly advertises in newspapers, magazines, and on radio and television about what it is doing to protect the environment and endangered species. At the same time, it is responsible for oil spills caused by carelessness both on land and at sea, which, of course, destroy all kinds of sea life and animals that live there. When such spills occur, unless they happen to hit the newspapers because they cannot be hidden from public view, employees are told to clean up the spills, but not to tell anyone outside of the company or even inside the company who does not already know about it. This, of course, would seem to be hypocrisy of the worst kind. Do you think the oil company should spend more time and money on preventing oil spills than on building shelters for some endangered species? Why or why not? What would make the company less hypocritical? Answer in detail. Should the company keep such spills secret when unknown to the public or do they owe the public the right to have that information as well as the advertisements about what they're doing to protect the environment? Why or why not? Is it all right to keep such spills secret because it's good for business? Why or why not?

CASE ◆ 4

A certain company that manufactures cosmetics uses rabbits to test the irritancy level of its products to their eyes for purposes of making nonirritating cosmetics for the eyes of women who will use such cosmetics. Large doses of any substance to be used are injected into one eye of the rabbits, while the other eye is left alone for comparison of any damage done. The test is painful and anesthetics are not used on rabbits. Since large doses have to be used in order to provide a greater margin of safety for possible eventual use on humans, permanent eye damage often occurs. No tests that avoid using animals have ever been developed. Is this type of testing moral? Why or why not? Would the use of rabbits for this purpose be more morally acceptable if they were given pain killers? Why or why not? Since the products are to be used on humans, should the company ask for human volunteers with the usual safeguards required of other types of human experimentation? Why or why not? Do you think animal experimentation is more morally justifiable if it's done for medical reasons—for example, to find a relief medication or cure for certain diseases? Why or why not?

CASE ◆ 5

A dam was proposed to be built on a certain river in a natural setting that would produce hydroelectric power and create recreational activities, such as boating, swimming, and waterskiing. The only problem, as environmentalists see it, is that there is a certain species of small fish found only in this river that will become extinct if the dam is built. The fish is not used for food or sport; in fact, no one knows what purpose it serves by being in the river. Should the dam be built? Why or why not? Would it make a difference to your answer if the small fish were a good food fish or could be used in some other commercial way, or is its extinction sufficient reason to not build the dam? Explain your answer in detail.

Chapter Summary

I. Key terms
   A. *Speciesism* is a prejudice for one's own species and against other species.
   B. *Sentientism* is the theory that only those beings with mental states should be the subject of moral concern.
   C. *Wholism* is a conception of nature where humans and nature together form a moral community.
   D. *Vegetarianism* is the refusal to eat the flesh of animals in favor of a diet of vegetables.

E. An *endangered species* is a species of animals in danger of becoming extinct because of the encroachment of civilization upon the natural environment and because of careless exploitation by human beings.

II. Nature and morality

A. Human beings have discovered in recent years that natural resources, including animals, plants, and trees, are not boundless but are subject to diminishment, destruction, and loss.

B. This will affect us in the social aspect of our morality (refer to Chapter 1 for a discussion of the four aspects), but many consider that nature also is valuable in itself.

III. Environmental ethical issues

A. We cannot continue the waste and destruction of natural resources, but must take action now to conserve and replenish what we use from nature.

B. Neither can we continue to exploit, misuse, and pollute the environment.

C. There is also the ethical issue of animal rights.

1. Many people feel that with our modern products and food availability, we no longer should be destroying animals for food and body parts (fur, skin, tusks).

2. Also we must be much more humane in the way we raise domestic animals for food.

3. We should either not use animals at all for scientific experimentation or use them only sparingly and again humanely.

4. We must also be more careful to ensure that various animal species are not decimated or made extinct.

IV. Our attitude toward nature and what lies behind it

A. These attitudes have not developed overnight.

B. Platonic dualism and the beginnings of Western philosophy, which essentially saw human beings as separate from and superior to the external world and nature, tended to split human beings off from nature.

C. Judeo-Christian teachings in the Bible taught that human beings are imbued with a soul whereas the rest of nature is not, and that human beings have dominion over all of nature and should "go forth and multiply."

D. With the advancement of science and technology nature has become, at least from the human point of view, more and more subservient to human beings.

E. Industrialization has not only increased the use of natural resources for its operation but also has polluted the environment with the disposing of waste.

    F. Through industrialization, population increases, and greater need for land and space, civilization has encroached on nature, destroying more and more of the natural environment.

V. Arguments for use and exploitation of the natural environment
    A. There are two types of dominion-over-nature arguments.
        1. Religious: Western religions seem to condone this type of dominion by what is stated in the Bible.
        2. Natural order and evolution: In this view, human beings are considered the highest evolved species in nature, so they should exercise power over the rest of it.
    B. Civilization is more important than nature. Because humans are the highest evolutionary and religious order, human civilization should take precedence over nature.
    C. Humans and only humans are deserving of moral rights and obligations.

VI. Arguments against the use and exploitation of nature
    A. Monistic wholism v. dominion and domination. Human beings and nature are parts of a whole and not separated into dominant and subordinate groups.
        1. Religious arguments about the superiority of humans have either been misinterpreted or are irrelevant.
        2. That humans have evolved to a higher level of intelligence does not mean that they are automatically entitled to dominion over nature. Someday they might be replaced by a more advanced species.
        3. The proper relationship between human beings and nature is wholistic rather than dominant and subordinate.
    B. Reasoning should not separate humans from nature but should unite them both more closely. Reasoning should lead to an acceptance of nature as intrinsically valuable.
    C. Nature, which contains most human needs and which relates to humans in a vital way, should never be made subordinate to civilization, which is human-constructed.

VII. The moderate position
    A. Nature is important and significant but not necessarily on the same footing with humans.
    B. It may therefore be used for human means but with care not to endanger or destroy it.
    C. This position generally agrees with the wholistic position but is not against using nature for the good of humans as long as it is done carefully, allowing for the preservation and protection of the environment.

VIII. Criteria for animal rights
    A. One criterion states that anything that is alive is deserving of moral consideration. Critics would argue against this.

1. It is too vague and unrealistic, and also it seems to violate the way nature itself works (e.g., the natural food chain).
2. Even human life is not valued merely for its own sake; the taking of human life can be declared moral under certain circumstances.

B. Those who have interests have rights. Therefore, because animals have interests (e.g., to survive, not to suffer pain), they have rights.

C. Attributes of soul, mind, and feelings. Some would argue that moral consideration is based on whether or not beings have these attributes.
   1. The difficulty of proving the existence of a soul is a problem with this argument as well as questioning why such an attribute should be the only criterion for moral consideration, and who knows whether or not animals have souls? Some religions believe they do.
   2. Animals have both minds and feelings and therefore satisfy this aspect of the criterion.

D. Proponents would state that animals seem to have reason, at least at the rudimentary level (e.g., chimpanzees and gorillas can learn sign language) and therefore should be considered as having moral rights.
   1. Some humans have severe mental impairment and can barely reason, if at all. If we have moral obligations toward them, why not toward animals?
   2. It would seem that having mental states at all (being sentient) would require at least the obligation not to inflict pain.
   3. Opponents to animal rights would argue that any mental states that animals may have are so far below those of humans that animals deserve little or no moral concern.

IX. Ways of dealing with animal rights
   A. Vegetarians do not use animals for food at all.
   B. There are arguments against vegetarianism.
      1. Even if animals have rights, they are less than the rights of humans, so the latter have a right to use the former for food, just as animals use other animals, according to nature.
      2. Sentientism, which states that animals should be morally respected because they have mental states, is criticized because it tends to eliminate non-animals, such as plants, flowers, and trees.
      3. Advocates of wholism would argue that sentientism and vegetarianism are too narrow and merely single out one aspect of nature for moral concern; they argue that all of nature is deserving of such respect. Critics of wholism, on the other hand, argue that it blurs proper distinctions in the hierarchy of beings in nature.

X. Use of animals for food
   A. Is it moral to kill sentient beings, with all of the attributes previously described, and use them for food?
   B. Ways of raising animals for food.

1. In the past domesticated animals were raised in the open air on ranches or farms.
2. Now with a greater demand for meat and other animal products (e.g., eggs, milk), factory farming, in which animals are often raised in narrow pens without light and air often separated from their mothers, is now used.

C. The vegetarian is absolutely against raising animals for food; moreover, vegetarians are aghast at the current methods used.

D. The carnivore (meat-eater) feels that the main purpose of raising animals is for food and that any method that will give human beings better quality meat more efficiently is certainly acceptable.

E. The moderate position condones using animals for food but does not accept wholesale slaughter, factory farming, or mistreatment of any kind where animals are concerned.

XI. Use of animals for experimentation

A. There are several arguments for animal experimentation.
1. Scientists argue that without the ability to use animals for experimentation, humans would have to be used and would be harmed or killed, or no cures for diseases could ever be found.
2. Because, by law, humans cannot be used for experimentation without their informed consent and the application of strict guidelines, scientific and medical progress would simply come to a standstill without animals.
3. They argue further that animals have much less value than human beings, so it is morally correct to use the former for experimentation.
4. Many of the animals used would just be put to sleep anyway because they are not wanted; therefore, why not have their deaths serve a purpose and help human beings?

B. Arguments against using animals for experimentation also exist.
1. Animals are thinking and feeling beings that suffer pain to the same extent and degree as do humans; therefore, it is immoral to make animals suffer and die merely so that humans can make progress in science and medicine.
2. Furthermore, many experiments are absolutely unnecessary to the health and well-being of human beings and are done out of scientific curiosity.
3. Animal rights activists feel that it is absolutely immoral to use animals for any experiments, and if other means cannot be found, then scientific progress will simply not be able to be made.

C. There is also a moderate position.
1. Moderates would not be opposed to using animals for experimentation but would insist that such experiments be absolutely neces-

sary to the health and well-being of humans and not be done merely to satisfy human curiosity.

    2. Care must be taken not to give animals more pain and suffering during the experiment than is absolutely necessary—every effort must be made to keep animals out of pain while experiments are going on.

XII. Killing animals for sport

    A. There are arguments for killing animals for sport.

        1. Hunting is an ancient activity that is a significant part of manhood. It was done in the earliest tribes and cultures and should continue even today.

        2. It is the best way of keeping the animal population under control; if not controlled, animals will destroy our crops, kill our domesticated animals, and encroach upon our cities.

        3. There is a need for wild animal meat and body parts.

            (a) Even though they have all the domesticated animal meat they wish, many people prefer wild game, such as venison and pheasant, and they should be allowed to indulge their tastes.

            (b) Even though clothes and other items can be made from the skins of domestic animals or from synthetic products, the more exotic skins and body parts (snakeskin, elephant tusks, fur) are prettier and rarer, and so valued more highly.

            (c) It is exciting to have the heads of wild animals a hunter has killed displayed on the walls, and it is unique to have such possessions as elephant-foot wastebaskets.

    B. There are also arguments against killing animals for sport.

        1. Hunting is an ancient activity that is, however, no longer required. Men originally hunted for food and clothes, but now both can be acquired without killing wild animals to do so.

        2. The animal population will control itself if humans will only let it. Killing animals such as the mountain lion has eliminated from nature predators that would control other animal populations by hunting and killing them for food.

        3. There is absolutely no further need for wild game or body parts because of the plethora of domesticated animal meat and wonderful human-made products, such as synthetic furs, that are now available.

    C. The moderate position seeks a midpoint between the extremes.

        1. Killing for sport can be allowed on a limited basis as long as endangered species are protected and other species don't become endangered.

        2. There is no reason to kill wild animals for meat or body parts except where and when it is allowed within the limits of (1) above.

XIII. Protection of endangered species
    A. An irreverence for even a small segment of life affects one's reverence for all life.
    B. Most species are beautiful or at least interesting and different, and they should be available not only for us but our children, grandchildren, and great-grandchildren to see.
    C. All animals seem to contribute in some way to the balance of nature and its food chain, and we should be careful not to upset that balance.

Exercises for Review

1. What do the following key terms mean, and how do they relate to environmental ethics: speciesism, sentientism, wholism, vegetarianism, endangered species?

2. Do you agree with the author's views that we have come to our destructive attitudes concerning the environment from our backgrounds in Western philosophy and Western religion? Why or why not? If you do not believe that either has had anything to do with these attitudes, then what has caused us to have them? Answer in detail.

3. If you believe the Judeo-Christian Bible really does not condone the way we control, waste, and destroy nature, then present evidence from the Bible or Judeo-Christian teachings that encourages reverence, protection, and preservation of nature.

4. Do you think the only and major reason for preserving and protecting nature is to protect our own good, or do you feel that we have a moral obligation toward nature because it is intrinsically valuable? Present arguments in detail.

5. Present arguments why we should protect endangered species. What difference does it really make if certain species become extinct? Doesn't nature make some species extinct? What difference does it make if human beings do the same thing? Answer in detail.

6. Which is more important—civilization and progress or the natural environment? Why?

7. Do you think animals have rights, and do you think that we have an obligation to see that these rights are protected? Why or why not? If you argue that they do have rights, what are they and why?

8. What is your position on vegetarianism and why? Defend or attack the vegetarian position, giving good reasons and arguments for whichever side you take.

9. Do you believe we should use animals for experimentation? Why or why not? Take a pro, con, or moderate position and say why you have chosen it.

10. Do you think it is moral to hunt animals for meat, body parts, or sport? Why or why not? Give good reasons for your answer.

Notes

1. Joel Feinberg, "The Rights of Animals and Unborn Generations," *Philosophical Environmental Crisis,* ed. W. Blackstone (Athens, Ga.: University of Georgia Press, 1974), 48–68.

2. James White, ed., *Contemporary Moral Problems,* 2nd ed. (St. Paul, Minn.: West, 1988): 315.

3. Ibid.

4. Ann Landers, "For Fur or Food, Killing's the Same," *The Bakersfield Californian* (27 March 1989, vol. 103, no. 86): D4.

Supplementary Reading

Artfield, Robin. *The Ethics of Environmental Concern.* New York: Columbia University Press, 1983.

Baird, Robert, and Stuart E Rosenbaum, eds. *Animal Experimentation: The Moral Issues.* Buffalo, N.Y.: Prometheus Books, 1991.

Calvin, DeWitt. *Environment and the Christian: What Can We Learn from the New Testament.* Grand Rapids, Mich.: Baker Books, 1991.

Cooper, David E., and Joy A. Palmer. *Environment in Question: Ethics and Global Issues.* New York: Routledge, 1992.

Daniels, Neil M. *The Morality Maze: An Introduction to Moral Ecology.* New York: Prometheus Books, 1991.

Frankena, William K. "Ethics and the Environment." In *Ethics and Problems of the 21st Century,* ed. Kenneth Goodpaster and K. M. Sayre. Notre Dame, Ind.: University of Notre Dame Press, 1979.

Frey, R. G. *Interests and Rights: The Case Against Animals.* Oxford: The Clarendon Press, 1980.

Garling, Tommy, and Gary Evans. *Environment, Cognition, and Action: A Multidisciplinary Approach.* New York: Oxford University Press, 1992.

Hargrove, Eugene C., ed. *Animal Rights—Environmental Ethics Debate: The Environmental Perspective.* Albany, N.Y.: State University of New York Press, 1992.

Hoffman, W. Michael, et al. *Business, Ethics, and the Environment: The Public Policy Debate.* Westport, Conn.: Quorum Books, 1990.

Leopold, Aldo. "The Land Ethic." In *A Sand County Almanac.* New York: Oxford University Press, 1966.

Mappes, Thomas A., and Jane S. Zembaty. *Social Ethics: Morality and Social Policy,* 3rd ed. New York: McGraw-Hill, 1987.

Regan, Tom. *The Case for Animal Rights.* Berkeley, Calif.: University of California Press, 1983.

————, ed. *Earthbound: New Introductory Essays in Environmental Ethics.* New York: Random House, 1984.

Regan, Tom, and Peter Singer, eds. *Animal Rights and Human Obligations.* Englewood Cliffs, N.J.: Prentice-Hall, 1976.

Rollin, Bernard E. *Animal Rights and Human Morality.* Buffalo, N.Y.: Prometheus, 1981.

Rolston, Holmes III. *Philosophy Gone Wild: Environmental Ethics.* New York: Prometheus Books, 1989.

Scherer, Donald, and Thomas Attig, eds. *Ethics and the Environment.* Englewood Cliffs, N.J.: Prentice-Hall, 1983.

Singer, Peter. *Animal Liberation.* New York: New York Review, 1975.

Stone, Christopher. *Should Trees Have Standing?* Los Altos, Calif.: Kaufman, 1974.

Villani, Jim, ed. *Environment: Essence and Issue.* Youngstown, Ohio: Pig Iron Press, 1992.

White, James E. *Contemporary Moral Problems,* 2nd ed. St. Paul, Minn.: West, 1988.

Appendixes

◆──

Introduction

My own views as to how the various moral issues discussed in this book might be dealt with and resolved are presented in the following appendixes. My views are based on Humanitarian Ethics, as outlined in Chapter 7, and the eight appendixes coincide with chapters 8 through 15 in the text.

Neither instructors nor students are in any way obligated to use these appendixes. However, they may find that after considering the issues themselves it may be interesting to get another point of view on the problems—one based on an ethical system that has been fully described to them. Furthermore, they may find it useful to analyze and critically evaluate a series of attempts to deal with and solve these problems.

Readers, of course, should not consider themselves bound by these opinions and theories. Instead, it is my hope that they will serve as a catalyst for exciting and profound discussion of the moral issues that we all find so crucial to our daily lives. Instructors may assign each appendix with its respective chapter, posing various discussion questions for students to deal with; they may hold off assigning the appendixes until after students have formed their own theories and solutions to the issues and problems discussed; or they need not assign the appendixes at all. No matter how they are used, I sincerely hope they will serve some useful educational purpose.

APPENDIX

1

Applying Humanitarian Ethics to the Moral Problems of the Taking of Human Life

---

Suicide

General Discussion of the Problem

In the matter of suicide, four of the basic principles—Value of Life, Goodness, Justice, and Freedom—are or may be directly involved. The Principle of Truth Telling and Honesty is only indirectly involved, if at all. For example, if telling a lie or being dishonest might cause someone to commit suicide, then of course the principle would come into play. In the discussion of the priority of the five principles in Chapter 7, I stated that Life and Goodness should come first, so let us begin our discussion of suicide by examining how they come into play in the suicide issue.

Because life is to be valued, every effort must be put forth, within reason, to avoid or prevent suicides, and certainly nothing should be done to cause them. However, as I have said, the value of life is determined most importantly by the person who holds or lives that life. This does not mean that the rest of society does not have some say in whether a person's life is valuable—obviously it does. Society often feels that it has the right to protect its members from others (by means of laws against murder and rape, for example) and even from themselves (through the prevention or stopping of suicides or self-mutilation wherever possible). But how far may we go in deciding for other people that they should go on living when they have decided that their lives are no longer of value to themselves and that they should therefore be ended? The Principle of Goodness also comes into play in that we generally hold that life is a good—according to many, the highest good—but we must ask ourselves who, in fact, decides that this is so. A general consensus that life is good is one thing; however, an individual's judgment that his or her own life is good is quite another. Who should be the final decision maker here?

It would seem empirically obvious that as long as people are rational, they should have the final decision over whether their lives are valuable or good and, therefore, whether they should continue or be ended. At this point, the Principle of Individual Freedom enters the discussion in a most significant way. Generally speaking, life should be revered, protected, and valued, but decisions concerning people's own lives or deaths should primarily be left up to them. Note that this in no way means that people have the right to make decisions about anyone else's life or death; it merely means that the freedom to decide whether life is good or valuable rests with the individual holding or living that life.

Conflicts can arise between this principle and the Principle of Justice, however, in that the taking of one's life quite often involves the lives and well-being of other people. Is it fair or just, for example, for a husband and father who decides this life is not worth living to commit suicide when doing so will obviously adversely affect his wife and children, his parents and relatives, his friends, and his coworkers? Though his life and death in the fullest sense are his own, can one dismiss that, because he has established significant relationships with others, in another sense his life belongs to these others to some extent or at least relates to them in a very important way?

This also involves the Principle of Goodness in a new way in that suicide may deprive the loved ones left behind of some goodness. It's true that this man's life may not have been good for him, but how much badness will now descend on the innocent people around him because of his actions? I see this—the conflict between the Principles of Freedom and Justice—as the major problem to be considered in deciding whether suicide is moral or immoral.

Generally, then, I would say that suicide is not in itself an immoral act because decisions about the goodness and value of life must be made freely by each person about his or her own life. However, I feel that every effort must be made to help suicidal people seek other alternatives and that help should be given to them in resolving their problems and improving their lives. I also feel that when others are involved, every effort ought to be made by the suicidal people to not cause harm or badness to these people through their act—in other words, the Principle of Justice should be observed.

However, the final decision about each person's own life must rest with the person involved, and severe punishment or incarceration should not be used to prevent people from making their own decisions freely. This does not mean that suicidal people cannot be temporarily hospitalized or given therapy, but punishment or incarceration or blame should not be heaped on them for deciding to commit suicide.

◆

Discussion of Specific Cases

C A S E ◆ 1

Many people would not call this act of Joe's a suicide, but I believe it is. Although the motives are different from those of many other suicides, one can still imagine other suicides in which these motives are employed. For example, what about the woman who no longer wants to be a burden on her family because she is sick and dying? Isn't she committing suicide for the good of others as she sees it? I would say that Joe's act is a moral one; he made the decision to sacrifice his life, committing suicide in order to protect and save the lives of his friends.

Note that no one would probably have thought any less of him had he not done this—if, for example, he had tried to protect himself from the grenade because he didn't want to die. Therefore, he made a free choice to do good (save his buddies' lives) rather than to save his own life. This decision raises an interesting question with regard to the Justice Principle. As far as his friends were concerned, Joe was fair and just toward them, but one could also ask, "What about justice and fairness to his wife, daughter, and family?" Obviously, Joe had to make a choice, and at that point he chose to save those with whom he was living at the time, even though it meant that his family would be harmed by his act of suicide. Therefore, I conclude that Joe's suicide was moral.

C A S E ◆ 2

William's act is a moral one. It might have been preferable if he had accepted the hospice approach to his care, but accepting or refusing medical treatment was his choice, and if he decided that his life should be ended, then I feel he had the right to make that decision. Furthermore, he generally eliminated any conflicts with the Justice principle as far as his family was concerned by discussing his desires with them. Under Humanitarian Ethics, then, he made a moral choice, even though not committing suicide would also have been a moral alternative in this instance.

I believe that Joan's decision to commit suicide was a moral one even though it probably would have been preferable for her to seek further help in making her life more worthwhile to her. However, I respect her feelings about her own life and her decision that, as far as she was concerned, nothing else could be done to help her. She didn't seem to be involving anyone close to her (family or friends) by committing suicide, so the Justice principle doesn't apply too closely. Because she made her decision "calmly," I feel that she had thought the situation over carefully and had made a choice between continuing what she considered to be a miserable existence and ending that existence. She chose a viable alternative and made a rational choice.

Defense of the Innocent (The Self Included)
General Discussion of the Problem

If one or more human beings unjustly threaten the lives of other human beings, then one is morally justified in defending oneself and others against the aggressor, who has violated the major ethical principle having to do with the value of life. Such aggressors have also violated or are threatening to violate three other principles in that they are depriving their victims of their individual freedom, they are taking away goodness in their victims' lives and replacing it with badness, and they are treating the victims unjustly and unequally because the victims have as much right to exist as they do.

In violating these principles, such aggressors forfeit their right to equal consideration under the five basic principles. Thus, according to the Value of Life principle, their prospective victims or others should attempt to stop them peacefully or by any means short of killing, but if no such means are possible, then they are justified in killing such aggressors.

Exactly what does "morally justified defense of other innocent people and self" mean, and what criteria are available to indicate when this condition prevails? To begin with, someone's life must *actually* be threatened; that is, there must be as little doubt as possible that an aggressor really intends to kill someone. That a person is insulting, aggravating, obnoxious, or mean is not sufficient reason to take his life. Even if a person steals from you, ruins your business, or slanders your good name, you are not justified in killing him; there must be an actual threat to your or someone else's life as signified by some overt action.

For example, if a man holds a gun on you and asks for your wallet or purse, you may or may not be justified in killing him, but if he says he will kill you regardless of what you do, then you have every right to kill him first. In any case, you do have the right to defend yourself against robbery or any other kind of lesser threat than death, and if in wrestling a gun from a robber the gun goes off and kills him, that is self-defense because there was an equal chance that either of you could have been killed, and the robber was responsible for bringing a deadly weapon onto the scene in the first place.

People also have the right to defend themselves against any physical violation of their person, such as rape or serious permanent injury, and are permitted to use any means, including killing, in this defense. They should always attempt to use peaceful means first, however, followed by any means short of killing. Once it is determined that a person intends to seriously injure or kill someone, however, then killing the aggressor is justified. Here the phrase "innocent people, including oneself" refers to the would-be victims or the victims of an unjust aggression.

The justification for defense of the innocent and of oneself is that a person who is threatening innocent people with death is violating all five ethical principles; therefore, the innocent have a right to defend themselves against one who has "proved himself morally unequal" through a willingness and desire to violate the ethical bases of all humanity and the lives and persons of others. As I have said before, the innocent have the right to kill in their defense, but they are not obligated to do so.

If people feel so strongly about the Value of Life principle that they cannot take a life under any circumstances, then they may, of course, forfeit their own lives rather than kill another. I am making allowances here for pacifists in Christianity as well as in other religions. It is difficult to say that "true Christians" could be anything other than pacifists after hearing and reading such statements by Jesus as "Love your enemies" and "Turn the other cheek." This would be an admirably consistent view of the Value of Life principle, which few Christians or any other human beings, for that matter, follow very closely. Nevertheless, people certainly ought to have the option of losing their own lives rather than taking the life of another, just as they have the right to commit suicide because only their lives are involved. Therefore, defense of the innocent including the self is morally justified as a right but not an obligation under the five basic ethical principles.

◆

Discussion of Specific Cases

CASE ◆ 1

In view of the general discussion just presented, I don't believe, under Humanitarian Ethics, that Ed was morally justified in killing the young man. I am not condoning the thief's actions, but I do not feel that the punishment Ed meted out fit the crime of stealing. In the case description, there is no evidence that the thief had the intention or even the capability of doing Ed bodily harm or killing him. Ed might have been justified in firing his pistol over the thief's head or even at his legs, but he was not morally justified in killing him. Since Ed got a good look at the thief, the proper moral approach to this problem would be to give this information to the police and let them deal with the thief.

C A S E ♦ 2

I believe that Mary was fully justified in trying to protect herself against rape and assault as well as possible death. Under such stressful circumstances, she could not fully judge whether or not the rapist intended to kill her, but she was fully justified in protecting herself against a threat of bodily harm or death. She was not in a position to reason with the man or to use gentler means than killing him to prevent him from attacking her; therefore, I believe her act was morally justified.

C A S E ♦ 3

I believe that the police officer's act is fully justified because innocent people have already been killed or injured and are still being threatened. The police have tried and pretty well exhausted other means to stop the sniper and bring him under control—all attempts have failed. Therefore, because the sniper has violated four of the five basic principles—life, goodness, justice, and freedom—he need not be granted any further ethical consideration and may be killed.

♦

War

General Discussion of the Problem

Especially in this century, because of the horrendous possibilities of total destruction when even small wars are waged, many pacifists have felt that war is totally wrong and that people should allow themselves or their country to be attacked without resisting. Some advocate that if settlements of grievances cannot be made peacefully, then any further resistance to invasion must also be made peacefully. However, most people favor at least "national self-defense," and some go so far as to extend such defense to aggressive acts against other countries who "might" threaten their nation with war, or anything else for that matter.

Generally speaking, war violates all five ethical principles: It seriously violates the Value of Life principle by killing millions, some of whom are not even combatants in the war; it causes a great deal more badness than goodness in most cases and usually distributes goodness and badness unequally; it almost always necessitates lies and dishonesty in propaganda on both sides and in dealings between or among warring factions; and it always encroaches on many people's freedom, from the involuntary drafting of civilians to the destruction of property and severe injury affecting millions of unwilling participants. With such serious violations of the five basic principles, one has cause to wonder if pacifism isn't the best solution to the problem of war.

I believe that many of the requirements that have been set down for defense of the innocent and self-defense can also be used to justify a limited war. A nation is morally justified in entering into a war if it is unjustly and overtly attacked by an aggressor nation, but only after all peaceful means to settle differences or stop aggression have failed. Few if any other reasons can justify such a destructive process. As the earlier Catholic version—a version with which I agree in part—has it, war should not be conducted for national prestige, influence, or the desire for territory or power.

In short, the defense of innocent human beings is the only valid reason for war. I believe that such a requirement was met in World War II, but not in the wars that followed it. During World War II, Germany, Italy, and Japan were set on a path of power, prestige, and mass killing rarely equaled in history. They were the aggressors, time and time again, and there can be no doubt that they carried out the torture and destruction of millions of innocent human beings. Therefore, I believe that the nations that entered the war to stop these three aggressor nations were justified in doing so.

The situations in Korea and Vietnam were a different matter, however. Both of these conflicts were essentially civil wars of ideology within particular countries, and the United State's part in these wars is rather difficult to justify. The Vietnam War is particularly difficult to justify because the reasons for U.S. involvement in it are muddy and suspiciously involved with national prestige, power, and protection of economic interests. Under the five basic ethical principles, war for these reasons cannot be justified.

Because wars are essentially immoral, the sooner all destructive weapons can be eliminated from human culture, the better off humanity will be. Perhaps it is not possible to stop all human beings from fighting one another, but if the most destructive means are no longer allowed to exist, then the intensity of such fighting will be significantly reduced.

I personally feel that firearms of all kinds should be destroyed and that the provision of the Constitution dealing with the right to bear arms ought to be amended to state that "no one has the right to bear arms," including law enforcement personnel. All firearms and explosives, especially the nuclear kind, should be banned throughout the world except for peaceful uses, and some method introduced to ensure that none are ever again manufactured. This is, of course, an ideal for which, I feel, we must continue to strive; in the meantime, the best we can do is keep attempting to reduce the armaments of war and do everything possible to ban wars themselves until the weapons can be eliminated.

Because war, except in defense of innocent people against clear aggression, is immoral, no one should be required to participate in an unjust war. If people can show by their lives and their actions that they are opposed to violence on a moral basis, they should not have to participate in any war that they consider unjust if they can give logical argument to support their contention. Furthermore, as in self-defense and defense of the innocent, if a person refuses on moral grounds to kill other human beings, even in a justified war, then this person's pacifistic viewpoint should be respected without recrimination of any kind.

◆

Discussion of Specific Cases

CASE ◆ 1

The large country is, of course, completely unjustified in attacking the small country. It has violated not only all five ethical principles but also the requirements we have discussed for a just war. The small country is morally justified in conducting war to defend itself and its innocent people; it has made every attempt to resolve the problem in a peaceful way, and the only choices it has now are to succumb to an immoral invasion or to try to ward off such an invasion by defending itself in as moral a way as it can.

CASE ◆ 2

The large, aggressive country is, of course, immoral, having violated every one of the five basic ethical principles and the requirements for a morally just war. Furthermore, it is continuing to conduct a campaign of death and destruction of innocent people. The alliance has attempted to negotiate and has failed; therefore, it is morally justified in trying to stop the large, aggressive power from continuing to wage war, especially considering that nuclear weapons are not involved.

CASE ◆ 3

It would seem that because the two halves of the small country have some ideological beliefs in common, they ought to make a greater attempt to negotiate a compromise or establish a coalition government. Therefore, their civil war does not seem to be morally justified. Instead of providing money, arms, and supplies, the larger powers, which have vested interests in the country, should do everything possible to encourage peace by assisting with negotiations.

Perhaps they can even supply nonmilitary goods such as medicines, food, and clothes, but they should not supply weapons or military assistance. They have a right to protect their vested interests in the country but not to the extent of waging or helping to wage war. The actions of country B were particularly questionable because it supplied its own armed forces, thus obviously escalating the war. The interference of the two outside powers merely prolongs the war, whereas without outside help the war might peter out, especially if the two outside powers push heavily for negotiation between the two sides.

Capital Punishment

General Discussion of the Problem

Innocent people have every moral right to be protected against those who kill or who seriously threaten to kill others. But how should this protection be gained? It can be gained most conclusively if one who has killed is also killed; in this way, at least, this person cannot kill again. Very little proof exists that killing such a person will prevent others from killing, however. The innocent can also protect themselves by separating such killers from them, whether in mental institutions (if the killer is insane) or in prisons.

The ideal situation would be to somehow correct or change the person who has killed so that we could know with certainty that he or she would never kill again except in self-defense or defense of the innocent; psychology and psychiatry have not been able to accomplish such a change, however. As a matter of fact, they have had a number of failures in their estimates of the rehabilitation of criminals who have killed, and such failures unfortunately have often resulted in the taking of more innocent human lives.

The major question here, of course, is "Are we morally justified in taking the life of someone who has committed a capital crime?" In previous discussions, I have certainly not accepted the Value of Life principle as an absolute that has no exception, and so I cannot with any consistency say that capital punishment is *never* justified. I have said that people have rights to their own lives and that no one should take people's lives against their will or free consent. I have also argued for taking life as a last resort to protect other innocent lives.

Therefore, would it not also be considered defense of the innocent to take the life of known killers, so that they cannot kill again? There is one major difference between killing another in defense of the innocent and taking the life of one who has already killed. In the first case, we presume that there are no other alternatives—the innocent person has either attempted to avoid killing by peaceful means or has attempted to stop the killer by injury rather than death and has failed, leaving only the choice of "kill or let innocent people be killed." Because, in a capital punishment case, we cannot stop the victim who is already dead from being killed, we can only decide, on the basis of the five basic ethical principles, the best and most moral method of protecting other innocent people from being killed.

What alternatives are available? Most drastic of all, of course, is the alternative of actually killing the person who has killed. As I have stated, this will ensure that this person will not kill again but it is, of course, a violation of the Value of Life principle. However, because the killer has already violated this principle, and probably the other four principles as well, are we not justified in taking his or her life?

We can attempt to rehabilitate such killers so that they will never kill again. This, as I have said, is still very difficult. Our present methods are to incarcerate killers, either in a prison or a mental institution. Sometimes in prison an attempt at rehabilitation is made, the seriousness of the attempt varying from prison system to prison system.

Very often killers are merely separated from the rest of society until they can get paroled for good behavior or until they die naturally or are killed in prison. In mental institutions, efforts are sometimes made to find out what caused such people to kill and various sorts of therapy are tried, some with success, some without. In many cases psychopathic killers have been declared sane and released, only to kill again.

One part of the problem with either of these two alternatives is that there are not enough qualified people to do a thorough job of rehabilitation in either kind of institution. The other part of the problem is that we are not psychologically advanced enough to be able to state unequivocally that people are "cured" of whatever caused them to kill in the first place and that now we can be certain they will never kill again. For now, at least, our only moral alternatives seem to be long-term imprisonment or death.

It is possible that we may in the future become psychologically advanced enough to state with certainty that people who have killed will never kill again. The way to do this, it seems to me, is to extensively study, both psychologically and physiologically, those who have already killed to find out what can be done to prevent other human beings from becoming killers.

For example, I have always felt that executing Caryl Chessman, the convicted so-called red-light bandit of California, after he had become more aware of himself as a human being as well as a criminal, was a real loss to the study of crime and the criminal. The present system of imprisonment is not satisfactory in that very little constructive study or rehabilitation is being done, partly because of society's views on the reason for imprisonment (punishment) and partly because of the lack of qualified social and medical scientists and facilities. The parole system is not totally effective either, as some known killers can be paroled from a life sentence early, thus endangering the lives of innocent people. Neither of these approaches works very well.

I make the following suggestions to improve the situation as it now exists. First, I feel that society is ethically justified in separating killers from innocent people and that because such people have violated the five basic ethical principles so completely, they have then forfeited their moral equality with those who have not. They have not, however, forfeited all rights as a human being. Therefore, I feel that ethically such killers should participate in the decision of what is to be done with them (within the limitations of protecting others from any of their future actions).

Second, I think that state and federal governments ought to liberally finance extensive studies of convicted killers to find out the causes of their actions with the view of completely rehabilitating them and also of preventing others from becoming killers in the future.

Third, known killers either should be given life imprisonment without parole or should be considered ineligible for parole for fifty years unless they become too sick or incapacitated to kill again or unless it can be stated with absolute certainty for some other reason that they will never kill again. This would provide society with more protection than it currently has and yet allow killers to live and contribute significantly to the study of humanity.

Fourth, killers should have the alternative of being administered a lethal dose of some painless drug rather than having to spend fifty or more years in prison. In other words, killers themselves should make the choice between long-term imprisonment or death.

There are several precautions to be observed here:

1. It must be known for certain that such killers have killed. If there are any doubts, then they ought to get a minimum of twenty years before they are eligible for parole, during which time they should be given every opportunity to appeal their case and prove their innocence.

2. The killing should either be a premeditated murder or a serious crime of passion, rather than an accidental death or a death caused by minor negligence. There should be penalties for these kinds of killings, too, but they should not be as stringent as those for "capital" crimes.

3. After killers serve fifty years, they ought to be *considered* for parole. If they are in any way still presumed to be dangerous, then parole should not be granted.

4. Every effort must be made to ensure that a killer's choice for death is not coerced in any way and that the chosen death will be administered painlessly and mercifully.

I feel that this approach to dealing with killers in our society is much more moral than the haphazard way we deal with them now. With this approach, we attempt to observe the Value of Life principle both for the innocent and for the killer; we attempt to bring about more good than bad by preventing the killers from killing again, by trying to discover the causes of human killing and the means to prevent it, and by protecting the innocent; we attempt to distribute the good justly; we are honest and truthful in allowing killers to decide their fate and making them aware of alternatives; and we try to allow for individual freedom within limitations both for the killer and for the innocent.

◆

Discussion of Specific Cases

CASE ◆ 1

The kidnapper-killer in this case who survives provides a very strong argument for not using capital punishment. Despite his terrible crime and all of the damage it caused to the victim and his family, this killer was able to contribute a great deal to society; yet society was still protected from him until he was deemed safe for parole. Not every killer is capable of reform, of course, but in this case I believe that capital punishment would certainly have yielded more bad than good. Perhaps such killers could be given a choice between a lethal injection or a fifty-year sentence, and if they chose the latter but killed again in prison or continually caused harm or injury, their choice for the sentence could be revoked, and they could then be put to death.

CASE ◆ 2

This man is obviously very dangerous to society and should never be let out of a penal or mental institution again. If he is truly as mentally ill as he seems to be, then he should be kept in an institution for life without parole; or, if he is judged capable of making a rational decision about his life or death, he should be given the alternative of painless execution. In any case, he must never again be released into society unless it can be *guaranteed* that he will never kill again.

CASE ◆ 3

Here, as in Case 1, this man has learned a great deal about himself, crime, and law while he has been in prison. It seems a shame to destroy all of his knowledge and talent. Wouldn't it be better to give him life imprisonment without parole, a twenty-to-fifty year sentence without parole (fifty if he cannot prove his innocence), or the choice of painless execution rather than destroying his life? Perhaps he could help teach or rehabilitate prisoners or aid scientists in studies of crime and criminal psychology. But, in any case, I think capital punishment would not be justified here.

Applying Humanitarian Ethics to the Moral Problems of Allowing Someone to Die, Mercy Death, and Mercy Killing

Allowing Someone to Die

General Discussion of the Problem

As long as malicious or criminal neglect or negligence is not involved and as long as patients aren't abandoned by health care personnel or their families, I believe that allowing someone to die is an appropriate form of action when dealing with patients who have terminal diseases. In fact, I believe it is just as appropriate as is all-out, aggressive treatment when there is a real chance that such treatment will save someone's life.

Furthermore, I am in total agreement with the hospice approach for care of the dying. In every terminal patient's case, there comes a point when treatment should no longer be concerned with curing and healing. Allowing people to die means that you care for and comfort them, giving them treatment that keeps them out of pain, but you do not heroically try to save them from their inevitable end. For example, if a very old patient dying of terminal cancer goes into cardiac arrest, the ethical medical treatment would be to let the person die rather than try to resuscitate her with heroic procedures such as radical heart surgery or open heart massage. Allowing someone to die at the appropriate time is both medically and morally sound.

What about cases, however, in which human beings are not terminally ill, such as in Cases 1 and 2 below, which deal with deformed newborn babies? In general, when people are not in terminal stages of illness, every effort must be made to cure, heal, or maintain them if they wish to accept treatment. The problem with newborn babies, of course, is that they do not have the ability to accept or refuse treatment, so it would seem that proper medical treatment must be given to help them to live.

One cannot, however, give a blanket commandment never to let them die because there certainly may be cases in which deformities are so severe that allowing the baby to die would be appropriate. I think that a baby born without a brain or a spinal cord, for example, should be allowed to die. This, it seems to me, is a clear-cut case, but in other cases, how do you determine what should be done? Do you count the number of deformities? Do you add up their severity? This becomes a very difficult decision, one that depends a great deal on the specific details of the case. However, I feel that the general ethical tendency should be to try to save such children with appropriate medical care and to give financial and emotional support to the children and their families whenever possible.

◆

Discussion of Specific Cases

CASES ✦ 1 AND 2

I feel that both of these cases were handled unethically to some degree. Even though a lifetime of mental retardation is extremely difficult for any child and family to face, I do not feel that this is sufficient justification to violate the Value of Life principle. However, neither do I feel that immediate families should have to bear the brunt of all of the difficulties. If society values life, as its members constantly say it does, then total and significant support at all levels must be given such children and their families. The lack of support is what I felt was unethical about Case 2. Society (through the hospital and the judge) overruled the mother and father in this case and then did nothing, or very little, to help them with their situation.

If parents do not feel that they can raise a mentally retarded child, with or without a defective heart, then society should provide this child with *significant*, homelike, and humane environments. If the family is willing to raise the child, then society should provide every assistance, if needed—financial, emotional, educational, and medical—that it can to ensure that the child's life is as meaningful and significant as it can be. That society is not doing its part in such cases is, of course, no excuse for oversimplifying the problem and letting the child die, but it does lend strength to the parents' argument that allowing the child to die would be better than having it live a minimal life and be unwanted besides. I think that the optimum solution in both cases would be to counsel the parents that the blockage should be removed and to promise to give any and all assistance that they need to raise the children. If they do not wish to raise the children, then the children should become wards of the state and be given the best care possible. All of this should be financially supported by the state through special tax monies set aside for unfortunate children of all types.

Because this "optimum" solution does not exist, however, we must still ask ourselves whether allowing babies to die in such instances remains a viable alternative. I still maintain that it is not. I feel that we must either strive to achieve the optimum solution or stop giving lip service to the value of human life. I can certainly sympathize with the problems faced by these children and their families, and I can only say that society must move toward the proper care and support of human beings in these circumstances.

Time and again, experience has shown that even severely mentally retarded people can live meaningful lives, albeit not at the same level as people who are not mentally retarded. When they are given stimulation, education, love, and friendship, they blossom and thrive and develop. When they are minimally "housed" and cared for, they live unsatisfactory existences, as would the rest of us under the same circumstances. In any case, I do not feel that a person's handicap can justify a violation of the Life principle.

Furthermore, when dealing with this type of problem, most ethicists generally agree with the foregoing. They feel that denying remedial surgery such as that described here would be tantamount to denying grown handicapped people simple appendectomies because their lives are considered meaningless by people without handicaps.

CASE ◆ 3

I believe that Louise's wishes should be respected and that she should be allowed to stay at home as long as she can. She and her family are perfect candidates for the hospice approach, and because one of the nurses is willing to work with the family at home, the doctor should allow Louise to go home to die. Furthermore, every support should be provided for her and her family. Her pain and other symptoms (nausea, constipation, difficulty in breathing, loss of appetite) should be ministered to, but the doctor should not worry, at this point in her disease, whether she will catch pneumonia or some other contagious disease and die. Rather than seeing nothing but eyes, masks, and gowns and being prevented from seeing her son and small daughter, Louise ought to have human company for the time she has left to live. This is the appropriate medical care for her now, not chemotherapy or protective isolation, which will do nothing more than intrude on her privacy and isolate her from her family and the more desirable aspects of her life.

CASE ♦ 4

Although Dr. Kevorkian's motives, in his eyes, may be humane, there are some serious moral problems with his actions. First, few of the people he helped to die were terminally ill. Rather, they had chronic diseases that could have been treated and which would have responded to pain control, which might have helped patients feel that life was worth living (see the hospice approach to pain control in Chapter 9). Therefore, his actions open the door for clinics or doctors or even unqualified others to administer death to any individual who desires it. If people wish to commit suicide, then that is a free choice on their part; I have already said this in Appendix 1.

The second problem that arises is that Dr. Kevorkian is operating outside the law, which means there is no control over what he does or how he does it. There have been cases in the past where relatives of terminally ill family members have gotten drugs illegally to help their family members die. In some cases, the terminally ill people did not die but instead were harmed by the mis-administration of drugs. Even though this problem has not happened to Dr. Kevorkian, because he obviously knows what is necessary to terminate people's lives, without legal controls it could certainly happen to others.

The third problem, related to the second, is determining who will be the terminator of people who want help in dying. Many doctors will not be willing to become known as death givers, especially because their profession urges them to help people to live. It is one thing to allow people to die; it is quite another to actively terminate their lives (see the difference between allowing to die and mercy death or mercy killing in Chapter 9). Doctors also worry about whether such actions will weaken the trust between patients and their doctors. Are patients who want to fight for life at all costs going to worry that their doctors might terminate their lives, maybe even without permission? And without legal observation, how will we know if patients really requested to die? Because of these problems, Humanitarian Ethics cannot approve of what Dr. Kevorkian has done and is doing. A new law was recently passed in Michigan that prohibits the assisting in a suicide, which implies that if Dr. Kevorkian assists anyone else in dying, he will be performing an illegal act and will be punished under the law.

◆————————————————————————————————————

Mercy Death

General Discussion of the Problem

As I have already mentioned, the hospice alternative should eliminate most of the need or desire for mercy death. If people are prevented from living lives of misery or suffering, then they won't ask to be "put out of their misery." The closer we come to establishing and using a hospice approach, the fewer situations will arise in which someone will request to be mercifully put to death. Therefore, we should work to establish such medical care rather than to establish laws that will allow for mercy death or mercy killing. However, we must also consider those people who are not hospice candidates or who want to die rather than live despite the availability of hospice. Should we allow mercy death for those people who have rationally chosen it after having been offered all other possible alternatives?

It seems to me that if we *clearly* receive a competent person's request to be allowed to die mercifully and every other alternative (possible cure, the hospice approach, and so forth) has been exhausted, then, in effect, we are being asked to assist in a suicide. Because I have already justified suicide within the five basic principles, the difficulties here have to do with making sure that people are competent and have truly given their consent, and deciding whether we are willing to participate directly in their dying.

The law has established very acceptable criteria for judging when a person is competent or incompetent to make decisions of this sort, and the law generally recognizes a person as competent. We would need to make very sure that people requesting mercy death are not just having momentary fits of depression and that they will not change their minds later. We would also, under the Principle of Truth Telling or Honesty, want to ensure that everyone involved—the person, the family, health care professionals, clergy, and so on—knew the situation as clearly as possible so that joint, rational decisions could be made concerning the death request and what to do about it.

Further, everything having to do with such a decision must be done completely in the open and be completely aboveboard. For instance, if the problem is a terminal illness, several doctors' opinions should be obtained; and where possible transplantation of organs is involved, no member of any transplant team should have anything to do with the decision-making process. People wishing to die should be represented by a qualified attorney and have their requests made obviously and openly legal, with a clause allowing them to change their minds at any time, even after the request has been legalized.

For some who argue against legalizing mercy death, there may never be enough safeguards to protect human life from being involuntarily taken by the state or by heirs of estates or by doctors who want organs for transplantation. However, if O. Ruth Russell's essay and book (cited in Chapter 9) do not convince those who are skeptical of mercy death that we should allow such a law, her work at least presents very clear ideas as to how we might form a law that would let people choose death if and when they want it.

With proper safeguards, then, and being absolutely sure that the person who wants a mercy death has explored all of the alternatives, is competent to decide, and has freely done so, it seems that all of the basic principles have been met in the same way as they would be in relation to suicide. I do feel, however, that every alternative should be examined first and every effort made to convince the person who is requesting mercy death that there are viable alternatives, such as hospice. If, after this, the person still requests it, then I believe it ought to be allowed, as long as all of the safeguards that have been described— and more, if necessary—are satisfied. I believe, as I have stated in my discussion of suicide, that people have the right to make rational and competent decisions concerning their own lives and deaths.

♦

Discussion of Specific Cases

CASE ♦ 1

I think that the officer would be justified, in this particular case, in shooting the driver to spare him the terrible pain and suffering of burning to death. Because there is absolutely no chance of saving the truck driver—unlike other cases where mercy death might be requested—the officer would be doing the man a great service. He, of course, need not answer the request if he feels that he cannot shoot an innocent man or that, as an officer of the law, he should not use his weapon in this way. But if he were able to do it, I feel he would be justified in giving the man mercy death. Unlike that of a dying cancer patient, the truck driver's suffering can in no way be alleviated; therefore, I feel that the officer would be performing a moral act, and that no court of law should indict him or her for committing such an act of mercy.

CASE ♦ 2

I feel that more efforts should have been made to help Robert adjust to his difficulties, at least until his prognosis was more certain. I also think that greater effort should have been given to controlling his pain and that psychiatric help should have been made immediately available to him and his family, especially the brother who eventually killed him. I believe that the brother did not commit a malicious act, but rather that he was under a great deal of emotional pressure and thought he was acting mercifully.

First, he must have felt very bad about Robert's condition, and, second, knowing his brother as he did, he must have thought he was doing "the least he could do" to end Robert's torment. However, only several days had gone by, and no one can be expected to adjust to such a tragic change in his life in so short a period. Perhaps Robert would never have been able to adjust, but he should have been given more time to find out, as well as much more psychological, sociological, and, if desired, religious assistance in making the adjustment.

Even though I feel that the young man who killed his brother was wrong, I believe that he should have been acquitted (as a young man was in a similar, real-life case) because of the tremendous strain he was under at the time. If he had had psychiatric help in dealing with these pressures, he might have tried to help his brother adjust rather than giving in to his request for mercy death. This is another example of a situation in which medical treatment in itself may not be enough—in which treatment must address the mental, emotional, sociological, and spiritual problems of both patients and their families.

CASE ♦ 3

Here again, I feel that this couple should have been given mental, emotional, sociological, and spiritual assistance as well as medical help. It is difficult to know whether the hospice approach could have been used to alleviate the wife's suffering in a more effective way than the treatment she had been receiving, but it is certainly the case that much more effort should have gone into relieving her pain and suffering.

Furthermore, her doctors should have recommended that she get psychiatric counseling for herself and also perhaps for her husband. It's difficult to understand why she insisted that her husband give her mercy death and why she herself didn't commit suicide, as she didn't seem to be too physically handicapped to perform such an act. If there had been a legal process, such as the one I have suggested, which she might have gone through in order to have her request for mercy death honored, perhaps many of the couple's needs would have come out into the open. And if they had gotten the assistance they needed, it might have been possible to eliminate the woman's desire to die before her illness overcame her.

Because the question of her mercy death had been discussed for two years previously and for four hours on the day it occurred, I believe we have to assume that the decision to die was a rational one. As I have implied, I believe she should not have burdened her husband with the guilt of having to decide to help her die, but I suppose she had the right to ask him; he also had the right to accept or refuse.

I do not believe, however, that he had an obligation to kill her. I feel he should have been arrested and tried, but that, given the circumstances, he should have been acquitted as the brother in Case 2 was. These two cases share two major similarities: (1) the acts, in my opinion, were immoral because all alternatives had not been explored and utilized and (2) the acts were performed under such strong emotional pressure that although the brother and the husband who performed mercy death should have been arrested, the extenuating circumstances of their acts would have to be taken into consideration. In Case 1, there was no alternative other than mercy death except to let the truck driver suffer horribly, and that's why I felt that the officer was justified.

◆

Mercy Killing

General Discussion of the Problem

The most difficult moral problems in the area of mercy killing—as well as abortion—arise because people's (or people's potential) consent cannot be obtained. Taking a life under these conditions would have to fall under the purview of ending people's lives against their wills or without their wills being exercised. With mercy killing, then, we must consider the quality of human life as well as its inherent value. I have tried to realistically state the Value of Life principle by including within it the acceptance of death, but this says nothing about what kind of life should be revered, preserved, or protected.

Because the quality of life is an extremely nebulous concept, its definition differing from individual to individual, for the most part it should be defined by the individuals themselves, because they are the ones who have to live their lives and the only ones who can really determine whether their lives are worth living. Some people can live what seems to them to be a meaningful existence with multiple deformities, whereas others would rather die than lose a limb, be paralyzed, or in any other way have their capacity for life decreased.

A larger problem exists, however, when one has to make the decision for someone else, such as in the case of unborn fetuses, newly born deformed babies, or older people who are sick and senile to the point of no longer being mentally competent. For example, a person in her late eighties who needs no artificial life support but remains in a fetal position during her sleeping and waking hours and has given no one an indication of whether she would rather be dead or alive presents a moral problem. Allowing her to die is not appropriate here because there is nothing to withdraw but food and drink, and these are only rarely considered artificial or extraordinary life supports.

If we decide to mercy kill, that is, "put her out of her misery," won't we be violating the basic moral principles? Can we determine for this person that the quality of her life is such that it should not be allowed to continue? Who can or should make such a decision? Similarly, can we determine for a newly born baby with serious multiple deformities whether the quality of his life will make it worth living? We can predict the fates of the senile old woman and the seriously deformed child to some extent because we know what has happened to those living under such conditions in the past, but should we be allowed to apply our knowledge and experience to beings who cannot give their permission for either dying or living under extremely limited conditions?

I have already said that allowing someone to die is, in certain situations, medically appropriate and perfectly legal and moral. I have also discussed the fact that after all alternatives have been exhausted, competent individuals may choose mercy death. I have even suggested that a request for mercy death could, with many legal safeguards, be legally authorized. However, mercy killing is different from allowing someone to die because it is a direct act to end someone's life; and it is different from mercy death because people who are to be mercy killed have not requested such an act, nor have they in any way been able to give their permission. And because it is a direct act to kill people against their wills or without their consent, I feel that mercy killing, except in the rarest of circumstances, is an immoral act that should not be performed.

◆

Discussion of Specific Cases

CASE ◆ 1

Because of the liberalization of abortion laws that followed the United States Supreme Court decision of 1973, situations similar to this have arisen several times in recent years. It seems that doctors who perform abortions feel that because an abortion has been decided on in a specific case, if the abortion procedure does not kill the fetus, then the living fetus delivered through the abortion procedure should either be allowed to die or be killed. I believe that this view is morally questionable. I will not at this time go into the morality or immorality of abortion; that will be discussed in the next appendix. However, I believe that any fetus/child that is born alive must be given every chance to live and must not be allowed to die or be mercy killed. California passed a law covering this situation after several questionable deaths of live fetuses had occurred. The law essentially states that any fetus born alive must be medically cared for in the same way as any other baby born alive through regular birth procedures. Therefore, because the fetus/baby was born alive, the doctor performed an immoral act in this case by purposely suffocating and killing the living child.

CASE ◆ 2

This is an extremely difficult case to deal with. The young woman is almost, but not quite, a brain death case. Such a person could live indefinitely at a minimal level of existence; nevertheless, she is alive and cannot be declared dead by any medical or legal criteria we have. One woman who died at the age of thirty-four had been in such a coma for twenty-eight years. Such situations must be very hard for the family to bear—and we don't know what the patients know or feel—but these difficulties do not justify the mercy killing of such patients. I think that such patients should be removed from acute care hospitals, taken off artificial life support systems, and placed in a hospice atmosphere.

If heart or kidney failure or pneumonia occurs, then I believe such patients should be allowed to die without any extraordinary measures to keep them alive (for example, CPR, dialysis, penicillin). When such patients can be cared for at home with full support, they should be; when this isn't possible they should be cared for in hospices. The expense for such care should be borne by the family to the extent it can afford it and by the state past that point. I feel that what the woman's sister did was wrong even though I sympathize with her feelings. I think that she probably ought to be arrested and brought to trial but that she probably should be acquitted by reason of temporary insanity.

CASE ◆ 3

This is the hardest of all of the cases to deal with, yet I feel that in this case mercy killing was justified. As you will see in the abortion chapter, Tay-Sachs carriers can now be warned of this problem in advance, and the fetus can also be tested in the uterus to see if it has Tay-Sachs disease. However, in this case, the child was already born and had no better chance for survival than the truck driver in the burning truck described in the mercy death section. Because the child could only get worse, suffer more, and die a horrible death, I feel that the father was justified in doing what he did. Now that Tay-Sachs disease can be determined prior to birth through amniocentesis or chorionic villus sampling, however, I feel that such children should not be allowed to be born. The father, of course, has the option of allowing the baby to die, and if this can be done while keeping the baby free from suffering and discomfort, then this would be the more moral action. If it cannot be done, however, I feel that the father is justified in mercy killing his child. Let me add that I don't believe this would be moral in just any case involving a deformed child—but definitely in the case of Tay-Sachs disease.

CASE ◆ 4

The main problems in this case are, first, that the husband did not explore all possible alternatives before killing his wife, and, second, that there was no evidence that his wife wanted to die. There are specialized facilities for Alzheimer's patients, but the husband evidently made little or no effort to find such a facility. He did try to get some help for her at home, but there were problems, as there often are with Alzheimer's disease patients, in getting his wife to accept this help. Since the couple was quite well off, it would seem he could have afforded to look for a more highly trained specialist if he could not find an acceptable facility. Many people with Alzheimer's do quite well when placed in a situation with optimal care. As in the Kevorkian cases, the man's wife was not terminally ill, which provides less of a reason to kill her than if she were in the end-stages of cancer, for example. Also, I think that the prosecuting attorney made a very good point that this case might set a precedent in a state where many people are retired, old, and infirm. I think that what the husband did was immoral even though he was obviously suffering emotionally and physically. The reason that the husband was sent to prison, in my opinion, is that he would not plead temporary insanity under the law and showed no remorse for what he had done. I think he should have been prosecuted, as he was, and I think that with the evidence available, his case was handled well. Considering his age and health, I think that commuting his sentence after serving some time was probably the humane thing to do. This case obviously differs from Cases 2, 3, and 4 under the mercy death section because in all of those cases, the people whose lives were terminated were clearly in favor of being put to death.

Applying Humanitarian Ethics to the Moral Problems of Abortion

◆──

The Moderate Position on Abortion

Before examining specifically how Humanitarian Ethics deals with and attempts to resolve the complex problem of abortion, I believe it is important to present more clearly and specifically the moderate position on abortion, which Humanitarian Ethics embodies, described only briefly in Chapter 10.

The Danger of Abortion

All of the research that has been done yields the conclusion that an abortion performed under normal medical conditions is generally not a dangerous procedure; neither, however, is it a minor procedure. Medically, repeated abortions and abortions in young women can cause later problems, but these problems are not so severe that laws prohibiting abortions are needed in order to protect women from bodily harm and death.[1]

Psychologically, it is quite difficult to generalize about the extent to which either going through an unwanted pregnancy or having an abortion will affect the mental and emotional well-being of a woman. Much less research has been done in this area than in the medical-physical sphere, and the data available about psychological trauma are certainly not as "hard" as the medical data. It would seem that each individual woman facing such a dilemma should be counseled carefully in an effort to discover how both abortion and unwanted pregnancy would affect her.[2] Concerning this aspect of the abortion problem, the more moderate position would tend to be quite permissive in allowing abortions for psychological reasons, whereas the less moderate position would be more restrictive.

The medical danger to the mother's life of going through a pregnancy (discussed in Chapter 10), has certainly been reduced by our medical and technological advances. By the same token, however, some danger does exist, and it should perhaps remain the most serious reason for allowing abortion.

Viable Alternatives to Abortion

The moderates in the abortion controversy definitely feel that there are some viable alternatives to abortion but that these alternatives are often lacking in both availability and quality. One alternative, adoption, is viable despite a number of problems, which were discussed in Chapter 10. But institutions offering quality care of unwanted and/or deformed children are definitely scarce.

Furthermore, even though economics shouldn't be the most important factor in a decision for or against the taking of human life, financial assistance simply doesn't exist in sufficient quantity either to help economically deprived parents to raise unplanned-for children or to establish and support humane, homelike institutions to substitute for parents who can't or won't take on the responsibility. The moderate position suggests that if we support the Value of Life principle, then we have an obligation to provide such financial assistance; not doing so is merely giving the principle lip service. As long as conditions do not improve, abortion will remain for many the most viable alternative.

Rape or Incest

The moderate position generally favors allowing a woman whose pregnancy is a result of rape or incest to have an abortion merely upon her request. She may, of course, also elect to go through with such a pregnancy. The feeling here is that the experience the woman has gone through may be so terrifying and brutalizing that allowing a child of such a union to be born would only extend the trauma. Almost everyone, except for the strongest prolife supporters, believes that abortion under these circumstances should be allowed upon the woman's request.

The Woman's Responsibility

The moderate position does not support the so-called revenge attitude directed against women who have become pregnant because they were careless in their use of contraceptives. To moderates, women in this situation merely illustrate the need for intensified contraceptive counseling to prevent such situations in the future. That a woman is now pregnant is the real problem, and recriminations concerning why she did not use contraceptives or why she wasn't more careful have no real value.

The Unwanted Child Argument

Although moderates are aware of the problems that ensue from going through with unwanted pregnancies, they generally feel that the prochoice people oversimplify a complex problem. First of all, there are two aspects to the argument: the interests of the child itself once it is born and the interests of society, which may have to bear the financial burden of supporting such children.

Several questions must be raised in relation to the question of unwanted children. First of all, does the fact that the child is unwanted by the natural mother necessarily mean that the child is not wanted by *somebody?* The overabundance of adoptive parents would certainly testify to the existence of many people who want, sometimes desperately, children who may be unwanted by their natural parents. Second, to what extent will the fact that children are not wanted be detrimental to them once they are born? There is no hard evidence to show that children who are unwanted don't become loved and wanted once they are born. There are many children, of course, who are not loved, and some who are even hated, but it is very difficult to predict in most cases what the effect on children will be.

There is no *necessary* connection between being unwanted and being abused after birth. In fact, many abused children were the result of planned pregnancies and were, in many instances, "wanted." Finally, does "being unwanted" mean the same thing as "having no value," and is destroying a conceptus more moral than allowing an unwanted child to be born? All of these questions should be asked, and when they are, the prochoice argument may lose a good deal of its force. This does not mean that consideration shouldn't be given to the possibility of abortion, but such consideration might reveal other alternatives besides abortion. For example, if the negative feelings of a mother toward her conceptus are not strong enough to be called hatred, then maybe psychological support therapy will help her deal with her feelings and overcome them enough to raise the child well.

The Conceptus as the Mother's Property

As we saw in Chapter 10, according to the prochoice argument the conceptus is the sole "property" of the woman in whose body it resides until birth, or at least until viability. This point of view does, however, present some problems. First of all, although the conceptus is certainly *in* the woman's body, it is not a *part* of her body in the same way that, for example, her finger is. Rather, the conceptus has separate genetic, circulatory, hormonal, and nervous systems; therefore, the mother and the conceptus can be distinguished clearly as two separate organisms. Moreover, how can the conceptus be merely a "woman's property" when it is separate, though dependent, and when it would not exist at all without a man's contribution of sperm? Furthermore, since when can one person "confer" personhood on another—what political or legal code gives this right to anyone?

Finally, if the conceptus is the sole property of the woman until it is born, then whose property is it at birth? Is it no longer the woman's property then? Does it become the property of the state? The whole property argument raises myriad problems. The moderate position would suggest that the woman must give some consideration to the conceptus, regarding it as a separate organism that is potentially a human being and whose potential grows with its development.

The Legal Right to Abortion

On the other hand, can we deny women the legal right to abortion, as the pro-life people say we should? Callahan suggests that we can do this only if legalizing abortion poses a threat to peace, security, and the safety of the whole society. One possible danger of legalizing abortion is that this could debase society's ideas of the value of life, which could lead to more extensive violations of the Value of Life principle. This is, of course, essentially the domino argument again, and, as we have seen, there is no clear evidence that legalizing abortion has ever led to such a situation. The only possible exception is Hitler's Third Reich, but here the motives for performing abortion, mercy killing, and genocide were quite different from the motives behind most abortions.

Legalizing abortion could also be considered a threat if one could show that the actual practice of abortion has been generally harmful to the lives of those already living; there is, however, no evidence to support this. Finally, one would have to show that *real* harm, not just predicted or asserted harm, has resulted from legalizing abortion, and no hard evidence exists to indicate that permissive abortion laws have been hazardous to members of societies in which such laws exist.[3]

One piece of evidence that might be of use here is Daniel Callahan's careful and extensive worldwide study of countries that had changed restrictive abortion laws to moderate or permissive ones. Callahan's study unquestionably revealed that there is no clear or conclusive evidence to indicate that allowing abortions to be performed has caused the reverence for life in other areas to diminish. On the contrary, in many countries where abortion laws had become moderate or permissive, laws against mercy killing and capital punishment remained in force or became even more restrictive.[4] The moderate position, then, would not oppose the legalization of abortion in general, but it might favor the restriction of abortions later in pregnancy.

Summary of the Moderate Position

Generally, the moderate position would allow and restrict abortions in roughly the same way that Sissela Bok has suggested. Supporters of this position would suggest that pregnant women should be counseled *objectively* about going through with their pregnancies or having abortions. Too much counseling today is one-sided—the advice a woman receives depends to a great extent on which agency she happens to call. If, for example, she calls an agency that is essentially prolife in philosophy, she is likely to get the advice to go through with pregnancy; if, on the other hand, she happens to call an abortion clinic, she may be advised to have an abortion. What is needed is objective counseling agencies whose only purpose is to furnish women with as much information and as many alternatives as possible. Such counseling should include

1. A determination of the woman's *true* wishes concerning pregnancy or abortion.
2. Information concerning abortion and birth procedures.
3. Information concerning alternatives to abortion (financial assistance, psychological counseling, day care for children, therapy and care for deformed children).
4. Full contraceptive counseling so that unwanted pregnancies can be avoided in the future.

Furthermore, real, viable alternatives *must* be available if women are to be encouraged to go through with pregnancies and to avoid abortion. Such alternatives should include

1. Financial assistance for pregnancy, child care, child rearing, and abortion.
2. Good and readily available adoptive situations.
3. Humane and homelike institutions for nonadoptive and/or severely deformed children.
4. Psychological and sociological therapy and assistance.

Most moderates believe that their position accomplishes three major objectives. First, it recognizes and deals with the conceptus's right to life. Second, it recognizes and deals with the freedom of women. Third, it expresses the serious concern of society for unborn life. Finally, it provides maximum freedom for everyone concerned with abortion decisions.

Before we go on to discuss the Humanitarian Ethics approach to abortion, two final points need to be made: first, that abortion decisions should essentially be private rather than public decisions and second, that the final decision to abort or keep the child must be left up to the women who are pregnant, with the exception of some restrictions on late abortions. Women should have the help and support of all aspects of society in making this very difficult decision, but in the final analysis, the decision is theirs.[5]

---◆

The Humanitarian Ethics Approach to the Problem

General Discussion of the Problem

In general, Humanitarian Ethics has an inherent bias in favor of protecting human life, even unborn human life, because the Value of Life principle is of primary importance in this ethical system. This would mean, then, that abortion should be a last resort, to be used only when there is strong justification. However, I tend to agree with the moderate choice position more than with either the strong prolife or the strong prochoice position described in Chapter 10. I believe that if abortions cannot be avoided—and women should try to avoid them to the best of their ability—they should be allowed on request up to the twelfth week. Needless to say, if they have to be performed, they should be done as soon as possible after pregnancy is discovered. Also, I agree with Bok's criteria for when taking a human life is most serious and also for when later abortions can be allowed.

I also feel very strongly that, with a few exceptions, the decision for or against abortion must finally rest with the woman who is carrying the conceptus. This does not mean that other opinions cannot or should not be brought to bear or that information, advice, and counseling cannot or should not be given. What it does mean is that the final decision rests with the pregnant woman unless someone wants to exert some kind of force and constraint to make her have the child—a difficult feat to accomplish and one that would probably be against all five ethical principles. For example, if a woman is Catholic and decides to have the child even if her own life may be lost, then she made the decision, not the Catholic Church. On the other hand, if she belongs to a Zero Population Growth organization and decides to have an abortion to help avoid overpopulation, then again it is her decision, not ZPG's.

Prior to the Supreme Court's abortion decision, when legislation prevented abortions, many women either tried to abort the fetus themselves or had illegal abortions. This sometimes caused disastrous results not only for the aborted fetuses but also for the women carrying them, and two lives were often lost instead of one.

However, that the final decision is the woman's does not make the decision any less a moral one, involving as it does the life and the quality of life of both the woman and her prospective child; nor should it eliminate a full presentation of alternatives and the information and counseling that go with them. Here again, I strongly advocate pointing out as many considerations as possible and providing as much assistance as we can to help the woman make this very crucial decision.

Of course, she really has only two ultimate alternatives—to abort or not to abort—but there are many important considerations that will affect which of these alternatives she chooses. The counseling and information that is offered must be fair, full, and objective on both sides of the issue so that the woman has enough correct information from which to make a rational moral decision.

A major difficulty with abortion, as with mercy killing, is that the being about whose life or death someone is deciding cannot give its free or informed consent. Therefore, the Value of Life principle is involved in a most serious and crucial way. Because we do not know what the will of the unborn is except in the strict biological sense—that is, once conceived most conceptuses strive to develop to the stage of birth—we must have the utmost justification before we take such a life. We must show that the other four principles will be met if we decide in favor of aborting the conceptus and that meeting them far outweighs the value of allowing the conceptus to develop and be born.

The best way of avoiding abortion altogether is, of course, to be meticulous about using the effective contraceptive devices that are currently available and to work very hard to develop more effective ones with minimal detrimental side effects. However, no contraceptive device is completely foolproof, and therefore if one fails or is not used for whatever reason, then we are faced with the abortion problem. There is also voluntary sterilization, which is almost entirely foolproof. This is a good solution provided that the person to be sterilized is sure he or she will never, at any time, want to have children. If this is the case, then voluntary sterilization—no matter how offensive such an operation may be to some people—is much better than having one abortion after another. However, until people are more educated and careful in methods of birth control, we will still be faced with the abortion problem.

In no other area of morality is there a greater need for many *real* and viable alternatives, with full information, counseling, and assistance available to the pregnant woman. If society wishes to strongly recommend that human life not be taken through abortion, then it must, as the moderate position suggests, provide the greatest medical, physical, financial, and moral support possible.

To respect the life of the conceptus is not to deny that its being unwanted makes it an imposition on a woman (from her point of view) for the nine months she must carry it within her. That the woman (and her partner) may have been careless or promiscuous or thoughtless should have no bearing on the kind of help she is given. A good deal of careful counseling should be given to her in reference to possible future pregnancies and how to avoid them, but the prime consideration in any counseling or assistance should be the lives of the woman and the conceptus. For this reason, all such counseling and assistance should be completely free from blame and recrimination.

It is very easy for some people to demand that a young woman carry an unplanned and unwanted conceptus to term, but it is not so easy if these people have to provide complete assistance to the woman and the conceptus so that she can successfully do so. As I have mentioned before, the information and counseling should present her with *all* of the alternatives—the psychological and medical effects of both abortion and of carrying a child to term, the actual possibilities of the child's being adopted, and the offer to give complete financial assistance and medical care during her pregnancy or during and after her abortion.

She must also be given time without pressure to decide for herself and the conceptus which decision would be the best one, given all of the alternatives and her particular circumstances. A great deal of attention must be paid to the kind of life that the prospective child will have if it is allowed to be born. Even though most children are born normal, sometimes the goodness of their lives is almost nonexistent because of the way they are treated by their inexperienced and unloving parents or by various uncaring personnel in the institutions or foster homes in which they live.

When alternatives and assistance can be provided, the prolife argument for the conceptus gains strength. I feel that every encouragement should be given to the woman *not* to decide to take another human life through abortion, *provided* that she is offered such assistance. All of this may be politically, socially, psychologically, and morally as well as economically expensive, but if the Value of Life principle is worth observing, then whatever sacrifices are needed must be made. They should not only be the sacrifices of the woman—her nine-month unwanted pregnancy is sacrifice enough, and those who wish to protect and preserve human life must alleviate any other sacrifices she might have to make.

We must also respect the fact that the final decision to abort or not to abort is the mother's. If she aborts, her act may be an immoral one, but as always, the decision to act morally or immorally is up to the individual. In this case, we have a duty, once she has made her decision, to help her acquire the best medical care available and to have the abortion performed as soon as possible so that the conceptus will be less rather than more of a developed human life.

♦

Discussion of Specific Cases

C A S E ♦ 1

This is a classic case of what happens to young unwed mothers. Everyone seems to be interested in what they want, but few are really concerned about what Janice wants. She is getting one-sided rather than objective counseling both from her priest and from the abortion clinic. Her mother is imposing her own religious beliefs on Janice, no matter how gently; her father, on the other hand, seems to be motivated, at least partly, by his own ego in wanting her to become a lawyer. The father of her baby does not want to marry her or to become a father at such an early age, nor does he want her to become a young mother. All the people involved, but especially Janice, are prime candidates for the careful pregnancy-abortion counseling I have suggested.

At this point in her pregnancy (eight weeks), an abortion would fit the Bok criterion of less than twelve weeks and therefore could be allowed. Because Janice is under seventeen years old, she should be informed about the hazards for future pregnancies that might ensue from an abortion, but she should also be informed that the risk is not high. In addition, she should be given all the information available about both abortion and carrying a child to term.

A sincere and concerted effort should be made to find out what Janice herself really wants to do about her pregnancy, and everyone involved should try to support her decision in every way they can rather than loading her with guilt or recrimination. If she really wishes to go through with her pregnancy, then she should get as much support for this decision as she would for an abortion. Last, but not least, she and Bob should have clear and complete contraceptive counseling so that future pregnancies and decisions concerning abortion can be avoided.

C A S E ♦ 2

Both Mary and her husband seem to be quite sure that they do not want another child, so waiting until the fourth month to have an amniocentesis does not seem to be a wise choice. Because they seem so sure that they really do not want to have a child—even one that is born without deformity—then now, when Mary is only one month pregnant, is the time to have the abortion. If they have doubts about having the abortion, then they should, of course, seek full counseling to help them clarify their decision, but they seem to have made up their minds, and because of this, I would say that their decision is moral.

CASES ♦ 3 AND 4

Before discussing each of these cases separately, I would like to make a general statement concerning abortion for "fetal reasons," or because the conceptus will be born with deformities. As I have already mentioned, the amniocentesis or chorionic villus sampling procedures make it possible for a prospective mother and father to know if their child will be born with, let us say, Down's syndrome and will be mentally retarded for its entire life.

The relationship of such information to the abortion question, of course, is that once a conceptus is discovered to have a deformity, a decision may be made to abort it, thereby avoiding both the difficult mercy-killing decision I described in Chapter 9 and also the kind of life that the prospective child and its family would have to live given its limitation. But the difficult decision to commit a mercy killing is replaced by the difficult decision to perform an abortion. Abortion, after all, ends a human life as surely as does mercy killing, except that in the abortion situation the human life would be less developed.

Can abortion be morally justified when it is discovered that the conceptus will be defective or deformed in some serious way? The final decision should still rest with the woman who is carrying it even though the prospective father should be given a chance to voice his opinion. The ideal situation would be to have the ability to eliminate the defect or deformity prior to the child's birth, and maybe someday this will be possible. Right now it is not, and the only alternatives are either to abort or give birth to a deformed child.

Even though the woman should make the final decision, what facts and opinions should she consider in making her decision? First, she should realize that abortion is the taking of a human life and therefore a violation of the Value of Life principle. She should next ask herself if an exception to this principle in her situation is morally justified and if so, why. She would need appropriate information and counseling on what her prospective child's limitations would be, and then she would need to determine whether, despite these limitations, she and her family would be able and willing to raise such a child so that their lives and the child's life would be as meaningful as possible.

If the family is unable or unwilling to raise the child, then she would need to consider whether a good adoption could be a certainty and whether such an adoption would bring a meaningful life to the child. She should also determine what help would be available to her if she and her family decided to raise the child, what institutional accommodations could be made, and whether such accommodations would be meaningful and enriching for the prospective child.

I have already discussed the general lack of assistance and of quality institutions and institutional care available today. Furthermore, even though there are parents who are willing to adopt retarded or deformed children, These are very few compared to the number of such children available for adoption. These facts would seem to put the emphasis on whether or not the mother is willing to give birth to the child and whether she and the father are willing to raise the child and give it as good a life as they can. As mentioned in Chapter 9, the life of a child with Down's syndrome, unless it is enhanced by a willing and loving family (real or institutional), will yield a minimum of satisfaction and excellence for all concerned; therefore, abortion in some cases—after all considerations have been taken into account—could be morally justified.

The severity of the prospective child's deformity should also be a factor in the woman's decision, for the deformities of deafness or blindness, although difficult to bear, are not as debilitating as extensive mental retardation due to Down's syndrome. A mother and her family would probably be able to cope better with the former limitations than with the latter.

At any rate, abortion ought to be allowed after all other choices have been examined and the woman can see no other alternative that would bring goodness and its just distribution to the prospective child and its family. In the final analysis, the goodness of the life of the prospective child and its family should be given the strongest consideration. Everything possible should be done to protect and preserve human life, even incipient human life. However, where the goodness of protecting that life is far outweighed by the goodness of terminating it for the reasons already suggested, then abortion may be justified.

C A S E ◆ 3

I would say that in the case of Tay-Sachs—considering what we know about the disease and what happens to infants who are born with it—an abortion even at five months of pregnancy can be more easily justified in a moral sense than going through with the pregnancy. After all, if the child were born, both it and the parents would suffer terribly for the short time the child would live. In Chapter 9, I described how the father of a Tay-Sachs child was driven to mercy killing in order to end the child's and the parents' suffering. I think that abortion is a far better means of dealing with this problem than mercy killing, even though if amniocentesis rather than CVS is used, the conceptus has developed further along than is usually the case in abortions on request, the very serious deformity of the child and the inevitability of its suffering justify a late abortion.

C A S E ◆ 4

Lupe and Robert have a very difficult decision to make and should be given full genetic counseling as well as counseling as to the nature and quality of the alternatives that are available to them and their prospective baby. I believe that in their situation, either going through with the pregnancy or having the abortion would be morally justified depending on the type of support that is available for them and their child. Because they are young and this is their first child, they ought not to have to raise a child with Down's syndrome unless they are willing to do so. I think that we ought to encourage them to do so by giving them complete support from all aspects (financial, sociological, emotional, and so on), but I also think even a late abortion in this case can be morally justified, especially if such support is not available to them and their prospective child.

C A S E ◆ 5

I do not think that an abortion can be justified for such a reason. It is one thing to abort a conceptus because it has Tay-Sachs disease or Down's syndrome, but to abort one because of its sex is capricious, inhumane, and immoral. If Bill and Isabel are even thinking about not wanting another daughter, Isabel should have had an early abortion and then be sterilized. I feel that they would be justified in giving their little girl up for adoption if they had wished to do so, but I would rather see them get intense counseling to help them adjust to having another daughter. I don't believe, however, that the life of a conceptus should count so little that it can be terminated simply because it happens to be the "wrong" sex.

Notes

1. See Callahan, 31–43, for results of research done all over the world on whether abortion is dangerous.
2. Ibid., 48–84.
3. Ibid., 474–80.
4. See Callahan, Section II, Chapters 5 to 8, for his exhaustive research on the effects of legalizing abortion.
5. Ibid., 493.

Applying Humanitarian Ethics to the Moral Problems of Lying, Cheating, Breaking Promises, and Stealing

◆―――――――――――――――――――――――――――――――――――――

Introduction

Because one of the five basic ethical principles in Humanitarian Ethics is the Principle of Honesty and Truth Telling, the Humanitarian Ethics position on these issues is that they generally shouldn't be done unless there is strong justification for doing them. As was shown throughout Chapter 11, doing any of them tends to break down the quality of human relationships and the trust that binds people together. If we cannot trust others to tell the truth, be honest, keep promises, and respect our possessions, then how can we maintain vital human relationships with them? In addition, lying, cheating, breaking promises, and stealing more often than not tend to injure individuals, thereby violating the Principle of Goodness. Further, most of the time they are unfair and unjust, violating the Principle of Justice or Fairness. They can even involve the lives of others and deny them freedom; therefore, the Humanitarian Ethics position is in general to oppose them.

◆

Lying

General Discussion of the Problem

For all of the reasons listed in Chapter 11 against lying, Humanitarian Ethics would state that lying is generally immoral. It would allow for exceptions where strong justification could be brought forth, such as when lying could save a human life or prevent serious harm from coming to another human being. Even "little white lies" should be avoided whenever possible because bringing in compassion and concern would allow one to tell the truth without harming someone else. Nowhere more than in lying does the domino argument have validity. It seems that whenever a lie is told it almost always follows that more and more lies are required to bolster the first, which often tends to make matters worse and break down trust even more than just one original lie.

Although this is an aphorism, honesty is indeed almost often "the best policy." As most of us know, we are highly respected for our truth telling and trustworthiness. Lying can only destroy this delicate reputation we all have. One of the finest statements one can make about another is to say that he or she is an honest person. Because of this and the harm lying causes to others, it should be avoided.

◆

Discussion of Specific Cases

CASE ◆ 1

In applying Humanitarian Ethics to this case, I will answer the four questions I asked at the end of the case description:

1. I feel that the family was wrong in not telling Jesusita the truth about her son. They might have justified delaying telling her if at the time she was in a very critical and unstable condition, but as soon as possible they should have told her. As Dr. Elisabeth Kübler-Ross has stated, the question should not be, "Should I tell the hurtful truth to someone?" but rather, "How should I share this important information with the

person?" Not telling her the truth in the beginning caused many more problems than if they had told her and given her loving support. We can't assume that we are going to "kill" someone who is seriously ill by telling her the truth. If we tell her gently and with compassion, and if we give her some hope and support, we will do her a much greater service than withholding information and playing all kinds of pretense games with her.

2. If she were my relative, I would tell her that her son died of a heart attack, giving her as much hope as I could, such as telling her that he had very little pain and that I and the rest of her family still love her and want her to keep trying to live as meaningfully as she can because we will not abandon her but will support and visit her often.

3. I definitely would advise now that she be told the truth in the manner described in answer 2, and I would advise the family to apologize to her, saying that at the time they thought they were doing the right thing, but that now they see that it was the wrong thing to do. If not, the longer the situation goes on, the worse it will get. What must Jesusita think of her son who used to visit her dutifully but does no longer for myriad reasons that seem to relegate her to last place on his list of priorities?

4. Yes, I feel that the situation would have been much better had she been told the truth from the very beginning and that the situation has been made much worse by not telling her, now requiring an apology and an elaborate explanation. If she had been told the truth from the beginning, all of this could have been avoided.

CASE ♦ 2

One way of handling this matter without lying is simply to tell Mike that you won't tell him because you fear for Barbara's and the children's safety. However, if you feel that he might go into a rage when told this and hurt you in some manner, then I would say that a lie would be justified because it seems quite obvious that both Barbara and the children could be seriously harmed and perhaps even lose their lives because of Mike's drinking and abusive behavior.

CASE ♦ 3

Situations like this one are always difficult to deal with. Many spouses know about their spouses' affairs and can deal with them as long as they are not brought into the open. Some spouses, on the other hand, would prefer to know the truth and why the affair happened and then attempt to resolve the problem. Some spouses can adjust to the information, especially if Tom, in this case, expressed remorse and fully intended not to have another affair. Some spouses cannot adjust, no matter what the adulterer says, and will immediately want to separate or get a divorce. It is important for Tom to know Carol and try to gauge her reaction to his revealing information about his affair.

As I see it, there are two viable alternatives, given the situation:

1. Tom could simply not tell Carol unless she asks him point blank. This would probably have to be considered as a lie of omission, but if he's sure she does not know and that she will never know, then not telling if not asked is certainly a possibility. This kind of lie of omission is certainly not as bad as not telling someone that there is a cliff at the end of the street so that they drive to the end and go over the cliff and die, but it is still a continuing of the dishonesty that has occurred all along. Further, Tom would have to be definite in his mind that the affair was over and that he would not enter into more affairs later. If Tom chooses this alternative, then he should get counseling to help him alleviate his guilt so that his behavior will not continue to raise Carol's suspicions. If Carol asks him directly about the affair, then I feel he is obliged to tell her the truth as gently as he can with remorse and promises never to have another affair. He can also offer to seek counseling with or without her.

2. The second alternative is to tell her as gently and compassionately as he can, emphasizing how guilty he feels and expressing sorrow for what has happened and also promising that it will never happen again. Here also he should volunteer for counseling both with their priest and any other counselor who may help. In telling her, he should avoid graphic details and not volunteer additional hurtful information.

◆

Cheating

General Discussion of the Problem

Cheating is mostly a violation of the Principle of Justice or Fairness and therefore should be avoided unless such an act might save a human life or prevent serious harm to someone. All three of the arguments for cheating are, I feel, grossly invalid and unjustified. That one needs to cheat in order to survive in a corrupt world only contributes to its continuing corruptness. The "everybody does it" argument was refuted in Chapter 1 in that you can't get an *ought* from an *is*. Further, honesty does not depend on whether or not one gets caught. Cheating is cheating regardless of being or not being caught. Here again, as in lying, a person who cheats and is known for his or her cheating cannot be trusted, and therefore relationships with that person are impossible.

♦

Discussion of Specific Cases

C A S E ♦ 1

Mike should definitely not cheat. Regardless of the importance of the grade to his career, he should have made more time for studying his history *all* semester. If he had, then his grade would not be as precarious as it was at the time of the final exam. He also should have allowed for more time to complete his studying for the exam so that he would not now be in the position where he has to consider cheating. Answers to the three questions following the case description are as follows:

1. It would make no difference to my answer if the test grade were or were not crucial. He has no more justification for cheating because the test grade is important. I have already stated how his not being prepared could have been avoided. He might now ask the instructor if he could do some extra credit work to improve his grade. This would be an act of honesty; cheating would be dishonest and immoral.

2. As I have already argued, whether or not one is caught does not dilute the immorality of cheating. Cheating is still cheating, even if the only person who knows is the cheater.

3. I have already presented arguments why Mike should not cheat. The reader may also refer to the arguments against cheating in Chapter 11, with which I concur.

C A S E ♦ 2

Dick and Lorraine should definitely not include the right fender in the claim. They could tell the body shop foreman about the right fender and offer to pay for it themselves. The foreman might even give them a discounted price because he has to repair so much of the car already under the rightful claim. Because the damage was not caused by the other car, they would be both cheating and lying if they included it in the claim. It is fallacious to argue that the insurance company has great monetary assets because of all of the premiums it collects and that it is okay to cheat it. Again, cheating is cheating whether you cheat a rich person or company or poor ones. Also, the "everybody does it" argument has already been refuted. It doesn't matter what their friends do or how many of them do it; what Dick and Lorraine would be doing is still immoral. I have already dealt with the argument of being or not being caught and its irrelevancy to the act of cheating.

C A S E ◆ 3

What Mark did was definitely immoral. He actually forged a letter for his own interests—he cheated in trying to get his book published. How does he know, for example, that the letter had that much to do with his book's being accepted by the publisher? At any rate, he should have been honest and taken his chances like all authors and worked to make his book the best he could. How he assumed that what he had done would never be discovered is unbelievable to me.

I think the publisher had every right to pull Mark's book off the market although he could have published it with an apology from Mark, perhaps even with a case study of what Mark did with his explanation of why he did it and why he now knows he was wrong. However, the publisher has to ensure that the book makes a profit, and if no teachers would adopt it for their classes because of bad publicity, then it could be a financial disaster for the publisher.

Not everyone would agree with me, but I think a dimension of intensity is added to a moral wrong if the person who commits it is especially expected to avoid it because of his or her profession or livelihood. I think that it is especially abhorrent for Mark as an ethicist and a teacher of ethics to so blatantly and directly commit an obvious moral wrong. A person who has studied and who teaches ethics, although no more perfect than any other human being, must try much harder not to commit an immoral act.

If the book were otherwise excellent and had something special to offer that other ethics books did not, then I might consider using it if the author did what I described in the previous paragraph. However, I probably would not use it, given his terrible breach of trust with his colleagues and students of ethics.

Breaking Promises

General Discussion of the Problem

Humanitarian Ethics generally rejects breaking promises as moral for all of the reasons listed in Chapter 11 in the arguments against it. People who break their promises cannot be trusted, making it very difficult to have a meaningful relationship with them. We all like to know that if a person promises to do or not do something, we can count on him or her to keep that promise. If someone breaks a promise even once then we cannot have a significant relationship with that person.

Promises may be broken only for good reasons, again such as to save someone from harm or death. In order to break a promise, one must have an exceedingly important reason to do so; otherwise, promises should be kept.

♦

Discussion of Specific Cases

CASE ♦ 1

No promise is ever too trivial for one to keep, and in this case keeping the promise was very important to Janice. That she made it a condition for her marrying Bernie also adds to its importance. I think all promises are important, but those made in connection with something as important as marriage are even more important, because breaking them tends to destroy an important relationship. It is quite possible to break only one promise or a few promises in one's life, but in my experience, one broken promise, like a lie, often leads to other broken promises. In other words, the domino theory is especially pertinent to this moral issue.

CASE ♦ 2

Such promises as David made to Harold should not be made. It is unfair of Harold to demand such a promise of David, and David should not have made such a promise if he had no intention of keeping it. Harold could have asked him to help and protect Doris in any way he could, but he had no right to demand that David promise to marry her. David, too, could have promised to take care of Doris as best as he could but not to marry her unless he wanted to anyway. One should try to keep reasonable promises one has made, of course, whether or not anyone else knows about them.

Sometimes there is unusual duress for promises to be made, and if David's was made under such conditions, he could be justified in breaking it rather than marry someone he didn't love. A lot would depend on the circumstances. If the circumstances were extenuating, then one honest way David could handle breaking his promise would be to tell Doris what happened and ask to be released by her from the promise while still offering to continue to be her friend.

CASE ♦ 3

Because Wanda had an agreement with Sandy, what she did was not a moral act. We shouldn't lie to children any more than to adults. We might not reveal to children everything that we know or are doing, but when asked specific questions, we should answer honestly but gently. Wanda is of course also entitled to her own life as an adult and does not have to govern her every action by what Sandy thinks, feels, or wants; however, she should deal with Sandy as fairly and honestly as possible. If Wanda's relationship with Howard is a serious one, which it seems to be, then what Wanda does will eventually affect

Sandy's life and cannot be merely relegated to Wanda's right to privacy. Wanda could have conducted her affair more discreetly and not at her home, which would have avoided Sandy's discovery. However, that Sandy actually asked her mother about the affair puts a stronger requirement on Wanda to be truthful with her. She of course need not and should not be graphic, but she can tell Sandy in a nice way about her feelings for Howard and give Sandy a chance and time to relate to the situation without being confronted with it. I feel that it's important to be as honest with children as is possible, because if adults lie or break promises, children will assume that these actions are acceptable.

I feel that Wanda's reasons for not telling Sandy and for reacting with anger are understandable but neither helpful nor really justifiable. As I said earlier, she should have attempted to be honest with Sandy, especially when she promised to and also because Sandy had asked her a direct question that required an honest answer. Rather than respond to Sandy's anger with her own anger, she should have apologized to her and explained why she didn't act as she said she would in this instance. She could then have gone on to explain her relationship with Howard more fully so that Sandy would understand better how her mother felt and where Sandy would fit into the situation.

◆

Stealing

General Discussion of the Problem

In most societies, people are entitled to what they have earned or inherited honestly, and no one has the right to take such possessions from them. People generally assume that their belongings are safe and that other people can be trusted not to steal them. Stealing violates mostly the Principle of Justice or Fairness, but also the Principles of Honesty and Truth Telling and Individual Freedom. Therefore, in Humanitarian Ethics, stealing is in general considered immoral. It is not fair, of course, to steal someone's fairly acquired earnings, possessions, ideas, or even reputation. Stealing is also dishonest even though it may be allowed in some extenuating situations. By stealing someone's possessions, material or otherwise, the thief limits that person's freedom. For example, if a couple has saved all year to go on a vacation and someone steals all of their money, then their freedom to enjoy that vacation has been denied. Therefore, the general view of stealing—like lying, cheating, and breaking promises—is that it is immoral unless strong justification can be brought forth, such as stealing in a disaster situation to prevent the starvation of innocent people.

♦

Discussion of Specific Cases

CASE ♦ 1

The theft of anything that is important to the owner is not a trivial wrong. This case presents beautifully the distinction between what is legal and what is moral as discussed in Chapter 1. Whether or not titles are protected by law, the moral principles previously described should be observed. That Victor has used this title for seven years and that his book has made it famous belies the title's theft. In addition to the outright stealing of the title, the publisher and the authors are obviously "cashing in" on the book's popularity, which is certainly unfair and unjust. That neither the publisher nor the authors even answered Victor's complaints is not only a blatant disregard for the seriousness of the situation but also a breach of good manners (see Chapter 1 on manners in relationship to morals).

Victor cannot merely assume that they stole his title on purpose, but it certainly seems implied that what happened was not merely an error on the part of either the publisher or the authors. For example, if the publisher had done this without the authors knowing it, then, of course, they wouldn't have been guilty. Because neither party responded to Victor's complaint, he could only presume that all parties knew what they were doing. Once a book has been published, there is not much anyone can do, but the parties responsible could have written Victor and said that any revised edition would use a different title and apologized for stealing his. What hurts here, as with the forged letter of recommendation in Case 3 under the section on cheating, is that teachers of ethics are supposed to know the difference between what is legal and what is moral, and so immoral actions on their part are even more reprehensible than those by people who have not been formally trained in ethics.

CASE ♦ 2

I believe that Katia is justified in stealing during the wartime emergency-type situation she was in. It would be better if some sort of rationing or control could be set up so that all survivors could receive equal shares, but such situations are not always possible. Therefore, I believe that she would be justified in taking only what is needed. She certainly would not be justified in looting for luxuries. When times were better, Katia could even offer to compensate the people whose house she had broken into.

Stealing during peacetime is of course a different matter. There are usually many agencies of both the state and federal governments that Katia could turn to, and only if all of these avenues had been fully explored and exhausted could stealing be condoned at all. It's not impossible that such a situation could occur, but most people can acquire some help, and even begging should be tried before one resorts to stealing.

C A S E ♦ 3

Stealing such items is immoral. One can understand how people felt during such riots and how their anger and frustration could have surfaced. However, even if their society were corrupt and even though it certainly suppressed and segregated them, they could not justify stealing things that did not belong to them, especially when most of the stolen goods were luxury items. These were not items needed for simple survival as was the food in Case 2, and therefore it cannot be condoned or justified.

C A S E ♦ 4

I do feel that Anne and Eric were guilty of theft. If they had felt that the will was unfair, then they should have sat down with the designated heirs and tried to get the will changed to be more equitable to their side of the family. Legally, of course, people may leave their estate to whomever they want; however, this does not always ensure justness or fairness. If after discussing the matter with the designated heirs, Anne and Eric received no satisfaction, they could then have announced that they were going to contest the will. At least they would have been honest and open and aboveboard with their actions. What they did was certainly highly questionable—getting Margaret, who was pretty much mentally incompetent, to change her will and then operating "under the table." On the face of it, they had no right to change Leroy's will unless they proceeded honestly and forthrightly. I feel also that they should have taken into consideration the effects of their actions—not just the immediate effects of gaining more money, but all of the hard feelings and loss of friendship that their actions caused. It would seem that friendship of long standing held very little importance for them.

A P P E N D I X

5

Applying Humanitarian Ethics to the Moral Problems of Human Sexuality

◆───────────────────────────────────

General Discussion of the Problem

Before discussing specific sexual activities and the moral considerations surrounding them, it is important to see how the five basic principles relate to human sexuality. The Value of Life principle should not be and very seldom is involved in matters of private sexuality; however, any act that is life threatening may be considered immoral unless people choose it for themselves, which is a rarity for example, cardiac patients who choose to risk their lives to have sexual relations). The Principle of Goodness is definitely involved in human sexual relationships in that sexual activity should cause pleasure and avoid pain, should strive for excellence, and should encourage harmony and foster creativity among all concerned.

There should always be a strong attempt to be honest and tell the truth in all aspects of any type of human relationship, but especially in matters of sexuality. Frankness and openness in the discussion of sexuality and sexual problems must also be encouraged. One of the absurdities in our culture is the obvious lack of education in or teaching about sexuality. There are, after all, experts available who have written books and who can supply clear empirical evidence and valid arguments concerning how to engage in meaningful sexual activity. Such information should be made available to all people at various stages of their development so that they can lead lives that are as full and rich as possible. Every effort should be made to distribute goodness and to be fair and just to all concerned, but especially toward the people immediately involved in the relationship.

Finally, in matters of private sexuality, individual freedom should be the guiding principle as long as the rights of the people immediately involved in the relationship are also observed. Humanitarian Ethics would consider rape, child molestation, sadism performed on unwilling victims, or any other kind of forced or coercive sexuality as immoral, and it would consider any other human sexual activities performed between or among consenting adults as moral as long as it can be shown that no direct harm comes to others because of these activities.

In other words, my ethical system is generally in agreement with the liberal point of view, which considers pornography, homosexuality, prostitution, masturbation, nonmonogamous marriages, and sex outside of marriage, except for adultery, as private sexual matters that should not be legislated against. As for "unnatural" sexuality, I would condone all forms of it performed by consenting adults except for bestiality.

Because I do not have a specific case to discuss for each aspect of human sexuality presented in Chapter 12, before going into a discussion of these cases I feel that I should describe the Humanitarian Ethics point of view on sexuality in general.

First, I feel that both nonmonogamous and group marriages are moral as long as the five basic principles are carefully observed—especially in relation to any children involved—and all people in these types of marriages have agreed to be involved. If no one outside them is harmed (other than that the group's style of living is not to a person's taste), then there seems to be nothing immoral about these marriages in themselves. Such arrangements are of a private nature pertaining only to those who have freely entered into them. Because people and their tastes and feelings differ so widely, voluntary experimentation may be allowed to take place as long as it is in consonance with the five basic principles.

Second, there is no evidence that masturbation leads to any harm either to the masturbater or to anyone else. It is, of course, generally prohibited as a public act under indecent exposure laws. However, assuming that it is a private act involving only one person, because it brings pleasure to that person without harming anyone else, and because it can help that person find out about and be at ease with his or her own body, then it should not be considered an immoral act.

Third, as far as so-called sexual perversion or unnatural sex acts are concerned, I would say that, except for bestiality, as long as these are private sexual matters entered into by consenting adults and they bring no harm to anyone else, then they should be considered as moral. In other words, many sexual activities—such as oral sex, anal sex, sadism and masochism, homosexual sex, and group sex—should be allowed under the Principle of Individual Freedom as long as none of the other four principles is violated. What adults freely consent to in private sexual relationships—as long as it does not harm anyone else—cannot be considered immoral under the five basic principles. In such relationships, the decision about what is perverted or unnatural must be left to the people involved. Of course, people must recognize that several of these types of sexual activities are high risk as far as developing AIDS and other sexually transmitted diseases (STDs) and should therefore practice safe sex to protect one another.

Bestiality, that is, sex acts between human beings and animals, is offensive to most but not all human beings. Because offensiveness to taste should not, in itself, be a determining factor and because adults are consenting in such acts, should they, like other private sex acts, be morally allowed? One factor here is that animals cannot consent, cannot resist, and probably would be unwilling participants in such acts. My basis so far for considering any private sexual activity as moral has been that the participants be consenting adult human beings. Because animals do not fall into this category—and even though they are not human beings, they would be denied their freedom and forced into a sexual act they cannot consent to—then bestiality could be considered immoral under the five basic principles.

Some people consider it hypocritical to raise animals to be killed for food without moral qualms yet do consider sexual activities with animals, even though they probably won't even be harmed, immoral. Whether killing animals for food is immoral or not, however, I would still say that bestiality should not be considered as moral, certainly not on the same basis as other acts between freely consenting adults.

Fourth, I believe as long as prostitution occurs between or among consenting adults, it is moral. In this regard, I am in favor of the "social acceptance and governmental control" argument presented as the last argument for prostitution in Chapter 12.

◆

Discussion of Specific Cases

CASE ◆ 1

It is my general feeling that premarital sex should be left entirely up to the individuals involved, provided that proper contraceptive precautions are taken so that the moral predicaments of abortion and the births of unwanted children, as well as the contraction of AIDS and other STDs, can be avoided. There is no legal or overriding moral requirement that people be legally married before they engage in sexual activity, but, to my way of thinking, there should certainly be a clear agreement—possibly even a personal contract—as to what people involved in such a relationship can expect from each other. Safe sex should be practiced for mutual protection.

Furthermore, as long as the five basic principles (most often four, because the Value of Life is seldom an issue in sexuality) are practiced by people involved in premarital sex, there would seem to be no need for any moral or legal sanctions against it. As I have mentioned, this type of sexual activity is usually referred to as "fornication" in the Bible, where it is considered immoral, but it need not be immoral as long as the people involved are consenting, free, honest, just, truthful, and good toward each other.

For example, if two single people consent to have sexual relations without any commitments or ties being implied—solely for the pleasure that they hope can be derived from their sexual relationship—I can see nothing overtly wrong in such a relationship. It is important for the people to be honest and truthful with each other so that one person is not led to think that the relationship means more than it does; it would be immoral for one person to lie to another about this matter in order to get the other to engage in a sexual relationship. As long as both people understand the situation, however, I can see no reason why immorality is *necessarily* involved.

People should be aware that sex is one of the most intimate of human relationships—one that can often lead to a greater commitment than is anticipated at the beginning of a relationship, so that either member of the relationship may be hurt by expecting more from it than was originally agreed on. However, this is a risk that both parties take, and if they have any intimations that such a situation might develop, then perhaps the person who might get hurt should avoid this type of relationship. This possibility can certainly be discussed in advance, and once a person knows himself or herself well enough, he or she should know whether such a situation should be avoided. However, merely because people may get more deeply involved than they originally planned is not enough reason to make all such relationships immoral.

Evidence and arguments are not conclusive enough to assert that this type of relationship by and in itself is detrimental or immoral to any human who might enter into it. Nor—because this is a matter of private sexual relations—should what other people think have any necessary bearing on whether or not such a relationship is entered into. The reactions of other people would certainly be one of the considerations people might want to make before engaging in such activity, especially if they cannot take criticism or any form of ostracism that they might receive from others in a culture that has frowned on premarital sexual relations for many years. But if people in such a relationship feel that they are not being immoral and can handle the reactions of others, then there should be no difficulty in having such a relationship.

In view of this, I obviously feel that Tom and Barbara, the two college teenagers, are not doing anything immoral. They seem to have arranged everything to avoid serious difficulties as much as possible (contraception and a clear agreement). For this reason, and because we are talking about a private sexual relationship that, as far as we can tell, will not directly harm anyone, I feel that their decision is moral.

C A S E ✦ 2

I tend to take a liberal point of view in terms of homosexuality also. There is no conclusive proof that homosexuality is a sickness, an abnormality, or a form of perversity. Moreover, there is no conclusive proof whether it is physiologically or culturally caused or merely a chosen sexual life-style. Given these ambiguities, we seem to be talking about private rather than public sexual matters, and the Principle of Individual Freedom should take precedence as long as the other principles are not violated and other people are not harmed (except by possible offense to their taste). The same principles and concerns apply here as in other marriage- or nonmarriage-type relationships such as practicing safe sex to avoid AIDS and other STDs. There is nothing in the relationship between Richard and Walter that poses harm to anyone outside the relationship. People around them might not want such a relationship or might not want to associate with them, but that is their privilege. Because the two men are not harming anyone, however, I would say that their relationship is moral.

C A S E ✦ 3

I see nothing immoral in the relationship between Sarah and Ben. They are both adults, and they have obviously entered freely into their live-in arrangement. The financial situation is certainly a factor, and it's too bad that our laws are structured so as to discourage legal marriage for people of this age, but even if they didn't want to marry for other reasons, what business is it of anyone's? Their children certainly do not have to accept the relationship, but these are matters of taste and should not be allowed to interfere with important life decisions of others when no harm to anyone is involved. I believe that what Ben and Sarah are involved in is a private matter between two freely consenting adults and, for this reason, that it is a moral act.

C A S E ✦ 4

Although adultery seldom violates the Value of Life principle, it does seem to involve a violation of the principles of Justice (in that it is an unfair and unjust treatment of another person—the other member of a marriage relationship) and Honesty or Truth Telling (in that it usually involves cheating on someone and not telling the truth about one's sexual affairs). It can also be said to violate the Principle of Goodness in that although it may bring pleasure to the two people involved in the adultery, it often causes extreme displeasure, unhappiness, and pain to the spouse who is being deceived and might infect him or her with AIDS or other STDs. Moreover, it obviously causes disharmony in the marriage relationship by destroying the unity of the family, perhaps resulting in separation and/or divorce, and often affecting innocent children who are members of the family unit. The adulterer or adulterers are exercising their own freedom, but at the cost of the freedom and rights of others. For all of these reasons, adultery is immoral and should be avoided.

The approach that should be used, but seldom is when an adulterous temptation arises, is to have an open and frank discussion with one's marriage partner about any problems before an adulterous relationship is entered into. Instead, most tempted unhappy marriage partners go ahead with an adulterous relationship or relationships until they are regularly practicing adultery. Because their mates have not been told and do not know about their affairs ("What they don't know won't hurt them"), the adulterers feel that the marriage is being maintained.

In addition to the fact that at least three basic principles are being violated, the unity and possible harmony and creativity of their marriage is constantly being undermined and, at least for one spouse, is actually destroyed. Very often the innocent marriage partner suspects, or even knows, but chooses to ignore what is happening. In this situation, however, nothing is really solved, and both partners continually live a lie. As mentioned in my justification for the Principle of Honesty or Truth Telling, if human relationships are to be meaningful and significant, they must be based on people telling each other the truth wherever possible and being honest with each other to the greatest degree possible. Once this basis is undermined, any human relationship will be weakened and eventually destroyed. Tempted spouses ought to admit their temptation to their mates, stressing that no adulterous act has yet been committed and that they feel the need to enter into a new human relationship that will very probably damage their marriage; then they should offer to openly and frankly discuss their marital problems with the idea of avoiding the adulterous relationship.

If the situation is brought into the open *before* any overt action has been taken and before any real commitments have been made to anyone other than the marriage partner, several alternatives are possible:

1. Both marriage partners can attempt to solve their marital problems, trying to discover why the adulterous act has been contemplated, with the idea of correcting, if possible, whatever is lacking in their marriage.

2. They can openly agree to and accept the practice of adultery with safe sex practices for *both* partners (as there should be no double standard) but continue their marriage under these conditions.

3. They can terminate their marriage either by separation or divorce if neither the first nor the second alternative can be worked out. In any of the three cases, however, the principles of Justice and Honesty or Truth Telling will have been observed, because whatever agreements are made will have been entered into with the full knowledge of both partners.

It is for these reasons and under these criteria that I feel that what Eric did was immoral; indeed, I feel that adultery in general is immoral unless it is agreed upon by all parties concerned because it tends to violate all of the basic ethical principles except for the Value of Life principle.

C A S E ◆ 5

In the matter of pornography, I agree with the liberal viewpoint. In Chapter 12, I discussed the public implications of pornography, stating that as long as no one is *forced* to engage in or view any activity that he or she feels is obscene, then pornography is a private matter. I also discussed the fact that there is no conclusive evidence that viewing or engaging in pornographic activities has any harmful effect on others or on the people engaging in such activities; in fact, there is evidence to the contrary. Therefore, if a person wishes to read or collect pornographic literature, art, or objects, or view or participate in pornographic activities, and provided others are not forced to do the same, then that person should be allowed to do whatever he or she wants.

There should be no attempt to ban or eliminate such activities or objects, but children and unwilling adult participants should be protected from any outward display of pornography. For example, the outside of a store that carries pornographic books should stress that minors are not allowed and should not display such books outside. In this way, those who wish to read and purchase such books may do so, but those who do not may avoid the bookstore altogether. Otherwise, matters of pornography should be left to the individual, and the Principle of Individual Freedom should take precedence.

It would seem in this case that the owners of the pornographic stores and theater have complied with all of these criteria; therefore, I think that in this situation pornography is a private sexual matter. No further laws should be enacted against these owners, and what they are doing should not be considered immoral.

Applying Humanitarian Ethics to Moral Problems in Medicine (Bioethics)

◆————————————————————————————————————

General Discussion of the Problem

The five basic ethical principles apply to bioethical issues in the same way they apply to the other moral issues I have discussed so far. In fact, all five of these principles come into play in almost all bioethical situations, as we have seen in our discussions of death and dying, abortion, and just distribution of scarce medical resources. Generally, in bioethics, we should value life but accept death as inevitable; strive for goodness at all times, mainly for patients and secondarily for families and others; be just and fair in our treatment of patients, families, and health care personnel despite any preconceptions we may have concerning their "guilt" or "innocence"; try to establish and maintain honest and truthful relationships and significant human communication; and allow for as much individual freedom as possible within the limits of the other four principles.

As for the rights and obligations of health care professionals and patients and families, I would favor the reciprocal, or collegial, approach because it maximizes freedom, equality, and justice, encouraging a free interchange of ideas. According to this approach, decisions are made collegially, with everyone having equal input, and the best interests of the patient are the main focus of discussion and decision making. In terms of truth telling and informed consent, I favor the moderate position. I feel that patients should be kept as informed as they wish to be and that they should be given information as they want and need to know it. In short, they should provide the guidelines for truth telling and informing. There are times when informed consent is necessary for tests and other procedures, and in such cases all information should be carefully gone over in person by the doctor, and all the patient's questions should be fully and clearly answered.

There are also other considerations involved in truth telling. First, most medical situations involve some ethical decisions, and doctors should not make such decisions alone. They need, rather, to be willing to share their expertise and their concern for and jurisdiction over their patients with other health care professionals, support professionals (such as social service workers and the clergy), and, of course, patients and their families themselves. Second, professionals must recognize that they are in their profession to serve patients and their families, not the other way around. Third, studies have shown that at some point most patients who are seriously ill and/or dying recognize the seriousness of their situation and want to know how they stand. In such cases, doctors should share the truth without destroying all hope, and they should do this with compassion for patients and their families rather than regarding them as numbers or personified diseases. Fourth, professionals should use all available means of communication—eye contact and touch, as well as oral and written language. Finally, professionals must realize that they can't make a blueprint for truth-telling approaches; methods will differ in relation to the patients, the families, and the situations. If patients and families wish or need to deny the truth, and if this denial is not destructive, then they should be allowed their temporary illusions. If they want to know part or all of the truth, then they should be allowed that, too. Generally speaking, however, I favor being honest with patients and their families.

Behavior Control

The Moderate Position. A more moderate position than the two views described in Chapter 13 states that behavior modification is justified provided that an individual is free and competent to consent to such modification (for example, people who join Weight Watchers or Alcoholics Anonymous). As long as these conditions are met, behavior controllers in all areas are justified in furnishing people with safe, ethical means and methods to accomplish what they want. According to this position, it is questionable whether a person incarcerated in a prison or a mental, institution is ever free or competent to make such decisions, especially where the change is strongly desired not by the person but by the institution or society at large.

The Humanitarian Ethics Approach. I agree with the moderate position in the area of behavior control. It seems to me that people who want to change their behavior should be allowed to do so in ethically permissible ways, which are not destructive to themselves or others. For example, brain surgery is justified if there is operable physiological brain disease or injury, but it generally should not be used to correct psychological problems that are not physiologically based because brain tissue cannot be replaced once it has been removed.

Of course, in some cases behavior is violent, destructive, vicious, or murderous and must be controlled. Here again, every ethically permissible method can generally be used provided that subjects will not be seriously injured or made ill by the behavior control procedures, although some "harm" may be necessary for the protection of innocent people. For example, life incarceration for a murderer might be considered harmful to the murderer, but that harm is outweighed by the danger to innocent people of releasing him.

I personally prefer conditioning techniques based on rewards to aversive techniques. Perhaps in some situations, such as when dealing with people who have committed serious crimes, some aversive conditioning (for example, a long period of incarceration, or solitary confinement) will need to be used. Generally, however, the reward approach is preferable unless subjects agree freely to aversive conditioning.

An example of reward conditioning is the method used by Weight Watchers. Everything is done to reinforce members staying on a diet and maintaining or losing weight, but nothing is done if weight is gained except to encourage members to keep trying to lose it. I also feel that no behavior control techniques for which side effects are not clearly known should be used except under extraordinary circumstances.

Finally, I feel that people who work as behavior controllers should be well qualified both medically and ethically. Moreover, they should be well versed in all methods of behavior control and should be willing to use the method that best suits the patient and the situation. For example, if patients need psychotherapy of some sort, they should have it; if they need certain psychotherapeutic drugs, they should have them; if they need operant conditioning, then they should have that, too. Generally, then, controllers or therapists should always consider first what is in the best interest of their patients, except when the latter could pose a serious danger to other innocent people.

Human Experimentation

The Moderate Position. From the moderate point of view, experimentation can be done on human beings, but only within strict guidelines. Any people to be experimented on must be competent adults and must be fully informed both in person and in writing of all the risks, side effects, and benefits of the experimentation. It can also be allowed as a last resort for therapeutic reasons provided that the people experimented on are fully informed and freely consent and that the risk or pain is no greater than any other procedure prescribed for their particular disease or injury. Such experimentation may even take place on children, with parents' consent. In such cases, however, it may be advisable to have a judge hear the case in order to provide the child with further protection.

Great care must be taken when an experiment has no benefit for the subject but, rather, is being done to benefit humanity in general or to advance knowledge. Subjects of such experiments must be fully consenting, competent adults; risks must be minimized; and subjects must be fully informed about the experiment. Mental incompetents and children should not be experimented on for these reasons.

The moderate position also accepts experimentation on incarcerated subjects, but only if they freely consent and are fully informed, just as they would be if they weren't incarcerated. They must not, in any case, be used as unknowing guinea pigs. Special bioethics committees should be established whenever and wherever *any* human experimentation is to be done, and all applications for human experimentation must be screened carefully before being approved.

Membership on such committees should not be limited to medical personnel but should also include ethicists, religious and nonreligious members, and other informed lay people, such as lawyers, sociologists, and psychologists. In such situations, the protection of subjects should have first priority. That is why experimentation for the therapeutic well-being of subjects is generally more acceptable than experimentation for "the good of humanity" or for the advancement of scientific knowledge. If such protection cannot be given, then experimentation must not be done.

The Humanitarian Ethics Approach. I generally favor the moderate position in relation to human experimentation. I feel that human experimentation can be done on freely consenting adults who are fully and clearly informed, especially when it is to be done for their own therapeutic well-being, but I also feel that it can be done for the benefit of others and for scientific advancement as long as the stated conditions are met.

Generally, however, I feel that prisoners should not be experimented on. Subjects of experiments should be completely free from coercion, and people who are incarcerated obviously don't have this freedom. I also feel that children should not be experimented on unless it is for their own therapeutic good and that it should be done only as a last resort, after nonexperimental therapies and procedures have all been tried to no avail. For example, if a child has cancer on which none of the usual therapies has been successful, if the child will die unless remission is attained, and if there is an experimental therapy that is not overly painful and that has some promise of success, then it may be tried. I also feel that any experiments to be done on children for any reason ought to be presented before a judge so that parents and doctors won't have to bear the whole burden of decision making and so that another, perhaps more objective, opinion may be obtained, thereby further safeguarding children's rights, health, and lives.

In any type of human experimentation, great care must be taken to see that coercion, either forcible or subtle, is fully eliminated. Finally, I am definitely in favor of clearing any and all human experimentation through the type of bioethics committee described in Chapter 13.

Genetics

The Moderate Position. Genetic experimentation and development should be allowed within careful guidelines. Amniocentesis, CVS, and genetic counseling have helped people make important decisions about pregnancy, childbearing, abortion, and sterilization, and as long as such matters are left to individual choice, they are ethically valid.

Other advances, however, must be made more carefully. Radical experimentation, such as cloning or the creation of life in a laboratory, should not proceed until we know with some certainty what its effects on the human species will be. Limited experimentation can be done in these areas; for example, the creation and cloning of animal life to increase food production would be justified and encouraged. The correction of genetic defects in conceptuses or in parents is also an area worthy of investigation and development. Even limited creation of human life or cloning may later be authorized, but only after its effects are known and safe guidelines have been established.

The Humanitarian Ethics Approach. I also favor the moderate position here. I feel that we should learn as much as we can about our genetic makeup but that we must have carefully drawn guidelines and safeguards to ensure that we know what the effects of applying genetic knowledge will be *before* we proceed with such techniques. I am definitely in favor of procedures such as amniocentesis and CVS and believe in full and complete counseling both before and after the birth of children in families where genetic problems are suspected or evident. I believe that genetic counselors play a very important role in this area and that they must be well qualified and suited for their jobs.

In addition, I believe that when we have the ability, we should encourage the correction of genetic defects in the conceptus, just as we now encourage such correction after the birth of children with genetic problems. Also, the correction or alteration of defective genes in adults should be encouraged when and if it becomes possible. I believe that we should proceed *very* carefully with the laboratory creation of human life and especially with the cloning of human life. I do feel that controlled experimentation can proceed in these areas, however. We have already made progress with artificial insemination and fertilized ovary implantation, so the creation in the laboratory of normal human life—to provide children for childless couples, for example—would seem to be a next and viable step. However, all of this experimentation should be kept on a small, individualistic, humanistic, and ethical level.

♦

Discussion of Specific Cases

CASE ♦ 1

The doctor seemed either to be very callous where Richard's feelings were concerned or to be unable to stop from expressing his own frustrations that he was no longer able to help his patient. I believe that he was right in telling Richard the truth but that he should not have done it so coldly and brutally, without offering Richard any hope. If he had listened carefully to Richard's questions, he would have known that Richard needed some hope, even if it only involved some medication to alleviate discomfort and pain.

To tell Richard that nothing more could be done was false (consider the hospice approach to care for the dying), and it eliminated all of Richard's hope, not just for a cure, but for being cared for as a significant human being. Once he had seen the extent of Richard's distress, the doctor could have prescribed the medication, telling Richard he couldn't promise any startling changes but also telling him that he would continue to look into other drugs and therapies for him. Finally, the doctor could have asked Richard about his pain, his ability to eat and sleep, and so on, really listening to him and trying to resolve or ease these difficulties for him.

CASE ♦ 2

I don't believe that counselors have the right to withhold any information that parents really desire and certainly none that they ask for. If parents don't ask for certain information, I don't feel that the counselors have the obligation to volunteer such information unless it will have some serious implication for the prospective child's health and well-being. A child's sex definitely does not fall into this category, so if parents did not specifically ask for this information, counselors are not obligated to reveal it. However, if parents do seek this information, then counselors are obligated to reveal it.

The only thing counselors can do if they discover that a couple will seek an abortion for such a questionable reason is to counsel them against the abortion. Counselors should make it clear that the child will otherwise be healthy and that late abortions, besides being more risky than earlier ones, are morally questionable because of the extent to which the fetus has developed. However, if the parents still wish to seek an abortion, and the law allows it, there is nothing more that the counselors can do. I stated in Appendix 3 that I feel that the parents are not ethically justified in aborting the fetus because of its sex, but despite this, I do not feel that counselors can withhold the truth if counselees directly ask for it.

CASE ◆ 3

The experimenter is in quite a quandary here because if he tells his subjects, the experiment will be ruined, but if he doesn't he will be invading their privacy, which should be guaranteed regardless of whether they are patients in or outside of an institution. In fact, as patients these people should be protected even more. There is, however, a third alternative, and that is to tape the patients without telling them, but not to use the tapes in any way unless patients agree to it. Patients should be informed clearly in person and in writing as to how the tape will be used, and they should be allowed to see it, after which they should have the right to refuse to have the tape used at all.

If this is their desire, then the tape must be immediately erased or destroyed to acquiesce to the patients' wishes. If patients will allow the tape to be used, then they ought to have the right to specify the purposes and limitations for its use; this also ought to be done in writing, and clear indications should be given as to how the tape may or may not be used. If this alternative is utilized, then tapes must be made totally secure until patients can give or refuse permission for their use. If this security cannot be guaranteed, then either the patients' permission must be acquired prior to taping or the experiment simply cannot be conducted. In all cases of experimentation, subjects' rights should come before the experiment, the desires of experimenters, or the advancement of science.

CASE ◆ 4

As I have already stated, I don't believe that experiments should be done on children—with or without their parents' permission—unless it is therapeutic for them and only when it is a last resort to save their lives. I think it is even more unforgivable to experiment on children in institutions, especially when those children are mentally retarded. There are acceptable cures for children who suffer from dysentery, and infecting otherwise healthy children with dysentery is completely unjustified, both medically and ethically.

The coercion of allowing only those children into the institution whose parents would agree to experimentation is also highly unethical and should not be permitted. A case such as this one makes it easy to see why it is important to require a court opinion prior to experimentation with children. If such a case had to be brought before a judge, it is very unlikely that the experiment would be allowed. In no way should the desire for experimentation be allowed to supersede the protection of the rights, bodies, and lives of children.

C A S E ♦ 5

I believe, as I have already stated, that a controller or therapist *generally* owes first allegiance or responsibility to the patient rather than to society, government, or an institution; therefore, in this situation, I feel that the therapist's first responsibility is to John, and that he must begin therapy by finding out what John really wants. This, of course, would take some preliminary therapy sessions.

If John is really happy as a homosexual, then the therapist should help him to adjust to his homosexuality; if, however, he would be happier being hetero-sexual or even bisexual, then the therapist's responsibility is to help him change his behavior and adjust to his new sexual orientation. The important thing is that the therapist not force John into some sort of mold, preconceived either by the therapist or society; rather, he should help John change his behavior once it is discovered what John really wants.

C A S E ♦ 6

As I mentioned earlier, I am generally not in favor of brain surgery to control behavior unless the behavior problem is physiologically based. It would seem to me that all other alternative therapies should be exhausted before the question of brain surgery ever arises. If there are no viable alternatives, then there is a question as to whether Mary should be subjected to a medical procedure with such great attendant risks and unknown effects. Related to this is the question of whether or not Mary is really in a position—given that she is in a mental institu-tion—to freely give an informed consent to such a procedure.

I believe that if all alternatives have been exhausted, including electrode implantation in the brain (the electrode could be removed if it didn't work or if it caused dangerous side effects), then the decision would first have to be made as to whether Mary was mentally competent to decide to have brain surgery.

I feel that several psychologists and psychiatrists, outside the institution where Mary is housed, should examine her and present their opinions before a judge qualified to hear competency cases. If Mary is adjudged to be mentally competent after a careful legal hearing, and if she is fully informed and aware that she might become very passive and suffer memory loss, then I feel she has a right to such surgery. I believe that no coercive methods should be used. The important thing for Mary to understand is the effect the surgery will have on her. Perhaps she could even be shown several brain surgery patients who have had the type of surgery she would undergo. In any case, she should not be promised that her violent episodes will cease or that she will be released from the institution.

APPENDIX
7

Applying Humanitarian Ethics to Moral Problems in Business (Business Ethics)

The Humanitarian Ethics Approach

General Discussion of the Problem

As in bioethics, the five basic ethical principles should generally apply in the area of business. One of the common ethical mistakes made in our society is to somehow separate business dealings from our moral activities. That is, we may generally believe that it is wrong to lie, cheat, and steal, for example, but may somehow see these behaviors as acceptable when done in the world of business. There is, of course, no logical or moral basis for such a separation.

In approaching business activities, therefore, people must value, protect, and preserve human life; strive for goodness in business and avoid badness and harm; strive to be just and fair in distributing good and bad from business activities; be as honest and truthful as they can in all of their business dealings, including agreements, contracts, advertising, and labor negotiations; and allow for as much individual freedom as possible for employers, employees, and consumers within the limits of the other four principles. These principles have as much meaning and application here as they have in dealing with any of the other moral issues or problems presented in this book.

In general I tend to support the moderate positions on discrimination and the environment and also the truthful approach in advertising described in Chapter 14. I feel that advertising should be based, as much as possible, on honesty and truth telling unless this principle would seriously conflict with the other principles—for example, if it would unnecessarily cost people their lives. It would seem that honesty and truth telling are generally the best policies to follow in business, as they are in other areas of our existence.

I also tend to lean more toward protecting and preserving the environment than allowing business to grow larger and more powerful because using up resources as if they will never run out and destroying our living environment have a more serious immediate and long-range effect on our lives and health than does the state of our economy. This policy does not have to mean the end of business; all it means is that business will now have to be conducted in harmony with our environment rather than in disregard of it. As I have mentioned, this policy will be expensive, and it may mean that economic progress may have to be slowed somewhat; however, we should all be willing to make the sacrifices necessary to preserve our world, our lives, and the lives of future generations.

I also lean toward a strong affirmative action program, not only in business, but also in all aspects of our society. I feel strongly that reverse discrimination should be avoided as much as possible, but for a while, anyway, I think it must remain as a necessary evil in some situations. My reason for this position is that although we have made strides as a nation toward righting wrongs resulting from discriminatory practices in the past, the immorality of racial, religious, and sexual prejudice has gone on for so long that gargantuan efforts are now needed to eliminate it. I feel that if we are strong in our resolve to make the necessary changes in this area, we can do so in a way that will avoid, for the most part, the additional harm of reverse discrimination.

As for rights and obligations, as I have mentioned in earlier chapters, no rights are absolute, but some do take precedence over others—the right to have one's life preserved and protected, for example. The rights of everyone involved in business activities should be established and carried out generally in accordance with the five principles and their priorities as described in Chapter 7. Conflicts of rights must not be resolved by arbitrarily establishing absolutes but, rather, by applying the basic ethical principles to specific situations, taking into consideration the particularities of that situation and the people involved in it.

Obligations, too, are to be established in accordance with the five basic ethical principles, and they must be fulfilled, whenever possible, in consonance with the Principle of Justice. Rights and obligations in any business should be clearly stated for everyone involved—employees, consumers, and employers—and they should be monitored and followed to the best of everyone's ability. In other words, in business—as in other aspects of our lives—being ethical and moral is all-important, and it must have priority over production, consumption, competition, and expansion. If everyone in business has this attitude, then we cannot help but create a better life for ourselves, not only economically, but in an overall human way as well.

◆

Discussion of Specific Cases

C A S E ◆ 1

This case is a good example of a situation in which production and profit in business take precedence over safety. Manufacturers are often loath to increase the cost of production in order to make their products safer; they would rather take the risk that no harm will result from this—that the product will be "safe enough." Obviously, as this case illustrates, this attitude often results not only in a threat to people's health and lives, but also in a higher cost in the long run to the manufacturers, in good public relations as well as in money.

This car company compounded its original mistake by ignoring the fact that the mistake was costing lives, making no effort to rectify it once it was discovered. Furthermore, the company even threatened to penalize the employee who was trying to rectify the problem. In this situation, public health and well-being should have been the main priority, not profit and loss. The design engineer was right in diligently attempting to correct the safety error, and for the car manufacturer to consistently penalize her for her ethics instead of rewarding her is a perfect example of misplaced values.

Susan's first ethical obligations were to the protection of innocent lives and to her own sense of right and wrong rather than loyalty to a company that was unethical in its actions toward others. By these unethical actions, in fact, the company nullified any obligations its employees might have had to be loyal to it; one need not and indeed should not be loyal to an organization that is unethical.

The engineer should have quit or allowed herself to be fired and then reported what she knew to public authorities. This action would have provoked an investigation, stopped production of the car until proper corrections were made, and forced the manufacturer to recall cars already sold so that their safety problems could be corrected. It obviously behooves every company to be exceptionally prudent when the safety of consumers is concerned, and in the long run such a policy will cost companies less. The research engineer cannot shirk her own ethical responsibility just because the company has removed direct responsibility from her because the lives of innocent people are involved here. Losing her job may be a hardship, but she really has no other choice if she wishes to act ethically.

C A S E ◆ 2

Steve's decision is wrong because he is ignoring an agreement made when he entered his union to abide by majority decisions in negotiations. It is also unethical to steal from one's business even if the company is insured against loss of tools and equipment and even if a worker thinks that the company can afford the loss because it makes so much money. Because a majority of Steve's coworkers and fellow union members approved the contract, he has no right to violate it unilaterally. Evidently, management and the union worked out what they both felt was a fair and just increase considering that the plant had lost profits in the last year.

Assuming that both sides negotiated in good faith, then Steve must also abide by the decision in good faith; his only other alternative is to resign and look for work elsewhere. Under the circumstances, Steve has no basis for stating that he was cheated out of his raise unfairly. Management does, I feel, have an obligation to help its workers meet the cost of living wherever it can do so, but this company seems to have done its best by coming within 2 percent of the cost of living increase. In short, all the parties involved except Steve seem to have done the best they could under the circumstances. What Steve did, however, was definitely unethical.

C A S E ◆ 3

No business is ethically justified in selling products or services that differ in content from what is advertised. It is ethically wrong for a company to switch major parts of its product in order to save money, and when such a practice is discovered, whether done inadvertently or deliberately, immediate restitution must be made without attempts to cover up, use bribery, or employ any other stalling tactics.

Because the price difference is one thousand dollars, the customers are entitled to the superior equipment that the higher price calls for—any other arrangement would be unethical. Whether the company is caught or not has absolutely nothing to do with the ethics of the situation; even if it knows it will never be caught, its basic policy should be to give consumers the right equipment for a fair price. Mike should, of course, refuse the bribe for not revealing what the company has done, no matter how enticing that bribe may be. Rather, he should report his discovery to the proper authorities and do everything he can to ensure that the company corrects all discrepancies and makes good its original claims.

CASE ♦ 4

As in the case of the research engineer for the car company, Myra has done the ethical thing up to this point and should persevere in her line of action. Her boss's version of what is and is not ethical in public relations and advertising serves only expediency; it is erroneous both logically and ethically. Advertising firms have an ethical obligation to tell the truth and to make sure that the products and services they are advertising are not dangerous, regardless of how large the account is. Since Myra cannot in good conscience create a campaign to promote a car that is endangering the lives of innocent people, she should not be required to do so. She certainly should not be coerced into doing so by being threatened with the denial of a just promotion.

As I have already said, the advertising firm should have a policy against representing unethical firms such as the car manufacturer, but even if it does decide to represent them, its employees should not be forced to violate their consciences by having to participate in such lies and misrepresentations. Like the research engineer, Myra owes her first loyalty to the people whose lives are endangered and also to her own conscience; she does not owe any loyalty to an organization that is not only being unethical but is also trying to coerce her into acting unethically. The position in which both Myra and Susan, the engineer, find themselves is very difficult—it is not easy to give up one's livelihood and job security—but how can they be happy in the long run working for firms that are so obviously unethical and that have such a total disregard for the rights and lives of others?

CASE ♦ 5

Because Denise and Bonnie are equally qualified, and because they are both women—which helps to fulfill one aspect of affirmative action—the decision to be made is how the difference between their personalities and their races should affect which one of them is hired. That Bonnie is more outgoing does not relate directly to the job, and its importance in terms of keeping office personnel happy is far outweighed by the mandate of affirmative action. If the two women were white, perhaps the more outgoing personality might be a factor in hiring, but it seems a factor of minimal importance in this situation.

My feeling is that, under these circumstances, the personnel manager should hire Denise. I don't feel that Bonnie could claim reverse discrimination because Denise is as well qualified as she is. It is also probably true that Bonnie, despite affirmative action, still has a better chance than Denise of finding a job elsewhere. Obviously, I feel that the personnel manager should be very conscious of affirmative action and reverse discrimination in making this decision, especially because the percentage of minority and women employees at the center is so low. I feel that the first criterion for hiring should be that the prospective employee has the qualifications for the job; once that criterion is met, however, I feel that affirmative action should have the greatest influence on the choice, at least until the ratio of minorities and women has been raised to an acceptable level.

CASE ✦ 6

I feel that every effort should be made by all parties to effect a series of compromises that will save the people and the environment, the town, and the company—in that order. I definitely feel that the government, as the representative of all people, does have a right—indeed, an obligation—to investigate businesses and communities to avoid destruction of the environment. The government's report is obviously very important to everyone in this area, and all parties should accept the following as their goals: to clean up the environment as soon as possible; to keep the town economically alive by maintaining the plant, even if at a reduced capacity until necessary changes can be made; and to allow the company to reap a reasonable profit from the plant's operations. Representatives of the company, the townspeople and their representatives (mayor, city council), and the federal government should meet together to see what can be done to accomplish the stated objectives.

The company must be willing to pay its fair share of the costs, but it should not be overburdened. The townspeople must also bear some of the burden, perhaps through higher taxes or the forgoing of raises for workers at the plant for one year. The government should also help financially by offering either low-interest government loans or part payment for the changes that the plant must undergo.

I feel that the mayor would be wrong in entering into collusion with the plant manager to stall environmental changes at the expense of the health and welfare of the entire community. I believe that the problem ought to be brought into the open so that the townspeople can be made aware of it and can help solve it in some way. I also feel the company that owns the plant ought to consider more than just a loss of profits in its decision making. After all, the company is contributing not only to the economic well-being of a town but also to the destruction of its environment and the possible ill-health of its people. The company should also consider the goodwill it can gain by maintaining the plant, even if it sustains some loss of profit. Instead of taking the either-or position, the company ought to present choices as to what can be done, and it should ask for help and cooperation from all involved parties.

The company must—as must everyone who is involved in this situation—accept the long-range necessity of protecting and preserving the environment; otherwise, there may not be a plant or many people around in years to come. I feel that all aspects of the situation are important, but I feel that the environmental aspect should be given first priority by all parties. If the plant maintains its rigid position and will only take the stalling route the manager has suggested to the mayor, I feel that the mayor has no choice but to refuse to go along with it.

Perhaps now that the town is better established, there will be time to encourage new, less environmentally destructive businesses to set themselves up in Farling. In any case, I feel that a decision to increase the danger to the health and well-being of the people and the environment would be the wrong decision for the mayor to make, even if it is the only way of saving the town economically. After all, if people have their health and lives, they can still move somewhere else and get other jobs; if, on the other hand, they are sick or dying, then the economics of the situation definitely becomes unimportant.

CASE ◆ 7

I think what happened to the first officer was abominable. True, she made a foolish mistake in having an affair with a higher ranking officer, but she did think that he loved her and believed him when he said he was divorcing his wife. Once she found out that he was not committed to her and just wanted to have sex with her, having no intention of divorcing his wife, she had every right to break off the affair and to have that be the end of it. Nothing she did deserved the treatment she received after breaking up with him. Despite an error in judgment, she should have been left alone by that officer once she said she wanted to end the affair, and in no way should she have received any harassment on her job. She definitely should have been able to count on backup while doing her police duties, regardless of what had gone on with the sergeant. Officers, especially the sergeant, should have been reprimanded, transferred to a different precinct, and perhaps even demoted, including those who did not back her up when she needed it.

CASE ◆ 8

The second officer was certainly unfairly treated because of her sex and should not have been discriminated against because she is female. She had successfully completed the difficult training that qualified her for the K9 corps and therefore should have been allowed to perform her duties without harassment, humiliation, or dehumanizing language and actions. That she was put in danger of being seriously injured when not only one but two male officers purposely gave their dogs the wrong commands is absolutely unacceptable and thoroughly unethical. Here again, I think that the officers responsible for her harassment should have been severely reprimanded, demoted, and transferred, and maybe even should have had their jobs terminated for their irresponsible behavior.

I think that both women should be offered their jobs back after the offenders have been removed from the precinct and should be paid full retroactive compensation whether they take their jobs back or not. I also think that any psychological therapy treatments should be paid for by the City of Long Beach. I also feel that they should receive the awards of their civil suits as soon as possible. These two cases are the worst cases of sexual harassment I have ever heard about. I'm sure that there are others equally bad or worse cases, but such actions must not be allowed to take place in any type of employment, according to Humanitarian Ethics.

Applying Humanitarian Ethics to Environmental Ethics

Environmental ethical issues have become quite significant and controversial in the last twenty years or so. When I was growing up in Los Angeles in the 1930s and 1940s, there was no concern about the diminution of resources. We believed our natural resources would last us forever. The air in Los Angeles was clean and pure, water was clear and delicious, and trees were plentiful. I don't need to describe what has happened since then all over our nation and the world, much less in Los Angeles, the smog capital of the world. Civilization and society have taken their toll on all aspects of our environment—animals, bodies of water, plants and trees, air, and land—to the extent that all human beings must realize that if the environment is not protected, the world as we know it will not exist for us, our children, or future generations.

However, problems with the environment have occurred as a result of our scientific and technological advances, which have made life better and more rich for human beings, and there is a battle between making progress and maintaining and even developing a beautiful natural environment and staying healthy in the process. In addition, many companies make their profit from the natural environment, such as lumber companies, chemical companies, mining firms, scientific research firms, and fur trapping organizations. It would seem that the best way to approach this ethical issue would be to seek a balance between protecting the environment in all of its aspects and allowing for the advancement of civilization and progress within reason.

As you might expect from the way Humanitarian Ethics has proceeded in the previous appendixes, it tends to favor the moderate position, which is to maintain the environment in its beauty and vitality, protect endangered species, and respect the lives of other living creatures (whether animals or plants and trees) and yet to allow for progress, scientific advancement, and scientific research for the betterment of all human beings.

Protection of the Environment: Recycling and Waste Disposal

Every effort must be made to protect and preserve the environment and yet allow for progress to continue to be made and businesses to flourish. These are not always easy tasks to accomplish, however. We obviously cannot continue with a willy-nilly, irresponsible destruction of the environment—laying waste to our forests and land; polluting our rivers, streams, and lakes; and burying waste that will not disintegrate and toxic chemicals that will destroy our lands, waters, and population.

Recycling

One of the most important actions we can take is to recycle our products and to use recycled materials in business. Where I once had two trash cans, I now have nine for the separation of various recyclable products. We need to make an even greater effort to recycle and to use recycled products so that we will not continue, for example, to decimate the trees throughout our land for paper and paper products.

Toxic Waste Disposal

We must also regulate the disposal of toxic wastes; otherwise, we ourselves and our children and grandchildren will not survive. Science and technology must come up with new ways to safely destroy such wastes without having to bury them in our land, dump them in our bodies of water, including our oceans, or let them escape into the atmosphere. There should be ways to accomplish this, and we must continue to develop them. I see no way around the governmental regulation of all of these things, and government must be reasonable and moderate in allowing businesses and people to flourish without destroying the environment.

♦───

Animal Rights

Humanitarianism believes that animals have rights because they are sentient and mental beings to varying degrees, but it does not put animals ultimately on the same level as human beings. It believes that animals may be used for food but not wastefully and that animals should not be killed painfully. It favors free range over factory farming or at least the careful concern for animals' well-being and treatment. It respects the vegetarian point of view but does not believe that people are immoral in any way if they choose to eat animal flesh as long as animals are not cruelly treated in the process. It also takes the view that since animals are killed for food, their skins and other parts can also be used as needed, but it is opposed to using endangered species for either food or body parts.

Animal Experimentation

Humanitarian Ethics believes that animals can be used for experimentation as long as they are treated humanely and not caused pain or needless suffering. Cures for diabetes, polio, heart disease, and many other diseases would never have been discovered without animal experimentation. This does not give researchers the right to torture or mutilate animals in any way, however, and there should be strict rules regulating this and safeguards against allowing animals to suffer pain. Any experiments must also be significant and not trivial or useless, as with the beagles and the strontium 90 testing. With such rules and safeguards it would seem that rather than being put to sleep, unwanted animals could be used for proper experimentation.

Killing Animals for Sport

Although I do not like to hunt or fish, I do not oppose allowing other people to do so, provided that they follow rules and regulations that protect animals and fish from becoming endangered or extinct. If hunting or fishing is indeed an ancient custom or ritual, then an unsportsmanlike approach to killing animals or fish should not be allowed. However, careful licensing, regulation, and quotas should be in effect to protect animals and fish and yet allow for the control of their overpopulation. The killing of exotic endangered animals for food and body parts should not be allowed, and laws protecting them should be duly enforced.

◆

Discussion of Specific Cases

CASE ◆ 1

The issues presented in the case of the baby harp seals or any other animal harvesting situation are very controversial and difficult to resolve. In the first place, I am opposed to killing animals for furs when there are perfectly good synthetic furs available that are just as beautiful as real furs. I don't think that people who wear fur coats that were made years ago should be looked down upon in any way, but I think we should stop using materials such as ivory, furs, or exotic skins unless they are acquired from animals who die naturally or who are hunted on a limited basis under strict quota regulation and licensing.

Perhaps a quota system could be applied to the harp seals, but only to adults. Just as fauns are protected from deer hunting, so also should other baby animals be allowed to grow up before being harvested. It should also be required that the harp seals be killed in the most painless way possible. Further, every effort should be made to find another industry for the people in that area so that they will not be deprived of their livelihood when killing of the harp seals is restricted or stopped.

CASE ◆ 2

Many of these distinctions seem to fall under the heading of "split-hairs." I would favor using parts of animals that were killed for food for clothing or shoes and accessories, thereby using natural animal resources efficiently. As I stated in Case 1, I see no reason for people to kill animals for furs, hides, or feathers unless the animals have already died or have been killed for food. Obviously, I think that killing animals for food is not unethical, whereas killing them merely for hides, furs, feathers, or body parts is. That's the distinction I find important. Again I stipulate that the killing of any wild animals should be done as humanely as possible and regulated by quota and licensing to avoid the endangerment of species. Therefore, I oppose raising animals just for their hides, furs, feathers, or body parts.

CASE ◆ 3

As I described in Chapter 14 on business ethics, industry has a powerful obligation to protect the environment to the greatest extent possible. Constant research should be done and safety procedures enacted to prevent such calamities as oil spills and to find effective methods of neutralizing and controlling spills when they do occur. This should be an oil company's first priority. It is also admirable to protect and preserve our natural environment and animal and plant species from destruction by the technology of oil drilling or strip mining, for example, but these actions should be real and extensive, and not just building a pipe here and there for a fox to hide in. Any and all destruction to the environment should be reported along with the causes and efforts being made to resolve whatever problem has occurred. Keeping the public informed is much better for a company's image than having people find out about the destruction of the environment after the fact. Advertisements and commercials that describe what the company is doing to preserve and protect the environment are fine as long as they're not distracting the public from the company's mistreatment of the environment.

C A S E ♦ 4

First of all, other tests that do not use animals or humans should be developed. It is difficult to understand why, with all of the scientific knowledge about chemistry, such experiments still have to be conducted. I believe it is hard to justify experimenting on animals or humans when pain and destruction is involved merely for cosmetic reasons. I do feel that experimenting on animals for significant medical developments, as I stated earlier in this appendix, is justified as long as these experiments are not trivial but benefit human beings. If it is absolutely necessary to test an important cosmetic on animals, then testing should be done painlessly, and such tests that might result in the loss of eyesight, for example, should be avoided. A company could also ask for human volunteers as long as the same protections and strict rules and regulations are followed that exist for human experimentation in general.

C A S E ♦ 5

One of the most difficult balances we have to achieve is that between preserving the environment and allowing scientific and technological progress. As I have said before, it is a balance that has to be achieved to the best of our abilities. We cannot stop the construction of necessary things like dams, roads, or hospitals because it will encroach upon the environment or a certain animal species. We can, however, make sure that we do our best to prevent excessive damage to the environment. The famous twentieth-century architect, Frank Lloyd Wright, set a good example. When designing a house or other building, he tried to fit it into its natural environment as much as possible, trying, for example, to maintain the forest around it. We should continue this practice. First of all, the project to be built must really be necessary to the well-being and progress to society (not the fourteenth shopping center in a two-mile area, for example). Second, everything must be done to protect the environment or animal species around it. Many things are possible, such as moving endangered animal species to safer environment, or trying to leave as much of the natural environment intact as possible so that the species will not be destroyed by the project. It would seem that moving this fish to a safer environment might be more acceptable than blocking building of the dam.

Glossary

Abortion: The termination of a pregnancy prior to birth. A *spontaneous abortion,* or *miscarriage,* is one that is not purposely caused by the potential mother or anyone else. An *induced abortion* is one that is caused by someone, usually a doctor or midwife. A *self-induced abortion* is caused by the pregnant woman without the aid of a doctor. A *therapeutic abortion* refers to abortion done for some medical reason, but this term is usually used interchangeably with induced abortion. An *illegal abortion* is one that is against the law, and a *legal abortion* is one that is in accordance with the law (abortions are presently legal in the United States). Generally there are three types of abortion: uterine aspiration, hysterotomy, and saline abortion (sometimes called amniocentesis abortion).

Absolute: Perfect in quality and complete; not to be doubted or questioned—positive, certain, unconditional; not limited by restrictions or exceptions. This term is usually applied to beings (for example, God), but most importantly to truth. *Absolutism* is the theory that morality is absolute rather than relative; that is, that there are absolute moral truths that we must adhere to and which particular situations, people, or places do not affect. *Near absolute* is a term coined by the author of this book to describe basic principles in ethics.

Abstinence: The act of forgoing or abstaining from something. As the term is used in this text, it means not engaging in sexual activities as one way of avoiding AIDS or STDs.

Acquired Immune Deficiency Syndrome (AIDS): A disease transmitted by various types of sexual activity, other means of ingesting bodily fluids, and injecting drugs with infected needles. The virus effectively destroys the infected person's immune system, making him or her susceptible to such diseases as Kaposi's sarcoma (a type of cancer) and pneumocystis carinii (a form of pneumonia).

Ad Hoc Committee: A committee formed to deal specifically with a single issue or problem—for example, the *ad hoc* committee on brain death, or irreversible coma.

Adultery: Sexual relations between a married person and a person other than the spouse. This is also known as *extramarital sex.*

Aesthetics (Esthetics): In philosophy, the study of values in art or beauty. Related to ethics because it involves values, although here the values apply to art or beauty.

Affective: That aspect of human beings that involves emotions and feelings.

Affirmative Action: That action taken to eliminate racial, religious, sexual, age, and handicap discrimination in employment practices.

Agent: A term in philosophy that means one who performs an act or action.

Allowing Someone to Die: The medical practice of deciding when treatment is no longer curing and healing and when artificial or extraordinary means of life support are to be discontinued. *See also* Euthanasia.

Amniocentesis: A test that is performed by withdrawing fluid from the amniotic sac and subjecting it to various tests through which any of about two hundred birth defects can be detected in a conceptus (fetus). This test can also determine other characteristics, such as sex. The term can also mean a form of abortion in which fluid is withdrawn from the amniotic sac and replaced with a saline, prostaglandin, or glucose solution that causes the uterus to contract and premature labor to begin. *See also* Amniotic Sac *and* Abortion.

Amniotic Sac: The sac containing fluid in which the conceptus floats during the entire period of gestation unless aborted.

Amoral: Indifferent to morality. This term applies only to human beings. Babies are considered amoral and, rarely, some adult human beings, such as the severely mentally disturbed, those who have had prefrontal lobotomies, and those with no moral education. Amoral can also mean not knowing the difference between right and wrong.

Analytic Ethics: *See* Metaethics.

Behavior Control: The alteration or manipulation of human behavior by various techniques, such as behavior modification, psychotherapy, drugs, brain surgery, and so on.

Behaviorism: A materialistic theory of human nature, developed originally by John Watson and further developed by B. F. Skinner, that states that human beings essentially *are* their behavior and that there is no such thing as mind, soul, spirit, or self but only body and brain, which react to external stimuli.

Beneficent: That which is good or which causes or brings about goodness, such as a beneficent act, which is a good act. The Principle of Beneficence is another name for the Principle of Goodness. *See also* Good or Right *and* Principle of Goodness or Rightness.

Bestiality: Sexual relations between human beings and animals.

Bioethics: Literally "life ethics." Essentially ethics having to do with medicine and medical aspects of human beings, such as human experimentation, abortion, mercy killing, and truth telling, among others.

Bisexual: Human beings who have sexual relations with either the opposite sex or their own sex. *See also* Homosexuality *and* Heterosexuality.

Brain Death: Refers to irreversible or irreparable brain damage determined by four criteria established by an *ad hoc* committee at Harvard Medical School in 1968: (1) unreceptivity and unresponsitivity, (2) no spontaneous movements or breathing, (3) no reflexes, and (4) a flat EEG. *See also* Electroencephalogram (EEG).

Capital Punishment: Usually punishment either by death or by a long jail sentence for having committed capital crimes such as premeditated murder, kidnapping, or torture and mutilation.

Cardinal Virtues: *See* Virtue.

Categorical Imperative: The key principle of Immanuel Kant's ethics, which states essentially that an act is immoral if the rule that would authorize it cannot be made into a rule for all human beings. *See also* Universal.

Cheat: To deceive by trickery: to swindle; to mislead; to act dishonestly or practice fraud.

Chemotherapy: Any therapy involving the introduction of chemicals into a person's body.

Chorionic Villus Sampling (CVS): A tool, like amniocentesis, that can be used to diagnose genetic defects in a fetus as early as the ninth week of pregnancy. A flexible catheter, inserted vaginally, is guided by ultrasound along uterine walls and extracts fetal cells from the threadlike projections (villi) on the chorion (outermost embryonic layer). Some studies have revealed that CVS may cause limb deformities in the fetus.

Cloning: A scientific technique, still in the experimental stages, by which a second human being or animal can be created from the cells of one already living. The new human being, for example, will be exactly like the one from whom he or she was "cloned" and will be called the first person's "clone."

Cognitive: That aspect of human beings that involves rationality and reason.

Collegial, Collegiality: An approach to doctor-patient relationships in which the patient and everyone having to do with the care of the patient are considered part of a team. All team members have significant input into how the patient should be cared for.

Conceptus: A term coined by Daniel Callahan in his book *Abortion: Law, Choice and Morality,* meaning "that which has been conceived." By using this term, one avoids the confusion of using the words *zygote, embryo,* and *fetus* to describe the conceptus at different stages of gestation because *conceptus* can be used from conception until birth. This term also eliminates the emotional connotations of calling unborn human life by the terms *child, baby, organism,* or *vegetating matter.*

Conditioning: A term used in behaviorism to describe the process by which human beings are caused to behave in certain ways, often as a "controller" wants them to. The term was first used by Pavlov in relation to the conditioned reflex and later by Skinner in his theory of operant conditioning.

Consequentialism: Ethical theories that are concerned with the consequences of actions or rules. The traditional philosophical name for this is *teleology* (from the Greek *telos,* meaning end or purpose). Examples of consequentialist theories are all forms of ethical egoism and utilitarianism.

Consistent: Compatible, not self-contradictory, harmonious; conforming to a set of rules or principles. *See also* Contradictory, Self-contradictory.

Contradictory, Self-contradictory: Inconsistent, contrary; for example, two statements so related that if one is true the other must be false. ("I am a human being" and "I am not a human being" are contradictory statements.) *Self-contradictory* refers to a proposition that contradicts itself, such as "A circle is a square." *See also* Consistent.

Cost-benefit Analysis: Also called "end-justifies-the-means" approach. The idea that one should strive for the greatest benefits deriving from the least cost expended. A possibility with any form of utilitarianism when "the greatest good for the greatest number" is stressed. Many ethicists question whether this approach is moral. *See also* End-justifies-the-means Approach.

CVS: *See* Chorionic Villus Sampling.

Declaration Pursuant to the Natural Death Act of California: A legalized "living will" type of document. This declaration is a part of California's Natural Death Act, which was signed into law on January 1, 1977 and revised in 1992. It purports to allow patients to state legally how they wish to be medically treated when they are dying or in other ways severely debilitated. *See also* Living Will and Durable Power of Attorney for Health Care.

Deontology: *See* Nonconsequentialism.

Determinism: Universal causation, the theory that everything in the universe has a cause. *Hard,* or *strong, determinism* states that freedom or free will is not compatible with universal causation. *Soft,* or *weak, determinism* states that everything is caused but that some causes originate with human beings;

therefore, freedom or free will is compatible with universal causation. Many theories of determinism come from the fields of the natural and physical sciences, the social sciences, and religion. *See also* Predestination *and* Fatalism.

Developmental View: That view of the beginning of human life, held by Daniel Callahan and others, that states that human life begins at conception but develops gradually through various stages until it reaches full human status. According to this view, the conceptus's biological and moral significance increases with its development.

Diagnosis: The medical examination of patients to discover what is wrong with them. The results of such examinations are also called the doctor's diagnosis.

Dialysis, Hemodialysis: The medical procedure whereby people who have no kidney function can still live by having the wastes removed from their blood. Dialysis machines are sometimes referred to as "artificial kidneys."

Domino Argument: Also called the "slippery slope," "the wedge," and "the camel's-nose-under-the-tent" argument. It essentially argues that if human beings allow one thing to be declared legal or moral, it will cause a flood of bad things to follow. For example, if we legalize abortion, then mercy killing and infanticide are sure to follow. Like a row of dominoes, if you push over the first one, the rest will fall over in turn.

Down's Syndrome: A type of congenital moderate to severe mental retardation that can occur in pregnancies of women of any age but most often in those thirty-five or older.

Durable Power of Attorney for Health Care: A legal document by which people can appoint an attorney-in-fact to make health care decisions for them in the event they become incompetent to do so.

Duty Ethics: The name sometimes attributed to Immanuel Kant's system of ethics because of his stress on performing a moral act out of a sense of duty, not inclination.

Eclectic: Selecting what is best from different systems or sources, having a wide range of tastes, desires, or likings. *See also* Synthesis.

Ectopic Pregnancy: A pregnancy that occurs in the fallopian tubes in which the ovum never moves down into the uterus. This is one of the two reasons for which the Roman Catholic church will allow abortion; the other is cancer of the uterus.

Egoism: That theory that is concerned with self-interest. *Psychological egoism* exemplifies the scientific, or descriptive, approach to morality, describing how human beings are thought to behave. *Strong psychological egoism* states that human beings *always* act in their own self-interest. *Weak psychological egoism* states that human beings *often* act in their own self-interest. Psychological egoism differs from *ethical egoism* in that the latter exemplifies the philosophical-normative approach to ethics. *Individual ethical egoism* says, "Everyone ought to act in *my* self-interest." *Personal ethical egoism* says, "I ought to act in my own self-interest but I make no claim concerning what others should do." *Universal ethical egoism* says, "Everyone ought to act in his or her own self-interest."

Electroencephalogram (EEG):   A test by which a record of brain waves can be acquired from electrical impulses produced by the brain; often used to confirm the results of other diagnostic techniques that indicate that a patient's brain has been severely or irreversibly damaged. *See also* Irreversible Coma.

Embryo: A term describing the conceptus between the second and the eighth weeks of gestation and development. *See also* Conceptus *and* Fetus.

Emotive Theory: That theory of morality that holds that morality is not based on reason and that moral statements simply mean (1) that the people uttering them are stating their approval or disapproval of someone or something or (2) that they are trying to evoke such approval or disapproval or actions of a certain type in others. *See also* Intuitionism.

Empirical: Reasoning from experience and sense observation, as opposed to "ideological," which has to do with reasoning from among ideas in the mind. The empirical approach to knowledge is a cornerstone of scientific investigation.

End-justifies-the-means Approach: A problem for consequentialist theories, especially utilitarianism, presenting the idea that as long as the end or consequences are good, then any means used to attain that good is justified, regardless of the morality of the means or any motives. *See also* Cost-benefit-analysis Approach.

Ethical: *See* Moral.

Ethical Egoism: *See* Egoism.

Ethical Monism: The theory that states that there is only one intrinsic good or value in life; that is, only one thing that is good in itself and worth having for its own sake. For example, hedonism states that pleasure or happiness is the only intrinsic good or value.

Ethical Pluralism: The theory that states there is more than one intrinsic good or value in life.

Ethics: From the Greek *ethos,* meaning character. In this book *ethics* is used interchangeably with *morality* except that in philosophy *ethics* means the study of morality. There are two approaches to ethics: the *scientific,* or *descriptive,* as used by the social sciences (for example, psychological egoism), and the *philosophical,* which includes the normative, or prescriptive, and metaethics (*see also* Normative, or Prescriptive, Ethics *and* Metaethics). When used in its ordinary sense, however, *ethics,* like *morality,* means the values by which human beings live in relation to other human beings, nature, God, and/or themselves. *See also* Moral.

Euthanasia: A Greek word originally meaning "happy death" or "death with dignity." To many people, however, this term refers to murder. *See also* Allowing Someone to Die, Mercy Death, *and* Mercy Killing.

Extramarital Sex: Sex outside of marriage. *See also* Adultery.

Extraordinary, or Heroic, Means: Any means used to treat a sick person or dying patient that is out of the ordinary, or heroic; that which will not cure or heal a patient but will only prolong his dying. This term was originally coined by Pope Pius XII, who said *extraordinary* would have to be defined according to particular persons, places, and times. *See also* Ordinary Means.

Falsity: Applies only to propositions. A proposition is false if it describes a state of affairs which was not, is not, or will not be actual. *See* Proposition *and* State of Affairs *and* Truth.

Fatalism: The view that all events are irrevocably fixed and predetermined so that they cannot be altered in any way by human beings—the future is always beyond their control. *See also* Predestination *and* Determinism.

Fetus: A term describing the conceptus between the eighth week of gestation or development and the time it is born. *See also* Conceptus *and* Embryo.

Free Love: The idea that anyone can freely engage in sex with anyone else within or outside of marriage as long as no coercion or force is used. *See also* Group Marriage.

Freudianism: Named after Sigmund Freud, the nineteenth-century founder of modern psychology. It is, among other things, a theory that states that human beings are determined by inner drives and unconscious motivations to behave the way they do. *See also* Determinism.

Gene Pool: The reproductive elements of all mating individuals, which comprise a "pool" from which the genes of the next generation are drawn.

Genetics: The biology of heredity; the study of heredity and its variation.

Genetic View: A view of the beginning of human life that says it begins at conception; that is, as soon as the genetic makeup of a conceptus is established. *See also* Developmental View.

Genocide: The deliberate and systematic destruction of a racial, political, or cultural group.

Gestation: The period of development of the conceptus from conception until birth; also called pregnancy. *See also* Conceptus *and* Embryo *and* Fetus *and* Zygote.

Good or Right: As defined in this book, that which has pleasure or happiness in it, involves excellence, creates harmony, and encourages creativity. A person can be said to be good, whereas an action can be said to be right.

Group Marriage: A communal type of living in which legally or nonlegally married couples and/or single people live together. Sexual relations in such a group may be monogamous or "free."

Hedonism: The theory that pleasure or happiness is the one intrinsic good or value in life; that an action is moral if it brings the greatest amount of pleasure or happiness with the least amount of pain or unhappiness. This is a basic tenet of the ethical theories of Epicurus (egoism) and Jeremy Bentham and J. S. Mill (utilitarianism).

Heterosexuality: The love or sexual orientation of a man for a woman or a woman for a man; the most approved and accepted form of sexuality and love in the Western world.

Homosexuality: Generally, the love and/or sexual orientation of a man for a man or a woman for a woman; commonly used to mean love and/or sexual relationships only between or among men. *Lesbianism* is used to describe love and/or sexual relationships between or among women.

Hospice Approach to Care for the Dying: *Hospice* literally means "a place of rest and refuge for strangers or pilgrims." The hospice approach to care for the dying was initiated at St. Christopher's Hospice in London by Dr. Cicely Saunders; there are now about 100 hospices all over England and many throughout the United States. The aim of the hospice approach is to provide comfort and care for the dying. Those involved in this approach have conducted advanced research on pain control and have provided a much more humane environment for dying patients and their families. Whenever possible, this approach stresses home care.

Human Being: A member of the species *homo sapiens. Potential human being* is sometimes applied to a human life from shortly after conception to about the twelfth or thirteenth week of development, after which the human life is called *actual*. This definition is not hard and fast, however, as some do not define a life as a human being until birth. *See also* Person, Personhood.

Humanism (Humanistic Ethics):   *Humanism* means many things, but in this text it refers to a nonreligious view of life essentially based on atheism or agnosticism and advocating a morality that excludes religion or religious belief.

Humanitarian Ethics: A system of ethics originated by the author that advocates five basic principles and a synthesized act-rules, consequentialism-non-consequentialism approach to morality (sometimes referred to as *mixed deontology*) that can include any moral system—religious or nonreligious—as long as the five basic moral principles are observed.

Immoral: That which is bad or wrong, such as a bad person or a wrong action; used interchangeably in this book with *unethical*.

Incest: Sexual relations between persons who are so closely related by blood that their marriage is illegal or forbidden by custom—usually between fathers and daughters, mothers and sons, or brothers and sisters.

Incipient Human Life: Life that is yet unborn; life during almost the entire period of gestation. *See also* Conceptus.

Inclinations: Those things that human beings are inclined to do usually by habit or emotions. Immanuel Kant opposed inclinations to duties, stating that to be moral, an act should be done out of a sense of duty, not from inclination.

Indeterminism: The theory that there is a certain amount of chance and freedom in the world, that not everything is caused, and that there is a real pluralism in reality. The opposite of determinism.

Informed Consent: Usually a formal written consent that patients give to health care professionals allowing them to conduct tests, procedures, or experimentation on the patients with patients' complete and "informed" knowledge and consent.

Intravenous (IV): Literally "within or into a vein." Refers to fluids pushed into the veins of human beings (for example, blood transfusion, glucose, or medications of various sorts).

Intuitionism: Morality based on feelings or emotions rather than on reason or rules; this is also known as *subjectivism.* Act nonconsequentialism is the best example of such a theory. Sayings such as "If it feels good, do it" and "Do your own thing" exemplify this approach to morality.

In Utero: Within the uterus.

Irreversible Coma: *See* Persistent Vegetative State (PVS).

Justice: Generally moral rightness, equity, fairness. There are four types of justice: *exchange justice,* which has to do with equal exchange of remuneration for products or services; *distributive justice,* which has to do with the distribution of good and bad based on merit or desert, need and ability, or according to the equality of human beings; *social justice,* which has to do with the obligation to be just and fair to all members of society or to society in general; and *retributive justice,* which is based on the "eye for an eye, tooth for a tooth" philosophy. *See also* Reward, Punishment.

Killing: To put to death, slay, or deprive of life.

Laissez-faire: The doctrine that government should not interfere with business.

Larceny: The felonious taking and removing of another's personal property with the intent of permanently depriving the owner. *Grand larceny* is stealing on a grand scale (e.g., a car); *petit* (or petty) *larceny* constitutes minor theft (e.g., stealing apples from a grocery store). *See also* Stealing.

Law of Nature: A term used to describe events in nature that occur consistently and without exception—for example, the law of gravity.

Lesbianism: *See* Homosexuality.

Leukemia: A form of cancer of the blood.

Lie: An intentionally deceptive message in the form of a statement; a piece of information deliberately presented as being true; anything meant to deceive or give a wrong impression. A *white lie* is a falsehood not meant to injure anyone and considered by many to be of little import.

Living Will: A will by which healthy and competent people can inform their relatives and others of how they want to be treated or not treated when they are too sick or incompetent to decide such things as whether to start or discontinue life-support systems, submit to surgery, and so on. It is not a legal document. *See also* Declaration Pursuant to the Natural Death Act of California *and* Durable Power of Attorney for Health Care.

Manners: The socially correct way of behaving; also, the prevailing systems or modes of social conduct of a specific society.

Masochism: The deriving of pleasure—including sexual pleasure—from being hurt, abused, or mistreated.

Mercy Death: Distinguished from mercy killing in that mercy death is a termination of life expressly requested by a dying patient who is competent to do so; distinguished from allowing someone to die in that a direct act (such as the administering of a massive overdose of drugs) is taken to end the patient's life. This is also known as *assisted suicide. See also* Allowing Someone to Die *and* Euthanasia *and* Mercy Killing.

Mercy Killing: A direct act taken to end someone's life with the motive of being merciful. The means include the administering of poison or a massive overdose of drugs, shooting, and so on. Mercy killing is distinguished from mercy death in that the former is done without the person's express consent; it is distinguished from allowing someone to die in that it is a direct act of termination. *See also* Allowing Someone to Die *and* Euthanasia *and* Mercy Death.

Metaethics: The second type of ethics under the philosophical approach. This word comes from the Greek, meaning "beyond or above ethics." In metaethics, also known as *analytic ethics,* the language and logic of ethics and ethical systems are studied, defined, and discussed, usually without the intent of setting up any kind of alternative ethical systems or of prescribing human behavior, as in *normative ethics. See also* Ethics *and* Normative, or Prescriptive, Ethics.

Metastasis: The spreading of bacteria or body cells (especially cancer cells) from one part of the body to another.

Missionary Position: The customarily accepted heterosexual position for sexual intercourse in which the man is on top of the woman.

Monogamy: Having only one spouse—the major form of marriage (legal or nonlegal) practiced in the Western world.

Moral: That which is good or right, such as a good person or a right action. Used interchangeably in this text with *ethical.*

Moral Import: That which has moral importance or significance, such as a proposition. "Human beings should not kill other human beings" has moral import, whereas "The house is green" does not. *See also* Proposition.

Morality: From the Latin *moralis,* meaning "customs or manners." In this book it is used interchangeably with *ethics* except when *ethics* is used specifically to note that area of philosophy that constitutes the study of morality. In the author's working definition, morality, or ethics, is how humans relate to or treat one another to promote mutual welfare, growth, and meaning in striving for good over bad and right over wrong. *See also* Ethics *and* Moral.

Moratorium: A temporary suspension of something—for example, certain scientific experiments.

Murder: The unlawful and immoral killing of one person by another, especially with malice aforethought. *See also* Killing *and* Mercy Death *and* Mercy Killing.

Nichomachean Ethics: The system of ethics established by Aristotle in the fourth century B.C., named after his son Nichomachus.

Nonconsequentialism: Ethical theories not based on consequences but on some other moral standard (usually considered "higher" by the nonconsequentialist); referred to in traditional philosophy as *deontology* (from the Greek, loosely meaning "ought"). Examples of such theories are Kant's Duty Ethics and the Divine Command Theory.

Nonmoral: That which is completely out of the sphere of morality. Animals, plants, and inanimate objects are essentially nonmoral.

Normative, or Prescriptive, Ethics: The first type of ethics under the philosophical approach. This is also known as *prescriptive ethics* because it is interested in setting up norms or value systems that *prescribe* how human beings ought to behave. All ethical systems, such as ethical egoism, utilitarianism, and Kant's Duty Ethics, are normative.

Objective: Outside of or external to human beings rather than within them. For example, objective values would be those outside of humans as opposed to those within them. *See also* Subjective.

Obligations: Responsibilities human beings have toward one another by law, morality, or tradition to see that their just rights are protected and accorded them. *See also* Right.

Oncology, Oncologist: *Oncology* is the branch of medicine dealing with tumors, especially cancerous tumors; an *oncologist* is a doctor who specializes in this branch of medicine.

Ordinary Means: Distinguished from extraordinary, or heroic, means of medical treatment of patients; refers to the appropriate treatment that would not be unusual or beyond what should be done for any particular patient given his or her specific illness, disease, or stage of dying. *See also* Extraordinary Means.

Paradigm, Paradigmatic: A *paradigm* is a pattern or model; *paradigmatic* means patternlike or model-like.

Paternalism: A type of human relationship in which one person acts as a father or father figure and another acts as a child. For example, in medicine, it is the attitude that doctors are father figures who know best, and their patients are their children.

Persistent Vegetative State (PVS):   A state that results from damage to the cerebral or neo-cortex, which controls the cognitive functions. Might also be called irreversible coma or cortical or cerebral death. *See also* Brain Death.

Person, Personhood: That point at which a human being can be considered as having a personality and being able to enter into meaningful human relationships—usually after birth and after some socialization; not clearly defined for those who are at various stages of minimal human being-ness (comatose and severely retarded people). *See also* Human Being.

Polygamy: Having more than one spouse. Less commonly, *polyandry* means having more than one husband, whereas *polygamy* means having more than one wife. *Bigamy* means having two spouses. Generally, polygamy is not legally or morally approved of in the Western world.

Pornography: Generally considered to be literature, art, film, or live display intended to incite lewd and lascivious feelings and without any redeeming social, literary, or artistic value. *Kiddie porn* refers to pornographic material depicting children. *Snuff porn* refers to pornographic material depicting murder.

Practical Imperative: Another name for Immanuel Kant's maxim that no human being should be treated merely as a means to someone else's end but, rather, that all human beings should be treated as unique ends in themselves.

Predestination: A religious version of determinism that states essentially that because God knows all, He has also foreordained everything to happen the way it has from the beginning. Human beings are completely determined by a supernatural power. *See also* Determinism *and* Fatalism.

Premarital Sex: Sexual relations that occur prior to marriage or without marriage; referred to in the Bible as *fornication*.

Prescriptive Ethics: *See* Normative, or Prescriptive, Ethics.

Prima Facie Duty: Literally, a duty "at first glance"; that is, all other things being equal, we ought to do it. This term, introduced by Sir William David Ross, means that some duties and obligations must come before others. For example, Ross believed that to avoid doing harm to someone is more important than to do good.

Principle of Goodness or Rightness: The ultimate principle of any moral system, because moral and ethical mean good or right. This principle requires three things: first, to promote goodness over badness; second, to cause no harm or badness; and third, to prevent badness or harm. *See also* Good or Right.

Principle of Individual Freedom (Equality Principle):   The principle that states that human beings ought to be free to pursue their own values and morality as long as these do not seriously conflict with or violate the other four basic moral principles (Value of Life, Goodness, Justice, and Truth Telling or Honesty).

Principle of Justice or Fairness: The principle that states that it is not enough to do good and avoid bad but that some effort must be made to distribute the good and bad resulting from actions. *See also* Justice *and* Punishment *and* Reward.

Principle of Truth Telling or Honesty: The principle that states that human beings always ought to strive to tell the truth or be honest except when it would interfere with or seriously violate the principles of Goodness, Value of Life, and Justice. This principle is necessary for meaningful communication and human relationships.

Prochoice or Abortion on Request: The position that abortion should be allowed at any time merely upon the woman's request or demand.

Procreation: Creating children mainly through human sexual intercourse although artificial insemination and laboratory, or test-tube, babies may also be included.

Prognosis: Prediction of the course and end of a disease and the outlook based on this prediction.

Prolife or Right to Life: The position that unborn conceptuses have an absolute right to life superseding all other rights, such as the woman's right to decide whether or not to go through with pregnancy.

Promise: A declaration that one will or will not do something; a vow. *Breaking a promise* is failing to conform to or acting contrary to or violating a promise.

Promulgate: To set forth or lay out something—for example, a set of ethical principles or a moral system.

Proponent: One who supports a particular point of view, position, or argument.

Proposition: A meaningful statement that asserts or claims something about reality and which has the characteristic of being either true or false. There are four types of propositions: *analytic,* such as "All triangles are three-sided"; *internal,* such as "I have a headache"; *external,* or *empirical,* such as "I see a table here before me"; and *moral,* such as "Human beings should not kill other human beings."

Proselytize: To try to convert someone from one point of view to one's own or to another.

Protective Isolation: In medicine, protecting patients and nonpatients from contagion. Reverse isolation is the means used to protect patients from contact with infections from the outside environment.

Psychological Egoism: *See* Egoism.

Punishment: The act of penalizing someone for a crime, fault, or misbehavior; a penalty for wrongdoing. There are three basic theories of punishment and reward: (1) retribution, or deserts, theory, which states that we ought to give people what they deserve, regardless of the consequences; (2) utilitarianism, or results, theory, which states that we ought to punish or reward only if it brings about good consequences; and (3) restitution, or compensation, theory, which states that proper reward or punishment is valid only when the victim is compensated for wrongs or harm done to him or her. *See also* Justice *and* Reward *and* Principle of Justice.

PVS: *See* Persistent Vegetative State.

Qualifying Rule: Rather than making an exception to a rule, one can qualify a rule so that the exception applies to all humanity. For example, "Never kill" can be qualified to read, "Never kill except in self-defense or defense of the innocent."

Radical Individualism: In health care, the view that patients have absolute rights over their own bodies and lives and therefore may reject all recommendations of health care personnel (especially doctors). *See also* Paternalism *and* Reciprocal, or Collegial, View.

Reciprocal, or Collegial, View: In health care, the view that decisions should not rest only with the doctor or only with the patient but must instead be made in a reciprocal (give-and-take), or collegial (team approach), way. *See also* Paternalism *and* Radical Individualism.

Relativism: The opposite of "absolutism" in that those who hold this point of view believe that there are no absolutes in morality but rather that morality is relative to particular cultures, groups, or even individuals, and further that everyone must decide his or her own values and ethics because there are no absolutes.

Reverse Discrimination: That type of discrimination and prejudice that works against the majority (usually young white men). In business employment practices this usually occurs as part of the effort to eliminate discrimination against minorities.

Reverse Isolation: *See* Protective Isolation.

Reversibility Criterion: An ethical principle that states that one should test the morality or immorality of an action by putting oneself in the other person's place, by reversing the situation in question. The Golden Rule ("Do unto others as you would have them do unto you") is one example of this criterion. Kant used this criterion in his system along with the criterion of universalizability.

Reward: Something given or received for worthy behavior, usually on the basis of merit, desert (what people deserve), or ability. *See also* Justice *and* Principle of Justice *and* Punishment.

Right: That which is due to anyone through law, morality, or tradition, such as the right to life or the right to freedom. *See also* Obligations.

Sadism: Enjoyment, including sexual enjoyment, gained from administering pain or hurt to another. *See also* Masochism.

Sanction: Authoritative permission or approval for some course of action; for example, a religious sanction of an action makes it moral for those who belong to that religion.

Sexually Transmitted Disease (STD): Any disease, such as chlamydia, syphilis, gonorrhea, herpes, and AIDs, which can be transmitted by sexual activity.

Situation Ethics: The theory invented by Joseph Fletcher that says that there are no moral rules or guides except for Christian love—what is moral in any situation is the loving thing to do in that situation. *See also* Relativism *and* Utilitarianism (specifically *act utilitarianism*).

Situationism: The theory that one's actions are governed strictly by the situation rather than by rules or principles. All act approaches to morality are situational.

State of Affairs: An occurrence or situation that either is or is not actual; the occurrence or situation in reality, as distinguished from our judgment or claims about it. States of affairs are either actual or not actual, never true or false. *See also* Proposition *and* Truth.

STD: *See* Sexually Transmitted Disease (STD).

Stealing: Taking something without right or permission, generally in a surreptitious way. *See also* Larceny.

Subject: As used in this book, one who is to be experimented upon.

Subjective: Coming from within human beings rather than outside of them. *See also* Objective.

Subjectivism: *See* Intuitionism.

Suicide: The act or instance of intentionally killing oneself. *See also* Killing *and* Mercy Death.

Synthesis: A bringing together of the best of a series of divergent ethical systems. A reasonable synthesis is a bringing together of the best of all of the systems or theories of ethics coupled with an attempt to eliminate their difficulties or faults. *See also* Eclectic.

Tay-Sachs Disease: A fatal disorder that is genetic in character and that is usually found in the infant offspring of Eastern European Jews.

Teleology: *See* Consequentialism.

Tenable: Capable of being held; workable, defensible. *See also* Viable.

Triage: In medicine, a disaster that requires decisions as to who gets treated first or at all; an emergency situation in which hospital facilities are taxed beyond their capabilities.

Truth: As applied to propositions, a proposition is true if it describes a state of affairs that was, is, or will be actual. Truth in this sense is absolute, not relative. *See* Falsity *and* Proposition *and* State of Affairs.

Unethical: *See* Immoral.

Unity in Diversity: The theory that attempts to resolve the absolutism-relativism controversy by stating that human beings are similar and also different; therefore, we should strive for a unity in such diversity. This can be accomplished if we allow freedom and diversity while accepting certain unifying principles (for example, allowing people freedom as long as they do not harm other people in the process).

Universal: Applicable to all human beings, situations, times, and places. A moral rule that is *universalizable* is one that can be applied to all human beings without self-contradiction. *Universalizability* is a principle in Kant's ethical system embodied in the Categorical Imperative, which states that a moral rule that cannot be universalized, or made applicable to all human beings, is not a true moral rule. *See also* Categorical Imperative *and* Absolute.

Universal Causation: *See* Determinism *and* Indeterminism.

Utilitarianism: A normative ethical theory originally established by Jeremy Bentham and John Stuart Mill that advocates bringing about good consequences or happiness to all concerned—sometimes stated as the greatest good for the greatest number. *Act utilitarianism* states that one should perform that act that will bring about the greatest good for all concerned. *Rule utilitarianism* states that one should always establish and/or follow that rule or those rules that will bring about the greatest good for all concerned.

Value of Life Principle: The first moral principle, which states that human life should be preserved, protected, and valued. This is sometimes referred to as the *Sanctity of Life Principle*. In this book it means a reverence for life and an acceptance of death.

Viable: Capable of working, such as a moral system. Also, in connection with pregnancy and abortion, a fetus that is able to exist outside of the mother's womb (usually after twenty-eight weeks of gestation). *See also* Tenable.

Virtue: The quality of moral excellence, righteousness, responsibility; a specific type of moral excellence or other exemplary quality considered meritorious. For example, the cardinal or natural virtues are justice, prudence, fortitude, and temperance.

Virtue Ethics: A moral theory that had its beginnings with Aristotle and which is based on human beings developing a moral or virtuous character by doing what an ideal good or virtuous person would do rather than being based on consequences, feelings, or rules.

Zero Population Growth (ZPG): A situation in which a man and a woman together produce no more than two children, one to replace each of them when they die, thereby ensuring no increase in the population.

Zygote: The term used to describe a conceptus immediately after the joining of the sperm and the egg—the fertilized ovum. *See also* Conceptus *and* Embryo *and* Fetus.

Index